NINTH EDITION

LANGE Q&A™

RADIOGRAPHY EXAMINATION

D.A. Saia, MA, RT(R) (M)
Director, Radiography Program
Stamford Hospital
Stamford, Connecticut

 **Medical**

New York   Chicago   San Francisco   Lisbon   London
Madrid   Mexico City   Milan   New Delhi
San Juan   Seoul   Singapore   Sydney   Toronto

2 3 4 5 6 7 8 9 0   QDB/QDB   17 16 15 14 13

Book ISBN	978-0-07-178720-8	Set ISBN	978-0-07-178721-5	CD ISBN	978-0-07-178722-2
Book MHID	0-07-178720-8	Set MHID	0-07-178721-6	CD MHID	0-07-178722-4

This book was set in Palatino by Aptara, Inc.
The editors were Catherine Johnson and Christie Naglieri.
The production supervisor was Sherri Souffrance.
Project management was provided by Indu Jawwad, Aptara, Inc.
Quad/Graphics was printer and binder.

This book is printed on acid-free paper.

Library of Congress Cataloging-in-Publication Data
Saia, D. A. (Dorothy A.)
    Lange Q & A radiography examination / D.A. Saia. — 9th ed.
        p. ; cm.
    Q & A radiography examination
    Radiography examination
    Includes bibliographical references and index.
    ISBN-13: 978-0-07-178721-5 (pbk.)
    ISBN-10: 0-07-178721-6 (pbk.)
    I. Title.   II. Title: Q & A radiography examination.   III. Title: Radiography examination.
    [DNLM: 1. Radiography–Examination Questions.   2. Technology, Radiologic–Examination
Questions. WN 18.2]
    616.07572076–dc23

                                                                2011040872

Please tell the author and publisher what you think of this book by sending your comments to radtech@mcgraw-hill.com. Please put the author and title of this book in the subject line.

The following figures were originally published in Saia DA, Radiography PREP: Program Review and Examination Preparation, 5th ed. New York: McGraw-Hill, 2009 and are reproduced with permission from McGraw-Hill: Figures 2-47, 2-49, 2-50, 2-52, 2-55, 2-58, 3-5, 4-19, 4-21, 4-22, 4-24, 5-1, 5-3, 5-10, 6-14, 6-15, 6-17, 6-22, and 7-24.

McGraw-Hill books are available at special quantity discounts to use as premiums and sales promotions, or for use in corporate training programs. To contact a representative please e-mail us at bulksales@mcgraw-hill.com.

To Tony
My love, my happiness

Contents

To the Student

Your feedback on the previous eight editions of this book has been encouraging; I appreciate all the comments and suggestions we have received, and I have greatly enjoyed my correspondence with so many of you. I hope that all who use this book, its companion Web site RadReviewEasy.com, and companion book PREP: Radiography—educators and students alike—will continue to provide me with their comments in order that both the books and Web site may continue to meet their needs. I invite and encourage you to contact me through McGraw-Hill or at dsaia@stamhealth.org with comments, questions, and suggestions for future editions. The ninth edition contains new and revised material to reflect changes in the American Registry of Radiologic Technologists (ARRT) Content Specifications published in August 2010 and to be implemented January 2012. It includes questions on digital/electronic imaging, including computed and direct digital radiography. Also included is the processing of electronic images including their acquisition, manipulation, and exposure indication. In recognition of the ever increasing importance and application of Computed Tomography in diagnostic imaging, this edition includes some fundamental CT questions and explanations.

You have provided us with a very favorable response to the companion Web site, RadReviewEasy.com. I was very excited about the implementation of this learning/preparation tool and your response has confirmed its usefulness. The Web site has given me the enjoyable opportunity to "meet" so many more of you. The new *RadReviewEasy 3.0* is an even more powerful tool (with more new features expected to be launched in 2012), and I hope that new users find it just as helpful as our first version.

RadReviewEasy.com's robust performance profile allows users to track their results performance by topic and test scores over time and to compare their scores to others using RadReviewEasy, including test-takers at the users' specific institutions.

Customization features allow you to:

- Choose the length and subject areas of a test or create a set of randomly selected questions.
- Retake tests composed of questions previously answered incorrectly so you can focus on weak areas.
- Time your tests or practice at your own pace.
- Take tests composed of questions that you are seeing for the first time.

Additionally, there is an Instructor Reporting Tool that can provide administrators/instructors with the ability to track individual student progress and generate reports on class activity or subject area performance.

The Web site affords the student an opportunity to practice CBT prior to taking the computerized ARRT examination. Visit RadReviewEasy.com for information on pricing and subscription terms.

I am sure you realize that a review book is not intended to be a "quick fix" preparation for the certification examination administered by the ARRT. It takes at least 2 years of didactic instruction and testing, and hours of clinical practice, to prepare oneself as an entry-level radiographer. During about the last 4 months of radiography education, the actual certification examination becomes a rather scary anticipation. Confident, competent, even cavalier students suddenly become sober when the "the Registry" is mentioned. They begin to question all they ever felt confident about. If you use this book the way it is designed to be used, and perhaps in conjunction with its companion Web site RadReviewEasy.com and the companion book, *Radiography PREP (Program Review and Examination Preparation)*, you should be able to set aside any fears you may have.

I believe that proper use of the materials presented here, online at RadReviewEasy, and in PREP will help you overcome your anxieties. First, read the introductory section carefully. It presents proven, sensible suggestions to help improve test-taking performance. It elaborates on simple processes to help selection of the correct answer, and several methods and strategies that may be employed while taking "the" test. Probably the most important key to reducing apprehension is to reduce the unknowns to the fewest number. You will also find an introduction to CBT with a description of what to expect, and helpful hints to enhance preparation and reduce anxiety. Second, the format and content of the book and the questions on RadReviewEasy.com have been specially designed to provide focus and direction for your review, and thus to help you do your very best on your certification examination. The ARRT has no secrets and springs no surprises on you. Just as your instructors have made known what is expected of you during your education, the ARRT has made known the content, question format, and terminology used on the certification examination. Each educational program receives the ARRT newsletter, *Educator Update*. The newsletter is published regularly by the ARRT and functions to keep educators and students current on the activities and policies of the ARRT. The Educator's Handbook is also published by the ARRT and serves as a source for general information, policies and procedures, and reprints of a number of documents, including *Content Specifications for the Examination in Radiography, Conventions Specific to the Radiography Examination*, and *Standard Terminology for Positioning and Protection*. These documents are revised periodically and advise educators of terminology, categories, content, and approximate weight of content areas on the ARRT examination. Although the *Content Specifications* by no means serves as a comprehensive radiography curriculum, it does serve as a suitable guide for examination review and preparation. It makes sense to design a review book in which the content, question format, and terminology are similar to that which students can expect to find on their certification examination.

The number of questions found in each chapter is proportional to the number found in that category on the actual ARRT examination. The questions are designed to test your problem-solving skills and your ability to integrate facts that fit the situation.

Most important and practical, I believe, are the detailed explanations found at the end of each chapter. *By themselves, the explanations are good reviews of essential material; they provide a "minilecture" for each question.* Use them to confirm your correct answers and to better understand your weaker areas. You will see that most explanations will tell you not only why the correct answer is correct, but also why the other answer choices (distractors) are incorrect. *Radiography PREP* can be used either *before* this book—as a review of the material this book will test you on—or it can be used *with* this book to help you strengthen particular essential areas of study.

Once you have finished reviewing the first five chapters, set aside special time for the practice tests in Chapters 6 and 7. Try to simulate the actual examination environment as much as possible. Choose a quiet place free from distractions and interruptions, gather the necessary materials, and arrange to be uninterrupted for up to 3 hours.

In summary, use this book as recommended to help ease your precertification examination jitters. Excessive anxiety can impair clear thinking and lower your score. Avoiding excessive stress can improve your concentration and information retrieval process. Remember, you have been well prepared by your program director and instructors, and you have studied and worked hard for at least 2 years. So follow the advice found in the Introduction: Prepare yourself sensibly and keep a positive attitude. I totally agree with a remark the famous automaker Henry Ford once said: *"Whether you think you can or whether you think you can't, you're right!"*

I wish you much satisfaction and success in your radiography career!

D.A. Saia

Acknowledgments

Once again, it is a pleasure to recognize and express my sincere appreciation to those who again have been so helpful and supportive during the preparation of this ninth edition.

Special recognition goes to my coworkers Olive Peart, MS, RT(R)(M) and Teresa Whiteside, AS, RT(R)(BD), (CDBT) for their generous support day-to-day and through the preparation of this project. Olive can always be depended upon to be there for me in times of "computer crisis." Teresa is a most welcome new addition to our faculty, and was very helpful in reviewing new CT material.

I am grateful to all the professional staff of McGraw-Hill. There would have never been an eighth edition without their expert direction and support. Special appreciation must be expressed to my editors Catherine A. Johnson and Christie Naglieri—I appreciate their calm patience during stressful periods. Thank you also to Sherri Souffrance in Production and to my wonderful Senior Project Manager, Indu Jawwad.

Tony Aiello and Jennifer Pollock deserve another special note of appreciation for their development and maintenance of the books' companion Web site, www.RadReviewEasy.com. Their foresight and expertise have brought a successful added dimension to this book.

Everyone at McGraw-Hill has been enormously helpful in the development and expansion of this project; it is always a pleasure to work with their creative and skilled staff.

I wish to express appreciation again to Philips Healthcare, Dunlee Division, and their Inside Sales Manager, Mr. Roger Flees, R.T. (Retired), for his assistance in granting permission to reproduce various tube rating charts. Thank you, Roger, for generously sharing your time and expertise. Our discussions of tube rating and heat storage were most helpful. Your patience in helping me obtain permission for use of tube rating charts is greatly appreciated.

The support and assistance offered in all previous editions by the late George Spahn of Fuji Medical Systems, USA will always be greatly appreciated. George was instrumental in the introduction and expansion of electronic imaging content in this book and especially in its companion text, PREP: Radiography. George Spahn is a great loss to Fuji Medical Systems, USA and the radiology community, and is missed by so many.

Many of the images are reproduced here through the courtesy of Stamford Hospital, Department of Radiology. A number of images found in Chapter 4, Image Acquisition and Evaluation, have been reproduced through the courtesy of American College of Radiology. A special thank you is also sent to Conrad P. Ehrlich, MD for the new images added to this book and to PREP.

Thank you to Mr. Joel R. Schenck, Marketing Product Manager of RMI, for permission to reproduce the mammographic phantom image found in Chapter 4.

Appreciative and affectionate acknowledgment is sent to all my students—past, present, and those still to come. Their questions, enthusiasm, and desire to learn not only make my job a most pleasant task, but also served as the original stimulus for the preparation of this text.

Finally, and most especially, a loving message of appreciation goes to my husband Tony. The preparation and revision of *two* books *and* a companion Web site is extraordinarily time consuming. His love, understanding, and encouragement were invaluable and deeply appreciated throughout the preparation of this, and every, edition.

D.A. Saia

Introduction

Completion of the ARRT radiography certification examination is often a high point in the career of a radiologic professional. Certification indicates that the individual has acquired a recognized level of knowledge and expertise and is qualified to deliver ionizing radiation in the performance of medical diagnostic testing. On what does success or failure depend?

Relax! It isn't as bad as it seems! As the student radiographer nears graduation, there is, understandably, an anxiety that begins to grow. It is a time when you wonder if you are smart enough and if you are skillful enough. Although there will always be room for growth, these concerns arise from the realization that an important landmark has been reached. Formal education will soon be at an end— no more written examinations and no more clinical competencies to complete. You will be on your own, proclaimed competent. How will you perform on the certification examination? How will you perform in the clinical arena? These are indeed sobering thoughts.

I believe that proper use of the materials presented here will help you overcome your anxieties. You will find several easy and effective suggestions for intelligent preparation and test taking. The suggestions are proven, sensible recommendations to help improve test-taking performance. Special focus has been placed on suggestions for the ARRT computer-based testing (CBT) system. They elaborate on simple processes to help in selection of the correct answer, and several methods and strategies that may be employed while taking your certification examination. Probably the most important key to reducing apprehension is to *reduce the unknowns to the fewest number*.

You will find that the format and content of this review book is very helpful and is specially designed to provide focus and direction for your review, thus helping you do your very best on the certification examination. The ARRT has no secrets and springs no surprises on you. Just as your instructors have made known what is expected of you during your education, the ARRT has made known the content, question format, and terminology used on the certification examination. The following are some tried-and-true tips and strategies for test taking in general, and specifics to help you through CBT. The later sections on Preparing for Success in CBT, Test-Taking Strategies, and Practice Tests will be particularly useful.

HOW THIS BOOK IS ORGANIZED

There are three primary sections in this book: a topic-by-topic *review* with 1,000 exam-type questions and paragraph-length *explanations*; two 200-question *practice* tests, also with paragraph-length explanations; and this *Introduction*, which includes information necessary to help you get the most out of the book and to do your best on the CBT system.

This is a current book of practice questions that are designed to mimic actual test questions. In addition, its companion Web site www. *RadReviewEasy. com* has additional questions and answers for further practice in simulated certification conditions; visit the site for pricing and subscription terms.

In summary, this book will provide you, the student, with a review that will better enable you to simulate and prepare for the certification examination by providing an excellent and comprehensive review of radiography.

ABOUT THE EXAMINATION

It is essential to carefully read the ARRT certification Handbook. It describes in detail all the essential testing information required before, during, and after the actual test. Failure to follow the required steps can result in forfeiture of test appointment, and re-application.

ARRT certification examinations are administered at Pearson VUE test centers. Several types of examinations are administered at these test centers. If you believe keyboard sounds might distract you, you are encouraged to request earplugs prior to entering the exam room.

As noted later in this section, you should plan to arrive at least 15 minutes early. Many test centers require you to be there 30 minutes ahead of the scheduled test time. If you are 15 minutes late, you run the risk of forfeiting your appointment time, and being required to re-apply.

Be prepared to show at least two forms of identification, one of which must be government-issued photo ID (e.g., driver's license, state ID card, passport).

Security requirements upon entry at the examination site include a photograph, digital signature, and palm vein scanning.

Paper, pencils, etc are not permitted in the exam room—an erasable board and pen are provided. A calculator is available on the test computer, or you may request a simple four function calculator from the test center. If you have any request/problem during the test, you should raise your hand for assistance (e.g., screen brightness needs adjustment, other problem with computer, need earplugs, etc).

There is a 20-minute tutorial before the start of the exam and a 10-minute survey after completion of the exam. Candidates are presented with multiple-choice questions on a computer screen and directed to select an answer using either the keyboard or a mouse. The process allows candidates to review or change any answers to any questions prior to submitting the completed examination for scoring.

The tutorial offered at the beginning of the examination allows the candidate to answer several practice questions. This ensures that the candidate is thoroughly familiar with the process.

The national certification examination for radiography is a standardized test administered by the ARRT and includes 220 multiple-choice questions; 200 questions are scored and 20 questions are unidentified pilot questions. The time allotted for the test is 3½ hours; passing score is 75%. Total time, including tutorial and survey, is four hours.

Beginning January 2000, the ARRT discontinued paper and pencil testing and began to use CBT for the administration of its radiography examinations. Pearson VUE testing centers will administer the ARRT examination. There is no postmarking deadline for ARRT applications for CBT. Applicants may apply for the examination prior to graduation, but will schedule their examination date within an assigned 90-day window that starts at graduation. Once the ARRT application is processed, and the applicant deemed eligible, the ARRT sends the candidate their CSR—Candidate Status Report. The CSR indicates the candidates ARRT number and their examination "window" dates. Most educators advise taking the certification examination shortly after completing all didactic and clinical requirements.

To gain admittance to the test center, the candidate must show two current identifications; at least one must show a photo, and both must show signatures. Positive identification will include photograph, digital signature, and palm vein scanning at the test site. A four-function nonprogrammable calculator is available on the computer, or can be provided to the examinee upon request. A tutorial of practice questions is offered at the start of the examination. This helps the candidate become familiar with the testing process. Test questions are administered in random order, that is, they are not grouped together by subject (and that is the way the two practice tests in this book are designed). *Multiple-choice* questions are presented on the computer screen and the candidate is directed to select the best answer—the mouse or keyboard may be used. There are other types of questions in addition to typical multiple-choice questions. *Select-multiple* questions require you to select all correct options from a list of four to eight possible responses. *Sorted-list* questions require you to place in order a given list of four to eight options. *Images with "hot spots"* require you to *click on* a particular spot or region. *Videos* require that you view a video, then answer the question that follows. Videos provide you with a control bar that allows to *play, pause,* and *stop.* The candidate is permitted to review or change answers to questions before indicating that he/she is finished with the examination.

STRATEGIES FOR STUDYING AND TEST TAKING

The purpose of a test strategy is to make the most of your knowledge, although no strategy, however elaborate, can help you if you do not know your subject.

A good test strategy can do the following:

1. Prevent you from making mistakes
2. Help you to use your time efficiently
3. Improve your odds of getting the right answer

The single most important trait of a good test strategy is *simplicity*. There are two ways to make and keep a procedure simple: The first way is to design it to be simple. The second is to practice the procedure as it is designed. The second part is up to you. If you use the following test strategies (particularly the elimination strategy) while using this review book, the strategies will become second nature to you, and you can then concentrate all your attention on passing your certification examination.

PREPARING FOR THE EXAMINATION

Designing a Study Schedule

It is important to establish a routine study schedule. This schedule should allow you to study at a time when you are at your optimum. Some students are more alert in the morning for this kind of work, while others have better success in the afternoon. It would not be a good plan to try and study late at night after a full day unless this is an optimum time for you.

There are several advantages to designing a schedule. The first is that it forces you to face the reality of your study load. Many students underplay the amount of time it will take to complete a thorough study, and this can adversely affect their performance. If you write out a schedule that includes both your daily responsibilities and the time you need to study, you will have a sense of the pace needed to complete your review. The second advantage to designing a schedule is that it will allow you to increase your concentration because the schedule defines the allotted amount of time for each topic you need to cover. Otherwise, a lot of time can be wasted in determining what to study during each session.

Setting up a Study Plan

After completing the best of radiography programs, even the best of students will have gaps in his or her knowledge, subjects that were somehow missed or forgotten, or that will not come to mind when needed. These gaps in your knowledge are often small; but since one piece of information often builds upon other pieces, a small gap in your knowledge can sometimes lead to a large drop in your test score. The best way to get around this problem is to use a well-defined study plan. Listed below are two alternative plans for you to consider. The first is *diagnosis and remediation*, and the second is *SQ3R*.

Diagnosis and Remediation

This is a two-step approach: *diagnosis* (finding out what you do not know) and *remediation* (learning the material).

Diagnosis. Many students graduate from their programs without a good idea of what they do or do not know. Fortunately, this book has been designed to make diagnosis simple. By following the steps listed below, you will know what you need to learn before you take the certifying examination.

Step 1. Begin with Chapter 1, Patient Care, or any of the other first five chapters. Go through the questions in one sitting, making the experience as similar to the actual examination as possible. Remember to practice test strategies while answering the questions. This will produce a more valid diagnosis.

While taking the test, you should note or highlight words and phrases from the questions that you do not understand. After you have finished the questions (but before you have graded your work) make a list of the terms you noted and the numbers of the questions that contained them.

Step 2. Analyze your results. Read the answers and make a list of the questions you missed. Compare this list with the subspecialty list at the end of the chapter. This will tell you if you are weak in a particular area. Once you have defined an area of weakness, pay special attention to the explanations provided. If the answer is still unclear, use the exact page references to your textbook for further study.

Anytime you go through your work, picking out and correcting your mistakes, you will gain a greater understanding of your strengths and weaknesses. However, by approaching the analysis systematically, the improvement can be dramatic. Concentrate on your areas of weakness, but be sure to read all the explanations at least once. This will allow you to compare your reasoning on right and wrong answers and to check for the possibility that you put down the right answer for the wrong reason.

Step 3. Repeat the process. The purpose of this study plan is to get important information into your long-term memory. The best way to ensure this is to begin your study plan early enough to allow yourself time to repeat your chapter study one more time before the examination. Keep and compare your results from each review and focus on any weaknesses still apparent from the comparison.

Remediation

Step 1. Read and cross read. Starting with the subspecialty that you missed most often, make a reading list. For those areas in which you missed three or four questions, a single reference will probably be enough, but if you missed more than four, you should cross read to cover the same information in more than one text. (You might also want to review these topics in your old class notes.)

When you study from texts, use the index and the table of contents to find the section you need. If you are using more than one text, compare and look for common ideas. Sometimes, writing a summary of your reading helps to clarify the information. This technique has been proven to improve retention and understanding, but it can be time consuming.

Step 2. Once you have finished your reading, go back to the questions that you missed. If they still are not clear, consult an expert. Most students are reluctant to approach an instructor with a question that does not relate directly to a class. However, most instructors are glad to answer questions that will improve the chances for their students to obtain a high passing score on the certification examination. Instructors appreciate questions that are specific, well thought out, and which show that the student has done some independent work.

SQ3R

The second method for study is best suited for reviewing your textbooks for further study once you have identified a weakness. It is called the SQ3R and

is presented by Frances P. Robinson in his book *Effective Study*. It makes study reading more efficient and long-term remembering more probable. *SQ3R* stands for *Survey, Question, Read, Recite,* and *Review.* The steps are as follows:

Survey. First, skim through an entire chapter.

1. Think about the title of the chapter. What do you already know about the subject? Write ideas in the margins. Read the conclusion. What better way is there to discover the main ideas of a chapter?
2. Read the headings. These are the main topics that have been developed by the author.
3. Read the captions under the diagrams, charts, and graphs.

Allow approximately 10 to 12 minutes for the survey step. Surveying will help increase your focus and interest in the material.

Question. Write out two or three questions relating to each heading. These should be questions that you believe will be answered within each section. Use the "who, what, when, where, why, and how" application when generating these questions.

Read. Now, read the first section. Keep in mind the questions you have created and read, with a purpose, as quickly as possible.

Recite. At the end of the section, look away from the book for a few seconds. Recite and think about what you have just learned. It is best to recite aloud because hearing the information will help increase your memorization.

Review. Reviewing is a key step if you want to retain the material you have read. Reviewing as you study results in less time needed for test preparation.

Learning to use the SQ3R method is a skill that takes practice. Often, students feel that it takes too long and is too complicated, but its use results in an increase in comprehension, interest, and memorization. The SQ3R method allows you to study at the same time that you are doing your course reading.

Summary

Everyone does not have the same learning style, and, as a result, effective study techniques are not the same for everyone. It is important to choose the method that is best for you, and this will take some experimentation. For instance, some students become frustrated when they cannot comprehend the textbook material while reading when seated at a desk. Sometimes, just getting up and pacing while memorizing can facilitate the learning process if you are having trouble at your desk. Other students learn faster with audio aids. If these are available to you and you are having trouble with learning just from your books, it may be worth the experiment to see if hearing the material will enhance your learning.

Study Groups

While preparing for an examination, properly organizing or attending a study group can be extremely helpful. However, a study group needs to be very focused with a specific agenda for each session. Otherwise, it can be a time waster. Listed below are some important points to keep in mind when organizing and conducting a study group:

1. Limit the group size to four or five people.
2. Select classmates who share your academic goals.
3. Meet the first time to discuss the meeting times, meeting place, and group goals.
4. Select a group leader and a time keeper. The group should meet for 2 to 3 hours for each session to ensure a thorough review.
5. Establish an agenda for each meeting that specifies the topics of discussion. This will save time and lend focus to the group. It ensures that the group reviews all pertinent topics by slotting time for all areas.
6. Establish group norms that define how the group will act. This would include things such as getting there on time, being prepared, and ending on time. It is important to emphasize that all members must do their fair share of the work for the group to gain the maximum benefit.

Study groups are useful to review and compare both lecture and reading notes, to review textbook information together, and to review examination topics. Group sessions are a good time to review the question types used on the certification examination, to discuss test-taking strategies, to help each other design study plans, and to drill or review together all material expected to be on the examination.

The support of a study group is extremely helpful in building self-confidence and in overall preparation for examinations. They are not intended to replace individual study time, but serve as a supplement. If properly utilized, study groups are an enormous asset for test preparation. Finally, when working within a group, many students are more likely to exert their best effort because they are accountable to the other members of the group.

Practice Tests

The practice tests (Chapters 6 and 7) can be used in one of the following two ways: (1) as a way of determining strengths and weaknesses before you go through the review book or (2) as a final preparation for the test after you have done your chapter-by-chapter review.

The practice tests have been designed in an effort to duplicate the experience of taking the certification examination. CBT administers test questions in *random order*, questions are not ordered according to topic. Therefore, the practice test questions in this book are in randomized sequence—just as you will find questions presented on the ARRT CBT. Taking the practice tests will make the process more familiar, so you would not be as nervous when you face the real test. The practice test will help you to determine whether or not you are answering the questions quickly enough, and whether your score is high enough to pass. In summary, the practice tests simply give you a chance to practice. Using these will give you the opportunity to practice for the ARRT CBT examination.

TEST-TAKING STRATEGIES

Time Management

Keeping track of your time and progress is harder than it might first appear. Most of us have been surprised while taking a test by how little time was left. This experience is even more upsetting in the middle of a certification examination. Knowing when there is a problem and knowing what to do about it are the objectives of time management.

Even with your eye on the clock, calculating the time you have left is not always easy. On the radiography examination, you have 3½ hours to finish 220 questions. That gives you about 57 seconds (0.9 minute) per question. In other words, you have to answer approximately 66 questions per hour.

Another way to look at this is by breaking the time into two blocks. If, when you are halfway through the allotted examination time, you have finished a minimum of 110 questions, you are working on time. However, there is one additional complication. Not all questions require equal time to work. It is quite possible to run across a string of difficult questions early in the test and fall behind, and then make up the time with easy questions later in the test. For this reason, being a few questions short at the halfway mark is not a cause for concern. However, if you have finished significantly less than 110 questions after 90 minutes, you may be starting to fall behind.

If you do fall behind, what can you do to catch up? Sometimes, simply seeing that you are behind and trying to work faster will be enough to motivate you to catch up. If not, you have other options. Try to read through the questions and answers a bit faster. If you have checked only one answer as likely to be right, put that choice down immediately; do not reconsider your answer. Always mark your best choice and move forward.

As a rule of thumb, if a fact question (one requiring you to recall a fact) takes more than a minute or two, select your best answer, "mark" the question (CBT has a "mark" button you can click), and go on. You may not skip a question; you must indicate an answer but you may mark the question and return to it later for further consideration. For a calculation problem (one requiring you to calculate some quantity), give yourself an extra minute or two. The CBT examination will indicate the number question you are currently answering, compared to the total number of questions (e.g., number 62 of 220). The computer counts down from your allotted time, and the computer screen will indicate the amount of time you have remaining.

Elimination: Finding the Correct Answer

Good test performance is sometimes determined by the ability to recognize the incorrect answers as well as the correct ones. *Eliminating incorrect answers* (termed *distractors*) not only improves your score, it actually makes the test a more accurate measure of your knowledge.

Eliminating a distractor reduces the possible wrong choices. If your knowledge allows you to eliminate two incorrect responses, your odds of a correct response would be increased from one out of four to one out of two. If you can eliminate three distractors, you would have a 100% probability of getting the right answer. Every distractor you elim-

inate increases your odds of picking the right answer.

Multiple-choice questions usually have one distractor that is obviously wrong, one distractor that is closer to the correct response, and one distractor that is very close to the correct answer. If you know the subject, you can eliminate the distractors that are most incorrect and improve your chances. If you prepare thoroughly, you will be able to eliminate the others. The more you know, the better you will do.

Many books on test-taking suggest complicated systems to eliminate bad answers and rank good ones, but in order to use elimination effectively, you need a procedure that is both quick and simple. For the ARRT CBT examination, you must select an answer in order for the next question to be displayed. If you are unsure of your selection, or just want to come back later to review it, you are able to *mark* the question. All the questions you have marked in this manner will be displayed one by one after you have completed all 220 questions. There is an optional tutorial that you may take prior to starting the examination. Taking the tutorial is a good way to become more familiar with navigating through the examination with greater ease and assurance.

Changing Answers

Everyone has had the experience of trying to remember the answer to a question without success and then *finding that piece of information further along in the test*. A problem that you stare at for an hour without progress might seem simple if you go on to other problems and come back to it later. Very often, another question will jog your memory; this technique can work for you during the CBT examination.

If you are unsure of the correct way to answer a question:

1. If one of the answers seems better than the rest, put it down and mark the question for future reference. Come back and check the question at the end if you have time.
2. If you can eliminate two of the possible answers, make an educated guess between the two remaining possibilities. Then, mark the question for future reference.
3. Ask yourself, "Will more time really help me answer this question?" If your answer is no, do the best you can with what you know,

using the process of elimination and making an educated guess. Again, mark the question for future reference so that you can reread it if there is time at the end.

Guessing

You have probably been given a great deal of information and advice about guessing on tests. Most of what you have been told may be confusing or contradictory. It may make the problem easier to think in terms of rolling a die. Imagine a game in which you get a point every time the number 1, for example, comes up. How could you improve your score in this game? One way would be to roll the die as many times as you could. Another way would be to reduce the number of sides on the die so the "right" side would be more likely to come up; this way is called *the process of elimination*, and it plays a good part in test taking when you are unsure of the correct response.

Although we do *not* suggest guessing as an effective method of test taking, we do recognize that there will be times when it can be effective for you. Keep in mind the following things if you need to use this method:

1. The process of elimination will help you significantly in determining the right answer. Use this technique to narrow down the possible choices.
2. *Mark* the question so that, if you have time, you can come back to it. It is possible that the correct response may reveal itself through a question further ahead on the test.
3. Remember that guessing really does not work as an effective strategy by itself. You will need to study hard and use guessing in conjunction with other methods for it to be effective.

PRACTICE TESTS

Taking the Practice Test

In order to use the practice test to determine how long the test will take you to complete or how high you will score, you must take it under conditions matching, as closely as possible, the actual test conditions. If you try to eat supper while taking the test, take a 5-hour break in the middle of the test, or stop after every question to look up the answer, you will not get a clear picture of your current standing or

potential to pass the examination. Following are some suggestions on how you can get the most out of the practice test:

1. Keep your schedule completely free. Find a time and a place that will guarantee that you will not be disturbed for the duration of the test. Most libraries work well for this purpose, as do unoccupied classrooms if you can get access to them. If you have to take the test at home, make sure that you would not be bothered by friends or family.
2. Minimize your distractions, do not take phone calls, and do not try to watch TV or concentrate on anything else other than the test.
3. Start at a predetermined time. You may choose to take the practice test at the same time of day your test will be given at the testing center.
4. Bring everything you will need to take the test. The CBT test center will supply you with scrap paper and a simple nonprogrammable calculator. You must remember to *request* a calculator from the testing center personnel during your check-in at the center.
5. Approach the practice tests with the same strategies and attitudes that you plan on using with the actual examination. (Rereading the section on test strategies would be a good idea.)
6. Note time-consuming questions. While taking the test, mark the questions that take longer than 2 or 3 minutes. Do not spend too much time on any one question.
7. Note how far you get. You should be able to finish the whole practice test in the allotted time, but if you do run out of time, draw a line across the test book to show how far you got and then finish the rest of the test.

Checking Your Results

You should be able to finish all of the questions with enough time left over to go back and check your answers on those problems you marked as difficult. Your score should be at least 160 correct answers (80%). If you fail at either of these two goals, you need to go over the test carefully and try to analyze your problem.

Two questions that you can address while analyzing a problem are "Was there a common factor in the questions that gave me trouble?" and "What were the subspecialties of the questions that I missed?" If you keep missing the same type of question, the problem could be easy to fix. Try going back and reworking the section of the book that corresponds to that topic.

Review your test-taking techniques. Did you spend too much time on a few questions? Did you spend too much time rereading answers that you had already eliminated as potential answers? If the answer to either of these questions is *yes*, you might want to review the earlier section on test strategies.

TEST STRATEGY CHECKLIST

1. ELIMINATE, CHOOSE, AND MARK
   Eliminate known incorrect answers, choose the best of the remaining, *mark* to return to later.
2. DO 50 EVERY 45
   Try to answer at least 50 questions every 45 minutes.
3. MARK UNCERTAIN ANSWERS
   Mark questions you guessed on so you can come back and double-check them.

PREPARING FOR SUCCESS IN CBT

Reducing the unknown to a minimum is one of the best ways to prepare for success in any endeavor. This will be discussed later in the stress-reduction section. Before proceeding to methods for improving your test performance, the following is a review of CBT facts that will help you better understand what to expect:

- You have the option to review a tutorial before starting your test, and it is a good idea to do that.
- Your responses can be given by using either the mouse or particular keystrokes that the tutorial will explain.
- The screen will show your name and the examination you are taking (e.g., radiography and advanced mammography).
- The computer screen will let you know what question you are currently working on, out of the total number of questions (e.g., number 62 of 220).
- The computer counts down your allotted time and the computer screen will indicate the amount of time you have remaining.
- One question at a time will appear on the computer screen.
- You will indicate your answer (A, B, C, or D) by clicking on a little circle in front of the corresponding letter.

- The bar along the bottom of the screen will probably have 4 or 5 buttons on which you may click.
- A click on the "Previous" button brings you back to the last question you answered.
- A click on the "Next" button advances you to the question that follows.
- A click on the "Mark" button will signal that you want to look at that question again after you have completed answering all 200 questions.
- You may change your answer while you are working on any one question, or when you return to the question later.
- You must indicate an answer to a question before you can advance to the next question.
- When your "marked" questions are returned to you for review, you may change the answer or leave it as it is. You will then click "unmark" to indicate that you are satisfied with your answer and do not need to see that question again.
- Once you have reviewed and unmarked all your marked questions, the screen will tell you that all your questions have been answered and give you the opportunity to return to review any and/or all questions.
- A "Comment" button appears with each question and allows you to communicate a comment to the ARRT about that particular question. Your comments will be welcome and can be useful and constructive, but any comment should be concise because you will be using your running time.

OPTIMIZING YOUR RESULTS

When you take the radiography examination, two factors determine your score:

- Your knowledge of the subject
- Your performance on the examination

Of the two, knowledge is the key element needed for success. *Performance is harder to guarantee.* For some people, it seems to come naturally. These people apply test-taking strategies almost unconsciously, concentrating all their attention on the test. For the rest of the population (which includes most people), standardized tests are some of the most stressful and unpleasant experiences that they will ever have to face.

Fortunately, it is possible to significantly improve your performance on tests, even if you have been taking tests all of your life with no apparent improvement. By mastering the following three areas, you can have better results and greatly reduce the trauma of test taking:

1. Know your test strategies
2. Learn to manage your stress
3. Avoid surprises on the day of the test

The important points for each of these areas are explained in detail in the following sections and are summarized in checklists included at the end of each part of the Introduction. These checklists are designed so that you can read them on the day of the test to reassure yourself that you have not forgotten anything.

Test-Taking Strategies

The strategies recommended earlier serve two purposes: (1) to give you a simple, systematic way of eliminating bad choices and improving your odds of getting a correct response and (2) to help you manage your time most efficiently during the test.

Managing Stress

Over the past 30 or so years, educators have become increasingly concerned about the problems of test anxiety and excessive stress that prevent students from doing their best on examinations. In the following sections, you will learn some basics about the nature of stress, the difference between good stress and bad stress, and some management techniques. All of the items listed will be helpful in reducing test anxiety, but the most important point for you to remember is that you are well prepared for the test you are about to take and the odds of your doing well are very good.

Where You Stand

The best way to reduce test anxiety is to address the following points:

1. Know the subject
2. Master a test-taking routine
3. Avoid surprises
4. Understand the role of stress in test taking
5. Practice relaxation techniques

The Stress Curve

Recently, stress has received national attention. Magazines discuss it, doctors warn against it, commercials promise to reduce it, and seminars claim to eliminate it. Stress is often treated as a psychological

cancer. There is, however, another aspect of stress that receives less attention. In demanding situations requiring optimal performance, moderate stress is not only natural, it is actually helpful. The relationship between stress and performance is called the stress curve; the most important aspect of the curve is the location of the maxima. The maxima is the point of optimal performance, which occurs somewhere between too much stress and no stress at all.

There are plenty of familiar examples of stress improving performance. Athletes often set personal records during pressure situations such as playoff games or international events. Actors give their best performances and musicians play or sing best before an audience. You can probably think of personal examples as well. Most of us have surprised ourselves at one time or another by doing better than we expected under pressure.

How to Recognize Good Stress

If everyone dealt with stress equally well and experienced the same level of stress in the same situation, setting up guidelines for optimal stress levels would be easy. Unfortunately, everyone handles stress differently, and determining what level of stress is best must be judged on an individual basis. Given the importance of the radiography examination and the amount of time you have spent preparing for it, there is little chance of your stress level being too low when you sit for the test.

How do you know if you have too much stress? Feeling nervous does not indicate excessive stress. You are just as likely to feel nervous when you are at your optimal stress level. Stress is excessive when it interferes with the test-taking process. If you have trouble reading the questions, if you lose your place because you are worrying about the test, or if you are too distracted to follow the test strategies you have been practicing, you are experiencing test anxiety.

Relaxation Techniques

Whether or not you anticipate problems with stress, it is a good idea to take a couple of minutes to relax before the test. Stretch your muscles, take deep, slow breaths, and try to think about something unrelated to the test. If, during the test, you have trouble working effectively because of stress, stop, close your eyes, and count to five while taking some deep, slow breaths. Remind yourself that you are extremely well prepared for this test. Not many people realize that breathing and anxiety are related, or that a deep-breathing relaxation exercise can be helpful in reducing anxiety.

When you feel anxious, you tend to tighten your chest muscles. This results in breathing changes, with movement predominantly in your upper chest rather than your lower abdomen. Breathing this way often leads to undesirable conditions:

1. A reduction of oxygen in your blood, which can affect the way you think and lead to anxiety or fatigue.
2. Too much oxygen in your blood, resulting in an uncomfortable condition called *hyperventilation*.

It is important, therefore, to learn how to control your breathing, which, in turn, will result in relaxation. When attempting the following breathing exercise, do not try too hard to relax—it can work against you. Instead, try to be as peaceful as possible.

First, take a deep, full breath and exhale fully and completely. Next, inhale again, mentally counting from 1 to 4 while breathing in. Hold this breath in while again counting from 1 to 4. Then, begin fully exhaling, while slowly counting from 1 to 8. Repeat this sequence four times. If you run out of breath before reaching number 8, take deeper breaths and exhale more slowly. If you can learn this technique ahead of time, you can use it while in the examination room without anyone else knowing.

If the stress continues, try to think less about what you are doing. After practicing on 1,200 questions, you have developed a kind of "automatic pilot," which will allow you to answer questions almost by reflex. Of course, this is not the best way to take the test, but if you are faced with serious stress problems, it is an option.

Avoiding Surprises
The Week Before the Test

You have spent the past 2 to 4 years studying radiography, and the past 2 to 4 months reviewing for this examination. You probably know a great deal more than you think you do. Your top priority now should be getting yourself up to your best testing performance. If you follow these suggestions, you should have a good start.

Take Care of Yourself. When you take the test, you want to be as healthy and well rested as possible. The time it takes to get enough sleep, take a walk, or prepare a balanced meal is better spent than hours of last-minute cramming.

Reread This Introduction. This may be unnecessary advice, but it is worth mentioning. Pay close attention to the figures and checklists.

Gather Your Supplies. You want to be sure to get everything you need, but, almost as importantly, you want everything organized so that you can avoid extra effort and worry. You might want to bring a sweater or light jacket. This may seem like a strange item, particularly if your test is taken in the summer, but an uncomfortably cold room is extremely distracting, and many public buildings have a wide variation in temperature from room to room. A sweater or windbreaker is a quick, easy solution. Avoid bringing a large purse or other large bundle. Lockers are available for stowing your personal items not allowed in the CBT room, but they are often fairly small lockers and will not accommodate a very large purse or other large package.

Scout the Location. It is a *very* good idea to visit the location of the examination if possible. Getting lost on the morning of a test will add unwanted stress. Keep in mind the following questions: (1) What is the best route to the examination? (2) Where is the parking? (3) Where are the doors to the building? If possible, go into the building and look around.

Treat Yourself. Go out and do something special. See a movie. Eat out. Go for a drive. Just let yourself unwind.

The Day of the Test

There are few things more irritating than being told not to worry when you feel like worrying, but not worrying is the best thing to do. To help you avoid worrying, two checklists have been included, one physical checklist (things you need to bring) and one mental checklist (things you need to remember). Check off each item and put it out of your mind. Knowing you have both mentally and physically prepared will help you to relax before the examination.

You should plan to arrive a few minutes early. Many test centers require you to be there 30 minutes ahead of the scheduled test time.

You will probably want to eat a light meal before taking the test. Digestion tends to slow down when a person is under stress, so a large meal is, in most cases, a bad idea. You will also want to avoid excessive stimulants (and caffeine is definitely considered a stimulant).

This brings up another point. Although you want to be well rested and alert, you should be careful not to disrupt your normal routine any more than necessary. Getting extra rest, eating light, and avoiding stimulants are relative suggestions—relative to your habits and lifestyle. *Do not make drastic changes on the day of the test.* Get an extra half hour or hour of sleep. Eat a lighter meal than you usually would. If you drink coffee, drink a little less than normal.

When you get to the testing center, take a few minutes to relax. Walk around. Stretch your muscles. Remind yourself that you have put a great deal of work into doing well on this test and that work is the main factor for determining success.

PHYSICAL CHECKLIST (What to Bring)

1. Your admission ticket
2. Two current IDs
3. Sweater or windbreaker

MENTAL CHECKLIST

1. Remind yourself that you are well prepared
2. Take the computer tutorial
3. Use your test-taking strategies
4. Focus on the test, not on the surroundings
5. After you have finished, use the same strategies to go over any questions you marked for review

---

REFERENCES

Benson H, Klipper M. *The Relaxation Response.* New York: Avon Books; 1990.

Bosworth S, Brisk M. *Learning Skills for the Science Student.* FL: H&H Publishing Company; 1986.

Bragstad B, Stumpf S. *A Guidebook for Teaching: Study Skills and Motivation.* Boston, MA: Allyn and Bacon; 1982.

Coffman S. *How to Survive at College.* IN: College Town Press; 1988.

Hamachek A. *Coping in College: A Guide for Academic Success.* Boston, MA: Allyn and Bacon; 1994.

Krantz H, Kemmelman J. *Keys to Reading and Study Skills.* New York: Holt, Rinehart & Winston; 1985.

Nieves L. *Coping in College.* Princeton, NJ: Educational Testing Service; 1984.

Palav S. *Learning Strategies for Allied Health Students.* Philadelphia: WB Saunders; 1995.

Robinson F. *Effective Study.* New York: Harper and Row; 1970.

Saia DA. *Radiography Program Review Exam Preparation.* 4th ed. New York: McGraw-Hill; 2006.

Vitale B, Nugent P. *Test Success: Test-Taking Techniques for the Health Care Student.* Philadelphia: FA Davis; 1996.

Master Bibliography

On the last line of each answer/explanation, there appears the last name of the author or editor of one of the publications listed here, along with a number or numbers indicating the correct page or range of pages where information relating to the correct answer may be found. For example, *(Bushong, p 45)* refers to page 45 of Bushong's *Radiologic Science for Technologists*.

Adler AM, Carlton RR. *Introduction to Radiologic Sciences and Patient Care*. 4th ed. St. Louis, MO: Saunders Elsevier; 2007.

ASRT Code of Ethics. http://www.asrt.org/content/RTs/CodeofEthics/Code_Of_Ethics.aspx.

BEIR Report VII. http://dels.nas.edu/dels/rpt_briefs/beir_vii_final.pdf.

Ballinger PW, Frank ED. *Merrill's Atlas of Radiographic Positions and Radiologic Procedures*, Vols 1, 2, and 3. 10th ed. St. Louis, MO: Mosby; 2004.

Bontrager KL, Lampignano JP. *Textbook of Radiographic Positioning and Related Anatomy*. 6th ed. St Louis, MO: Mosby; 2005.

Bontrager KL, Lampignano JP. *Textbook of Radiographic Positioning and Related Anatomy*. 7th ed. St Louis, MO: Mosby; 2010.

Bontrager KL. *Textbook of Radiographic Positioning and Related Anatomy*. 6th ed. St. Louis, MO: Mosby; 2005.

Bushong SC. *Radiologic Science for Technologists*. 8th ed. St. Louis, MO: Mosby; 2004.

Bushong SC. *Radiologic Science for Technologists*. 9th ed. St. Louis, MO: Mosby; 2008.

Bushberg JT, Seibert JA, Leidholdt EM, Boone JM. *The Essential Physics of Medical Imaging*. 2nd ed. Baltimore, MD: Lippincott Williams & Wilkins; 2002.

Carlton RR, Adler AM. *Principles of Radiographic Imaging*. 4th ed. Albany, NY: Delmar; 2006.

Carter C, Vealé B. *Digital Radiography and PACS*. 1st ed revised. Mosby Elsevier; 2010.

Chen MYM, Pope TL, Ott DJ. *Basic Radiology*. 1st ed. McGraw-Hill; 2004.

Dowd SB, Tilson ER. *Practical Radiation Protection and Applied Radiobiology*. 2nd ed. Philadelphia: WB Saunders; 1999.

Ehrlich RA, Daly JA. *Patient Care in Radiography*. 7th ed. St. Louis, MO: Mosby; 2009.

Ehrlich RA, McCloskey ED. *Patient Care in Radiography*. 6th ed. St. Louis, MO: Mosby; 2004.

Fauber TL. *Radiographic Imaging and Exposure*. 2nd ed. St. Louis, MO: Mosby; 2004.

Fauber TL. *Radiographic Imaging and Exposure*. 3rd ed. Mosby; 2009.

Fosbinder RA, Kelsey CA. *Essentials of Radiologic Science*. 1st ed. New York: McGraw-Hill; 2002.

Fosbinder R, Orth D. *Essentials of Radiologic Science*. Baltimore, MD: Lippincott Williams & Wilkins; 2012.

Frank ED, Long BW, Smith BJ. *Merrill's Atlas of Radiographic Positioning and Procedures*. Vols 1, 2, and 3. 11th ed. St. Louis, MO: Mosby; 2007.

Fuji Medical Systems, CR Users Guide, 1999.

Fuji Photo Film Co., Ltd *(FCR) Fuji Computed Radiography*, Minato-Ku, Japan, 2002.

Gurley LT, Callaway WJ. *Introduction to Radiologic Technology*. 6th ed. St. Louis, MO: Mosby; 2006.

Haus AG, Jaskulski SM. *Basics of Film Processing in Medical Imaging*. 1st ed. Madison, WI: Medical Physics Publishing; 1997.

Hendee WR, Ritenour ER. *Medical Imaging Physics*. 4th ed. New York: Wiley-Liss, Inc; 2002.

Lazo DL. *Fundamentals of Sectional Anatomy: An Imaging Approach* 1sdt ed. Thomson, Delmar Learning; 2005.

Laudicina P. *Applied Pathology for Radiographers*. Philadelphia: WB Saunders; 1989.

Martini FH, Bartholomew EF. *Essentials of Anatomy & Physiology*. 4th ed. San Francisco, CA: Pearson Education, Inc; 2007.

Mills WR. The relation of bodily habitus to visceral form, tonus, and motility. *Am J Roentgenol* 1917;4: 155–169.

McKinney WEJ. *Radiographic Processing and Quality Control*. Philadelphia: Lippincott; 1988.

NCRP Report No 116. *Recommendations on Limits for Exposure to Ionizing Radiation*. NCRP; 1987.

NCRP Report No 99. *Quality Assurance for Diagnostic Imaging*. NCRP, 1990.

ARRT. *New Test Item Format for Radiography Examination*. http://www.arrt.org/index.html?content= eduguide/news.htm. Accessed August 2, 2007.

Peart O. *A&L Mammography Review*. 1st ed. New York: McGraw-Hill; 2002.

Peart O. *Mammography and Breast Imaging: Just the Facts*. New York: McGraw-Hill; 2005.

Publication Dissemination, Education and Information Division, National Institute for Occupational Safety and Health, 4676 Columbia Parkway, Cincinnati, OH 45226; 1998.

Purtilo R. *Ethical Dimensions in the Health Professions*. 4th ed. Philadelphia: WB Saunders; 2005.

Romans, LE. *Computed Tomography for Technologists, A Comprehensive Text*. Baltimore, MD: Wolters Kluwer Health/Lippincott Williams & Wilkins, 2011.

Saia DA. *Radiography PREP*. 4th ed. New York: McGraw-Hill; 2006.

Saia DA. *Radiography PREP*. 5th ed. New York: McGraw-Hill; 2009.

Seeram E. *Digital Radiography: An Introduction*. Delmar: CENGAGE Learning, 2011.

Selman J. *The Fundamentals of Imaging Physics and Radiobiology*. 9th ed. Springfield, IL: Charles C Thomas; 2000.

Shephard CT. *Radiographic Image Production and Manipulation*. 1st ed. New York: McGraw-Hill; 2003.

Statkiewicz-Sherer MA, Visconti PJ. *Radiation Protection in Medical Radiography*. 5th ed. St. Louis, MO: Mosby; 2006.

Statkiewicz-Sherer MA, Visconti PJ, Ritenour ER. *Radiation Protection in Medical Radiography*. 6th ed. St. Louis, MO: Mosby; 2011.

Thomas CL, ed. *Taber's Cyclopedic Medical Dictionary*. 20th ed. Philadelphia: F A Davis; 2005.

Thompson MA, Hattaway MP, Hall JD, et al. *Principles of Imaging Science and Protection*. 1st ed. Philadelphia: WB Saunders; 1994.

Torres LS, Linn-Watson Norcutt TA, Dutton AG. *Basic Medical Techniques and Patient Care in Imaging Technology*. 6th ed. Philadelphia: Lippincott; 2003.

Tortora GJ, Derrickson B. *Principles of Anatomy and Physiology*. 11th ed. Hoboken, NJ: John Wiley & Sons, Inc; 2006.

Tortora GJ, Derrickson B. *Principles of Anatomy and Physiology*. 12th ed. Hoboken, NJ: John Wiley & Sons, Inc; 2009.

Tortora GJ, Derrickson B. *Introduction to the Human Body*. 8th ed. Hoboken, NJ: Wiley, 2010.

Towsley-Cook DM, Young TA. *Ethical and Legal Issues for Imaging Professionals*. 2nd ed. St. Louis, MO: Mosby; 2007.

Travis EL. *Primer of Medical Radiobiology*. 3rd ed. Chicago, IL: Year Book; 1997.

Wilson BG. *Ethics and Basic Law for Medical Imaging Professionals*. Philadelphia: FA Davis; 1997.

Wolbarst AB. *Physics of Radiology*. Stamford, CT: Appleton & Lange; 2003.

Wolbarst AB. *Physics of Radiology*. 2nd ed. Madison, WI: Medical Physics Publishing; 2005.

CHAPTER 1

Patient Care and Education
Questions

DIRECTIONS (Questions 1 through 130): Each of the numbered items or incomplete statements in this section is followed by answers or by completions of the statement. Select the *one* lettered answer or completion that is *best* in each case.

1. When a patient with one strong side and one weak side is being assisted onto an x-ray table, the radiographer should

   (A) position the weaker side closer to the table
   (B) position the stronger side closer to the table
   (C) let the patient manage without assistance
   (D) lift the patient carefully onto the table

2. Honor Code violations that can prevent a radiography student from meeting ARRT certification requirements include

   1. failing one or more courses in the radiography program
   2. being suspended from the radiography program
   3. being dismissed/expelled from a radiography program

   (A) 1 only
   (B) 1 and 2 only
   (C) 2 and 3 only
   (D) 1, 2, and 3

3. For medicolegal reasons, radiographic images are required to include all the following information *except*

   (A) the patient's name and/or identification number
   (B) the patient's birth date
   (C) a right- or left-side marker
   (D) the date of the examination

4. A radiographer who discloses confidential patient information to unauthorized individuals can be found guilty of

   (A) libel
   (B) invasion of privacy
   (C) slander
   (D) defamation

5. An iatrogenic infection is one caused by

   (A) physician intervention
   (B) blood-borne pathogens
   (C) chemotherapy
   (D) infected droplets

6. A vasomotor effect experienced after injection of a contrast agent is characterized by all of the following symptoms *except*

   (A) nausea
   (B) syncope
   (C) hypotension
   (D) anxiety

7. The higher the gauge number of an intravenous (IV) needle,

   (A) the larger is its diameter
   (B) the greater is its length
   (C) the smaller is its diameter
   (D) the shorter its length

8. Demonstration of which anatomic structures require(s) ingestion of barium sulfate suspension?

   1. Duodenum
   2. Pylorus
   3. Ilium

   (A) 1 only
   (B) 1 and 2 only
   (C) 2 and 3 only
   (D) 1, 2, and 3

9. Which of the following drugs is used to treat dysrhythmias?

   (A) Epinephrine
   (B) Lidocaine
   (C) Nitroglycerin
   (D) Verapamil

10. Examples of COPD include

    1. bronchitis
    2. pulmonary emphysema
    3. asthma

    (A) 1 only
    (B) 1 and 2 only
    (C) 2 and 3 only
    (D) 1, 2, and 3

11. Administration of contrast agents for radiographic demonstration of the spinal canal is performed by which of the following parenteral routes?

    (A) Subcutaneous
    (B) Intravenous
    (C) Intramuscular
    (D) Intrathecal

12. Accidental injection of medication or contrast medium into tissues around a vein is termed

    (A) extravasation
    (B) hematoma
    (C) venipuncture
    (D) collateral circulation

13. Which of the following can be transmitted via infected blood?

    1. HBV
    2. AIDS
    3. TB

    (A) 1 only
    (B) 1 and 2 only
    (C) 2 and 3 only
    (D) 1, 2, and 3

14. The mechanical device used to correct an ineffectual cardiac rhythm is a

    (A) defibrillator
    (B) cardiac monitor
    (C) crash cart
    (D) resuscitation bag

15. You have encountered a person who is apparently unconscious. Although you open his airway, there is no rise and fall of the chest, and you can hear no breath sounds. You should

    (A) begin mouth-to-mouth rescue breathing, giving two full breaths
    (B) proceed with the Heimlich maneuver
    (C) begin external chest compressions at a rate of 80 to 100 compressions/min
    (D) begin external chest compressions at a rate of at least 100 compressions/min

16. In classifying IV contrast agents, the total number of dissolved particles in solution per kilogram of water defines

    (A) osmolality
    (B) toxicity
    (C) viscosity
    (D) miscibility

17. Which of the following is a violation of correct sterile technique?

   (A) Gowns are considered sterile in the front down to the waist, including the arms.
   (B) Sterile gloves must be kept above the waist level.
   (C) Persons in sterile dress should pass each other face to face.
   (D) A sterile field should not be left unattended.

18. Misunderstandings between cultures can happen as a result of

   1. looking directly into someone's eyes
   2. the use of certain gestures
   3. standing too close while speaking to another

   (A) 1 only
   (B) 1 and 2 only
   (C) 2 and 3 only
   (D) 1, 2, and 3

19. The legal doctrine *respondeat superior* means which of the following?

   (A) A matter settled by precedent.
   (B) A thing or matter settled by justice.
   (C) The thing speaks for itself.
   (D) Let the master answer.

20. Some proteins in latex can produce mild to severe allergic reactions. Medical equipment that could contain latex includes

   1. tourniquets
   2. enema tips
   3. catheters

   (A) 1 only
   (B) 1 and 2 only
   (C) 2 and 3 only
   (D) 1, 2, and 3

21. Conditions in which there is a lack of normal bone calcification include

   1. rickets
   2. osteomalacia
   3. osteoarthritis

   (A) 1 only
   (B) 1 and 2 only
   (C) 2 and 3 only
   (D) 1, 2, and 3

22. A quantity of medication introduced intravenously over a period of time is termed

   (A) an IV push
   (B) an infusion
   (C) a bolus
   (D) a hypodermic

23. Anaphylactic shock manifests early symptoms that include

   1. dysphagia
   2. itching of palms and soles
   3. constriction of the throat

   (A) 1 only
   (B) 2 only
   (C) 2 and 3 only
   (D) 1, 2, and 3

24. The legal document or individual authorized to make an individual's health care decisions, should the individual be unable to make them for himself or herself, is the

   1. advance health care directive
   2. living will
   3. health care proxy

   (A) 1 only
   (B) 1 and 2 only
   (C) 2 and 3 only
   (D) 1, 2, and 3

25. In which stage of infection do the infective microbes begin to multiply?

(A) Latent period
(B) Incubation period
(C) Disease phase
(D) Convalescent phase

26. When performing cardiopulmonary resuscitation (CPR) on an infant, it is recommended that the number of compressions per minute, compared with that for an adult,

(A) remain the same
(B) double
(C) decrease
(D) increase

27. All the following statements regarding hand hygiene and skin care are correct *except*

(A) hands should be cleansed before and after each patient examination
(B) faucets should be opened and closed with paper towels
(C) hands should be smooth and free from chapping
(D) any cracks or abrasions should be left uncovered to facilitate healing

28. A patient suffering from orthopnea would experience the *least* discomfort in which body position?

(A) Fowler
(B) Trendelenburg
(C) Recumbent
(D) Erect

29. When a patient arrives in the radiology department with a urinary Foley catheter bag, it is important to

(A) place the drainage bag above the level of the bladder
(B) place the drainage bag at the same level as the bladder
(C) place the drainage bag below the level of the bladder
(D) clamp the Foley catheter

30. Instruments required to assess vital signs include

1. a stethoscope
2. a sphygmomanometer
3. a watch with a second hand

(A) 1 only
(B) 1 and 2 only
(C) 1 and 3 only
(D) 1, 2, and 3

31. Hirschsprung disease, or congenital megacolon, is related to which of the following age groups?

(A) Neonate
(B) Toddler
(C) Adolescent
(D) Adult

32. Possible side effects of an iodinated contrast medium that is administered intravenously include all the following *except*

1. a warm, flushed feeling
2. altered taste
3. rash and hives

(A) 1 only
(B) 3 only
(C) 2 and 3 only
(D) 1, 2, and 3

33. In the blood pressure reading 145/75 mm Hg, what does 145 represent?

1. The phase of relaxation of the cardiac muscle tissue
2. The phase of contraction of the cardiac muscle tissue
3. A higher-than-average diastolic pressure

(A) 1 only
(B) 2 only
(C) 1 and 3 only
(D) 2 and 3 only

34. Facsimile transmission of health information is

1. not permitted
2. permitted for urgently needed patient care
3. permitted for third-party payer hospitalization certification

(A) 1 only
(B) 2 only
(C) 2 and 3 only
(D) 1, 2, and 3

35. Forms of intentional misconduct include

1. slander
2. invasion of privacy
3. negligence

(A) 1 only
(B) 2 only
(C) 1 and 2 only
(D) 1, 2, and 3

36. Which of the following statements is correct with regard to assisting a patient from a wheelchair to an x-ray table?

(A) The wheelchair should be parallel with the x-ray table.
(B) The patient's weaker side should be closer to the x-ray table.
(C) The wheelchair should directly face the x-ray table.
(D) The patient's stronger side should be closer to the x-ray table.

37. In her studies on death and dying, Dr. Elizabeth Kubler-Ross described the first stage of the grieving process as

(A) denial
(B) anger
(C) bargaining
(D) depression

38. You and a fellow radiographer have received an unconscious patient from a motor vehicle accident. As you perform the examination, it is important that you

1. refer to the patient by name
2. make only those statements that you would make with a conscious patient
3. reassure the patient about what you are doing

(A) 1 only
(B) 1 and 2 only
(C) 2 and 3 only
(D) 1, 2, and 3

39. A cathartic is used to

(A) inhibit coughing
(B) promote elimination of urine
(C) stimulate defecation
(D) induce vomiting

40. When radiographing the elderly, it is helpful to

1. move quickly
2. address them by their full name
3. give straightforward instructions

(A) 1 only
(B) 1 and 2 only
(C) 2 and 3 only
(D) 1, 2, and 3

41. What is the needle angle usually recommended for intramuscular injections?

(A) 90 degrees
(B) 75 degrees
(C) 45 degrees
(D) 15 degrees

42. How should the wheelchair footrests be positioned as a patient is assisted into or out of a wheelchair?

(A) Accessible to the foot
(B) Moved aside
(C) Parallel to the floor
(D) Available for support

43. An esophagram would most likely be requested for patients with which of the following esophageal disorders/symptoms?

   1. Varices
   2. Achalasia
   3. Dysphasia

   (A) 1 only
   (B) 1 and 2 only
   (C) 1 and 3 only
   (D) 1, 2, and 3

44. Which of the following may be used to effectively reduce the viscosity of contrast media?

   (A) Warming
   (B) Refrigeration
   (C) Storage at normal room temperature
   (D) Storage in a cool, dry place

45. The type of shock often associated with pulmonary embolism or myocardial infarction is classified as

   (A) neurogenic
   (B) cardiogenic
   (C) hypovolemic
   (D) septic

46. Which of the following must be included in a patient's medical record or chart?

   1. Diagnostic and therapeutic orders
   2. Medical history
   3. Informed consent

   (A) 1 and 2 only
   (B) 1 and 3 only
   (C) 2 and 3 only
   (D) 1, 2, and 3

47. What type of precautions prevent the spread of infectious agents in droplet form?

   (A) Contact precautions
   (B) Airborne precautions
   (C) Protective isolation
   (D) Strict isolation

48. Which of the following conditions must be met in order for patient consent to be valid?

   1. The patient must sign the consent form before receiving sedation.
   2. The physician named on the consent form must perform the procedure.
   3. All the blanks on the consent form must be filled in before the patient signs the form.

   (A) 1 and 2 only
   (B) 1 and 3 only
   (C) 2 and 3 only
   (D) 1, 2, and 3

49. The Heimlich maneuver is used if a patient is

   (A) in cardiac arrest
   (B) choking
   (C) having a seizure
   (D) suffering from hiccups

50. Each of the following is an example of a fomite *except*

   (A) a doorknob
   (B) a tick
   (C) a spoon
   (D) an x-ray table

51. Which of the following legal phrases defines a circumstance in which both the health care provider's and the patient's actions contributed to an injurious outcome?

   (A) Intentional misconduct
   (B) Contributory negligence
   (C) Gross negligence
   (D) None of the above

52. What is the *first* treatment for extravasation of contrast media during an IV injection?

   (A) Apply a hot compress.
   (B) Apply a cold compress.
   (C) Apply pressure to the vein until bleeding stops.
   (D) Remove the needle and locate a sturdier vein immediately.

53. Which of the following diastolic pressure readings might indicate hypertension?

    (A) 40 mm Hg
    (B) 60 mm Hg
    (C) 80 mm Hg
    (D) 100 mm Hg

54. To reduce the back strain that can result from moving heavy objects, the radiographer should

    (A) hold the object away from his or her body when lifting
    (B) bend at the waist and pull
    (C) pull the object
    (D) push the object

55. All the following statements regarding oxygen delivery are true *except*

    (A) oxygen is classified as a drug and must be prescribed by a physician
    (B) the rate of delivery and mode of delivery must be part of a physician order for oxygen
    (C) oxygen may be ordered continuously or as needed by the patient
    (D) none of the above; they are all true

56. If an emergency trauma patient experiences hemorrhaging from a leg injury, the radiographer should

    1. apply pressure to the bleeding site
    2. call the emergency department for assistance
    3. apply a pressure bandage and complete the examination

    (A) 1 and 2 only
    (B) 1 and 3 only
    (C) 2 and 3 only
    (D) 1, 2, and 3

57. Gas-producing powder or crystals usually are ingested preliminary to which of the following examinations?

    (A) Double-contrast barium enema (BE)
    (B) Double-contrast gastrointestinal (GI) series
    (C) Oral cholecystogram
    (D) IV urogram (IVU)

58. According to the CDC, all the following precaution guidelines are true *except*

    (A) airborne precautions require that the patient wear a mask
    (B) masks are indicated when caring for patients on MRSA precautions
    (C) patients under MRSA precautions require a negative-pressure room
    (D) gloves are indicated when caring for a patient on droplet precautions

59. When disposing of contaminated needles, they are placed in a special container using what procedure?

    (A) Recap the needle, remove the syringe, and dispose of the needle.
    (B) Do not recap the needle, remove the syringe, and dispose of the needle.
    (C) Recap the needle and dispose of the entire syringe.
    (D) Do not recap the needle and dispose of the entire syringe.

60. You are working in the outpatient department and receive a patient who is complaining of pain in the right hip joint; however, the requisition asks for a left femur examination. What should you do?

    (A) Perform a right hip examination.
    (B) Perform a left femur examination.
    (C) Perform both a right hip and a left femur examination.
    (D) Check with the referring physician.

61. While performing mobile radiography on a patient, you note that the requisition is for a chest image to check placement of a Swan–Ganz catheter. A Swan–Ganz catheter is a(n)

    (A) pacemaker
    (B) chest tube
    (C) IV catheter
    (D) urinary catheter

62. Which of the following examinations require(s) restriction of a patient's diet?

    1. Barium enema
    2. Pyelogram
    3. Metastatic survey

    (A) 1 only
    (B) 1 and 2 only
    (C) 1 and 3 only
    (D) 2 and 3 only

63. The radiographer must perform which of the following procedures prior to entering a contact isolation room with a mobile x-ray unit?

    1. Put on gown and gloves only.
    2. Put on gown, gloves, mask, and cap.
    3. Clean the mobile x-ray unit.

    (A) 1 only
    (B) 2 only
    (C) 1 and 3 only
    (D) 2 and 3 only

64. Examples of nasogastric (NG) tubes include

    1. Swan–Ganz
    2. Salem-sump
    3. Levin

    (A) 1 and 2 only
    (B) 1 and 3 only
    (C) 2 and 3 only
    (D) 1, 2, and 3

65. All the following are central venous lines *except*

    (A) a Port-a-Cath
    (B) a PICC
    (C) a Swan–Ganz catheter
    (D) a Salem-sump

66. The *most* effective method of sterilization is

    (A) dry heat
    (B) moist heat
    (C) pasteurization
    (D) freezing

67. The condition in which pulmonary alveoli lose their elasticity and become permanently inflated, causing the patient to consciously exhale, is

    (A) bronchial asthma
    (B) bronchitis
    (C) emphysema
    (D) TB

68. Chest drainage systems should always be kept

    1. below the level of the patient's chest
    2. above the patient's chest
    3. at the level of the patient's diaphragm

    (A) 1 only
    (B) 1 and 2 only
    (C) 2 and 3 only
    (D) 1, 2, and 3

69. What venous device can be used for a patient requiring IV injections at frequent or regular intervals?

    (A) Butterfly needle
    (B) Heparin lock
    (C) IV infusion
    (D) Hypodermic needle

70. Which of the following statements is (are) true regarding the proper care of a patient with a tracheostomy?

    1. Employ sterile technique if you must touch a tracheostomy for any reason.
    2. Before you suction a tracheostomy, the patient should be well aerated.
    3. Never suction for longer than 15 seconds, permitting the patient to rest in between.

    (A) 1 and 2 only
    (B) 1 and 3 only
    (C) 2 and 3 only
    (D) 1, 2, and 3

71. In which of the following situations should a radiographer wear protective eye gear (goggles)?

    1. When performing an upper GI radiographic examination
    2. When assisting the radiologist during an angiogram
    3. When assisting the radiologist in a biopsy/aspiration procedure

    (A) 1 and 2 only
    (B) 1 and 3 only
    (C) 2 and 3 only
    (D) 1, 2, and 3

72. In reviewing a patient's blood chemistry, which of the following blood urea nitrogen (BUN) ranges is considered normal?

    (A) 0.6 to 1.5 mg/100 mL
    (B) 4.5 to 6 mg/100 mL
    (C) 8 to 25 mg/100 mL
    (D) Up to 50 mg/100 mL

73. Particulate matter entering the respiratory bronchi can cause

    (A) emphysema
    (B) empyema
    (C) pneumothorax
    (D) pneumoconiosis

74. All the following are forms of *mechanical* obstruction seen in neonates or infants *except*

    (A) paralytic ileus
    (B) meconium ileus
    (C) volvulus
    (D) intussusception

75. The pain experienced by an individual whose coronary arteries are not conveying sufficient blood to the heart is called

    (A) tachycardia
    (B) bradycardia
    (C) angina pectoris
    (D) syncope

76. A MRI procedure is contraindicated for a patient who has

    (A) a herniated disk
    (B) aneurysm clips
    (C) dental fillings
    (D) subdural bleeding

77. An inanimate object that has been in contact with an infectious microorganism is termed a

    (A) vector
    (B) fomite
    (C) host
    (D) reservoir

78. The advantages of using nonionic, water-soluble contrast media include

    1. cost-containment benefits
    2. low toxicity
    3. fewer adverse reactions

    (A) 1 only
    (B) 1 and 2 only
    (C) 2 and 3 only
    (D) 1, 2, and 3

79. A radiographer should recognize that gerontologic patients often have undergone physical changes that include loss of

    1. muscle mass
    2. bone calcium
    3. mental alertness

    (A) 1 only
    (B) 1 and 2 only
    (C) 1 and 3 only
    (D) 1, 2, and 3

80. Which of the following statements is (are) true regarding a two-member team performing mobile radiography on a patient with MRSA precautions?

1. One radiographer remains "clean"—that is, he or she has no physical contact with the patient.
2. The radiographer who positions the mobile unit also makes the exposure.
3. The radiographer who positions the cassette also retrieves the cassette and removes it from its plastic protective cover.

(A) 1 and 2 only
(B) 1 and 3 only
(C) 2 and 3 only
(D) 1, 2, and 3

81. Symptoms associated with a respiratory reaction to contrast media include

1. sneezing
2. hoarseness
3. wheezing

(A) 1 and 2 only
(B) 1 and 3 only
(C) 2 and 3 only
(D) 1, 2, and 3

82. While in your care for a radiologic procedure, a patient asks to see his chart. Which of the following is the *appropriate* response?

(A) Inform the patient that the chart is for health care providers to view, not for the patient.
(B) Inform the patient that you do not know where the chart is.
(C) Inform the patient that he has the right to see his chart but that he should request to view it with his physician so that it is interpreted properly.
(D) Give the patient the chart and leave him alone for a few minutes to review it.

83. Skin discoloration owing to cyanosis may be observed in the

1. gums
2. earlobes
3. tongue

(A) 1 only
(B) 1 and 2 only
(C) 3 only
(D) 1, 2, and 3

84. Diseases spread by direct or close contact include

1. MRSA
2. Conjunctivitis
3. Hepatitis A

(A) 1 only
(B) 1 and 2 only
(C) 2 and 3 only
(D) 1, 2, and 3

85. You receive an ambulatory patient for a GI series. As the patient is being seated on the x-ray table, he tells you he feels faint. You should

1. lay the patient down on the x-ray table
2. elevate the patient's legs or place the table slightly Trendelenburg
3. leave quickly and call for help

(A) 1 only
(B) 1 and 2 only
(C) 1 and 3 only
(D) 1, 2, and 3

86. The medical term for *hives* is

(A) vertigo
(B) epistaxis
(C) urticaria
(D) aura

87. Blood pressure is measured in units of

(A) millimeters of mercury (mm Hg)
(B) beats per minute
(C) degrees Fahrenheit (°F)
(D) liters per minute (L/min)

88. Which blood vessels are best suited for determination of pulse rate?

    (A) Superficial arteries
    (B) Deep arteries
    (C) Superficial veins
    (D) Deep veins

89. Which ethical principle is related to sincerity and truthfulness?

    (A) Beneficence
    (B) Autonomy
    (C) Veracity
    (D) Fidelity

90. The medical term for *congenital clubfoot* is

    (A) coxa plana
    (B) osteochondritis
    (C) talipes
    (D) muscular dystrophy

91. In what order should the following examinations be performed?

    1. Upper GI series
    2. IVU
    3. BE

    (A) 3, 1, 2
    (B) 1, 3, 2
    (C) 2, 1, 3
    (D) 2, 3, 1

92. Hypochlorite bleach (Clorox) and Lysol are examples of

    (A) antiseptics
    (B) bacteriostatics
    (C) antifungal agents
    (D) disinfectants

93. The condition that allows blood to shunt between the right and left ventricles is called

    (A) patent ductus arteriosus
    (B) coarctation of the aorta
    (C) atrial septal defect
    (D) ventricular septal defect

94. *Logrolling* is a method of moving patients having suspected

    (A) head injury
    (B) spinal injury
    (C) bowel obstruction
    (D) extremity fracture

95. The cycle of infection includes which of the following components?

    1. Reservoir of infection
    2. Susceptible host
    3. Means of transmission

    (A) 1 only
    (B) 1 and 2 only
    (C) 2 and 3 only
    (D) 1, 2, and 3

96. The act of inspiration will cause elevation of the

    1. sternum
    2. ribs
    3. diaphragm

    (A) 1 only
    (B) 1 and 2 only
    (C) 2 and 3 only
    (D) 1, 2, and 3

97. A radiologic technologist can be found guilty of a *tort* in which of the following situations?

    1. Failure to shield a patient of childbearing age from unnecessary radiation
    2. Performing an examination on a patient who has refused the examination
    3. Discussing a patient's condition with a third party

    (A) 1 only
    (B) 1 and 2 only
    (C) 2 and 3 only
    (D) 1, 2, and 3

98. Guidelines for cleaning contaminated objects or surfaces include which of the following?

1. Clean from the least contaminated to the most contaminated areas.
2. Clean in a circular motion, starting from the center and working outward.
3. Clean from the top down.

(A) 1 only
(B) 1 and 2 only
(C) 1 and 3 only
(D) 1, 2, and 3

99. If a radiographer performed a lumbar spine examination on a patient who was supposed to have an elbow examination, which of the following charges may be brought against the radiographer?

(A) Assault
(B) Battery
(C) False imprisonment
(D) Defamation

100. Types of inflammatory bowel disease include

1. ulcerative colitis
2. Crohn's disease
3. intussusception

(A) 1 only
(B) 1 and 2 only
(C) 2 and 3 only
(D) 1, 2, and 3

101. Which of the following statements would be true regarding tracheostomy patients?

1. Tracheostomy patients have difficulty speaking.
2. A routine chest x-ray requires the tracheostomy tubing to be rotated out of view.
3. Audible rattling sounds indicate a need for suction.

(A) 1 only
(B) 1 and 2 only
(C) 1 and 3 only
(D) 1, 2, and 3

102. When caring for a patient with an IV line, the radiographer should keep the medication

(A) 18 to 20 inches above the level of the vein
(B) 18 to 20 inches below the level of the vein
(C) 28 to 30 inches above the level of the vein
(D) 28 to 30 inches below the level of the vein

103. Diseases that require droplet precautions include

1. rubella
2. mumps
3. influenza

(A) 1 only
(B) 1 and 2 only
(C) 2 and 3 only
(D) 1, 2, and 3

104. Protective or "reverse" isolation is required in which of the following conditions?

1. TB
2. Burns
3. Leukemia

(A) 1 only
(B) 1 and 2 only
(C) 2 and 3 only
(D) 1, 2, and 3

105. When a GI series has been requested on a patient with a suspected perforated ulcer, the type of contrast medium that should be used is

(A) a thin barium sulfate suspension
(B) a thick barium sulfate suspension
(C) water-soluble iodinated media
(D) oil-based iodinated media

106. Nitroglycerin is used

(A) to relieve pain from angina pectoris
(B) to prevent a heart attack
(C) as a vasoconstrictor
(D) to increase blood pressure

107. A patient experiencing an episode of syncope should be placed in which of the following positions?

(A) Dorsal recumbent with head elevated

(B) Dorsal recumbent with feet elevated

(C) Lateral recumbent

(D) Seated with feet supported

108. The diameter of a needle's lumen is referred to as its

(A) bevel

(B) gauge

(C) hub

(D) length

109. A patient in a recumbent position with the head lower than the feet is said to be in which of the following positions?

(A) Trendelenburg

(B) Fowler

(C) Sims

(D) Stenver

110. The normal average rate of respiration for a healthy adult patient is

(A) 5 to 7 breaths/min

(B) 8 to 12 breaths/min

(C) 12 to 20 breaths/min

(D) 20 to 30 breaths/min

111. Which of the following is a vasopressor and may be used for an anaphylactic reaction or a cardiac arrest?

(A) Nitroglycerin

(B) Epinephrine

(C) Hydrocortisone

(D) Digitoxin

112. Examples of means by which infectious microorganisms can be transmitted via indirect contact include

1. a fomite
2. a vector
3. nasal or oral secretions

(A) 1 only

(B) 1 and 2 only

(C) 2 and 3 only

(D) 1, 2, and 3

113. All the following rules regarding proper hand washing technique are correct *except*

(A) keep hands and forearms lower than elbows

(B) use paper towels to turn water on

(C) avoid using hand lotions whenever possible

(D) carefully wash all surfaces and between fingers

114. The following instructions should be given to a patient following a barium sulfate contrast examination:

1. Increase fluid and fiber intake for several days.
2. Changes in stool color will occur until all barium has been evacuated.
3. Contact a physician if no bowel movement occurs in 24 hours.

(A) 1 only

(B) 2 only

(C) 1 and 3 only

(D) 1, 2, and 3

115. The medical abbreviation meaning "after meals" is

(A) tid

(B) qid

(C) qh

(D) pc

116. Symptoms of inadequate oxygen supply include

1. dyspnea
2. cyanosis
3. retraction of intercostal spaces

(A) 1 only
(B) 1 and 2 only
(C) 2 and 3 only
(D) 1, 2, and 3

117. A patient whose systolic blood pressure is consistently greater than 140 mm Hg usually is considered

(A) hypertensive
(B) hypotensive
(C) average/normal
(D) baseline

118. In which of the following conditions is a double-contrast BE essential for demonstration of the condition?

1. Polyps
2. Colitis
3. Diverticulosis

(A) 1 only
(B) 1 and 2 only
(C) 1 and 3 only
(D) 1, 2, and 3

119. When a radiographer is obtaining a patient history, both subjective and objective data should be obtained. An example of *subjective* data is that

(A) the patient appears to have a productive cough
(B) the patient has a blood pressure of 130/95 mm Hg
(C) the patient states that she experiences extreme pain in the upright position
(D) the patient has a palpable mass in the right upper quadrant of the left breast

120. Symptoms of impending diabetic coma include

1. increased urination
2. sweet-smelling breath
3. extreme thirst

(A) 1 and 2 only
(B) 1 and 3 only
(C) 2 and 3 only
(D) 1, 2, and 3

121. Diseases that require contact precautions include

1. MRSA
2. *Clostridium difficile* (C-diff)
3. TB

(A) 1 only
(B) 1 and 2 only
(C) 2 and 3 only
(D) 1, 2, and 3

122. Which of the following is (are) symptom(s) of shock?

1. Pallor and weakness
2. Increased pulse
3. Fever

(A) 1 only
(B) 1 and 2 only
(C) 1 and 3 only
(D) 1, 2, and 3

123. Increased pain threshold, breakdown of skin, and atrophy of fat pads and sweat glands are all important considerations when working with which of the following groups of patients?

(A) Infants
(B) Children
(C) Adolescents
(D) Geriatric patients

124. The practice that is used to retard the growth of pathogenic bacteria is termed

(A) antisepsis
(B) disinfection
(C) sterilization
(D) medical asepsis

125. The usual patient preparation for an upper GI examination is

    (A) nothing by mouth (NPO) 8 hours before the examination
    (B) light breakfast only on the morning of the examination
    (C) clear fluids only on the morning of the examination
    (D) 2 oz of castor oil and enemas until clear

126. When reviewing patient blood chemistry levels, what is considered the normal creatinine range?

    (A) 0.6 to 1.5 mg/100 mL
    (B) 4.5 to 6 mg/100 mL
    (C) 8 to 25 mg/100 mL
    (D) Up to 50 mg/100 mL

127. Which of the following medical equipment is used to determine blood pressure?

    1. Pulse oximeter
    2. Stethoscope
    3. Sphygmomanometer

    (A) 1 and 2 only
    (B) 1 and 3 only
    (C) 2 and 3 only
    (D) 1, 2, and 3

128. Diseases whose mode of transmission is through the air include

    1. TB
    2. mumps
    3. rubella

    (A) 1 only
    (B) 1 and 2 only
    (C) 1 and 3 only
    (D) 1, 2, and 3

129. A small container holding several doses of medication is termed

    (A) an ampoule
    (B) a vial
    (C) a bolus
    (D) a carafe

130. Tracheostomy is indicated in cases of tracheal obstruction when the obstruction is located

    (A) below the level of the larynx
    (B) above the level of the larynx
    (C) inferior to the carina
    (D) in the right primary bronchus

Answers and Explanations

1. **(B)** When transferring patients, always help the patient transfer toward the *strong* side. Be certain that the wheels of stretchers and wheelchairs are locked during transfer. When assisting a patient in changing, first remove clothing from the unaffected side. If this is done, removing clothing from the affected side will require less movement and effort. (*Adler and Carlton, 4th ed., p. 168*)

2. **(C)** The word *honor* implies regard for the standards of one's profession, a refusal to lie/deceive, an uprightness of character or action, a trustworthiness and incorruptibility. Other words used to describe these qualities are *honesty*, *integrity*, and *probity*.

   These are qualities required of students and health care professionals. This honor/integrity can only be achieved in an environment where intellectual honesty and personal integrity are highly valued—and where the responsibility for communicating and maintaining these standards is widely shared. The ARRT publishes an important document regarding Honor Code violations. In order to meet ARRT certification requirements, candidates for the ARRT examination must answer the question: "Have you ever been suspended, dismissed, or expelled from an educational program that you have attended?" . . . in addition to reading and signing the "Written Consent under FERPA," allowing the ARRT to obtain specific parts of their educational records concerning violations to an honor code if the student has ever been suspended, dismissed, or expelled from an educational program attended. If the applicant answers "yes" to that question he or she must include an explanation and documentation of the situation with the completed application for certification. If the applicant has any doubts, he or she should contact the ARRT Ethics Requirements Department at (651) 687-0048, ext. 8580. [Source: The American Registry of Radiologic Technologists Standards of Ethics. (Reproduced, with permission, from the ARRT Standards of Ethics. ARRT: 2008. Copyright © 2008 The American Registry of Radiologic Technologists.)]

3. **(B)** Every radiographic image *must* include (1) the patient's name or ID number, (2) the side marker, right or left; (3) the date of the examination; and (4) the identity of the institution or office. Additional information *may* be included: the patient's birth date or age, name of the attending physician, and the time of day. When multiple examinations (e.g., chest examinations or small bowel images) of a patient are made on the same day, it becomes crucial that the time the radiographs were taken be included on the image. This allows the physician to track the patient's progress. (*Frank et al., 11th ed., vol. 1, p. 25*)

4. **(B)** A radiographer who discloses confidential information to unauthorized individuals may be found guilty of *invasion of privacy*. If the disclosure is in some way detrimental or otherwise harmful to the patient, the radiographer

may also be accused of *defamation*. Spoken defamation is *slander*; written defamation is *libel. (Adler and Carlton, 4th ed., pp. 374–375)*

5. **(A)** The prefix *iatr-* is from the Greek *iatros*, meaning "physician." An iatrogenic infection is one caused by physician intervention or by medical or diagnostic treatment/procedures. Examples include infection following surgery and nausea or other illness following prescribed drug use. *(Adler and Carlton, 4th ed., pp. 226–227)*

6. **(C)** Reactions to contrast agents are named and categorized according to the body system(s) affected, the nature of the reaction (i.e., allergic vs. nonallergic), and its severity (i.e., mild, moderate, or severe). These reactions are categorized as *vasomotor* (a nonallergic reaction), *anaphylactic* (allergic reaction), *vasovagal* (life-threatening), and *acute renal failure* (renal shutdown). *Vasomotor* effects are principally emotional and anxiety-based. They are characterized by anxiety, syncope, nausea, lightheadedness, and sometimes, a few hives. The patient usually just requires reassurance and not medical attention. An *anaphylactic* reaction is a true allergic reaction to e.g. iodinated media and can lead to a life-threatening situation. Immediate medical attention is required. Symptoms of anaphylactic reaction include laryngo/bronchospasm, hypotension, moderate to severe urticaria, angioedema, and tachycardia. A *vasovagal* reaction is life-threatening and requires a declared emergency ("code"). Symptoms of a vasovagal reaction include bradycardia, hypotension, and no detectable pulse. The fourth type of reaction, *acute renal failure*, may not manifest for up to 48 hours following injection of the contrast agent. Patients should notify their physician if they experience any changes in their urinary habits or any other atypical symptoms. Treatment would include hydration, dispensation of a diuretic (e.g., Lasix), and possibly even renal dialysis. *(Bontrager and Lampignano, 6th ed., p. 558)*

7. **(C)** The *diameter* of a needle is the needle's *gauge*. The higher the gauge number, the smaller is the diameter and the thinner is the needle.

For example, a very tiny-gauge needle (25 gauge) may be used on a pediatric patient for an IV injection, whereas a large-gauge needle (16 gauge) may be used for donating blood. The *hub* of a needle is the portion of the needle that attaches to a syringe. The *length* of the needle varies depending on its use. A longer needle is needed for intramuscular injections, whereas a shorter needle is used for subcutaneous injections. The *bevel* of the needle is the slanted tip of the needle. For IV injections, the bevel always should face up. *(Adler and Carlton, 4th ed., p. 308)*

8. **(B)** Oral administration of barium sulfate is used to demonstrate the upper digestive system—the esophagus, fundus, body, and pylorus of the stomach—and barium progression through the small bowel. The small bowel includes the duodenum, jejunum, and ileum (ilium is part of the pelvis). *(Gurley and Callaway, 6th ed., pp. 131–132)*

9. **(B)** *Lidocaine* (Xylocaine) is an antiarrhythmic used to prevent or treat cardiac arrhythmias (dysrhythmia). *Epinephrine* (Adrenalin) is a bronchodilator. Bronchodilators may be administered in a spray mister, such as for asthma, or by injection to relieve severe bronchospasm. *Nitroglycerin* and *verapamil* are vasodilators. Vasodilators permit increased blood flow by relaxing the walls of the blood vessels. *(Adler and Carlton, 4th ed., p. 304)*

10. **(D)** Chronic obstructive pulmonary disease (COPD) is the abbreviation for *chronic obstructive pulmonary disease;* it refers to a group of disorders, including bronchitis, emphysema, asthma, and bronchiectasis. COPD is irreversible and decreases the ability of the lungs to perform their ventilation functions. There is often less than half the normal expected maximal breathing capacity. *(Taber, 20th ed., p. 416)*

11. **(D)** A parental route of drug administration is one that bypasses the digestive system. The five parenteral routes require different needle placements: under the skin (*subcutaneous*), through the skin and into the muscle (*intramuscular*), between the layers of the skin (*intradermal*), into a vein (*intravenous*), and into

the subarachnoid space (*intrathecal*). (*Adler and Carlton, 4th ed., p. 307*)

12. **(A)** *Extravasation* occurs when medication or contrast medium is injected into the tissues surrounding a vein rather than into the vein itself. It can happen when the patient's veins are particularly deep and/or small. If this happens, the needle should be removed, pressure applied to prevent formation of a *hematoma*, and then hot packs applied to relieve pain. The antecubital vein is the most commonly used *venipuncture* site for contrast medium administration. (*Adler and Carlton, 4th ed., p. 322*)

13. **(B)** Epidemiologic studies indicate that *HIV* and acquired immunodeficiency syndrome (*AIDS*) can be transmitted only by intimate contact with blood or body fluids of an infected individual. This can occur through the sharing of contaminated needles, through sexual contact, from mother to baby at childbirth, and from transfusion of contaminated blood. *HIV* and *AIDS* cannot be transmitted by inanimate objects. Hepatitis B virus (*HBV*) is another blood-borne infection that affects the liver. It is thought that more than 1 million people in the United States have chronic hepatitis B and, as such, can transmit the disease to others. Acid-fast bacillus (AFB) isolation is employed with patients suspected or known to be infected with tuberculosis (*TB*). AFB isolation requires that the patient wear a mask to avoid the spread of acid-fast bacilli (in bronchial secretions) during coughing. (*Adler and Carlton, 4th ed., p. 227*)

14. **(A)** The mechanical device used to correct an ineffectual cardiac ventricular rhythm is a *defibrillator*. The two paddles attached to the unit are placed on a patient's chest and used to introduce an electric current in an effort to correct the dysrhythmia. *Automatic implantable cardioverter defibrillators* (AICDs) are devices that are implanted in the body and that deliver a small shock to the heart if a life-threatening dysrhythmia occurs. A *cardiac monitor* is used to display, and sometimes record, electrocardiographic (ECG) readings and some pressure readings. A *crash cart* is a supply cart with various medications and equipment necessary for treating a

patient who is suffering from a myocardial infarction or some other serious medical emergency. It is checked and restocked periodically. A *resuscitation bag* is used for ventilation, such as during CPR. (*Torres et al., 6th ed., pp. 173–175*)

15. **(A)** The victim's airway should first be opened. This is accomplished by tilting back the head and lifting the chin. However, if the victim may have suffered a spinal cord injury, the spine should not be moved, and the airway should be opened using the jaw-thrust method. The rescuer next listens to breathing sounds and watches for the rise and fall of the chest to indicate breathing. If there is no breathing, the rescuer pinches the victim's nose and delivers two full breaths via mouth-to-mouth rescue breathing. If rise and fall of the chest still are not present, the Heimlich maneuver is instituted. If ventilation does not take place during the two full breaths, the victim's circulation is checked next (using the carotid artery). If there is no pulse, external chest compressions are begun at a rate of 80 to 100 compressions/min for adults and at least 100 compressions/min for infants. (*Torres et al., 6th ed., p. 172*)

16. **(A)** In classifying contrast agents, the total number of dissolved particles in solution per kilogram of water defines the *osmolality* of the contrast agent. The *toxicity* defines how noxious or harmful a contrast agent is. Contrast agents with low osmolality have been found to cause less tissue toxicity than the ionic IV contrast agents. The *viscosity* defines the thickness or concentration of the contrast agent. The viscosity of a contrast agent can affect its injection rate. A thicker, or more viscous, contrast agent will be more difficult to inject (more pressure is needed to push the contrast agent through the syringe and needle or the angiocatheter). The *miscibility* of a contrast agent refers to its ability to mix with body fluids, such as blood. Miscibility is an important consideration in preventing thrombus formation. It is generally preferable to use a contrast agent with low osmolality and low toxicity because such an agent is safer for the patient and less likely to cause any untoward reactions. When ionic and nonionic contrast agents are compared, a nonionic contrast agent has a

lower osmolality. To further understand osmolality, remember that whenever IV contrast media are introduced, there is a notable shift in fluid and ions. This shift is caused by an inflow of water from interstitial regions into the vascular compartment, which increases the blood volume and cardiac output. Consequently, there will be an increase in systemic arterial pressure and peripheral vascular resistance with peripheral *vasodilation*. In addition, the pulmonary pressure and heart rate increase. When the effects of osmolality on the patient are understood, it becomes clear that an elderly patient or one with cardiac disease or impaired circulation would greatly benefit from the use of an agent with lower osmolality. *(Adler and Carlton, 4th ed., p. 331)*

17. **(C)** Persons in sterile dress should not pass each other face to face. Rather, they should pass each other *back to back* to avoid contaminating each other. Gowns are considered sterile in the front down to the waist, including the arms. Sterile gloves must be kept above the waist level. If the hands are accidentally lowered or placed behind the back, they are no longer sterile. A sterile field should not be left unattended. Sterile fields should be set up immediately prior to a procedure and should be covered with a sterile drape if a few moments are to elapse before the procedure can begin. A sterile field should be monitored constantly to be certain that it has not been contaminated. *(Adler and Carlton, 4th ed., p. 247)*

18. **(D)** Misunderstandings between cultures can occur as a result of the use of gestures, which have different meanings in different countries. In the US and Europe, the "thumbs up" gesture has a positive implication. However, it is considered rude in Australia and obscene in the Middle East. Other examples of potentially misunderstood gestures include: if you compliment a Mexican child, you must touch the head, while in Asia it is not acceptable to touch the head of a child; in the Philippines, it is rude to beckon with the index finger; furthermore, in the US, people are comfortable speaking about 18 inches apart, while in the Middle East, people stand much closer together when they talk; in England, people stand further apart. *(Ehrlich and Daly, 7th ed.)*

19. **(D)** *Respondeat superior* is a phrase meaning "let the master answer" or "the one ruling is responsible." If a radiographer were negligent, there may be an attempt to prove that the radiologist was responsible because the radiologist oversees the radiographer. The legal doctrine *res ipsa locquitur* relates to a thing or matter that speaks for itself. For instance, if a patient went into the hospital to have a kidney stone removed and ended up with an appendectomy, that speaks for itself, and negligence can be proven. *Res judicata* means a thing or matter settled by justice. *Stare decisis* refers to a matter settled by precedent. *(Gurley and Callaway, 6th ed., p. 200)*

20. **(D)** Medical equipment that could contain latex includes disposable gloves, *tourniquets*, blood pressure cuffs, stethoscopes, IV tubing, oral and nasal airways, *enema tips*, endotracheal tubes, syringes, electrode pads, *catheters*, wound drains, and injection ports. It should be noted that when powdered latex gloves are changed, latex protein/powder particles get into the air, where they can be inhaled and come in contact with body membranes. Studies have indicated that when unpowdered gloves are worn, there are extremely low levels of the allergy-producing proteins present. *(OSHA/latex, www.sbaa.org/atf/cf/%7B99DD789C-904D-467E-A2E4-DF1D36E381C0%7D/Latex_2006.pdf)*

21. **(B)** *Rickets* and *osteomalacia* are disorders in which there is softening of bone. Rickets results from a deficiency of vitamin D and usually is found affecting the growing bones of young children. The body's weight on the soft bones of the legs results in bowed and misshapen legs. Osteomalacia is an adult condition in which new bone fails to calcify. It is a painful condition and can result in easily fractured bones, especially in the lower extremities. *Osteoarthritis* is seen often in the elderly and is characterized by degeneration of articular cartilage in adjacent bones. The resulting rubbing of bone against bone results in pain and deterioration. *(Tortora and Derrickson, 11th ed., p. 190)*

22. **(B)** Quantities of medication can be dispensed intravenously over a period of time via an *IV infusion*. A special infusion pump may be used to precisely regulate the quantity received by the patient. An *IV push* refers to a rapid injection; the term *bolus* refers to the quantity of material being injected. The term *hypodermic* refers to administration of medication by any route other than oral. (*Adler and Carlton, 4th ed., p. 316*)

23. **(D)** Adverse reactions to the intravascular administration of iodinated contrast media are not uncommon, and although the risk of a life-threatening reaction is relatively low, the radiographer must be alert to recognize the situation and deal with it effectively should a serious reaction occur. A minor reaction is characterized by flushed appearance and nausea and, occasionally, by vomiting and a few hives. *Early* symptoms of a possible anaphylactic reaction include constriction of the throat, possibly because of laryngeal edema, dysphagia (difficulty swallowing), and itching of the palms and soles. The radiographer must maintain the patient's airway, summon the radiologist, and call a "code." (*Adler and Carlton, 4th ed., p. 279*)

24. **(D)** The patient's rights can be exercised on the patient's behalf by a *designated surrogate or proxy* decision maker if the patient lacks decision-making capacity, is legally incompetent, or is a minor. Many people believe that potential legal and ethical issues can be avoided by creating an *advance health care directive* or *living will*. Since all persons have the right to make decisions regarding their own health care, this legal document preserves that right in the event an individual is unable to make those decisions. An advance health care directive, or living will, names the health care proxy authorized to make all health care decisions and can include specifics regarding DNR (Do not resuscitate), DNI (Do not intubate), and/or other end-of-life decisions. (*Adler and Carlton, 4th ed., p. 155*)

25. **(B)** There are four stages of infection. In the initial phase, the *latent period*, the infection is introduced and lies dormant. As soon as the microbes begin to shed, the infection becomes communicable. The microbes reproduce (during the *incubation* period), and during the actual disease period, signs and symptoms of the infection may begin. The infection is most active and communicable at this point. As the patient fights off the infection and the symptoms regress, the *convalescent (recovery) phase* occurs. (*Torres et al., 6th ed., p. 56*)

26. **(D)** The heart rate of an infant is much faster than that of an adult; therefore, the number of compressions per minute is also greater. Infant CPR requires five compressions to one breath. There should be at least 100 compressions/min. (*Adler and Carlton, 4th ed., p. 285*)

27. **(D)** Today we know that *the most important precaution in the practice of aseptic technique is proper hand hygiene*. The radiographer's hands should be thoroughly washed with soap and warm running water for at least 15 seconds before and after each patient examination, or by using an alcohol sanitizer. If the faucet cannot be operated with the knee, it should be opened and closed using paper towels (to avoid contamination of or by the faucet). The radiographer's uniform should not touch the sink. The hands and forearms should always be kept lower than the elbows; care should be taken to wash all surfaces and between fingers. Hand lotions should be used to prevent hands from chapping; broken skin permits the entry of microorganisms. *Disinfectants, antiseptics, and germicides are substances used to kill pathogenic bacteria*; they are frequently used in hand hygiene substances. Alcohol-based hand sensitizers have been recommended as an alternative to handwashing with soap and water, except when there is visible soiling or after caring for a patient with *Clostridium difficile* infection. (*Torres et al., 6th ed., pp. 61–62*)

28. **(D)** *Orthopnea* is a respiratory condition in which the patient has difficulty breathing (dyspnea) in any position other than erect. The patient is usually comfortable in the erect, standing, or seated position. The *Trendelenburg* position places the patient's head lower than the rest of the body, the *Fowler* position is

a semierect position, and the *recumbent* position is lying down. *(Taber, 20th ed., p. 1,535)*

29. **(C)** When caring for a patient with an indwelling Foley catheter, place the drainage bag and tubing *below the level of the bladder* to maintain the gravity flow of urine. Placement of the tubing or bag above or level with the bladder will allow backflow of urine into the bladder. This reflux of urine can increase the chance of a urinary tract infection (UTI). *(Adler and Carlton, 4th ed., p. 253)*

30. **(D)** The four *vital signs* are *temperature, pulse, respiration,* and *blood pressure.* Because radiographers may be required to take vital signs in an emergency, they should practice these skills. A *thermometer* is required to measure a patient's temperature. A *watch with a second hand* is required to measure a patient's pulse and respiration. To measure blood pressure, a *blood pressure cuff, sphygmomanometer,* and *stethoscope* are required. This is the skill that the radiographer should practice most frequently because it is the one most likely to be needed in an emergency situation. *(Torres et al., 6th ed., p. 139)*

31. **(A)** Hirschsprung disease, or congenital megacolon, is caused by the absence of some or all of the bowel ganglion cells—usually in the rectosigmoid area but occasionally more extensively. Hirschsprung disease is the most common cause of lower GI obstruction in *neonates* and is treated surgically by excision of the affected area followed by reanastomosis with normal, healthy bowel. Hirschsprung disease is diagnosed by barium enema or, in mild cases, by rectal biopsy. *(Bontrager and Lampignano, 6th ed., p. 660)*

32. **(B)** Nonionic, low-osmolality iodinated contrast agents are associated with far fewer side effects and reactions than ionic, higher osmolality contrast agents. A *side effect* is an effect that is unintended but possibly expected and fundamentally *not harmful.* An *adverse reaction* is a *harmful* unintended effect. Possible *side effects* of iodinated contrast agents include a warm, flushed feeling, a metallic taste in the mouth, nausea, headache, and pain at the injection site. *Adverse reactions* include itching, anxiety, rash or hives, vomiting, sneezing, dyspnea, and hypotension. *(Adler and Carlton, 4th ed., p. 279)*

33. **(B)** The normal blood pressure range for men and women is a 110 to 140 mm Hg *systolic* reading (left number) and a 60 to 80 mm Hg *diastolic* reading (right number). Systolic pressure is the contraction phase of the left ventricle, and diastolic pressure is the relaxation phase in the heart cycle. *(Torres et al., 6th ed., pp. 148–149)*

34. **(C)** Facsimile transmission of health information is convenient but should be used only to address immediate and urgent patient needs—and every precaution must be taken to ensure its confidentiality. It should be used only with prior patient authorization, when urgently needed for patient care, or when required for third-party payer ongoing hospitalization certification. These recommendations are made by the American Health Information Management Association (AHIMA). *(Adler and Carlton, 4th ed., p. 368)*

35. **(C)** Verbal defamation of another, or *slander,* is a type of intentional misconduct. *Invasion of privacy* (i.e., public discussion of privileged and confidential information) is intentional misconduct. However, if a radiographer leaves a weak patient standing alone to check images or get supplies and that patient falls and sustains an injury, that would be considered unintentional misconduct, or *negligence. (Adler and Carlton, 4th ed., pp. 375–376)*

36. **(D)** When helping a patient in or out of a wheelchair, *it must first be locked.* Then, the footrests must be moved up and aside to prevent the patient from tripping over them or tilting the wheelchair forward. The wheelchair should be placed at a 45-degree angle with the x-ray table or bed, with the patient's *stronger side closest* toward the x-ray table or bed. Once the patient is seated, the footrests should be lowered into place for the patient's comfort. *(Adler and Carlton, 4th ed., p. 169)*

37. **(A)** Dr. Elizabeth Kubler-Ross explains that loss requires gradual adjustment and involves

several steps. The first is denial or isolation, where the individual often refuses to accept the thought of loss or death. The second step is anger, as the individual attempts to deal with feelings of helplessness. The next is bargaining, in which the patient behaves as though "being good" like a "good patient" will be rewarded by a miraculous cure or return of the loss. Once the individual acknowledges that this is not likely to happen, depression is the next step. This depression precedes acceptance, where the individual begins to deal with fate or loss. (*Adler and Carlton, 4th ed., p. 155*)

38. **(D)** An unconscious patient frequently is able to hear and understand all that is going on, even though he or she is unable to respond. Therefore, while performing the examination, the radiographer always should refer to the patient by name and take care to continually explain what is being done and reassure the patient. (*Adler and Carlton, 4th ed., pp. 148–149*)

39. **(C)** *Cathartics* stimulate defecation and are used in preparation for radiologic examinations of the large bowel. *Diuretics* are used to promote urine elimination in individuals whose tissues are retaining excessive fluid. *Emetics* induce vomiting, and *antitussives* are used to inhibit coughing. (*Torres et al., 6th ed., p. 283*)

40. **(C)** Elderly patients (actually, most people) dislike being rushed or hurried along. They appreciate the radiographer who is caring and respectful enough to take the extra few moments necessary to progress at a slower speed. Some elderly patients are easily confused, and it is best to address them by their full name and keep instructions simple and direct. The elderly require the same respectful, dignified care as all other patients. (*Adler and Carlton, 4th ed., pp. 152–153*)

41. **(A)** Medications can be administered in a number of ways. *Parenteral* administration refers to drugs administered via intramuscular, subcutaneous, IV, or intrathecal routes—that is, any way other than by mouth. Intramuscular drug injections usually require that the needle form a 90-degree angle of in-

jection. For subcutaneous injections, the needle should form a 45-degree angle. *Intravenous* injections generally require that the needle form about a 15-degree angle with the arm. (*Adler and Carlton, 4th ed., pp. 313–316*)

42. **(B)** When helping a patient into or out of a wheelchair, *it must first be locked*. Then, the footrests must be moved up and aside to prevent the patient from tripping over them or tilting the wheelchair forward. The wheelchair should be placed at a 45-degree angle with the x-ray table or bed, with the patient's *stronger side closest* to the x-ray table or bed. Once the patient is seated, the footrests should be lowered into place for the patient's comfort. (*Adler and Carlton, 4th ed., p. 169*)

43. **(B)** Dilated, twisted veins, or *varices*, of the esophagus are frequently associated with obstructive liver disease or cirrhosis of the liver. These esophageal veins enlarge and can rupture, causing serious hemorrhage. *Achalasia* is dilation of the esophagus as a result of the cardiac sphincter's failure to relax and allow food to pass into the stomach. *Dysphasia* is a speech impairment resulting from a brain lesion; it is unrelated to the esophagus. *Dysphagia* refers to difficulty swallowing and is the most common esophageal complaint. *Hiatal hernia* is another common esophageal problem; it is characterized by protrusion of a portion of the stomach through the cardiac sphincter. It is a common condition, and many individuals with the condition are asymptomatic. Each of these conditions of the esophagus may be evaluated with an esophagogram. Positions usually include the posteroanterior, right anterior oblique, and right lateral positions. (*Bontrager and Lampignano, 6th ed., pp. 463–464*)

44. **(A)** Iodinated contrast material can become somewhat *viscous* (i.e., thick and sticky) at normal room temperatures. This makes injection much more difficult. Warming the contrast medium to body temperature serves to reduce viscosity. This may be achieved by placing the vial in warm water or putting it into a special warming oven. (*Adler and Carlton, 4th ed., p. 331*)

45. **(B)** *Cardiogenic shock* is related to cardiac failure and results from interference with heart function. It can occur in cases of cardiac tamponade, pulmonary embolus, or myocardial infarction. *Hypovolemic shock* is related to loss of large amounts of blood, either from internal bleeding or from hemorrhage associated with trauma. The type of shock associated with the pooling of blood in the peripheral vessels is classified as *neurogenic shock.* This occurs in cases of trauma to the central nervous system that result in decreased arterial resistance and pooling of blood in peripheral vessels. *Septic shock,* along with *anaphylactic shock,* generally is classified as *vasogenic shock.* (*Adler and Carlton, 4th ed., p. 278*)

46. **(D)** The Joint Commission [formerly the Joint Commission on the Accreditation of Health-care Organizations (JCAHO)] is the organization that accredits health care organizations in the United States. The Joint Commission sets forth certain standards for medical records. In keeping with these standards, all diagnostic and therapeutic orders must appear in the patient's medical record or chart. In addition, patient identification information, medical history, consent forms, and any diagnostic and therapeutic reports should be part of the patient's permanent record. The patient's chart is a means of communication between various health care providers. (*Torres et al., 6th ed., p. 19*)

47. **(B)** Category-specific isolations have been replaced by *transmission-based precautions: airborne, droplet,* and *contact.* Under these guidelines, some conditions or diseases can fall into more than one category. *Airborne precautions* are employed with patients suspected or known to be infected with *tubercle bacillus* (TB), *chickenpox* (*varicella*), or *measles* (*rubeola*). Airborne precautions *require that the patient wear a mask* to avoid the spread of bronchial secretions or other pathogens during coughing. If the patient is unable or unwilling to wear a mask, the radiographer must wear one. The radiographer should wear gloves, but a gown is required only if flagrant contamination is likely. Patients under *airborne precautions* require a *private, specially ventilated (negative-pressure)*

room. A private room is also indicated for all patients on *droplet precautions,* that is, with diseases transmitted via *large droplets* expelled from the patient while speaking, sneezing, or coughing. The pathogenic droplets can infect others when they come in contact with mouth or nasal mucosa or conjunctiva. *Rubella* ("German measles"), *mumps,* and *influenza* are among the diseases spread by droplet contact; a *private room is required* for the patient, and health care practitioners should use *gowns and gloves.* Any diseases spread by direct or close *contact,* such as *MRSA, conjunctivitis,* and *hepatitis A,* require *contact precautions. Contact precautions* require a *private patient room* and the use of *gloves, masks, and gowns* for anyone coming in direct contact with the infected individual or his or her environment. (*Adler and Carlton, 4th ed., pp. 232–233*)

48. **(D)** All the statements in the question are true and necessary in order for patient consent to be valid. The patient must sign the consent form before receiving sedation. The physician named on the consent form must perform the procedure; no other physician should perform it. Also, the consent form should be complete prior to being signed; there should be no blank spaces on the consent form when the patient signs it. In the case of a minor, a parent or guardian is required to sign the form. If a patient is not competent, then the legally appointed guardian should sign the consent form. Remember that obtaining consent is the physician's responsibility, so the explanation of the procedural risks should be performed by the physician, not by the radiographer. (*Ehrlich and Daly, 7th ed., pp. 67–68*)

49. **(B)** The Heimlich maneuver is used when a person is choking. If you suspect that an individual is choking, be certain that the airway is indeed obstructed before attempting the Heimlich maneuver. A person with a completely obstructed airway will not be able to speak or cough. If the person cannot speak or cough, then the airway is obstructed, and the Heimlich maneuver should be performed. The proper method is to stand behind the choking victim with one hand in a fist, thumb side in, midway between the navel and the xiphoid tip. Place

the other hand over the closed fist with the palm open and apply pressure in and up. Repeat the thrust several times until the object is dislodged. For an infant, the procedure is modified. Four back blows are given midway between the scapulae using the heel of the hand. If the object is not dislodged, the baby is turned over (being very careful to support the baby's head and spine), and four chests thrusts are performed just below the nipple line using several fingers. *(Adler and Carlton, 4th ed., p. 280)*

50. **(B)** Many microorganisms can remain infectious while awaiting transmission to another host. A contaminated inanimate object such as a food utensil, doorknob, or IV pole is referred to as a *fomite*. A *vector* is an insect or animal carrier of infectious organisms, such as a rabid animal, a mosquito that carries malaria, or a mouse/deer tick that carries Lyme disease. They can transmit disease through either direct or indirect contact. *(Adler and Carlton, 4th ed., p. 226)*

51. **(B)** A circumstance in which both the health care provider's and the patient's actions contribute to an injurious outcome is termed *contributory negligence*. An example would be a patient who fails to follow the physician's orders or fails to show up for follow-up care and then sues when the condition causes permanent damage. Another example would be a patient who deliberately gives false information about the ingestion of drugs, leading to adverse effects from medications administered. Most states do not completely dismiss injury if there has been negligence on the part of the health care institution, even if the patient's actions contributed substantially to the injury. Rather, *comparative negligence* is applied, where the percentage of the injury owing to the patient's actions is compared with the total amount of injury. A jury may decide that a physician was negligent in his or her actions, but because the patient lied about using an illegal street drug that contributed to the injurious outcome, the patient is 80% responsible for his or her condition. The party suing may be awarded $100,000 for injuries but actually would receive only $20,000. *Gross negligence* occurs when there is willful or deliberate neglect of the patient. Assault, battery, invasion of pri-

vacy, false imprisonment, and defamation of character all fall under the category of *intentional misconduct. (Ehrlich and Daly, 7th ed., p. 70)*

52. **(C)** *Extravasation* of contrast media into surrounding tissue is potentially very painful. If it does occur, the needle should be removed and the extravasation cared for immediately (before looking for another vein). First, *pressure* should be applied to the vein until bleeding stops. Application of *a cold pack* to the affected area helps to relieve pain. Application of a *warm towel* at the injection site can hasten absorption of the contrast medium. *(Ehrlich and Daly, 7th ed., pp. 248–249; Bontrager and Lampignano, 6th ed., p. 559)*

53. **(D)** The *diastolic* number is the bottom (right) number in a blood pressure reading. The normal range for diastolic pressure is considered to be 60 to 80 mm Hg. A diastolic pressure reading of 110 mm Hg might indicate hypertension. A diastolic pressure of 50 mm Hg might indicate shock. The *systolic* number is the top (left) number in a blood pressure reading. The normal systolic pressure range is 110 to 140 mm Hg. *(Torres et al., 6th ed., p. 148)*

54. **(D)** When moving heavy objects, there are several rules that will reduce back strain. When carrying a heavy object, hold it close to your body. Your back should be kept straight; avoid twisting. When lifting an object, bend at the knees and use leg and abdominal muscles to lift (rather than your back muscles). Whenever possible, push or roll heavy objects (i.e., mobile unit), rather than pulling or lifting. *(Torres et al., 6th ed., p. 82)*

55. **(D)** None of the statements in the question is false; all are true. Oxygen is classified as a drug and must be prescribed by a physician. The rate and mode of delivery of oxygen must be specified in the physician's orders. It can be ordered to be delivered continuously or as needed. *(Adler and Carlton, 4th ed., p. 203)*

56. **(A)** It is unlikely that the radiographer will be faced with a wound hemorrhage because bleeding from wounds is controlled before the patient is seen for x-ray examination. However,

if a patient does experience hemorrhaging from a wound, you should apply pressure to the bleeding site and call for assistance. Delay can lead to serious blood loss. *(Adler and Carlton, 4th ed., pp. 287–288)*

57. **(B)** A *double-contrast GI* examination requires that the patient ingest gas-producing powder, crystals, pills, or beverage followed by a small amount of high-density barium. The patient then may be asked to roll in the recumbent position in order to coat the gastric mucosa while the carbon dioxide expands. This procedure provides optimal visualization of the gastric walls. Although a double-contrast BE uses a negative contrast agent, it is not ingested but rather is delivered rectally. An *oral cholecystogram* can be performed approximately 3 hours after ingestion of special ipodate calcium granules. An IVU requires an IV injection of iodinated contrast medium. *(Frank et al., 11th ed., vol. 2, p. 142)*

58. **(C)** Category-specific isolations have been replaced by *transmission-based precautions: airborne, droplet,* and *contact.* Under these guidelines, some conditions or diseases can fall into more than one category. *Airborne precautions* are employed with patients suspected or known to be infected with *tubercle bacillus (TB), chickenpox (varicella),* or *measles (rubeola).* Airborne precautions *require that the patient wear a mask* to avoid the spread of bronchial secretions or other pathogens during coughing. If the patient is unable or unwilling to wear a mask, the radiographer must wear one. The radiographer should wear gloves, but a gown is required only if flagrant contamination is likely. Patients under *airborne precautions* require a *private, specially ventilated (negative-pressure) room.* A private room is also indicated for all patients on *droplet precautions,* that is, with diseases transmitted via *large droplets* expelled from the patient while speaking, sneezing, or coughing. The pathogenic droplets can infect others when they come in contact with mouth or nasal mucosa or conjunctiva. *Rubella* ("German measles"), *mumps,* and *influenza* are among the diseases spread by droplet contact; a *private room is required* for the patient, and health care practitioners should use *gowns and gloves.* Any dis-

eases spread by direct or close *contact,* such as methicillin-resistant Staphylococcus aureus (MRSA), *conjunctivitis,* and *hepatitis A,* require *contact precautions.* Contact precautions require a *private patient room* and the use of *gloves, masks, and gowns* for anyone coming in direct contact with the infected individual or his or her environment. *(Adler and Carlton, 4th ed., pp. 232–233)*

59. **(D)** Most needle sticks occur during attempts to recap a needle. Proper disposal of contaminated needles and syringes is becoming more vital as HIV infection, AIDS, and HBV infection reach epidemic proportions. To prevent the spread of any possible infection, handle contaminated materials as little as possible. Therefore, do not attempt to recap a needle; instead, dispose of the entire syringe with the needle attached in the special container that is available. *(Torres et al., 6th ed., p. 309)*

60. **(D)** Although it is never the responsibility of the radiographer to diagnose a patient, it is the responsibility of every radiographer to be alert. The patient should not be subjected to unnecessary radiation from an unwanted examination. Rather, it is the radiographer's responsibility to check with the referring physician and report the patient's complaint. *(Ehrlich and Daly, 7th ed., p. 74)*

61. **(C)** A *Swan–Ganz catheter* is a specific type of IV catheter used to measure the pumping ability of the heart, to obtain pressure readings, and to introduce medications and IV fluids. A *pacemaker* is a device that is inserted under the patient's skin to regulate heart rate. Pacemakers may be permanent or temporary. *Chest tubes* are used to remove fluid or air from the pleural cavity. Any of these items may be identified on a chest radiograph, provided that the cassette is properly positioned and the correct exposure factors are employed. If the physician is interested in assessing the proper placement of a Swan–Ganz catheter, the lungs may have to be slightly overexposed to clearly delineate the proper placement of the tip of the Swan–Ganz catheter, which will overlap the denser cardiac silhouette. A *urinary catheter* will not

appear on a chest radiograph. *(Adler and Carlton, 4th ed., p. 214)*

62. **(B)** A patient who is having a *BE* generally is required to have a low-residue diet for 1 or 2 days, followed by cathartics and cleansing enemas prior to the examination. Any retained fecal material can simulate or obscure pathology. A patient who is scheduled for a *pyelogram* must have the preceding meal withheld to avoid the possibility of aspirating vomitus in case of an allergic reaction. A *metastatic survey* does not require the use of contrast media, and no patient preparation is necessary. *(Torres et al., 6th ed., p. 234)*

63. **(A)** When performing bedside radiography in a contact isolation room, the radiographer should wear a gown and gloves. The IPs are prepared for the examination by placing a pillowcase over them to protect them from contamination. Whenever possible, one person should manipulate the mobile unit and remain "clean," whereas the other handles the patient. The mobile unit should be cleaned with a disinfectant on exiting the patient's room, not prior to entering. *(Torres et al., 6th ed., p. 69)*

64. **(C)** The Levin and Salem-sump tubes are NG tubes used for gastric decompression. The *Salem-sump* tube is radiopaque and has a double lumen. One lumen is for gastric air compression, and the other is for removal of fluids. The *Levin* tube is a single-lumen tube that is used to prevent accumulation of intestinal liquids and gas during and following intestinal surgery. The *Swan–Ganz* IV catheter is advanced to the pulmonary artery and used to measure various heart pressures. *(Adler and Carlton, 4th ed., p. 260)*

65. **(D)** A catheter placed in a large vein is called a *central venous line*. It can be used to deliver frequent medications or nutrition or to monitor cardiac pressures. Catheters can vary in size and number of lumens depending on intended use. The *Port-a-Cath* is a totally implanted access port, and the peripherally inserted central catheter (*PICC*) is a peripherally inserted central catheter—they both per-

mit long-term intravenous treatment. The *Swan–Ganz* catheter is advanced to the pulmonary artery and is used to measure the pumping ability of the heart, to obtain pressure readings, and to introduce medications and IV fluids. The *Levin* and *Salem-sump* tubes are NG tubes used for gastric decompression. The *Salem-sump* tube is radiopaque and has a double lumen. One lumen is for gastric air compression, and the other is for removal of fluids. *(Adler and Carlton, 4th ed., p. 213)*

66. **(B)** The most effective method of sterilization is moist heat, using steam under pressure. This is known as *autoclaving*. Sterilization with dry heat requires higher temperatures for longer periods of time than sterilization with moist heat. *Pasteurization* is moderate heating with rapid cooling; it is used frequently in the commercial preparation of milk and alcoholic beverages such as wine and beer. It is not a form of sterilization. *Freezing* also can kill some microbes, but it is not a form of sterilization. *(Torres et al., 6th ed., pp. 116–117)*

67. **(C)** *Emphysema* is a progressive disorder caused by long-term irritation of the bronchial passages, such as by air pollution or cigarette smoking. Emphysema patients are unable to exhale normally because of loss of elasticity of alveolar walls. If emphysema patients receive oxygen, it is usually administered at a very slow flow rate because their respirations are controlled by the level of carbon dioxide in the blood. *(Bontrager and Lampignano, 6th ed., p. 92)*

68. **(A)** The chest drainage system unit always should be kept below the level of the patient's chest. Chest tubes are used to remove air, blood, or fluid from the pleural cavity. By draining fluid from the pleural cavity, a collapsed lung, or *atelectasis*, may be relieved. By relieving the pressure from air in the pleural cavity, a *pneumothorax* may be reduced. Radiographers must take care that the tubes of the chest drainage unit do not kink and do not get caught on IV poles or radiographic equipment. It is imperative that the unit remain below the level of the chest. The chest drainage

system has several components. One component is a chamber that collects the draining fluid. Another component is the suction control chamber. A third component is the water-seal chamber, which prevents air from the atmosphere from entering the system. The last component is the water-seal venting chamber, which allows air to leave the system, thus preventing pressure buildup. In order for the unit to work properly, it must remain below the level of the chest. *(Adler and Carlton, 4th ed., pp. 211–212)*

69. **(B)** Another name for an *intermittent injection port* is a *heparin lock*. Heparin locks are used for patients who will require frequent or regular injections. An intravenous catheter is placed in the vein, and an external adapter with a diaphragm allows for repeated injections. This helps to prevent the formation of scarred, sclerotic veins as a result of frequent injections at the same site. Heparin locks provide more freedom than an *IV infusion*, which also allows for repeated access. *Hypodermic needles* usually are used for drawing blood or drawing up fluids, whereas a *butterfly needle* usually is used for venipuncture. *(Torres et al., 6th ed., p. 318)*

70. **(D)** All the statements in the question are true regarding the proper care of a patient with a tracheostomy. If a tracheostomy needs to be touched for any reason, sterile technique should be employed to avoid the possibility of infection. Patients with tracheostomies require frequent suction. This is usually not performed by the technologist, but radiographers may be called on to assist with suctioning, especially for patients who must be in the radiology department for lengthy procedures. Patients who are to be suctioned should be aerated beforehand (i.e., oxygen should be administered prior to suctioning). It is also important that patients be permitted to rest during suctioning. Never suction for longer than 15 seconds; check breath sounds with a stethoscope to ensure that the airway is clear. It is the radiographer's responsibility to check the work area and ensure that the suction is working and that ample ancillary supplies (i.e., suction kit, catheters, and tubing) are available. *(Adler and Carlton, 4th ed., pp. 249–250)*

71. **(C)** It is recommended that a radiographer wear protective eye gear (goggles) during any procedure in which there might be splattering of blood or body fluids. This includes both angiography and biopsy/aspiration procedures. This would not be expected during a routine upper GI examination. *(Torres et al., 6th ed., p. 64)*

72. **(C)** The BUN level indicates the quantity of *nitrogen in the blood in the form of urea*. The normal concentration is 8 to 25 mg/100 mL. *BUN* and *creatinine* blood chemistry levels should be checked prior to beginning an IVU. An increase in the BUN level often indicates decreased renal function. Increased BUN and/or creatinine levels may forecast an increased possibility of contrast media–induced renal effects and poor visualization of the renal collecting systems. The normal creatinine range is 0.6 to 1.5 mg/100 mL. *(Bontrager and Lampignano, 6th ed., p. 556)*

73. **(D)** *Pneumoconiosis* is a condition of the lungs characterized by particulate matter having been deposited in lung tissue; it sometimes results in emphysema. Overdistension of the alveoli with air is *emphysema*. The condition is often a result of many years of smoking and is characterized by *dyspnea*, especially when recumbent. *Empyema* is pus in the thoracic cavity; *pneumothorax* is air or gas in the pleural cavity. *(Bontrager and Lampignano, 6th ed., pp. 92–93)*

74. **(A)** *Volvulus* and *intussusception* both involve a mechanical "closure" or obstruction of the intestinal lumen by a change in the continuous pathway of the GI tract—volvulus by a twisting of the bowel on itself causing obstruction and intussusception by "telescoping" of the bowel causing obstruction. *Meconium ileus* is another form of mechanical obstruction where meconium (first feces of a newborn) becomes hardened and impacted, causing obstruction. *Paralytic* (or *adynamic*) *ileus*, however, is an obstruction caused by loss of peristaltic movement of the intestine. *(Bontrager and Lampignano, 6th ed., p. 660)*

75. **(C)** An individual whose coronary arteries are not carrying enough blood to the heart muscle (myocardium) as a result of partial or

complete blockage of a cardiac vessel experiences crushing pain in the chest, frequently radiating to the left jaw and arm. This is termed *angina pectoris*. It may be relieved by the drug nitroglycerin, which dilates the coronary arteries, thus facilitating circulation. *Tachycardia* refers to rapid heart rate, and *bradycardia*, to slow heart rate. *Syncope* is fainting. *(Adler and Carlton, 4th ed., p. 290)*

76. **(B)** The presence of aneurysm clips is contraindication for magnetic resonance imaging (MRI); even a slight shift can cause damage. MRI can be performed for a herniated disk and subdural bleeding. Dental fillings do not contraindicate MRI. *(Torres et al., 6th ed., p. 363)*

77. **(B)** A *fomite* is an inanimate object that has been in contact with an infectious microorganism. A *reservoir* is a site where an infectious organism can remain alive and from which transmission can occur. Although an inanimate object can be a reservoir for infection, living objects (such as humans) also can be reservoirs. For infection to spread, there must be a *host* environment. Although an inanimate object may serve as a temporary host where microbes can grow, microbes flourish on and in the human host, where there are plenty of body fluids and tissues to nourish and feed the microbes. A *vector* is an animal host of an infectious organism that transmits the infection via bite or sting. *(Torres et al., 6th ed., p. 54)*

78. **(C)** The relatively low osmolality and non-ionic, water-soluble contrast media available to radiology departments have outstanding advantages, especially for patients with a history of allergic reaction. They were used originally for intrathecal injections (myelography), but they were quickly accepted for intravascular injections as well. *Side effects and allergic reactions are less likely and less severe with these media.* Their one very significant disadvantage is their high cost compared with that of ionic contrast media. *(Adler and Carlton, 4th ed., p. 329)*

79. **(B)** *Gerontology*, or geriatrics, is the study of the elderly. Although bone demineralization and loss of muscle mass occur to a greater or lesser degree in most elderly individuals, the radiographer must not assume that all gerontologic patients are hard of hearing, clumsy, or not mentally alert. Today, many elderly people remain very active, staying mentally and physically agile well into their so-called golden years. The radiographer must keep this in mind as he or she provides age-specific care to the gerontologic patient. *(Torres et al., 6th ed., p. 211)*

80. **(A)** When a two-member team of radiographers is performing mobile radiography on a patient with contact precautions, such as an MRSA patient, one radiographer remains "clean"—that is, he or she has no physical contact with the patient. The clean radiographer will position the mobile unit and make the exposure. The other member of the team will position the cassette and retrieve the cassette. As the two radiographers fold down the cassette's protective plastic cover, the "clean" radiographer will remove the cassette from the plastic. Both radiographers should be protected with gowns, gloves, and masks if the patient is on contact precautions. In addition, after the examination is completed, the mobile unit should be cleaned with a disinfectant. Conditions requiring the use of contact precautions also include hepatitis A and varicella infection. *(Adler and Carlton, 4th ed., p. 233)*

81. **(D)** All these symptoms are related to a respiratory reaction. There also may be dyspnea, asthma attack, or cyanosis. The patient who has received contrast media should be watched closely. If any symptoms arise, the radiologist should be notified immediately. *(Adler and Carlton, 4th ed., p. 331)*

82. **(C)** If a patient in your care asks to see his or her chart, the appropriate response is to refer the patient to his or her physician. A patient *does* have the right to review his or her own medical record; however, the patient should do so in the presence of the physician so that the patient does not misinterpret the information and so that the physician can address concerns or answer questions. It is not appropriate to hand over the chart to a patient, nor is it appropriate to deceive the patient into

believing that the chart is not available for viewing or that the patient has no right to review the chart. *(Adler and Carlton, 4th ed., p. 368)*

83. **(B)** *Cyanosis* is a condition resulting from a deficiency of oxygen circulating in the blood. It is characterized by bluish discoloration of the gums, nailbeds, earlobes, and the area around the mouth. Cyanosis may be accompanied by labored breathing or other types of respiratory distress. *(Torres et al., 6th ed., p. 147)*

84. **(D)** Category-specific isolations have been replaced by *transmission-based precautions: airborne, droplet,* and *contact.* Under these guidelines, some conditions or diseases can fall into more than one category. Any diseases spread by direct or close *contact,* such as *MRSA, conjunctivitis,* and *hepatitis A,* require *contact precautions. Contact precautions* require a *private patient room* and the use of *gloves, masks, and gowns* for anyone coming in direct contact with the infected individual or his or her environment. *Airborne precautions* are employed with patients suspected or known to be infected with *tubercle bacillus* (TB), *chickenpox* (*varicella*), or *measles* (*rubeola*). Airborne precautions *require that the patient wear a mask* to avoid the spread of bronchial secretions or other pathogens during coughing. If the patient is unable or unwilling to wear a mask, the radiographer must wear one. The radiographer should wear gloves, but a gown is required only if flagrant contamination is likely. Patients under *airborne precautions* require a *private, specially ventilated* (*negative-pressure*) *room.* A private room is also indicated for all patients on *droplet precautions,* that is, with diseases transmitted via *large droplets* expelled from the patient while speaking, sneezing, or coughing. The pathogenic droplets can infect others when they come in contact with mouth or nasal mucosa or conjunctiva. *Rubella* ("German measles"), *mumps,* and *influenza* are among the diseases spread by droplet contact; a *private room is required* for the patient, and health care practitioners should use *gowns and gloves.* (*Adler and Carlton, 4th ed., pp. 232–233*)

85. **(B)** A patient who has been NPO since midnight or who is anxious, frightened, or in pain

may suffer an episode of syncope (fainting) on exertion. The patient should be helped to a recumbent position with feet elevated to increase blood flow to the head. A patient who feels like fainting should never be left alone. *(Adler and Carlton, 4th ed., p. 287)*

86. **(C)** *Urticaria* is a vascular reaction resulting in dilated capillaries and edema and causing the patient to break out in hives. The medical term for *nosebleed* is *epistaxis. Vertigo* refers to a feeling of "whirling" or a sensation that the room is spinning. Some possible causes of vertigo include inner ear infection and acoustic neuroma. An *aura* may be classified as either a feeling or a sensory response (such as flashing lights, tasting metal, or smelling coffee) that precedes an episode such as a seizure or a migraine headache. *(Adler and Carlton, 4th ed., p. 286)*

87. **(A)** Blood pressure is measured in *millimeters of mercury* (mm Hg). Heart rate, or pulse, is measured in units of *beats per minute.* Temperature is measured in *degrees Fahrenheit* (°F). Oxygen delivery is measured in units of *liters per minute* (L/min). Table 1–1 outlines the normal ranges for vital signs in healthy adults. *(Torres et al., 6th ed., p. 147)*

TABLE 1–1. NORMAL RANGES FOR VITAL SIGNS IN ADULTS

Blood pressure	110–140 mm Hg/60–80 mm Hg
Pulse rate	60–100 beats/min
Temperature	97.7°F–99.5°F
Respiration rate	12–20 breaths/min

88. **(A)** *Superficial arteries* are best suited for determination of pulse rate. The five most easily palpated pulse points are the radial, carotid, temporal, femoral, and popliteal pulses. The radial pulse is used most frequently. The apical pulse, at the apex of the heart, is most accurate and can be determined with the use of a stethoscope. *(Adler and Carlton, 4th ed., p. 198)*

89. **(C)** *Veracity* (i.e., sincerity) is not only telling the truth but also not practicing deception. *Autonomy* is the ethical principle that is related to the theory that patients have the right to decide what will or will not be done to them. *Beneficence* is related to the idea of doing

good and being kind. *Fidelity* is faithfulness and loyalty. *(Adler and Carlton, 4th ed., p. 253)*

90. **(C)** *Talipes* is the term used to describe congenital clubfoot. There are several types of talipes, generally characterized by a deformed talus and a shortened Achilles tendon, giving the foot a *clubfoot* appearance. *Osteochondritis* (Osgood–Schlatter disease) is a painful incomplete separation of the tibial tuberosity from the tibial shaft. It is often seen in active adolescent boys. *Coxa plana* (Legg–Calvé–Perthes disease) is ischemic necrosis leading to flattening of the femoral head. *Muscular dystrophy* is a congenital disorder characterized by wasting of skeletal muscles. *(Frank et al., 11th ed., vol. 1, p. 273)*

91. **(D)** When scheduling patient examinations, it is important to avoid the possibility of residual contrast medium covering areas that will be of interest on later examinations. The IVU [also referred to as an *intravenous pyelogram* (IVP)] should be scheduled first because the contrast medium used is excreted rapidly. The BE should be scheduled next. Finally, the upper GI series is scheduled. There should not be enough barium remaining from the previous BE to interfere with the examination of the stomach or duodenum, although a preliminary scout image should be taken in each case. *(Torres et al., 6th ed., p. 234)*

92. **(D)** Hypochlorite bleach (Clorox) and Lysol are examples of *disinfectants*. Disinfectants are used in radiology departments to clean equipment and to remove microorganisms from areas such as radiographic tables. *Antiseptics* are also used to stop the growth of microorganisms, but they are often applied to the skin, not to radiographic equipment. *Antifungal* medications can be administered systemically or topically to treat or prevent fungal infections. *Antibacterial* medications (*bacteriostatics*) also can be administered systemically or externally. Tetracycline is a systemic antibacterial medication. *(Torres et al., 6th ed., p. 116)*

93. **(D)** *Ventricular septal defect* is a congenital heart condition characterized by a hole in the interventricular septum that allows oxy-

genated and unoxygenated blood to mix. Some interventricular septal defects are small and close spontaneously; others require surgery. *Coarctation of the aorta* is a narrowing or constriction of the aorta. *Atrial septal defect* is a small hole (the remnant of the fetal foramen ovale) in the interatrial septum. It usually closes spontaneously in the first months of life; if it persists or is unusually large, surgical repair is necessary. The ductus arteriosus is a short fetal blood vessel connecting the aorta and pulmonary artery that usually closes within 10 to 15 hours after birth. A *patent ductus arteriosus* is one that persists and requires surgical closure. *(Taber, 20th ed., p. 2,323)*

94. **(B)** Patients arriving at the emergency department (ED) with suspected *spinal injury* should not be moved. Anteroposterior (AP) and horizontal lateral projections of the suspected area should be evaluated and a decision made about the advisability of further images. For a lateral projection, the patient should be moved along one plane, that is, rolled like a log. It is imperative that twisting motions be avoided. *(Torres et al., 6th ed., p. 87)*

95. **(D)** The cycle of infection includes four components: a susceptible host, a reservoir of infection, a pathogenic organism, and a means of transmission. *Pathogenic organisms* are microscopic and include bacteria, fungi, and viruses. The *reservoir of infection* is the environment in which the microorganism thrives; this can be the human body. A *susceptible host* may have reduced resistance to infection. The *means of transmission* is either direct (i.e., touch) or indirect (i.e., vector, fomite, or airborne). *(Adler and Carlton, 4th ed., p. 225)*

96. **(B)** The diaphragm is the major muscle of respiration. On inspiration/inhalation, the diaphragm and abdominal viscera are depressed, enabling filling and expansion of the lungs, accompanied by upward movement of the sternum and ribs. During expiration/exhalation, air leaves the lungs, and they deflate while the diaphragm relaxes and moves to a more superior position along with the abdominal viscera. As the diaphragm relaxes and moves up, the sternum

and ribs move inferiorly. *(Frank et al., 11th ed., vol. 1, pp. 503–504)*

97. **(D)** A *tort* is an *intentional* or *unintentional* act that involves personal injury or damage to a patient. Allowing a patient to be exposed to unnecessary radiation, either by neglecting to shield the patient or by performing an unwanted examination, would be considered a tort, and the radiographer would be legally accountable. Discussing a patient's condition with a third party undoubtedly would be considered a serious intentional tort. *(Torres et al., 6th ed., p. 15)*

98. **(C)** Because hospitals are the refuge of the sick, they can also be places of disease transmission unless proper infection control guidelines are followed. When cleaning contaminated objects or surfaces such as the radiographic table, it is important to *clean from the least contaminated to the most contaminated area* and *from the top down*. Soiled gowns and linens should be folded from the outside in and disposed of properly. When the patient's skin is being prepared for surgery, it is often cleaned in circular motion starting from the center and working outward; however, this motion is not used for objects or surfaces. *(Torres et al., 6th ed., p. 66)*

99. **(B)** A radiographer who performs the wrong examination on a patient may be charged with battery. *Battery* refers to the unlawful laying of hands on a patient. The radiographer also could be charged with battery if a patient is moved about roughly or touched in a manner that is inappropriate or without the patient's consent. *Assault* is the *threat* of touching or laying hands on someone. If a patient feels threatened by a practitioner, either because of the tone or pitch of the practitioner's voice or because the practitioner uses words that are threatening, the practitioner can be accused of assault. *False imprisonment* may be considered if a patient is ignored after stating that she no longer wishes to continue with the procedure or if restraining devices are used improperly or used without a physician's order. The accusation of *defamation* can be upheld when patient confidentiality is not

respected and, as a result, the patient suffers embarrassment or mockery. *(Adler and Carlton, 4th ed., p. 374)*

100. **(B)** The two most common types of chronic inflammation of the intestines are ulcerative colitis and Crohn's disease. The latter can attack any part of the GI tract and extends through all layers of the intestinal wall (therefore the possibility of forming fistulous tracks to contiguous structures). Ulcerative colitis attacks only the large bowel and only the mucosal layer of the intestinal wall. Curiously, cigarette smoking increases the risk for Crohn's disease and decreases the risk for ulcerative colitis. Intussusception is an obstructive disorder. *(Tortora and Derrickson, 11th ed., p. 944)*

101. **(C)** The tracheostomy patient will have difficulty speaking as a result of redirection of the air past the vocal cords. Gurgling or rattling sounds coming from the trachea indicate an excess accumulation of secretions, requiring suction with sterile catheters. Any rotation or movement of the tracheostomy tube may cause the tube to become dislodged, and an obstructed airway could result. *(Torres et al., 6th ed., p. 239)*

102. **(A)** It is generally recommended that the IV bottle/bag be kept 18 to 20 inches above the level of the vein. If the container is too high, the pressure of the IV fluid can cause it to pass through the vein into surrounding tissues, causing a painful and potentially harmful condition. If the IV container is too low, blood may return through the needle into the tubing, form a clot, and obstruct the flow of IV fluid. *(Torres et al., 6th ed., p. 323)*

103. **(D)** A private room is indicated for all patients on *droplet precaution*; that is, diseases transmitted via large droplets expelled from the patient while speaking, sneezing, or coughing. The pathogenic droplets can infect others when they come in contact with mouth or nasal mucosa or conjunctiva. *Rubella* ("German measles"), *mumps,* and *influenza* are among the diseases spread by droplet contact; a *private room is required* for the patient, and health care practitioners must wear a regular

(string) *mask* to enter a droplet precautions isolation room. *(Adler and Carlton, 4th ed., p. 233)*

104. **(C)** Protective or "reverse" isolation is used to keep the susceptible patient from becoming infected. Patients who have suffered burns have lost a very important means of protection, their skin, and therefore have increased susceptibility to bacterial invasion. Patients whose immune systems are depressed have lost the ability to combat infection and hence are more susceptible to infection. Active TB requires airborne precautions, not protective isolation. *(Torres et al., 6th ed., p. 69)*

105. **(C)** Whenever a perforation of the GI tract is suspected, a water-soluble contrast agent (such as Gastrografin or oral Hypaque) should be used because it is easily absorbed from within the peritoneal cavity. Leakage of barium sulfate into the peritoneal cavity can have serious consequences. Water-soluble contrast agents also may be used in place of barium sulfate when the possibility of barium impaction exists. Oil-based contrast agents are used rarely today. *(Frank et al., 11th ed., vol. 2, pp. 166–167)*

106. **(A)** *Angina pectoris* is a crushing chest pain caused by a circulatory disturbance of the coronary arteries. Nitroglycerin is used to dilate blood vessels (vasodilation) and decrease blood pressure in the treatment of pain from angina pectoris. Nitroglycerin usually is given sublingually and thus is absorbed directly into the bloodstream. *(Torres et al., 6th ed., p. 280)*

107. **(B)** *Syncope,* or fainting, is the result of a drop in blood pressure caused by insufficient blood (oxygen) flow to the brain. The patient should be helped into a dorsal recumbent position with feet elevated to facilitate blood flow to the brain. *(Ehrlich and Daly, 7th ed., p. 286)*

108. **(B)** The diameter of a needle is the needle's *gauge.* The higher the gauge number, the smaller is the diameter and the thinner is the needle. For example, a very tiny-gauge needle

(25 gauge) may be used on a pediatric patient for an IV injection, whereas a large-gauge needle (16 gauge) may be used for donating blood. The *hub* of a needle is the portion of the needle that attaches to a syringe. The *length* of the needle varies depending on its use. A longer needle is needed for intramuscular injections, whereas a shorter needle is used for subcutaneous injection. The *bevel* of the needle is the slanted tip of the needle. For IV injections, the bevel always should face up. *(Adler and Carlton, 4th ed., p. 308)*

109. **(A)** The patient is said to be in the *Trendelenburg* position when the head is positioned lower than the feet. This position is helpful in several radiographic procedures, such as separating redundant bowel loops and demonstration of hiatal hernias. It is also used in treating shock. In the *Fowler* position, the head is higher than the feet. The *Sims* position is the left posterior oblique (LPO) position with the right leg flexed up for insertion of the enema tip. The *Stenver* position is a radiographic position for radiographing the mastoids. *(Taber, 20th ed., p. 2,234)*

110. **(C)** The normal average rate of respiration for a healthy adult patient is between 12 and 20 breaths/min. For children, the rate is higher, averaging between 20 and 30 breaths/min. In addition to monitoring the respiratory rate, it is also important to monitor the depth (shallow or labored) and pattern (regularity) of respiration. A respiratory rate greater than 20 breaths/min in an adult would be considered *tachypnea. (Adler and Carlton, 4th ed., p. 198)*

111. **(B)** *Epinephrine* (Adrenalin) is the vasopressor used to treat an anaphylactic reaction or cardiac arrest. *Nitroglycerin* is a vasodilator. *Hydrocortisone* is a steroid that may be used to treat bronchial asthma, allergic reactions, and inflammatory reactions. *Digitoxin* is used to treat cardiac fibrillation. *(Adler and Carlton, 4th ed., p. 305)*

112. **(B)** Infectious microorganisms can be transmitted from patients to other patients or to health care workers and from health care workers to patients. They are transmitted by means of either direct or indirect contact. *Direct contact* involves *touch.* Diseases transmitted by direct contact include skin infections such as boils and sexually transmitted diseases such as syphilis and AIDS. Direct contact with droplets of nasal or oral secretions from a sneeze or cough is referred to as *droplet contact.* *Indirect contact* involves transmission of microorganisms via *airborne* contamination, *fomites,* and *vectors. Pathogenic microorganisms* expelled from the respiratory tract through the mouth or nose can be carried as evaporated droplets through the air or dust and settle on clothing, utensils, or food. Patients with respiratory tract infections or disease transported to the radiology department therefore should wear a mask to prevent such transmission during a cough or sneeze; it is not necessary for the health care worker to wear a mask (as long as the patient does). Many microorganisms can remain infectious while awaiting transmission to another host. A contaminated inanimate object such as a food utensil, doorknob, or IV pole is referred to as a *fomite.* A *vector* is an insect or animal carrier of infectious organisms, such as a rabid animal, a mosquito that carries malaria, or a tick that carries Lyme disease. They can transmit disease through either direct or indirect contact. *(Adler and Carlton, 4th ed., pp. 225–226)*

113. **(C)** Frequent and correct hand hygiene is an essential part of medical asepsis; it is the best method for avoiding the spread of microorganisms. If the faucet cannot be operated with the knee or a foot pedal, it should be opened and closed using paper towels. Care should be taken to wash all surfaces of the hand and between the fingers thoroughly. The hands and forearms always should be kept below the elbows. Hand lotions should be used frequently to keep hands from chapping. Unbroken skin prevents the entry of microorganisms; dry, cracked skin breaks down that defense and permits the entry of microorganisms. *(Ehrlich and Daly, 7th ed., p. 158)*

114. **(D)** Physicians often prescribe a mild laxative to aid in the elimination of barium sulfate. If a laxative is not given, the patient should be instructed to increase dietary fluid and fiber and to monitor bowel movements (the patient should have at least one within 24 hours). Patients should also be aware of the white appearance of their stool that will be present until all barium is expelled. *(Torres et al., 6th ed., p. 222)*

115. **(D)** The medical abbreviation *pc* means "after meals." "Three times a day" is indicated by the abbreviation *tid.* The abbreviation *qid* means "four times a day." "Every hour" is represented by *qh. (Adler and Carlton, 4th ed., p. 319)*

116. **(D)** Oxygen is taken into the body and supplied to the blood to be delivered to all body tissues. Any tissue(s) lacking in or devoid of an adequate blood supply can suffer permanent damage or die. Oxygen may be required in cases of severe anemia, pneumonia, pulmonary edema, and shock. Symptoms of inadequate oxygen supply include *dyspnea, cyanosis, diaphoresis, retraction of intercostal spaces, dilated nostrils,* and *distension of the veins of the neck.* The patient who experiences any of these symptoms will be very anxious and must not be left unattended. The radiographer must call for help, assist the patient to a sitting or semi-Fowler position (the recumbent position makes breathing more difficult), and have oxygen and emergency drugs available. *(Taber, 20th ed., p. 653)*

117. **(A)** *Systolic* blood pressure describes the pressure during *contraction* of the heart. It is expressed as the top (left) number when recording blood pressure. *Diastolic* blood pressure is the reading during *relaxation* of the heart and is placed on the bottom (right) when recording blood pressure. A patient is considered *hypertensive* when the systolic pressure is consistently above 140 mm Hg and *hypotensive* when the systolic pressure is lower than 90 mm Hg. *(Adler and Carlton, 4th ed., p. 194)*

118. **(B)** Double-contrast studies of the large bowel are particularly useful for demonstration of the *bowel wall* and anything projecting into it, for example, polyps. *Polyps* are projections of the bowel wall mucous membrane into the bowel lumen. *Colitis* is inflammation of the

large bowel, often associated with ulcerations of the mucosal wall. A single-contrast study most likely would obliterate these mucosal conditions, but coating of the bowel mucosa with barium and subsequent filling of the bowel with air (double contrast) provide optimal delineation. Single-contrast studies will demonstrate projections/outpouchings from the intestinal wall such as diverticulitis. *(Frank et al., 11th ed., vol. 2, p. 142)*

119. **(C)** Obtaining a complete and accurate history from the patient for the radiologist is an important aspect of a radiographer's job. Both subjective and objective data should be collected. *Objective* data include signs and symptoms that can be observed, such as a cough, a lump, or elevated blood pressure. *Subjective* data relate to what the patient feels and to what extent. A patient may experience pain, but is it mild or severe? Is it localized or general? Does the pain increase or decrease under different circumstances? A radiographer should explore this with the patient and document the information on the requisition for the radiologist. *(Adler and Carlton, 4th ed., p. 158)*

120. **(D)** When a diabetic patient misses an insulin injection, the body loses its ability to metabolize glucose, and ketoacidosis can occur. If this is not corrected quickly, the patient may become comatose. Symptoms of impending coma include increased urination, sweet (fruity) breath, and extreme thirst. Other symptoms are weakness and nausea. *(Torres et al., 6th ed., p. 170)*

121. **(B)** Any disease spread by direct or close *contact,* such as MRSA and *Clostridium difficile* (C-diff), and *some wounds* require *contact precautions.* Contact precaution procedures require a private patient room and the use of gloves and gowns for anyone coming in direct contact with the infected individual or the infected person's environment. Some facilities require health care workers to wear a mask when caring for a patient with MRSA infection. *(Adler and Carlton, 4th ed., p. 233)*

122. **(B)** A patient who is going into shock may exhibit *pallor and weakness,* a significant *drop in blood pressure,* and an *increased pulse.* The patient may also experience *apprehension and restlessness* and may have *cool, clammy skin.* A radiographer recognizing these symptoms should call them to the physician's attention immediately. Fever is not associated with shock. *(Torres et al., 6th ed., p. 163)*

123. **(D)** Increased pain threshold, breakdown of skin, and atrophy of fat pads and sweat glands are all important considerations when working with *geriatric patients.* Many changes occur as our bodies age. Although muscle is replaced with fat, the amount of subcutaneous fat is decreased, and the skin atrophies. Therefore, the geriatric patient requires *extragentle treatment.* A mattress pad should always be placed on the radiographic table to help prevent *skin injury* or abrasions. If tape is required, paper tape should be used instead of adhesive tape. Geriatric patients are also more sensitive to *hypothermia* because of the breakdown of the sweat glands and always should be kept covered both to preserve modesty and for extra warmth. *Loss of sensation* in the skin increases pain tolerance, so the geriatric patient may not be aware of excessive stress on bony prominences such as the elbow, wrist, coccyx, and ankles. *(Dowd and Tilson, 2nd ed., vol. 2, p. 1026)*

124. **(A)** *Antisepsis* is the practice that retards the growth of pathogenic bacteria. *Medical asepsis* refers to the destruction of pathogenic microorganisms through the process of *disinfection.* Examples of disinfectants include hydrogen peroxide, chlorine, and boric acid. *Surgical asepsis* (i.e., sterilization) refers to the removal of all microorganisms *and* their spores (reproductive cells) and is practiced in the surgical suite. Health care practitioners must practice medical asepsis at all times. *(Adler and Carlton, 4th ed., pp. 230–231)*

125. **(A)** To obtain a diagnostic examination of the stomach, it must first be empty. The usual preparation is NPO (nothing by mouth) after midnight (approximately 8 hours before the examination). Any material in the stomach can simulate the appearance of disease. *(Torres et al., 6th ed., p. 233)*

126. (A) *Creatinine* is a normal alkaline constituent of urine and blood, but increased quantities of creatinine are present in advanced stages of renal disease. Creatinine and BUN blood chemistry levels should be checked prior to beginning an IVU. Increased levels may forecast an increased possibility of contrast media–induced renal effects and poor visualization of the renal collecting systems. The normal creatinine range is 0.6 to 1.5 mg/100 mL. The normal BUN range is 8 to 25 mg/100 mL. *(Bontrager and Lampignano, 6th ed., p. 556)*

127. (C) A *stethoscope* and a *sphygmomanometer* are used together to measure blood pressure. The first sound heard is the systolic pressure, and the normal range is 110 to 140 mm Hg. When the sound is no longer heard, the diastolic pressure is recorded. The normal diastolic range is 60 to 90 mm Hg. Elevated blood pressure is called *hypertension. Hypotension,* or low blood pressure, is not of concern unless it is caused by injury or disease; in that case, it can result in shock. A *pulse oximeter* is used to measure a patient's pulse rate and oxygen saturation level. *(Adler and Carlton, 4th ed., p. 202)*

128. (D) Diseases that are transmitted through the air include TB, rubella ("German measles"), mumps, and influenza. Airborne precautions *require the patient to wear a mask* to avoid the spread of acid-fast bacilli (in the bronchial secretions of TB patients) or other pathogens during coughing. If the patient is unable or unwilling to wear a mask, the radiographer must wear one. The radiographer should wear gloves, but a gown is required only if flagrant contamination is likely. Pa-tients infected with diseases calling for *airborne precautions* require a *private, specially ventilated (negative-pressure) room.* A private room is also indicated for all patients on *droplet precautions,* that is, with diseases that are transmitted via large droplets expelled from the patient while speaking, sneezing, or coughing. The pathogenic droplets can infect others when they come in contact with the mouth or nasal mucosa or conjunctiva. *Rubella* ("German measles"), *mumps,* and *influenza* are among the diseases spread by droplet contact; a *private room is required* for the patient, and health care practitioners must use *gowns and gloves. (Adler and Carlton, 4th ed., pp. 232–233)*

129. (B) Injectable medications are available in two different kinds of containers. An *ampoule* is a small container that usually holds a single dose of medication. A *vial* is a somewhat larger container that holds a number of doses of medication. The term *bolus* is used to describe an amount of fluid to be injected. A *carafe* is a narrow-mouthed container; it is not likely to be used for medical purposes. *(Adler and Carlton, 4th ed., p. 309)*

130. (B) Tracheostomy is the surgical opening of the trachea to provide and secure an open airway. A tracheostomy is often performed in emergency situations when there is *upper* airway obstruction, that is, *above* the level of the larynx. Conditions requiring a tracheostomy include crushing injury of the tracheal rings, inflamed and swollen tracheal mucous membranes, and aspiration of foreign body. *(Tortora and Derrickson, 13th ed., p. 928)*

Subspecialty List

65. Medical emergencies
66. Infection control
67. Medical emergencies
68. Physical assistance and transfer
69. Ethical and legal aspects
70. Medical emergencies
71. Infection control
72. Physical assistance and transfer
73. Contrast media
74. Interpersonal communication
75. Contrast media
76. Interpersonal communication
77. Infection control
78. Contrast media
79. Medical emergencies
80. Infection control
81. Contrast media
82. Interpersonal communication
83. Medical emergencies
84. Ethical and legal aspects
85. Physical assistance and transfer
86. Medical emergencies
87. Physical assistance and transfer
88. Contrast media
89. Infection control
90. Physical assistance and transfer
91. Medical emergencies
92. Infection control
93. Medical emergencies
94. Contrast media
95. Infection control
96. Physical assistance and transfer
97. Ethical and legal aspects
98. Infection control
99. Ethical and legal aspects
100. Interpersonal communication
101. Medical emergencies
102. Contrast media
103. Contrast media
104. Infection control
105. Contrast media
106. Medical emergencies
107. Medical emergencies
108. Contrast media
109. Physical assistance and transfer
110. Medical emergencies
111. Medical emergencies
112. Infection control
113. Infection control
114. Infection control
115. Interpersonal communication
116. Medical emergencies
117. Medical emergencies
118. Contrast media
119. Interpersonal communication
120. Interpersonal communication
121. Infection control
122. Physical assistance and transfer
123. Interpersonal communication
124. Interpersonal communication
125. Ethical and legal aspects
126. Physical assistance and transfer
127. Physical assistance and transfer
128. Infection control
129. Physical assistance and transfer
130. Medical emergencies

CHAPTER 2

Image Procedures
Questions

DIRECTIONS (Questions 1 through 300): Each of the numbered items or incomplete statements in this section is followed by answers or by completions of the statement. Select the *one* lettered answer or completion that is *best* in each case.

1. The term *varus* refers to

   (A) turned outward
   (B) turned inward
   (C) rotated medially
   (D) rotated laterally

2. Demonstration of the posterior fat pad on the lateral projection of the adult elbow can be caused by

   1. trauma or other pathology
   2. greater than 90-degree flexion
   3. less than 90-degree flexion

   (A) 1 only
   (B) 3 only
   (C) 1 and 2 only
   (D) 1 and 3 only

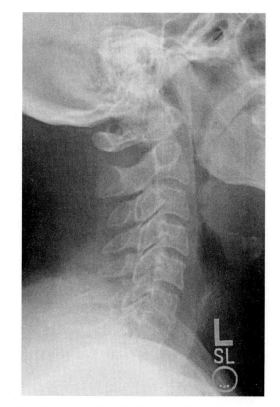

Figure 2–1. Courtesy of Stamford Hospital, Department of Radiology.

3. Critique the lateral cervical spine seen in Figure 2–1 and select the most correct statement below.

   (A) The chin has been depressed too much.
   (B) The chin needs to be extended more.
   (C) The head is tilted.
   (D) The shoulders are not depressed enough.

4. The coronoid process should be visualized in profile in which of the following positions?

   (A) Scapular Y
   (B) AP scapula
   (C) Medial oblique elbow
   (D) Lateral oblique elbow

5. The male bony pelvis differs from the female bony pelvis in which of the following way(s)?

1. The male pelvis has a larger pelvic inlet.
2. The female pubic arch is greater than 90 degrees.
3. The male ilium is more vertical.

(A) 1 only
(B) 1 and 2 only
(C) 2 and 3 only
(D) 1, 2, and 3

6. Which of the following techniques would provide a posteroanterior (PA) projection of the gastroduodenal surfaces of a barium-filled high and transverse stomach?

(A) Place the patient in a 35- to 40-degree right anterior oblique (RAO) position.
(B) Place the patient in a lateral position.
(C) Angle the CR 35 to 45 degrees cephalad.
(D) Angle the CR 35 to 45 degrees caudad.

7. With the patient and the x-ray tube positioned as illustrated in Figure 2–2, which of the following will be visualized?

1. Intercondyloid fossa
2. Patellofemoral articulation
3. Tangential patella

(A) 1 only
(B) 1 and 2 only
(C) 2 and 3 only
(D) 1, 2, and 3

8. All the following statements regarding respiratory structures are true *except*

(A) the right lung has three lobes.
(B) the inferior portion of the lung is the apex.
(C) each lung is enclosed in serous membrane.
(D) the main stem bronchi enter the lung hilum.

9. All the following statements regarding an exact PA projection of the skull are true *except*

(A) the orbitomeatal line is perpendicular to the IR.
(B) the petrous pyramids fill the orbits.
(C) the midsagittal plane (MSP) is parallel to the IR.
(D) the central ray is perpendicular to the IR and exits at the nasion.

10. What could be done to improve the mediolateral projection of the knee seen in Figure 2–3?

(A) Rotate the pelvis slightly forward.
(B) Rotate the pelvis slightly backward.
(C) Angle the x-ray tube 5 degrees cephalad.
(D) Angle the x-ray tube 5 degrees caudad.

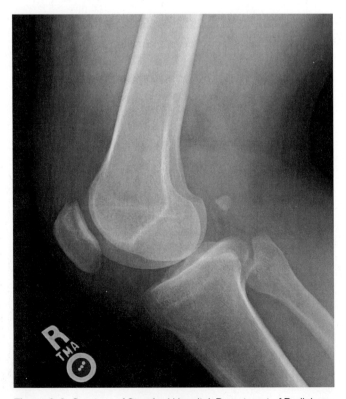

Figure 2–3. Courtesy of Stamford Hospital, Department of Radiology.

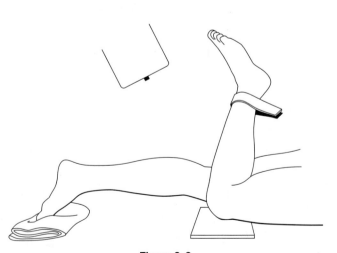

Figure 2–2.

11. Pacemaker electrodes can be introduced through a vein in the chest or upper extremity, from where they are advanced to the

(A) left atrium
(B) right atrium
(C) left ventricle
(D) right ventricle

12. Widening of the intercostal spaces is characteristic of which of the following conditions?

(A) Pneumothorax
(B) Emphysema
(C) Pleural effusion
(D) Pneumonia

13. Which of the following structures is (are) located in the right upper quadrant (RUQ)?

1. Hepatic flexure
2. Gallbladder
3. Ileocecal valve

(A) 1 only
(B) 1 and 2 only
(C) 2 and 3 only
(D) 1, 2, and 3

14. Which of the following statements regarding the image in Figure 2–4 is correct?

(A) The left kidney is more parallel to the IR.
(B) The image was made in the left posterior oblique position.
(C) The left ureter is better visualized.
(D) The image was made postvoid.

15. During an upper gastrointestinal (GI) examination, a stomach of average shape demonstrates a barium-filled fundus and double contrast of the pylorus and duodenal bulb. The position used is most likely

(A) AP erect
(B) PA
(C) RAO
(D) LPO

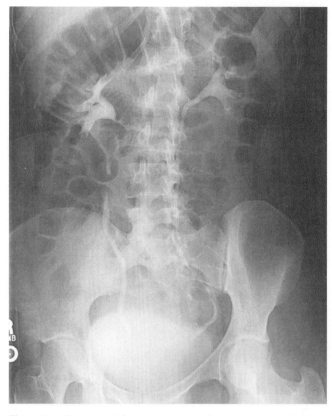

Figure 2-4. Courtesy of Stamford Hospital, Department of Radiology.

16. Which of the following articulations participate(s) in formation of the ankle mortise?

1. Talotibial
2. Talocalcaneal
3. Talofibular

(A) 1 only
(B) 1 and 3 only
(C) 2 and 3 only
(D) 3 only

17. Which projection of the foot will best demonstrate the longitudinal arch?

(A) Mediolateral
(B) Lateromedial
(C) Lateral weight-bearing
(D) 30-degree medial oblique

18. Graves disease is associated with

(A) thyroid underactivity
(B) thyroid overactivity
(C) adrenal underactivity
(D) adrenal overactivity

19. To *best* visualize the lower ribs, the exposure should be made

   (A) on normal inspiration
   (B) on inspiration, second breath
   (C) on expiration
   (D) during shallow breathing

20. In the AP axial projection (Towne method) of the skull, with the CR directed 30 degrees caudad to the orbitomeatal line (OML) and passing midway between the external auditory meati, which of the following is best demonstrated?

   (A) Occipital bone
   (B) Frontal bone
   (C) Facial bones
   (D) Basal foramina

21. The right posterior oblique position (Judet method) of the right acetabulum will demonstrate the

   1. anterior rim of the right acetabulum
   2. right iliac wing
   3. right anterior iliopubic column

   (A) 1 only
   (B) 1 and 2 only
   (C) 2 and 3 only
   (D) 1, 2, and 3

22. Figure 2–5 demonstrates which of the following conditions?

   (A) Right upper lobe atelectasis
   (B) Left upper lobe atelectasis
   (C) Pneumothorax
   (D) Dextrocardia

23. A frontal view of the sternum is *best* accomplished in which of the following positions?

   (A) AP
   (B) PA
   (C) RAO
   (D) LAO

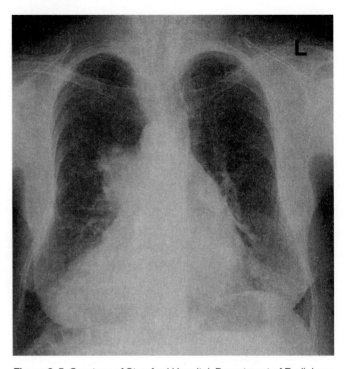

Figure 2–5. Courtesy of Stamford Hospital, Department of Radiology.

24. What is the name of the condition that results in the forward slipping of one vertebra on the one below it?

   (A) Spondylitis
   (B) Spondylolysis
   (C) Spondylolisthesis
   (D) Spondylosis

25. During atrial systole, blood flows into the

   1. right ventricle via the mitral valve
   2. left ventricle via the bicuspid valve
   3. right ventricle via the tricuspid valve

   (A) 1 only
   (B) 1 and 2 only
   (C) 2 and 3 only
   (D) 1, 2, and 3

26. How should a chest examination to rule out air–fluid levels be obtained on a patient having traumatic injuries?

    (A) Perform the examination in the Trendelenburg position.
    (B) Erect inspiration and expiration images should be obtained.
    (C) Include a lateral chest examination performed in dorsal decubitus position.
    (D) Perform the examination AP supine at 44 inches SID.

27. All the following statements regarding the use of iodinated contrast agents with patients taking metformin hydrochloride are true *except*

    (A) metformin is used to help lower blood sugar levels in type 2 diabetic patients.
    (B) patients on metformin who have intravenous (IV) iodinated contrast agent administration are at risk for renal failure.
    (C) metformin should be withheld for 48 hours before IV iodinated contrast studies.
    (D) metformin should be withheld for 48 hours after IV iodinated contrast studies.

28. Which of the following methods was used to obtain the image seen in Figure 2–6?

    (A) Erect PA, chin extended, OML forming 37 degrees to IR
    (B) Erect PA, OML, and CR perpendicular to IR
    (C) Erect PA, chin extended, OML 15 degree from horizontal
    (D) Erect PA, chin extended, OML 30 degree from horizontal

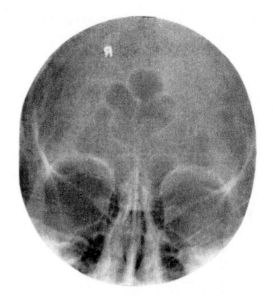

Figure 2–6. Courtesy of Stamford Hospital, Department of Radiology.

29. Which of the following statements regarding the radiograph in Figure 2–6 is (are) true?

    1. The position is used to demonstrate the frontal and ethmoid sinuses.
    2. The ethmoid sinuses are seen near the medial aspect of the orbits.
    3. The perpendicular plate is visualized in midline of the nasal cavity.

    (A) 1 only
    (B) 1 and 2 only
    (C) 1 and 3 only
    (D) 1, 2, and 3

30. Which of the following is an important consideration to avoid excessive metacarpophalangeal joint overlap in the oblique projection of the hand?

    (A) Oblique the hand no more than 45 degrees.
    (B) Use a support sponge for the phalanges.
    (C) Clench the fist to bring the carpals closer to the IR.
    (D) Use ulnar flexion.

31. All the following positions are used frequently to demonstrate the sternoclavicular articulations *except*

    (A) weight-bearing
    (B) RAO
    (C) LAO
    (D) PA

32. Which of the following positions is most likely to place the right kidney parallel to the IR?

    (A) AP
    (B) PA
    (C) RPO
    (D) LPO

33. When examining a patient whose elbow is in partial flexion, how should an AP projection be obtained?

    1. With humerus parallel to IR, CR perpendicular
    2. With forearm parallel to IR, CR perpendicular
    3. Through the partially flexed elbow, resting on the olecranon process, CR perpendicular

    (A) 1 only
    (B) 1 and 2 only
    (C) 2 and 3 only
    (D) 1, 2, and 3

34. Which of the following positions is required to demonstrate small amounts of air in the peritoneal cavity?

    (A) Lateral decubitus, affected side up
    (B) Lateral decubitus, affected side down
    (C) AP Trendelenburg
    (D) AP supine

35. Which of the anatomic structures listed below is seen most anteriorly in a lateral projection of the chest?

    (A) Esophagus
    (B) Trachea
    (C) Cardiac apex
    (D) Superimposed scapular borders

36. For an AP projection of the knee on a patient whose measurement from ASIS to tabletop is 21 cm, which CR direction will best demonstrate the knee joint?

    (A) 5 degrees caudad
    (B) 10 degrees caudad
    (C) 5 degrees cephalad
    (D) 0 degrees (perpendicular)

37. In which of the following projections was the image in Figure 2–7 made?

    (A) AP
    (B) Medial oblique
    (C) Lateral oblique
    (D) Acute flexion

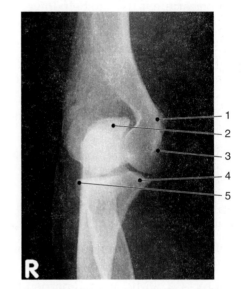

Figure 2–7. Courtesy of Stamford Hospital, Department of Radiology.

38. Which of the following anatomic structures is indicated by the number 2 in Figure 2–7?

    (A) Medial epicondyle
    (B) Trochlea
    (C) Capitulum
    (D) Olecranon process

39. Which of the following is (are) well demonstrated in the lumbar spine pictured in Figure 2–8?

1. Apophyseal articulations
2. Intervertebral foramina
3. Pedicles

(A) 1 only
(B) 1 and 2 only
(C) 2 and 3 only
(D) 1, 2, and 3

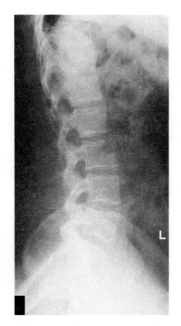

Figure 2–8. Courtesy of Stamford Hospital, Department of Radiology.

40. In which of the following tangential axial projections of the patella is complete relaxation of the quadriceps femoris required for an accurate diagnosis?

1. Supine flexion 45 degrees (Merchant)
2. Prone flexion 90 degrees (Settegast)
3. Prone flexion 55 degrees (Hughston)

(A) 1 only
(B) 1 and 2 only
(C) 2 and 3 only
(D) 1, 2, and 3 only

41. Which of the following projections can be used to supplement the traditional "open-mouth" projection when the upper portion of the odontoid process cannot be well demonstrated?

(A) AP or PA through the foramen magnum
(B) AP oblique with right and left head rotation
(C) Horizontal beam lateral
(D) AP axial

42. The floor of the cranium includes all the following bones *except*

(A) the temporal bones
(B) the occipital bone
(C) the ethmoid bone
(D) the sphenoid bone

43. A lateral projection of the hand in extension is often recommended to evaluate

1. a fracture
2. a foreign body
3. soft tissue

(A) 1 only
(B) 2 only
(C) 2 and 3 only
(D) 1 and 3 only

44. In which of the following positions was the radiograph in Figure 2–9 taken?

(A) RPO
(B) LPO
(C) AP axial
(D) Right lateral decubitus

45. The structure indicated as number 4 in Figure 2–9 is the

(A) terminal ilium
(B) appendix
(C) cecum
(D) sigmoid

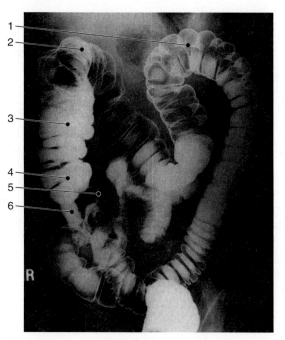

Figure 2–9. Courtesy of Stamford Hospital, Department of Radiology.

46. The condition that results from a persistent fetal foramen ovale is

    (A) an atrial septal defect
    (B) a ventricular septal defect
    (C) a patent ductus arteriosus
    (D) coarctation of the aorta

47. Which of the following projections or positions will best demonstrate subacromial or subcoracoid dislocation?

    (A) Tangential
    (B) AP axial
    (C) Transthoracic lateral
    (D) PA oblique scapular Y

48. With the patient recumbent on the x-ray table with the head lower than the feet, the patient is said to be in the

    (A) Trendelenburg position
    (B) Fowler position
    (C) decubitus position
    (D) Sims position

49. Which of the following positions can be used to demonstrate the axillary ribs of the right thorax?

    1. RAO
    2. LAO
    3. RPO

    (A) 1 only
    (B) 1 and 2 only
    (C) 2 and 3 only
    (D) 1, 2, and 3

50. In which projection of the foot are the interspaces between the first and second cuneiforms best demonstrated?

    (A) Lateral oblique foot
    (B) Medial oblique foot
    (C) Lateral foot
    (D) Weight-bearing foot

51. The sternal angle is at approximately the same level as the

    (A) T2–3 interspace fifth thoracic vertebra
    (B) T9–10 interspace
    (C) T5
    (D) costal margin

52. Which of the following structures is (are) located in the right upper quadrant (RUQ)?

    1. Spleen
    2. Gallbladder
    3. Hepatic flexure

    (A) 1 only
    (B) 1 and 2 only
    (C) 2 and 3 only
    (D) 1, 2, and 3

53. To demonstrate esophageal varices, the patient must be examined in

    (A) the recumbent position
    (B) the erect position
    (C) the anatomic position
    (D) the Fowler position

54. Which of the following statements regarding Figure 2–10 is (are) true?

1. Correct degree of rotation is present.
2. Midphalanges are foreshortened.
3. Fingers are parallel to the IR.

(A) 1 only
(B) 1 and 2 only
(C) 2 and 3 only
(D) 1, 2, and 3

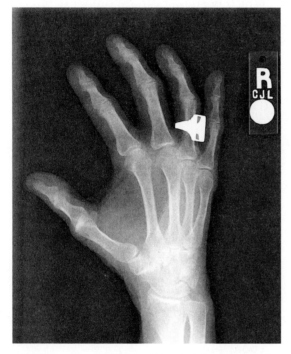

Figure 2–10. Courtesy of Stamford Hospital, Department of Radiology.

55. The tissue that occupies the central cavity within the shaft of a long bone in an adult is

(A) red marrow
(B) yellow marrow
(C) cortical tissue
(D) cancellous tissue

56. All the following structures are associated with the posterior femur *except*

(A) popliteal surface
(B) intercondyloid fossa
(C) intertrochanteric line
(D) linea aspera

57. Which of the following projections of the ankle would *best* demonstrate the mortise?

(A) Medial oblique 15 to 20 degrees
(B) Lateral oblique 15 to 20 degrees
(C) Medial oblique 45 degrees
(D) Lateral oblique 45 degrees

58. Which of the following statements with respect to the PA chest seen in Figure 2–11 is (are) correct?

1. Adequate inspiration is demonstrated.
2. The shoulders are rolled forward adequately.
3. Rotation is demonstrated.

(A) 1 only
(B) 1 and 2 only
(C) 2 and 3 only
(D) 1, 2, and 3

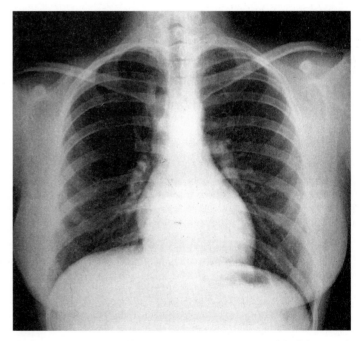

Figure 2–11. Courtesy of Stamford Hospital, Department of Radiology.

59. Which of the following bony landmarks is in the same transverse plane as the symphysis pubis?

    (A) Ischial tuberosity
    (B) Prominence of the greater trochanter
    (C) Anterosuperior iliac spine
    (D) Anteroinferior iliac spine

60. A radiolucent sponge can be placed under the patient's waist for a lateral projection of the lumbosacral spine to

    1. make the vertebral column parallel with the IR
    2. place the intervertebral disk spaces perpendicular to the IR
    3. decrease the amount of SR reaching the IR

    (A) 1 only
    (B) 1 and 2 only
    (C) 2 and 3 only
    (D) 1, 2, and 3

61. To reduce the amount of scattered radiation reaching the IR in CR/DR imaging of the lumbosacral region, which of the following is (are) recommended?

    1. Close collimation
    2. Lead mat on table posterior to the patient
    3. Decreased SID

    (A) 1 only
    (B) 1 and 2 only
    (C) 2 and 3 only
    (D) 1, 2, and 3

62. Which of the following is (are) distal to the tibial plateau?

    1. Intercondyloid fossa
    2. Tibial condyles
    3. Tibial tuberosity

    (A) 1 only
    (B) 1 and 2 only
    (C) 2 and 3 only
    (D) 1, 2, and 3

63. Evaluation criteria for a lateral projection of the humerus include

    1. epicondyles parallel to the IR
    2. lesser tubercle in profile
    3. superimposed epicondyles

    (A) 1 only
    (B) 1 and 3 only
    (C) 2 and 3 only
    (D) 1, 2, and 3

64. Which position of the shoulder demonstrates the lesser tubercle in profile medially?

    (A) AP
    (B) External rotation
    (C) Internal rotation
    (D) Neutral position

65. With the patient in the PA position, which of the following tube angle and direction combinations is correct for an axial projection of the clavicle?

    (A) 5 to 15 degrees caudad
    (B) 5 to 15 degrees cephalad
    (C) 15 to 30 degrees cephalad
    (D) 15 to 30 degrees caudad

66. Which of the following fracture classifications describes a small bony fragment pulled from a bony process?

    (A) Avulsion fracture
    (B) Torus fracture
    (C) Comminuted fracture
    (D) Compound fracture

67. What portion of the humerus articulates with the ulna to help form the elbow joint?

    (A) Semilunar/trochlear notch
    (B) Radial head
    (C) Capitulum
    (D) Trochlea

68. Movement of a part toward the midline of the body is termed

(A) eversion

(B) inversion

(C) abduction

(D) adduction

69. During myelography, contrast medium is introduced into the

(A) subdural space

(B) subarachnoid space

(C) epidural space

(D) epidermal space

70. The junction of the sagittal and coronal sutures is the

(A) diploe

(B) lambda

(C) bregma

(D) pterion

71. Which of the following statements is (are) true regarding the radiograph in Figure 2–12?

1. The patient is placed in an RAO position.
2. The midcoronal plane is about 60 degrees to the IR.
3. The acromion process is free of superimposition.

(A) 1 only

(B) 1 and 2 only

(C) 2 and 3 only

(D) 1, 2, and 3

72. Examples of synovial pivot articulations include the

1. atlantoaxial joint
2. radioulnar joint
3. temporomandibular joint

(A) 1 only

(B) 1 and 2 only

(C) 2 and 3 only

(D) 1, 2, and 3 only

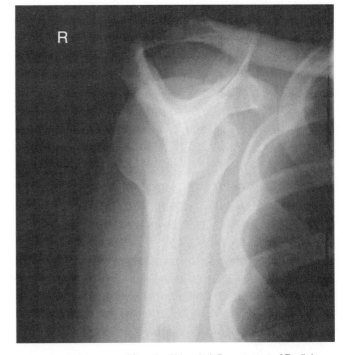

Figure 2–12. Courtesy of Stamford Hospital, Department of Radiology.

73. The lumbar transverse process is represented by what part of the "Scotty dog" seen in a correctly positioned oblique lumbar spine?

(A) Eye

(B) Nose

(C) Body

(D) Ear

74. An injury to a structure located on the side opposite that of the primary injury is referred to as

(A) blowout

(B) Le Fort

(C) contracture

(D) contrecoup

75. In which of the following positions can the sesamoid bones of the foot be demonstrated to be free of superimposition with the metatarsals or phalanges?

(A) Dorsoplantar metatarsals/toes

(B) Tangential metatarsals/toes

(C) 30-degree medial oblique foot

(D) 30-degree lateral oblique foot

76. Which of the following conditions is limited specifically to the tibial tuberosity?

    (A) Ewing sarcoma
    (B) Osgood–Schlatter disease
    (C) Gout
    (D) Exostosis

77. AP stress studies of the ankle may be performed

    1. to demonstrate fractures of the distal tibia and fibula
    2. following inversion or eversion injuries
    3. to demonstrate a ligament tear

    (A) 1 only
    (B) 1 and 2 only
    (C) 2 and 3 only
    (D) 1, 2, and 3

78. Which of the following is (are) part of the bony thorax?

    1. Manubrium
    2. Clavicles
    3. 24 ribs

    (A) 1 only
    (B) 1 and 2 only
    (C) 1 and 3 only
    (D) 1, 2, and 3

79. Aspirated foreign bodies in older children and adults are *most likely* to lodge in the

    (A) right main stem bronchus
    (B) left main stem bronchus
    (C) esophagus
    (D) proximal stomach

80. The PA chest radiograph shown in Figure 2–13 demonstrates

    1. rotation
    2. scapulae removed from lung fields
    3. adequate inspiration

    (A) 1 only
    (B) 1 and 3 only
    (C) 2 and 3 only
    (D) 1, 2, and 3

81. The letter *B* in Figure 2–13 indicates

    (A) a left anterior rib
    (B) a right posterior rib
    (C) a left posterior rib
    (D) a right anterior rib

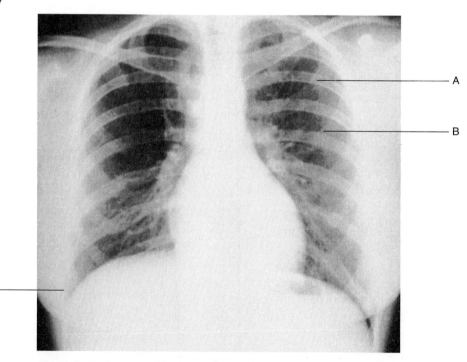

Figure 2–13. Courtesy of Stamford Hospital, Department of Radiology.

82. With the patient seated at the end of the x-ray table, elbow flexed 80 degrees, and the CR directed 45 degrees laterally *from the shoulder to the elbow joint*, which of the following structures will be demonstrated best?

    (A) Radial head
    (B) Ulnar head
    (C) Coronoid process
    (D) Olecranon process

83. The structures forming the brain stem include

    1. the pons
    2. the medulla oblongata
    3. the midbrain

    (A) 1 and 2 only
    (B) 1 and 3 only
    (C) 2 and 3 only
    (D) 1, 2, and 3

84. The CR will parallel the intervertebral foramina in which of the following projections?

    1. Lateral cervical spine
    2. Lateral thoracic spine
    3. Lateral lumbar spine

    (A) 1 only
    (B) 1 and 2 only
    (C) 2 and 3 only
    (D) 1, 2, and 3

85. What structure can be located midway between the anterosuperior iliac spine (ASIS) and pubic symphysis?

    (A) Dome of the acetabulum
    (B) Femoral neck
    (C) Greater trochanter
    (D) Iliac crest

86. The structure labeled 3 in Figure 2–14 is the

    (A) maxillary sinus
    (B) sphenoidal sinus
    (C) ethmoidal sinus
    (D) frontal sinus

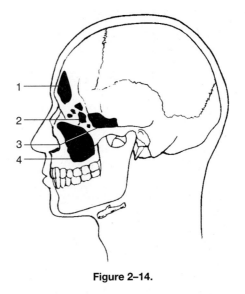

Figure 2–14.

87. Which of the following would *best* evaluate the structure labeled 4 in Figure 2–14?

    (A) PA axial projection (Caldwell method)
    (B) Parietoacanthal projection (Waters method)
    (C) Lateral projection
    (D) Submentovertical projection

88. Which of the following positions demonstrates the sphenoid sinuses?

    1. Modified Waters (mouth open)
    2. Lateral
    3. PA axial

    (A) 1 only
    (B) 1 and 2 only
    (C) 2 and 3 only
    (D) 1, 2, and 3

89. The radiograph shown in Figure 2–15 demonstrates the articulation between the

    1. talus and the calcaneus
    2. calcaneus and the cuboid
    3. talus and the navicular

    (A) 1 only
    (B) 1 and 2 only
    (C) 2 and 3 only
    (D) 1, 2, and 3

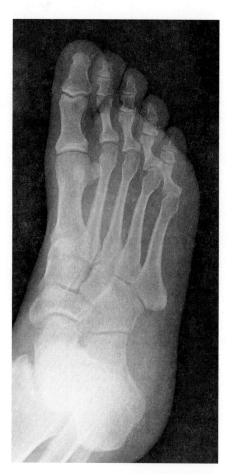

Figure 2–15. Courtesy of Stamford Hospital, Department of Radiology.

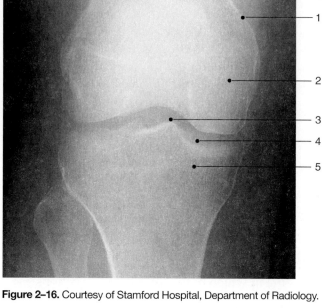

Figure 2–16. Courtesy of Stamford Hospital, Department of Radiology.

90. Identify the structure labeled 1 in the AP projection of the knee shown in Figure 2–16.

(A) Lateral condyle
(B) Lateral epicondyle
(C) Medial condyle
(D) Medial epicondyle

91. The articular facets of L5-S1 are best demonstrated in a(n)

(A) AP projection
(B) 30-degree oblique
(C) 45-degree oblique
(D) AP axial

92. The patient's chin should be elevated during chest radiography to

(A) permit the diaphragm to move to its lowest position
(B) avoid superimposition on the apices
(C) assist in maintaining an upright position
(D) keep the MSP parallel

93. The secondary center of ossification in long bones is the

(A) diaphysis
(B) epiphysis
(C) metaphysis
(D) apophysis

94. Medial displacement of a tibial fracture would be best demonstrated in the

(A) AP projection
(B) lateral projection
(C) medial oblique projection
(D) lateral oblique projection

95. The lumbar lamina is represented by what part of the "Scotty dog" seen in a correctly positioned oblique lumbar spine view?

    (A) Eye
    (B) Nose
    (C) Body
    (D) Neck

96. All the following statements regarding the position shown in Figure 2–17 are true *except*

    (A) a left pleural effusion could be demonstrated.
    (B) a right pneumothorax could be demonstrated.
    (C) a left lateral decubitus position is illustrated.
    (D) the CR is directed vertically to the level of T7.

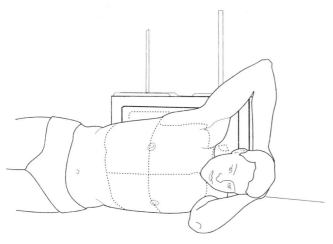

Figure 2–17.

97. Which of the following positions would *best* demonstrate the proximal tibiofibular articulation?

    (A) AP
    (B) 90 degrees mediolateral
    (C) 45-degree internal rotation
    (D) 45-degree external rotation

98. At what level do the carotid arteries bifurcate?

    (A) Foramen magnum
    (B) Trachea
    (C) Pharynx
    (D) C4

99. During a double-contrast BE, which of the following positions would afford the *best* double-contrast visualization of the lateral wall of the descending colon and the medial wall of the ascending colon?

    (A) AP or PA erect
    (B) Right lateral decubitus
    (C) Left lateral decubitus
    (D) Ventral decubitus

100. What is the structure indicated by the number 8 in Figure 2–18?

    (A) Common hepatic duct
    (B) Common bile duct
    (C) Cystic duct
    (D) Pancreatic duct

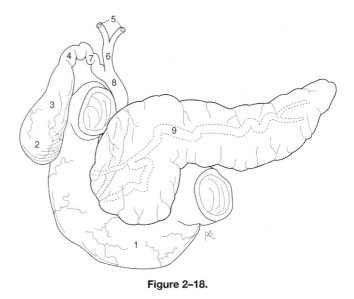

Figure 2–18.

101. What is the structure indicated by the number 7 in Figure 2–18?

    (A) Common hepatic duct
    (B) Common bile duct
    (C) Cystic duct
    (D) Pancreatic duct

102. Which of the following conditions is often the result of ureteral obstruction or stricture?

    (A) Pyelonephrosis
    (B) Nephroptosis
    (C) Hydronephrosis
    (D) Cystourethritis

103. Which of the following examinations involves the introduction of a radiopaque contrast medium through a uterine cannula?

    (A) Retrograde pyelogram
    (B) Voiding cystourethrogram
    (C) Hysterosalpingogram
    (D) Myelogram

104. All the following statements regarding large bowel radiography are true *except*

    (A) the large bowel must be completely empty prior to examination.
    (B) retained fecal material can obscure pathology.
    (C) single-contrast studies help to demonstrate intraluminal lesions.
    (D) double-contrast studies help to demonstrate mucosal lesions.

105. In a lateral projection of the normal knee, the

    1. fibular head should be somewhat superimposed on the proximal tibia.
    2. patellofemoral joint should be visualized.
    3. femoral condyles should be superimposed.

    (A) 1 only
    (B) 2 only
    (C) 1 and 3 only
    (D) 1, 2, and 3

106. All elbow fat pads are best demonstrated in which position?

    (A) AP
    (B) Lateral
    (C) Acute flexion
    (D) AP partial flexion

107. The term used to describe expectoration of blood from the bronchi is

    (A) hemoptysis
    (B) hematemesis
    (C) chronic obstructive pulmonary disease (COPD)
    (D) bronchitis

108. Double-contrast examinations of the stomach or large bowel are performed to better visualize the

    (A) position of the organ
    (B) size and shape of the organ
    (C) diverticula
    (D) gastric or bowel mucosa

109. Which of the following are mediastinal structures?

    1. Heart
    2. Trachea
    3. Esophagus

    (A) 1 only
    (B) 1 and 2 only
    (C) 2 and 3 only
    (D) 1, 2, and 3

110. Which of the following statements is (are) true regarding the position illustrated in Figure 2–19?

    1. The right (adjacent to the table) ureter is parallel to the IR.
    2. The left (elevated) kidney is parallel to the IR.
    3. The degree of obliquity should be about 30 degrees.

    (A) 1 only
    (B) 1 and 2 only
    (C) 2 and 3 only
    (D) 1, 2, and 3

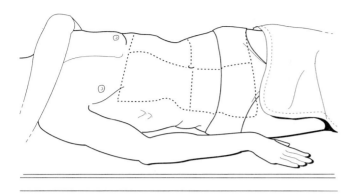

Figure 2–19.

111. In which position of the shoulder is the greater tubercle seen superimposed on the humeral head?

(A) AP
(B) External rotation
(C) Internal rotation
(D) Neutral position

112. With the patient positioned as illustrated in Figure 2–20, which of the following structures is best demonstrated?

(A) Patella
(B) Patellofemoral articulation
(C) Intercondyloid fossa
(D) Tibial tuberosity

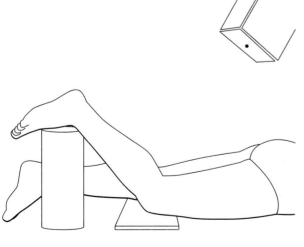

Figure 2–20.

113. Which of the following structures is illustrated by the number 2 in Figure 2–21?

(A) Maxillary sinus
(B) Coronoid process
(C) Zygomatic arch
(D) Coracoid process

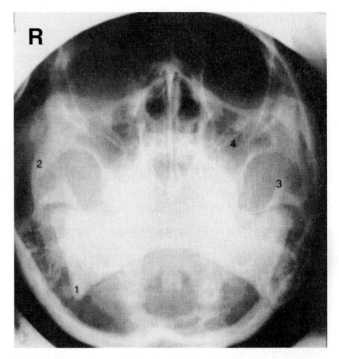

Figure 2–21. Courtesy of Stamford Hospital, Department of Radiology.

114. Which of the following articulations may be described as diarthrotic?

1. Knee
2. Intervertebral joints
3. Temporomandibular joint (TMJ)

(A) 1 only
(B) 2 only
(C) 1 and 3 only
(D) 1, 2, and 3

115. Ulnar flexion/deviation will *best* demonstrate which carpal(s)?

    1. Medial carpals
    2. Lateral carpals
    3. Scaphoid

    (A) 1 only
    (B) 1 and 2 only
    (C) 2 and 3 only
    (D) 1, 2, and 3

116. What should be done to better demonstrate the coracoid process shown in Figure 2–22?

    (A) Use a perpendicular CR.
    (B) Angle the CR about 30 degrees cephalad.
    (C) Angle the CR about 30 degrees caudad.
    (D) Angle the MSP 15 degrees toward the affected side.

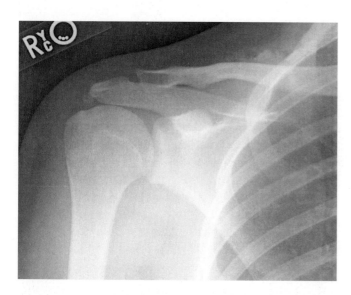

Figure 2–22. Courtesy of Stamford Hospital, Department of Radiology.

117. Structures comprising the neural, or vertebral, arch include

    1. pedicles
    2. laminae
    3. body

    (A) 1 only
    (B) 1 and 2 only
    (C) 2 and 3 only
    (D) 1, 2, and 3

118. In which type of fracture are the splintered ends of bone forced through the skin?

    (A) Closed
    (B) Compound
    (C) Compression
    (D) Depressed

119. The thoracic apophyseal joints are demonstrated with the

    (A) coronal plane 90 degrees to the IR
    (B) midsagittal plane 90 degrees to the IR
    (C) coronal plane 20 degrees to the IR
    (D) midsagittal plane 20 degrees to the IR.

120. Which of the following may be used to evaluate the glenohumeral joint?

    1. Scapular Y projection
    2. Inferosuperior axial
    3. Transthoracic lateral

    (A) 1 only
    (B) 1 and 2 only
    (C) 2 and 3 only
    (D) 1, 2, and 3

121. The long, flat structures that project posteromedially from the pedicles are the

    (A) transverse processes
    (B) vertebral arches
    (C) laminae
    (D) pedicles

122. The type of ileus characterized by cessation of peristalsis is termed

    (A) mechanical
    (B) paralytic
    (C) asymptomatic
    (D) sterile

123. Radiography of which of the following structure(s) in the AP or PA position will inherently result in an image demonstrating shape distortion of the anatomic part?

1. Kidney
2. Scaphoid
3. Sigmoid

(A) 1 only
(B) 1 and 2 only
(C) 2 and 3 only
(D) 1, 2, and 3

124. Which of the following procedures will *best* demonstrate the cephalic, basilic, and subclavian veins?

(A) Aortofemoral arteriogram
(B) Upper-limb venogram
(C) Lower-limb venogram
(D) Renal venogram

125. Which of the following statements is (are) correct with respect to the images shown in Figure 2–23?

1. Image A was made with cephalad angulation.
2. Image B was made with cephalad angulation.
3. Images A and B were made with CR directed 15 degrees cephalad.

(A) 1 only
(B) 2 only
(C) 2 and 3 only
(D) 1, 2, and 3

126. The body habitus characterized by a long and narrow thoracic cavity and low midline stomach and gallbladder is the

(A) asthenic
(B) hyposthenic
(C) sthenic
(D) hypersthenic

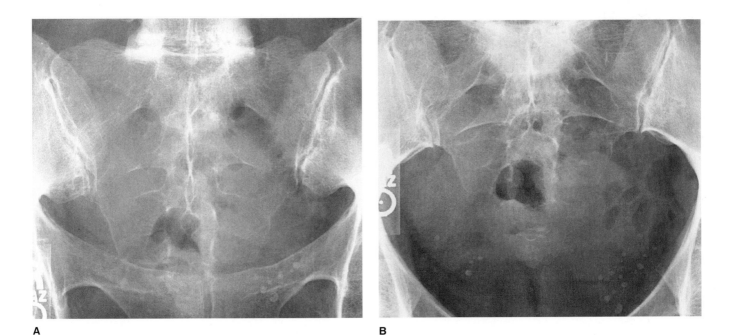

A   B

Figure 2–23A&B. Courtesy of Stamford Hospital, Department of Radiology.

127. Which of the following should be performed to rule out subluxation or fracture of the cervical spine?

    (A) Oblique cervical spine, seated
    (B) AP cervical spine, recumbent
    (C) Horizontal beam lateral
    (D) Laterals in flexion and extension

128. Which of the following is proximal to the carpal bones?

    (A) Distal interphalangeal joints
    (B) Proximal interphalangeal joints
    (C) Metacarpals
    (D) Radial styloid process

129. Which of the following statements regarding the scapular Y projection of the shoulder is (are) true?

    1. The midsagittal plane should be about 60 degrees to the IR.
    2. The scapular borders should be superimposed on the humeral shaft.
    3. An oblique projection of the shoulder is obtained.

    (A) 1 only
    (B) 1 and 2 only
    (C) 2 and 3 only
    (D) 1, 2, and 3

130. Which of the following are characteristics of the hypersthenic body type?

    1. Short, wide, transverse heart
    2. High and peripheral large bowel
    3. Diaphragm positioned low

    (A) 1 and 2 only
    (B) 1 and 3 only
    (C) 2 and 3 only
    (D) 1, 2, and 3

131. *Glossitis* refers to inflammation of the

    (A) epiglottis
    (B) salivary glands
    (C) tongue
    (D) ossicles

132. With the patient's head in a PA position and the CR directed 20 degrees cephalad, which part of the mandible will be *best* visualized?

    (A) Symphysis
    (B) Rami
    (C) Body
    (D) Angle

133. During IV urography, the prone position generally is recommended to demonstrate

    1. the filling of the ureters
    2. the renal pelvis
    3. the superior calyces

    (A) 1 only
    (B) 1 and 2 only
    (C) 1 and 3 only
    (D) 1, 2, and 3

134. The plane that passes vertically through the body, dividing it into anterior and posterior halves, is termed the

    (A) median sagittal plane (MSP)
    (B) midcoronal plane
    (C) sagittal plane
    (D) transverse plane

135. To demonstrate a profile view of the glenoid fossa, the patient is AP recumbent and obliqued 45 degrees

    (A) toward the affected side
    (B) away from the affected side
    (C) with the arm at the side in the anatomic position
    (D) with the arm in external rotation

136. Which of the following anatomic structures is indicated by the number 1 in Figure 2–24?

    (A) Body of L3
    (B) Body of L4
    (C) Spinous process
    (D) Transverse process

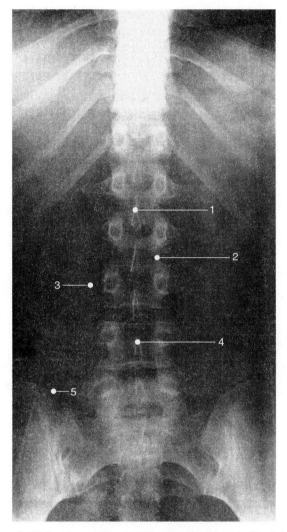

Figure 2–24. Courtesy of Stamford Hospital, Department of Radiology.

137. During an air-contrast BE, in what part of the colon is air most likely to be visualized with the body in the AP recumbent position?

    (A) Transverse colon
    (B) Descending colon
    (C) Ascending colon
    (D) Left and right colic flexures

138. Central ray angulation may be required for

    1. magnification of anatomic structures
    2. foreshortening or self-superimposition
    3. superimposition of overlying structures

    (A) 1 only
    (B) 1 and 2 only
    (C) 2 and 3 only
    (D) 1, 2, and 3

139. Which of the following is recommended to better demonstrate the tarsometatarsal joints in a dorsoplantar projection of the foot?

    (A) Invert the foot.
    (B) Evert the foot.
    (C) Angle the CR 10 degrees posteriorly.
    (D) Angle the CR 10 degrees anteriorly.

140. Valid evaluation criteria for a lateral projection of the forearm requires that

    1. the epicondyles be parallel to the IR.
    2. the radius and ulna be superimposed distally.
    3. the radial tuberosity should face anteriorly.

    (A) 1 only
    (B) 1 and 2 only
    (C) 2 and 3 only
    (D) 1, 2, and 3

141. Which of the following positions will provide an AP projection of the L5-S1 interspace?

    (A) Patient AP with 30- to 35-degree angle cephalad
    (B) Patient AP with 30- to 35-degree angle caudad
    (C) Patient AP with 0-degree angle
    (D) Patient lateral, coned to L5

142. Subject/object unsharpness can result from all of the following *except* when

    (A) object shape does not coincide with the shape of x-ray beam
    (B) object plane is not parallel with x-ray tube and/or IR
    (C) anatomic object(s) of interest is/are in the path of the CR
    (D) anatomic object(s) of interest is/are at a distance from the IR

143. Patients are instructed to remove all jewelry, hair clips, metal prostheses, coins, and credit cards before entering the room for an examination in

    (A) sonography
    (B) computed tomography (CT)
    (C) magnetic resonance imaging (MRI)
    (D) nuclear medicine

144. The true lateral position of the skull uses which of the following principles?

    1. Interpupillary line perpendicular to the IR
    2. MSP perpendicular to the IR
    3. Infraorbitomeatal line (IOML) parallel to the transverse axis of the IR

    (A) 1 only
    (B) 1 and 2 only
    (C) 1 and 3 only
    (D) 1, 2, and 3

145. In which of the following positions was the radiograph shown in Figure 2–25 probably made?

    (A) Supine recumbent
    (B) Prone recumbent
    (C) PA upright
    (D) Supine Trendelenburg

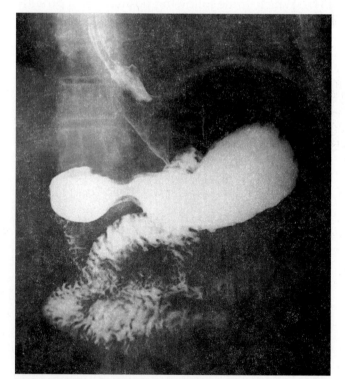

Figure 2–25. Courtesy of Stamford Hospital, Department of Radiology.

146. A kyphotic curve is formed by which of the following?

    1. Sacral vertebrae
    2. Thoracic vertebrae
    3. Lumbar vertebrae

    (A) 1 only
    (B) 1 and 2 only
    (C) 3 only
    (D) 1 and 3 only

147. Which of the following is (are) required for a lateral projection of the skull?

    1. The IOML is parallel to the IR.
    2. The MSP is parallel to the IR.
    3. The CR enters ¾ inch superior and anterior to the EAM.

    (A) 1 only
    (B) 1 and 2 only
    (C) 2 and 3 only
    (D) 1, 2, and 3

148. That ossified portion of a long bone where cartilage has been replaced by bone is known as the

    (A) diaphysis
    (B) epiphysis
    (C) metaphysis
    (D) apophysis

149. Which of the following positions will *most* effectively move the gallbladder away from the vertebrae in an asthenic patient?

    (A) LAO
    (B) RAO
    (C) LPO
    (D) Erect

150. The ileocecal valve normally is located in which of the following body regions?

    (A) Right iliac
    (B) Left iliac
    (C) Right lumbar
    (D) Hypogastric

151. Which of the following is (are) true regarding radiographic examination of the acromioclavicular joints?

    1. The procedure is performed in the erect position.
    2. Use of weights can improve demonstration of the joints.
    3. The procedure should be avoided if dislocation or separation is suspected.

    (A) 1 only
    (B) 1 and 2 only
    (C) 1 and 3 only
    (D) 2 and 3 only

152. A type of cancerous bone tumor occurring in children and young adults and arising from bone marrow is

    (A) Ewing sarcoma
    (B) multiple myeloma
    (C) enchondroma
    (D) osteochondroma

153. Arteries and veins enter and exit the medial aspect of each lung at the

    (A) root
    (B) hilus
    (C) carina
    (D) epiglottis

154. Which of the following skull positions will demonstrate the cranial base, sphenoidal sinuses, atlas, and odontoid process?

    (A) AP axial
    (B) Lateral
    (C) Parietoacanthial
    (D) Submentovertical (SMV)

155. Which of the following statements is (are) true with respect to the radiograph shown in Figure 2–26?

    1. The acromion process is seen partially superimposed on the third rib.
    2. This projection is performed to evaluate the scapula.
    3. This projection is performed to evaluate the acromioclavicular articulation.

    (A) 1 only
    (B) 2 only
    (C) 1 and 2 only
    (D) 2 and 3 only

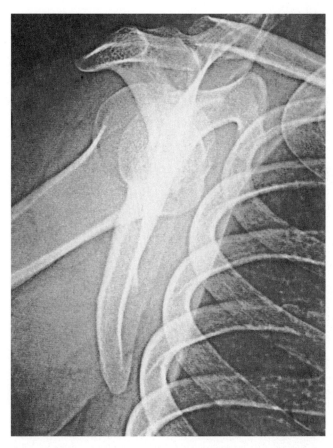

Figure 2–26. Courtesy of Stamford Hospital, Department of Radiology.

156. Which of the following is (are) located on the anterior aspect of the femur?

1. Patellar surface
2. Intertrochanteric crest
3. Linea aspera

(A) 1 only
(B) 1 and 2 only
(C) 2 and 3 only
(D) 1, 2, and 3

157. An intrathecal injection is associated with which of the following examinations?

(A) Intravenous urogram
(B) Retrograde pyelogram
(C) Myelogram
(D) Cystogram

158. In Figure 2–27, the structure indicated as number 7 is which of the following?

(A) Neck of rib
(B) Tubercle of rib
(C) Transverse process
(D) Head of rib

159. Which of the following statements is (are) correct with respect to evaluation criteria for a PA projection of the chest for lungs?

1. Sternal extremities of clavicles are equidistant from vertebral borders.
2. Ten posterior ribs are demonstrated above the diaphragm.
3. The esophagus is visible in the midline.

(A) 1 only
(B) 1 and 2 only
(C) 2 and 3 only
(D) 1, 2, and 3

160. In which of the following positions/ projections will the talocalcaneal joint be visualized?

(A) Dorsoplantar projection of the foot
(B) Plantodorsal projection of the os calcis
(C) Medial oblique position of the foot
(D) Lateral foot

161. In the lateral projection of the ankle, the

1. talotibial joint is visualized.
2. talofibular joint is visualized.
3. tibia and fibula are superimposed.

(A) 1 only
(B) 1 and 2 only
(C) 1 and 3 only
(D) 1, 2, and 3

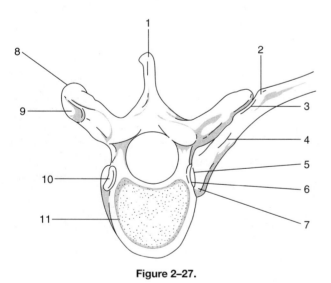

Figure 2–27.

162. The position illustrated in the radiograph in Figure 2–28 may be obtained with the patient

1. supine and the CR angled 30 degrees caudad.
2. supine and the CR angled 30 degrees cephalad.
3. prone and the CR angled 30 degrees cephalad.

(A) 1 only
(B) 2 only
(C) 1 and 3 only
(D) 2 and 3 only

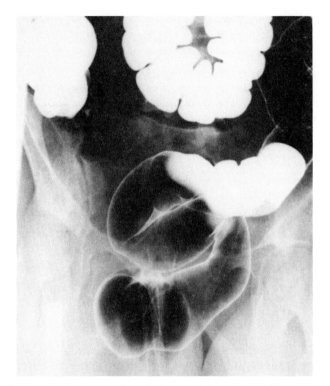

Figure 2–28. Courtesy of Stamford Hospital, Department of Radiology.

163. All the following positions are likely to be employed for both single- and double-contrast examinations of the large bowel *except*

(A) lateral rectum.
(B) AP axial rectosigmoid.
(C) right and left lateral decubitus abdomen.
(D) RAO and LAO abdomen.

164. Which of the following statements regarding the Norgaard method, "Ball-Catcher's position," is (are) correct?

1. Bilateral AP oblique hands are obtained.
2. It is used for early detection of rheumatoid arthritis.
3. The hands are obliqued about 45 degrees, palm up.

(A) 1 only
(B) 1 and 2 only
(C) 2 and 3 only
(D) 1, 2, and 3

165. Which of the following can be used to demonstrate the intercondyloid fossa?

1. Prone, knee flexed 40 degrees, CR directed caudad 40 degrees to the popliteal fossa
2. Supine, IR under flexed knee, CR directed cephalad to knee, perpendicular to tibia
3. Prone, patella parallel to IR, heel rotated 5 to 10 degrees lateral, CR perpendicular to knee joint

(A) 1 only
(B) 1 and 2 only
(C) 2 and 3 only
(D) 1, 2, and 3

166. The scapula shown in Figure 2–29 demonstrates

1. its posterior aspect
2. its costal surface
3. its sternal articular surface

(A) 1 only
(B) 1 and 2 only
(C) 1 and 3 only
(D) 1, 2, and 3

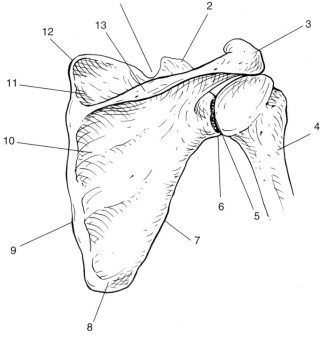

Figure 2–29.

167. In Figure 2–29, which of the following is represented by the number 3?

(A) Acromion process
(B) Scapular spine
(C) Coracoid process
(D) Acromioclavicular joint

168. In Figure 2–29, which of the following is represented by the number 7?

(A) Medial border
(B) Lateral border
(C) Inferior angle
(D) Superior angle

169. With the patient in the PA position and the OML and CR perpendicular to the IR, the resulting radiograph will demonstrate the petrous pyramids

(A) below the orbits
(B) in the lower third of the orbits
(C) completely within the orbits
(D) above the orbits

170. When evaluating a PA axial projection of the skull with a 15-degree caudal angle, the radiographer should see

1. petrous pyramids in the lower third of the orbits
2. equal distance from the lateral border of the skull to the lateral rim of the orbit bilaterally
3. symmetrical petrous pyramids

(A) 1 and 2 only
(B) 1 and 3 only
(C) 2 and 3 only
(D) 1, 2, and 3

171. Which of the following barium-filled anatomic structures is *best* demonstrated in the LPO position?

(A) Hepatic flexure
(B) Splenic flexure
(C) Sigmoid colon
(D) Ileocecal valve

172. The uppermost portion of the iliac crest is at approximately the same level as the

(A) costal margin
(B) umbilicus
(C) xiphoid tip
(D) fourth lumbar vertebra

173. What is the position of the stomach in a hypersthenic patient?

(A) High and vertical
(B) High and horizontal
(C) Low and vertical
(D) Low and horizontal

174. In the anterior oblique position of the cervical spine, the structures best seen are the

(A) intervertebral foramina nearest the IR
(B) intervertebral foramina furthest from the IR
(C) interarticular joints
(D) intervertebral joints

175. During chest radiography, the act of inspiration

1. elevates the diaphragm
2. raises the ribs
3. depresses the abdominal viscera

(A) 1 only
(B) 1 and 2 only
(C) 2 and 3 only
(D) 1, 2, and 3

176. In the lateral projection of the scapula, the

1. vertebral and axillary borders are superimposed.
2. acromion and coracoid processes are superimposed.
3. inferior angle is superimposed on the ribs.

(A) 1 only
(B) 1 and 2 only
(C) 1 and 3 only
(D) 1, 2, and 3

177. Which of the following statements is (are) true regarding Figure 2–30?

1. The image was made in the LAO position.
2. The CR should enter more inferiorly.
3. The sternum is projected onto the left side of the thorax.

(A) 1 only
(B) 2 only
(C) 2 and 3 only
(D) 1, 2, and 3

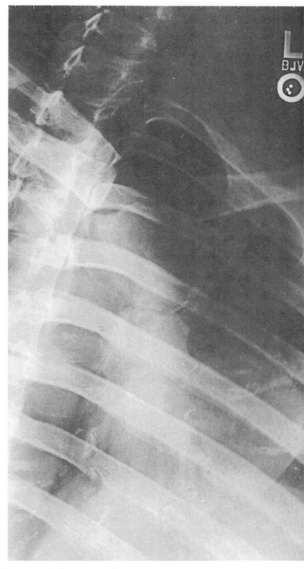

Figure 2–30. Courtesy of Stamford Hospital, Department of Radiology.

178. To better visualize the knee-joint space in the radiograph in Figure 2–31, the radiographer should

   (A) flex the knee more acutely
   (B) flex the knee less acutely
   (C) angle the CR 5 to 7 degrees cephalad
   (D) angle the CR 5 to 7 degrees caudad

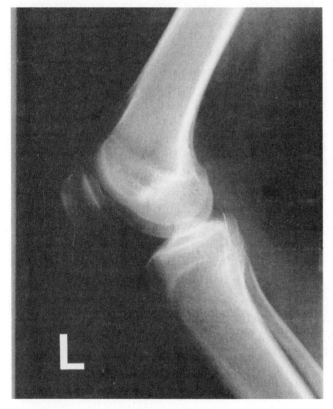

Figure 2–31. Courtesy of Stamford Hospital, Department of Radiology.

179. Which of the following is (are) demonstrated in an AP projection of the cervical spine?

   1. Intervertebral disk spaces
   2. C3–7 cervical bodies
   3. Apophyseal joints

   (A) 1 only
   (B) 1 and 2 only
   (C) 2 and 3 only
   (D) 1, 2, and 3

180. With which of the following does the trapezium articulate?

   (A) Fifth metacarpal
   (B) First metacarpal
   (C) Distal radius
   (D) Distal ulna

181. Which of the following statements is (are) true regarding a PA axial projection of the paranasal sinuses?

   1. The OML is elevated 15 degrees from the horizontal.
   2. The petrous pyramids completely fill the orbits.
   3. The frontal and ethmoidal sinuses are visualized.

   (A) 1 only
   (B) 1 and 2 only
   (C) 1 and 3 only
   (D) 1, 2, and 3

182. Tracheotomy is an effective technique used to restore breathing when there is

   (A) respiratory pathway obstruction above the larynx
   (B) crushed tracheal rings owing to trauma.
   (C) respiratory pathway closure owing to inflammation and swelling
   (D) all the above

183. To demonstrate the first two cervical vertebrae in the AP projection, the patient is positioned so that

   (A) the glabellomeatal line is vertical.
   (B) the acanthiomeatal line is vertical.
   (C) a line between the mentum and the mastoid tip is vertical.
   (D) a line between the maxillary occlusal plane and the mastoid tip is vertical.

184. For which of the following conditions is operative cholangiography a useful tool?

    1. Patency of the biliary ducts
    2. Biliary tract calculi
    3. Gallbladder calculi

    (A) 1 only
    (B) 1 and 2 only
    (C) 2 and 3 only
    (D) 1, 2, and 3

185. For the average patient, the CR for a lateral projection of a barium-filled stomach should enter

    (A) midway between the midcoronal line and the anterior abdominal surface
    (B) midway between the vertebral column and the lateral border of the abdomen
    (C) at the midcoronal line at the level of the iliac crest
    (D) perpendicular to the level of L2

186. Which of the following positions is obtained with the patient lying supine on the radiographic table with the CR directed horizontally to the iliac crest?

    (A) Left lateral decubitus position
    (B) Right lateral decubitus position
    (C) Ventral decubitus position
    (D) Dorsal decubitus position

187. Which of the following is (are) appropriate technique(s) for imaging a patient with a possible traumatic spine injury?

    1. Instruct the patient to turn slowly and stop if anything hurts.
    2. Maneuver the x-ray tube instead of moving the patient.
    3. Call for help and use the log-rolling method to turn the patient.

    (A) 1 and 2 only
    (B) 1 and 3 only
    (C) 2 and 3 only
    (D) 1, 2, and 3

188. Which of the following positions is used to demonstrate vertical patellar fractures and the patellofemoral articulation?

    (A) AP knee
    (B) Lateral knee
    (C) Tangential patella
    (D) Tunnel view

189. The structure labeled 5 in Figure 2–32 is the

    (A) body of C1
    (B) body of C2
    (C) odontoid process
    (D) anterior arch of C1

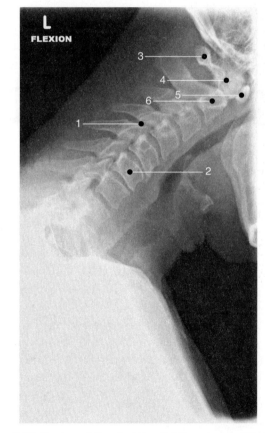

Figure 2–32. Courtesy of Stamford Hospital, Department of Radiology.

190. The structure labeled 4 in Figure 2–32 is the

    (A) body of C1
    (B) body of C2
    (C) odontoid process
    (D) anterior arch of C1

191. Which of the following examinations is used to demonstrate vesicoureteral reflux?

(A) Retrograde urogram
(B) Intravenous urogram (IVU)
(C) Voiding cystourethrogram
(D) Retrograde cystogram

192. Which of the following should be demonstrated in a true AP projection of the clavicle?

1. Clavicular body
2. Acromioclavicular joint
3. Sternocostal joint

(A) 1 only
(B) 1 and 2 only
(C) 2 and 3 only
(D) 1, 2, and 3

193. In which of the following projections is the talofibular joint *best* demonstrated?

(A) AP
(B) Lateral oblique
(C) Medial oblique
(D) Lateral

194. Free air in the abdominal cavity is *best* demonstrated in which of the following positions?

(A) AP projection, left lateral decubitus position
(B) AP projection, right lateral decubitus position
(C) PA recumbent position
(D) AP recumbent position

195. Which of the following sequences correctly describes the path of blood flow as it leaves the left ventricle?

(A) Arteries, arterioles, capillaries, venules, veins
(B) Arterioles, arteries, capillaries, veins, venules
(C) Veins, venules, capillaries, arteries, arterioles
(D) Venules, veins, capillaries, arterioles, arteries

196. Which of the following projections of the elbow should demonstrate the radial head free of ulnar superimposition?

(A) AP
(B) Lateral
(C) Medial oblique
(D) Lateral oblique

197. Which of the following projections will *best* demonstrate acromioclavicular separation?

(A) AP recumbent, affected shoulder
(B) AP recumbent, both shoulders
(C) AP erect, affected shoulder
(D) AP erect, both shoulders

198. Which of the following statements regarding myelography is (are) correct?

1. Spinal puncture may be performed in the prone or flexed lateral position.
2. Contrast medium distribution is regulated through x-ray tube angulation.
3. The patient's neck must be in extension during Trendelenburg positions.

(A) 1 only
(B) 1 and 2 only
(C) 1 and 3 only
(D) 1, 2, and 3

199. The term that refers to parts away from the source or beginning is

(A) cephalad
(B) proximal
(C) distal
(D) lateral

200. With the patient PA, the MSP centered to the grid, the OML forming a 37-degree angle with the IR, and the CR perpendicular and exiting the acanthion, which of the following is *best* demonstrated?

(A) Occipital bone
(B) Frontal bone
(C) Facial bones
(D) Basal foramina

201. The inhalation of liquid or solid particles into the nose, throat, or lungs is referred to as

(A) asphyxia
(B) aspiration
(C) atelectasis
(D) asystole

202. Endoscopic retrograde cholangiopancreatography (ERCP) usually involves

1. cannulation of the hepatopancreatic ampulla
2. introduction of contrast medium into the common bile duct
3. introduction of barium directly into the duodenum

(A) 1 only
(B) 1 and 2 only
(C) 1 and 3 only
(D) 1, 2, and 3

203. Which of the following is (are) associated with a Colles' fracture?

1. Transverse fracture of the radial head
2. Chip fracture of the ulnar styloid
3. Posterior or backward displacement

(A) 1 only
(B) 1 and 3 only
(C) 2 and 3 only
(D) 1, 2, and 3

204. The axiolateral, or horizontal beam, projection of the hip requires the IR to be placed

1. parallel to the central ray (CR)
2. parallel to the long axis of the femoral neck
3. in contact with the lateral surface of the body

(A) 1 only
(B) 1 and 2 only
(C) 2 and 3 only
(D) 1, 2, and 3

205. Which of the following guidelines should be followed when performing radiographic examinations on pediatric patients?

(A) Use restraint only when necessary.
(B) Always use physical or mechanical restraint.
(C) Use physical restraint only.
(D) Use mechanical restraint only.

206. Which of the following interventional procedures can be used to increase the diameter of a stenosed vessel?

1. Percutaneous transluminal angioplasty (PTA)
2. Stent placement
3. Peripherally inserted central catheter (PICC line)

(A) 1 only
(B) 1 and 2 only
(C) 1 and 3 only
(D) 1, 2, and 3

207. Important considerations for radiographic examinations of traumatic injuries to the upper extremity include

1. the joint closest to the injured site should be supported during movement of the limb.
2. both joints must be included in long bone studies.
3. two views, at 90 degrees to each other, are required.

(A) 1 only
(B) 1 and 2 only
(C) 2 and 3 only
(D) 1, 2, and 3

208. Correct preparation for a patient scheduled for an upper gastrointestinal (GI) series is most likely to be

(A) iodinated contrast administration evening before examination; water only in the morning
(B) NPO after midnight
(C) cathartics and cleansing enemas
(D) NPO after midnight, cleansing enemas, and empty bladder before scout image

209. The contraction and expansion of arterial walls in accordance with forceful contraction and relaxation of the heart are called

(A) hypertension
(B) elasticity
(C) pulse
(D) pressure

210. The AP Trendelenburg position is often used during an upper GI examination to demonstrate

(A) the duodenal loop
(B) filling of the duodenal bulb
(C) hiatal hernia
(D) hypertrophic pyloric stenosis

211. Which of the following positions would be the *best* choice for a right shoulder examination to rule out fracture?

(A) Internal and external rotation
(B) AP and tangential
(C) AP and AP axial
(D) AP and scapular Y

212. Which of the following projections will best demonstrate the tarsal navicular free of superimposition?

(A) AP oblique, medial rotation
(B) AP oblique, lateral rotation
(C) Mediolateral
(D) Lateral weight-bearing

213. Which of the following bones participate(s) in the formation of the obturator foramen?

1. Ilium
2. Ischium
3. Pubis

(A) 1 and 2 only
(B) 1 and 3 only
(C) 2 and 3 only
(D) 1, 2, and 3

214. Which of the following radiologic procedures requires that a contrast medium be injected into the renal pelvis via a catheter placed within the ureter?

(A) Nephrotomography
(B) Retrograde urography
(C) Cystourethrography
(D) IVU

215. The AP projection of the coccyx requires that the CR be directed

1. 15 degrees cephalad
2. 2 inches superior to the pubic symphysis
3. to a level midway between the ASIS and pubic symphysis

(A) 1 only
(B) 2 only
(C) 1 and 2 only
(D) 1 and 3 only

216. Which of the following views would *best* demonstrate arthritic changes in the knees?

(A) AP recumbent
(B) Lateral recumbent
(C) AP erect
(D) Medial oblique

217. Which of the following positions will demonstrate the lumbosacral apophyseal articulation?

(A) AP
(B) Lateral
(C) 30-degree RPO
(D) 45-degree LPO

218. Which of the following statements is (are) true regarding the images shown in Figure 2–33?

1. Image A is positioned in internal rotation.
2. Image B is positioned in internal rotation.
3. The greater tubercle is better demonstrated in image A.

(A) 1 only
(B) 2 only
(C) 1 and 3 only
(D) 2 and 3 only

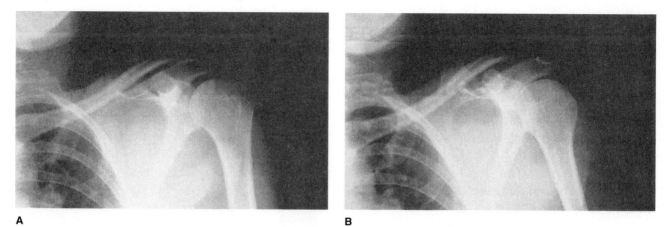

A   B

Figure 2–33A&B. Courtesy of Stamford Hospital, Department of Radiology.

219. Which of the following will best demonstrate the size and shape of the liver and kidneys?

(A) Lateral abdomen

(B) AP abdomen

(C) Dorsal decubitus abdomen

(D) Ventral decubitus abdomen

220. Correct preparation for a patient scheduled for a lower GI series is *most likely* to be

(A) iodinated contrast evening before examination; water only in the morning.

(B) NPO after midnight.

(C) cathartics and cleansing enemas.

(D) NPO after midnight, cleansing enemas, and empty bladder before scout image.

221. The AP axial projection, or "frog leg" position, of the femoral neck places the patient in a supine position with the affected thigh

(A) adducted 25 degrees from the horizontal

(B) abducted 25 degrees from the vertical

(C) adducted 40 degrees from the horizontal

(D) abducted 40 degrees from the vertical

222. Which of the following precautions should be observed when radiographing a patient who has sustained a traumatic injury to the hip?

1. When a fracture is suspected, manipulation of the affected extremity should be performed by a physician.
2. The AP axiolateral projection should be avoided.
3. To evaluate the entire region, the pelvis typically is included in the initial examination.

(A) 1 only

(B) 1 and 3 only

(C) 2 and 3 only

(D) 1, 2, and 3

223. Which of the following projections require(s) that the humeral epicondyles be perpendicular to the IR?

1. AP humerus
2. Lateral forearm
3. Internal rotation shoulder

(A) 1 only

(B) 1 and 2 only

(C) 2 and 3 only

(D) 1, 2, and 3

224. Prior to the start of an IVU, which of the following procedures should be carried out?

1. Have patient empty the bladder.
2. Review the patient's allergy history.
3. Check the patient's creatinine level.

(A) 1 only
(B) 2 only
(C) 1 and 2 only
(D) 1, 2, and 3

225. To demonstrate the entire circumference of the radial head, exposure(s) must be made with the

1. epicondyles perpendicular to the cassette
2. hand pronated and supinated as much as possible
3. hand lateral and in internal rotation

(A) 1 only
(B) 1 and 2 only
(C) 1 and 3 only
(D) 1, 2, and 3

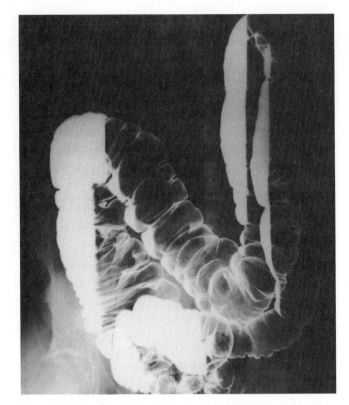

Figure 2–34. Courtesy of Stamford Hospital, Department of Radiology.

226. The image shown in Figure 2–34 was made in what position?

(A) AP or PA erect
(B) Dorsal decubitus
(C) Left lateral decubitus
(D) Right lateral decubitus

227. In myelography, the contrast medium generally is injected into the

(A) cisterna magna
(B) individual intervertebral disks
(C) subarachnoid space between the first and second lumbar vertebrae
(D) subarachnoid space between the third and fourth lumbar vertebrae

228. To evaluate the interphalangeal joints in the oblique and lateral positions, the fingers

(A) rest on the cassette for immobilization
(B) must be supported parallel to the IR
(C) are radiographed in natural flexion
(D) are radiographed in palmar flexion

229. Which of the following is (are) effective in reducing exposure to sensitive tissues for frontal views during scoliosis examinations?

1. Use of PA position
2. Use of breast shields
3. Use of compensating filtration

(A) 1 only
(B) 1 and 2 only
(C) 2 and 3 only
(D) 1, 2, and 3

230. Which type of articulation is evaluated in arthrography?

(A) Synarthrodial
(B) Diarthrodial
(C) Amphiarthrodial
(D) Cartilaginous

231. The laryngeal prominence is formed by the

    (A) thyroid gland
    (B) thyroid cartilage
    (C) vocal cords
    (D) pharynx

232. In the AP projection of the ankle, the

    1. plantar surface of the foot is vertical.
    2. fibula projects more distally than the tibia.
    3. calcaneus is well visualized.

    (A) 1 only
    (B) 1 and 2 only
    (C) 2 and 3 only
    (D) 1, 2, and 3

233. Which of the following examinations most likely would be performed to diagnose Wilm's tumor?

    (A) BE
    (B) Upper GI
    (C) IVU
    (D) Bone survey

234. To visualize or "open" the right sacroiliac joint, the patient is positioned

    (A) 30 to 40 degrees LPO
    (B) 30 to 40 degrees RPO
    (C) 25 to 30 degrees LPO
    (D) 25 to 30 degrees RPO.

235. Deoxygenated blood from the head and thorax is returned to the heart by the

    (A) pulmonary artery
    (B) pulmonary veins
    (C) superior vena cava
    (D) thoracic aorta

236. Which of the following women is likely to have the most homogeneous glandular breast tissue?

    (A) A postpubertal adolescent
    (B) A 20-year-old with one previous pregnancy
    (C) A menopausal woman
    (D) A postmenopausal 65-year-old

237. Standard radiographic protocols may be reduced to include two views, at right angles to each other, in which of the following situations?

    (A) Barium examinations
    (B) Spine radiography
    (C) Skull radiography
    (D) Emergency and trauma radiography

238. Which of the following is a condition in which an occluded blood vessel stops blood flow to a portion of the lungs?

    (A) Pneumothorax
    (B) Atelectasis
    (C) Pulmonary embolism
    (D) Hypoxia

239. Following the ingestion of a fatty meal, what hormone is secreted by the duodenal mucosa to stimulate contraction of the gallbladder?

    (A) Insulin
    (B) Cholecystokinin
    (C) Adrenocorticotropic hormone
    (D) Gastrin

240. Which of the following projections is *most likely* to demonstrate the carpal pisiform free of superimposition?

    (A) Radial flexion/deviation
    (B) Ulnar flexion/deviation
    (C) AP (medial) oblique
    (D) AP (lateral) oblique

241. Myelography is a diagnostic examination used to demonstrate

    1. internal disk lesions.
    2. posttraumatic swelling of the spinal cord.
    3. posterior disk herniation.

    (A) 1 only
    (B) 2 only
    (C) 2 and 3 only
    (D) 1, 2, and 3

242. Which of the following blood chemistry levels must the radiographer check prior to excretory urography?

1. Creatinine
2. Blood urea nitrogen (BUN)
3. Red blood cells (RBCs)

(A) 1 only
(B) 1 and 2 only
(C) 2 and 3 only
(D) 1, 2, and 3

243. Which of the following are components of a trimalleolar fracture?

1. Fractured lateral malleolus
2. Fractured medial malleolus
3. Fractured posterior tibia

(A) 1 only
(B) 1 and 3 only
(C) 2 and 3 only
(D) 1, 2, and 3

244. The functions of which body system include mineral homeostasis, protection, and triglyceride storage?

(A) Endocrine
(B) Integumentary
(C) Skeletal
(D) Muscular

245. The four major arteries supplying the brain include the

1. brachiocephalic artery
2. common carotid arteries
3. vertebral arteries

(A) 1 and 2 only
(B) 1 and 3 only
(C) 2 and 3 only
(D) 1, 2, and 3

246. Ingestion of barium sulfate is contraindicated in which of the following situations?

1. Suspected perforation of a hollow viscus
2. Suspected large bowel obstruction
3. Preoperative patients

(A) 1 only
(B) 1 and 3 only
(C) 2 and 3 only
(D) 1, 2, and 3

247. Which of the following is a major cause of bowel obstruction in children?

(A) Appendicitis
(B) Intussusception
(C) Regional enteritis
(D) Ulcerative colitis

248. Which of the following is (are) well demonstrated in the lumbar spine shown in Figure 2–35?

1. Apophyseal articulations
2. Intervertebral foramina
3. Inferior articular processes

(A) 1 only
(B) 1 and 2 only
(C) 1 and 3 only
(D) 1, 2, and 3

249. Which of the following statements is (are) correct, with respect to a left lateral projection of the chest?

1. The MSP must be perfectly vertical and parallel to the IR.
2. The right posterior ribs will be projected slightly posterior to the left posterior ribs.
3. Arms must be raised high to prevent upper-arm soft-tissue superimposition on lung field.

(A) 1 only
(B) 1 and 2 only
(C) 1 and 3 only
(D) 1, 2, and 3

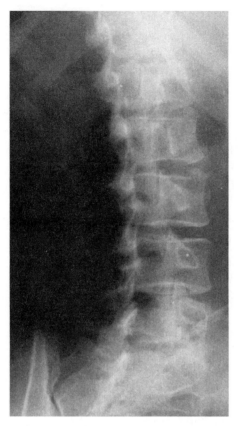

Figure 2–35. Courtesy of Stamford Hospital, Department of Radiology.

250. Which of the following is represented by the number 3 in Figure 2–36?

(A) Inferior vena cava
(B) Aorta
(C) Gallbladder
(D) Psoas muscle

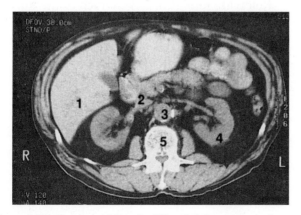

Figure 2–36. Courtesy of Stamford Hospital, Department of Radiology.

251. Which of the following bones participate(s) in the formation of the knee joint?

1. Femur
2. Tibia
3. Patella

(A) 1 and 2 only
(B) 1 and 3 only
(C) 2 and 3 only
(D) 1, 2, and 3

252. All the following are palpable bony landmarks used in radiography of the pelvis *except*

(A) the femoral neck
(B) the pubic symphysis
(C) the greater trochanter
(D) the iliac crest

253. Lateral deviation of the nasal septum may be *best* demonstrated in the

(A) lateral projection
(B) PA axial (Caldwell method) projection
(C) parietoacanthal (Waters method) projection
(D) AP axial (Towne method) projection

254. Which of the following structures should be visualized through the foramen magnum in an AP axial projection (Towne method) of the skull for occipital bone?

1. Posterior clinoid processes
2. Dorsum sella
3. Posterior arch of C1

(A) 1 only
(B) 2 only
(C) 1 and 2 only
(D) 2 and 3 only

255. What is the structure labeled number 5 in Figure 2–37?

   (A) Base of the 2nd metacarpal
   (B) Pisiform
   (C) Trapezium
   (D) Trapezoid

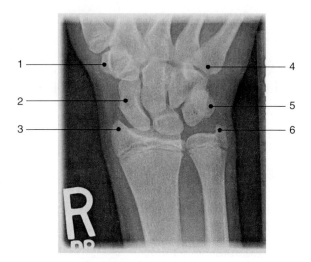

Figure 2–37. Courtesy of Stamford Hospital, Department of Radiology.

256. What is the structure labeled number 3 in Figure 2–37?

   (A) Trapezium
   (B) Scaphoid
   (C) Ulnar styloid
   (D) Radial styloid

257. In the anterior oblique position of the cervical spine, the CR should be directed

   (A) parallel to C4
   (B) perpendicular to C4
   (C) 15 degrees cephalad to C4
   (D) 15 degrees caudad to C4.

258. Which of the following is a functional study used to demonstrate the degree of AP motion present in the cervical spine?

   (A) Open-mouth projection
   (B) Moving-mandible AP
   (C) Flexion and extension laterals
   (D) Right and left bending AP

259. If a patient's zygomatic arch has been traumatically depressed or the patient has flat cheekbones, the arch may be demonstrated by modifying the SMV projection and rotating the patient's head

   (A) 15 degrees toward the side being examined
   (B) 15 degrees away from the side being examined
   (C) 30 degrees toward the side being examined
   (D) 30 degrees away from the side being examined

260. Which of the following factors can contribute to hypertension?

   1. Obesity
   2. Smoking
   3. Stress

   (A) 1 only
   (B) 1 and 2 only
   (C) 2 and 3 only
   (D) 1, 2, and 3

261. What is the degree of difference between the baselines numbered 2 and 3 in Figure 2–38 and used for various projections of the skull?

   (A) 7 degrees
   (B) 8 degrees
   (C) 15 degrees
   (D) 23 degrees

262. Referring to Figure 2–38, which of the following positions requires that baseline number 3 be parallel to the IR?

   (A) Parietoacanthial
   (B) PA axial (Caldwell)
   (C) AP axial (Towne)
   (D) SMV

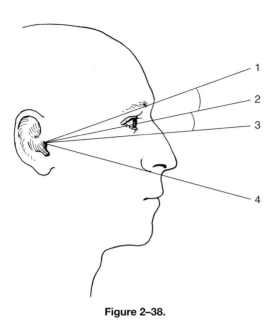

Figure 2–38.

263. Orthoroentgenography, or radiographic measurement of long bones of an upper or lower extremity, requires which of the following accessories?

    1. Bell-Thompson scale
    2. Bucky tray
    3. Cannula

    (A) 1 only
    (B) 1 and 2 only
    (C) 1 and 3 only
    (D) 1, 2, and 3

264. Which of the following is (are) demonstrated in a lateral projection of the cervical spine?

    1. Intervertebral foramina
    2. Apophyseal joints
    3. Intervertebral joints

    (A) 1 only
    (B) 1 and 2 only
    (C) 2 and 3 only
    (D) 1, 2, and 3

265. In a lateral projection of the nasal bones, the CR is directed

    (A) ½ inch posterior to the anterior nasal spine
    (B) ¾ inch posterior to the glabella
    (C) ¾ inch distal to the nasion
    (D) ½ inch anterior to the EAM

266. To make a patient as comfortable as possible during a single-contrast barium enema (BE), the radiographer should

    1. instruct the patient to relax the abdominal muscles to prevent intra-abdominal pressure
    2. instruct the patient to concentrate on breathing deeply to reduce colonic spasm
    3. prepare a warm barium suspension (98–105°F) to aid in retention

    (A) 2 only
    (B) 1 and 2 only
    (C) 2 and 3 only
    (D) 1, 2, and 3

267. Which of the following positions will *best* demonstrate the right apophyseal articulations of the lumbar vertebrae?

    (A) PA
    (B) Left lateral
    (C) RPO
    (D) LPO

268. Structures involved in blowout fractures include the

    1. orbital floor
    2. inferior rectus muscle
    3. zygoma

    (A) 1 only
    (B) 1 and 2 only
    (C) 2 and 3 only
    (D) 1, 2, and 3

269. Inspiration and expiration projections of the chest are performed to demonstrate

1. partial or complete collapse of pulmonary lobe(s)
2. air in the pleural cavity
3. foreign body

(A) 1 only
(B) 1 and 2 only
(C) 1 and 3 only
(D) 1, 2, and 3

270. Shoulder arthrography is performed to

1. evaluate humeral luxation
2. demonstrate complete or partial rotator cuff tear
3. evaluate the glenoid labrum

(A) 1 only
(B) 1 and 2 only
(C) 2 and 3 only
(D) 1, 2, and 3

271. Which of the following positions will separate the radial head, neck, and tuberosity from superimposition on the ulna?

(A) AP
(B) Lateral
(C) Medial oblique
(D) Lateral oblique

272. The most significant risk factor for breast cancer is

(A) age
(B) gender
(C) family history
(D) personal history

273. Which of the following structures is located at the level of the interspace between the second and third thoracic vertebrae?

(A) Manubrium
(B) Jugular notch
(C) Sternal angle
(D) Xiphoid process

274. For the AP projection of the scapula, the

1. patient's arm is abducted at right angles to the body.
2. patient's elbow is flexed with the hand supinated.
3. exposure is made during quiet breathing.

(A) 1 and 2 only
(B) 1 and 3 only
(C) 3 only
(D) 1, 2, and 3

275. The innominate bone is located in the

(A) middle cranial fossa
(B) posterior cranial fossa
(C) foot
(D) pelvis.

276. The sternoclavicular joints are best demonstrated with the patient PA and

(A) in a slight oblique position, affected side adjacent to the IR
(B) in a slight oblique position, affected side away from the IR
(C) erect and weight-bearing
(D) erect with and without weights

277. Which of the following sinus groups is demonstrated with the patient positioned as for a parietoacanthal projection (Waters method) with the CR directed through the patient's open mouth?

(A) Frontal
(B) Ethmoidal
(C) Maxillary
(D) Sphenoidal

278. Below-diaphragm ribs are better demonstrated when

(A) respiration is suspended at the end of full exhalation.
(B) exposed using shallow breathing technique.
(C) the patient is in the recumbent position.
(D) the patient is in the AP erect position.

279. Which of the following positions is essential in radiography of the paranasal sinuses?

(A) Erect
(B) Recumbent
(C) Oblique
(D) Trendelenburg

280. What projection of the os calsis is obtained with the leg extended, the plantar surface of the foot vertical and perpendicular to the IR, and the CR directed 40 degrees cephalad?

(A) Axial plantodorsal projection
(B) Axial dorsoplantar projection
(C) Lateral projection
(D) Weight-bearing lateral projection

281. During GI radiography, the position of the stomach may vary depending on

1. the respiratory phase
2. body habitus
3. patient position

(A) 1 and 2 only
(B) 1 and 3 only
(C) 2 and 3 only
(D) 1, 2, and 3

282. With a patient in the PA position and the OML perpendicular to the table, a 15- to 20-degree caudal angulation would place the petrous ridges in the lower third of the orbit. To achieve the same result in a baby or a small child, it is necessary for the radiographer to modify the angulation to

(A) 10 to 15 degrees caudal
(B) 25 to 30 degrees caudal
(C) 15 to 20 degrees cephalic
(D) 3 to 5 degrees caudal

283. The structure labeled number 6 in Figure 2–39 is the

(A) left subclavian artery
(B) brachiocephalic artery
(C) right common carotid artery
(D) left vertebral artery

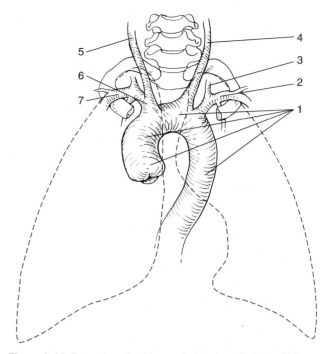

Figure 2–39. Reproduced, with permission, from Doherty GM, ed. *Current Surgical Diagnosis & Treatment*, 12th ed. New York: McGraw-Hill, 2006:824.

284. The structure labeled number 3 in Figure 2–39 is the

(A) left subclavian artery
(B) brachiocephalic artery
(C) right common carotid artery
(D) left vertebral artery

285. In the lateral projection of the foot, the

1. plantar surface should be perpendicular to the IR.
2. metatarsals are superimposed.
3. talofibular joint should be visualized.

(A) 1 only
(B) 1 and 2 only
(C) 2 and 3 only
(D) 1, 2, and 3

286. Hysterosalpingography may be performed for demonstration of

    1. uterine tubal patency
    2. mass lesions in the uterine cavity
    3. uterine position

    (A) 1 and 2 only
    (B) 1 and 3 only
    (C) 2 and 3 only
    (D) 1, 2, and 3

287. The number 2 in Figure 2–40 represents which of the following structures?

    (A) Body
    (B) Pedicle
    (C) Inferior articular process
    (D) Superior articular process

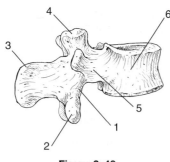

Figure 2–40.

288. To demonstrate the mandibular body in the PA position, the

    (A) CR is directed perpendicular to the IR.
    (B) CR is directed cephalad to the IR.
    (C) skull is obliqued away from the affected side.
    (D) skull is obliqued toward the affected side.

289. Which of the following equipment is necessary for ERCP?

    1. A fluoroscopic unit with imaging device and tilt-table capabilities
    2. A fiberoptic endoscope
    3. Polyethylene catheters

    (A) 1 and 2 only
    (B) 1 and 3 only
    (C) 2 and 3 only
    (D) 1, 2, and 3

290. All the following statements regarding pediatric positioning are true *except*

    (A) for radiography of the kidneys, the CR should be directed midway between the diaphragm and the symphysis pubis.
    (B) if a pediatric patient is in respiratory distress, a chest radiograph should be obtained in the AP projection rather than in the standard PA projection.
    (C) chest radiography on a neonate should be performed in the supine position.
    (D) radiography of pediatric patients with a myelomeningocele defect should be performed in the supine position.

291. The act of expiration will cause the

    1. diaphragm to move inferiorly
    2. sternum and ribs to move inferiorly
    3. diaphragm to move superiorly

    (A) 1 only
    (B) 1 and 2 only
    (C) 2 and 3 only
    (D) 1, 2, and 3

292. A patient unable to extend his or her arm is seated at the end of the x-ray table, elbow flexed 90 degrees. The CR is directed 45 degrees medially. Which of the following structures will be demonstrated *best*?

    1. Radial head
    2. Capitulum
    3. Coronoid process

    (A) 1 only
    (B) 1 and 2 only
    (C) 2 and 3 only
    (D) 1, 2, and 3

293. Which of the following articulate(s) with the bases of the metatarsals?

1. The heads of the first row of phalanges
2. The cuboid
3. The cuneiforms

(A) 1 only
(B) 1 and 2 only
(C) 2 and 3 only
(D) 1, 2, and 3

294. Which of the following statements regarding knee x-ray arthrography is (are) true?

1. Ligament tears can be demonstrated.
2. Sterile technique is observed.
3. MRI can follow x-ray.

(A) 1 and 2 only
(B) 1 and 3 only
(C) 2 and 3 only
(D) 1, 2, and 3

295. What projection was used to obtain the image seen in Figure 2–41?

(A) AP, internal rotation
(B) AP, external rotation
(C) AP, neutral position
(D) AP axial

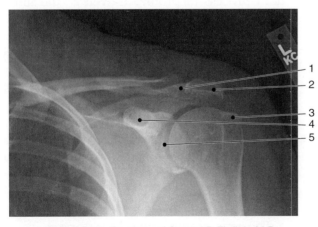

Figure 2–41. Courtesy of Conrad P. Ehrlich, M.D.

296. The structure labeled number 4 in Figure 2–41 is the

(A) acromion process
(B) coracoid process
(C) coronoid process
(D) glenoid process

297. The structure labeled number 5 in Figure 2–41 is the

(A) sternoclavicular joint
(B) acromioclavicular joint
(C) glenohumeral joint
(D) acromiohumeral joint

298. Which of the following is demonstrated in a 25-degree RPO position with the CR entering 1 inch medial to the elevated ASIS?

(A) Left sacroiliac joint
(B) Right sacroiliac joint
(C) Left ilium
(D) Right ilium

299. The relationship between the ends of fractured long bones is referred to as

(A) angulation
(B) apposition
(C) luxation
(D) sprain

300. A lateral projection of the larynx is occasionally required to rule out foreign body, polyps, or tumor. The CR should be directed

(A) just below the EAM
(B) to the level of the mandibular angles
(C) to the level of the laryngeal prominence
(D) to the level of C7

Answers and Explanations

1. **(B)** The term *varus* refers to bent or turned *inward*. In genu varus, the tibia or femur turns inward causing bowlegged deformity; in talipes varus, the foot turns inward (clubfoot deformity). The term *valgus* refers to a part turned/deformed *outward*—as in hallux valgus and talipes valgus. Hallux valgus is angulation of the great toe away from the midline; talipes valgus is a foot deformity with the heel turned outward—a component of clubfoot. *(Bontrager and Lampignano, 6th ed., p. 26)*

2. **(D)** There are three important fat pads associated with the elbow, best demonstrated in the *true* lateral projection. They cannot be demonstrated in the AP projection because of their superimposition on bony structures. The *anterior* fat pad is located just anterior to the distal humerus. The *posterior* fat pad is located within the olecranon fossa at the distal posterior humerus. The *supinator* fat pad/stripe is located at the proximal radius just anterior to the head, neck, and tuberosity. The *posterior* fat pad *is not visible* radiographically in the *normal* elbow. The posterior fat pad is visible in cases or trauma or other pathology and when the elbow is insufficiently flexed. *(Bontrager and Lampignano, 7th ed., p. 133)*

3. **(D)** The lateral projection of the cervical spine requires that the MSP be parallel to the IR and the MCP be perpendicular to the IR. The chin must be elevated enough so as not to superimpose the mandibular angles on cervical structures—yet not so much that the base of the skull obscures cervical structures. The degree of flexion/extension is appropriate in this image; no cervical structures are obscured. The vertebrae are symmetrical—no rotation is present. However, C7 is not clearly delineated, and its all-important articulation with T1 is not visible. This indicates that the shoulders are not sufficiently depressed. *(Frank, Long, and Smith, 11th ed., vol. 1, p. 401)*

4. **(C)** The coronoid process is located on the proximal anterior ulna. The *medial oblique* projection of the elbow demonstrates the coronoid process in profile, as well as the ulnar olecranon process within the humeral olecranon fossa. The *lateral oblique* elbow projection demonstrates the proximal radius and ulna free of superimposition. The coracoid *process* is located on the scapula. *(Frank, Long, and Smith, 11th ed., vol. 1, p. 146)*

5. **(C)** The male and female bony pelves have several differing characteristics. An overview of comparisons is listed below.

Male pelvis
- The general structure is heavy and thick.
- The greater, or false, pelvis is deep.
- The pelvic brim, or inlet, is small and heart-shaped.
- The acetabulum is large and faces laterally.
- The pubic angle is less than 90 degrees.
- The ilium is more vertical.

Female pelvis
- The general structure is light and thin.
- The greater, or false, pelvis is shallow.
- The pelvic brim, or inlet, is large and oval.
- The acetabulum is small and faces anteriorly.
- The pubic angle is more than 90 degrees.
- The ilium is more horizontal.

(Tortora and Derrickson, 11th ed., p. 244)

6. **(C)** In the PA position, portions of the barium-filled hypersthenic stomach superimpose on themselves. Thus, patients with a hypersthenic body habitus usually present a high transverse stomach with poorly defined curvatures. If the PA stomach is projected with a *35- to 45-degree cephalad* CR, the stomach "opens up." That is, the curvatures, the antral portion, and the duodenal bulb all appear as a sthenic habitus stomach would appear. A 35- to 40-degree *RAO* position is used to demonstrate many of these structures in the average, or sthenic, body habitus. A *lateral* position is used to demonstrate the anterior and posterior gastric surfaces and retrogastric space. *(Bontrager and Lampignano, 6th ed., p. 480)*

7. **(C)** Note the relationship between the thigh, lower leg, patella, and CR. The CR is directed *parallel to the plane of the patella,* thereby providing a *tangential* projection of the patella (i.e., patella in profile) and an unobstructed view of the *patellofemoral articulation* (Figure 2–42). A tunnel view is required to demonstrate the intercondyloid fossa and the articulating surfaces of the tibia and femur. *(Frank, Long, and Smith, 11th ed., vol. 1, p. 325)*

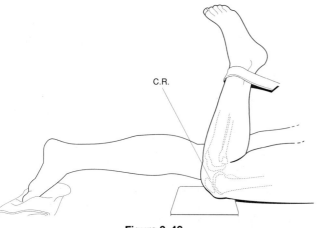

C.R.

Figure 2–42.

8. **(B)** The trachea (windpipe) bifurcates into left and right *main stem bronchi,* each entering its respective lung hilum. The *left* bronchus divides into *two* portions, one for each lobe of the left lung. The *right* bronchus divides into *three* portions, one for each lobe of the right lung (Figure 2–43). The lungs are conical in shape, consisting of upper pointed portions, termed the *apices* (plural of apex), and broad lower portions (or *bases*). The lungs are enclosed in a double-walled serous membrane called the *pleura.* *(Bontrager and Lampignano, 6th ed., p. 80)*

9. **(C)** In the exact PA projection of the skull, the perpendicular CR exits the nasion and the petrous pyramids should *fill* the orbits (Figure 2–44). As the CR is angled caudally, the petrous ridges/pyramids are projected lower in the orbits. At about 25 to 30 degrees caudad they are projected *below* the orbits. The OML must be *perpendicular* to the IR for the petrous pyramids to be projected into the expected location, that is, superimposed within the orbits. The MSP must be *perpendicular* to the IR, or the skull will be rotated and left/right symmetry will be lost. *(Frank, Long, and Smith, 11th ed., vol. 2, p. 312)*

10. **(B)** The figure illustrates a mediolateral projection of the knee. The femoral condyles are not superimposed posteriorly, indicating incorrect degree of forward/backward rotation. Because the magnified medial femoral condyle is obscuring the femoropatellar articulation, the radiographer should rotation the pelvis backward a bit. This will superimpose the femoral condyles, place the patella perpendicular to the tabletop, and open the femoropatellar joint space. *(Frank, Long, and Smith, 11th ed., vol. 1, p. 306)*

11. **(D)** Pacemakers are electromechanical devices that help to regulate the heart rate. They consist of a pulse generator connected to a lead that has an electrode at its tip. The lead is introduced under fluoroscopic guidance into the subclavian vein, then moved to the right atrium, and finally positioned at the apex of the *right ventricle.* *(Bontrager and Lampignano, 6th ed., p. 647)*

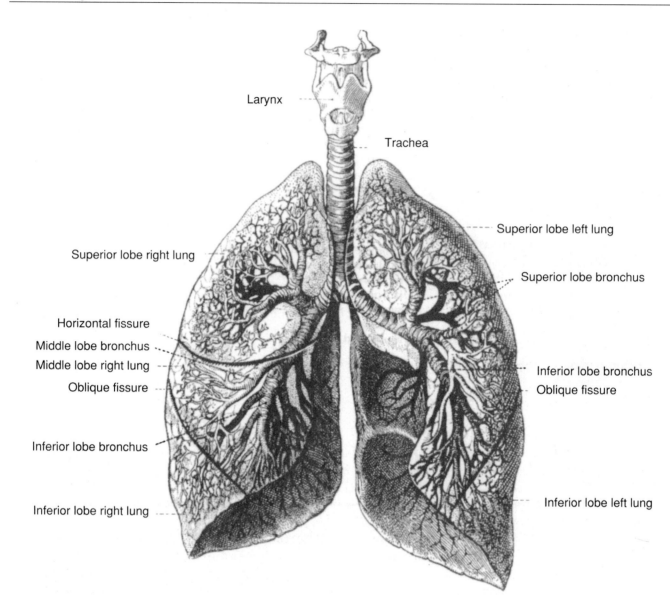

Larynx

Trachea

Superior lobe left lung

Superior lobe right lung

Superior lobe bronchus

Horizontal fissure
Middle lobe bronchus
Middle lobe right lung
Oblique fissure

Inferior lobe bronchus
Oblique fissure

Inferior lobe bronchus

Inferior lobe left lung

Inferior lobe right lung

Figure 2–43. Reproduced, with permission, from Montgomery RL. *Appleton & Lange's Review of Anatomy for the USMLE Step I.* East Norwalk, CT: Appleton & Lange, 1995:27.

12. **(B)** Chest radiographs demonstrating *emphysema* will show the characteristic irreversible trapping of air that increases gradually and overexpands the lungs. This produces the characteristic "flattening" of the hemidiaphragms and widening of the intercostal spaces. The increased air content of the lungs requires a compensating decrease in technical factors. *Pneumonia* is inflammation of the lungs, usually caused by bacteria, virus, or chemical irritant. *Pneumothorax* is a collection of air or gas in the pleural cavity (outside the lungs), with an accompanying collapse of the lung. *Pleural effusion* is excessive fluid between the parietal and visceral layers of pleura. *(Bontrager and Lampignano, 6th ed., p. 92)*

13. **(B)** The *gallbladder* is located on the posterior surface of the liver in the right upper quadrant (RUQ). The *hepatic* (right colic) *flexure*, so named because of its close proximity to the liver, is also in the RUQ. The cecum, located in the right lower quadrant (RLQ), is continuous with the terminal ilium—forming the *ileocecal valve. (Bontrager and Lampignano, 6th ed., p. 112)*

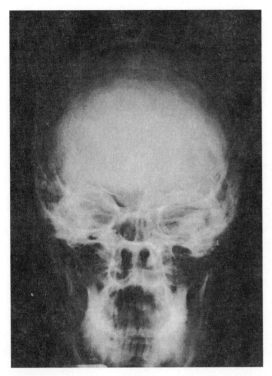

Figure 2–44. Courtesy of Stamford Hospital, Department of Radiology.

14. **(A)** The image shown is one of a series of IVU images taken 15 minutes after injection of the contrast medium. The urinary collecting system is well demonstrated. An RPO position is illustrated, with the right marker indicating the right side; also, the right ilium is more "open" than the left. The RPO position places the *left kidney* and *right ureter* parallel to the IR. The urinary bladder contains considerable contrast, indicating that it is most likely a *prevoid* image. *(Bontrager and Lampignano, 6th ed., p. 574)*

15. **(D)** With the body in the AP recumbent position (or LPO position), *barium* flows easily into the *fundus* of the stomach (from the more distal portions of the stomach), displacing/drawing the stomach somewhat superiorly. The fundus, then, is filled with barium, whereas the *air* that had been in the fundus is now displaced into the *gastric body, pylorus,* and *duodenum,* illustrating them in *double contrast.* Double-contrast delineation of these structures allows us to see *through* the stomach to the retrogastric areas and structures. The RAO position demonstrates a

barium-filled pylorus and duodenum. *Anterior and posterior aspects* of the stomach are visualized in the *lateral* position; medial and lateral aspects of the stomach are visualized in the AP projection. *(Frank, Long, and Smith, 11th ed., vol. 2, p. 142)*

16. **(B)** The ankle mortise, or ankle joint, is formed by the articulation of the tibia, fibula, and talus (Figure 2–45). Two articulations form the ankle mortise: the talotibial and talofibular articulations. The calcaneus is not associated with formation of the ankle mortise. *(Frank, Long, and Smith, 11th ed., vol. 1, p. 233)*

17. **(C)** The bones of the foot are arranged to form a number of longitudinal and transverse *arches.* The longitudinal arch facilitates walking and is evaluated radiographically in lateral weight-bearing (erect) projections. Recumbent laterals would not demonstrate any structural change that occurs when the

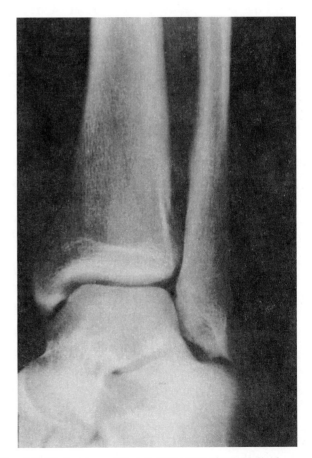

Figure 2–45. Courtesy of Stamford Hospital, Department of Radiology.

individual is weight-bearing erect. *(Frank, Long, and Smith, 11th ed., vol. 1, p. 268)*

18. **(B)** Graves disease is the most frequently occurring form of *hyperthyroidism.* Graves disease is an autoimmune disorder whose symptoms include enlargement of the thyroid gland and exophthalmos (protrusion of the eyes resulting from fluid buildup behind them). Hypothyroidism can result in cretinism in the child and myxedema in the adult. Adrenal overactivity produces Cushing syndrome; underactivity causes Addison disease. *(Tortora and Derrickson, 11th ed., p. 659)*

19. **(C)** *Full* or *forced expiration* is used to elevate the diaphragm and demonstrate the ribs *below* the diaphragm to best advantage (with exposure adjustment). *Deep inspiration* is used to depress the diaphragm and demonstrate as many ribs *above the diaphragm* as possible. Shallow breathing is used occasionally to visualize the ribs above the diaphragm while obliterating pulmonary vascular markings. *(Frank, Long, and Smith, 11th ed., vol. 1, p. 490)*

20. **(A)** The AP axial projects the anterior structures (frontal and facial bones) downward, thus permitting visualization of the *occipital bone* without superimposition (Towne method). The dorsum sella and posterior clinoid processes of the sphenoid bone should be visualized within the foramen magnum. This projection may also be obtained by angling the CR 30 degrees caudad to the OML (Figure 2–46). The *frontal bone* is best shown with the patient PA and with a perpendicular CR. The parietoacanthal projection is the single best position for *facial bones. Basal foramina* are well demonstrated in the submentovertical projection. *(Frank, Long, and Smith, 11th ed., vol. 2, p. 316)*

21. **(B)** The posterior oblique projection of the acetabulum (Judet method) requires a 45-degree obliquity of the entire MSP. In the RPO position, the *down* side (the *right* side in this case) will demonstrate the *anterior rim of the right acetabulum,* the *right posterior ilioischial column,* and the *right iliac wing.* When centered to the *up* side (left in this case), the structures

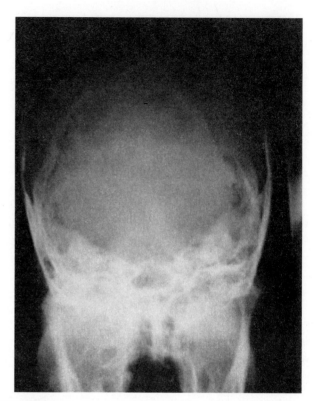

Figure 2–46. Courtesy of Stamford Hospital, Department of Radiology.

demonstrated are the posterior rim of the left acetabulum, left anterior iliopubic column, and the left obturator foramen. *(Bontrager and Lampignano, 6th ed., p. 279)*

22. **(D)** The figure illustrates a PA projection of the chest and the side marker correctly placed. The heart is seen on the *right* side— this is termed *dextrocardia.* Atelectasis (partial or complete collapse of lung) would be demonstrated as increased *tissue* density in the affected area. A classic pneumothorax (air within the thoracic cavity) would demonstrate an absence of lung markings in the affected area and flattening of the hemidiaphragm on the affected side. A small pneumothorax can be easily missed on a chest image having excessive density *(Taber, p. 579).*

23. **(C)** Because the sternum and vertebrae would be superimposed in a direct PA or AP projection, a slight oblique (just enough to separate the sternum from superimposition on the vertebrae) is used instead of a direct frontal projection. In the RAO position, the heart superimposes a homogeneous density over the

sternum, thereby providing more clear radiographic visualization of its bony structure. If the *LAO* position were used to project the sternum to the *right* of the thoracic vertebrae, the posterior ribs and pulmonary markings would cast confusing shadows over the sternum because of their differing densities. *(Frank, Long, and Smith, 11th ed., vol. 1, pp. 472–473)*

24. **(C)** The forward slipping of one vertebra on the one below it is called *spondylolisthesis*. *Spondylolysis* is the breakdown of the pars interarticularis; it may be unilateral or bilateral and results in forward slipping of the involved vertebra—the *condition* of spondylolisthesis. Inflammation of one or more vertebrae is called *spondylitis*. *Spondylosis* refers to degenerative changes occurring in the vertebra. *(Frank, Long, and Smith, 11th ed., vol. 1, p. 388)*

25. **(C)** Venous blood is returned to the right atrium via the superior (from the upper body) and inferior (from the lower body) venae cavae (see Figure 2–47). During atrial systole, blood passes from the right atrium through the tricuspid valve into the right ventricle and from the left atrium through the bicuspid/mitral valve into the left ventricle. During ventricular systole, the pulmonary artery (the only artery to carry deoxygenated blood) carries blood from the right ventricle to the lungs for oxygenation, whereas the left ventricle moves oxygenated blood through the aortic semilunar valve into the aorta and to all body tissues. *(Tortora and Derrickson, 11th ed., pp. 716–718)*

26. **(C)** One of the most important principles in chest radiography is that it be performed, whenever possible, in the erect position. It is in this position that the diaphragm can descend to its lowest position during inspiration, and any air–fluid levels can be detected. However, patients having traumatic injuries frequently must be examined in the supine position. An AP supine chest is performed first. If the examination is also being performed to rule out air–fluid levels, this can be

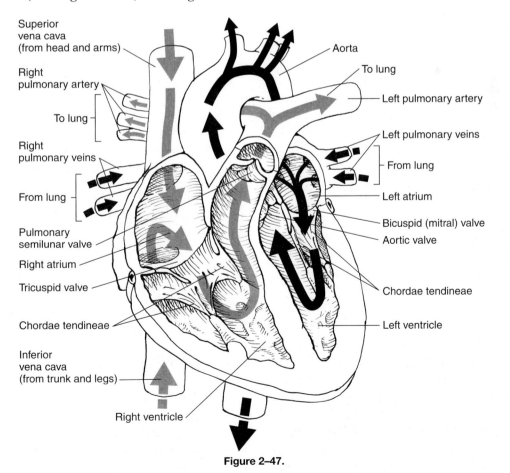

Figure 2–47.

determined by performing the *lateral projection in the dorsal decubitus position*. The patient is lying supine, and a *horizontal* (cross-table) x-ray beam is used. (*Frank, Long, and Smith, 11th ed., vol. 2, p. 40*)

27. **(C)** *Metformin hydrochloride* (Glucophage) is used as an adjunct to appropriate diet to lower blood glucose levels in patients who have type 2 diabetes and whose hyperglycemia is not being managed satisfactorily with diet alone. Patients on Glucophage who are having intravascular iodinated contrast studies can develop an acute alteration of renal function or acute acidosis. It is recommended that patients on Metformin hydrochloride (Glucophage) have it withheld 48 hours *after* the examination (*Bontrager and Lampignano, 7th ed., p. 542*)

28. **(C)** The radiograph shown is a PA projection (Caldwell method) of the frontal and anterior ethmoidal sinuses. The frontal sinuses are seen centrally in the vertical plate of the frontal bone behind the glabella and extending laterally over the superciliary arches. The ethmoidal sinuses are seen adjacent and inferior to the medial aspect of the orbits. The patient is positioned PA erect with the chin extended so that the OML is 15 degrees from the horizontal. With the OML perpendicular to the IR, the petrous pyramids would fill the orbits (true PA).

    In the PA position with chin extended (choice A) and OML 37 degrees to the IR (parietoacanthial projection, Waters method), the petrous pyramids are projected below the maxillary sinuses. (*Bontrager and Lampignano, 7th ed., p. 439*)

29. **(D)** The radiograph shown is a PA projection (Caldwell method) of the *frontal and anterior ethmoid sinuses*. The frontal sinuses are seen centrally in the vertical plate of the frontal bone behind the glabella and extending laterally over the superciliary arches. The ethmoid sinuses are seen adjacent and inferior to the medial aspect of the orbits. The nasal cavity is seen, with the perpendicular plate and vomer, in the midline. The patient is positioned PA

erect with the chin extended so that the OML is 15 degrees from the horizontal. (*Bontrager and Lampignano, 7th ed., p. 439*)

30. **(A)** The oblique projection of the hand should demonstrate minimal overlap of the third, fourth, and fifth metacarpals. Excessive overlap of these metacarpals is caused by obliquing the hand *more than 45 degrees*. The use of a 45-degree foam wedge ensures that the fingers will be extended and parallel to the IR, thus permitting visualization of the interphalangeal joints and avoiding foreshortening of the phalanges. Clenching of the fist and ulnar flexion are maneuvers used to better demonstrate the carpal scaphoid. (*Frank, Long, and Smith, 11th ed., vol. 1, p. 118*)

31. **(A)** Sternoclavicular articulations may be examined with the patient PA, either bilaterally with the patient's head resting on the chin or unilaterally with the patient's head turned toward the side being examined. The sternoclavicular articulations also may be examined in the oblique position, with either the patient rotated slightly or the CR angled slightly medialward. Weight-bearing positions are used frequently for evaluation of acromioclavicular joints. (*Frank, Long, and Smith, 11th ed., vol. 1, p. 480*)

32. **(D)** Since the kidneys do not lie parallel to the IR in the AP position, the oblique positions are used during IVU to visualize them better. With the AP oblique projections (RPO and LPO positions), the kidney that is *farther* away is placed *parallel* to the IR, and the kidney that is *closer* is placed *perpendicular* to the IR. Therefore, in the LPO position, the *left kidney*, being closer, is *perpendicular* to the IR. The *right kidney*, the one farther away, is placed *parallel* to the IR. (*Frank, Long, and Smith, 11th ed., vol. 2, p. 180*)

33. **(B)** When a patient's elbow needs to be examined in partial flexion, the lateral projection offers little difficulty, but the AP projection requires special attention. If the AP radiograph is made with a perpendicular CR and the olecranon process resting on the tabletop, the articulating surfaces are obscured. With the

elbow in partial flexion, *two exposures are necessary.* One is made with the forearm parallel to the IR (humerus elevated), which demonstrates the proximal forearm. The other is made with the humerus parallel to the IR (forearm elevated), which demonstrates the distal humerus. In both cases, the CR is perpendicular if the degree of flexion is not too great or is angled slightly into the joint space with greater degrees of flexion. *(Frank, Long, and Smith, 11th ed., vol. 1, pp. 148–149)*

34. **(A)** Air or fluid levels will be clearly delineated only if the CR is directed parallel to them. Therefore, to demonstrate air or fluid levels, the erect or decubitus position should be used. Small amounts of *fluid* within the peritoneal or pleural space are best demonstrated in the lateral decubitus position, *affected side down.* Small amounts of air within the peritoneal or pleural space are best demonstrated in the lateral decubitus position, *affected side up. (Frank, Long, and Smith, 11th ed., vol. 1, p. 538)*

35. **(C)** The relationship of these three structures is easily appreciated in a lateral projection of the chest. The *heart* is seen in the anterior half of the thoracic cavity, with its apex extending inferior and anterior. The air-filled *trachea* can be seen in about the center of the chest, and the air-filled *esophagus* is seen just posterior to the trachea (Figure 2–48). The superimposed vertebral and axillary borders of the scapulae would be seen most posteriorly. *(Bontrager and Lampignano, 6th ed., p. 98)*

36. **(D)** The knee is formed by the proximal tibia, the patella, and the distal femur, which articulate to form the *femorotibial* and *femoropatellar* joints. Body habitus will change the relationship of the knee-joint space with the tabletop/IR considerably. The CR should be directed to ½ inch below patellar apex (knee joint). The direction of CR depends on distance between the ASIS and tabletop/IR. When this distance is up to 19 cm (thin pelvis), the CR should be directed 3 to 5 degrees caudad; when the distance is between 19 to 24 cm, the CR is directed vertically/ perpendicular (0 degrees); when the distance

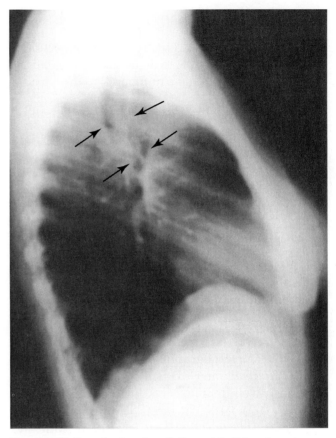

Figure 2–48. From the American College of Radiology Learning File. Courtesy of the ACR.

is greater than 24 cm (thick pelvis), the CR is directed 3 to 5 degrees cephalad. *(Frank, Long, and Smith, 11th ed., vol. 1, p. 302)*

37. **(B)** The image illustrates a *medial oblique (internal rotation)* projection of the elbow with epicondyles 45 degrees to the IR. An oblique view of the proximal radius and ulna and the distal humerus is obtained. This projection is particularly useful to demonstrate the *coronoid process* in profile, the *trochlea*, and the *medial epicondyle.* The external oblique (lateral rotation) projection demonstrates the radial head free of superimposition as well as the radial neck and the humeral capitulum. The acute flexion projection (Jones Method) of the elbow is a two-projection method demonstrating the elbow anatomy when the part cannot be extended for an AP projection. *(Bontrager and Lampignano, 7th ed., p. 165)*

38. **(D)** The image illustrates a *medial oblique (internal rotation)* projection of the elbow with

epicondyles 45 degrees to the IR. An oblique view of the proximal radius and ulna and the distal humerus is obtained. This projection is particularly useful to demonstrate the *coronoid process* in profile (number 4), the *trochlea* (number 3), and the *medial epicondyle* (number 1). The olecranon process (number 2) fits into the olecranon fossa during extension of the elbow. A small portion of the radial head (number 5) not superimposed on the ulna can be seen. The external oblique (lateral rotation) projection demonstrates the entire radial head free of superimposition as well as the radial neck and the humeral capitulum..*(Bontrager and Lampignano, 7th ed., pp. 131–133, 165)*

39. **(C)** A *lateral* projection of the lumbar spine is illustrated. The *intervertebral articulations* (disk spaces) are well demonstrated. Because the *intervertebral foramina,* which are formed by the *pedicles,* are 90 degrees to the MSP, they are also well demonstrated in the lateral projection. The articular facets, forming the *apophyseal joints,* lie 30 to 50 degrees to the MSP and are visualized in the oblique position. *(Frank, Long, and Smith, 11th ed., vol. 1, pp. 428–429)*

40. **(A)** The tangential axial projections of the patella are also often referred to as *sunrise* or *skyline views.* The supine flexion 45-degree (Merchant) position requires a *special apparatus,* and the patellae can be examined bilaterally. This position also requires patient comfort *without muscle tension*—muscle tension can cause a subluxed patella to be pulled into the intercondyler sulcus, giving the appearance of a normal patella. The two prone positions differ according to the degree of flexion employed. The 90-degree flexion (Settegast) position must not be employed with suspected patellar fracture. *(Bontrager and Lampignano, 6th ed., pp. 254, 255)*

41. **(A)** A diagnostic image of C1–2 depends on adjusting the flexion of the neck *so that the maxillary occlusal plane and the base of the skull are superimposed.* Accurate adjustment of these structures usually will allow good visualization of the odontoid process and the atlantoaxial articulation. Should patient anatomy

occasionally prevent the usual visualization, the odontoid process can be visualized through the foramen magnum, either AP or PA. In the AP position (Fuchs method) or the PA position (Judd method), the patient's chin is extended to be in line vertically with the mastoid tip (similar to a Waters' or reverse Waters' position). The CR is directed to the midline and perpendicularly at the level of the mastoid tip. The resulting image demonstrates the odontoid process through the foramen magnum. These positions should not be attempted if the patient has a suspected, new, or healing fracture or destructive disease. *(Frank, Long, and Smith, 11th ed., vol. 1, pp. 392–394)*

42. **(B)** The skull is divided into two parts—the cranial bones and the facial bones. There are eight cranial bones. Four of them comprise the *calvarium*—the frontal, the two parietals, and the occipital. The bones that comprise the *floor* of the cranium are the *two temporals,* the *ethmoid,* and the *sphenoid. (Bontrager and Lampignano, 6th ed., p. 368)*

43. **(C)** The lateral hand in extension, with appropriate technique adjustment, is recommended to evaluate foreign-body location in soft tissue. A small lead marker frequently is taped to the spot thought to be the point of entry. The physician then uses this external marker and the radiograph to determine the exact foreign-body location. Extension of the hand in the presence of a fracture would cause additional and unnecessary pain and possibly additional injury. *(Frank, Long, and Smith, 11th ed., vol. 1, p. 121)*

44–45. **(44, A; 45, C)** The radiograph shown is an oblique position of a double contrast study of the large bowel, illustrating an "open" view of the splenic/left colic flexure (number 1) and descending colon, with the hepatic/right colic flexure (number 2) somewhat superimposed on the transverse and ascending (number 3) colon. Therefore, the radiograph must have been made in either an *RPO* (if the patient was supine) or an *LAO* (if the patient was prone) position. The LPO and RAO positions are used to demonstrate the hepatic flexure and ascending colon free of self-superimposition. The distal ilium is well visualized (number 6), as well as the commencement of the large bowel—the cecum (number 4)—and its vermiform appendix (number 5). The AP or PA axial position generally is used to visualize the rectosigmoid colon. *(Frank, Long, and Smith, 11th ed., vol. 2, p. 184)*

46. **(A)** *Atrial septal defect* is a small hole (the remnant of the fetal foramen ovale) in the interatrial septum. It usually closes spontaneously in the first months of life; if it persists or is unusually large, surgical repair is necessary. The ductus arteriosus is a short fetal blood vessel connecting the aorta and pulmonary artery that usually closes within 10 to 15 hours after birth. A *patent ductus arteriosus* is one that persists and requires surgical closure. *Ventricular septal defect* is a congenital heart condition characterized by a hole in the interventricular septum that allows oxygenated and unoxygenated blood to mix. Some interventricular septal defects are small and close spontaneously; others require surgery. *Coarctation of the aorta* is a narrowing or constriction of the aorta. *(Tortora and Derrickson, 11th ed., p. 794)*

47. **(D)** The *scapular Y* refers to the characteristic Y formed by the humerus, acromion, and coracoid processes. The patient is placed in a PA oblique position—an RAO or LAO position depending on which is the affected side. The midcoronal plane is adjusted approximately 60 degrees to the IR, and the affected arm remains relaxed at the patient's side. The scapular Y position is employed *to demonstrate anterior (subcoracoid) or posterior (subacromial) humeral dislocation*. The humerus normally is superimposed on the scapula in this position; any deviation from this may indicate dislocation. *(Frank, Long, and Smith, 11th ed., vol. 1, pp. 179–191)*

48. **(A)** When the patient is recumbent with the head lower than the feet, he or she is said to be in the *Trendelenburg position*. The *decubitus position* is used to describe the patient who is recumbent (prone, supine, or lateral) with the CR directed horizontally. In the *Fowler position*, the patient's head is positioned higher than the feet. The *Sim position* is the (LAO) position assumed for enema tip insertion. *(Bontrager and Lampignano, 6th ed., pp. 18, 20)*

49. **(C)** The axillary portion of the ribs is best demonstrated in a 45-degree oblique position. The axillary ribs are demonstrated in the AP oblique projection with the affected side *adjacent to* the IR and in the PA oblique projection with the affected side *away from* the IR. Therefore, the *right* axillary ribs would be demonstrated in the RPO (AP oblique with affected side *adjacent to* the IR) and LAO (PA oblique with affected side *away from* the IR) positions. *(Frank, Long, and Smith, 11th ed., vol. 1, pp. 492–495)*

50. **(A)** The *lateral oblique* demonstrates the interspaces between the first and second metatarsals and between the first and second cuneiforms. To best demonstrate *most* of the tarsals and intertarsal spaces (including the cuboid, sinus tarsi, and tuberosity of the fifth metatarsal), a *medial oblique projection* is required (plantar surface and IR form a 30-degree angle). A *weight-bearing lateral projection* of the feet is used to demonstrate the longitudinal arches. *(Frank, Long, and Smith, 11th ed., vol. 1, pp. 260–263)*

51. **(C)** Surface landmarks, prominences, and depressions are very useful to the radiographer in locating anatomic structures that are not visible externally. The fifth thoracic vertebra is at approximately the same level as the sternal angle. The T2–3 interspace is about at the same level as the manubrial (suprasternal) notch. The costal margin is about the same level as L3. *(Frank, Long, and Smith, 11th ed., vol. 1, p. 63)*

52. **(C)** The abdomen can be divided into four quadrants or nine regions. The liver, gallbladder, and hepatic/right colic flexure are all located in the RUQ. The stomach and spleen are both normally located in the LUQ. *(Frank, Long, and Smith, 11th ed., vol. 1, p. 62)*

53. **(A)** Esophageal varices are tortuous dilatations of the esophageal veins. They are much less pronounced in the erect position and

always must be examined with the patient recumbent. The recumbent position affords more complete filling of the veins because blood flows against gravity. *(Frank, Long, and Smith, 11th ed., vol. 2, p. 138)*

54. **(B)** A PA oblique projection of the hand is shown. The correct degree of obliquity (45 degrees) is evidenced by no overlap of midshaft third, fourth, and fifth metacarpals and minimal overlap of their heads. The interphalangeal joint spaces are not visualized because the fingers are not elevated to be parallel to the IR. *(Bontrager and Lampignano, 6th ed., p. 154)*

55. **(B)** The central cavity of a long bone is the medullary canal. It contains *yellow* bone marrow, the most abundant type of marrow in the body. *Red* marrow is found within the cancellous tissue forming the extremities of long bones. *(Frank, Long, and Smith, 11th ed., vol. 1, p. 68)*

56. **(C)** The femur is the longest and strongest bone in the body. The femoral shaft is bowed slightly anteriorly and presents a long, narrow ridge posteriorly called the *linea aspera*. The distal femur is associated with two large condyles; the deep depression separating them posteriorly is the *intercondyloid fossa* (Figure 2–49). Just superior to the large condyles are the smaller medial and lateral epicondyles. The posterior distal femoral surface presents the *popliteal surface*, whereas the distal anterior surface presents the patellar surface. Proximally, the femur presents a head, neck, and greater and lesser trochanters. The intertrochanteric crest is a prominent ridge of bone between the trochanters posteriorly; *anteriorly the intertrochanteric line* is seen. The femoral head presents a roughened prominence, the fovea capitis femoris—ligaments attached here secure the femoral head to the acetabulum. *(Tortora and Derrickson, 11th ed., p. 249)*

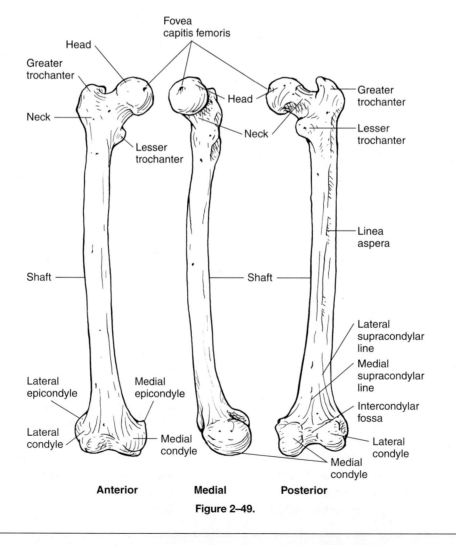

Figure 2–49.

57. **(A)** The *15-degree medial oblique projection* is used to demonstrate the ankle mortise (joint). Although the joint is well demonstrated in the 15-degree medial oblique projection, there is some superimposition of the distal tibia and fibula, and greater obliquity is required to separate the bones. To best demonstrate the distal tibiofibular articulation, a *45-degree medial oblique projection* of the ankle is required. *(Frank, Long, and Smith, 11th ed., vol. 1, pp. 289–290)*

58. **(D)** A PA projection of the chest is illustrated. Adequate inspiration is present because the diaphragm is depressed enough to demonstrate 10 posterior ribs. The shoulders are rolled forward sufficiently; the scapulae are completely removed from superimposition on the lung fields. The major fault with this image is the obvious rotation, as evidenced by the asymmetry between the medial extremities of the clavicles and the vertebral borders. Note that the medial extremity of the right clavicle is completely visible, whereas the left is not seen at all. *(Bontrager and Lampignano, 6th ed., p. 96)*

59. **(B)** The most prominent part of the greater trochanter is at the same level as the pubic symphysis—both are valuable positioning landmarks. The ASIS is in the same transverse plane as S2. The ASIS and the pubic symphysis are the bony landmarks used to locate the hip joint, which is located midway between the two points. *(Bontrager and Lampignano, 6th ed., p. 38)*

60. **(B)** When placed in the recumbent lateral position, the average adult's lumbar spine will not be parallel to the x-ray tabletop. Because the shoulders and hips generally are wider than the waist, the vertebral column slopes downward in the central areas—making the lower thoracic and upper lumbar spine closer to the tabletop than the upper thoracic and lower lumbar spine. One solution is to place a radiolucent sponge under the patient's waist. This will elevate the sagging spinal area and make the *vertebral column parallel to the x-ray tabletop and IR.* It will also open the intervertebral disks better, placing more of them

parallel to the path of the x-ray photons and *perpendicular to the IR.* This position also places the intervertebral foramina parallel with the path of the CR. The radiolucent sponge is strictly a positioning aid and has no impact on the amount of SR reaching the IR. *(Bontrager and Lampignano, 6th ed., p. 335)*

61. **(B)** Electronic imaging (CR and DR) uses image-capture devices that have greater sensitivity compared with film/screen imaging. Therefore, special consideration must be given to the SR emerging from the patient and striking the IR. To reduce the amount of SR that reaches the IR, the x-ray beam should be tightly collimated, and a lead mat should be placed on the x-ray table just posterior to the patient's lumbosacral area. The x-ray photons that would have extended posterior to the patient's skin and simply struck the x-ray table—causing increased SR to reach the IR—will be absorbed by the lead mat. Of course, these same methods are used successfully in improving image quality in screen/film technology as well. The SID is unrelated to scattered radiation production. *(Bontrager and Lampignano, 6th ed., p. 330)*

62. **(C)** The knee joint is formed by the femur, tibia, and patella. The most superior aspect of the tibia is the *tibial plateau*—formed by the *tibial condyles just distal to it.* The proximal tibia also presents the *tibial tuberosity* on its anterior surface, just distal to the condyles. *Proximal* to the tibial plateau, and articulating with it, are the *femoral condyles*—the deep notch separating them is the *intercondyloid fossa.* The term *proximal* refers to a part located closer to the point of attachment; the term *distal* refers to a part located farther away from the point of attachment. *(Bontrager and Lampignano, 6th ed., p. 216)*

63. **(C)** The greater and lesser tubercles are prominences on the proximal humerus separated by the intertubercular (bicipital) groove. The lateral projection of the humerus places the shoulder in extreme internal rotation with the epicondyles perpendicular to the IR and superimposed. The lateral projection of the humerus should demonstrate the lesser

tubercle in profile. The AP projection of the humerus/shoulder places the *epicondyles parallel to the IR* and the shoulder in *external rotation* and demonstrates the *greater tubercle in profile*. (*Frank, Long, and Smith, 11th ed., vol. 1, p. 176*)

64. **(C)** The *external rotation* position is the true *AP position* and places the greater tubercle in profile laterally and places the lesser tubercle anteriorly. The *internal rotation* position demonstrates the lesser tubercle in profile medially and places the humerus in a true lateral position; the greater tubercle is seen superimposed on the humeral head. The epicondyles should be superimposed and perpendicular to the IR. The *neutral position* places the epicondyles about 45 degrees to the IR and places the greater tubercle anteriorly but still lateral to the lesser tubercle. (*Bontrager and Lampignano, 6th ed., pp. 187, 192*)

65. **(D)** When the clavicle is examined in the PA recumbent position, the CR must be directed 15 to 30 degrees caudad to project most of the clavicle's length above the ribs. The direction of the CR is reversed when examining the patient in the AP position. (*Bontrager and Lampignano, 6th ed., p. 202*)

66. **(A)** An *avulsion* fracture is a small bony fragment pulled from a bony process as a result of a forceful pull of the attached ligament or tendon. A *comminuted* fracture is one in which the bone is broken or splintered into pieces. A *torus* fracture is a greenstick fracture with one cortex buckled and the other intact. A *compound* fracture is an open fracture in which the fractured ends have perforated the skin. (*Bontrager and Lampignano, 6th ed., p. 602*)

67. **(D)** The distal humerus articulates with the proximal radius and ulna to form the elbow joint. Specifically, the *semilunar/trochlear notch* of the proximal ulna articulates with the *trochlea* of the distal medial humerus. The *capitulum* is lateral to the trochlea and articulates with the *radial head* (Figure 2–50). (*Frank, Long, and Smith, 11th ed., vol. 1, p. 99*)

68. **(D)** These are all terms used to describe particular body movements. *Eversion* refers to movement of the foot caused by turning the ankle outward. *Inversion* is foot motion caused by turning the ankle inward. *Abduction* is movement of a part away from the midline. *Adduction* is movement of a part toward the midline. (*Bontrager and Lampignano, 6th ed., pp. 26–27*)

69. **(B)** The central nervous system (brain and spinal cord) is located within three protective membranes, the *meninges*. The inner membrane is the *pia mater*, the middle membrane is

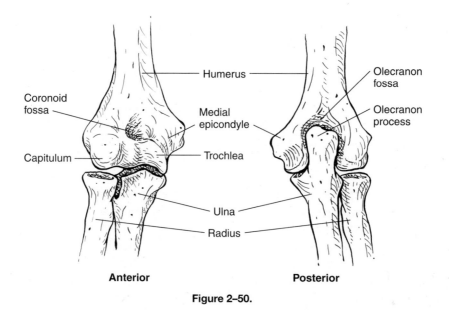

Anterior   **Posterior**

Figure 2–50.

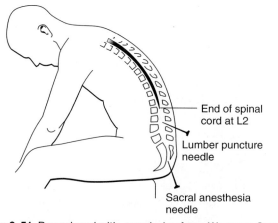

End of spinal
cord at L2

Lumber puncture
needle

Sacral anesthesia
needle

Figure 2–51. Reproduced with, permission from, Waxman: *Correlative Neuroanatomy*, 24th ed. 2000. McGraw-Hill, Inc. p 75; Fig 6-11

the *arachnoid,* and the outer membrane is the *dura mater.* The *subarachnoid space* is located between the pia and arachnoid mater and contains cerebrospinal fluid (CSF). During myelography, the needle is introduced into the subarachnoid space (L3–4 or L4–5), a small amount of CSF is removed, and the contrast medium is introduced (Figure 2–51). The *subdural space* is located between the arachnoid and dura mater. The *epidural space* is

located between the two layers of the dura mater. *(Bontrager and Lampignano, 6th ed., p. 721)*

70. **(C)** The skull has two major parts: the *cranium,* which is composed of 8 bones and houses the brain, and the 14 irregularly shaped *facial bones* (Figure 2–52). The inner and outer compact tables of the cranial skull are separated by cancellous tissue called *diploe.* The internal table has a number of branching meningeal grooves and larger sulci that house blood vessels. The bones of the skull are separated by immovable (synarthrotic) joints called *sutures.* The major sutures of the cranium are the *sagittal,* which separates the parietal bones; the *coronal,* which separates the frontal and parietal bones; the *lambdoidal,* which separates the parietal and occipital bones; and the *squammosal,* which separates the temporal and parietal bones. The sagittal and coronal sutures meet at the *bregma,* which corresponds to the fetal anterior fontanel. The sagittal and lambdoidal sutures meet posteriorly at the *lambda,* which corresponds to the fetal posterior fontanel. The

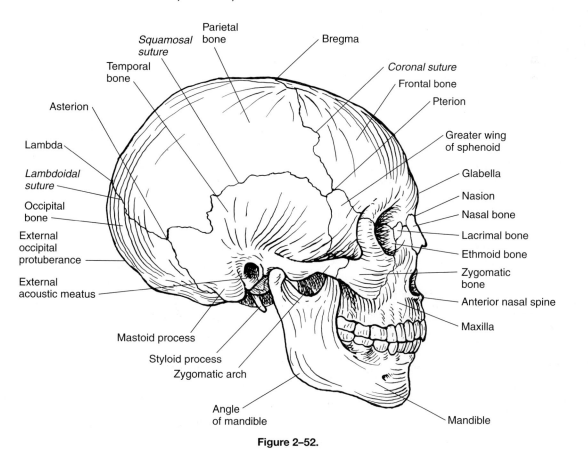

Figure 2–52.

parietal, frontal, and sphenoid bones meet at the *pterion*, the location of the anterolateral fontanel. The highest point of the skull is called the *vertex*. (*Frank, Long, and Smith, 11th ed., vol. 2, pp. 278–279*)

71. **(D)** A right scapular Y is illustrated; this refers to the characteristic Y formed by the clearly visible humerus, acromion, and coracoid. The patient is positioned in a PA oblique position—in this case, an RAO projection to demonstrate the right side. The MCP is adjusted to approximately 60 degrees to the IR, and the affected arm is left relaxed at the patient's side. The scapular Y position is employed *to demonstrate anterior or posterior humeral dislocation.* The humerus is superimposed on the scapula in this position; any deviation from this may indicate dislocation. (*Frank, Long, and Smith, 11th ed., vol. 1, pp. 189–191*)

72. **(B)** Synovial pivot joints are diarthrotic, that is, freely movable. Pivot joints permit rotation motion. Examples include the proximal radioulnar joint that permits supination and pronation of the hand. The atlantoaxial joint is the articulation between C1 and C2 and permits rotation of the head. The temporomandibular joint is diarthrotic, having both hinge and planar movements. (*Tortora and Derrickson, 11th ed., p. 269*)

73. **(B)** The *45-degree oblique projection* of the lumbar spine generally is performed for demonstration of the *apophyseal joints*. In a correctly positioned oblique lumbar spine, "Scotty dog" images are demonstrated (Figures 2–53 and 2–54). The Scotty's ear corresponds to the

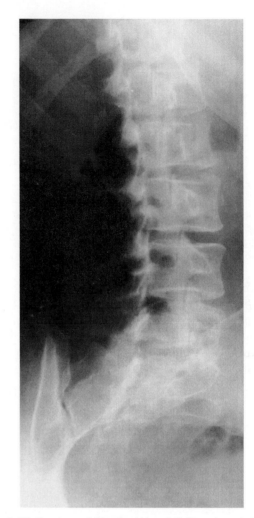

Figure 2–54. Courtesy of Stamford Hospital, Department of Radiology.

superior articular process, his nose to the transverse process, his eye to the pedicle, his neck to the pars interarticularis, his body to the lamina, and his front foot to the inferior articular process. (*Bontrager and Lampignano, 6th ed., p. 334*)

74. **(D)** An injury to a structure located on the side opposite of the primary injury is called a *contrecoup* injury. For example, a blow to the back of the head will injure frontal and temporal lobes because they are forced forward against the irregularly shaped bones of the anterior cranial vault. *Blowout* fractures occur to the floor of the orbit on a direct blow. A *Le Fort* fracture involves severe bilateral maxillary fractures. *Contracture* refers to shortening of muscle fibers. (*Bontrager and Lampignano, 6th ed., p. 417*)

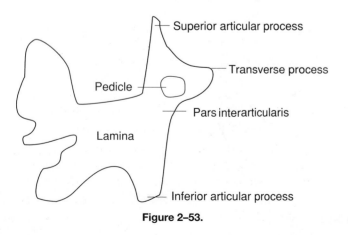

Figure 2–53.

75. (B) The tangential projection projects the sesamoid bones separate from adjacent structures. The patient is best examined in the prone position because this places the parts of interest closest to the IR. The affected foot is dorsiflexed so as to place its plantar surface 15 to 20 degrees with the vertical. The CR is directed perpendicular to the posterior surface of the foot (near the metatarsophalangeal joints). The dorsoplantar and oblique projections of the foot will demonstrate the sesamoid bones superimposed on adjacent bony structures. *(Bontrager and Lampignano, 6th ed., p. 231)*

76. (B) *Osgood-Schlatter disease* is most common in adolescent boys, involving osteochondritis of the tibial tuberosity epiphysis. The large patellar tendon actually will pull the tibial tuberosity away from the tibia. Immobilization generally will resolve the issue. *Ewing sarcoma* is a malignant bone tumor most common in young children. It attacks long bones and presents a characteristic "onion peel" appearance. *Gout* is a type of arthritis that most commonly attacks the knee and first metatarsophalangeal joint, although other joints also can be involved. High levels of uric acid in the blood are deposited in the joint. *Exostosis* is a bony growth arising from the surface of a bone and growing away from the joint. It is a benign and sometimes painful condition. *(Bontrager and Lampignano, 6th ed., p. 225)*

77. (C) After forceful eversion or inversion injuries of the ankle, *AP stress studies* are valuable to confirm the presence of a ligament tear. Keeping the ankle in an AP position, the physician guides the ankle into inversion and eversion maneuvers. Characteristic changes in the relationship of the talus, tibia, and fibula will indicate ligament injury. Inversion stress demonstrates the lateral ligament, whereas eversion stress demonstrates the medial ligament. A fractured ankle would not be manipulated in this manner. *(Frank, Long, and Smith, 11th ed., vol. 1, p. 293)*

78. (C) The bony thorax consists of *12 pairs of ribs* and the structures to which they are attached anteriorly and posteriorly: the *sternum* (consisting of manubrium, body/gladiolus, and xiphoid/ensiform process) and the 12 *thoracic vertebrae* (Figure 2–55). These structures form a bony cage that surrounds and protects the vital organs within (the heart, lungs, and great vessels). The scapulae, together with the clavicles, form the shoulder (pectoral) girdle of the upper extremity. *(Bontrager and Lampignano, 6th ed., p. 350)*

79. (A) Because the *right* main stem bronchus is *wider and more vertical*, aspirated foreign bodies are more likely to enter it than the left main stem bronchus, which is narrower and angles more sharply from the trachea. An *aspirated* foreign body does not enter the esophagus or the stomach because they are not respiratory structures. The esophagus and stomach are *digestive* structures; a foreign body would most likely be *swallowed* to enter these structures. *(Tortora and Derrickson, 11th ed., p. 857)*

80. (D) A PA projection of the chest is shown. Adequate *inspiration* is demonstrated by visualization of 10 posterior ribs above the diaphragm. The shoulders are rolled forward, removing the scapulae from the lung fields. *Rotation* of the chest is demonstrated by the unequal distance between the sternum and medial extremities of the clavicles. *Pulmonary apices* and *costophrenic angles* are demonstrated adequately. An *air-filled* trachea is seen in the lower cervical and upper thoracic region as a midline area of increased density. Adequate *long-scale contrast* has been achieved, as indicated by visualization of pulmonary vascular markings. *(Bontrager and Lampignano, 6th ed., p. 87)*

81. (A) A PA projection of the chest is shown. Adequate *inspiration* is demonstrated by visualization of 10 posterior ribs above the diaphragm. *Rotation* of the chest is demonstrated by asymmetrical sternoclavicular joints. The apices and costophrenic angles should be included on every chest radiograph. The letter *A* indicates a left posterior rib, *B* represents a left anterior rib, and *C* represents the right costophrenic angle. *(Frank, Long, and Smith, 11th ed., vol. 1, pp. 518–521)*

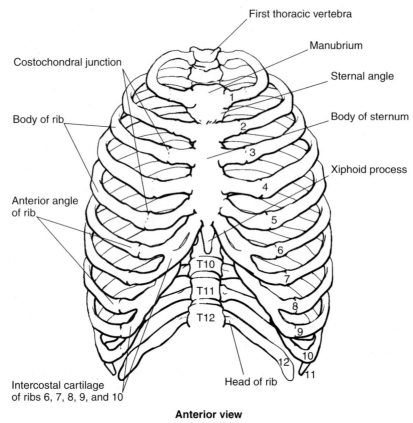

First thoracic vertebra

Manubrium

Sternal angle

Costochondral junction

Body of sternum

Body of rib

Xiphoid process

Anterior angle
of rib

Intercostal cartilage
of ribs 6, 7, 8, 9, and 10

Head of rib

Anterior view

Figure 2–55.

82. **(C)** The axial trauma lateral (Coyle) position is described. If routine elbow projections in extension are not possible because of limited part movement, these positions can be used to demonstrate the coronoid process and/or radial head. With the elbow flexed *90 degrees* and the CR directed to the elbow joint at an angle of 45 degrees medially (i.e., toward the shoulder), the joint space between the *radial head* and capitulum should be revealed. With the elbow flexed *80 degrees* and the CR directed to the elbow joint at an angle of 45 degrees laterally (i.e., from the shoulder toward the elbow), the elongated *coronoid process* will be visualized. *(Bontrager and Lampignano, 6th ed., p. 174)*

83. **(D)** The brain generally is described as having three divisions. The *forebrain* is composed of the cerebrum, the thalamus, and the hypothalamus. The *midbrain* is a short, constricted portion connecting the forebrain to the hindbrain and containing the corpora quadrigemina and the aqueduct of Sylvius. The *hindbrain* is composed of the pons, medulla oblongata, and cerebellum. The *brain stem* is defined as the midbrain, pons, and medulla oblongata. *(Bontrager and Lampignano, 6th ed., p. 721)*

84. **(C)** If the x-ray photons can pass through/between structures such as joint spaces and foramina, these joint spaces and foramina must be situated perpendicular to the IR and parallel to the CR. The intervertebral foramina of the thoracic and lumbar vertebrae are perpendicular to the IR and, therefore, *parallel to the CR* in the *lateral* projection. The cervical intervertebral foramina are well demonstrated when placed 45 degrees to the IR and CR. *(Bontrager and Lampignano, 6th ed., pp. 292, 295, 322)*

85. **(A)** The dome of the acetabulum lies midway between the ASIS and the symphysis pubis. On an adult of average size, a line perpendicular to this point will parallel the plane of the

femoral neck. In an AP projection of the hip, the CR should be directed to a point approximately 2 inches down that perpendicular line so as to enter the distal portion of the femoral head. *(Frank, Long, and Smith, 11th ed., vol. 1, p. 341)*

86–87. **(86, B; 87, B)** Figure 2–14 illustrates an anatomic lateral view of the paranasal sinuses. Number 1 points to the *frontal* sinuses and number 2 to the *ethmoidal* sinuses; both can be visualized using the PA axial projection (Caldwell method). Number 3 is the *sphenoidal* sinuses, which are well demonstrated in the SMV projection. Number 4 is the *maxillary* sinuses, which are best demonstrated using the parietoacanthal projection (Waters method). The lateral projection demonstrates the four pairs of paranasal sinuses superimposed on each other. *(Bontrager and Lampignano, 6th ed., pp. 438–441)*

88. **(B)** The parietoacanthal (Waters method) projection demonstrates the *maxillary* sinuses. The modified Waters position, with the CR directed through the open mouth, will demonstrate the sphenoid sinuses through the open mouth. The PA axial projection demonstrates the *frontal and ethmoidal* sinus groups. The lateral projection, with the CR entering 1 inch posterior to the outer canthus, demonstrates *all* the paranasal sinuses. X-ray examinations of the sinuses always should be performed *erect* to demonstrate leveling of any fluid present. *(Bontrager and Lampignano, 6th ed., pp. 438–442)*

89. **(C)** The radiograph shown is that of a *medial oblique foot*. With the foot rotated medially so that the plantar surface forms a *30-degree oblique* with the IR, the *sinus tarsi*, the *tuberosity* of the fifth metatarsal, and several *articulations* should be demonstrated—the articulations between the talus and the navicular, between the calcaneus and the cuboid, between the cuboid and the bases of the fourth and fifth metarsals, and between the cuboid and the lateral (third) cuneiform. *(Frank, Long, and Smith, 11th ed., vol. 1, pp. 260–261)*

90. **(D)** Figure 2–16 shows an AP projection of the knee. The distal femur and proximal tibia and fibula are seen. The femorotibial joint space is open, and the tibial articular facets of the tibial plateau (number 4) are demonstrated. The intercondylar eminence (number 3) is seen. Number 2 is the medial femoral condyle; number 1 is the medial femoral epicondyle; and number 5 is the medial tibial condyle. *(Bontrager and Lampignano, 6th ed., p. 217)*

91. **(B)** Lumbar articular facets, forming the apophyseal joints, are demonstrated in the *oblique* position. L1 through L4 are best demonstrated in a 45-degree oblique, while L5-S1 are best seen in the 30-degree oblique. The AP axial projection is used to demonstrate an AP projection of L5-S1. *(Bontrager and Lampignano, 7th ed., p. 334)*

92. **(B)** Chest positioning must be correct and accurate; thoracic structures are easily distorted. To avoid *superimposition on the upper medial apices,* the patient's chin should be sufficiently elevated. Movement of the diaphragm to its lowest position is a function of the erect position and of making the exposure after the second inspiration. The MSP is perpendicular to the IR in the PA projection and parallel to the IR in the lateral projection. The position of the chin has little to do with the MSP. *(Bontrager and Lampignano, 6th ed., pp. 86–87)*

93. **(B)** Long bones are composed of a shaft, or diaphysis, and two extremities. The *diaphysis* is referred to as the *primary ossification center.* In the growing bone, the cartilaginous *epiphyseal plate* (located at the extremities of long bones) is gradually replaced by bone. For this reason, the epiphyses are referred to as the *secondary ossification centers.* The ossified growth area of long bones is the *metaphysis. Apophysis* refers to vertebral joints formed by articulation of superjacent articular facets. *(Bontrager and Lampignano, 6th ed., p. 7)*

94. **(A)** A *frontal* projection (AP or PA) demonstrates the *medial* and *lateral* relationships of

structures. A *lateral* projection demonstrates the anterior and posterior relationships of structures. Two views, at right angles to each other, generally are taken of most structures. *(Bontrager and Lampignano, 6th ed., p. 36)*

95. **(C)** The 45-degree oblique projection of the lumbar spine generally is performed for demonstration of the apophyseal joints. In a correctly positioned oblique lumbar spine, "Scotty dog" images are demonstrated. The Scotty's ear corresponds to the superior articular process, his nose to the transverse process, his eye to the pedicle, his neck to the pars interarticularis, his body to the lamina, and his front foot to the inferior articular process (Figure 2–56). *(Bontrager and Lampignano, 6th ed., p. 334)*

96. **(D)** The illustration shows the patient positioned on his left side with the cassette behind his back. This is a *left lateral decubitus* position. The x-ray beam is directed *horizontally* in decubitus positions to demonstrate air–fluid levels. Air or fluid levels will be clearly delineated only if the CR is directed parallel to them. Fluid levels will be best detected on the *down* side (in this case, *left*); air levels will be best detected on the *up* side (in this case, *right*). If the patient were lying on the right side, it would be a *right lateral decubitus position*. If the patient were lying on his or her back with a horizontal x-ray beam, it would be a *dorsal decubitus position*. Lying prone with a horizontal x-ray beam is termed a *ventral*

decubitus position. (Bontrager and Lampignano, 6th ed., p. 101)

97. **(C)** In the *AP* projection, the proximal fibula is at least partially superimposed on the lateral tibial condyle. *Medial rotation* of 45 degrees will "open" the proximal tibiofibular articulation. *Lateral rotation* will obscure the articulation even more. *(Frank, Long, and Smith, 11th ed., vol. 1, p. 289)*

98. **(D)** The common carotid arteries function to supply oxygenated blood to the head and neck. Major branches of the common carotid arteries (internal carotids) function to supply the anterior brain, whereas the posterior brain is supplied by the vertebral arteries (branches of the subclavian). The carotid arteries bifurcate into internal and external carotid arteries at the level of C4. The foramen magnum and pharynx are superior to the level of bifurcation, and the larynx is inferior to the level of bifurcation. *(Frank, Long, and Smith, 11th ed., vol. 3, p. 55)*

99. **(B)** A right lateral decubitus position will demonstrate a double-contrast visualization of left-sided bowel structures, that is, the lateral side of the descending colon and the medial side of the ascending colon. A left lateral decubitus position will demonstrate a double-contrast visualization of right-sided bowel structures, that is, the lateral side of the ascending colon and the medial side of the descending colon. With the patient in the erect position, barium moves inferiorly and air rises to provide double-contrast visualization of the hepatic and splenic flexures. *(Frank, Long, and Smith, 11th ed., vol. 2, p. 190)*

100–101. **(100, B; 101, C)** Figure 2–18 illustrates a portion of the *biliary system*. Bile leaves the liver through the right and left *hepatic ducts* (number 5), which join to form the *common hepatic duct* (number 6). Bile enters the gallbladder through the *cystic duct* (number 7). The *neck* of the gallbladder is indicated by the number 4, its *body* by the number 3, and its *fundus* by the number 2. The gallbladder stores and concentrates bile, and when it contracts, bile flows out through the cystic duct

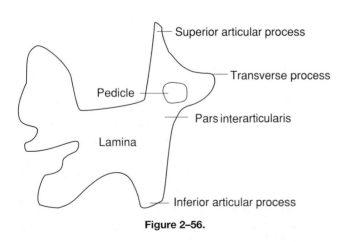

Superior articular process

Transverse process

Pedicle

Pars interarticularis

Lamina

Inferior articular process

Figure 2–56.

and down the *common bile duct* (number 8). The common bile duct and *pancreatic duct* (number 9) unite to form the short *hepatopancreatic ampulla* (of Vater), which empties into the *duodenum* (number 1). *(Tortora and Derrickson, 11th ed., p. 917)*

102. **(C)** *Hydronephrosis* is a collection of urine in the renal pelvis owing to obstructed outflow, such as from a stricture or obstruction. If the obstruction occurs at the level of the bladder or along the course of the ureter, it will be accompanied by the condition of hydroureter above the level of obstruction. These conditions may be demonstrated during IVU. The term *pyelonephrosis* refers to some condition of the renal pelvis. *Nephroptosis* refers to drooping or downward displacement of the kidneys. This may be demonstrated using the erect position during IVU. *Cystourethritis* is inflammation of the bladder and urethra. *(Taber, p. 1022)*

103. **(C)** Hysterosalpingography involves the introduction of a radiopaque contrast medium through a uterine cannula into the uterus and uterine (Fallopian) tubes. This examination is often performed to document patency of the uterine tubes in cases of infertility. A retrograde pyelogram requires cystoscopy and involves introduction of contrast medium through the vesicoureteral orifices and into the renal collecting system. A voiding cystourethrogram also requires cystoscopy and involves filling the bladder with contrast medium and documenting the voiding mechanism. A myelogram is performed to investigate the spinal canal. *(Frank, Long, and Smith, 11th ed., vol. 2, p. 262)*

104. **(C)** Perhaps the most important prerequisite to a successful BE examination is a thoroughly clean large bowel. Any retained fecal material can simulate or obscure pathology. A single-contrast examination demonstrates the anatomy and contour of the large bowel, as well as anything that may project out *from* the bowel wall (e.g., diverticula). In a double-contrast examination, the bowel wall (*mucosa*) is coated with barium, and then the lumen is filled with air. This enables visualization of

any *intraluminal lesions* such as polyps and tumor masses. *(Bontrager and Lampignano, 6th ed., p. 501)*

105. **(D)** To better visualize the joint space in the lateral projection of the knee, 20 to 30 degrees of flexion is recommended. The *femoral condyles are superimposed* so as to demonstrate the *patellofemoral joint* and the articulation between the femur and the tibia. The head of the fibula will be slightly superimposed on the proximal tibia. The correct degree of forward or backward body rotation is responsible for visualization of the patellofemoral joint. Cephalad tube angulation of 5 to 7 degrees is responsible for demonstrating the articulation between the femur and the tibia (by removing the magnified medial femoral condyle from superimposition on the joint space). *(Frank, Long, and Smith, 11th ed., vol. 1, p. 306)*

106. **(B)** There are three important fat pads associated with the elbow. The anterior fat pad is located just anterior to the distal humerus. The posterior fat pad is located within the olecranon fossa at the distal posterior humerus. The supinator fat pad/stripe is located at the proximal radius just anterior to the head, neck, and tuberosity. The posterior fat pad is not visible radiographically in the *normal* elbow. All three fat pads can be demonstrated only in the lateral projection of the elbow. *(Bontrager and Lampignano, 6th ed., p. 139)*

107. **(A)** The expectoration of blood from the larynx, trachea, bronchi, or lungs is termed *hemoptysis*. Hemoptysis can occur in several diseases, including pneumonia, bronchitis, pulmonary tuberculosis, and others. *Hematemesis* is vomiting of blood—this can occur with gastric ulcers, gastritis, esophageal varices, and other conditions. *(Taber, p. 971)*

108. **(D)** Double-contrast studies of the stomach or large intestine involve coating the organ with a thin layer of barium sulfate and then introducing air. This allows the operator to see through the organ to structures behind it and, most especially, allows visualization of the *mucosal lining* of the organ. A barium-filled stomach or large bowel demonstrates the

position, size, and shape of the organ and any lesion that projects *out* from its walls, such as diverticula. Polypoid lesions, which project *inward* from the wall of an organ, may go unnoticed unless a double-contrast examination is performed. *(Frank, Long, and Smith, 11th ed., vol. 2, p. 144)*

109. **(D)** The mediastinum is the space between the lungs that contains the heart, great vessels, trachea, esophagus, and thymus gland. It is bounded anteriorly by the sternum and posteriorly by the vertebral column, and extends from the upper thorax to the diaphragm. *(Frank, Long, and Smith, 11th ed., vol. 1, p. 505)*

110. **(D)** An *RPO* position is illustrated. The oblique IVU projections should be approximately *30 degrees;* this position significantly changes the position of the kidneys and ureters. When the abdomen is obliqued, the kidney of the "down" side is *perpendicular* to the IR and its ureter is *parallel* to the IR. The kidney of the "up" side is *parallel* to the IR. *(Frank, Long, and Smith, 11th ed., vol. 2, p. 220)*

111. **(C)** The *external rotation* position is the true *AP* position and places the greater tubercle in profile laterally and places the lesser tubercle anteriorly. The *internal rotation* position demonstrates the lesser tubercle in profile medially and places the humerus in a true lateral position; the greater tubercle is seen superimposed on the humeral head. The epicondyles should be superimposed and perpendicular to the IR. The *neutral position* places the epicondyles about 45 degrees to the IR and places the greater tubercle anteriorly but still lateral to the lesser tubercle. *(Bontrager and Lampignano, 6th ed., pp. 187, 192)*

112. **(C)** The PA axial projection (Camp-Coventry method) of the *intercondyloid fossa* (tunnel view) is shown. The knee is flexed about 40 degrees, and the CR is directed caudally 40 degrees and perpendicular to the tibia (Figure 2–57). The patella and patellofemoral articulation are demonstrated in the axial/tangential view of the patella. *(Frank, Long, and Smith, 11th ed., vol. 1, p. 314)*

113. **(C)** The parietoacanthal projection (Waters method) demonstrates a distorted view of the frontal and ethmoidal sinuses. The *maxillary sinuses* (number 4) are well demonstrated, projected free of the petrous pyramids. This is also the best single position for the demonstration of *facial bones.* The *mandibular angle* is illustrated by the number 1, the *zygomatic arch* by number 2, and the *coronoid process* by number 3. *(Bontrager and Lampignano, 6th ed., p. 440)*

114. **(C)** *Diarthrotic,* or synovial, joints, such as the knee and the TMJ, are freely movable. Most diarthrotic joints are associated with a joint capsule containing synovial fluid. Diarthrotic joints are the most numerous in the body and are subdivided according to *type* of movement. *Amphiarthrotic* joints are partially movable joints whose articular surfaces are connected by cartilage, such as intervertebral joints. *Synarthrotic* joints, such as the cranial sutures, are immovable. *(Bontrager and Lampignano, 6th ed., pp. 10–13)*

115. **(C)** The carpal scaphoid is somewhat curved and consequently foreshortened radiographically in the PA position. To better separate it from the adjacent carpals, the ulnar flexion (ulnar deviation) maneuver is employed frequently. In addition to correcting foreshortening of the scaphoid, ulnar flexion/deviation opens the interspaces between adjacent lateral carpals. Radial flexion/deviation

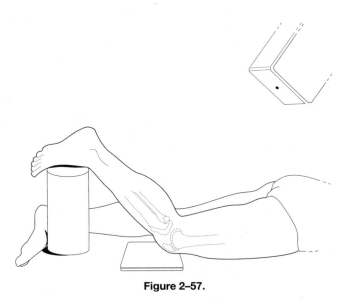

Figure 2–57.

is used to better demonstrate *medial* carpals. (*Frank, Long, and Smith, 11th ed., vol. 1, p. 130*)

116. **(B)** The figure shows an AP projection of the shoulder. A plane passing through the epicondyles is parallel to the IR (and perpendicular to the CR). To project the coracoid process with less self-superimposition, the CR must be angled cephalad 15 degrees. The amount of cephalad angulation depends on the degree of thoracic kyphosis; the greater the degree of kyphosis, the greater is the degree of cephalad angulation required. A 30-degree angle is used for the average patient. (*Frank, Long, and Smith, 11th ed., vol. 1, p. 204*)

117. **(B)** The typical vertebra has a *body* and a *neural/vertebral arch* surrounding the vertebral foramen (Figure 2–58). The neural arch is composed of two *pedicles* and two *laminae* that support four articular processes, two transverse processes, and one spinous process. The pedicles are short, thick processes extending back from the posterior aspect of the vertebral body, each one sustaining a *lamina*. The laminae extend posteriorly to the midline and join to form the spinous process. Each pedicle has notches superiorly and inferiorly (superior and inferior vertebral notches) that—with adjacent vertebrae—form the intervertebral foramina, through which the spinal nerves pass. The neural arch also has lateral transverse processes for muscle attachment and superior and inferior articular processes for the formation of apophyseal joints (classified as diarthrotic). The vertebral column permits flexion, extension, and lateral and rotary

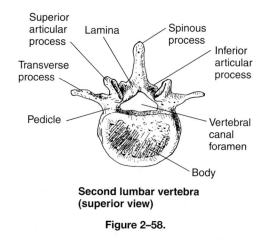

Second lumbar vertebra (superior view)

Figure 2–58.

motions through its various articulations. (*Frank, Long, and Smith, 11th ed., vol. 1, p. 376*)

118. **(B)** The type of fracture in which the splintered ends of bone are forced through the skin is a *compound* fracture. In a *closed* fracture, no bone protrudes through the skin. *Compression* fractures are seen in stressed areas, such as the vertebrae. A *depressed* fracture would not protrude but rather would be pushed in. (*Bontrager and Lampignano, 6th ed., pp. 600–602*)

119. **(D)** The thoracic apophyseal joints are demonstrated in an oblique position with the coronal plane 70 degrees to the IR (MSP 20 degrees to the IR). This may be accomplished by first placing the patient lateral and then obliquing the patient 20 degrees "off lateral." The apophyseal joints closest to the IR are demonstrated in the PA oblique projection and those remote from the IR in the AP oblique projection. Comparable detail is obtained using either method because the OID is about the same. The thoracic intervertebral foramina are demonstrated in the lateral projection. This places the MSP of the patient parallel to the IR, and the coronal plane perpendicular to the IR. (*Frank, Long, and Smith, 11th ed., vol. 1, pp. 421–423*)

120. **(D)** The *scapular Y* projection is an oblique projection of the shoulder that is used to demonstrate anterior or posterior shoulder dislocation. The *inferosuperior axial* projection may be used to evaluate the glenohumeral joint when the patient is able to abduct the arm. The *transthoracic lateral* projection is used to evaluate the glenohumeral joint and upper humerus when the patient is unable to abduct the arm. (*Frank, Long, and Smith, 11th ed., vol. 1, p. 189*)

121. **(C)** The typical vertebra has two parts—the body and the vertebral arch. The body is the dense, anterior bony mass. Posteriorly attached is the vertebral arch, a ring-like structure. The vertebral arch is formed by two *pedicles* (short, thick processes projecting posteriorly from the body) and two *laminae* (broad, flat processes projecting posteriorly and medially from the pedicles). (*Bontrager and Lampignano, 6th ed., p. 290*)

122. **(B)** Obstruction of the small bowel is termed *ileus*; there are two types of ileus—paralytic/adynamic and mechanical. *Paralytic* or *adynamic ileus* is characterized by an absence of peristalsis. This can be caused by infection (e.g., appendicitis or peritonitis) or postoperative difficulty. *Mechanical ileus* is caused by some sort of physical obstruction such as tumor or adhesions. *(Bontrager and Lampignano, 6th ed., p. 493)*

123. **(D)** Accurate *positioning skills* require knowledge of *anatomy* (the position of the structure with respect to the IR) and *geometric principles* (how the x-ray tube angle will project or distort the anatomic structure). *Shape distortion* is related to the *alignment* of the x-ray tube, the object being examined, and the IR. When all three are parallel to one another, shape distortion is minimal. If one or more are out of alignment, shape distortion occurs. The two types of shape distortion are *foreshortening* and *elongation*. *Foreshortening* occurs as a result of the anatomic structure within the body being at an angle with the IR. For example, in the supine position, the kidneys are not parallel to the IR: Their lower pole is anterior to their upper pole. Another example is the curved carpal scaphoid: Its full length will not be appreciated in the PA projection because it will be self-superimposed and foreshortened owing to its curve. *Elongation* occurs as a result of x-ray tube angulation. Elongation is often used intentionally to see structures better. The axial projection of the sigmoid colon during BE "opens" the S-shaped sigmoid to allow visualization of its entire length—which could not be appreciated on the direct AP or PA projection. The AP axial skull (Towne) projection pushes the facial bones inferiorly to better see the occipital bone. *The greater the tube angulation, the greater is the elongation (distortion) produced.* *(Shephard, pp. 228–232)*

124. **(B)** The cephalic, basilic, and subclavian veins should be demonstrated on an upper limb venogram. Venography of the upper limb usually is performed to rule out venous obstruction or thrombosis. The injection site is usually in the hand or wrist, and images should be obtained up to the area of the superior vena cava. *(Frank, Long, and Smith, 11th ed., vol. 3, p. 51)*

125. **(A)** There are five fused sacral vertebrae; the fused transverse processes form the alae. The anterior and posterior sacral foramina transmit spinal nerves. The sacrum articulates superiorly with the fifth lumbar vertebra, forming the L5-S1 articulation, and inferiorly with the coccyx, forming the sacrococcygeal joint. The *sacrum curves posteriorly* and inferiorly, whereas the *coccyx curves anteriorly*; thus, they require different tuble angles to "open them up." Image A demonstrates an AP axial projection of the sacrum with CR angulation of 15 degrees *cephalad*. Image B is an AP axial projection of the coccyx using the required 10-degree *caudal* CR angle. *(Frank, Long, and Smith, 11th ed., vol. 1, pp. 444–445)*

126. **(A)** The four types of body habitus describe differences in visceral shape, position, tone, and motility. One body type is *hypersthenic*, characterized by the very large individual with short, wide heart and lungs, high transverse stomach and gallbladder, and peripheral colon. The *sthenic individual* is the average, athletic, most predominant type. The *hyposthenic* patient is somewhat thinner and a little frailer, with organs positioned somewhat lower. The *asthenic* type is smaller in the extreme, with a long thorax, a very long, almost pelvic stomach, and a low medial gallbladder. The colon is medial and redundant. Hypersthenic patients usually demonstrate the greatest motility. *(Frank, Long, and Smith, 11th ed., vol. 1, p. 65)*

127. **(C)** When a cervical spine radiograph is requested to rule out subluxation or fracture, the patient will arrive in the radiology area on a stretcher. The patient should *not* be moved before a subluxation is ruled out. Any movement of the head and neck could cause serious damage to the spinal cord. A horizontal beam lateral projection is performed and evaluated. The physician then will decide what further images are required. *(Frank, Long, and Smith, 11th ed., vol. 2, p. 35)*

128. **(D)** The term *proximal* refers to structures closer to the point of attachment. For example, the elbow is described as being *proximal* to the wrist; that is, the elbow is closer to the point of attachment (the shoulder) than is the wrist. Referring to the question, then, the interphalangeal joints (both proximal and distal) and the metacarpals are both *distal* to the carpal bones. The radial styloid process is *proximal* to the carpals. *(Bontrager and Lampignano, 6th ed., p. 23)*

129. **(C)** The scapular Y projection requires that the *coronal* plane be about 60 degrees to the IR (MSP is about 30 degrees), thus resulting in an *oblique* projection of the shoulder. The vertebral and axillary *borders of the scapula are superimposed on the humeral shaft*, and the resulting relationship between the glenoid fossa and humeral head will demonstrate anterior or posterior dislocation. Lateral or medial dislocation is evaluated on the AP projection. *(Frank, Long, and Smith, 11th ed., vol. 1, p. 189)*

130. **(A)** The hypersthenic body type is large and heavy. The thoracic cavity is short, the lungs are short with broad bases, and the heart is usually in an almost transverse position. The diaphragm is high; the stomach and gallbladder are high and transverse. The large bowel is positioned high and peripheral (and often requires that 14 × 17 inch cassettes be placed cross-wise for imaging a BE). *(Frank, Long, and Smith, 11th ed., vol. 1, p. 65)*

131. **(C)** Inflammation of the tongue is called *glossitis*. Inflamed salivary glands are usually referred to with reference to the affected gland, as in *parotitis* (inflammation of the parotid gland). Inflammation of the epiglottis is termed *epiglottitis*.

132. **(B)** With the patient in the PA position, the *rami* are well visualized with a perpendicular ray or with 20 to 25 degrees of cephalad angulation. A portion of the mandibular body is demonstrated in this position, but most of it is superimposed over the cervical spine. *(Frank, Long, and Smith, 11th ed., vol. 2, p. 370)*

133. **(B)** The kidneys lie obliquely in the posterior portion of the trunk with their superior portion angled posteriorly and their *inferior portion and ureters angled anteriorly.* Therefore, to facilitate filling of the most anteriorly placed structures, the patient is examined in the prone position. Opacified urine then flows to the most dependent part of the kidney and ureter—*the ureteropelvic region, inferior calyces, and ureters. (Saia, 4th ed., p. 191)*

134. **(B)** The *median sagittal*, or *midsagittal*, plane (MSP) passes vertically through the midline of the body, dividing it into left and right halves. Any plane parallel to the MSP is termed a *sagittal* plane. The *midcoronal* plane is perpendicular to the MSP and divides the body into anterior and posterior halves. A *transverse* plane passes through the body at right angles to a sagittal plane. These planes, especially the MSP, are very important reference points in radiographic positioning (Figure 2–59). *(Frank, Long, and Smith, 11th ed., vol. 1, p. 58)*

135. **(A)** In an AP projection of the shoulder, there is superimposition of the humeral head and glenoid fossa. With the patient obliqued 45 degrees toward the affected side, the glenohumeral joint is open, and the glenoid fossa is seen in profile. The patient's arm is abducted somewhat and placed in internal rotation. *(Frank, Long, and Smith, 11th ed., vol. 1, pp. 192–193)*

136. **(C)** The radiograph shown illustrates an AP projection of the lumbar spine. The intervertebral disk spaces (number 2) are well visualized because the patient's knees were flexed with feet flat on the table. Number 1 points out the spinous process; number 3 is the transverse process. Number 4 points out the body of the fourth lumbar vertebra, and number 5 is the medial border of the iliac crest. The prominent border of the psoas muscle is well demonstrated. *(Bontrager and Lampignano, 6th ed., p. 333)*

137. **(A)** During a double-contrast BE, barium and air will distribute themselves according to the position of parts of the colon within the body and according to body position. When the body is in the AP recumbent position, the most anterior structures will be air filled. Anterior structures include the transverse colon

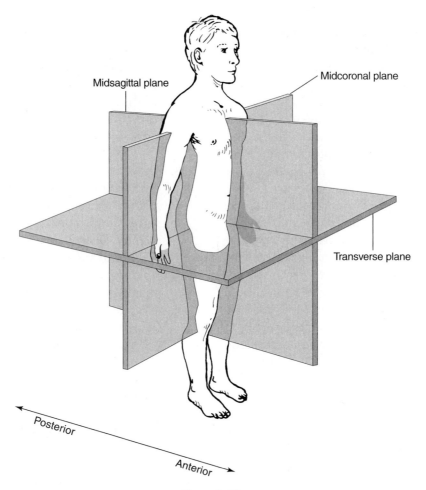

Midsagittal plane

Midcoronal plane

Transverse plane

Posterior

Anterior

Figure 2–59.

and a portion of the sigmoid colon. Both flexures would be air filled in the erect position. *(Bontrager and Lampignano, 6th ed., p. 489)*

138. **(C)** If structures are overlying or underlying the area to be demonstrated (e.g., the medial femoral condyle obscuring the joint space in the lateral knee projection), CR angulation is used (e.g., 5-degree cephalad angulation to see the joint space in the lateral knee).

If structures are likely to be foreshortened or self-superimposed (e.g., the scaphoid in a PA wrist), CR angulation may be employed to place the structure more closely parallel with the IR.

Another example is the oblique cervical spine, where cephalad or caudad angulation is required to "open" the intervertebral foramina.

Magnification is controlled by object-to-image-receptor distance (OID) and SID; it is unrelated to CR angulation. *(Frank, Long, and Smith, 11th ed., vol. 1, p 307)*

139. **(C)** In the dorsoplantar projection of the foot, the CR may be directed perpendicularly or angled 10 degrees posteriorly. Angulation serves to "open" the tarsometatarsal joints that are not well visualized on the dorsoplantar projection with perpendicular ray. Inversion and eversion of the foot do not affect the tarsometatarsal joints. *(Frank, Long, and Smith, 11th ed., vol. 1, p. 256)*

140. **(C)** To accurately position a lateral forearm, the elbow must form a 90-degree angle with the humeral epicondyles perpendicular to the IR and superimposed. The radius and ulna are superimposed distally. Proximally, the coronoid process and radial head are superimposed, and the radial head faces anteriorly. Failure of the elbow to form a 90-degree angle or the hand to be lateral results in a less than satisfactory lateral projection of the forearm. *(Frank, Long, and Smith, 11th ed., vol. 1, p. 142)*

141. **(A)** The routine AP projection of the lumbar spine demonstrates the intervertebral disk spaces between the first four lumbar vertebrae. The space between L5 and S1, however, is angled with respect to the other disk spaces. Therefore, the CR must be directed 30 to 35 degrees cephalad to parallel the disk space and thus project it open onto the IR. *(Frank, Long, and Smith, 11th ed., vol. 1, p. 436)*

142. **(C)** A certain amount of object unsharpness is an inherent part of every radiographic image because of the position and shape of anatomic structures within the body. Structures within the three-dimensional human body lie in different *planes*. Additionally, the three-dimensional *shape* of solid anatomic structures rarely coincides with the shape of the divergent beam. Consequently, some structures are imaged with more inherent distortion than others, and shapes of anatomic structures can be entirely misrepresented. Structures *farther* from the IR will be distorted (i.e., *magnified*) more than those *closer* to the IR; structures *closer* to the x-ray source will be distorted (i.e., *magnified*) more than those *farther* from the x-ray source.

For the *shape* of anatomic structures to be accurately recorded, the structures must be parallel to the x-ray tube and the IR, and aligned with the central ray (CR). *The shape of anatomic structures lying at an angle within the body or placed away from the CR will be misrepresented on the IR.* There are two types of shape distortion. If a linear structure is angled within the body, that is, not parallel with the long axis of the part/body and not parallel to the IR, then that anatomic structure will appear *smaller*—it will be *foreshortened*. On the other hand, *elongation* occurs when the x-ray tube is angled.

Image details placed away from the *path* of the CR will be exposed by more divergent rays, resulting in *rotation distortion*. This is why the CR must be directed to the part of greatest interest.

Unless the edges of a three-dimensional *object* conform to the shape of the x-ray beam, blur or unsharpness will occur at the partially attenuating edge of the object. This can be accompanied by changes in radiographic/image density, according to the thickness of areas traversed by the x-ray beam. *(Bushong, 9th ed., pp. 286–290)*

143. **(C)** Patients are instructed to remove all jewelry, hair clips, metal prostheses, coins, and credit cards before entering the room for MRI. MRI does not use radiation to produce images but instead uses a very strong magnetic field. All patients must be screened prior to entering the magnetic field to be sure that they do not have any metal on or within them. Proper screening includes questioning the patient about any eye injury involving metal, cardiac pacemakers, aneurysm clips, insulin pumps, heart valves, shrapnel, or any metal in the body. This is extremely important, and if there is any doubt, the patient should be rescheduled for a time after it has been determined that it is safe for him or her to enter the room. Patients who have done metalwork or welding are frequently sent to diagnostic radiology for screening images of the orbits to ensure that there are no metal fragments near the optic nerve. Any external metallic objects, such as bobby pins, hair clips, or coins in the pocket, must be removed, or they will be pulled by the magnet and can cause harm to the patient. Credit cards and any other plastic cards with a magnetic strip will be wiped clean if they come in contact with the magnetic field. *(Torres et al., 6th ed., pp. 362–363)*

144. **(C)** A lateral projection generally is included in a routine skull series. The patient is placed in a PA oblique position. The *MSP* is positioned parallel to the IR, and the *IOML* is adjusted so as to be parallel to the long axis of the cassette. The *interpupillary line* must be perpendicular to the IR. In a routine lateral projection of the skull, the CR should enter approximately 2 inches superior to the EAM. *(Frank, Long, and Smith, 11th ed., vol. 2, p. 306)*

145. **(B)** The radiograph shown in Figure 2–25 is a *prone recumbent* projection. If the patient were in the *supine recumbent* position, barium would be located in the fundus of the stomach because the fundus is more posterior, and barium would flow down to fill the posterior structure. If the patient were in the supine *Trendelenburg* position, barium flow to the fundus would be facilitated even more. If the patient were *erect*, air–fluid levels would be clearly defined. In addition, the barium-filled stomach tends to spread more horizontally in the prone position (as is seen in the radiograph). *(Frank, Long, and Smith, 11th ed., vol. 2, p. 144)*

146. **(B)** The *lordotic* curves are *secondary* curves; that is, they develop sometime after birth. The cervical and lumbar vertebrae form lordotic curves. The thoracic and sacral vertebrae exhibit the *primary kyphotic* curves, those that are present at birth. *(Frank, Long, and Smith, 11th ed., vol. 1, p. 375)*

147. **(B)** In the lateral position of the skull, the *midsagittal plane* must be *parallel* to the IR and the interpupillary line vertical. Flexion of the head is adjusted until the *IOML* is *parallel* to the IR. The CR should enter about *2 inches superior* to the EAM. The centering point for a lateral sella turcica is ¾ inch anterior and superior to the EAM. *(Frank, Long, and Smith, 11th ed., vol. 2, p. 306)*

148. **(C)** Long bones are composed of a shaft, or diaphysis, and two extremities, or epiphyses. In growing bone, the cartilaginous *epiphyseal plate* is gradually replaced by bone. The ossified growth area of long bones is the *metaphysis*. Apophysis refers to vertebral joints formed by articulation of superjacent articular facets. *(Bontrager and Lampignano, 6th ed., p. 9)*

149. **(A)** The position of the gallbladder varies with the body habitus of the patient. *Hypersthenic* patients are more likely to have their gallbladder located *high and lateral*. The *asthenic* patient's gallbladder is most likely to occupy a *low and medial* position, occasionally superimposed on the vertebrae or iliac fossa. The *LAO* position is used most often to move the gallbladder away from the spine. The erect position would make the gallbladder move even more inferior and medial. *(Frank, Long, and Smith, 11th ed., vol. 2, p. 96)*

150. **(A)** The abdomen is divided into nine regions. The upper lateral regions are the left and right hypochondriac, with the epigastric separating them. The middle lateral regions are the left and right lumbar, with the umbilical region between them. The lower lateral regions are the left and right iliac, with the hypogastric region between them. The *ileocecal valve*, cecum, and

appendix (if present) are located in the lower right abdomen—therefore, the *right iliac region.* *(Frank, Long, and Smith, 11th ed., vol. 1, p. 62)*

151. **(B)** Evaluation of the acromioclavicular joints requires *bilateral* AP or PA *erect* projections *with and without the use of weights.* Weights are used to emphasize the minute changes within a joint caused by *separation* or *dislocation.* Weights should be anchored from the patient's wrists rather than held in the patient's hands because this encourages tightening of the shoulder muscles and obliteration of any small separation. *(Frank, Long, and Smith, 11th ed., vol. 1, p. 202)*

152. **(A)** *Ewing sarcoma* is a (primary) malignant bone tumor that arises from bone marrow and occurs in children and young adults. The disease is characterized by new bone formation in a layering effect—giving the bone the characteristic "onion peel" appearance radiographically. *Multiple myeloma* is also a cancerous bone tumor usually affecting adults between the ages of 40 and 70 years. Bone undergoes osteolytic changes, and radiographic demonstration appears as circular areas of bone loss. As their name implies (*chondr*), *enchondroma* and *osteochondroma* involve cartilage—they are both benign conditions. *(Bontrager and Lampignano, 6th ed., p. 143)*

153. **(B)** The *hilus* (hilum) is the slit-like opening on the medial aspect of the lung through which arteries, veins, lymphatics, and so forth enter and exit. The *carina* is an internal ridge located at the bifurcation of the trachea into right and left primary, or main stem, bronchi. The *epiglottis* is a flap of elastic cartilage that functions to prevent fluids and solids from entering the respiratory tract during swallowing. The *root* of the lung attaches the lung, via dense connective tissue, to the mediastinum. The root of the left lung is at the level of T6, and the root of the right is at T5. *(Bontrager and Lampignano, 6th ed., p. 80)*

154. **(D)** The *SMV* projection is made with the patient's head resting on the vertex and the CR directed perpendicular to the IOML. This position may be used as part of a sinus survey to demonstrate the sphenoidal sinuses or as a view of the cranial base for the basal foramina

(especially the foramina ovale and spinosum). It also demonstrates the bony part of the auditory (eustachian) tubes. *AP* or *PA axial* projections are used frequently to demonstrate the occipital region or evaluate the sellar region. A *lateral* projection is usually part of a routine skull evaluation. The *parietoacanthal* projection is the single best position to demonstrate facial bones. *(Frank, Long, and Smith, 11th ed., vol. 2, p. 324)*

155. **(B)** The radiograph in Figure 2–26 illustrates a lateral projection of the *scapula*. The axillary and vertebral borders are superimposed. The acromion and coracoid process are visualized; the *coracoid* process is partially superimposed on the axillary portion of the third rib. A scapular Y projection is often performed to demonstrate shoulder dislocation, but the affected arm is left to rest at the patient's side; the arm in this radiograph is abducted somewhat to better view the body of the scapula. *(Frank, Long, and Smith, 11th ed., vol. 1, p. 214)*

156. **(A)** The femur is the longest and strongest bone in the body. The femoral shaft is bowed slightly anteriorly and presents a long, narrow ridge *posteriorly* called the *linea aspera*. The proximal femur consists of a head that is received by the pelvic acetabulum. The femoral neck, which joins the head and shaft, normally angles upward about 120 degrees and forward (in anteversion) about 15 degrees. The greater and lesser trochanters are large processes on the *posterior* proximal femur. The *intertrochanteric crest* runs obliquely between the trochanters; the intertrochanteric line parallels the intertrochanteric crest on the anterior femoral surface. The intercondyloid fossa, a deep notch, is found on the distal posterior femur between the large femoral condyles, and the *popliteal surface* is a smooth surface just superior to the intercondyloid fossa. Just opposite the popliteal surface, on the distal *anterior* femur is the *patellar surface*— a smooth surface for patellar motion during flexion and extension of the knee. *(Frank, Long, and Smith, 11th ed., vol. 1, pp. 234–235)*

157. **(C)** An *intrathecal* injection is one made within the spinal meninges. A myelogram requires an intrathecal injection to introduce contrast medium into the subarachnoid space. An IVU requires an intravenous injection; a retrograde pyelogram requires that contrast medium be introduced into the ureters by way of cystoscopy. A cystogram requires that contrast medium be introduced via catheter into the urinary bladder. *(Frank, Long, and Smith, 11th ed., vol. 1, p. 286)*

158. **(D)** The typical vertebra is divided into two portions—the (anterior) *body* (number 11) and the (posterior) *vertebral arch*. The vertebral arch supports seven processes: two transverse (number 8), one spinous (number 1), two superior articular processes, and two inferior articular processes. A thoracic vertebra is shown. The thoracic vertebrae are unique in that they have downward-angling spinous processes and articulations for ribs. Numbers 5 and 10 illustrate the facets where the heads of ribs (number 7) articulate to form the costovertebral articulations (number 6). Number 2 illustrates the ribs' tubercle—it articulates with the transverse process facet (number 9) to form the costotransverse articulation (number 3). *(Frank, Long, and Smith, 11th ed., vol. 1, pp. 380–381)*

159. **(B)** In a PA projection of the chest, there should be no rotation, as evidenced by *symmetry* of sternal extremities of clavicles equidistant from vertebral borders. The shoulders are rolled forward to remove the scapulae from the lung fields. Inspiration should be adequate to demonstrate 10 *posterior* ribs above the diaphragm. The air-filled *trachea* should be seen midline; the esophagus is unlikely to be visualized without a contrast agent. *(Frank, Long, and Smith, 11th ed., vol. 1, p. 521)*

160. **(B)** The talocalcaneal, or subtalar, joint is a three-faceted articulation formed by the talus and the os calcis (calcaneus). The plantodorsal and dorsoplantar projections of the os calcis should exhibit sufficient density to visualize the talocalcaneal joint (Figure 2–60). This is the only "routine" projection that will demonstrate the talocalcaneal joint. If evaluation of the talocalcaneal joint is desired, special views (such as the Broden and Isherwood methods)

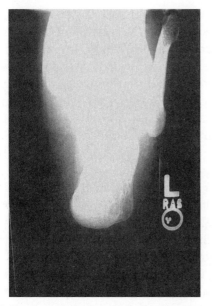

Figure 2–60. Courtesy of Stamford Hospital, Department of Radiology.

are required. *(Frank, Long, and Smith, 11th ed., vol. 1, pp. 278–279)*

161. **(C)** In a lateral projection of the ankle, the tibia and fibula are superimposed, and the foot is somewhat dorsiflexed to better demonstrate the talotibial joint. The talofibular joint is not visualized because of superimposition with other bony structures. It may be well visualized in the medial oblique projection of the ankle. *(Frank, Long, and Smith, 11th ed., vol. 1, p. 286)*

162. **(B)** A double-contrast examination of the large bowel is performed to see through the bowel to its posterior wall and to visualize any intraluminal lesions or masses. Oblique projections are used to "open up" the flexures—the RAO for the hepatic flexure and the LAO for the splenic flexure. To view the redundant S-shaped sigmoid in the AP position, the CR is directed 30 to 40 degrees cephalad. The CR is reversed when the patient is in the PA position; that is, the CR is directed 30 to 40 degrees caudad. *(Frank, Long, and Smith, 11th ed., vol. 2, pp. 178, 183)*

163. **(C)** Radiographic examinations of the large bowel generally include the AP or PA axial position to "open" the S-shaped sigmoid colon, the lateral position especially for the rectum, and the LAO and RAO (or LPO and RPO) positions to "open" the colic flexures. The left and right decubitus positions usually are employed only in double-contrast barium enemas to better demonstrate double contrast of the medial and lateral walls of the ascending and descending colon. *(Frank, Long, and Smith, 11th ed., vol. 2, p. 186)*

164. **(D)** Bilateral AP oblique hands are obtained using the Norgaard method or "Ball-Catcher position." The method is used to detect early rheumatoid arthritis changes or fracture to the base of the fifth metacarpal. The hands are positioned and supported in a 45-degree oblique, palm-up position. The CR is directed to the level of the fifth metacarpophalangeal joint (MPJ) midway between the hands—both hands are exposed simultaneously. *(Bontrager and Lampignano, 6th ed., p. 157)*

165. **(B)** Statement number 1 describes the PA axial projection (Camp-Coventry method) for demonstration of the intercondyloid fossa. Statement number 2 describes the AP axial projection (Béclère method) for demonstration of the intercondyloid fossa. The positions are actually the reverse of each other. Statement number 3 describes the method of obtaining a PA projection of the patella. *(Frank, Long, and Smith, 11th ed., vol. 1, pp. 314–317)*

166. **(A)** Visualization of the scapular spine (number 13) indicates that this is a view of the *posterior* aspect of the scapula. The scapula's *anterior*, or *costal*, surface is that which is adjacent to the ribs. The scapula has no sternal articulation. *(Tortora and Derrickson, 11th ed., p. 234)*

167–168. **(167, A; 168, B)** Figure 2–29 depicts a posterior view of the right scapula and its articulation with the humerus (number 4). The scapula presents two borders—the lateral or axillary border (number 7) and the medial or vertebral border (number 9). It also presents three angles—the inferior angle (number 8), the superior angle (number 12), and the lateral angle (number 6). The processes of the scapula are the coracoid (number 2), the acromion (number 3), and the scapular spine (number 13). The scapula has a (supra) scapular notch (number 1), a supraspinatus fossa (number 11), and an infraspinatus fossa (number 10). Number 5 identifies the glenoid fossa—the articular surface for the humeral head, forming the glenohumeral articulation. *(Tortora and Derrickson, 11th ed., p. 234)*

169. **(C)** For the PA projection of the skull, the OML is adjusted perpendicular to the IR, and the MSP must be perpendicular to the IR. The CR is directed so as to exit the nasion. In this position, the petrous pyramids should completely *fill* the orbits. When caudal angulation is used with this position, the petrous pyramids are projected in the *lower portion*, or out of, the orbits. If cephalad angulation is used with this position, the petrous pyramids are projected up toward the occipital region (as in the nuchofrontal projection). *(Frank, Long, and Smith, 11th ed., vol. 2, p. 310)*

170. **(D)** A PA axial projection of the skull with a 15-degree caudad angle will show the petrous pyramids in the lower third of the orbits. If *no* angulation is used, the petrous pyramids will fill the orbits. Either PA projection should demonstrate symmetrical petrous pyramids and an equal distance from the lateral border of the skull to the lateral border of the orbit on both sides. This determines that there is no rotation of the skull. *(Frank, Long, and Smith, 11th ed., vol. 2, p. 314)*

171. **(A)** The AP oblique positions (RPO and LPO) demonstrate the colonic structures farther from the IR. The LPO position will demonstrate the hepatic flexure and ascending colon, whereas the RPO position demonstrates the splenic flexure and descending colon. In the prone oblique positions (RAO and LAO), the flexure disclosed is the one closer to the IR. Therefore, the LAO position will "open up" the left colic, or splenic, flexure, and the RAO position will demonstrate the right colic, or hepatic, flexure. *(Bontrager and Lampignano, 6th ed., pp. 515–517)*

172. **(D)** Surface landmarks, prominences, and depressions are very useful to the radiographer in locating anatomic structures that are not visible externally. The *costal margin* is at about the same level as L3. The *umbilicus* is at approximately the same level as the L3–4 interspace. The *xiphoid tip* is at about the same level as T10. The *fourth lumbar vertebra* is at approximately the same level as the iliac crest. *(Frank, Long, and Smith, 11th ed., vol. 1, p. 63)*

173. **(B)** The position, shape, and motility of various organs can differ greatly from one body habitus to another. The *hypersthenic* individual is large and heavy; the lungs and heart are high, the stomach is high and transverse, the gallbladder is high and lateral, and the colon is high and peripheral. In contrast, the other habitus extreme is the *asthenic* individual. This patient is slender and light and has a long and narrow thorax, a low and long stomach, a low and medial gallbladder, and a low medial and redundant colon. The radiographer must consider these characteristic differences when radiographing individuals of various body types. *(Frank, Long, and Smith, 11th ed., vol. 1, p. 65)*

174. **(A)** The cervical intervertebral foramina lie 45 degrees to the MSP and 15 to 20 degrees to a transverse plane. When the *anterior oblique* position (LAO or RAO) is used, the cervical intervertebral foramina demonstrated are those *closer to* the IR. In the posterior oblique position (LPO or RPO), the foramina disclosed are those *farther from* the IR. There is, therefore, some magnification of the foramina in the posterior oblique positions. The interarticular (apophyseal) joints and intervertebral joints are best visualized in the lateral projection. *(Frank, Long, and Smith, 11th ed., vol. 1, p. 405)*

175. **(C)** With inspiration, the diaphragm moves inferiorly and depresses the abdominal viscera. The ribs and sternum are elevated. As the ribs are elevated, their angle is decreased. Radiographic density can vary considerably in appearance depending on the phase of respiration during which the exposure is made. *(Bontrager and Lampignano, 6th ed., p. 84)*

176. **(A)** A lateral projection of the scapula superimposes its medial and lateral borders (vertebral and axillary, respectively). The coracoid

and acromion processes should be readily identified separately (not superimposed) in the lateral projection. The entire scapula should be free of superimposition with the ribs. The erect position is probably the most comfortable position for a patient with scapular pain. *(Frank, Long, and Smith, 11th ed., vol. 1, p. 214)*

177. **(C)** The image demonstrates the sternum made in the *RAO* position. This position projects the sternum to the *left* side of the thorax. Superimposition of the sternum onto the heart and other mediastinal structures promotes more uniform density. The CR for this image should have been directed more inferiorly, that is, midway between the jugular (manubrial) notch and the xiphoid process. *(Frank, Long, and Smith, 11th ed., vol. 1, pp. 472–475)*

178. **(C)** In the lateral projection of the knee, the joint space is obscured by the magnified medial femoral condyle unless the CR is angled 5 to 7 degrees cephalad. The degree of flexion of the knee is important when evaluating the knee for possible transverse patellar fracture. In such a case, the knee should not be flexed more than 10 degrees. The knee normally should be flexed 20 to 30 degrees in the lateral position. *(Frank, Long, and Smith, 11th ed., vol. 1, p. 307)*

179. **(B)** The AP projection of the cervical spine demonstrates the bodies and intervertebral spaces of the last five vertebrae (C3–7). The cervical apophyseal joints are 90 degrees to the MSP and, therefore, are demonstrated in the lateral projection. *(Frank, Long, and Smith, 11th ed., vol. 1, pp. 398–399)*

180. **(B)** The *first metacarpal,* on the lateral side of the hand, articulates with the most lateral carpal of the distal carpal row, the greater *multangular/ trapezium.* This articulation forms a rather unique and very versatile *saddle joint* named for the shape of its articulating surfaces. *(Bontrager and Lampignano, 6th ed., p. 136)*

181. **(C)** The PA axial (Caldwell) projection of the paranasal sinuses is used to demonstrate the frontal and ethmoidal sinuses. The patient's skull is placed PA, and the OML is elevated 15 degrees from the horizontal. This projects the petrous pyramids into the lower third of the orbits, thus permitting optimal visualization of the frontal and ethmoidal sinuses. *(Bontrager and Lampignano, 6th ed., p. 439)*

182. **(A)** The respiratory passageways include the nose, pharynx, larynx (upper respiratory structures), trachea, bronchi, and lungs (lower structures). If obstruction of the breathing passageways occurs in the *upper* respiratory tract, above the larynx (i.e., in the nose or pharynx), *tracheotomy* may be performed to restore breathing. *Intubation* can be done into the *lower* structures, larynx, and trachea, moving aside any soft obstruction and restoring the breathing passageway. *(Tortora and Derrickson, 11th ed., p. 856)*

183. **(D)** To clearly demonstrate the atlas and axis without superimposition of the teeth or the base of the skull, a line between the maxillary occlusal plane (edge of upper teeth) and mastoid tip must be vertical. If the head is flexed too much, the teeth will be superimposed. If the head is extended too much, the cranial base will be superimposed on the area of interest. A line between the mentum and the mastoid tip is used to demonstrate the odontoid process only through the foramen magnum (Fuchs method). *(Frank, Long, and Smith, 11th ed., vol. 1, p. 393)*

184. **(B)** Operative cholangiography plays a vital role in biliary tract surgery. The contrast medium is injected, and imaging occurs *following* a cholecystectomy so that gallbladder calculi will not be visualized. This procedure is used to investigate the patency of the bile ducts, the function of the hepatopancreatic sphincter (of Oddi), and the presence of previously undetected biliary tract calculi. *(Frank, Long, and Smith, 11th ed., vol. 3, p. 273)*

185. **(A)** Lateral projections of the barium-filled stomach (Figure 2–61) may be performed recumbent or upright for demonstration of the retrogastric space. With the patient in the (usually right) lateral position, the CR is

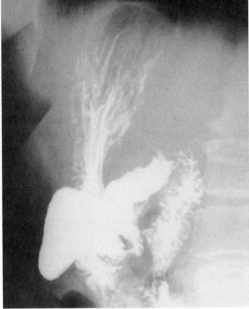

Figure 2–61. Courtesy of Stamford Hospital, Department of Radiology.

directed to a point midway between the midcoronal line and the anterior surface of the abdomen at the level of L1. When the patient is in the LPO or RAO position, the CR should be directed midway between the vertebral column and the lateral border of the abdomen. For the PA projection, the CR is directed perpendicular to the IR at the level of L2. *(Frank, Long, and Smith, 11th ed., vol. 2, pp. 152–153)*

186. **(D)** A decubitus projection is obtained using a horizontal x-ray beam. The type of decubitus projection is dependent on the patient's recumbent position. When the patient is lying *AP recumbent* (i.e., *supine*), the patient is said to be in the dorsal decubitus position. When the patient is lying *prone*, he or she is in the ventral decubitus position. If the patient is lying in the *left or right lateral recumbent* position with the x-ray beam directed horizontally, the patient is said to be in the left or right lateral decubitus position, respectively. *(Bontrager and Lampignano, 6th ed., p. 20)*

187. **(C)** When imaging a patient with a possible traumatic spine injury, it is appropriate to either maneuver the x-ray tube head or, if the patient must be moved, to use the log-rolling method. This cannot be done by one person;

the radiographer must summon assistance. If the patient is on a backboard and in a neck collar, as most patients with suspected spine injury are, it is never appropriate to ask the patient to turn, scoot, or slide over. The only movement that should be permitted is movement of the entire spine, body, and head together, as in log-rolling. Any twisting could cause severe and permanent damage to the spinal cord, resulting in paralysis or even death. *(Torres et al., pp. 77–79)*

188. **(C)** In the tangential (sunrise) projection of the patella, the CR is directed parallel to the longitudinal plane of the patella, thereby demonstrating a vertical fracture and providing the best view of the patellofemoral articulation. The AP knee projection could demonstrate a vertical fracture through the superimposed femur, but it does not demonstrate the patellofemoral articulation. The tunnel view of the knee is used to demonstrate the intercondyloid fossa. *(Frank, Long, and Smith, 11th ed., vol. 1, pp. 324–325)*

189–190. **(189, D; 190, C)** The radiograph shown is a lateral projection of the cervical spine taken in flexion. Flexion and extension views are useful in certain cervical injuries, such as whiplash, to indicate the degree of anterior and posterior motion. The structure labeled number 1 is an *apophyseal joint;* because apophyseal joints are positioned 90 degrees to the MSP, they are well visualized in the lateral projection. The structure labeled number 2 is a *vertebral body.* Numbers 3 through 6 are various components of C1 (atlas) and C2 (axis). The large *body of C2* (number 6) is has a process superiorly, the *odontoid process/dens* (number 4). The odontoid process fits into, and articulates with. C1. The superimposed *posterior arch of C1* is indicated by number 3. The dens is articulated with the *anterior arch of C1* (number 5). *(Frank, Long, and Smith, 11th ed., vol. 1, p. 397)*

191. **(C)** The voiding cystourethrogram (*VCUG*) is a functional study performed to evaluate the physiology of urination to demonstrate possible *vesicoureteral reflux* (backup of urine from bladder into ureters, causing repeated urinary tract infections). The retrograde urogram and retrograde cystogram demonstrate the anatomy (not function) of the urinary tract. The intravenous/excretory urogram does demonstrate function of the urinary tract but does not evaluate the urethra. *(Bontrager and Lampignano, 6th ed., p. 578)*

192.   **(B)** The AP projection of the clavicle should demonstrate the clavicular *body*/shaft and its two extremities: the sternal extremity and its associated *sternoclavicular* articulation, and the acromial extremity and its associated *acromioclavicular* articulation. The sternocostal joint is the articulation between the sternum and rib and is not delineated in the AP clavicle image. *(Bontrager and Lampignano, 6th ed., p. 202)*

193.   **(C)** The AP projection demonstrates superimposition of the distal fibula on the talus; the joint space is not well seen. The 15- to 20-degree medical oblique position shows the entire mortise joint; the talofibular joint is well visualized, as well as the talotibial joint. There is considerable superimposition of the talus and fibula in the lateral and lateral oblique projections. *(Frank, Long, and Smith, 11th ed., vol. 1, p. 291)*

194.   **(A)** The erect position is employed most often to demonstrate air–fluid levels in the chest or abdomen or both. However, patients having traumatic injuries frequently must be examined in the recumbent position. The recumbent position will not demonstrate air–fluid levels unless it is a decubitus position. If free air is being questioned, we will look for that quantity of air on the "up" side because air rises. However, because liver tissue is so homogeneous, a small amount of air will be perceived more easily superimposed on it rather than on left-sided structures. Thus, an AP projection obtained in the left lateral decubitus position will best demonstrate a small amount of free air because that air will be superimposed on the liver. *(Frank, Long, and Smith, 11th ed., vol. 2, p. 44)*

195.   **(A)** Blood is oxygenated in the lungs and carried to the left atrium by the four pulmonary veins. From the left atrium, blood flows through the bicuspid (mitral) valve into the left ventricle. Blood leaving the left ventricle is bright red, oxygenated blood that travels through the systemic circulation, which delivers oxygenated blood via arteries and returns deoxygenated blood to the lungs via veins. From the left ventricle, blood first goes through the largest arteries and then goes to progressively smaller arteries (arterioles), to the capillaries, to the smallest veins (venules), and on to progressively larger veins. *(Tortora and Derrickson, 11th ed., p. 737)*

196.   **(D)** On the *AP* projection of the elbow, the radial head and ulna normally are somewhat superimposed. The *lateral oblique* projection demonstrates the radial head free of ulnar superimposition. The *lateral* projection demonstrates the olecranon process in profile. The *medial oblique* projection demonstrates considerable overlap of the proximal radius and ulna but should clearly demonstrate the coronoid process free of superimposition and the olecranon process within the olecranon fossa. *(Frank, Long, and Smith, 11th ed., vol. 1, pp. 143–147)*

197.   **(D)** Acromioclavicular (AC) joints usually are examined when separation or dislocation is suspected. They must be examined in the erect position because in the recumbent position a separation appears to reduce itself. Both AC joints are examined simultaneously for comparison because separations may be minimal. *(Frank, Long, and Smith, 11th ed., vol. 1, p. 202)*

198.   **(C)** Myelography is radiologic examination of the structures within the spinal canal. Opaque contrast medium is usually used. Following injection, the contrast medium is distributed to the vertebral region of interest by *gravity;* the *table* is angled Trendelenburg for visualization of the cervical region and in the Fowler position for visualization of the thoracic and lumbar regions. Although the table is Trendelenburg, care must be taken that the patient's neck is kept in acute *extension* to compress the cisterna magna and keep contrast medium from traveling into the ventricles of the brain. *(Bontrager and Lampignano, 6th ed., p. 763)*

199. (C) There are many terms (with which the radiographer must be familiar) that are used to describe radiographic positioning techniques. *Cephalad* refers to that which is toward the head, and *caudad* refers to that which is toward the feet. Structures close to the source or beginning are said to be *proximal*, whereas those lying away from the source or origin are *distal*. Parts close to the midline are said to be *medial*, and those away from the midline are *lateral*. *(Bontrager and Lampignano, 6th ed., p. 23)*

200. (C) The parietoacanthal projection (Waters position) provides an oblique frontal projection of the facial bones. The maxilla (and antra), zygomatic arches, and orbits are well demonstrated. The patient is positioned PA with the head resting on the extended chin so that the OML forms a 37-degree angle with the IR. The position may be reversed if the patient is positioned AP and the CR is directed 30 degrees cephalad to the IOML. This position is not preferred, however, because the facial bones are significantly magnified as a result of increased OID. *(Bontrager and Lampignano, 6th ed., p. 420)*

201. (B) Inhalation of a foreign substance such as water or food particles into the airway and/or bronchial tree is called *aspiration*. *Asphyxia* is caused by deprivation of oxygen as a result of interference with ventilation from trauma, electric shock, and so on. *Atelectasis* is incomplete expansion of a lung or portion of a lung. *Asystole* is cardiac standstill—failure of the heart muscle to contract and pump blood to vital organs. *(Tortora and Derrickson, 11th ed., p. 889)*

202. (B) ERCP may be performed to investigate abnormalities of the biliary system or pancreas. The patient's throat is treated with a local anesthetic in preparation for the passage of the endoscope. The hepatopancreatic ampulla (of Vater) is located, and a cannula is passed through it so that contrast medium may be introduced into the common bile duct. Spot images of the common bile duct and pancreatic duct are taken frequently in the oblique position. Direct injection of barium mixture into

the duodenum occurs during an enteroclysis procedure of the small bowel. *(Frank, Long, and Smith, 11th ed., vol. 2, p. 116)*

203. (C) A Colles fracture usually is caused by a fall onto an outstretched (extended) hand to "brake" a fall. The wrist then suffers an impacted transverse fracture of the *distal* inch of the *radius* with an accompanying chip fracture of the *ulnar* styloid process. Because of the hand position at the time of the fall, the fracture usually is *displaced backward* approximately 30 degrees. *(Bontrager and Lampignano, 6th ed., pp. 142, 601)*

204. (C) The cassette for a cross-table (axiolateral or horizontal beam) lateral projection of the hip is placed in a vertical position. The top edge of the cassette should be placed directly above the iliac crest and adjacent to the *lateral surface* of the affected hip. The cassette is positioned *parallel* to the femoral neck; the CR is *perpendicular* to the femoral neck and cassette. *(Frank, Long, and Smith, 11th ed., vol. 1, p. 358)*

205. (A) No hard and fast rule can be applied to restraining pediatric patients. Much depends on the child's age and emotional temperament and the type of examination. Children never should be restrained routinely; many are capable of understanding a clear and simple explanation of why their cooperation is needed. Physical restraint is almost always frightening to the older child, and unnecessary restraint is inexcusable. When a parent or other individual (never a radiation worker!) must be in the radiographic room with the patient, remember to provide proper protection. *(Adler and Carlton, 4th ed., p. 187)*

206. (B) Radiologic interventional procedures function to *treat* pathologic conditions as well as provide diagnostic information. *Percutaneous transluminal angioplasty* (PTA) uses an inflatable balloon catheter under fluoroscopic guidance to increase the diameter of a plaque-stenosed vessel. A *stent* is a cage-like metal device that can be placed in the vessel to provide support to the vessel wall. A *peripherally inserted central catheter* (PICC) is also placed under fluoroscopic control. It is simply a venous access catheter that can be left in place for several months. It provides convenient venous access for patients requiring frequent blood tests, chemotherapy, or large amounts of antibiotics. (*Bontrager and Lampignano, 6th ed., pp. 711–712*)

207. **(C)** All traumatic injuries require the radiographer to be particularly alert and observant. Patient status must be observed and monitored continually. The radiographer must speak calmly to the patient, *explaining the procedure even if the patient appears unconscious or unresponsive.* In the case of an injured limb, *both joints must be supported* if any movement is required. *Both joints also must be included* when examining long bones. The injured limb need not be placed in exact AP and lateral positions, but any two views of the part *at right angles to each other* must be obtained. (*Frank, Long, and Smith, 11th ed., vol. 2, pp. 32–33*)

208. **(B)** Diagnostic x-ray examinations that require contrast agents include upper gastrointestinal (GI) series, lower GI series (BE), intravenous urogram (IVU), and the occasional gallbladder (GB) series. Patient preparation is somewhat different for each of these examinations. An iodinated contrast agent, usually in the form of several pills, is taken by the patient the evening before a scheduled GB examination, and only water is allowed the morning of the examination. The patient scheduled for an upper GI series must receive NPO (nothing by mouth) after midnight. A lower GI series (BE) requires that the large bowel be very clean prior to the administration of barium; this requires the administration of *cathartics* (laxatives) and cleansing enemas. Preparation for an IVU requires that the patient be NPO after midnight; some institutions also require that the large bowel be cleansed of gas and fecal material. Aftercare for barium examinations is very important. Patients typically are instructed to take milk of magnesia, increase their intake of fiber, drink plenty of water, and expect changes in stool color until all barium is evacuated and to call their physician if they do not have a bowel movement within 24 hours. Because water is removed from the barium sulfate

suspension in the large bowel, it is essential to make patients understand the importance of these instructions to avoid barium impaction in the large bowel. The use of barium sulfate suspensions is contraindicated when ruling out *visceral perforation*. (*Bontrager and Lampignano, 6th ed., p. 471*)

209. **(C)** Since the heart contracts and relaxes while functioning to pump blood from the heart, arteries that are large and those that are in closest proximity to the heart will feel the effect of the heart's forceful contractions in their walls. The arterial walls pulsate in unison with the heart's contractions. This movement may be detected with the fingers in various parts of the body and is referred to as the *pulse*. (*Tortora and Derrickson, 11th ed., p. 754*)

210. **(C)** Placing the patient in a 20- to 30-degree AP Trendelenburg position during an upper GI examination helps to demonstrate the presence of a *hiatal hernia*. A 10- to 15-degree Trendelenburg position with the patient rotated slightly to the right also will help demonstrate regurgitation and hiatal hernia. Filling of the *duodenal bulb* and demonstration of the *duodenal loop* are best seen in the RAO position. *Congenital hypertrophic pyloric stenosis* is caused by excessive thickening of the pyloric sphincter. It is noted in infancy and characterized by projectile vomiting. The pyloric valve will let very little pass through, and as a result, the stomach becomes enlarged (hypertrophied). (*Frank, Long, and Smith, 11th ed., vol. 2, p. 154*)

211. **(D)** The AP projection will give a general survey and show mediolateral and inferosuperior joint relationships. The scapular Y position (LAO or RAO) is employed to demonstrate anterior (subcoracoid) or posterior (subacromial) humeral dislocation. The humerus normally is superimposed on the scapula in this position; any deviation from this may indicate dislocation. Rotational views must be avoided in cases of suspected fracture. The AP and scapular Y combination is the closest to two views at right angles to each other. (*Frank, Long, and Smith, 11th ed., vol. 1, pp. 178, 189*)

212. **(A)** The medial oblique projection requires that the leg be rotated medially until the plantar surface of the foot forms a 30-degree angle with the cassette. This position demonstrates the navicular with minimal bony superimposition. The lateral oblique projection of the foot superimposes much of the navicular on the cuboid. The navicular is also superimposed on the cuboid in lateral projections. (*Frank, Long, and Smith, 11th ed., pp. 260–261*)

213. **(C)** The *obturator foramen* is a large oval foramen below each acetabulum and is formed by the *ischium and pubis*. The acetabulum is the bony socket that receives the head of the femur to form the hip joint. The upper two-fifths of the acetabulum is formed by the ilium, the lower anterior one-fifth is formed by the pubis, and the lower posterior two-fifths is formed by the ischium. Thus, the acetabulum is formed by all three of the bones that form the pelvis—the ilium, the ischium, and the pubis. (*Frank, Long, and Smith, 11th ed., vol. 1, p. 335*)

214. **(B)** Retrograde urography requires ureteral catheterization so that a contrast medium can be introduced directly into the pelvicalyceal system. This procedure provides excellent opacification and structural information but does not demonstrate the function of these structures. IV studies such as the IVU demonstrate function. Cystourethrography is an examination of the bladder and urethra, frequently performed during voiding. Nephrotomography is performed after IV administration of a contrast agent; it may be used to evaluate small intrarenal lesions and renal hypertension. (*Frank, Long, and Smith, 11th ed., vol. 2, p. 228*)

215. **(B)** The AP projection of the coccyx requires the CR to be directed *10 degrees caudally* and centered *2 inches superior to the pubic symphysis*. The AP projection of the *sacrum* requires a 15-degree cephalad angle centered at a point midway between the pubic symphysis and the ASIS. (*Bontrager and Lampignano, 6th ed., p. 344*)

216. **(C)** Arthritic changes in the knee result in changes in the joint bony relationships. These bony relationships are best evaluated in the AP position. *Narrowing of the joint spaces is* readily detected more on AP *weight-bearing* projections than on recumbent projections. (*Frank, Long, and Smith, 11th ed., vol. 1, p. 308*)

217. **(C)** The articular facets (apophyseal joints) of the L5-S1 articulation form a 30-degree angle with the MSP; they are, therefore, well demonstrated in a 30-degree oblique position. The 45-degree oblique position demonstrates the apophyseal joints of L1–4. (*Frank, Long, and Smith, 11th ed., vol. 1, p. 432*)

218. **(D)** When the shoulder is placed in *internal rotation*, a greater portion of the glenoid fossa is superimposed by the humeral head, and the *lesser tubercle* is visualized, as in image B. The *external rotation* position (image A) removes the humeral head from a large portion of the glenoid fossa and better demonstrates the *greater tubercle*. (*Frank, Long, and Smith, 11th ed., vol. 1, p. 178*)

219. **(B)** The AP projection provides a general survey of the abdomen showing the size and shape of the liver, spleen, and kidneys. When performed erect, it should demonstrate both hemidiaphragms. The lateral projection is sometimes requested and is useful for evaluating the prevertebral space occupied by the aorta. Ventral and dorsal decubitus positions provide a lateral view of the abdomen that is useful for demonstration of air–fluid levels. (*Frank, Long, and Smith, 11th ed., vol. 2, p. 101*)

220. **(C)** Diagnostic x-ray examinations that require contrast agents include upper GI series, lower GI series (BE), IVU, and the occasional GB series. Patient preparation is somewhat different for each of these examinations. An iodinated contrast agent, usually in the form of several pills, is taken by the patient the evening before a scheduled GB examination, and only water is allowed the morning of the examination. The patient scheduled for an upper GI series must receive NPO (nothing by mouth) after midnight. A lower GI series (BE) requires that the large bowel be very clean prior to the administration of barium; this requires the administration of *cathartics* (laxatives) and cleansing enemas.

Preparation for an IVU requires that the patient be NPO after midnight; some institutions also require that the large bowel be cleansed of gas and fecal material. Aftercare for barium examinations is very important. Patients typically are instructed to take milk of magnesia, increase their intake of fiber, drink plenty of water, and expect changes in stool color until all barium is evacuated and to call their physician if they do not have a bowel movement within 24 hours. Because water is removed from the barium sulfate suspension in the large bowel, it is essential to make patients understand the importance of these instructions to avoid barium impaction in the large bowel. The use of barium sulfate suspensions is contraindicated when ruling out *visceral perforation*. (*Bontrager and Lampignano, 6th ed., p. 501*)

221. **(D)** The patient is supine with the leg *abducted* (drawn away from the midline) approximately 40 degrees. This 40-degree abduction from the vertical places the long axis of the femoral neck parallel to the IR. *Adduction* is drawing the extremity closer to the midline of the body. (*Frank, Long, and Smith, 11th ed., vol. 1, p. 350*)

222. **(B)** Typically, traumatic injury to the hip requires a cross-table (axiolateral) lateral projection, as well as an AP projection of the entire pelvis. Both of these are performed using minimal manipulation of the affected extremity, reducing the possibility of further injury. A physician should perform any required manipulation of the traumatized hip. (*Frank, Long, and Smith, 11th ed., vol. 1, pp. 355, 358*)

223. **(C)** When the arm is placed in the *AP* position, the epicondyles are parallel to the plane of the IR, and the shoulder is placed in external rotation. In this position, an AP projection of the humerus, elbow, and forearm can be obtained; it places the greater tubercle of the humerus in profile. For the *lateral* projection of the humerus and the internal rotation projection of the shoulder, the arm is *internally* rotated, elbow somewhat flexed, with the back of the hand against the thigh, and the *epicondyles are superimposed and perpendicular to the IR*. The lateral projections of the humerus, elbow, and forearm all require that the epicondyles be perpendicular to the plane of the cassette. (*Frank, Long, and Smith, 11th ed., vol. 1, pp. 159–160*)

224. **(D)** Prior to the start of an IVU, the patient should be instructed to empty the bladder. This is advised to avoid dilution of the contrast agent. Diluted contrast within the bladder will not affect the diagnosis of *renal* abnormalities but may obscure bladder abnormalities. The patient's allergy history should be reviewed to avoid the possibility of a severe reaction to the contrast agent. The patient's creatinine level and blood urea nitrogen (BUN) should be checked; significant elevation of these blood chemistry levels often suggests renal dysfunction. The normal BUN level is 8 to 25 mg/100 mL; normal creatinine range is 0.6 to 1.5 mg/100 mL. (*Frank, Long, and Smith, 11th ed., vol. 2, p. 216*)

225. **(D)** Although routine elbow projections may be essentially negative, conditions may exist (such as an elevated fat pad) that seem to indicate the presence of a small fracture of the radial head. To demonstrate the entire circumference of the radial head, four exposures are made with the elbow flexed 90 degrees and with the humeral epicondyles superimposed and perpendicular to the cassette—one with the hand supinated as much as possible, one with the hand lateral, one with the hand pronated, and one with the hand in internal rotation, thumb down. Each maneuver changes the position of the radial head, and a different surface is presented for inspection. (*Frank, Long, and Smith, 11th ed., vol. 1, pp. 152–153*)

226. **(D)** The radiograph shown is made in the right lateral decubitus position. It is part of a series of radiographs made during an air contrast (double-contrast) BE examination. A double-contrast examination of the large bowel is performed to see *through* the bowel to its posterior wall and to visualize any *intraluminal* (e.g., polypoid) *lesions* or *masses*. Various body positions are used to redistribute the barium and air. To demonstrate the medial and lateral walls of the bowel, decubitus positions are used. The radiograph shows a right lateral decubitus position because the *barium has gravitated* to the right side (the side of the hepatic flexure). The *air rises* and delineates the medial side of the ascending colon and the lateral side of the descending colon. The

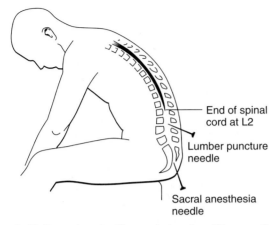

End of spinal
cord at L2

Lumber puncture
needle

Sacral anesthesia
needle

Figure 2–62. Reproduced, with permission, from Waxman: *Correlative Neuroanatomy*, 24th ed. 2000. McGraw-Hill, Inc. p 75; Fig 6-11

posterior wall of the rectum could be visualized using the ventral decubitus position and a horizontal beam lateral to the rectum. *(Frank, Long, and Smith, 11th ed., vol. 2, p. 187)*

227. **(D)** Generally, contrast medium is injected into the subarachnoid space between the third and fourth lumbar vertebrae (Figure 2–62). Because the spinal cord ends at the level of the first or second lumbar vertebra, this is considered to be a relatively safe injection site. The cisterna magna can be used, but the risk of contrast medium entering the ventricles and causing side effects increases. Diskography requires injection of contrast medium into the individual intervertebral disks. *(Tortora and Derrickson, 11th ed., p. 440)*

228. **(B)** The fingers must be supported parallel to the IR (e.g., on a finger sponge) in order that the joint spaces parallel the x-ray beam. When the fingers are flexed or resting on the cassette, the relationship between the joint spaces and the IR changes, and the joints appear "closed." *(Frank, Long, and Smith, 11th ed., vol. 1, pp. 118–119)*

229. **(D)** Spinal column studies often are required for evaluation of adolescent scoliosis, thus presenting a twofold problem—radiation exposure to youthful gonadal and breast tissues and significantly differing tissue densities/thicknesses. Electronic imaging (CR/DR) helps to reduce the exposure required for the examination. Exposure–dose concerns are also addressed with the use of a compensating

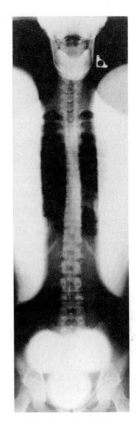

Figure 2–63. Courtesy of Nuclear Associates.

filter (for uniform density) that incorporates lead shielding for the breasts and gonads (Figure 2–63). *(Bontrager and Lampignano, 6th ed., p. 338)*

230. **(B)** *Diarthrodial* joints are freely movable joints that distinctively contain a joint capsule. Contrast medium is injected into this joint capsule to demonstrate the menisci, articular cartilage, bursae, and ligaments of the joint under investigation. *Synarthrodial* joints are immovable joints composed of either cartilage or fibrous connective tissue. *Amphiarthrodial* joints allow only slight movement. *(Frank, Long, and Smith, 11th ed., vol. 1, p. 73)*

231. **(B)** The laryngeal prominence, or "Adam's apple," is formed by the *thyroid cartilage*—the principal cartilage of the larynx. The thyroid *gland*, one of the endocrine glands, is lateral and inferior to the thyroid cartilage. The *vocal cords* are within the laryngeal cavity. Portions of the *pharynx* serve as passages for both air and food. *(Frank, Long, and Smith, 11th ed., vol. 2, p. 76)*

232. **(B)** To demonstrate the ankle joint space to best advantage, the plantar surface of the foot should be vertical in the AP projection of the ankle. Note that the fibula is the more distal of the two long bones of the lower leg and forms the lateral malleolus. The calcaneus is not well visualized in this projection because of super-imposition with other tarsals. *(Frank, Long, and Smith, 11th ed., vol. 1, p. 285)*

233. **(C)** Wilm's tumor is a rapidly developing tumor of the kidney(s). It is the most common childhood renal tumor, usually affecting only one kidney. Newer treatments are effective in controlling about 90% of these tumors. As the kidneys are affected, an *IVU* would be the most appropriate of the examinations listed. Other useful examinations would be CT scan and sonography. *(Bontrager and Lampignano, 6th ed., p. 660)*

234. **(C)** Sacroiliac joints lie obliquely within the pelvis and open anteriorly at an angle of 25 to 30 degrees to the midsagittal plane. A 25- to 30-degree oblique position places the joints perpendicular to the IR. The right sacroiliac joint may be demonstrated in the LPO and RAO positions with little magnification varia-tion. *(Frank, Long, and Smith, 11th ed., vol. 1, pp. 438–441)*

235. **(C)** Deoxygenated (venous) blood from the *upper* body (i.e., head, neck, thorax, and upper extremities) empties into the *superior vena cava.* Deoxygenated (venous) blood from the *lower* body (i.e., abdomen, pelvis, and lower extremities) empties into the *inferior vena cava.* The superior and inferior venae cavae empty into the right atrium. The coronary sinus, which returns venous blood from the heart, also empties into the right atrium. Deoxy-genated blood passes from the right atrium through the tricuspid valve into the right ven-tricle. From the right ventricle, blood is pumped (during ventricular systole) through the pulmonary semilunar valve into the pul-monary artery—the only artery that carries deoxygenated blood. From the pulmonary ar-tery, blood travels to the lungs, picks up oxy-gen, and is carried by the four pulmonary veins (the only veins carrying oxygenated blood) to the left atrium. The oxygenated blood passes through the mitral (or bicuspid) valve during atrial systole and into the left ventricle. During ventricular systole, oxygenated blood from the left ventricle passes through the aortic semilunar valve into the aorta and into the systemic circulation. *(Tortora and Derrickson, 11th ed., p. 758)*

236. **(A)** Breast tissue is most dense, glandular, and radiographically homogeneous in appearance in the postpubertal adolescent. Following pregnancy and lactation, changes occur within the breast that reduce the glandular tissue and replace it with fatty tissue (a process called *fatty infiltration*). Menopause causes further at-rophy of glandular tissue. *(Frank, Long, and Smith, 11th ed., vol. 2, pp, 411–413)*

237. **(D)** Standard radiographic protocols may be reduced to include two views, at right angles to each other, in emergency and trauma radi-ography. Department policy and procedure manuals include protocols for radiographic examinations. In the best interest of the pa-tient, and to enable the radiologist to make an accurate diagnosis, standard radiographic protocols should be followed. If the radiogra-pher must deviate from the protocol or be-lieves that additional projections may be helpful, then this should be discussed with the radiologist. Emergency and trauma radi-ography occasionally is an exception to this rule. If the emergency department physician's request varies from the department protocol, the radiographer must respect this. A note should be added to the request so that the ra-diologist is informed of the reason for a change in protocol. For example, a patient who has been involved in a motor vehicle ac-cident may need many radiographic studies, but the emergency department physician may order an AP chest and an AP and cross-table lateral C-spine only. Standard protocol may include a lateral chest and a cone-down view of the atlas and axis, as well as cervical oblique views. The emergency department physician has made a decision based on expe-rience and expertise that overrules standard protocols. At a later time, when the patient has been stabilized, the patient may be sent back to radiology for additional views. *(Dowd and Tilson, 2nd ed., vol. 2, pp. 1056–1057)*

238. **(C)** Blood pressure in the pulmonary circulation is relatively low, and therefore, pulmonary vessels can easily become blocked by blood clots, air bubbles, or fatty masses, resulting in a *pulmonary embolism*. If the blockage stays in place, it results in an extra strain on the right ventricle, which is now unable to pump blood. This can result in congestive heart failure. *Pneumothorax* is air in the pleural cavity. *Atelectasis* is a collapsed lung or part of a lung. *Hypoxia* is a condition of low tissue oxygen. *(Tortora and Derrickson, 11th ed., p. 685)*

239. **(B)** About 30 minutes after the ingestion of fatty foods, cholecystokinin is released from the duodenal mucosa and absorbed into the bloodstream. As a result, the gallbladder is stimulated to contract, releasing bile into the intestine. *(Frank, Long, and Smith, 11th ed., vol. 2, p. 96)*

240. **(C)** In the direct PA projection of the wrist, the carpal pisiform is superimposed on the carpal triquetrum. The AP oblique projection (medial surface adjacent to the IR) separates the pisiform and triquetrum and projects the pisiform as a separate structure. The pisiform is the smallest and most palpable carpal. *(Frank, Long, and Smith, 11th ed., vol. I, p. 129)*

241. **(C)** Myelography is used to demonstrate encroachment on and compression of the spinal cord as a result of disk herniation, tumor growth, or posttraumatic swelling of the cord. This is accomplished by placing positive or negative contrast medium into the subarachnoid space. Myelography will demonstrate posterior protrusion of herniated intervertebral disks or spinal cord tumors. Anterior protrusion of a herniated intervertebral disk does not impinge on the spinal cord and is not demonstrated in myelography. Internal disk lesions can be demonstrated only by injecting contrast medium into the individual disks (*diskography*). *(Bontrager and Lampignano, 6th ed., p. 762)*

242. **(B)** The radiographer must check blood chemistry levels that are associated with renal function prior to beginning excretory urography.

These levels are blood urea nitrogen (BUN) and creatinine. Normal BUN range is 8–25 mg/100 mL. Normal creatinine range is 0.6–1.5 mg/100 mL. Elevated levels can indicate poor renal function. *(Bontrager and Lampignano, 6th ed., p. 556)*

243. **(D)** A trimalleolar fracture involves three separate fractures. The lateral malleolus is fractured in the "typical" fashion, but the medial malleolus is fractured on both its medial and posterior aspects. The trimalleolar fracture frequently is associated with subluxation of the articular surfaces. *(Laudicina, p. 184)*

244. **(C)** The skeleton's design functions to *protect* vital internal organs such as the heart and lungs. Bone stores important *minerals* (e.g., calcium and phosphorus) and releases them into the blood as needed. Yellow bone marrow is composed mainly of fat cells and stores triglycerides for use as an energy reserve. The endocrine system is associated with hormone production; the integumentary system includes the skin that is important in protection and excretion; the muscular system is responsible for movement and heat production. *(Tortora and Derrickson, 11th ed., p. 172)*

245. **(C)** Major branches of the common carotid arteries (internal carotids) function to supply the anterior brain, whereas the posterior brain is supplied by the vertebral arteries (branches of the subclavian artery). The brachiocephalic (innominate) artery is unpaired and is one of the three branches of the aortic arch, from which the right common carotid artery is derived. The left common carotid artery comes directly off the aortic arch. *(Tortora and Derrickson, 11th ed., pp. 761–762)*

246. **(D)** Barium sulfate suspension is the usual contrast medium of choice for investigation of the alimentary tract. There are, however, a few exceptions. Whenever there is the possibility of escape of contrast medium into the peritoneal cavity, barium sulfate is contraindicated, and a water-soluble iodinated medium is recommended because it is easily aspirated before surgery (or resorbed and excreted by the kidneys). Patients with a ruptured hollow

viscus (e.g., perforated ulcer, diverticulitis, etc.), those with suspected large bowel obstruction, and those who are scheduled for surgery are examples of patients who should ingest only water-soluble iodinated media. (*Frank, Long, and Smith, 11th ed., vol. 2, p. 140*)

247. **(B)** *Intussusception* is the telescoping of one part of the intestinal tract into another. It is a major cause of bowel obstruction in children, usually in the region of the ileocecal valve, and is much less common in adults. Radiographically, intussusception appears as the classic "coil spring," with barium trapped between folds of the telescoped bowel. The diagnostic BE procedure occasionally can reduce the intussusception, although care must be taken to avoid perforation of the bowel. *Appendicitis* occurs when an obstructed appendix becomes inflamed. Distension of the appendix occurs, and if the appendix is left untended, gangrene and perforation can result. *Regional enteritis* (Crohn disease) is a chronic granulomatous inflammatory disorder that can affect any part of the GI tract but generally involves the area of the terminal ilium. Ulceration and formation of fistulous tracts often occur. *Ulcerative colitis* occurs most often in young adults; its etiology is unknown, although psychogenic or autoimmune factors seem to be involved. (*Bontrager and Lampignano, 6th ed., p. 119*)

248. **(C)** An oblique projection of the lumbar spine is shown. This is a 45-degree LPO projection demonstrating the apophyseal joints closest to the IR. The apophyseal joints are formed by the articulation of the inferior articular facets of one vertebra with the superior articular facets of the vertebra below. Note the "Scotty dog" images that appear in the oblique lumbar spine. Intervertebral foramina are best visualized in the lateral lumbar position. (*Bontrager and Lampignano, 6th ed., p. 334*)

249. **(D)** The chest should be examined in the upright position whenever possible to demonstrate any air–fluid levels. For the lateral projection, the patient elevates the arms well enough to avoid upper-arm soft-tissue superimposition on the lung fields. In the left lateral position, the right posterior ribs, being remote

from the IR, will be somewhat magnified and *very slightly* posterior to the left posterior ribs. The MSP must remain vertical to avoid "tilt" distortion, and the coronal plane must be vertical to avoid rotation distortion. (*Bontrager and Lampignano, 6th ed., p. 88*)

250. **(B)** A cross-sectional image of the abdomen is shown in Figure 2–36. The large structure on the right, labeled number 1, is the liver. The gallbladder is seen as a somewhat darker density on the medial border of the liver. The left kidney is labeled number 4; the right kidney is seen clearly on the other side. The vertebra is labeled number 5, and the psoas muscles are seen just posterior to the vertebra. Just anterior to the body of the vertebra is the circular aorta, labeled number 3 (some calcification can be seen as brighter densities). The somewhat flattened inferior vena cava (number 2) is seen to the left of and slightly anterior to the aorta. (*Bontrager and Lampignano, 6th ed., p. 114*)

251. **(A)** The knee (tibiofemoral joint) is the largest joint of the body, formed by the articulation of the femur and tibia. However, it actually consists of three articulations—the patellofemoral joint, the lateral tibiofemoral joint (lateral femoral condyle with tibial plateau), and the medial tibiofemoral joint (medial femoral condyle with tibial plateau). Although the knee is classified as a synovial (diarthrotic) hinge-type joint, the patellofemoral joint actually is a gliding joint, and the medial and lateral tibiofemoral joints are hinge type. (*Frank, Long, and Smith, 11th ed., vol. 1, p. 238*)

252. **(A)** Femoral necks are nonpalpable bony landmarks. The ASIS, pubic symphysis, and greater trochanter are palpable bony landmarks used in radiography of the pelvis and for localization of the femoral necks. (*Frank, Long, and Smith, 11th ed., vol. 1, p. 341*)

253. **(C)** The full length of the nasal septum is best demonstrated in the parietoacanthal (Waters method) projection. This is also the single best view for facial bones. The PA axial (Caldwell method) projection superimposes the petrous structures over the nasal septum, whereas the lateral projection superimposes and obscures good visualization of the septum. The AP axial projection is used to demonstrate the occipital bone. *(Frank, Long, and Smith, 11th ed., vol. 2, pp. 398–399)*

254. **(C)** The AP axial projection (Towne method) of the skull requires that the CR be angled 30 degrees caudad if the OML is perpendicular to the IR (37 degrees caudad if the IOML is perpendicular to the IR). The frontal and facial bones are projected down and away from superimposition on the occipital bone. If positioning is accurate, the *dorsum sella* and *posterior clinoid processes* will be demonstrated within the foramen magnum. If the CR is angled excessively, the *posterior aspect of the arch of C1* will appear in the foramen magnum. *(Frank, Long, and Smith, 11th ed., vol. 2, p. 316)*

255. **(B)** 256. **(D)** The image illustrates a PA projection of the wrist. This projection best demonstrates visualization of the distal radioulnar joint, the proximal and distal rows of carpals, and the proximal metacarpals (more of the metacarpals should be seen here). The base of the fifth metacarpal is number 4. The trapezium (lateral carpal, distal row) is number 1; the base of the first metacarpal is seen articulating with the trapezium forming the (saddle) carpometacarpal articulation. Number 2 is the scaphoid – the most lateral carpal of the proximal carpal row. Number 3 is the radial styloid process. Number 5 is the pisiform, seen just lateral to, and partially superimposed upon, the triquetrum. Number 6 is the ulnar styloid process. *(Frank, Long, and Smith, 11th ed., vol. 1, p. 93 and 124)*

257. **(D)** The *anterior oblique* positions (LAO and RAO) of the cervical spine require a 15-degree caudal angulation and demonstrate the intervertebral foramina *closest* to the IR. The *posterior oblique* positions (LPO and RPO) require that the CR be directed 15 degrees to C4. The posterior oblique positions demonstrate the intervertebral foramina *farther* away from the IR. *(Frank, Long, and Smith, 11th ed., vol. 1, pp. 404–406)*

258. **(C)** The degree of anterior and posterior motion occasionally is diminished with a whiplash type of injury. Anterior (forward, flexion) and posterior (backward, extension) motion is evaluated in the lateral position, with the patient assuming the best possible flexion and extension. Left- and right-bending images of the thoracic and lumbar vertebrae are obtained frequently when evaluating scoliosis. *(Frank, Long, and Smith, 11th ed., vol. 1, pp. 402–403)*

259. **(A)** When one cheekbone is depressed, a tangential projection is required to "open up" the zygomatic arch and draw it away from the overlying cranial bones. This is accomplished by placing the patient in the SMV position, rotating the head 15 degrees toward the affected side, and centering to the zygomatic arch. A 30-degree rotation places the mandibular shadow over the zygomatic arch. *(Frank, Long, and Smith, 11th ed., vol. 2, pp. 364–365)*

260. **(D)** Normal blood pressure is 110 to 140 mmHg systolic and 60 to 80 mmHg diastolic. High blood pressure (hypertension) is indicated by systolic pressure higher than 140 mmHg and diastolic pressure higher than 90 mmHg. Hypertension can be identified as extreme or moderate. Extreme hypertension can result in brain damage within just a few minutes. Moderate hypertension can cause damage to organs: the lungs, kidneys, brain, heart, and so on. Various disease processes can produce hypertension as well as contributing factors such as medications, obesity, smoking, and stress. *(Adler and Carlton, 4th ed., p. 201)*

261. **(A)** Accurate positioning of the skull requires the use of several baselines. In the figure, line 1 represents the *glabellomeatal line* (GML), line 2 is the *orbitomeatal line* (OML), line 3 is the *infraorbitomeatal line* (IOML), and line 4 is the *acanthomeatal line* (AML). The OML and the IOML usually are separated by 7 degrees. The OML and the GML usually are separated by 8 degree (therefore, there is a 15-degree difference between the GML and the IOML). It is useful to remember these differences because CR angulation must be adjusted when using a baseline other than the one recommended for a particular position. For example, if it is recommended that the CR be angled *30 degrees to the OML*, then the CR would be angled *37 degrees to the IOML*. *(Bontrager and Lampignano, 6th ed., p. 382)*

262. **(D)** The SMV (Schüller method) projection of the skull requires that the patient's neck be extended, placing the vertex adjacent to the IR holder/upright Bucky so that the IOML is *parallel* with the IR. This projection is useful for demonstrating the ethmoidal and sphenoidal sinuses, pars petrosae, mandible, and foramina ovale and spinosum. The lateral projection of the skull requires that the patient be in the prone oblique position with the MSP parallel to the IR and the interpupillary line perpendicular to the IR. This position also requires that the IOML (line 3) be parallel to the long axis of the IR. The AP and PA axial projections of the skull require the OML or IOML to be *perpendicular* to the IR. *(Bontrager and Lampignano, 6th ed., p. 389)*

263. **(B)** Orthoroentgenography is the radiographic measurement of long-bone length. It can be required on adults or children having extremity length (especially leg) discrepancies. This can be performed most easily with the use of the metallic *Bell-Thompson scale* secured to the x-ray tabletop adjacent to the limb being examined (or between both limbs for simultaneous bilateral examination). A 14 × 17 inch cassette is in the Bucky tray (to permit movement of the cassette between exposures), and three well-collimated exposures are made—at the hip joint, the knee joint, and the ankle joint. A *cannula* is a tube placed in a cavity to introduce or withdraw material and is unrelated to orthoroentgenography. *(Bontrager and Lampignano, 6th ed., p. 770)*

264. **(C)** *Intervertebral joints* (occupied by the intervertebral disks) are well visualized in the lateral projection of all the vertebral groups. Cervical articular facets (forming *apophyseal/interarticular joints*) are 90 degrees to the midsagittal plane and, therefore, are well demonstrated in the *lateral* projection. The cervical *intervertebral foramina* lie 45 degree to the midsagittal plane (and 15–20 degrees to a transverse plane) and, therefore, are demonstrated in the *oblique* position. *(Bontrager and Lampignano, 6th ed., p. 292)*

265. **(C)** The patient is placed in a true lateral position, and the CR is directed perpendicular to a point ¾ inch distal to the nasion. An 8 × 10 inch cassette divided in half may be used for this procedure. *(Frank, Long, and Smith, 11th ed., vol. 2, p. 360)*

266. **(B)** To reduce anxiety prior to the examination, the radiographer should give the patient a full explanation of the enema procedure. This explanation should include keeping the anal sphincter tightly contracted, relaxing the abdominal muscles, and deep breathing. The barium suspension should be either just below body temperature (at 85–90°F) to prevent injury and bowel irritation *or* cold (at 41°F) to produce less colonic irritation and to stimulate contraction of the anal sphincter. *(Bontrager and Lampignano, 6th ed., p. 503)*

267. **(C)** The posterior oblique positions (LPO and RPO) of the lumbar vertebrae demonstrate the apophyseal joints closer to the IR. The left apophyseal joints are demonstrated in the LPO position, whereas the right apophyseal joints are demonstrated in the RPO position. The lateral position is useful to demonstrate the intervertebral disk spaces, intervertebral foramina, and spinous processes. *(Frank, Long, and Smith, 11th ed., vol. 1, p. 458)*

268. **(B)** *Blowout fractures* of the orbital floor are caused by a direct blow to the eye. The orbital floor is caused to collapse; this carries the *inferior rectus muscle* through the fracture site and into the *maxillary sinus*. Diplopia (double vision) often results. Blowout fractures are well demonstrated with the Waters method (parietoacanthal projection) and by using tomographic studies. A parietoacanthal projection with the OML perpendicular and the CR angled 30 degrees caudad also will demonstrate the orbital floor in profile. The *zygoma* usually is not involved with a blowout fracture but rather with a *tripod* fracture. *(Bontrager and Lampignano, 6th ed., p. 417)*

269. **(D)** The phase of respiration is exceedingly important in thoracic radiography because lung expansion and the position of the diaphragm strongly influence the appearance of the finished radiograph. Inspiration and expiration radiographs of the chest are taken to

demonstrate air in the pleural cavity (*pneumothorax*), to demonstrate *atelectasis* (partial or complete collapse of one or more pulmonary lobes) or the degree of *diaphragm excursion,* or to detect the presence of a *foreign body.* The expiration image will require a somewhat greater exposure (6–8 kV more) to compensate for the diminished quantity of air in the lungs. *(Frank, Long, and Smith, 11th ed., vol. 1, p. 520)*

270. **(C)** Shoulder arthrograms (Figure 2–64) are used to evaluate rotator cuff tear, glenoid labrum (a ring of fibrocartilaginous tissue around the glenoid fossa), and frozen shoulder. Routine radiographs demonstrate arthritis, and the addition of a transthoracic humerus or scapular Y projection would be used to demonstrate luxation (dislocation). *(Frank, Long, and Smith, 11th ed., vol. 2, p. 16)*

271. **(D)** In the *AP* projection of the elbow, the proximal radius and ulna are partially superimposed. In the *lateral* projection, the radial head is partially superimposed on the coronoid process, facing anteriorly. In the *medial oblique* projection, there is even greater superimposition. The *lateral oblique* projection completely separates the proximal radius and ulna, projecting the radial head, neck, and tuberosity free of superimposition with the proximal ulna. *(Frank, Long, and Smith, 11th ed., vol. 1, pp. 143–147)*

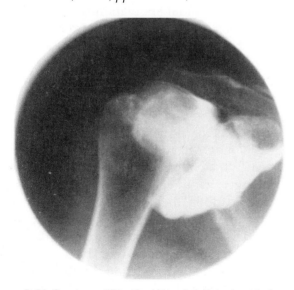

Figure 2–64. Courtesy of Stamford Hospital, Department of Radiology.

272. **(B)** Changes in hormone levels affect changes in the glandular tissue of the breast. These breast tissue changes are seen during breast development, during pregnancy and lactation, and during menopause. Women at higher risk of developing breast cancer include those having experienced early menses (before age 12 years), late menopause (after age 52 years), and nulliparity (no full- or late-term pregnancies). Risks other than hormonal include family and personal history and age. The greatest single risk factor for breast cancer is gender—being female. Although occurrence of breast cancer in men is not unknown, it is fairly rare. *(Peart, p. 1)*

273. **(B)** There are several surface landmarks and localization points that can help the radiographer in positioning various body structures. The *jugular notch,* located at the superior aspect of the manubrium, is approximately opposite the T2–3 interspace. The *sternal angle* is located opposite the T4–5 interspace. The *xiphoid* (or ensiform) *process* is located opposite T10. *(Frank, Long, and Smith, 11th ed., vol. 1, p. 63)*

274. **(D)** With the patient in the AP position, the scapula and upper thorax are normally superimposed. With the arm abducted, the elbow flexed, and the hand supinated, much of the scapula is drawn away from the ribs. The patient should not be rotated toward the affected side because this causes superimposition of ribs on the scapula. The exposure is made during quiet breathing to obliterate pulmonary vascular markings. *(Frank, Long, and Smith, 11th ed., vol. 1, pp. 212–213)*

275. **(D)** The two *innominate* bones (os coxae) make up the *pelvis.* Each innominate bone is made three bones: ilium, ischium, and pubis. These three bones contribute to form the formation of the acetabulum. When the interior of the acetabulum is viewed, the ilium comprises its upper two-thirds, the ischium comprises its lower posterior two-thirds, and the pubis comprises the lower anterior one-third of the acetabulum. *(Bontrager and Lampignano, 6th ed., p. 263)*

276. **(A)** Sternoclavicular joints should be imaged in the PA position whenever possible to keep the object-to-image-receptor distance (OID) to a minimum. The *oblique* position (about 15 degrees) opens the joint *closest* to the IR. The erect position may be used but is not required. Weight-bearing images are not recommended for sternoclavicular joints because they often are for acromioclavicular joints. *(Frank, Long, and Smith, 11th ed., vol. 1, p. 480)*

277. **(D)** This is a modification of the parietoacanthal projection (Waters method) in which the patient is requested to open the mouth, and then the skull is positioned so that the OML forms a 37-degree angle with the IR. The CR is directed through the sphenoidal sinuses and exits the open mouth. The routine parietoacanthal projection (with mouth closed) is used to demonstrate the maxillary sinuses projected above the petrous pyramids. The frontal and ethmoidal sinuses are best visualized in the PA axial position (modified Caldwell method). *(Bontrager and Lampignano, 6th ed., p. 442)*

278. **(C)** The ribs below the diaphragm are best demonstrated with the diaphragm elevated. This is accomplished by placing the patient in a *recumbent* position and by taking the exposure at the end of *exhalation.* Conversely, the ribs above the diaphragm are best demonstrated with the diaphragm depressed. Placing the patient in the erect position and taking the exposure at the end of deep inspiration accomplishes this. *(Frank, Long, and Smith, 11th ed., vol. 1, p. 490)*

279. **(A)** Because sinus examinations are performed to evaluate the presence or absence of fluid, they must be performed in the *erect position with a horizontal x-ray beam.* The PA axial (Caldwell) projection demonstrates the frontal and ethmoidal sinus groups, and the parietoacanthal projection (Waters method) shows the maxillary sinuses. The lateral position demonstrates all the sinus groups, and the SMV position is used frequently to demonstrate the sphenoidal sinuses. *(Frank, Long, and Smith, 11th ed., vol. 2, p. 391)*

280. **(A)** The *plantodorsal* projection of the os calsis/calcaneus is described. It is performed

supine and requires cephalad angulation. The CR enters the plantar surface and exits the dorsal surface. The axial *dorsoplantar* projection requires that the CR enter the dorsal surface of the foot and exit the plantar surface. *(Frank, Long, and Smith, 11th ed., vol. 1, p. 278)*

281. **(D)** During GI radiography, the position of the stomach may vary depending on the respiratory phase, the body habitus, and the patient position. *Inspiration* causes the lungs to fill with air and the diaphragm to descend, thereby pushing the abdominal contents downward. On *expiration,* the diaphragm will rise, allowing the abdominal organs to ascend. Body *habitus* is an important factor in determining the size and shape of the stomach. An asthenic patient may have a long, J-shaped stomach, whereas the stomach of a hypersthenic patient may be transverse. The body habitus is an important consideration in determining the positioning and placement of the cassette. The patient *position* also can alter the position of the stomach. If a patient turns from the RAO position into the AP position, the stomach will move into a more horizontal position. Although the cardiac sphincter and the pyloric sphincter are relatively fixed, the fundus is quite mobile and will vary in position. *(Dowd and Tilson, 2nd ed., vol. 2, p. 778)*

282. **(A)** With a patient in the PA position and the OML perpendicular to the table, a 15- to 20-degree caudal angulation would place the petrous ridges in the lower third of the orbit. To achieve the same result in a baby or a small child, it is necessary for the radiographer to decrease the angulation or modify the angulation to 10 to 15 degrees caudal. The reason for this can be understood by examining the baselines for skull positioning. In the adult skull, the OML and IOML are about 7 degrees apart. In a baby or small child, the difference is larger, about 15 degrees apart. Remember that in adults, the head makes up about one-seventh the length of the body. In children, the head is about one-fourth the length of the body. These differences must be considered in radiographic examination of the skull for babies. *(Frank, Long, and Smith, 11th ed., vol. 3, p. 193)*

283. (B) 284. (D) The figure illustrates the aortic arch (number 1) and its three main branches—the brachiocephalic artery (number 6), the left common carotid artery (number 4), and the left subclavian artery (number 2). The right common carotid artery (number 5) and the right subclavian artery (number 7) are branches of the brachiocephalic. The vertebral arteries are the first main branch of the subclavian arteries. The left vertebral artery is labeled number 3. *(Tortora and Derrickson, 12th ed., p. 787)*

285. (B) When the foot is positioned for a lateral projection, the plantar surface should be perpendicular to the IR so as to superimpose the metatarsals. This may be accomplished with the patient lying on either the affected or the unaffected side (usually the affected), that is, mediolateral or lateromedial. The talofibular articulation is best demonstrated in the medial oblique projection of the ankle. *(Frank, Long, and Smith, 11th ed., vol. 1, p. 264)*

286. (D) Hysterosalpingography may be performed for demonstration of uterine tubal patency, mass lesions in the uterine cavity, and uterine position. Although hysterosalpingography is often performed to check tubal patency, the uterine anatomy, position, and morphology are also exhibited. In addition, polyps, fibroids, or space-occupying lesions within the uterus are well demonstrated. *(Frank, Long, and Smith, 11th ed., vol. 2, p. 262)*

287. (C) The typical vertebra, shown in Figure 2–65, is divided into two portions—the *body* (anteriorly) and the *vertebral arch* (posteriorly). The vertebral arch supports seven processes—two transverse, one spinous (number 3), two superior articular (number 4), and two inferior articular (number 2). The superior articular processes and the superjacent inferior articular processes join to form apophyseal joints. Pedicles (number 5) project posteriorly from the vertebral body (number 6). Their upper and lower surfaces form vertebral notches. Superjacent vertebral notches form intervertebral foramina. The *lamina* is represented by number 1. The transverse and spinous processes serve as attachments for

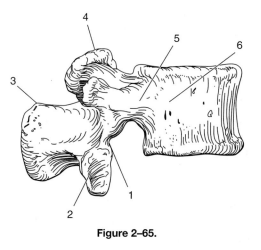

Figure 2–65.

muscles or articulations for ribs in the thoracic region. The superior and inferior surfaces of the vertebral body are covered with articular cartilage, and between the vertebral bodies lie the intervertebral disks. *(Frank, Long, and Smith, 11th ed., vol. 1, pp. 380–381)*

288. (A) The straight PA projection (0 degrees), with CR directed perpendicular to the IR, effectively demonstrates the mandibular body. In this position, the rami and condyles are superimposed on the occipital bone and petrous portion of the temporal bone. To better visualize the rami and condyles, the CR is directed cephalad 20 to 30 degrees. *(Bontrager and Lampignano, 6th ed., p. 430)*

289. (D) A fluoroscopic unit with spot device and tilt table should be used for endoscopic retrograde pancreatography. The Trendelenburg position is sometimes necessary to fill the interhepatic ducts, and a semierect position may be necessary to fill the lower end of the common bile duct. Also necessary are a fiberoptic endoscope for locating the hepatopancreatic ampulla and polyethylene catheters for the introduction of contrast medium. *(Frank, Long, and Smith, 11th ed., vol. 2, p. 116)*

290. (D) Radiography of pediatric patients with a myelomeningocele defect should be performed in the prone position rather than in the routine supine position. The supine position would put unnecessary pressure on the protrusion of the meninges and spinal cord.

All the other statements in the question are true. The anatomic dimensions of children are different from those of adults, and this must be kept in mind when performing pediatric radiography. The liver occupies a larger area of the abdominal cavity in a child than in an adult. This causes the kidneys to be in a lower position. Generally, the kidneys will be midway between the diaphragm and the symphysis pubis. Chest radiography for the pediatric patient varies depending on the age of the child. Neonates are routinely radiographed in the supine position. Although infants also may be examined in the supine position, it is preferable to examine them by placing the infant securely in a support device to obtain a good PA erect radiograph. Exceptions to this rule are made if the infant is in respiratory distress. To avoid aggravating the respiratory distress, an erect AP radiograph usually is obtained. *(Dowd and Tilson, 2nd ed., vol. 2, pp. 1004–1005, 1013)*

291. **(C)** The diaphragm is the major muscle of respiration. On inspiration/inhalation, the diaphragm and abdominal viscera are depressed, enabling the filling and expansion of the lungs, accompanied by upward movement of the sternum and ribs. During expiration/exhalation, air leaves the lungs and they deflate, and the diaphragm relaxes and moves to a more superior position along with the abdominal viscera. As the diaphragm relaxes and moves up, the sternum and ribs move inferiorly. *(Frank, Long, and Smith, vol. 1, p. 512)*

292. **(B)** The axial trauma lateral (Coyle) position is described. If routine elbow projections in extension are not possible because of limited part movement, this position can be used to demonstrate the coronoid process and/or radial head. With the elbow flexed *90 degrees* and the CR directed to the elbow joint at an angle of 45 degrees medially (i.e., toward the shoulder), the joint space between the *radial head* and capitulum should be revealed. With the elbow flexed *80 degrees* and the CR directed to the elbow joint at an angle of 45 degrees laterally (i.e., from the shoulder toward the elbow), the elongated *coronoid process* will

be visualized. *(Bontrager and Lampignano, 6th ed., p. 174)*

293. **(C)** The foot is composed of the 7 tarsal bones, 5 metatarsals, and 14 phalanges. The metatarsals and phalanges are miniature long bones; each has a shaft, base (proximal), and head (distal). The bases of the first to third metatarsals articulate with the three cuneiforms. The bases of the fourth and fifth metatarsals articulate with the cuboid. The heads of the metatarsals articulate with the bases of the first row of phalanges. *(Bontrager and Lampignano, 6th ed., p. 210)*

294. **(D)** X-ray arthrography requires the use of local anesthesia; sterile technique must be observed to avoid introducing infection into the joint. Fluoroscopy is used for proper placement of the needle and to obtain images immediately after the introduction of contrast medium. Many physicians follow up the x-ray arthrogram with an magnetic resonance (MR) arthrogram to visualize additional soft tissue structures. Arthrography is performed to detect compromised knee capsule structures, meniscal damage, ligament tears, and Baker cysts. *(Bontrager and Lampignano, 6th ed., p. 754)*

295. **(B) 296. (B) 297. (C)** An AP, external rotation, projection of the shoulder is pictured. The hand is supinated, and the arm is in the anatomical position. Therefore, the greater tubercle (number 3) is well visualized. The greater portion of the clavicle is seen, the acromioclavicular joint (number 1), the acromion process (number 2), the coracoid process (number 4), and the glenohumeral joint (number 5). The coronoid process is located on the ulna. *(Bontrager and Lampignano, 7th ed., p. 185)*

298. **(A)** The sacroiliac joints angle posteriorly and medially 25 degrees to the MSP. Therefore, to demonstrate the sacroiliac joints with the patient in the AP position, the *affected* side must be elevated 25 degrees. This places the joint space perpendicular to the IR and parallel to the CR. Therefore, the RPO position will demonstrate the *left sacroiliac joint*, and the

LPO position will demonstrate the *right sacroiliac joint*. When the examination is performed with the patient in the PA position, the *unaffected* side will be elevated 25 degrees. *(Frank, Long, and Smith, 11th ed., vol. 1, pp. 438–441)*

299. **(B)** Various terms are used to describe the position of fractured ends of long bones. The term *apposition* is used to describe the *alignment*, or *misalignment*, between the ends of fractured long bones. The term *angulation* describes the *direction* of misalignment. The term *luxation* refers to a dislocation. A *sprain* refers to a wrenched articulation with ligament injury. *(Bontrager and Lampignano, 6th ed., p. 600)*

300. **(C)** AP and lateral projections of the airway and larynx are required occasionally to rule out *foreign body, polyps, tumors,* or any other condition suspected of causing some airway obstruction. The AP projection is positioned as for an AP cervical spine projection with the CR perpendicular to the laryngeal prominence. The lateral projection is positioned as for a lateral cervical spine projection and is centered to the coronal plane passing through the trachea (anterior to the cervical spine) at the *level of the laryngeal prominence*. Centering just below the EAM would demonstrate the nasopharynx. Centering at the mandibular angles would demonstrate the oropharynx. Exposures are made on slow inspiration to visualize air-filled structures. *(Frank, Long, and Smith, 11th ed., vol. 2, p. 88)*

Subspecialty List

57. Extremity imaging
58. Thorax imaging
59. General procedural considerations
60. General procedural considerations
61. General procedural considerations
62. Extremity imaging
63. Extremity imaging
64. Extremity imaging
65. Thorax imaging
66. Extremity imaging
67. Extremity imaging
68. General procedural considerations
69. Cardiovascular/neurologic/ miscellaneous imaging
70. General procedural considerations
71. Extremity imaging
72. Extremity imaging
73. Spine and pelvis imaging
74. General procedural considerations
75. Extremity imaging
76. Extremity imaging
77. Extremity imaging
78. Thorax imaging
79. Thorax imaging
80. Thorax imaging
81. Thorax imaging
82. Extremity imaging
83. General procedural considerations
84. Cardiovascular/neurologic/ miscellaneous imaging
85. Spine and pelvis imaging
86. Cranium imaging
87. Cranium imaging
88. Cranium imaging
89. Extremity imaging
90. Extremity imaging
91. Spine and pelvis imaging
92. Thorax imaging
93. Extremity imaging
94. Extremity imaging
95. Spine and pelvis imaging
96. Thorax imaging
97. Extremity imaging
98. Cranium imaging
99. Abdomen and GI studies
100. Abdomen and GI studies
101. Abdomen and GI studies
102. Urologic studies
103. Urologic studies
104. Abdomen and GI studies
105. Extremity imaging
106. Extremity imaging
107. General procedural considerations
108. Abdomen and GI studies
109. Thorax imaging
110. Urologic studies
111. Extremity imaging
112. Extremity imaging
113. Cranium imaging
114. Extremity imaging
115. Extremity imaging
116. Extremity imaging
117. Spine and pelvis imaging
118. General procedural considerations
119. Spine and pelvis imaging
120. Extremity imaging
121. Spine and pelvis imaging
122. Abdomen and GI studies
123. General procedural considerations
124. Cardiovascular/neurologic/ miscellaneous imaging
125. Spine and pelvis imaging
126. General procedural considerations
127. Spine and pelvis imaging
128. Extremity imaging
129. Extremity imaging
130. General procedural considerations
131. General procedural considerations
132. Cranium imaging
133. Urologic studies
134. General procedural considerations
135. Extremity imaging
136. Spine and pelvis imaging
137. Abdomen and GI studies
138. General procedural considerations
139. Extremity imaging
140. Extremity imaging
141. Spine and pelvis imaging
142. Cardiovascular/neurologic/ miscellaneous imaging
143. Other Procedures
144. Cranium imaging
145. Abdomen and GI studies
146. Spine and pelvis imaging
147. Cranium imaging
148. Extremity imaging
149. Abdomen and GI studies
150. Abdomen and GI studies
151. Extremity imaging
152. Other procedures

249. Thorax imaging
250. Other procedures
251. Extremity imaging
252. Spine and pelvis imaging
253. Cranium imaging
254. Cranium imaging
255. Extremity imaging
256. Extremity imaging
257. Spine and pelvis imaging
258. Spine and pelvis imaging
259. Cranium imaging
260. Other procedures
261. Cranium imaging
262. Cranium imaging
263. Extremity imaging
264. Spine and pelvis imaging
265. Cranium imaging
266. Abdomen and GI studies
267. Spine and pelvis imaging
268. Head and neck imaging
269. Thorax imaging
270. Other procedures
271. Extremity imaging
272. Other procedures
273. Spine and pelvis imaging
274. Extremity imaging
275. Spine and pelvis imaging
276. Thorax imaging
277. Cranium imaging
278. Thorax imaging
279. Cranium imaging
280. Extremity imaging
281. Abdomen and GI studies
282. Cranium imaging
283. Cardiovascular/neurologic/ miscellaneous imaging
284. Cardiovascular/neurologic/ miscellaneous imaging
285. Extremity imaging
286. Other procedures
287. Spine and pelvis imaging
288. Cranium imaging
289. Abdomen and GI studies
290. Other procedures
291. General procedural considerations
292. Extremity imaging
293. Extremity imaging
294. Other procedures
295. Extremity imaging
296. Extremity imaging
297. Extremity imaging
298. Spine and pelvis imaging
299. Spine and pelvis imaging
300. Thorax imaging

CHAPTER 3

Radiation Protection
Questions

DIRECTIONS (Questions 1 through 200): Each of the numbered items or incomplete statements in this section is followed by answers or by completions of the statement. Select the *one* lettered answer or completion that is *best* in each case.

1. What is used to account for the differences in tissue sensitivity to ionizing radiation when determining effective dose *E*?

    1. Tissue weighting factors (W_t)
    2. Radiation weighting factors (W_r)
    3. Absorbed dose

    (A) 1 only
    (B) 1 and 2 only
    (C) 2 and 3 only
    (D) 1, 2, and 3

2. According to the National Council on Radiation Protection and Measurements (NCRP), the monthly gestational dose-equivalent limit for embryo/fetus of a pregnant radiographer is

    (A) 1 mSv
    (B) 5 mSv
    (C) 15 mSv
    (D) 50 mSv

3. A time of 1.5 minutes is required for a particular fluoroscopic examination, whose exposure rate is 275 mR/h. What is the approximate radiation exposure for the radiologic staff present in the fluoroscopy room during the examination?

    (A) 183 mR
    (B) 68.7 mR
    (C) 18.33 mR
    (D) 6.87 mR

4. If the exposure rate to an individual standing 4.0 m from a source of radiation is 10 mR/h, what will be the dose received after 20 minutes at a distance of 6 m from the source?

    (A) 22.5 mR
    (B) 7.5 mR
    (C) 4.44 mR
    (D) 1.48 mR

5. All the following statements regarding mobile radiographic equipment are true *except*

    (A) the exposure cord must permit the operator to stand at least 6 ft from the patient, x-ray tube, and useful beam
    (B) exposure switches must be the two-stage type
    (C) a lead apron should be carried with the unit and worn by the radiographer during exposure
    (D) the radiographer must alert individuals in the area before making the exposure

6. Which of the following cell types has the greatest radiosensitivity in the adult human?

   (A) Nerve cells
   (B) Muscle cells
   (C) Spermatids
   (D) Lymphocytes

7. Guidelines for the use of protective shielding state that gonadal shielding should be used

   1. if the patient has reasonable reproductive potential
   2. when the gonads are within 5 cm of the collimated field
   3. when tight collimation is not possible

   (A) 1 only
   (B) 1 and 2 only
   (C) 1 and 3 only
   (D) 2 and 3 only

8. The interaction between ionizing radiation and the target molecule that is *most likely* to occur is the

   (A) direct effect
   (B) indirect effect
   (C) target effect
   (D) random effect

9. What is the approximate entrance skin exposure (ESE) for the average anteroposterior (AP) supine abdomen radiograph?

   (A) 300 rad
   (B) 300 mrad
   (C) 35 rad
   (D) 35 mrad

10. All of the following device(s) are generally used to help reduce patient dose, *except*

   1. grid
   2. collimator
   3. gonad shield

   (A) 1 only
   (B) 1 and 2 only
   (C) 2 and 3 only
   (D) 1, 2, and 3

11. How will x-ray photon intensity be affected if the source-to-image distance (SID) is doubled?

   (A) Its intensity increases two times.
   (B) Its intensity increases four times.
   (C) Its intensity decreases two times.
   (D) Its intensity decreases four times.

12. What is the established annual occupational dose-equivalent limit for the lens of the eye?

   (A) 10 mSv
   (B) 50 mSv
   (C) 150 mSv
   (D) 250 mSv

13. Occupational radiation monitoring is required when it is possible that the individual might receive more than

   (A) 5 mrem
   (B) 10 mrem
   (C) one-tenth the annual dose limit
   (D) one-fourth the annual dose limit

14. Sources of natural background radiation contributing to whole-body radiation dose include

   1. dental x-rays
   2. terrestrial radionuclides
   3. internal radionuclides

   (A) 1 only
   (B) 1 and 2 only
   (C) 2 and 3 only
   (D) 1, 2, and 3

15. Irradiation of water molecules within the body and their resulting breakdown is termed

   (A) epilation
   (B) radiolysis
   (C) proliferation
   (D) repopulation

16. Which of the following contributes *most* to occupational exposure?

    (A) The photoelectric effect
    (B) Compton scatter
    (C) Classic scatter
    (D) Thompson scatter

17. Which of the following is (are) used to account for the differences in tissue characteristics when determining effective dose to biologic material?

    1. Tissue weighting factors (W_t)
    2. Radiation weighting factors (W_r)
    3. Absorbed dose

    (A) 1 only
    (B) 1 and 2 only
    (C) 2 and 3 only
    (D) 1, 2, and 3

18. The x-ray interaction with matter that is responsible for the majority of scattered radiation reaching the image receptor (IR) is

    (A) the photoelectric effect
    (B) Compton scatter
    (C) classical scatter
    (D) Thompson scatter

19. The exposure rate to a body 4 ft from a source of radiation is 16 R/h. What distance from the source would be necessary to decrease the exposure to 6 R/h?

    (A) 5 ft
    (B) 7 ft
    (C) 10 ft
    (D) 14 ft

20. With milliamperes (mA) increased to maintain output intensity, how is the ESE affected as the source-to-skin distance (SSD) is increased?

    (A) The ESE increases.
    (B) The ESE decreases.
    (C) The ESE remains unchanged.
    (D) ESE is unrelated to SSD.

21. Late radiation-induced somatic effects include

    1. thyroid cancers
    2. cataractogenesis
    3. genetic mutations

    (A) 1 only
    (B) 1 and 2 only
    (C) 2 and 3 only
    (D) 1, 2, and 3

22. Each time an x-ray beam scatters, its intensity at 1 m from the scattering object is what fraction of its original intensity?

    (A) 1/10
    (B) 1/100
    (C) 1/500
    (D) 1/1,000

23. According to the NCRP, the annual occupational whole-body dose-equivalent limit is

    (A) 1 mSv
    (B) 50 mSv
    (C) 150 mSv
    (D) 500 mSv

24. A thermoluminescent dosimetry system would use which of the following crystals?

    (A) Silver halide
    (B) Sodium thiosulfate
    (C) Lithium fluoride
    (D) Aluminum oxide

25. Sources of secondary radiation include

    1. background radiation
    2. leakage radiation
    3. scattered radiation

    (A) 1 only
    (B) 1 and 2 only
    (C) 2 and 3 only
    (D) 1, 2, and 3

26. All the following have an effect on patient dose *except*

    (A) kilovoltage
    (B) milliampere-seconds
    (C) focal spot size
    (D) inherent filtration

27. The photoelectric effect is more likely to occur with

    1. absorbers having a high Z number
    2. high-energy incident photons
    3. positive contrast media

    (A) 1 and 2 only
    (B) 1 and 3 only
    (C) 2 and 3 only
    (D) 1, 2, and 3

28. All the following radiation-exposure responses exhibit a nonlinear threshold dose–response relationship *except*

    (A) skin erythema
    (B) hematologic depression
    (C) radiation lethality
    (D) leukemia

29. In radiation protection, the product of absorbed dose and the correct modifying factor (rad × QF) is used to determine

    (A) roentgen (C/kg)
    (B) rem (Sv)
    (C) curie (Cu)
    (D) radiation quality

30. Which of the following is recommended for the pregnant radiographer?

    (A) Change dosimeters weekly.
    (B) Wear a second dosimeter under the lead apron.
    (C) Wear two dosimeters and switch their positions appropriately.
    (D) The pregnant radiographer must leave radiation areas for duration of the pregnancy.

31. The annual dose limit for medical imaging personnel includes radiation from

    1. occupational exposure
    2. background radiation
    3. medical x-rays

    (A) 1 only
    (B) 1 and 2 only
    (C) 2 and 3 only
    (D) 1, 2, and 3

32. Which of the following anomalies is (are) possible if an exposure dose of 40 rad (400 mGy) were delivered to a pregnant uterus in the third week of pregnancy?

    1. Skeletal anomaly
    2. Organ anomaly
    3. Neurologic anomaly

    (A) 1 only
    (B) 2 only
    (C) 2 and 3 only
    (D) 1, 2, and 3

33. The effects of radiation on biologic material depend on several factors. If a quantity of radiation is delivered to a body over a long period of time, the effect

    (A) will be greater than if it were delivered all at one time
    (B) will be less than if it were delivered all at one time
    (C) has no relation to how it is delivered in time
    (D) depends solely on the radiation quality

34. Medical and dental radiation accounts for what percentage of the general public's exposure to human-made radiation?

    (A) 10%
    (B) 50%
    (C) 75%
    (D) 90%

35. Which of the following is (are) composed of nondividing, differentiated cells?

    1. Neurons and neuroglia
    2. Epithelial tissue
    3. Lymphocytes

    (A) 1 only
    (B) 1 and 2 only
    (C) 1 and 3 only
    (D) 1, 2, and 3

36. How does filtration affect the primary beam?

    (A) It increases the average energy of the primary beam.
    (B) It decreases the average energy of the primary beam.
    (C) It makes the primary beam more penetrating.
    (D) It increases the intensity of the primary beam.

37. What is the minimum lead requirement for lead aprons, according to the NCRP?

    (A) 0.05 mm Pb
    (B) 0.50 mm Pb
    (C) 0.25 mm Pb
    (D) 1.0 mm Pb

38. An optically stimulated luminescence dosimeter contains which of the following detectors?

    (A) Gadolinium
    (B) Aluminum oxide
    (C) Lithium fluoride
    (D) Photographic film

39. Immature cells are referred to as

    1. undifferentiated cells
    2. stem cells
    3. genetic cells

    (A) 1 only
    (B) 1 and 2 only
    (C) 1 and 3 only
    (D) 1, 2, and 3

40. What is the term used to describe x-ray photon interaction with matter and the transference of part of the photon's energy to matter?

    (A) Absorption
    (B) Scattering
    (C) Attenuation
    (D) Divergence

41. What is the approximate ESE for the average upright PA chest radiograph using 115 kVp and a grid?

    (A) 20 rad
    (B) 20 mrad
    (C) 200 rad
    (D) 200 mrad

42. To be in compliance with radiation safety standards, the fluoroscopy exposure switch must

    (A) sound during fluoro-on time
    (B) be on a 6-ft-long cord
    (C) terminate fluoro after 5 minutes
    (D) be the "dead man" type

43. Primary radiation barriers must be *at least* how high?

    (A) 5 ft
    (B) 6 ft
    (C) 7 ft
    (D) 8 ft

44. The annual dose limit for occupationally exposed individuals is valid for

    (A) alpha, beta, and x-radiations
    (B) x- and gamma radiations only
    (C) beta, x-, and gamma radiations
    (D) all ionizing radiations

45. The interaction between x-ray photons and matter shown in Figure 3–1 is associated with

   1. total energy transfer from photon to electron
   2. an outer-shell electron
   3. Compton scatter

   (A) 1 only
   (B) 1 and 2 only
   (C) 1 and 3 only
   (D) 2 and 3 only

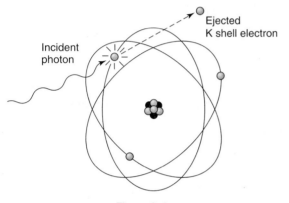

Figure 3–1.

46. Patient dose increases as fluoroscopic

   (A) FOV increases
   (B) FOV decreases
   (C) FSS increases
   (D) FSS decreases

47. Types of gonadal shielding include which of the following?

   1. Flat contact
   2. Shaped contact (contour)
   3. Shadow

   (A) 1 only
   (B) 1 and 2 only
   (C) 2 and 3 only
   (D) 1, 2, and 3

48. What unit of measure is used to express ionizing radiation dose to biologic material?

   (A) Roentgen (C/kg)
   (B) Rad (Gy)
   (C) Rem (Sv)
   (D) RBE

49. LET is best defined as

   1. a method of expressing radiation quality
   2. a measure of the rate at which radiation energy is transferred to soft tissue
   3. absorption of polyenergetic radiation

   (A) 1 only
   (B) 1 and 2 only
   (C) 1 and 3 only
   (D) 1, 2, and 3

50. For exposure to 1 rad of each of the following ionizing radiations, which would result in the greatest dose to the individual?

   (A) External source of 1-MeV x-rays
   (B) External source of diagnostic x-rays
   (C) Internal source of alpha particles
   (D) External source of beta particles

51. The skin response to radiation exposure that appears as hair loss is known as

   (A) dry desquamation
   (B) moist desquamation
   (C) erythema
   (D) epilation

52. Biologic material is *least* sensitive to irradiation under which of the following conditions?

   (A) Anoxic
   (B) Hypoxic
   (C) Oxygenated
   (D) Deoxygenated

53. The reduction in the intensity of an x-ray beam as it passes through material is termed

   (A) absorption
   (B) scattering
   (C) attenuation
   (D) divergence

54. Which type of dose–response relationship represents radiation-induced leukemia and genetic effects?

    (A) Linear, threshold
    (B) Nonlinear, threshold
    (C) Linear, nonthreshold
    (D) Nonlinear, nonthreshold

55. A dose of 25 rad to the fetus during the seventh or eighth week of pregnancy is likely to cause which of the following?

    (A) Spontaneous abortion
    (B) Skeletal anomalies
    (C) Neurologic anomalies
    (D) Organogenesis

56. Late effects of radiation, whose incidence is dose related and for which there is no threshold dose, are referred to as

    (A) nonstochastic
    (B) stochastic
    (C) chromosomal aberration
    (D) hematologic depression

57. Which of the following methods can be used to reduce radiation exposure to a recently fertilized ovum?

    1. Elective booking
    2. Patient questionnaire
    3. The 10-day rule

    (A) 1 only
    (B) 1 and 2 only
    (C) 2 and 3 only
    (D) 1, 2, and 3

58. Classify the following tissues in order of *increasing* radiosensitivity:

    1. Liver cells
    2. Intestinal crypt cells
    3. Muscle cells

    (A) 1, 3, 2
    (B) 2, 3, 1
    (C) 2, 1, 3
    (D) 3, 1, 2

59. The largest amount of diagnostic x-ray absorption is most likely to occur in which of the following tissues?

    (A) Lung
    (B) Adipose
    (C) Muscle
    (D) Bone

60. According to NCRP regulations, leakage radiation from the x-ray tube must not exceed

    (A) 10 mR/h
    (B) 100 mR/h
    (C) 10 mR/min
    (D) 100 mR/min

61. Which of the following *most effectively* minimizes radiation exposure to the patient?

    (A) Small focal spot
    (B) Low-ratio grids
    (C) Increased SID
    (D) High-speed intensifying screens

62. Which of the following statements is (are) true with respect to radiation safety in fluoroscopy?

    1. Tabletop radiation intensity must not exceed 2.1 R/min/mA.
    2. Tabletop radiation intensity must not exceed 10 R/min.
    3. In high-level fluoroscopy, tabletop intensity up to 20 R/min is permitted.

    (A) 1 only
    (B) 1 and 2 only
    (C) 2 and 3 only
    (D) 1, 2, and 3

63. The symbols $^{130}_{56}$ Ba and $^{138}_{56}$ Ba are examples of which of the following?

    (A) Isotopes
    (B) Isobars
    (C) Isotones
    (D) Isomers

64. Which of the following account(s) for an x-ray beam's heterogeneity?

  1. Incident electrons interacting with several layers of tungsten target atoms
  2. Energy differences among incident electrons
  3. Electrons moving to fill different shell vacancies

  (A) 1 only
  (B) 1 and 2 only
  (C) 1 and 3 only
  (D) 1, 2, and 3

65. Which of the following factors will affect both the quality and the quantity of the primary beam?

  1. Half-value layer (HVL)
  2. Kilovolts (kV)
  3. Milliamperes (mA)

  (A) 1 only
  (B) 1 and 2 only
  (C) 1 and 3 only
  (D) 1, 2, and 3

66. Diagnostic x-radiation may be correctly described as

  (A) low energy, low LET
  (B) low energy, high LET
  (C) high energy, low LET
  (D) high energy, high LET

67. Primary radiation barriers usually require which thickness of shielding?

  (A) ¼-in. lead
  (B) ⅛-in. lead
  (C) ¹⁄₁₆-in. lead
  (D) ¹⁄₃₂-in. lead

68. Which of the following groups of exposure factors will deliver the least patient dose?

  (A) 300 mA, 250 ms, 70 kVp
  (B) 300 mA, 125 ms, 80 kVp
  (C) 400 mA, 90 ms, 80 kVp
  (D) 600 mA, 30 ms, 90 kVp

69. For radiographic examinations of the skull, it is generally preferred that the skull be examined in the

  (A) AP projection
  (B) PA projection
  (C) erect position
  (D) supine position

70. According to the NCRP, the annual occupational dose-equivalent limit (50 rem) to the thyroid, skin, and extremities is

  (A) 50 mSv
  (B) 150 mSv
  (C) 500 mSv
  (D) 1,500 mSv

71. The skin response to radiation exposure, which appears as reddening of the irradiated skin area, is known as

  (A) dry desquamation
  (B) moist desquamation
  (C) erythema
  (D) epilation

72. Which of the dose–response curve(s) shown in Figure 3–2 illustrate(s) a linear threshold response to radiation exposure?

  1. Dose–response curve A
  2. Dose–response curve B
  3. Dose–response curve C

  (A) 1 only
  (B) 2 only
  (C) 1 and 2 only
  (D) 2 and 3 only

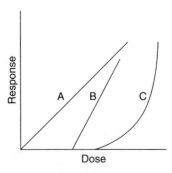

Figure 3–2.

73. What is the intensity of scattered radiation perpendicular to and 1 m from a patient compared with the useful beam at the patient's surface?

(A) 0.01%
(B) 0.1%
(C) 1.0%
(D) 10.0%

74. Which of the following formulas is a representation of the inverse-square law of radiation used to determine x-ray intensity at different distances?

(A) $\dfrac{I_1}{I_2} = \dfrac{D_2^2}{D_1^2}$

(B) $\dfrac{I_1}{I_2} = \dfrac{D_1^2}{D_2^2}$

(C) $\dfrac{kVp_1}{kVp_2} = \dfrac{D_2^2}{D_1^2}$

(D) $\dfrac{kVp_1}{kVp_2} = \dfrac{D_1^2}{D_2^2}$

75. An increase of 1.0 mm added aluminum filtration of the x-ray beam would have which of the following effects?

1. Increase in average energy of the beam
2. Increase in patient skin dose
3. Increase in milliroentgen output

(A) 1 only
(B) 1 and 2 only
(C) 2 and 3 only
(D) 1, 2, and 3

76. Aluminum filtration has its greatest effect on

(A) low-energy x-ray photons
(B) high-energy x-ray photons
(C) low-energy scattered photons
(D) high-energy scattered photons

77. The amount of time that x-rays are being produced and directed toward a particular wall is referred to as the

(A) workload
(B) use factor
(C) occupancy factor
(D) controlling factor

78. The operation of personnel radiation monitoring devices can depend on which of the following?

1. Ionization
2. Luminescence
3. Thermoluminescence

(A) 1 only
(B) 1 and 2 only
(C) 2 and 3 only
(D) 1, 2, and 3

79. Which of the following result(s) from restriction of the x-ray beam?

1. Less scattered radiation production
2. Less patient hazard
3. Less radiographic contrast

(A) 1 only
(B) 1 and 2 only
(C) 2 and 3 only
(D) 1, 2, and 3

80. Which acute radiation syndrome requires the largest exposure before any effects become apparent?

(A) Hematopoietic
(B) Gastrointestinal
(C) Central nervous system (CNS)
(D) Skeletal

81. Early symptoms of acute radiation syndrome include

    1. leukopenia
    2. nausea and vomiting
    3. cataracts

    (A) 1 and 2 only
    (B) 2 only
    (C) 1 and 3 only
    (D) 2 and 3 only

82. Referring to the nomogram in Figure 3–3, what is the approximate patient ESE from an AP projection of the abdomen made at 105 cm using 70 kVp, 300 mA, 200 ms, and 2.5 mm Al total filtration?

    (A) 5 mR
    (B) 166 mR
    (C) 245 mR
    (D) 288 mR

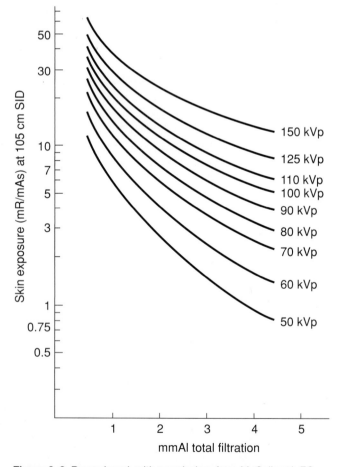

Figure 3–3. Reproduced, with permission, from McCullough EC, Cameron JR. Exposure rates from diagnostic x-ray units. *Br J Radiol* 1970;43:448–451.

83. The unit of measurement used to express occupational exposure is the

    (A) roentgen (C/kg)
    (B) rad (Gy)
    (C) rem (Sv)
    (D) relative biologic effectiveness (RBE)

84. Possible responses to irradiation in utero include

    1. spontaneous abortion
    2. congenital anomalies
    3. childhood malignancies

    (A) 1 only
    (B) 1 and 2 only
    (C) 2 and 3 only
    (D) 1, 2, and 3 only

85. The Bucky slot cover is in place to protect the

    1. patient
    2. fluoroscopist
    3. technologist

    (A) 1 only
    (B) 1 and 2 only
    (C) 2 and 3 only
    (D) 1, 2, and 3

86. Which type of personnel radiation monitor can provide an immediate reading?

    (A) Thermoluminescent dosimeter (TLD)
    (B) Optically stimulated luminescence (OSL)
    (C) Film badge
    (D) Ionization chamber

87. Which of the following terms is correctly used to describe x-ray beam quality?

    (A) mA
    (B) HVL
    (C) Intensity
    (D) Dose rate

88. The *most* efficient type of male gonadal shielding for use during fluoroscopy is

    (A) flat contact
    (B) shaped contact (contour)
    (C) shadow
    (D) cylindrical

89. Isotopes are atoms that have the same

    (A) mass number but a different atomic number
    (B) atomic number but a different mass number
    (C) atomic number but a different neutron number
    (D) atomic number and mass number

90. If the ESE for a particular exposure is 25 mrad, what will be the intensity of the scattered beam perpendicular to and 1 m from the patient?

    (A) 25 mrad
    (B) 2.5 mrad
    (C) 0.25 mrad
    (D) 0.025 mrad

91. The likelihood of adverse radiation effects to any radiographer whose dose is kept below the recommended guideline is

    (A) very probable
    (B) possible
    (C) very remote
    (D) zero

92. Factors that contribute to the amount of scattered radiation produced include

    1. radiation quality
    2. field size
    3. grid ratio

    (A) 1 only
    (B) 1 and 2 only
    (C) 2 and 3 only
    (D) 1, 2, and 3

93. The SSD in mobile fluoroscopy must be

    (A) a minimum of 15 in.
    (B) a maximum of 15 in.
    (C) a minimum of 12 in.
    (D) a maximum of 12 in.

94. The automatic exposure device that is located immediately under the x-ray table is the

    (A) ionization chamber
    (B) scintillation camera
    (C) photomultiplier
    (D) photocathode

95. The law of Bergonié and Tribondeau states that cells are more radiosensitive if they are

    1. highly proliferative
    2. highly differentiated
    3. immature

    (A) 1 only
    (B) 1 and 2 only
    (C) 1 and 3 only
    (D) 1, 2, and 3

96. It is necessary to question a female patient of childbearing age regarding her

    1. date of last menstrual period
    2. possibility of being pregnant
    3. age at her first pregnancy

    (A) 1 only
    (B) 1 and 2 only
    (C) 1 and 3 only
    (D) 2 and 3 only

97. Which of the dose–response curves seen in Figure 3–4 represents possible genetic effects of ionizing radiation?

   (A) Dose–response curve *A*
   (B) Dose–response curve *B*
   (C) Dose–response curve *C*
   (D) None of these

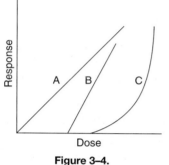

Figure 3–4.

98. What is the effect on RBE as LET increases?

   (A) As LET increases, RBE increases.
   (B) As LET increases, RBE decreases.
   (C) As LET increases, RBE stabilizes.
   (D) LET has no effect on RBE.

99. Which of the following would *most likely* result in the greatest skin dose?

   (A) Short SID
   (B) High kVp
   (C) Increased filtration
   (D) Increased mA

100. Which of the following radiation-induced conditions is most likely to have the *longest* latent period?

   (A) Leukemia
   (B) Temporary infertility
   (C) Erythema
   (D) Acute radiation lethality

101. Which of the following ionizing radiations is described as having an RBE of 1.0?

   (A) 10 MeV protons
   (B) 5 MeV alpha particles
   (C) Diagnostic x-rays
   (D) Fast neutrons

102. If an individual receives 50 mR while standing 4 ft from a source of radiation for 2 minutes, which of the following option(s) will *most effectively* reduce his or her radiation exposure to that source of radiation?

   (A) Standing 3 ft from the source for 2 minutes
   (B) Standing 8 ft from the source for 2 minutes
   (C) Standing 5 ft from the source for 1 minute
   (D) Standing 6 ft from the source for 2 minutes

103. The most radiosensitive portion of the GI tract is the

   (A) upper esophagus
   (B) stomach
   (C) small bowel
   (D) cecum and ascending colon

104. How do fractionation and protraction affect radiation dose effects?

   1. They reduce the effect of radiation exposure.
   2. They permit cellular repair.
   3. They allow tissue recovery.

   (A) 1 only
   (B) 1 and 2 only
   (C) 2 and 3 only
   (D) 1, 2, and 3

105. The photoelectric effect is an interaction between an x-ray photon and

   (A) an inner-shell electron
   (B) an outer-shell electron
   (C) a nucleus
   (D) another photon

106. Filters used in radiographic x-ray tubes generally are composed of

   (A) aluminum
   (B) copper
   (C) tin
   (D) lead

107. All the following function to reduce patient dose *except*

(A) beam restriction

(B) high kVp, low mAs factors

(C) a high-speed grid

(D) a high-speed imaging system

108. In the production of Bremsstrahlung radiation

(A) the incident photon ejects an inner-shell tungsten electron

(B) the incident photon is deflected, with resulting energy loss

(C) the incident electron ejects an inner-shell tungsten electron

(D) the incident electron is deflected, with resulting energy loss

109. An increase in total filtration of the x-ray beam will increase

(A) patient skin dose

(B) beam HVL

(C) image contrast

(D) milliroentgen (mR) output

110. Which of the following is considered the unit of exposure in air?

(A) Roentgen (C/kg)

(B) Rad (Gy)

(C) Rem (Sv)

(D) RBE

111. The purpose of filters in a film badge is

(A) to eliminate harmful rays

(B) to measure radiation quality

(C) to prevent exposure by alpha particles

(D) as a support for the film contained within

112. How many HVLs are required to reduce the intensity of a beam of monoenergetic photons to less than 15% of its original value?

(A) 2

(B) 3

(C) 4

(D) 5

113. Which of the following has (have) an effect on the amount and type of radiation-induced tissue damage?

1. Quality of radiation
2. Type of tissue being irradiated
3. Fractionation

(A) 1 only

(B) 1 and 2 only

(C) 1 and 3 only

(D) 1, 2, and 3

114. Radiation dose to personnel is reduced by which of the following exposure control cord guidelines?

1. Exposure cords on fixed equipment must be very short.
2. Exposure cords on mobile equipment should be fairly long.
3. Exposure cords on fixed and mobile equipment should be of the coiled, expandable type.

(A) 1 only

(B) 1 and 2 only

(C) 2 and 3 only

(D) 1, 2, and 3

115. Any wall that the useful x-ray beam can be directed toward is called a

(A) secondary barrier

(B) primary barrier

(C) leakage barrier

(D) scattered barrier

116. Which of the following body parts is (are) included in whole-body dose?

1. Gonads
2. Blood-forming organs
3. Extremities

(A) 1 only

(B) 1 and 2 only

(C) 1 and 3 only

(D) 1, 2, and 3

117. Which of the following projections would deliver the largest thyroid dose?

 (A) AP skull
 (B) PA skull
 (C) PA esophagus
 (D) PA chest

118. Which of the following personnel monitoring devices used in diagnostic radiography is considered to be the *most* sensitive and accurate?

 (A) TLD
 (B) Film badge
 (C) OSL dosimeter
 (D) Pocket dosimeter

119. Irradiation of macromolecules in vitro can result in

 1. main-chain scission
 2. cross-linking
 3. point lesions

 (A) 1 only
 (B) 1 and 2 only
 (C) 2 and 3 only
 (D) 1, 2, and 3

120. Which of the following radiation situations is potentially the *most* harmful?

 (A) A large dose to a specific area all at once
 (B) A small dose to the whole body over a period of time
 (C) A large dose to the whole body all at one time
 (D) A small dose to a specific area over a period of time

121. How much protection is provided from a 100-kVp x-ray beam when using a 0.50-mm lead-equivalent apron?

 (A) 40%
 (B) 75%
 (C) 88%
 (D) 99%

122. Occupational radiation monitoring is required when it is likely that an individual will receive more than what fraction of the annual dose limit?

 (A) ½
 (B) ¼
 (C) ⅒
 (D) ¹⁄₄₀

123. The interaction illustrated in Figure 3–5

 1. can pose a safety hazard to personnel
 2. can have a negative impact on image quality
 3. occurs with low-energy incident photons

 (A) 1 only
 (B) 1 and 2 only
 (C) 2 and 3 only
 (D) 1, 2, and 3

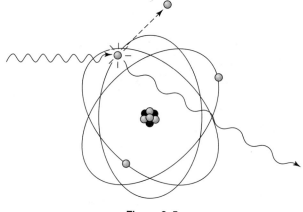

Figure 3–5.

124. Examples of late effects of ionizing radiation on humans include

 1. leukemia
 2. local tissue damage
 3. malignant disease

 (A) 1 only
 (B) 1 and 2 only
 (C) 1 and 3 only
 (D) 1, 2, and 3

125. Which of the following cells are the *most* radiosensitive?

    (A) Myelocytes
    (B) Erythroblasts
    (C) Megakaryocytes
    (D) Myocytes

126. Which of the following statements regarding the pregnant radiographer is (are) true?

    1. She should declare her pregnancy to her supervisor.
    2. She should be assigned a second personnel monitor.
    3. Her radiation history should be reviewed.

    (A) 1 only
    (B) 1 and 2 only
    (C) 2 and 3 only
    (D) 1, 2, and 3

127. What is (are) the major effect(s) of deoxyribonucleic acid (DNA) irradiation?

    1. Malignant disease
    2. Chromosome aberration
    3. Cell death

    (A) 1 only
    (B) 1 and 2 only
    (C) 2 and 3 only
    (D) 1, 2, and 3

128. Which of the following contributes *most* to patient dose?

    (A) The photoelectric effect
    (B) Compton scatter
    (C) Classic scatter
    (D) Thompson scatter

129. Which of the following statements is (are) true with respect to the dose–response curve shown in Figure 3–6?

    1. The quantity of radiation is directly related to the dose received.
    2. No threshold is required for effects to occur.
    3. A minimum amount of radiation is required for manifestation of effects.

    (A) 1 only
    (B) 1 and 2 only
    (C) 1 and 3 only
    (D) 2 and 3 only

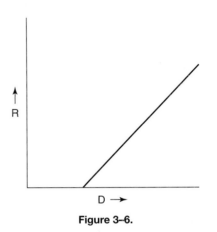

Figure 3–6.

130. The classifications of acute radiation syndrome include all the following *except*

    (A) central nervous system
    (B) gastrointestinal
    (C) neonatal
    (D) hematologic

131. In the production of characteristic radiation at the tungsten target, the incident electron

    (A) ejects an inner-shell tungsten electron
    (B) ejects an outer-shell tungsten electron
    (C) is deflected, with resulting energy loss
    (D) is deflected, with resulting energy gain

132. Which of the following defines the gonadal dose that, if received by every member of the population, would be expected to produce the same total genetic effect on that population as the actual doses received by each of the individuals?

    (A) Genetically significant dose
    (B) Somatically significant dose
    (C) Maximum permissible dose
    (D) Lethal dose

133. If an exposure dose of 50 mR/h is delivered from a distance of 3 ft, what would be the dose delivered after 20 minutes at a distance of 5 ft from the source?

    (A) 6 mR
    (B) 18 mR
    (C) 46 mR
    (D) 138 mR

134. The term *effective dose* refers to

    (A) whole-body dose
    (B) localized organ dose
    (C) genetic effects
    (D) somatic and genetic effects

135. Which of the following is (are) possible long-term somatic effects of radiation exposure?

    1. Blood changes
    2. Cataractogenesis
    3. Embryologic effects

    (A) 1 only
    (B) 1 and 2 only
    (C) 2 and 3 only
    (D) 1, 2, and 3

136. The operation of personal radiation monitoring can be based on stimulated luminescence. Which of the following personal radiation monitors function(s) in that manner?

    1. OSL dosimeter
    2. TLD
    3. Pocket dosimeter

    (A) 1 only
    (B) 1 and 2 only
    (C) 1 and 3 only
    (D) 1, 2, and 3

137. If a patient received 1,400 mrad during a 7-minute fluoroscopic examination, what was the dose rate?

    (A) 200 rad/min
    (B) 5 rad/min
    (C) 2.0 rad/min
    (D) 0.2 rad/min

138. Biologic material irradiated under hypoxic conditions is

    (A) more sensitive than when irradiated under oxygenated conditions
    (B) less sensitive than when irradiated under anoxic conditions
    (C) less sensitive than when irradiated under oxygenated conditions
    (D) unaffected by the presence or absence of oxygen

139. Which interaction between ionizing radiation and the target molecule involves formation of a free radical?

    (A) Direct effect
    (B) Indirect effect
    (C) Target effect
    (D) Random effect

140. The single most important scattering object in both radiography and fluoroscopy is the

    (A) x-ray table
    (B) x-ray tube
    (C) patient
    (D) IR

141. All the following statements regarding TLDs are true *except*

   (A) TLDs are reusable
   (B) a TLD is a personal radiation monitor
   (C) TLDs use a lithium fluoride phosphor
   (D) after x-ray exposure, TLDs emit heat in response to stimulation by light

142. A student radiographer who is under 18 years of age must not receive an annual occupational dose of greater than

   (A) 0.1 rem (1 mSv)
   (B) 0.5 rem (5 mSv)
   (C) 5 rem (50 mSv)
   (D) 10 rem (100 mSv)

143. What is the approximate ESE for the average AP lumbar spine radiograph?

   (A) 30 rad
   (B) 30 mrad
   (C) 300 rad
   (D) 300 mrad

144. Which of the following is (are) likely to improve image quality *and* decrease patient dose?

   1. Beam restriction
   2. Low kilovolt and high microampere-second factors
   3. Grids

   (A) 1 only
   (B) 1 and 3 only
   (C) 2 and 3 only
   (D) 1, 2, and 3

145. Types of secondary radiation barriers include

   1. the control booth
   2. lead aprons
   3. the x-ray tube housing

   (A) 2 only
   (B) 1 and 2 only
   (C) 2 and 3 only
   (D) 1, 2, and 3

146. Lead aprons are worn during fluoroscopy to protect the radiographer from exposure to radiation from

   (A) the photoelectric effect
   (B) Compton scatter
   (C) classic scatter
   (D) pair production

147. Types of structural damage to a DNA molecule by ionizing radiation include which of the following?

   1. Single-side-rail scission
   2. Double-side-rail scission
   3. Cross-linking

   (A) 1 only
   (B) 2 only
   (C) 1 and 2 only
   (D) 1, 2, and 3

148. Which of the following can be an effective means of reducing radiation exposure?

   1. Barriers
   2. Distance
   3. Time

   (A) 1 only
   (B) 2 only
   (C) 1 and 2 only
   (D) 1, 2, and 3

149. The effects of radiation on biologic material depend on several factors. If a large quantity of radiation is delivered to a body over a short period of time, the effect

   (A) will be greater than if it were delivered in increments
   (B) will be less than if it were delivered in increments
   (C) has no relation to how it is delivered in time
   (D) solely depends on the radiation quality

150. *Somatic effects* of radiation refer to effects that are manifested

 (A) in the descendants of the exposed individual
 (B) during the life of the exposed individual
 (C) in the exposed individual and his or her descendants
 (D) in the reproductive cells of the exposed individual

151. What minimum total amount of filtration (inherent plus added) is required in x-ray equipment operated above 70 kVp?

 (A) 2.5 mm Al equivalent
 (B) 3.5 mm Al equivalent
 (C) 2.5 mm Cu equivalent
 (D) 3.5 mm Cu equivalent

152. The dose of radiation that will cause a noticeable skin reaction is referred to as the

 (A) LET
 (B) SSD
 (C) SED
 (D) SID

153. The NCRP recommends an annual effective occupational dose-equivalent limit of

 (A) 2.5 rem (25 mSv)
 (B) 5 rem (50 mSv)
 (C) 10 rem (100 mSv)
 (D) 20 rem (200 mSv)

154. Some patients, such as infants and children, are unable to maintain the necessary radiographic position without assistance. If mechanical restraining devices cannot be used, which of the following should be requested or permitted to hold the patient?

 (A) Transporter
 (B) Patient's father
 (C) Patient's mother
 (D) Student radiographer

155. A *controlled area* is defined as one

 1. that is occupied by people trained in radiation safety
 2. that is occupied by people who wear radiation monitors
 3. whose occupancy factor is 1

 (A) 1 and 2 only
 (B) 2 only
 (C) 1 and 3 only
 (D) 1, 2, and 3

156. Which of the following terms refers to the period between conception and birth?

 (A) Gestation
 (B) Congenital
 (C) Neonatal
 (D) In vitro

157. Somatic effects resulting from radiation exposure can

 1. have possible consequences on the exposed individual
 2. have possible consequences on future generations
 3. cause temporary infertility

 (A) 1 only
 (B) 1 and 3 only
 (C) 2 and 3 only
 (D) 1, 2, and 3

158. How does the use of rare earth intensifying screens contribute to lowering the patient dose?

 1. It permits the use of lower milliampere-seconds.
 2. It permits the use of lower kilovolts peak (kVp).
 3. It eliminates the need for patient shielding.

 (A) 1 only
 (B) 1 and 2 only
 (C) 1 and 3 only
 (D) 2 and 3 only

159. In which type of monitoring device do photons release electrons by their interaction with air?

(A) Film badge
(B) TLD
(C) Pocket dosimeter
(D) OSL dosimeter

160. The advantages of beam restriction include which of the following?

1. Less scattered radiation is produced.
2. Less biologic material is irradiated.
3. Less total filtration will be necessary.

(A) 1 only
(B) 1 and 2 only
(C) 2 and 3 only
(D) 1, 2, and 3

161. The person responsible for ascertaining that all radiation guidelines are adhered to and that personnel understand and employ radiation safety measures is the

(A) radiology department manager
(B) radiation safety officer
(C) chief radiologist
(D) chief technologist

162. The dose–response curve that appears to be valid for genetic and some somatic effects is the

1. linear
2. nonlinear
3. nonthreshold

(A) 1 only
(B) 1 and 3 only
(C) 2 and 3 only
(D) 1, 2, and 3

163. Which of the following statements regarding the human gonadal cells is (are) true?

1. The female oogonia reproduce only during fetal life.
2. The male spermatogonia reproduce continuously.
3. Both male and female stem cells reproduce only during fetal life.

(A) 1 only
(B) 2 only
(C) 1 and 2 only
(D) 3 only

164. Protective devices such as lead aprons function to protect the user from

1. scattered radiation
2. the primary beam
3. remnant radiation

(A) 1 only
(B) 1 and 2 only
(C) 1 and 3 only
(D) 1, 2, and 3

165. The primary function of filtration is to reduce

(A) patient skin dose
(B) operator dose
(C) image noise
(D) scattered radiation

166. Which of the following factors can affect the amount or the nature of radiation damage to biologic tissue?

1. Radiation quality
2. Absorbed dose
3. Size of irradiated area

(A) 1 only
(B) 2 only
(C) 1 and 2 only
(D) 1, 2, and 3

167. Examples of stochastic effects of radiation exposure include

    1. radiation-induced malignancy
    2. genetic effects
    3. leukemia

    (A) 1 only
    (B) 1 and 2 only
    (C) 2 and 3 only
    (D) 1, 2, and 3

168. Which of the following tissues is (are) considered to be particularly radiosensitive?

    1. Intestinal mucous membrane
    2. Epidermis of extremities
    3. Optic nerves

    (A) 1 only
    (B) 1 and 2 only
    (C) 2 and 3 only
    (D) 1, 2, and 3

169. Which of the following groups of exposure factors will deliver the *least* amount of exposure to the patient?

    (A) 400 mA, 0.25 second, 100 kVp
    (B) 600 mA, 0.33 second, 90 kVp
    (C) 800 mA, 0.5 second, 80 kVp
    (D) 800 mA, 1.0 second, 70 kVp

170. Stochastic effects of radiation are those that

    1. have a threshold
    2. may be described as "all-or-nothing" effects
    3. are late effects

    (A) 1 only
    (B) 1 and 2 only
    (C) 2 and 3 only
    (D) 1, 2, and 3

171. To within what percentage of the SID must the collimator light and actual irradiated area be accurate?

    (A) 2%
    (B) 5%
    (C) 10%
    (D) 15%

172. Under what circumstances might a radiographer be required to wear two dosimeters?

    1. During pregnancy
    2. While performing vascular procedures
    3. While performing mobile radiography

    (A) 1 and 2 only
    (B) 2 only
    (C) 2 and 3 only
    (D) 1, 2, and 3

173. What quantity of radiation exposure to the reproductive organs is required to cause temporary infertility?

    (A) 100 rad
    (B) 200 rad
    (C) 300 rad
    (D) 400 rad

174. Which of the following personnel radiation monitors will provide an immediate reading?

    (A) TLD
    (B) Film badge
    (C) Lithium fluoride chips
    (D) Pocket dosimeter

175. The tabletop exposure rate during fluoroscopy shall *not* exceed

    (A) 5 mR/min
    (B) 10 R/min
    (C) 10 mR/h
    (D) 5 R/h

176. Which of the dose–response curves shown in Figure 3–7 is representative of radiation-induced skin erythema?

1. Dose–response curve *A*
2. Dose–response curve *B*
3. Dose–response curve *C*

(A) 1 only

(B) 1 and 2 only

(C) 3 only

(D) 2 and 3 only

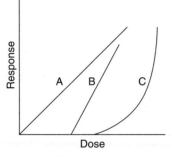

Figure 3–7.

177. If the exposure rate at 3 ft from the fluoroscopic table is 40 mR/h, what will be the exposure rate for 30 minutes at a distance of 5 ft from the table?

(A) 7 mR

(B) 12 mR

(C) 14 mR

(D) 24 mR

178. Which of the following radiation protection measures is (are) appropriate for mobile radiography?

1. The radiographer must be at least 6 ft from the patient and the x-ray tube during the exposure.
2. The radiographer must announce in a loud voice that an exposure is about to be made and wait for personnel, visitors, and patients to temporarily leave the area.
3. The radiographer must try to use the shortest practical SID.

(A) 1 and 2 only

(B) 1 and 3 only

(C) 2 and 3 only

(D) 1, 2, and 3

179. Radiation that passes through the tube housing in directions other than that of the useful beam is termed

(A) scattered radiation

(B) secondary radiation

(C) leakage radiation

(D) remnant radiation

180. The presence of ionizing radiation may be detected in which of the following ways?

1. Ionizing effect on air
2. Photographic effect on film emulsion
3. Fluorescent effect on certain crystals

(A) 1 only

(B) 1 and 2 only

(C) 1 and 3 only

(D) 1, 2, and 3

181. Which of the following refers to a regular program of evaluation that ensures the proper functioning of x-ray equipment, thereby protecting both radiation workers and patients?

(A) Sensitometry

(B) Densitometry

(C) Quality assurance

(D) Modulation transfer function

182. What should be the radiographer's main objective regarding personal radiation safety?

(A) Not to exceed his or her dose limit

(B) To keep personal exposure as far below the dose limit as possible

(C) To avoid whole-body exposure

(D) To wear protective apparel when "holding" patients for exposures

183. Referring to the nomogram in Figure 3–8, what is the approximate patient ESE from a particular projection made at 105 cm using 125 kVp, 400 mA, 8 ms, and 3.0 mm Al total filtration ?

(A) 23 mR

(B) 48 mR

(C) 230 mR

(D) 480 mR

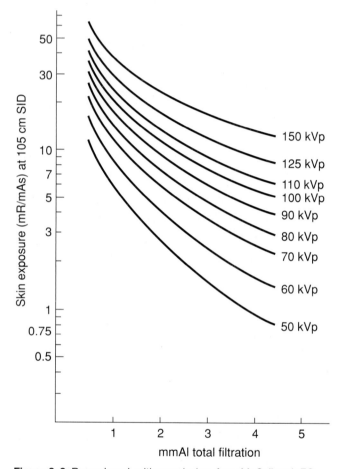

Figure 3–8. Reproduced, with permission, from McCullough EC, Cameron JR. Exposure rates from diagnostic x-ray units. *Br J Radiol* 1970;43:448–451.

184. If the exposure rate to a body standing 7 ft from a radiation source is 140 mR/h, what will be the dose to that body at a distance of 8 ft from the source in 30 minutes?

(A) 182.8 mR

(B) 107 mR

(C) 91.4 mR

(D) 53.6 mR

185. Which of the following types of radiation is (are) considered electromagnetic?

1. X-ray
2. Gamma
3. Beta

(A) 1 only

(B) 1 and 2 only

(C) 2 and 3 only

(D) 1, 2, and 3

186. Which of the following features of fluoroscopic equipment is (are) designed especially to eliminate unnecessary radiation exposure to the patient and/or personnel?

1. Bucky slot cover
2. Exposure switch/foot pedal
3. Cumulative exposure timer

(A) 1 only

(B) 1 and 2 only

(C) 2 and 3 only

(D) 1, 2, and 3

187. Radiation output from a diagnostic x-ray tube is measured in which of the following units of measurement?

(A) Rad

(B) Rem

(C) Roentgen

(D) Becqueral

188. Which of the following is (are) considered especially radiosensitive tissues?

1. Bone marrow
2. Intestinal crypt cells
3. Erythroblasts

(A) 1 and 2 only

(B) 1 and 3 only

(C) 2 and 3 only

(D) 1, 2, and 3

189. Which of the following safeguards is (are) taken to prevent inadvertent irradiation in early pregnancy?

1. Patient postings
2. Patient questionnaire
3. Elective booking

(A) 1 and 2 only
(B) 1 and 3 only
(C) 2 and 3 only
(D) 1, 2, and 3

190. The interaction between x-ray photons and tissue that is responsible for radiographic contrast but that also contributes significantly to patient dose is

(A) the photoelectric effect
(B) Compton scatter
(C) coherent scatter
(D) pair production

191. Which of the following is (are) acceptable way(s) to monitor the radiation exposure of those who are occupationally employed?

1. TLD
2. OSL dosimeter
3. Quarterly blood cell count

(A) 1 only
(B) 1 and 2 only
(C) 1 and 3 only
(D) 1, 2, and 3

192. The genetic dose of radiation borne by each member of the reproductive population is called the

(A) genetically related dose
(B) genetically significant dose
(C) somatic related dose
(D) somatic significant dose

193. According to the NCRP, the pregnant radiographer's gestational dose-equivalent limit for a 1-month period is

(A) 1 mSv
(B) 5 mSv
(C) 0.1 mSv
(D) 0.5 mSv

194. Which of the following projections is most likely to deliver the largest dose to the ovaries?

(A) AP lumbar spine, 7×17 in. cassette, 80 kVp
(B) AP lumbar spine, 14×17 in. cassette, 80 kVp
(C) AP abdomen, 80 kVp
(D) AP abdomen, 70 kVp

195. The correct way(s) to check for cracks in lead aprons is (are)

1. to fluoroscope them once a year
2. to radiograph them at low kilovoltage twice a year
3. by visual inspection

(A) 1 only
(B) 1 and 2 only
(C) 2 and 3 only
(D) 1, 2, and 3

196. The *target theory* applies to

(A) spermatagonia
(B) oocytes
(C) lymphocytes
(D) DNA molecules

197. Which of the following is (are) features of fluoroscopic equipment designed especially to eliminate unnecessary radiation to patient and personnel?

1. Protective curtain
2. Filtration
3. Collimation

(A) 1 only
(B) 1 and 2 only
(C) 1 and 3 only
(D) 1, 2, and 3

198. Which of the following has(have) been identified as source(s) of radon exposure?

1. Indoors, in houses
2. Smoking cigarettes
3. Radiology departments

(A) 1 only
(B) 1 and 2 only
(C) 2 and 3 only
(D) 1, 2, and 3

199. What is the relationship between LET and RBE?

(A) As LET increases, RBE increases.
(B) As LET increases, RBE decreases.
(C) As LET decreases, RBE increases.
(D) There is no direct relationship between LET and RBE.

200. The biologic effect on an individual depends on which of the following?

1. Type of tissue interaction(s)
2. Amount of interactions
3. Biologic differences

(A) 1 and 2 only
(B) 1 and 3 only
(C) 2 and 3 only
(D) 1, 2, and 3

Answers and Explanations

1. **(A)** The *tissue weighting factor* (W_t) represents the relative tissue radiosensitivity of irradiated material (e.g., muscle vs. intestinal epithelium vs. bone). The *radiation weighting factor* (W_r) is a number assigned to different types of ionizing radiations in order to better determine their effect on tissue (e.g., x-ray vs. alpha particles). The W_r of different ionizing radiations depends on the LET of that particular radiation. The following formula is used to determine *effective dose E:*

   Effective dose E = radiation weighting factor W_r
   $\times$ tissue weighting factor W_t
   $\times$ absorbed dose

   (Bushong, 8th ed., p. 556)

2. **(B)** The pregnant radiographer poses a special radiation protection consideration, for the safety of the unborn individual. It must be remembered that the developing fetus is particularly sensitive to radiation exposure. Therefore, established guidelines state that the occupational gestational dose-equivalent limit for *embryo/fetus* of a pregnant radiographer is 5 mSv (500 mrem), not to exceed 0.5 mSv in 1 month. According to the NCRP, the annual occupational *whole-body* dose-equivalent limit is 50 mSv (5 rem or 5,000 mrem). The annual occupational whole-body dose-equivalent limit for *students* under the age of 18 years is 1 mSv (100 mrem or 0.1 rem). The annual occupational dose-equivalent limit for the *lens of eye* is 150 mSv (15 rem). The annual occupational dose-equivalent limit for the *thyroid, skin,* and *extremities* is 500 mSv (50 rem). *(Bushong, 8th ed., p. 557)*

3. **(D)** If the exposure rate for the examination is 250 mR/h (60 minutes), then a 3-minute examination would be proportionally less—as the following equation illustrates:

   $$\frac{275 \ (mR)}{60 \ (min)} = \frac{x \ (mR)}{1.5 \ (min)}$$
   $$60 \ x = 412.5$$

   Thus, $x = 6.87$-mR dose in 1.5 minutes. *(Bushong, 8th ed., p. 570)*

4. **(D)** The relationship between x-ray intensity and distance from the source is expressed in the inverse-square law of radiation. The formula is

   $$\frac{I_1}{I_2} = \frac{D_2^2}{D_1^2}$$

   Substituting known values:

   $$\frac{10}{x} = \frac{36}{16}$$
   $$36x = 160$$
   $$x = 4.44$$

   Thus, $x = 4.44$ mR in *60 minutes* and, therefore, 1.48 mR in *20 minutes*. Distance has a profound effect on dose received and, therefore, is one of the cardinal rules of radiation protection. As distance from the source increases, dose received decreases. *(Bushong, 8th ed., pp. 68–70)*

5. **(B)** NCRP Report No. 102 states that the exposure switch on mobile radiographic units shall be so arranged that the operator can stand at least 2 m *(6 ft)* from the patient, the x-ray tube, and the useful beam. An appropriately long exposure cord accomplishes this requirement. The fluoroscopic and/or radiographic exposure switch or switches must be of the "dead man" type; that is, the exposure will terminate should the switch be released. A lead apron should be carried with every mobile x-ray unit for the operator to wear during the exposure. Lastly, the radiographer must be certain to alert individuals in the area, enabling unnecessary occupants to move away, before making the exposure. *(NCRP Report No. 102, p. 25)*

6. **(D)** *Lymphocytes*, a type of white blood cell concerned with the immune system, have the *greatest* radiosensitivity of all body cells. *Spermatids* are also highly radiosensitive, although not to the same degree as lymphocytes. *Muscle* cells have a fairly low radiosensitivity, and *nerve* cells are the *least* radiosensitive in the body (in fetal life, however, nerve cells are highly radiosensitive). *(Dowd and Tilson, 2nd ed., p. 135)*

7. **(B)** It is our professional responsibility to minimize exposure dose to both patients and ourselves, and one of the most important ways is with a closely collimated radiation field. Gonadal shielding should be used when the patient is of reproductive age or younger, when the gonads are in or near the collimated field, and when the clinical objectives will not be compromised. *(Frank, Long, and Smith, 11th ed., vol. 1, p. 33)*

8. **(B)** The principal interactions that occur between x-ray photons and body tissues in the diagnostic x-ray range, the photoelectric effect and Compton scatter, are ionization processes producing photoelectrons and recoil electrons that traverse tissue and subsequently ionize molecules. These interactions occur randomly but can lead to molecular damage in the form of *impaired function* or *cell death*. The *target theory* specifies that DNA molecules are the targets of greatest importance and sensitivity; that is, DNA is the key sensitive molecule. However, since the body has 65 to 80% water, most interactions between ionizing radiation and body cells will involve radiolysis of water rather than direct interaction with DNA. The two major types of effects that occur are the *direct effect* and the *indirect effect*. The direct effect usually occurs with high-LET radiations and when ionization occurs at the DNA molecule itself. The indirect effect, which occurs most frequently, happens when ionization takes place away from the DNA molecule in cellular water. However, the energy from the interaction can be transferred to the molecule via a *free radical* (formed by *radiolysis of cellular water*). Possible damage to the DNA molecule is diverse. A single main-chain/side-rail scission (break) on the DNA molecule is *repairable*. A double main-chain/side-rail scission may repair with difficulty or may result in *cell death*. A double main-chain/side-rail scission on the same "rung" of the DNA ladder results in *irreparable* damage or *cell death*. Faulty repair of main-chain breakage can result in *cross-linking*. Damage to the nitrogenous bases, that is, damage to the base itself or to the rungs connecting the main chains, can result in alteration of base sequences, causing a *molecular lesion/point mutation*. Any subsequent divisions result in daughter cells with incorrect genetic information. *(Bushong, 8th ed., p. 507)*

9. **(B)** Patients occasionally will question the radiographer regarding the amount of radiation they are receiving during their examination. Most of these patients are merely curious because they have heard a recent news report about x-rays or have perhaps studied about x-rays in school recently. It is a good idea for radiographers to have some knowledge of average exposure doses for patients who desire this information. The curious patient also can be referred to the medical physicist for more detailed information. The average anteroposterior (AP) supine lumbar spine radiograph

delivers an ESE of about 350 mrad (0.35 rad). The average AP supine abdomen radiograph delivers about 300 mrad; the average AP cervical spine radiograph delivers about 80 mrad. *(Dowd and Tilson, 2nd ed., p. 247)*

10. **(A)** Collimators or other kinds of *beam restrictors* limit the amount of tissue being irradiated and, therefore, can reduce patient dose significantly. The use of *gonadal shielding* protects the reproductive organs from unnecessary radiation exposure and should be employed whenever possible. *Grids* function to absorb scattered radiation before it reaches the image to cause fog. Grids improve the radiographic image considerably; however, their use requires a significant *increase in milliampere-seconds*, that is, patient dose. *(Frank, Long, and Smith, 11th ed., vol. 1, pp. 32–33)*

11. **(D)** Source-to-image-receptor distance (SID) has a significant impact on x-ray beam *intensity* (other terms we could use are *exposure rate* and *dose*). *As the distance between the x-ray tube and IR increases, exposure rate/intensity/dose (and, therefore, radiographic density) decreases according to the inverse-square law.* According to the inverse-square law, the exposure rate is *inversely* proportional to the *square* of the distance; that is, if the SID is *doubled*, the resulting beam intensity will be one-fourth the original intensity; if the SID is cut in half, the resulting beam intensity will be 4 times the original intensity. *(Dowd and Tilson, 2nd ed., p. 199)*

12. **(C)** According to the NCRP, the annual occupational *whole-body* dose-equivalent limit is 50 mSv (5 rem or 5,000 mrem). The annual occupational whole-body dose-equivalent limit for *students* under the age of 18 years is 1 mSv (100 mrem or 0.1 rem). The annual occupational dose-equivalent limit for the *lens of eye* is 150 mSv (15 rem). The annual occupational dose-equivalent limit for the *thyroid*, *skin*, and *extremities* is 500 mSv (50 rem). *(Bushong, 8th ed., p. 557)*

13. **(C)** Different types of monitoring devices are available for the occupationally exposed, and anyone who might receive more than *one-tenth the annual dose limit* must be monitored. Ionization is the fundamental principle of operation of both the film badge and the pocket dosimeter. In the film badge, the film's silver halide emulsion is ionized by x-ray photons. The pocket dosimeter contains an ionization chamber (containing air), and the number of ions formed (of either sign) is equated to exposure dose. TLDs are radiation monitors that use lithium fluoride crystals. Once exposed to ionizing radiation and then heated, these crystals give off light in proportion to the amount of radiation received. OSL dosimeters are radiation monitors that use aluminum oxide crystals. These crystals, once exposed to ionizing radiation and then subjected to a laser, give off luminescence proportional to the amount of radiation received. *(Bushong, 8th ed., p. 593)*

14. **(C)** The entire population of the world is exposed to varying amounts of background (environmental) radiation. Sources of background radiation are either *natural* or *human-made*. Exposure to *natural* background radiation is a result of cosmic radiation from space (*external terrestrial*) and naturally radioactive elements *within the earth's crust (internal terrestrial) and our own bodies (internal sources, from ingested materials)*. Naturally, the closer we are to the *cosmic radiations* from space, the greater our personal exposure will be; living at higher elevations and air travel expose us to greater amounts of radiation. Living or working in a building made of materials derived from the ground exposes us to some background radiation from the naturally radioactive elements found in the earth's crust. The food we eat, the water we drink, and the air we breathe all contribute to the quantity of radiation we ingest and inhale. Human-made radiation, however, is the type of background radiation over which we have some control. Medical and dental x-rays, nuclear power plant environs, and nuclear medicine contribute to our exposure to *human-made* background radiation. *(Selman, 9th ed., p. 501)*

15. **(B)** *Radiolysis* has to do with the irradiation of water molecules and the formation of free

radicals. Free radicals contain enough energy to damage other molecules some distance away. They can migrate to and damage a DNA molecule (indirect hit theory). *(Bushong, 8th ed., pp. 506, 507)*

16. **(B)** In the *photoelectric effect*, a relatively low-energy photon uses all its energy to eject an inner-shell electron, leaving a vacancy. An electron from the shell above drops down to fill the vacancy and in so doing gives up a characteristic ray. This type of interaction is most harmful to the patient because all the photon energy is transferred to tissue. In *Compton scatter*, a high-energy incident photon uses some of its energy to eject an outer-shell electron. In so doing, the incident photon is deflected with reduced energy, but it usually retains most of its energy and exits the body as an energetic scattered ray. *This scattered ray will either contribute to image fog or pose a radiation hazard to personnel* depending on its direction of exit; thus, Compton scatter contributes the most to occupational exposure. In *classic scatter*, a low-energy photon interacts with an atom but causes no ionization; the incident photon disappears into the atom and then is released immediately as a photon of identical energy but with changed direction. *Thompson scatter* is another name for classic scatter. *(Selman, 9th ed., p. 128)*

17. **(A)** The *tissue weighting factor* (W_t) represents the relative tissue radiosensitivity of irradiated material (e.g., muscle vs. intestinal epithelium vs. bone). The *radiation weighting factor* (W_r) is a number assigned to different types of ionizing radiations in order to better determine their effect on tissue (e.g., x-ray vs. alpha particles). The W_r of different ionizing radiations depends on the LET of that particular radiation. The following formula is used to determine *effective dose E:*

Effective dose E = radiation weighting
factor W_r
× tissue weighting factor W_t
× absorbed dose

(Bushong, 8th ed., p. 556)

18. **(B)** In the *photoelectric effect*, a relatively low-energy photon uses all its energy to eject an

inner-shell electron, leaving a vacancy. An electron from the shell above drops down to fill the vacancy and in so doing gives up a characteristic ray. This type of interaction is most harmful to the patient because all the photon energy is transferred to tissue. In *Compton scatter*, a high-energy incident photon ejects an outer-shell electron. In doing so, the incident photon is deflected with reduced energy, but it *usually retains most of its energy and exits the body as an energetic scattered ray.* This scattered ray will either contribute to image fog or pose a radiation hazard to personnel depending on its direction of exit. In *classic scatter*, a low-energy photon interacts with an atom but causes no ionization; the incident photon disappears into the atom and then is released immediately as a photon of identical energy but with changed direction. *Thompson scatter* is another name for classic scatter. *(Bushong, 8th ed., pp. 176–178)*

19. **(B)** The relationship between x-ray intensity and distance from the source is expressed by the inverse-square law of radiation. The formula is

$$\frac{I_1}{I_2} = \frac{D_2^2}{D_1^2}$$

Substituting known values:

$$\frac{16 \text{ R/h}}{6 \text{ R/h}} = \frac{x^2}{16}$$
$$6x^2 = 256$$
$$x^2 = 42.66$$

Thus, $x = 6.5$ ft (necessary to decrease the exposure to 6 R/h). Note that in order for the exposure rate to decrease, the distance from the source of radiation must increase. *(Bushong, 8th ed., p. 68)*

20. **(A)** As an x-ray source moves away from an absorber, the x-ray intensity (quantity) decreases. Conversely, as the source of x-rays moves closer to the absorber, the intensity increases. In fluoroscopy, the source of x-rays is 12 to 15 inches below the x-ray tabletop. Since the source-to-object distance (SOD) is so short, patient skin dose can be quite high. Simply increasing the SID will decrease ESE, but mA will

have to be increased to maintain the required exit exposure. Although mA is increased to maintain required exit exposure, because of the characteristic *divergence* of the x-ray beam, ESE will *still* be less at longer SIDs.

Distance has a profound effect on dose received and, therefore, is one of the cardinal rules of radiation protection. *As distance from the source increases, dose received decreases.* (*Bushong, 9th ed., p. 582*)

21. **(D)** Late somatic effects are those that can occur years after initial exposure and are caused by low, chronic exposures. Occupationally exposed personnel are concerned with the late effects of radiation exposure. Bone malignancies, thyroid cancers, leukemia, and skin cancers are examples of *carcinogenic* somatic effects of radiation. Another example of somatic effects of radiation is *cataract* formation to the lenses of eyes of individuals accidentally exposed to sufficient quantities of radiation. The lives of many of the early radiation workers were several years shorter than the lives of the general population. Statistics revealed that radiologists, for example, had a shorter life span than physicians of other specialties. *Life-span shortening*, then, *was* another somatic effect of radiation. Certainly, these effects should *never be experienced today.* The human reproductive organs are particularly radiosensitive. *Fertility* and *heredity* can be greatly affected by the *germ cells* produced within the testes (*spermatogonia*) and ovaries (*oogonia*). Excessive radiation exposure to the gonads can cause *temporary or permanent sterility* and/or *genetic mutations.* (*Bushong, 8th ed., pp. 532–534*)

22. **(D)** One of the radiation protection guidelines for the occupationally exposed is that the x-ray beam should scatter twice before reaching the operator. Each time the x-ray beam scatters, its intensity at 1 m from the scattering object is *one-thousandth* of its original intensity. Of course, the operator should be behind a shielded booth while making the exposure, but multiple scatterings further reduce the danger of exposure from scattered radiation. (*Bushong, 8th ed., p. 572*)

23. **(B)** According to the NCRP, the annual occupational *whole-body* dose-equivalent limit is 50 mSv (5 rem or 5,000 mrem). The annual occupational whole-body dose-equivalent limit for *students* under the age of 18 years is 1 mSv (100 mrem or 0.1 rem). The annual occupational dose-equivalent limit for the *lens of eye* is 150 mSv (15 rem). The annual occupational dose-equivalent limit for the *thyroid, skin, and extremities* is 500 mSv (50 rem). The total gestational dose-equivalent limit for embryo/fetus of a pregnant radiographer is 5 mSv (500 mrem), not to exceed 0.5 mSv in 1 month. (*Bushong, 8th ed., p. 557*)

24. **(C)** TLDs are personnel radiation monitors that use *lithium fluoride* crystals. Once exposed to ionizing radiation and then heated, these crystals give off light proportional to the amount of radiation received. TLDs are very accurate personal monitors. Even more accurate are optically stimulated luminescence (OSL) dosimeters. OSL dosimeters use *aluminum oxide* as their sensitive crystal. Silver halide is in film emulsion and sodium thiosulfate is in fixer solution. (*Bushong, 8th ed., p. 593*)

25. **(C)** *Secondary* radiation consists of *leakage and scattered* radiation. Leakage radiation can be emitted when a defect exists in the tube housing. A significant quantity of scattered radiation is generated within, and emitted from, the patient. *Background* radiation is naturally occurring radiation that is emitted from the earth and that also exists within our bodies. (*Sherer et al., 4th ed., p. 240*)

26. **(C)** The selected milliampere-seconds is directly related to patient dose. That is, if milliampere-seconds are doubled, patient dose is doubled. Similarly, if milliampere-seconds are cut in half, patient dose is cut in half. The selected kilovolts peak is inversely related to patient dose. That is, if the kilovolts peak is increased, patient dose can be decreased because more x-ray photons are transmitted through the patient rather than being absorbed. Inherent filtration is provided by materials that are a permanent part of the tube housing, that is, the glass envelope of the x-ray tube and the oil coolant. Added filtration, usually thin sheets of aluminum, is present to make a total of 2.5 mm Al equivalent for

equipment operated above 70 kVp. Filtration is used to decrease patient dose by removing the weak x-rays that have no value but contribute to the skin dose. The effect of focal spot size is principally on radiographic sharpness; it has no effect on patient dose. *(Bushong, 8th ed., pp. 137, 138)*

27. **(B)** The photoelectric effect is the interaction between x-ray photons and matter that is largely responsible for patient dose. The photoelectric effect occurs when a relatively *low-energy* photon uses *all* its energy to eject an *inner-shell* electron. That electron is ejected from the atom, leaving a hole in, for example, the K shell. An L-shell electron then drops down to fill the K vacancy and in so doing emits a characteristic ray whose energy equals the difference in binding energies for the K and L shells. The photoelectric effect occurs with *high*-atomic-number (Z) absorbers such as bone and with positive contrast media. *(Bushong, 8th ed., p. 176)*

28. **(D)** The genetic effects of radiation and some somatic effects, such as leukemia, are plotted on a *linear* dose–response curve. The linear dose–response curve has *no threshold;* that is, *there is no dose below which radiation is absolutely safe.* The *nonlinear/sigmoidal* dose–response curve has a *threshold* and is thought to be generally correct for most *somatic* effects—such as *skin erythema, epilation, hematologic depression,* and *radiation lethality* (death). *(Bushong, 8th ed., pp. 498–499)*

29. **(B)** *Rem (dose-equivalent) is the only unit of measurement that expresses the dose–effect relationship.* The product of rad (absorbed dose) and the quality factor appropriate for the radiation type is expressed as rem or dose equivalent (DE) and may be used to predict the type and extent of response to radiation. *(Sherer et al., 5th ed., p. 11)*

30. **(B)** Special arrangements are required for occupational monitoring of the pregnant radiographer. The pregnant radiographer will wear two dosimeters—one in its usual place at the collar and the other, a baby/fetal dosimeter, worn over the abdomen and *under* the lead apron during fluoroscopy. The baby/fetal dosimeter must be identified as such and always must be worn in the same place. Care must be taken not to mix the positions of the two dosimeters. The dosimeters are read monthly, as usual. The pregnant radiographer may not be made to leave the radiation area/department because of her pregnancy. *(Bushong, 8th ed., p. 560)*

31. **(A)** Occupationally exposed individuals are required to use devices that will record and provide documentation of the radiation they receive over a given period of time, traditionally 1 month. The most commonly used personal dosimeters are the OSL, the TLD, and the film badge. These devices must be worn *only* for documentation of occupational exposure. They must not be worn for any medical or dental x-rays one receives as a patient, and they are not used to measure naturally occurring background radiation. *(Thompson et al., p. 459)*

32. **(B)** Irradiation during *pregnancy*, especially in early pregnancy, must be avoided. The fetus is particularly radiosensitive during the first trimester, during much of which time pregnancy may not even be suspected. High-risk examinations include pelvis, hip, femur, lumbar spine, cystograms and urograms, and upper and lower gastrointestinal (GI) series. During the first trimester, specifically the 2nd to 10th weeks of pregnancy (i.e., during major organogenesis), if the radiation dose is sufficient, fetal anomalies can be produced. *Skeletal and/or organ anomalies* can appear if irradiation occurs in the early part of this time period, and *neurologic anomalies* can be formed in the latter part; *mental retardation* and childhood *malignant diseases*, such as cancers or leukemia, and retarded growth/development also can result from irradiation during the first trimester. Fetal irradiation during the second and third trimesters is not likely to produce anomalies but rather, with sufficient dose, some type of childhood malignant disease. Fetal irradiation during the first 2 weeks of gestation can result in *embryonic resorption* or *spontaneous abortion*. It must be

emphasized, however, that the likelihood of producing fetal anomalies at doses below 20 rad is exceedingly small and that most general diagnostic examinations are likely to deliver fetal doses of less than 1 to 2 rad. *(Bushong, 8th ed., pp. 544–546)*

33. **(B)** The effects of a quantity of radiation delivered to a body depend on the amount of radiation received, the size of the irradiated area, and how the radiation is delivered in time. If the radiation is delivered in portions over a period of time, it is said to be *fractionated* and has a less harmful effect than if it were delivered all at once because cells have an opportunity to repair, and some recovery occurs between doses. *(Bushong, 8th ed., p. 496)*

34. **(D)** Artificial/human-made sources of radiation include radioactive fallout, industrial radiation, and medical and dental x-rays. About 90% of the general public's exposure to artificial radiation is from medical and dental x-rays. It is our professional obligation, therefore, to keep our patient's radiation dose to a minimum. *(Bushong, 8th ed., p. 6)*

35. **(A)** Nondividing, differentiated cells are specialized, mature cells that *do not undergo mitosis.* Having these qualities, they are rendered radioresistant, according to the theory proposed by Bergonié and Tribondeau. The adult nervous system is composed of nondividing, differentiated cells and thus is the most radioresistant system in the adult. Epithelial tissue and lymphocytes contain many precursor stem cells and hence are among the most radiosensitive cells in the body. *(Bushong, 8th ed., p. 492)*

36. **(A)** X-rays produced at the tungsten target make up a heterogeneous primary beam. Filtration serves to eliminate the softer, less penetrating photons, leaving an x-ray beam of higher average energy. Filtration is important in patient protection because unfiltered, low-energy photons that are not energetic enough to reach the IR stay in the body and contribute to total patient dose. *(Bushong, 8th ed., p. 157)*

37. **(B)** Lead aprons are secondary radiation barriers and *must* contain *at least 0.25 mm Pb* equivalent (according to CFR 20), usually in the form of lead-impregnated vinyl. Many radiology departments routinely use lead aprons containing 0.5 mm Pb (*the NCRP recommends 0.5 mm Pb equivalent minimum*). These aprons are heavier, but they attenuate a higher percentage of scattered radiation. *(Bushong, 8th ed., p. 560)*

38. **(B)** Different types of monitoring devices are available for the occupationally exposed. The film badge has *photographic film*; the pocket dosimeter contains an ionization chamber; TLDs use *lithium fluoride* crystals. *OSL dosimeters* are personnel radiation monitors that use *aluminum oxide* crystals. These crystals, once exposed to ionizing radiation and then subjected to a laser, give off luminescence proportional to the amount of radiation received. *(Bushong, 8th ed., p. 594)*

39. **(B)** Cells are frequently identified by their stage of development. *Immature* cells may be referred to as *undifferentiated* or *stem cells.* Immature cells are much more radiosensitive than mature cells. *(Bushong, 8th ed., pp. 591, 592)*

40. **(B)** *Scattering* occurs when there is partial transfer of the proton's energy to matter, as in the Compton effect. *Absorption* occurs when an x-ray photon interacts with matter and disappears, as in the photoelectric effect. The reduction in the intensity (quantity) of an x-ray beam as it passes through matter is termed *attenuation. Divergence* refers to a directional characteristic of the x-ray beam as it is emitted from the focal spot. *(Bushong, 8th ed., p. 241)*

41. **(B)** Patients occasionally will question the radiographer about the amount of radiation they are receiving during their examination. Most of these patients are merely curious because they have heard a recent news report about x-rays or have perhaps studied about x-rays in school recently. It is a good idea for radiographers to have some knowledge of average exposure doses for patients who desire this information. The curious patient can also

be referred to the medical physicist for more detailed information. The average high-kilovolt-age chest radiograph with grid delivers an ESE of about 20 mrad (0.020 rad). The same chest radiograph done without a grid at 80 kVp would deliver an ESE of about 12 mrad (0.012 rad). The average AP supine lumbar spine radiograph delivers an ESE of about 350 mrad (0.35 rad). The average AP supine abdomen radiograph delivers about 300 mrad; the average AP cervical spine radiograph delivers about 80 mrad. *(Dowd and Tilson, 2nd ed., p. 247)*

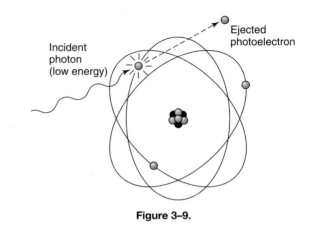

Figure 3–9.

42. **(D)** For radiation safety, the fluoroscopy exposure switch must be of the *"dead man"* type. When the foot is removed from the fluoro pedal, the "dead man" switch will terminate the exposure immediately. There must also be a fluoroscopy timer that will either sound or interrupt exposure after 5 minutes of fluoroscopy. *(Bushong, 8th ed., p. 570)*

43. **(C)** Radiation protection guidelines have established that primary radiation barriers must be 7 ft high. Primary radiation barriers are walls that the primary beam might be directed toward. They usually contain 1.5 mm of lead (¹⁄₁₆ in.), but this may vary depending on use factor, and so on. *(Bushong, 8th ed., pp. 571–572)*

44. **(C)** The occupational dose limit is valid for beta, x-, and gamma radiations. Because alpha radiation is so rapidly ionizing, traditional personnel monitors will not record alpha radiation. However, because alpha particles are capable of penetrating only a few centimeters of air, they are practically harmless as an external source. *(Bushong, 8th ed., p. 596)*

45. **(A)** Diagnostic x-ray photons interact with tissue in a number of ways, but most frequently they are involved in the *photoelectric effect* or in the production of *Compton scatter*. The photoelectric effect is shown in Figure 3–9; it occurs when a relatively *low-energy* x-ray photon *uses all its energy* to eject an *inner-shell electron*. That electron is ejected (photoelectron) from the innermost (K) shell, leaving a "hole" in the K shell and producing a positive ion. An

L-shell electron then drops down to fill the K vacancy and in so doing emits a *characteristic ray* whose energy is equal to the difference between the binding energies of the K and L shells. The photoelectric effect occurs with high-atomic-number absorbers such as bone and positive contrast media and is responsible for the production of contrast. Therefore, its occurrence is helpful for the production of the radiographic image, but it contributes significantly to the dose received by the patient (because it involves complete absorption of the incident photon). Scattered radiation, which produces a radiation hazard to the radiographer (as in fluoroscopy), is a product of the Compton scatter interaction occurring with higher energy x-ray photons. *(Selman, 9th ed., pp. 125–126)*

46. **(B)** During fluoroscopic procedures, as field of view (FOV) decreases, magnification of the output screen image increases, and contrast and resolution improve. The focal point on an image intensifier's 6-in. field/mode is further away from the output phosphor than the focal point on the normal mode; therefore, the output image is magnified. Because less minification takes place, the *image is not as bright. Exposure factors are increased automatically to compensate for the loss in brightness with smaller FOVs.* Focal spot size (FSS) is unrelated to patient dose. *(Fosbinder, p. 285)*

47. **(D)** Gonadal shielding should be used whenever appropriate and possible during radiographic and fluoroscopic examinations. *Flat*

contact shields are useful for simple recumbent (AP, PA) studies, but when the examination necessitates obtaining oblique, lateral, or erect projections, they become less efficient. *Shaped contact (contour)* shields are best because they enclose the male reproductive organs and remain in position in oblique, lateral, and erect positions. *Shadow* shields that attach to the tube head are particularly useful for surgical sterile fields. *(Sherer et al., 5th ed., pp. 177–181)*

48. **(C)** *Rad* is an acronym for *radiation absorbed dose*; it measures the energy deposited in any material. *Roentgen* is the unit of exposure; it measures the quantity of ionizations in air. *Rem* is an acronym for *radiation-equivalent man*; it includes the RBE specific to the tissue irradiated and, therefore, is a valid unit of measurement for the *dose* to biologic tissue. *(Bushong, 8th ed., p. 23)*

49. **(B)** When biologic material is irradiated, there are a number of modifying factors that determine what kind and how much response will occur in the material. One of these factors is LET, which expresses the *rate at which particulate or photon energy is transferred to the absorber.* Because different kinds of radiation have different degrees of penetration in different materials, it is also a useful way of expressing the quality of the radiation. *(Thompson et al., p. 419)*

50. **(C)** Electromagnetic radiations such as x-rays and gamma rays are considered low-LET radiations because they produce fewer ionizations than the highly ionizing particulate radiations such as alpha particles. *Alpha particles* are large and heavy (two protons and two neutrons), and although they possess a great deal of kinetic energy (approximately 5 MeV), their energy is lost rapidly through multiple ionizations (approximately 40,000 atoms/cm of air). As an *external* source, alpha particles are almost harmless because they ionize the air very quickly and never reach the individual. As *internal sources*, however, they ionize tissues and are potentially the most harmful. It may be stated that the alpha particle has one of the highest LETs of all ionizing radiations. *(Bushong, 8th ed., p. 496)*

51. **(D)** The various skin responses to irradiation include all four choices. The first noticeable response would be *erythema*, a reddening of the skin very much like sunburn. *Dry desquamation* could follow; it is a dry peeling of the skin. *Moist desquamation* is peeling with associated pus-like fluid. *Epilation* is hair loss; it can be temporary or permanent depending on sensitivity and dose. *(Bushong, 8th ed., p. 522)*

52. **(A)** Tissue is most sensitive to radiation when it is oxygenated *and least sensitive when it is devoid of oxygen. Anoxic* refers to tissue without oxygen; *hypoxic* refers to tissue with little oxygen. Anoxic and hypoxic tumors typically are avascular (with little or no blood supply) and, therefore, more radioresistant. *(Bushong, 8th ed., pp. 496–497)*

53. **(C)** The reduction in the intensity (quantity) of an x-ray beam as it passes through matter as a result of absorption and scatter is called *attenuation. Absorption* occurs when an x-ray photon interacts with matter and disappears, as in the *photoelectric effect. Scattering* occurs when there is partial transfer of energy to matter, as in the *Compton effect. (Bushong, 8th ed., pp. 185–186)*

54. **(C)** Radiation-induced malignancy, leukemia, and genetic effects are late effects (or stochastic effects) of radiation exposure. These can occur years after survival of an acute radiation dose or after exposure to low levels of radiation over a long period of time. Radiation workers need to be especially aware of the late effects of radiation because their exposure to radiation is usually low level over a long period of time. Occupational radiation protection guidelines, therefore, are based on late effects of radiation according to a linear, nonthreshold dose–response curve. *(Bushong, 8th ed., p. 499)*

55. **(C)** During the first trimester, specifically the second through eighth weeks of pregnancy (during major organogenesis), if the radiation dose is at least 20 rad, fetal anomalies can be produced. *Skeletal anomalies* usually appear if irradiation occurs in the early part of this time period, and *neurologic anomalies* are formed in

the latter part; mental retardation and childhood malignant diseases, such as cancers or leukemia, also can result from irradiation during the first trimester. Fetal irradiation during the second and third trimesters is not likely to produce anomalies but rather, with sufficient dose, some type of childhood malignant disease. Fetal irradiation during the first 2 weeks of gestation can result in *spontaneous abortion*. It must be emphasized that the likelihood of producing fetal anomalies at doses below 20 rad is exceedingly small and that most general diagnostic examinations are likely to deliver fetal doses of less than 1 to 2 rad. (*Bushong, 8th ed., p. 546*)

56. **(B)** *Late* or *long-term effects* of radiation can occur in tissues that have survived a previous irradiation months or years earlier. These late effects, such as carcinogenesis and genetic effects, are "all-or-nothing" effects—either the organism develops cancer or it does not. Most late effects *do not have a threshold dose;* that is, any dose, however small, can induce an effect. Increasing that dose will increase the *likelihood* of the occurrence but will not affect its severity; these effects are termed *stochastic. Nonstochastic effects* are those that will not occur below a particular threshold dose and that increase in severity as the dose increases. *Early* effects of radiation exposure are in response to relatively high radiation doses. These should never occur in diagnostic radiology; they occur only in response to doses much greater than those used in diagnostic radiology. One of the effects that may be noted in such a circumstance is the *hematologic effect*—reduced numbers of white blood cells, red blood cells, and platelets in the circulating blood. Immediate local tissue effects can include effects on the gonads (temporary infertility) and on the skin (epilation, erythema). Acute radiation lethality, or radiation death, occurs after an acute exposure and results in death in weeks or days. (*Bushong, 8th ed., pp. 517, 532*)

57. **(D)** In consideration of the potential risk, female patients of childbearing age should be questioned regarding their last menstrual period (LMP) and the possibility of their being pregnant. Facilities offering radiologic services should make inquiries of their female patients regarding LMP and advise them of the risk associated with radiation exposure during pregnancy and the advisability of *elective booking.* The *10-day rule* identifies the first 10 days following the onset of menses as the safest time to schedule elective procedures of the abdomen/pelvis. In addition to supporting the as low as reasonably achievable (ALARA) concept, many institutions also use a *patient questionnaire* as a guide for scheduling elective abdominal x-ray examinations on women of reproductive age. The patient completes a form that requests information concerning her LMP and the possibility of her being pregnant. In place of either or both of the preceding—or in addition to them— posters can be obtained or signs can be made that caution the patient to tell the radiologic technologist if she suspects that she might be pregnant. Most facilities will post these signs in waiting rooms, dressing rooms, and radiographic rooms. (*Sherer, Visconti, and Ritenour, p. 216*)

58. **(D)** According to Bergonié and Tribondeau, the most radiosensitive cells are undifferentiated, rapidly dividing cells, such as lymphocytes, intestinal crypt (of Lieberkühn) cells, and spermatogonia. Liver cells are among the types of cells that are somewhat differentiated and capable of mitosis. These characteristics render them somewhat radiosensitive. Muscle cells, as well as nerve cells and red blood cells, are highly differentiated and do not divide. Therefore, in order of *increasing* sensitivity (from least to greatest sensitivity), the cells are muscle, liver, and then intestinal crypt cells. (*Selman, 9th ed., pp. 374–375*)

59. **(D)** Our bodies contain a variety of tissues having a variety of *tissue densities*. These tissues densities afford differing degrees of resistance to the passage of x-ray photons. Tissues having *greater density absorb more* of the x-ray beam (recall the photoelectric effect). Soft tissues are fairly easily penetrated to varying degrees; that is, lung and adipose are easier to penetrate than muscle. *Bone* has much higher tissue mass density and,

therefore, absorbs more of the x-ray beam. *(Bushong, 8th ed., p. 183)*

60. **(B)** X-ray photons produced in the x-ray tube can radiate in directions other than the one desired. The *tube housing*, therefore, is constructed so that very little of this leakage radiation is permitted to escape. The regulation states that leakage radiation must not exceed 100 mR/h at 1 m while the tube is operated at maximum potential. *(Bushong, 8th ed., p. 130)*

61. **(D)** Focal spot size affects recorded detail and x-ray tube heat limits—it has no effect on patient dose. Low-ratio grids, although they require fewer milliampere-seconds than high-ratio grids, are not a means of patient protection. Long SIDs usually require the use of higher milliampere-seconds and so would not be an effective means of patient protection. The use of high-speed intensifying screens enables the use of lower milliampere-second values and, therefore, is an important consideration in limiting patient dose. Limiting the irradiated field size, through collimation or other beam restriction, is perhaps the most effective way of controlling patient exposure dose. *(Bushong, 8th ed., p. 12)*

62. **(D)** In fluoroscopy, the source of x-rays is 12 to 15 in. below the x-ray tabletop. Since the source to object distance (SOD) is so short, patient skin dose can be quite high. Consequently, the x-ray intensity at the tabletop is limited to keep patient dose (ESE) within safe limits. The radiation protection guidelines state that x-ray intensity at tabletop must not exceed *2.1 R/min/mA at 80 kVp*. In equipment without *high-level fluoroscopy* capability, the guideline can be expressed as *10 R/min* tabletop limit. In equipment with high-level fluoroscopy capability, the tabletop limit is *20 R/min*. *(Bushong, 8th ed., p. 570)*

63. **(A)** $^{130}_{56}$Ba and $^{138}_{56}$Ba are isotopes of the same element, barium (Ba), because they have the *same atomic number* but different mass numbers (numbers of neutrons). *Isobars* are atoms with the same mass number but different atomic numbers. *Isotones* have the *same number of neutrons* but different atomic numbers.

Isomers have the *same atomic number and mass number;* they are identical atoms existing at different energy states. *(Bushong, 8th ed., p. 49)*

64. **(D)** The x-ray photons produced at the tungsten target make up a heterogeneous beam, a spectrum of photon energies. This is accounted for by the fact that the incident electrons have differing energies. Also, the incident electrons travel through several layers of tungsten target material, lose energy with each interaction, and, therefore, produce increasingly weaker photons. During characteristic x-ray production, vacancies may be filled in the K, L, or M shells, which differ from each other in binding energies, and, therefore, photons with varying amounts of energy are emitted. *(Bushong, 8th ed., pp. 144–146)*

65. **(B)** Kilovoltage (kV) and the half-value layer (HVL) effect a change in both the quantity and the quality of the primary beam. *The principal qualitative factor of the primary beam is kilovoltage*, but an increase in kilovoltage will also increase the *number* of photons produced at the target. HVL, defined as the *amount of material necessary to decrease the intensity of the beam to one-half*, therefore changes both beam quality and beam quantity. Milliamperage is directly proportional to x-ray intensity (quantity) but is unrelated to the quality of the beam. *(Thompson et al., p. 405)*

66. **(A)** X-radiation used for diagnostic purposes is of relatively *low energy*. Kilovoltages of up to 150 kV are used, as compared with radiations having energies of up to several million volts. *Linear energy transfer* (LET) refers to the rate at which energy is transferred from ionizing radiation to soft tissue. Particulate radiations, such as alpha particles, have mass and charge and, therefore, lose energy rapidly as they penetrate only a few centimeters of air. X- and gamma radiations, having no mass or charge, are *low-LET* radiations. *(Bushong, 8th ed., p. 495)*

67. **(C)** Examples of *primary* barriers are the lead walls and doors of a radiographic room, that is, any surface that could be struck by the

useful beam. Primary protective barriers of typical installations generally consist of walls with $\frac{1}{16}$ *in.* (1.5 mm) of lead and 7 ft high. *Secondary radiation* is defined as leakage and/or scattered radiation. The x-ray tube housing protects from leakage radiation, as stated earlier. The patient is the source of most scattered radiation. *Secondary radiation barriers* include that portion of the walls *above* 7 ft in height; this area requires only $\frac{1}{32}$ *in.* of lead. The control booth is also a secondary barrier, toward which the primary beam must never be directed. *(Bushong, 8th ed., p. 572)*

68. **(D)** Selection of exposure factors has a significant impact on patient dose. Remember that milliampere-seconds (mAs) are used to regulate the *quantity* of radiation delivered to the patient and kilovolts peak (kVp) determines the *penetrability* of the x-ray beam. As kilovoltage is increased, more high-energy photons are produced, and the overall average energy of the beam is increased. An increase in milliampere-seconds increases the number of photons produced at the target, but milliampere-seconds are unrelated to photon energy. Generally speaking, then, in an effort to keep radiation dose to a minimum, it makes sense to use the lowest mAs setting and the highest kVp setting that will produce the desired radiographic results. An added benefit is that at high kilovolts peak and low milliampere-second values, the heat delivered to the x-ray tube is lower, and tube life is extended. In this example, (A) = 75 mAs, (B) = 37.5 mAs, (C) = 36 mAs, and (D) = 18 mAs. Decreasing the milliampere-seconds and increasing the kilovolts peak appropriately is the most effective combination for reducing patient dose. *(Bushong, 8th ed., pp. 162–163)*

69. **(B)** Because the primary x-ray beam has a poly-energetic (heterogeneous) nature, *the entrance or skin dose is significantly greater than the exit dose.* This principle may be employed in radiation protection by placing particularly radiosensitive organs away from the primary beam. To place the gonads further from the primary beam and reduce gonadal dose, abdominal radiography should be performed in the posteroanterior (PA) position whenever possible. Dose to the *lens* is decreased significantly when skull radiographs are performed in the PA position.

70. **(C)** According to the NCRP, the annual occupational *whole-body* dose-equivalent limit is 50 mSv (5 rem or 5,000 mrem). The annual occupational whole-body dose-equivalent limit for *students* under the age of 18 years is 1 mSv (100 mrem or 0.1 rem). The annual occupational dose-equivalent limit for the *lens of eye* is 150 mSv (15 rem). The annual occupational dose-equivalent limit for the *thyroid, skin,* and *extremities* is 500 mSv (50 rem). The total gestational dose-equivalent limit for *embryo/fetus* of a pregnant radiographer is 5 mSv (500 mrem), not to exceed 0.5 mSv in 1 month. *(Bushong, 8th ed., p. 557)*

71. **(C)** The first noticeable skin response to excessive irradiation would be *erythema*, a reddening of the skin very much like sunburn. *Dry desquamation*, a dry peeling of the skin, may follow. *Moist desquamation* is peeling with associated puslike fluid. *Epilation*, or hair loss, may be temporary or permanent depending on sensitivity and dose. *(Bushong, 8th ed., p. 521)*

72. **(B)** Figure 3–2 illustrates three dose–response curves. *Curve A* begins at zero, indicating that there is no safe dose, that is, *no threshold*. Even one x-ray photon theoretically can cause a response. It is a straight *(linear)* line, indicating that *response is proportional to dose*. That is, as dose increases, response increases. *Curve B* is another *linear* curve, but this one illustrates a situation in which a particular dose of radiation must be received before the response will occur. That is, there is a *threshold dose*, and this is a linear threshold curve. *Curve C* is another threshold curve, but this curve is nonlinear. It illustrates that once the minimum dose is received, a response occurs slowly initially and then increases sharply as exposure increases. *(Bushong, 8th ed., p. 499)*

73. **(B)** The patient is the most important radiation scatterer during both radiography and fluoroscopy. In general, at 1 m from the

patient, *the intensity is reduced by a factor of 1,000* to about 0.1% of the original intensity. Successive scatterings can reduce the intensity to unimportant levels. *(Bushong, 8th ed., p. 572)*

74. **(A)** As an x-ray source moves away from a detector, the x-ray intensity (quantity) decreases. Conversely, as the source of x-rays moves closer to the detector, the intensity increases. This is a predictable relationship that may be calculated using the inverse-square law, which states that the intensity (exposure rate) of radiation at a given distance from a point source is inversely proportional to the square of the distance. For example, if the distance from an x-ray source were doubled, the intensity of x-rays at the detector would be one-fourth its original value. This relationship is represented by the formula

$$\frac{I_1}{I_2} = \frac{D_2^2}{D_1^2}$$

(Bushong, 8th ed., pp. 68–70)

75. **(A)** Aluminum filters are used to *decrease* patient skin dose by absorbing the low-energy photons (therefore, *decreased* milliroentgen output) that *do not contribute to the image* but *do contribute to patient skin dose.* HVL is defined as that thickness of any absorber that will decrease the intensity of a particular beam to one-half its original value. As filtration of an x-ray beam is increased, the overall *average energy of the resulting beam is greater* (because the low-energy photons have been removed) and, therefore, the HVL thickness required would be greater. *(Bushong, 8th ed., p. 165)*

76. **(A)** X-ray photons emerging from the focal spot comprise a *heterogeneous* primary beam. There are many low-energy x-rays that, if not removed, would contribute significantly to patient *skin dose.* These low-energy photons are too weak to penetrate the patient and expose the IR; they simply penetrate a small thickness of tissue before being absorbed. Filters, usually made of aluminum, are used in radiography to reduce patient dose by removing this low-energy radiation (i.e., *decreased* beam intensity) and resulting in an x-ray

beam of *higher average energy. Total filtration* is composed of *inherent filtration* plus *added filtration.* X-ray photons scatter only after they have interacted with the absorber/patient; scatter is unrelated to filtration. *(Bushong, 8th ed., p. 165)*

77. **(B)** *Use factor* describes the percentage of time that the primary beam is directed toward a particular wall. The use factor is one of the factors considered in determining protective barrier thickness. Another is *workload,* which is determined by the number of x-ray exposures made per week. *Occupancy factor* is a reflection of who occupies particular areas (radiation workers or nonradiation workers) and is another factor used in determining radiation barrier thickness. *(Bushong, 8th ed., p. 573)*

78. **(D)** *Ionization* is the fundamental principle of operation of both the film badge and the pocket dosimeter. In the film badge, the film's silver halide emulsion is ionized by x-ray photons. The pocket dosimeter contains an ionization chamber, and the number of ionizations taking place may be equated to the exposure dose. TLDs contain lithium fluoride crystals that undergo characteristic changes on irradiation. When the crystals are subsequently *heated,* they emit a quantity of visible (thermo) *luminescence/light* in proportion to the amount of radiation absorbed. OSL dosimeters contain aluminum oxide crystals that also undergo characteristic changes on irradiation. When the Al_2O_3 crystals are *stimulated by a laser,* they emit (optically stimulated) *luminescence/light* in proportion to the amount of radiation absorbed. *(Bushong, 8th ed., p. 593)*

79. **(B)** As the size of the irradiated field decreases, scattered radiation production and patient hazard decrease. If the amount of scattered radiation decreases, then radiographic contrast is higher (shorter scale). *(Selman, 9th ed., p. 247)*

80. **(C)** Radiation effects that appear days or weeks following exposure (early effects) are in response to high radiation doses; this is called *acute radiation syndrome.* These effects should

never occur in diagnostic radiology; they occur only in response to much greater doses. Sufficient exposure of the *hematologic* system to ionizing radiation can result in nausea, vomiting, diarrhea, decreased blood cells count, and infection. Very large exposure of the *GI system* (1,000–5,000 rad) causes severe damage to the (stem) cells lining the GI tract. This can result in nausea, vomiting, diarrhea, blood changes, and hemorrhage. Exposure greater than 5,000 rad is required to affect the normally resilient CNS. (*Bushong, 8th ed., pp. 517–518*)

81. **(A)** Occupationally exposed individuals generally receive small amount of low-energy radiation over a long period of time. These individuals, therefore, are concerned with the potential *long-term* effects of radiation, such as *carcinogenesis* (including *leukemia*) and *cataractogenesis*. However, if a large amount of radiation is delivered to the whole body at one time, the short-term early somatic effects must be considered. If the whole body receives 600 rad at one time, *acute radiation syndrome* is likely to occur. Early signs of acute radiation syndrome include *nausea, vomiting, diarrhea, fatigue,* and *leukopenia* (decreased white blood cells count); these occur in the first (*prodromal*) stage of acute radiation syndrome. (*Bushong, 8th ed., p. 524*)

82. **(D)** An approximate ESE can be determined using the illustrated nomogram. First, mark 2.5 mm Al on the *x* (horizontal) axis. Next, mark where a line drawn up from that point intersects the 70-kVp line. Draw a line straight across to the *y* (vertical) axis; this should approximately reach the 4.8 mR/mAs point. Because 60 mAs was used for the exposure, the approximate ESE is 288 mR (60 × 4.8). (*Bushong, 8th ed., p. 587*)

83. **(C)** *Roentgen* is the unit of exposure; it measures the quantity of ionizations in air. *Rad* is an acronym for *radiation absorbed dose*; it measures the energy deposited in any material. *Rem* is an acronym for *radiation-equivalent man*; it includes the RBE specific to the tissue irradiated and, therefore, is a valid unit of measurement for the *dose to biologic material*. (*Bushong, 8th ed., pp. 24–25*)

84. **(D)** Irradiation during pregnancy, especially in early pregnancy, is avoided because the fetus is particularly radiosensitive during the first trimester. Especially high-risk examinations include pelvis, hip, femur, lumbar spine, cystograms and urograms, upper GI series, and barium enema (BE) examinations. During the 2nd through 10th weeks of pregnancy (i.e., during major organogenesis), fetal anomalies can be produced. *Skeletal and/or organ anomalies* can appear if irradiation occurs early on, and *neurologic* anomalies can be formed in the latter part; *mental retardation* and *childhood malignant diseases* can also result from irradiation during the first trimester. Fetal irradiation during the second and third trimesters, with sufficient dose, can cause some type of childhood malignant disease. Fetal irradiation during the first 2 weeks of gestation most likely will result in *embryonic resorption* or *spontaneous abortion*. It must be emphasized that the likelihood of producing fetal anomalies at doses below 20 rad is exceedingly small and that most general diagnostic examinations are likely to deliver fetal doses of less than 1 to 2 rad. (*Bushong, 8th ed., pp. 544–546*)

85. **(C)** All *fluoroscopic* equipment has protective devices and protocols to protect the patient and user. Fluoroscopic equipment must provide at least 12 in. (30 cm) and preferably 15 in. (38 cm) between the x-ray source (focal spot) and the x-ray tabletop (patient), according to NCRP Report No. 102. The tabletop intensity of the fluoroscopic beam must not exceed 10 R/min or 2.1 R/min/mA. With under-table fluoroscopic tubes, a *Bucky slot closer/cover* having at least the equivalent of 0.25 mm Pb must be available to attenuate scattered radiation coming from the patient, *posing a radiation hazard to the fluoroscopist and radiographer*. Fluoroscopic milliamperes must not exceed 5 mA. Because the image intensifier functions as a primary barrier, it must have a lead equivalent of at least 2.0 mm. A cumulative timing device must be available to signal the fluoroscopist when a maximum of 5 minutes of fluoroscopy time has elapsed. Because occupational exposure to scattered radiation is of considerable importance in fluoroscopy, a protective curtain/drape of at least 0.25 mm Pb equivalent

must be placed between the patient and fluoroscopist. *(Bushong, 8th ed., p. 570)*

86. **(D)** The pocket dosimeter, or *pocket ionization chamber*, resembles a penlight. Within the dosimeter is a thimble ionization chamber. In the presence of ionizing radiation, a particular quantity of air will be ionized and cause the fiber indicator to register radiation quantity in milliroentgen (mR). The self-reading type may be "read" by holding the dosimeter up to the light and, looking through the eyepiece, observing the fiber indicator, which indicates a quantity of 0 to 200 mR. Although it provides an immediate reading while other personnel monitors require "processing," the disadvantage of the pocket dosimeter is that it does not provide a permanent legal record of exposure. *(Adler and Carlton, 4th ed., p. 124)*

87. **(B)** Kilovoltage (kV) and the HVL effect a change in both the quantity and the quality of the primary beam. *The principal qualitative factor of the primary beam is kilovoltage,* but an increase in kilovoltage will also increase the *number* of photons produced at the target. HVL, defined as *the amount of material necessary to decrease the intensity of the beam to one-half,* therefore changes both beam quality and beam quantity. Milliamperage is directly proportional to x-ray intensity (i.e., quantity/dose rate) but is unrelated to the quality of the beam. *(Bushong, 8th ed., p. 165)*

88. **(B)** Gonadal shielding should be used whenever appropriate and possible during radiographic and fluoroscopic examinations. *Flat contact shields* are useful for simple recumbent studies, but when the examination necessitates obtaining oblique, lateral, or erect projections, flat contact shields are easily displaced and become less efficient. *Shaped contact (contour) shields* are best because they enclose the male reproductive organs and remain in position for oblique, lateral, and erect projections. *Shadow shields* that attach to the tube head are particularly useful for surgical sterile fields. *(Bushong, 8th ed., pp. 598–599)*

89. **(B)** *Isotopes* are atoms of the same element (the same atomic number or number of protons)

but a different mass number. They differ, therefore, in their number of neutrons. Atoms having the same mass number but different atomic number are *isobars.* Atoms having the same neutron number but different atomic number are *isotones.* Atoms with the same atomic number and mass number are *isomers.* *(Bushong, 8th ed., p. 47)*

90. **(D)** The patient is the most important radiation scatterer during both radiography and fluoroscopy. In general, at 1 m from the patient, *the intensity is reduced by a factor of 1,000* to about 0.1% of the original intensity. Successive scatterings can reduce the intensity to unimportant levels. Calculate that 0.1% of 25 mrad is 0.025 mrad. *(Bushong, 8th ed., p. 572)*

91. **(C)** The likelihood of radiation effects to occupationally exposed individuals whose dose is kept below the recommended limits is very remote. Exposure to ionizing radiation always carries some risk, but studies have indicated that the risk is a very small one if established guidelines are followed. Potential hazards must be understood and proper precautions taken. *(Bushong, 8th ed., p. 555)*

92. **(B)** The amount of scattered radiation produced depends first on the kilovoltage (beam quality) selected; *the higher the kilovolts peak, the more scattered radiation is produced.* The size of the irradiated field also has a great deal to do with the amount of scattered radiation produced; *the larger the field size,* the greater is the amount of scattered radiation. Thickness and condition of tissue also are important considerations; *the thicker and/or more dense the tissue,* the more scatter is produced. If the condition of the tissue is such that *pathology* makes it more difficult to penetrate, more scattered radiation will be produced. Grid ratio has no effect on the amount of scattered radiation *produced* but does significantly impact the amount of scattered radiation *reaching the IR. (Thompson et al., pp. 280, 282)*

93. **(C)** Lead and distance are the two most important ways to protect from radiation exposure. Fluoroscopy can be particularly hazardous because the *source-to-skin distance*

(SSD) is so much shorter than in overhead radiography. Therefore, it has been established that *fixed* (stationary) *and mobile* fluoroscopic equipment must provide at least 12 in. (30 cm) of SSD for protection of the patient. *(Bushong, 8th ed., p. 569)*

94. **(A)** Automatic exposure control (AEC) devices are used in today's equipment and serve to produce consistent and comparable radiographic results. In one type of AEC, there is an *ionization chamber* just beneath the tabletop above the cassette. The part to be examined is centered on it (the sensor) and radiographed. When a predetermined quantity of ionization has occurred (equal to the correct density), the exposure terminates automatically. In the other type of AEC, the *phototimer/photomultiplier*, a small fluorescent screen is positioned beneath the cassette. When remnant radiation emerging from the patient exposes the IR and exits the cassette, the fluorescent screen emits light. Once a predetermined amount of fluorescent light is "seen" by the photocell sensor, the exposure is terminated. A *scintillation camera* is used in nuclear medicine. A *photocathode* is an integral part of the image intensification system. *(Bushong, 8th ed., p. 116)*

95. **(C)** Bergonié and Tribondeau were French scientists who, in 1906, theorized what has now become verified law. Cells are more radiosensitive if they are *immature* (undifferentiated or stem) cells, if they are *highly mitotic* (having a high rate of proliferation), and if the irradiated tissue is young. Cells and tissues that are still undergoing development are more radiosensitive than fully developed tissues. *(Bushong, 8th ed., p. 495)*

96. **(B)** It is our ethical responsibility to minimize radiation exposure to ourselves and our patients, particularly during early pregnancy. One way to do this is to inquire about the *possibility of* our female patients *being pregnant* or for the *date of their last menstrual* period (to determine the possibility of irradiating a newly fertilized ovum). The safest time for a woman of childbearing age to have elective radiographic examinations is during the first 10 days following the onset of menstruation. *(Thompson et al., p. 487)*

97. **(A)** Figure 3–4 illustrates three dose–response curves. *Curve A* begins at zero, indicating that there is no safe dose, that is, *no threshold*. Even one x-ray photon theoretically can cause a response. It is a straight (*linear*) line, indicating that *response is proportional to dose;* as dose increases, response increases. *Radiation-induced cancer, leukemia,* and *genetic effects* follow a linear nonthreshold dose–response relationship. *Curve B* is another linear curve (*response is proportional to dose*), but this one illustrates that a particular dose of radiation must be received before a response will occur. That is, there is a *threshold dose;* this is called a *linear threshold curve. Curve C* is another threshold curve, but this curve is nonlinear. It illustrates that once the minimum dose is received, a response occurs slowly initially and then increases sharply as exposure increases. This threshold, nonlinear (sigmoid) dose–response curve, illustrates the effect to skin from exposure to high levels of ionizing radiation. *(Bushong, 8th ed., p. 499)*

98. **(A)** LET expresses the rate at which photon or particulate energy is transferred to (absorbed by) biologic material (through ionization processes); it depends on the type of radiation and the characteristics of the absorber. RBE describes the degree of response or amount of biologic change one can expect of the irradiated material. *As the amount of transferred energy (LET) increases* (from interactions occurring between radiation and biologic material), *the amount of biologic effect/damage will also increase. (Thompson et al., pp. 419–420)*

99. **(A)** *The shorter the SID, the greater is the skin dose.* That is why there are specific SSD restrictions in fluoroscopy. High kilovolt peak produces more penetrating photons, thereby decreasing skin dose. Filtration is used to remove the low-energy photons from the primary beam, which contribute to skin dose. *(Thompson et al., pp. 293–294)*

100. **(A)** Radiation effects that appear days or weeks following exposure (early effects) are

in response to relatively high radiation doses. These should never occur in diagnostic radiology today; they occur only in response to doses much greater than those used in diagnostic radiology. One of the effects that may be noted in such a circumstance is the hematologic effect—reduced numbers of white blood cells, red blood cells, and platelets in the circulating blood. Immediate local tissue effects can include effects on the gonads (i.e., temporary infertility) and on the skin (e.g., epilation and erythema). Acute radiation lethality, or radiation death, occurs after an acute exposure and results in death in weeks or days. Radiation-induced malignancy, leukemia, and genetic effects are late effects (or stochastic effects) of radiation exposure. These can occur years after survival of an acute radiation dose or after exposure to low levels of radiation over a long period of time. Radiation workers need to be especially aware of the late effects of radiation because their exposure to radiation is usually low level over a long period of time. Occupational radiation protection guidelines, therefore, are based on late effects of radiation according to a linear, nonthreshold dose–response curve. *(Bushong, 8th ed., p. 537)*

101. **(C)** LET increases with the *ionizing* potential of the radiation; for example, alpha particles are more ionizing than x-radiation, and, therefore, they have a higher LET. As ionizations and LET increase, there is greater possibility of an effect on living tissue; therefore, the RBE increases. The RBE [sometimes called *quality factor* (QF)] of diagnostic x-rays is 1, the RBE of fast neutrons is 10, the RBE of 5-MeV alpha particles is 20, and the RBE of 10-MeV protons is 5.0. *(Bushong, 8th ed., p. 496)*

102. **(B)** A quick survey of the distractors reveals that option (A) will increase exposure dose and thus is eliminated as a possible correct answer. Options (B), (C), and (D) will serve to reduce radiation exposure because in each case either time is decreased or distance is increased. It remains to be seen, then, which is the more effective. Using the inverse-square law of radiation, at a distance of 8 ft, the individual will receive *12.5 mR in 2 minutes*

(double distance from source = one-fourth the original intensity). At 5 ft, the individual will receive 16 mR in 1 minute:

$$\frac{50\ (I_1)}{x\ (I_2)} = \frac{25\ D_2^2}{16\ (D_1^2)}$$
$$25x = 800$$

Thus, $x = 32$ mR in 2 minutes and, therefore, 16 mR in 1 minute at 5 ft. At 6 ft, the individual will receive 22.2 mR in 2 minutes:

$$\frac{50\ (I_1)}{x\ (I_2)} = \frac{36\ D_2^2}{16\ (D_1^2)}$$
$$36x = 800$$

Thus, $x = 22.22$ mR in 2 minutes at 6 ft. Therefore, the most effective option is (B), *12.5 mR in 2 minutes at 8 ft. (Bushong, 8th ed., p. 66)*

103. **(C)** The most radiosensitive portion of the GI tract is the small bowel. Projecting from the lining of the small bowel are villi, from the intestinal crypt cells of Lieberkühn, which are responsible for the absorption of nutrients into the bloodstream. Because the cells of the villi are continually being cast off, new cells must continually arise from the crypts of Lieberkühn. Being highly mitotic undifferentiated stem cells, they are very radiosensitive. Thus, the small bowel is the most radiosensitive portion of the GI tract. *(Dowd and Tilson, 2nd ed., p. 155)*

104. **(D)** Fractionation and protraction influence the effect of radiation on tissue. Larger quantities, of course, increase tissue effect. The energy (i.e., quality and penetration) of the radiation determines whether the effects will be superficial (erythema) or deep (organ dose). Certain tissues (such as blood-forming organs and the gonads) are more radiosensitive than others (such as muscle and nerve). If the dose is delivered in *portions (fractionation)* and/or delivered over a *length of time (protraction)*, the *less the tissue effects*. *(Bushong, 8th ed., p. 496)*

105. **(A)** In the *photoelectric effect*, a relatively low-energy incident photon uses all its energy to

eject an inner-shell electron, leaving a vacancy. An electron from the next shell will drop to fill the vacancy, and *a characteristic ray is given up* in the transition. This type of interaction is more harmful to the patient because all the photon energy is transferred to tissue. *(Bushong, 8th ed., pp. 176–178)*

106. **(A)** Filters are used in radiography to remove soft (low-energy) radiation that contributes only to patient dose. The filters usually are made of aluminum. Equipment operating above 70 kVp must have *total filtration* of 2.5 mm Al equivalent (inherent + added). *(Bushong, 8th ed., p. 11)*

107. **(C)** The use of a *grid* requires an increase in milliampere-seconds and, therefore, patient dose; the higher the grid ratio, the greater is the increase in milliampere-seconds required. *Collimation* (beam restriction) restricts the amount of tissue being irradiated and, therefore, reduces patient dose. *High kilovoltage* reduces the amount of radiation absorbed by the patient's tissues (recall the photoelectric effect), and low milliampere-seconds reduces the quantity of radiation delivered to the patient. The higher the speed of the *imaging system* (e.g., film–screen combination), the less are the required milliampere-seconds. *(Bushong, 8th ed., pp. 11, 248)*

108. **(D)** Bremsstrahlung (or Brems) radiation is one of the two kinds of x-rays produced at the tungsten target of the x-ray tube during interaction between high-speed electrons coming from the filament and the anodes' tungsten atoms. The incident high-speed electron, passing through a tungsten atom, is attracted by the positively charged nucleus and, therefore, is *deflected from its course, with a resulting loss of energy.* This energy is given up in the form of an x-ray photon. *(Bushong, 8th ed., pp. 151–152)*

109. **(B)** Aluminum filters are used to decrease patient skin dose by absorbing the low-energy photons (therefore, *decreased* milliroentgen output) that *do not contribute to the image* but *do contribute to patient skin dose.* HVL is defined as that thickness of any absorber that will decrease the intensity of a particular beam to one-half its original value. As filtration of an x-ray beam is increased, the overall *average energy of the resulting beam is greater* (because the low-energy photons have been removed)— and, therefore, the HVL thickness required would be greater. *(Bushong, 8th ed., p. 165)*

110. **(A)** The *roentgen* measures ionization in air and is referred to as the *unit of exposure. Rad* is an acronym for radiation *a*bsorbed *d*ose, and *rem* is an acronym for radiation-equivalent *m*an. RBE is used to determine biologic damage in living tissue. *(Thompson et al., p. 456)*

111. **(B)** The filters (usually aluminum and copper) serve to help measure radiation quality (i.e., energy). Only the most energetic radiation will penetrate the copper; radiation of lower levels of energy will penetrate the aluminum, and the lowest energy radiation will pass readily through the unfiltered area. Thus, radiation of different energy levels can be recorded, measured, and reported. *(Bushong, 8th ed., p. 593)*

112. **(B)** An HVL may be defined as the amount and thickness of absorber necessary to reduce the radiation intensity to half its original value. Thus, the first HVL would reduce the intensity to 50% of its original value, the second to 25%, the third to 12.5%, and the fourth to 6.25% of its original value. *(Bushong, 8th ed., p. 54)*

113. **(D)** All the factors listed influence the effect of radiation on tissue. Larger *quantities,* of course, increase radiation's effect on tissue. The *energy* (i.e., quality and penetration) of the radiation determines whether the effects will be superficial (erythema) or deep (organ dose). *Certain tissues* (such as blood-forming organs and the gonads) are more radiosensitive than others (such as muscle and nerve). The *length of time* over which the exposure is spread (*fractionation*) is important; the longer the period of time, the less are the tissue effects. *(Bushong, 8th ed., pp. 496–497)*

114. **(B)** Radiographic and fluoroscopic equipment is designed to help decrease the exposure

dose to patient and operator. One of the design features is the exposure cord. Exposure cords on *fixed* equipment must be short enough to prevent the exposure from being made outside the control booth. Exposure cords on *mobile* equipment must be long enough to permit the operator to stand at least 6 ft from the x-ray tube. *(Bushong, 8th ed., p. 569)*

115. **(B)** Protective barriers are classified as either primary or secondary. Primary barriers protect from the useful, or primary, x-ray beam and consist of a certain thickness of lead. They are located anywhere that the primary beam can possibly be directed, for example, the walls of the x-ray room. The walls of the x-ray room usually require a 1/16-in. (1.5-mm) thickness of lead and should be 7 ft high. Secondary barriers protect from secondary (scattered and leakage) radiation. Secondary barriers are control booths, lead aprons, gloves, and the wall of the x-ray room above 7 ft. Secondary barriers require much less lead than primary barriers. *(Bushong, 8th ed., p. 571)*

116. **(B)** Whole-body dose is calculated to include all the especially radiosensitive organs. The gonads and the blood-forming organs are particularly radiosensitive. Some body parts, such as the skin and extremities, have a higher annual dose limit. *(Bushong, 8th ed., p. 555)*

117. **(A)** Exposure dose to patients can be expressed as *entrance skin exposure* (ESE), sometimes referred to as *skin entrance exposure* (SEE). Exposure can also be expressed in terms of *organ dose*. Organ doses to the gonads, bone marrow, breast, thyroid, lens, and lung can be determined. Patient position and beam restriction often make a significant difference in patient dose. Examinations performed PA, rather than AP, often decrease exposure to sensitive organs. This is so because the lower energy x-ray photons will be absorbed by the anatomic structures closer to the x-ray source, and the higher energy photons will penetrate and exit the part (penetrating the sensitive part rather than being absorbed by it). PA abdomen radiographs

deliver less quantity dose to the reproductive organs than do AP abdomen radiographs. An AP skull projection (80 kVp) delivers about 90 mrad to the thyroid, whereas a PA skull (80 kVp) radiograph delivers 8 mrad; the PA esophagus (110 kVp) radiograph delivers 9 mrad, and the PA chest (120 kVp) radiograph delivers about 1 mrad. *(Bontrager and Lampignano, 6th ed., p. 67)*

118. **(C)** Ionization is the fundamental principle of operation of both the film badge and the pocket dosimeter. In the film badge, the film's silver halide emulsion is ionized by x-ray photons. The pocket dosimeter contains an ionization chamber, and the number of ionizations taking place may be equated to exposure dose; it is accurate, but it is used only to detect larger amounts of radiation exposure. The TLD can measure exposures as low as 5 mrem, whereas film badges will measure a minimum exposure only as low as 10 mrem. TLDs contain lithium fluoride crystals that undergo characteristic changes on irradiation. When the crystals are subsequently heated, they emit a quantity of visible (thermo) luminescence/light in proportion to the amount of radiation absorbed. The relatively new OSL dosimeters contain aluminum oxide crystals that also undergo characteristic changes on irradiation. When the Al_2O_3 crystals are stimulated by a laser, they emit (optically stimulated) luminescence/light in proportion to the amount of radiation absorbed. OSL dosimeters can measure exposures as low as 1 mrem. *(Thompson et al., p. 461)*

119. **(D)** Irradiation damage is a result of either the effects of irradiation on water (radiolysis) or its effects on macromolecules. Effects on macromolecules include main-chain scission, cross-linking, and point lesions. *Main-chain scission* breaks the DNA molecule into two or more pieces. *Cross-linking* is incorrect joining of broken DNA fragments. A *point lesion* is the disruption of a single chemical bond as a result of irradiation. Because 80% of the body is made up of water, radiolysis of water is the predominant radiation interaction in the body. *(Bushong, 8th ed., p. 503)*

120. **(C)** The greatest effect–response from irradiation is brought about by a *large dose of radiation to the whole body delivered all at one time.* Whole-body radiation can depress many body functions. With a fractionated dose, the effects would be less severe because the body would have an opportunity to repair between doses. *(Bushong, 8th ed., p. 464)*

121. **(B)** Lead aprons are worn by occupationally exposed individuals during fluoroscopic procedures. Lead aprons are available with various lead equivalents; 0.25, 0.5, and 1.0 mm of lead are the most common. The 1.0-mm lead equivalent apron will provide close to 100% protection at most kilovoltage levels, but it is rarely used because it weighs anywhere from 12 to 24 lb. A 0.25-mm lead-equivalent apron will attenuate about 97% of a 50-kVp x-ray beam, 66% of a 75-kVp beam, and 51% of a 100-kVp beam. A 0.5-mm apron will attenuate about 99% of a 50-kVp beam, 88% of a 75-kVp beam, and 75% of a 100-kVp beam. *(Thompson et al., p. 457)*

122. **(C)** Different types of monitoring devices are available for the occupationally exposed, and anyone who might receive more than *one-tenth the annual dose limit* must be monitored. Ionization is the fundamental principle of operation of both the film badge and the pocket dosimeter. In the film badge, the film's silver halide emulsion is ionized by x-ray photons. The pocket dosimeter contains an ionization chamber (containing air), and the number of ions formed (of either sign) is equated to exposure dose. TLDs are radiation monitors that use lithium fluoride crystals. Once exposed to ionizing radiation and then heated, these crystals give off light proportional to the amount of radiation received. OSL dosimeters are radiation monitors that use aluminum oxide crystals. These crystals, once exposed to ionizing radiation and then subjected to a laser, give off luminescence proportional to the amount of radiation received. *(Bushong, 8th ed., p. 593)*

123. **(B)** The principal interactions that occur between x-ray photons and body tissues in the diagnostic x-ray range, the *photoelectric effect* and *Compton scatter*, are ionization processes producing photoelectrons and recoil electrons that traverse tissue and subsequently ionize molecules. In the *illustrated Compton* scatter, a fairly *high*-energy x-ray photon ejects an *outer-shell* electron. Although the x-ray photon is deflected with reduced energy (modified scatter), it retains most of its original energy and exits the body as an energetic scattered photon. Because the scattered photon exits the body, it does not pose a radiation hazard to the patient. It can, however, contribute to *image fog* and pose a *radiation hazard to personnel* (as in fluoroscopic procedures). In the photoelectric effect, a *low-* energy x-ray photon uses all its energy to eject an *inner-shell* electron, leaving an orbital vacancy. An electron from the shell above fills the vacancy and in so doing gives up energy in the form of a characteristic ray. The photoelectric effect is more likely to occur in absorbers having high atomic number and contributes significantly to patient dose because all the photon energy is absorbed by the patient. Coherent (unmodified) scatter does not involve ionization. *(Bushong, 8th ed., p. 174)*

124. **(D)** Occupationally exposed individuals are concerned principally with *late* (i.e., *long-term* or *delayed*) effects of ionizing radiation such as radiation-induced *genetic effects, leukemia,* and *cancers* (e.g., bone, lung, thyroid, and breast), as well as *local effects,* such as skin erythema, infertility, and cataracts—these can occur many years following initial exposure to low levels of ionizing radiation. The long-term/delayed effects usually are *chronic,* and many are represented by the linear, non-threshold dose–response curve. *(Bushong, 8th ed., p. 484)*

125. **(B)** Bergonié and Tribondeau theorized in 1906 that all precursor cells are particularly radiosensitive (e.g., stem cells found in bone marrow). There are several types of stem cells in bone marrow, and the different types differ in degree of radiosensitivity. Of these, red blood cell precursors, or erythroblasts, are the most radiosensitive. White blood cell precursors, or myelocytes, follow. Platelet precursor cells, or megakaryocytes, are the least radiosensitive. Myocytes are mature muscle cells that are fairly radioresistant. *(Bushong, 8th ed., p. 495)*

126. **(D)** The pregnant radiographer *should declare her pregnancy* to her supervisor; at that time, her radiation exposure history can be reviewed and appropriate assignments made. Special arrangements are required for occupational monitoring of the pregnant radiographer. The pregnant radiographer will wear two dosimeters—one in its usual place at the collar and the other, a baby/fetal dosimeter, worn over the abdomen and *under* the lead apron during fluoroscopy. The baby/fetal dosimeter must be identified as such and always must be worn in the same place. Care must be taken not to mix the positions of the two dosimeters. The dosimeters are read monthly as usual. *(Bushong, 8th ed., p. 560)*

127. **(D)** *Chromosome aberration, cell death,* and *malignant disease* are major effects of DNA irradiation, often as a result of abnormal metabolic activity. If the damage happens to the DNA of a germ cell, the radiation response may not occur until one or more generations later. *(Bushong, 8th ed., pp. 404–405)*

128. **(A)** In the *photoelectric effect,* a relatively low-energy photon uses all its energy to eject an inner-shell electron, leaving a vacancy. An electron from the shell above drops down to fill the vacancy and in so doing emits a characteristic ray. This type of interaction is most harmful to the patient because *all the photon energy is transferred to tissue.* In *Compton scatter,* a high-energy incident photon uses some of its energy to eject an outer-shell electron. In so doing, the incident photon is deflected with reduced energy but usually retains most of its energy and exits the body as an energetic scattered ray. The scattered radiation will either contribute to image fog or pose a radiation hazard to personnel depending on its direction of exit. In *classic scatter,* a low-energy photon interacts with an atom but causes no ionization; the incident photon disappears in the atom and then reappears immediately and is released as a photon of identical energy but with changed direction. *Thompson scatter* is another name for classic scatter. *(Bushong, 8th ed., p. 176)*

129. **(C)** Figure 3–6 shows a linear threshold dose–response curve. Its linear aspect indicates that the response/effect is related directly to the dose received; that is, as the dose increases, the response increases. The fact that this is a threshold curve indicates that a particular dose is required before any response/effect will occur. *(Bushong, 8th ed., p. 498)*

130. **(C)** Early somatic effects are manifested within minutes, hours, days, or weeks of irradiation and occur only following a very large dose of ionizing radiation. It must be emphasized that doses received from diagnostic radiologic procedures are not sufficient to produce these early effects. An exceedingly *high dose of radiation delivered to the whole body in a short period of time* is required to produce early somatic effects. These whole-body responses are grouped into three categories—reflecting the system(s) affected and the resulting symptoms: *hematologic, gastrointestinal,* and *central nervous system.* *(Bushong, 8th ed., p. 484)*

131. **(A)** Characteristic radiation is one of two kinds of x-rays produced at the tungsten target of the x-ray tube. The incident, or incoming, high-speed electron ejects a K-shell tungsten electron. This leaves a hole in the K shell, and an L-shell electron drops down to fill the K vacancy. Because L electrons are at a higher energy level than K-shell electrons, the L-shell electron gives up the difference in binding energy in the form of a photon, a *characteristic x-ray* (characteristic of the K shell). *(Selman, 9th ed., p. 115)*

132. **(A)** The genetically significant dose (GSD) illustrates that large exposures to a few people are cause for little concern when diluted by the total population. On the other hand, we all share the burden of that radiation received by the total population, especially as the use of medical radiation increases, so each individual's share of the total exposure increases. *(Selman, 9th ed., pp. 386–387)*

133. **(A)** The relationship between x-ray intensity and distance from the source is expressed by the *inverse-square law of radiation*. The formula is

$$\frac{I_1}{I_2} = \frac{D_2^2}{D_1^2}$$

Substituting known values:

$$\frac{50}{x} = \frac{25}{9}$$
$$25x = 450$$

Thus, $x = 18$ mR/h (60 minutes) and, therefore, 6 mR in 20 minutes. Distance has a profound effect on dose received and, therefore, is one of the cardinal rules of radiation protection. *As distance from the source increases, dose received decreases.* (Bushong, 8th ed., pp. 68–70)

134. **(A)** Every radiographic examination involves an ESE, which can be determined fairly easily. It also involves a gonadal dose and a marrow dose, which, if needed, can be calculated by the radiation physicist. If the ESE of a particular examination were calculated to determine the *equivalent whole-body dose*, this would be termed the *effective dose*. For example, the ESE of a PA chest radiograph is approximately 70 mrem, whereas the effective dose is 10 mrem. The effective (whole body) dose is much less because much of the body is not included in the primary beam. (Fosbinder and Kelsey, p. 390)

135. **(C)** *Somatic effects* are those induced in the irradiated body. *Genetic effects* of ionizing radiation are those that may not appear for many years (generations) following exposure. Formation of cataracts or cancer (such as leukemia) and embryologic damage are all possible *long-term somatic effects* of radiation exposure. A fourth is life-span shortening. Blood changes are generally *early* effects of exposure to large quantities of ionizing radiation. (Bushong, 9th ed., pp. 551–558)

136. **(B)** Occupationally exposed individuals are required to use devices to record and document the radiation they receive over a given period of time, traditionally 1 month. The most commonly used personal dosimeters are the OSL dosimeter, the TLD, and the film badge. These devices are worn *only* for documentation of occupational exposure, not for any medical or dental x-rays received as a patient. TLDs are radiation monitors that use lithium fluoride crystals. Once exposed to ionizing radiation and then heated, these crystals give off light proportional to the amount of radiation received. OSL dosimeters are radiation monitors that use aluminum oxide crystals. These crystals, once exposed to ionizing radiation and then subjected to a laser, give off luminescence proportional to the amount of radiation received. The pocket dosimeter contains an ionization chamber (containing air), and the number of ions formed (of either sign) is equated to exposure dose. (Bushong, 9th ed., p. 594)

137. **(D)** A measure 1,400 mrad is equal to 1.4 rad. If 1.4 rad were delivered in 7 minutes, then the dose rate would be 0.2 rad/min:

$$\frac{1.4 \text{ rad}}{7 \text{ min}} = \frac{x \text{ rad}}{1 \text{ min}}$$
$$7x = 1.4$$
$$x = 0.2 \text{ rad/min}$$

(Selman, 9th ed., p. 117)

138. **(C)** Biologic tissue is more sensitive to radiation when it is in an oxygenated state. A characteristic of many avascular (and, therefore, hypoxic) tumors is their resistance to treatment with radiation. Hyperbaric (high-pressure oxygen) therapy is used in some therapy centers in an effort to increase the sensitivity of the tissues being treated. (Bushong, 8th ed., pp. 496–497)

139. **(B)** The principal interactions that occur between x-ray photons and body tissues in the diagnostic x-ray range, the photoelectric effect and Compton scatter, are ionization processes producing photoelectrons and recoil electrons that traverse tissue and subsequently ionize molecules. These interactions occur randomly but can lead to molecular damage in the form of *impaired function* or *cell death*. The *target theory* specifies that DNA molecules are the targets of greatest importance and sensitivity; that is, DNA is the key sensitive molecule. However, since the body is 65% to 80% water, most interactions between ionizing radiation and body cells will involve radiolysis of water rather than direct interaction with DNA. The two major types of effects that occur are the direct effect and the indirect effect. The *direct effect* usually occurs with high-LET radiations and when ionization occurs at the DNA molecule itself. The *indirect effect*, which occurs most frequently, happens when ionization takes place away from the DNA molecule in cellular water. However, the energy from the interaction can be transferred to the molecule via a free radical (formed by radiolysis of cellular water).

Possible damage to the DNA molecule is diverse. A single main-chain/side-rail scission (break) on the DNA molecule is repairable. A double main-chain/side-rail scission may be repaired with difficulty or may result in cell death. A double main-chain/side-rail scission on the same rung of the DNA ladder results in irreparable damage or cell death. Faulty repair of main-chain breakage can result in cross-linking. Damage to the nitrogenous bases, that is, damage to the base itself or to the rungs connecting the main chains, can result in alteration of base sequences, causing a molecular lesion/point mutation. Any subsequent divisions result in daughter cells with incorrect genetic information. (*Bushong, 9th ed., p. 541*)

140. (C) The patient, as the first scatterer, is the most important scatterer. At 1 m from the patient, the intensity of the scattered beam is 0.1% of the intensity of the primary beam. Compton scatter emerging from the patient is almost as energetic as the primary beam entering the patient. (*Selman, 9th ed., p. 535*)

141. (D) A TLD is a sensitive and accurate device used in radiation dosimetry. It may be used as a personal dosimeter or to measure patient dose during radiographic examinations and therapeutic procedures. The TLD uses a thermoluminescent phosphor, usually lithium fluoride. When used as a personal monitor, the TLD is worn for 1 month.

During this time, it stores information regarding the radiation to which it has been exposed. It is then returned to the commercial supplier. In the laboratory, the phosphors are heated. They respond by emitting a particular quantity of light (not heat) that is in proportion to the quantity of radiation delivered to it. After they are cleared of stored information, they are returned for reuse. (*Bushong, 9th ed., p. 593*)

142. (A) Because the established dose-limit formula guideline is used for occupationally exposed persons 18 years of age and older, guidelines had to be established to cover the event that a student entered the clinical component of a radiography educational program prior to age 18. The guideline states that the occupational dose limit for students *under 18* years of age is 0.1 rem (100 mrem or 1 mSv) in any given year. (*Bushong, 9th ed., p. 620*)

143. (D) Patients occasionally will question the radiographer regarding the amount of radiation they are receiving during their examination. Most of these patients are merely curious because they have heard a recent news report about x-rays or have perhaps studied about x-rays in school recently. It is a good idea for radiographers to have some knowledge of average exposure doses for patients who desire this information. The curious patient also can be referred to the medical physicist for more detailed information. The average AP cervical spine radiograph delivers about 80 mrad (0.080 rad). The average AP supine lumbar spine radiograph delivers an ESE of about 350 mrad (0.35 rad). The average AP supine abdomen radiograph delivers about 300 mrad. (*Dowd and Tilson, 2nd ed., p. 247*)

144. (A) The use of beam restrictors limits the amount of tissue being irradiated, thus decreasing patient dose *and* decreasing the production of scattered radiation. High milliampere-second factors increase patient dose. Patient dose is reduced by using high-kilovolt and low-milliampere-second combinations. Although the use of a grid improves image quality by decreasing the amount of scattered radiation reaching the IR, it always requires an increase in exposure factor (usually milliampere-seconds) and, therefore, results in increased patient dose. *(Bushong, 9th ed., pp. 229–233)*

145.   **(D)** *Secondary* radiation includes *leakage and scattered radiation.* The control booth wall is a secondary barrier; therefore, the primary beam must never be directed toward it. The x-ray tube housing must reduce leakage radiation to less than 100 mR/h at a distance of 1 m from the housing. Lead aprons, lead gloves, portable x-ray barriers, and so on are also designed to protect the user from exposure to *scattered* radiation and will not protect her or him from the primary beam. *(Selman, 9th ed., p. 403)*

146.   **(B)** In the *photoelectric effect*, a relatively low-energy photon uses all its energy to eject an inner-shell electron, leaving a vacancy. An electron from the shell above drops down to fill the vacancy and in so doing gives up a characteristic ray. This type of interaction is most harmful to the patient because all the photon energy is transferred to tissue. In *Compton scatter*, a high-energy incident photon ejects an outer-shell electron. The incident photon is deflected with reduced energy, but it usually retains most of its energy and exits the body as an energetic scattered ray. This scattered ray either will contribute to image fog or will *pose a radiation hazard to personnel* depending on its direction of exit. In *classic scatter*, a low-energy photon interacts with an atom but causes no ionization; the incident photon disappears into the atom and then is released immediately as a photon of identical energy but with changed direction. *Pair production* is an interaction that occurs only at energies of 1.02 MeV, and therefore, it does not occur in diagnostic radiography. *(Bushong, 8th ed., pp. 174–175)*

147.   **(D)** The principal interactions that occur between x-ray photons and body tissues in the diagnostic x-ray range, the photoelectric effect and Compton scatter, are ionization processes producing photoelectrons and recoil electrons

that traverse tissue and subsequently ionize molecules. These interactions occur randomly but can lead to molecular damage in the form of *impaired function* or *cell death*. The *target theory* specifies that DNA molecules are the targets of greatest importance and sensitivity; that is, DNA is the key sensitive molecule. However, since the body is 65% to 80% water, most interactions between ionizing radiation and body cells will involve radiolysis of water rather than direct interaction with DNA. The two major types of effects that occur are the direct effect and the indirect effect. The *direct effect* usually occurs with high-LET radiations and when ionization occurs at the DNA molecule itself. The *indirect effect*, which occurs most frequently, happens when ionization takes place away from the DNA molecule in cellular water. However, the energy from the interaction can be transferred to the molecule via a free radical (formed by radiolysis of cellular water).

Possible damage to the DNA molecule is diverse. A single main-chain/side-rail scission (break) on the DNA molecule is repairable. A double main-chain/side-rail scission may be repaired with difficulty or may result in cell death. A double main-chain/side-rail scission on the same rung of the DNA ladder results in irreparable damage or cell death. Faulty repair of main-chain breakage can result in cross-linking. Damage to the nitrogenous bases, that is, damage to the base itself or to the rungs connecting the main chains, can result in alteration of base sequences, causing a molecular lesion/point mutation. Any subsequent divisions result in daughter cells with incorrect genetic information. *(Bushong, 9th ed., p. 523)*

148.   **(D)** As the amount of time one spends in a controlled area decreases, radiation exposure should decrease. Radiation exposure is affected considerably by one's proximity to the radiation source, as defined by the inverse-square law. Barriers (shielding) are an effective means of reducing radiation exposure; primary barriers, such as walls, protect one from the primary beam, and secondary barriers, such as lead aprons, are used to protect one from secondary radiation. *(Bushong, 9th ed., p. 620)*

149. **(A)** The effects of a quantity of radiation delivered to a body depend on a few factors, including the amount of radiation received, the size of the irradiated area, and how the radiation is delivered in time. If the radiation is delivered in portions over a period of time, it is said to be *fractionated* and has a less harmful effect than if the radiation were delivered all at once. Cells have an opportunity to repair, and some recovery occurs between doses. *(Bushong, 9th ed., p. 514)*

150. **(B)** *Somatic effects* of radiation refer to those effects experienced directly by the exposed individual, such as erythema, epilation, and cataracts. *Genetic effects* of radiation exposure are caused by irradiation of the reproductive cells of the exposed individual and are transmitted from one generation to the next. *(Selman, 9th ed., p. 382)*

151. **(A)** The x-ray tube's glass envelope and oil coolant are considered inherent (built-in) filtration. Thin sheets of aluminum are added to make *a total of at least 2.5 mm Al-equivalent filtration in equipment operated above 70 kVp.* This is done to remove the low-energy photons that serve only to contribute to patient skin dose. *(Bushong, 8th ed., p. 168)*

152. **(C)** *Erythema* is the reddening of skin as a result of exposure to large quantities of ionizing radiation. It was one of the first somatic responses to irradiation demonstrated to the early radiology pioneers. The effects of radiation exposure to the skin follow a *nonlinear, threshold dose–response relationship.* An individual's response to skin irradiation depends on the dose received, the period of time over which it was received, the size of the area irradiated, and the individual's sensitivity. The dose that it takes to bring about a noticeable erythema is referred to as the *SED.* *(Bushong, 8th ed., p. 521)*

153. **(B)** In the past few decades, ICRP and NCRP studies have indicated that radiation-induced cancer risks are greater than radiation-induced genetic risks—contrary to previous thought. Their philosophy then grew to be concerned with the probability of radiation-induced cancer mortality in the occupational radiation industry in comparison with annual accidental mortality in "safe" (radiation-free) industries. The NCRP reexamined its 1987 recommendations, and in NCRP Report No. 116, it reiterates its *annual effective occupational dose limit as 50 mSv (5 rem). (NCRP Report NO. 116, pp. 1, 4, 12)*

154. **(B)** If mechanical restraint is impossible, a friend or relative accompanying the patient should be requested to hold the patient. If a parent is to perform this task, it is preferable to elect the father so as to avoid the possibility of subjecting a newly fertilized ovum to even scattered radiation. If a friend or relative is not available, a nurse or transporter may be asked for help. Protective apparel, such as lead apron and gloves, must be provided to the person(s) holding the patient. *Radiology personnel must* never *assist in holding patients, and the individual assisting must* never *be in the path of the primary beam. (Thompson et al., p. 484)*

155. **(D)** A *controlled area* is one that is occupied by radiation workers who are trained in radiation safety and who wear radiation monitors. The exposure rate in a controlled area must not exceed 100 mR/week; its occupancy factor is considered to be 1, indicating that the area may always be occupied and, therefore, requires maximum shielding. An *uncontrolled area* is one occupied by the general population; the exposure rate there must not exceed 10 mR/week. Shielding requirements vary according to several factors, one being *occupancy factor. (Bushong, 9th ed., p. 586)*

156. **(A)** The length of time from conception to birth, that is, pregnancy, is referred to as *gestation.* The term *congenital* refers to a condition existing at birth. *Neonatal* relates to the time immediately after birth and the first month of life. *In vitro* refers to something living outside a living body (as in a test tube), as opposed to *in vivo* (within a living system). *(Bushong, 8th ed., p. 544)*

157. **(B)** It is well established that sufficient quantities of ionizing radiation can cause a number of serious somatic and/or genetic effects.

Somatic effects of radiation are those that affect the *irradiated body itself*. Somatic effects are described as being *early* or *late* depending on the length of time between irradiation and manifestation of effects. The human reproductive organs are particularly radiosensitive. *Fertility* and *heredity* are greatly affected by the *germ cells* produced within the testes (spermatogonia) and ovaries (oogonia). Excessive radiation exposure to the gonads can cause *temporary or permanent infertility* and/or *genetic mutations*. Infertility is somatic because it affects the exposed individual; genetic mutations affect future generations. (*Dowd and Tilson, 2nd ed., p. 117*)

158. **(A)** The faster the intensifying screens used, the fewer are the required milliampere-seconds. Decreasing the intensity (i.e., mAs or quantity) of photons significantly contributes to reducing total patient dose. Decreasing the kilovoltage would increase patient dose because the primary beam would be made up of fewer penetrating photons, so the milliampere-seconds would have to be increased. The importance of patient shielding is never diminished. (*Bushong, 9th ed., p. 216*)

159. **(C)** Different types of monitoring devices are available for the occupationally exposed. Ionization is the fundamental principle of operation of both the film badge and the pocket dosimeter. In the film badge, the film's silver halide emulsion is ionized by x-ray photons. The pocket dosimeter contains an ionization chamber (containing air), and the number of ions formed (of either sign) is equated to exposure dose. TLDs are radiation monitors that use lithium fluoride crystals. Once exposed to ionizing radiation and then heated, these crystals give off light proportional to the amount of radiation received. OSL dosimeters are radiation monitors that use aluminum oxide crystals. These crystals, once exposed to ionizing radiation and then subjected to a laser, give off luminescence proportional to the amount of radiation received. (*Selman, 9th ed., p. 400*)

160. **(B)** With greater beam restriction, less biologic material is irradiated, thereby reducing the possibility of harmful effects. If less tissue is irradiated, less scattered radiation is produced, resulting in improved IR contrast. The total filtration is not a function of beam restriction but rather is a radiation protection guideline aimed at reducing patient skin dose. (*Selman, 9th ed., p. 247*)

161. **(B)** Radiation safety guidelines are valuable only if they are followed by radiation personnel. The radiation safety officer (RSO) is responsible for being certain that established guidelines are enforced and that personnel understand and employ radiation safety measures to protect themselves and their patients. The RSO is also responsible for performing routine equipment checks to ensure that all equipment meet radiation safety standards. (*NCRP Report No. 405, p. 34*)

162. **(B)** The genetic effects of radiation and some somatic effects, such as leukemia, are plotted on a linear dose–response curve. The linear dose–response curve has *no threshold; that is, there is no dose below which radiation is absolutely safe.* The nonlinear/sigmoidal dose–response curve has a threshold and is thought to be generally correct for most somatic effects. (*Bushong, 9th ed., pp. 516–517*)

163. **(C)** The development of male and female reproductive stem cells has important radiation protection implications. Male stem cells reproduce continuously. However, female stem cells develop only during fetal life; women are born with all the reproductive cells they will ever have. It is exceedingly important to shield children whenever possible because they have their reproductive futures ahead of them. (*Bushong, 9th ed., pp. 540–541*)

164. **(A)** Protective apparel functions to protect the occupationally exposed person *from scattered radiation only*. Lead aprons and lead gloves do not protect from the primary beam. No one in the radiographic room except the patient must ever be exposed to the primary beam. The occupationally exposed and those (family and friends) who might assist a patient during an examination must wear protective apparel and keep out of the way of the primary beam. (*Bushong, 9th ed., pp. 624–625*)

165. (A) It is our ethical responsibility to minimize the radiation dose to our patients. X-rays produced at the tungsten target make up a heterogeneous primary beam. There are many "soft" (low-energy) photons that, if not removed by filters, would only contribute to greater patient skin dose. They are too weak to penetrate the patient and contribute to the image-forming radiation; they penetrate a small thickness of tissue and are absorbed. *(Bushong, 8th ed., p. 11)*

166. (D) *Radiation quality* determines degree of penetration and the amount of energy transferred to the irradiated tissue (LET). Certainly, the larger the absorbed radiation dose, the greater is the effect. Biologic effect is increased as the size of the irradiated area is increased. The nature of the effect is influenced by the location of irradiated tissue (bone marrow vs. gonads). *(Bushong, 8th ed., pp. 520–521)*

167. (D) Radiation effects that appear days or weeks following exposure (early effects) are in response to relatively high radiation doses. These should never occur in diagnostic radiology today; they occur only in response to doses much greater than those used in diagnostic radiology. One of the effects that may be noted in such a circumstance is the hematologic effect—reduced numbers of white blood cells, red blood cells, and platelets in the circulating blood. Immediate local tissue effects can include effects on the gonads (i.e., temporary infertility) and on the skin (e.g., epilation and erythema). Acute radiation lethality, or radiation death, occurs after an acute exposure and results in death in weeks or days. Radiation-induced malignancy, leukemia, and genetic effects are late effects (or stochastic effects) of radiation exposure. These can occur years after survival of an acute radiation dose or after exposure to low levels of radiation over a long period of time. Radiation workers need to be especially aware of the late effects of radiation because their exposure to radiation is usually low level over a long period of time. Occupational radiation protection guidelines, therefore, are based on late effects of radiation according to a linear, nonthreshold dose–response curve. *(Bushong, 8th ed., p. 537)*

168. (A) The most radiosensitive portion of the GI tract is the small bowel. Projecting from the lining of the small bowel are villi, from the crypts of Lieberkühn, which are responsible for the absorption of nutrients into the bloodstream. Because the cells of the villi are continually being cast off, new cells must continually arise from the crypts of Lieberkühn. Being highly mitotic, undifferentiated stem cells, they are very radiosensitive. Thus, the small bowel is the most radiosensitive portion of the GI tract. In the adult, the CNS is the most radioresistant system, and the epidermis is composed of radioresistant-mature, postmitotic cells. *(Dowd and Tilson, 2nd ed., p. 155)*

169. (A) The mAs setting regulates the quantity of radiation delivered to the patient, and the kVp setting regulates the quality (i.e., penetration) of the radiation delivered to the patient. Therefore, higher energy (i.e., more penetrating) radiation (which is more likely to exit the patient), accompanied by lower milliampere-seconds (mAs), is the safest combination for the patient. *(Thompson et al., p. 275)*

170. (C) Late effects of radiation can occur in cells that have survived a previous irradiation months or years earlier. These late effects, such as carcinogenesis and genetic effects, are "all-or-nothing" effects—either the organism develops cancer or it does not. Most late effects do not have a threshold dose; that is, *any* dose, however small, theoretically can induce an effect. Increasing that dose *will* increase the *likelihood* of the occurrence but *will not* affect its *severity*; these effects are termed *stochastic*. *Nonstochastic effects* are those that will not occur below a particular threshold dose and that increase in severity as the dose increases. *(Bushong, 8th ed., p. 532)*

171. (A) Restriction of field size is one important method of patient protection. However, the accuracy of the light field must be evaluated periodically as part of a quality assurance (QA) program. Guidelines for patient protection state that the collimator light and actual irradiated area must be accurate to within 2% of the SID. (*Thompson et al., p. 403*)

172. **(A)** Radiographers usually are required to wear one dosimeter, positioned at their collar and worn *outside* a lead apron. Special circumstances, however, warrant the use of a second monitor. During pregnancy, a second "baby monitor" is worn at the abdomen, *under* any lead apron. During special vascular procedures, the dose to the radiographer can increase significantly. This is so because the leaded protective curtain is often absent from the fluorotower and because of the extensive use of cineradiography. As a result, the radiographer's upper extremities can receive a greater exposure (e.g., when assisting during catheter introduction), and a *ring* or *bracelet badge* is often recommended. A second dosimeter is not required when performing mobile radiography. (*Bushong, 8th ed., p. 525*)

173. **(B)** The reproductive cells are considered among the most radiosensitive cells in the body. The immature female sex cells are the oogonia; they mature to ova. The immature male sex cells are the spermatogonia; they mature to sperm. Different amounts of ionizing radiation to these cells can cause differing levels/degrees of response. Doses as low as 10 rad can cause menstrual changes in women and decrease the number of sperm in men. At 200 rad, temporary infertility is likely, and at 500 rad, sterility will result. (*Bushong, 8th ed., p. 523*)

174. **(D)** A TLD is used to measure monthly exposure to radiation, as is the film badge. Lithium fluoride chips are the thermoluminescent material used in TLDs. A pocket dosimeter (a small personal ionization chamber) measures the quantity of ionizations occurring during the period worn and reads out in millirem; it is used primarily when working with large quantities of radiation. (*Selman, 9th ed., p. 400*)

175. **(B)** It is important to limit tabletop exposure during fluoroscopy because the SSD is so much less than in overhead radiography, so a much higher skin dose is delivered to the patient. For this reason, the tabletop exposure

rate during fluoroscopy should not exceed 10 R/min. (*Selman, 9th ed., p. 415*)

176. **(C)** Figure 3–7 illustrates three dose–response curves. *Curve A* begins at zero, indicating that there is no safe dose, that is, *no threshold*. Even one x-ray photon theoretically can cause a response. It is a straight (linear) line, indicating that *response is directly related to dose;* as dose increases, response increases. *Radiation-induced cancer, leukemia,* and *genetic effects* follow a linear nonthreshold dose–response relationship. *Curve B* is another linear curve (response is *directly related* to dose), but this one illustrates that a particular dose of radiation must be received before a response will occur. That is, there is a *threshold dose;* this is called a *linear threshold curve.* *Curve C* is another threshold curve, but this curve is nonlinear. It illustrates that once the minimum dose is received, a response occurs slowly initially and then increases sharply as exposure increases. This threshold, nonlinear (sigmoid) dose–response curve, illustrates the effect to *skin* from exposure to high levels of ionizing radiation. (*Bushong, 8th ed., p. 499*)

177. **(A)** The intensity/exposure rate of radiation at a given distance from a point source is inversely proportional to the square of the distance. This is the inverse-square law of radiation, and it is expressed in the following equation:

$$\frac{I_1}{I_2} = \frac{D_2^2}{D_1^2}$$

Substituting known values:

$$\frac{40 \text{ mR/h}}{x \text{ mR/h}} = \frac{25}{9}$$
$$25x = 360$$

Thus, $x = 14.4$ mR/h and, therefore, *7.2 mR in 30 minutes.* (*Bushong, 8th ed., pp. 68–70*)

178. **(A)** Mobile radiography (along with fluoroscopy and special procedures) is an area of *higher occupational exposure.* With no lead barrier to retreat behind, distance becomes the best source of protection. The exposure switch of mobile equipment must be manufactured to allow the technologist to stand *at least 6 ft* away from the patient and the x-ray tube. Hospital personnel, visitors, and patients also must be protected from unnecessary radiation exposure. Therefore, the radiographer must request that these people leave the immediate area until after the exposure is made and *announce* in a loud voice when the exposure is about to be made, allowing time for individuals to leave the area. The use of a short SID increases patient exposure and produces poor recorded detail. *(Carlton and Adler, 4th ed., p. 558)*

179.   (C) *Scattered and secondary radiations* are those that have deviated in direction while passing through a part. *Leakage radiation* is radiation that emerges from the leaded tube housing in directions other than that of the useful beam. Tube head construction must keep leakage radiation to less than 0.1 R/h at 1 m from the tube. *Remnant radiation* is the radiation that emerges from the patient to form the radiographic image. *(Bushong, 8th ed., p. 130)*

180.   (D) The presence of ionizing radiation may be detected in several ways. It has an *ionizing* effect on air, which is the basic principle of the roentgen as unit of measurement. X-rays have a *photographic* effect on film emulsion, which is readily observable on radiographic images. The *fluorescent* effect on certain crystals, such as calcium tungstate and lanthanum, accounts for our use of these phosphors in intensifying screens. Radiation's *physiologic* effects have been demonstrated to be genetic damage, erythema, and cataractogenesis; many of these were noted by the early radiology pioneers. *(Selman, 9th ed., pp. 115, 116)*

181.   (C) *Sensitometry* and *densitometry* are used in evaluation of the film processor; they are just one portion of a complete QA program. *Modulation transfer function* (MTF) is used to express spatial resolution—another component of the QA program. A complete QA program includes testing of all components of the imaging system—processors, focal spot, x-ray timers, filters, intensifying screens, beam alignment, and so on. *(Thompson et al., pp. 399–400)*

182.   (B) Even the smallest exposure to radiation can be harmful. It, therefore, must be every radiographer's objective to keep his or her occupational exposure as far below the dose limit as possible. Radiology personnel never should hold patients during an x-ray examination. *(Bushong, 8th ed., pp. 9–10)*

183.   (B) An approximate ESE can be determined using the illustrated nomogram. First, mark 3.0 mm Al on the x (horizontal) axis. Next, mark where a line drawn up from that point intersects the 125-kVp line. Draw a line straight across to the y (vertical) axis; this should approximately reach the 15 mR/mAs point. Because 3.2 mAs was used for the exposure, the approximate ESE is 4.8 mR (15 × 3.2). *(Bushong, 8th ed., p. 587)*

184.   (D) The relationship between x-ray intensity and distance from the source is expressed in the inverse-square law of radiation. The formula is

$$\frac{I_1}{I_2} = \frac{D_2^2}{D_1^2}$$

Substituting known values,

$$\frac{104}{x} = \frac{64}{49}$$
$$64x = 6860$$

Thus, $x = 107$ mR in *1 hour (60 minutes)* and, therefore, 53.6 mR in *30 minutes*. Note the inverse relationship between distance and dose. *As distance from the source of radiation increases, dose rate decreases significantly.* *(Bushong, 8th ed., pp. 68–70)*

185.   (B) *Alpha and beta radiation are particulate radiations;* alpha is composed of two protons and two neutrons, and beta is identical to an electron. *Gamma and x-radiation are electromagnetic,* having wave-like fluctuations like other radiations of the electromagnetic spectrum (e.g., visible light and radio waves). *(Bushong, 8th ed., p. 60)*

186.   (D) The *Bucky slot cover* shields the opening at the side of the table because the Bucky tray is parked at the end of the table for the fluoroscopy procedure; this is important because

the opening created otherwise would allow scattered radiation to emerge at approximately the level of the operator's gonads. The *exposure switch* (usually a foot pedal) must be of the "dead man" type; that is, when the foot is released from the switch, there is immediate termination of exposure. The *cumulative exposure timer* sounds or interrupts the exposure after 5 minutes of fluoro time, thus making the fluoroscopist aware of accumulated fluoro time. In addition, *source-to-tabletop distance* is restricted to at least 15 in. for stationary equipment and at least 12 in. for mobile equipment. Increased source-to-tabletop distance increases source-to-patient distance, thereby decreasing patient dose. *(Bushong, 8th ed., p. 570)*

187.   **(C)** As x-ray photons emerge from the x-ray tube they immediately encounter air—before being intercepted by any material. The *roentgen* is the unit of exposure; it measures the quantity of ionizations in air. The roentgen is, therefore, the unit of choice for measuring x-ray tube output—and an ion-chamber dosimeter instrument is used for this purpose. *Rad* is an acronym for *radiation absorbed dose*; it measures the energy deposited in any material. *Rem* is an acronym for *radiation-equivalent man*; it includes the relative biologic effectiveness. *Becqueral* is the SI unit of measurement for radioactivity. *(Bushong, 8th ed., p. 588)*

188.   **(D)** All the tissues listed are considered especially radiosensitive. The intestinal *crypt cells of Lieberkühn* are responsible for the absorption of nutrients into the bloodstream. Because these cells are continually being cast off, new cells must continually arise. Being highly mitotic undifferentiated stem cells, they are very radiosensitive. Excessive radiation to the *blood-forming organs* (such as *bone marrow*) can cause leukemia or life-span shortening. Young, immature embryonic cells such as *erythroblasts* are listed among the most radiosensitive. Lymphocytes are the most radiosensitive cells in the body. *(Bushong, 8th ed., p. 492)*

189.   **(D)** Elective booking of a radiologic examination after inquiring about the patient's

previous menstrual cycle is the most effective means of preventing accidental exposure of a recently fertilized ovum. Patient questionnaires obtain this information from the patient and are also used often in an informed consent form. Patient postings in waiting and changing areas alert patients to advise the radiographer if there is any chance of pregnancy. These three safeguards replace the earlier 10-day rule, which is now obsolete. *(Bushong, 8th ed., p. 559)*

190.   **(A)** In the photoelectric effect, the incident (low-energy) photon is completely absorbed and thus is responsible for producing contrast and contributing to patient dose. The photoelectric effect is the interaction between x-ray and tissue that predominates in the diagnostic range. In Compton scatter, only partial absorption occurs, and most energy emerges as scattered photons. In coherent scatter, no energy is absorbed by the part; it all emerges as scattered photons. Pair production occurs only at very high energy levels, at least 1.02 MeV. *(Bushong, 8th ed., p. 176)*

191.   **(B)** The OSL dosimeter and TLD are used frequently to measure the radiation exposure of radiographers. The pocket dosimeter may be employed by radiation workers who are exposed to higher doses of radiation and need a daily reading. A blood test is an unacceptable method of monitoring radiation dose effects because a very large dose would have to be received before blood changes would occur. *(Sherer et al., 5th ed., pp. 257–261)*

192.   **(B)** The genetically significant dose (GSD) illustrates that large exposures to a few people are cause for little concern when diluted by the total population. On the other hand, we all share the burden of that radiation received by the total population, especially as the use of medical radiation increases, so each individual's share of the total exposure increases. *(Selman, 9th ed., pp. 386–387)*

193.   **(D)** According to the NCRP, the annual occupational *whole-body* dose-equivalent limit is 50 mSv (5 rem or 5,000 mrem). The annual occupational whole-body dose-equivalent limit

for *students* under the age of 18 years is 1 mSv (100 mrem or 0.1 rem). The annual occupational dose-equivalent limit for the *lens of the eye* is 150 mSv (15 rem). The annual occupational dose-equivalent limit for the *thyroid*, *skin*, and *extremities* is 500 mSv (50 rem). The total gestational dose-equivalent limit for the *embryo/fetus* of a pregnant radiographer is 5 mSv (500 mrem), not to exceed 0.5 mSv in 1 month. *(Bushong, 8th ed., p. 557)*

194. **(C)** Exposure dose to patients can be expressed as *entrance skin exposure* (ESE), sometimes referred to as *skin entrance exposure* (SEE). Exposure can also be expressed in terms of *organ dose*. Organ doses to the gonads, bone marrow, breast, thyroid, lens, and lung can be determined. Patient position and beam restriction often make a significant difference in patient dose. Examinations performed PA rather than AP often decrease exposure to sensitive organs. This is so because the lower energy x-ray photons will be absorbed by the anatomic structures closer to the x-ray source, and the higher energy photons will penetrate and exit the part (penetrating the sensitive part rather than being absorbed by it). PA abdomen radiographs deliver less quantity dose to the reproductive organs than AP abdomen radiographs do. An AP lumbar spine radiograph, 7 × 17 in. cassette, 80 kVp delivers about 74 mrad to the ovaries, whereas the same projection using a 14 × 17 in. cassette delivers 92 mrad. An AP abdomen radiograph with 70 kVp delivers 80 mrad, whereas at 80 kVp, the ovarian dose is 68 mrad. *(Bontrager and Lampignano, 6th ed., p. 67)*

195. **(A)** Lead aprons require certain maintenance and care if they are to continue to provide protection from ionizing radiation. They can be kept clean with a damp cloth. It is very important that they be hung when not in use rather than being folded or left in a heap between examinations. A folded or crumpled position encourages the formation of cracks in the leaded vinyl. Lead aprons should be fluoroscoped (at about 120 kVp) at least once a year

to check for development of any cracks. *(Bushong, 8th ed., p. 464)*

196. **(D)** The principal interactions that occur between x-ray photons and body tissues in the diagnostic x-ray range, the photoelectric effect and Compton scatter, are ionization processes producing photoelectrons and recoil electrons that traverse tissue and subsequently ionize molecules. These interactions occur randomly but can lead to molecular damage in the form of *impaired function* or *cell death*. The *target theory* specifies that DNA molecules are the targets of greatest importance and sensitivity; that is, DNA is the key sensitive molecule. However, since the body is 65% to 80% water, most interactions between ionizing radiation and body cells will involve radiolysis of water rather than direct interaction with DNA. The two major types of effects that occur are the direct effect and the indirect effect. The *direct effect* usually occurs with high-LET radiations and when ionization occurs at the DNA molecule itself. The *indirect effect*, which occurs most frequently, happens when ionization takes place away from the DNA molecule in cellular water. However, the energy from the interaction can be transferred to the molecule via a free radical (formed by radiolysis of cellular water). *(Bushong, 8th ed., p. 507)*

197. **(D)** The *protective curtain*, which is usually made of leaded vinyl with at least 0.25 mm Pb equivalent, must be positioned between the patient and the fluoroscopist to greatly reduce the exposure of the fluoroscopist to energetic scatter from the patient. As with overhead equipment, fluoroscopic total *filtration* must be at least 2.5 mm Al equivalent to reduce excessive exposure to soft radiation. *Collimator–beam* alignment must be accurate to within 2%. *(Bushong, 8th ed., p. 570)*

198. **(B)** Because minerals in rocks and the earth can emanate radioactivity, high levels of radon gas inside homes have been of recent concern. Another source of radon gas is from burning cigarettes, whether as a smoker or as passive exposure. Uranium miners have been identified with a much higher incidence of lung cancer; many of these individuals also

were smokers. Radiology departments are not known as a source of radon gas exposure. *(Dowd and Tilson, 2nd ed., p. 147)*

199.   **(A)** LET increases with the *ionizing* potential of the radiation; for example, alpha particles are more ionizing than x-radiation; therefore, they have a higher LET. As ionizations and LET increase, there is greater possibility of an effect on living tissue; therefore, the RBE increases. The RBE (sometimes called the *quality factor*) of diagnostic x-rays is 1, the RBE of fast neutrons is 10, and the RBE of 5-MeV alpha particles is 20. *(Bushong, 8th ed., p. 496)*

200.   **(D)** *Photoelectric interaction* in tissue involves complete absorption of the incident photon, whereas *Compton interactions* involve only partial transfer of energy. The larger the quantity of radiation and the greater the number of photoelectric interactions, the greater is the patient dose. Radiation to more radiosensitive tissues such as gonadal tissue or blood-forming organs is more harmful than the same dose to muscle tissue. *(Selman, 9th ed., pp. 513–514)*

Subspecialty List

65. Minimizing patient exposure
66. Biologic aspects of radiation
67. Personnel protection
68. Minimizing patient exposure
69. Minimizing patient exposure
70. Radiation exposure and monitoring
71. Biologic aspects of radiation
72. Biologic aspects of radiation
73. Personnel protection
74. Personnel protection
75. Minimizing patient exposure
76. Minimizing patient exposure
77. Personnel protection
78. Radiation exposure and monitoring
79. Minimizing patient exposure
80. Biologic aspects of radiation
81. Biologic aspects of radiation
82. Minimizing patient exposure
83. Radiation exposure and monitoring
84. Biologic aspects of radiation
85. Personnel protection
86. Radiation exposure and monitoring
87. Minimizing patient exposure
88. Minimizing patient exposure
89. Biologic aspects of radiation
90. Personnel protection
91. Personnel protection
92. Biologic aspects of radiation
93. Minimizing patient exposure
94. Minimizing patient exposure
95. Biologic aspects of radiation
96. Minimizing patient exposure
97. Biologic aspects of radiation
98. Biologic aspects of radiation
99. Minimizing patient exposure
100. Biologic aspects of radiation
101. Biologic aspects of radiation
102. Personnel protection
103. Biologic aspects of radiation
104. Biologic aspects of radiation
105. Biologic aspects of radiation
106. Minimizing patient exposure
107. Minimizing patient exposure
108. Biologic aspects of radiation
109. Minimizing patient exposure
110. Radiation exposure and monitoring
111. Radiation exposure and monitoring
112. Minimizing patient exposure
113. Minimizing patient exposure
114. Personnel protection
115. Radiation exposure and monitoring
116. Personnel protection
117. Minimizing patient exposure
118. Radiation exposure and monitoring
119. Biologic aspects of radiation
120. Minimizing patient exposure
121. Personnel protection
122. Personnel protection
123. Minimizing patient exposure
124. Biologic aspects of radiation
125. Biologic aspects of radiation
126. Personnel protection
127. Biologic aspects of radiation
128. Minimizing patient exposure
129. Biologic aspects of radiation
130. Biologic aspects of radiation
131. Personnel protection
132. Biologic aspects of radiation
133. Personnel protection
134. Radiation exposure and monitoring
135. Biologic aspects of radiation
136. Radiation exposure and monitoring
137. Minimizing patient exposure
138. Biologic aspects of radiation
139. Biologic aspects of radiation
140. Personnel protection
141. Radiation exposure and monitoring
142. Personnel protection
143. Minimizing patient exposure
144. Minimizing patient exposure
145. Radiation exposure and monitoring
146. Personnel protection
147. Minimizing patient exposure
148. Personnel protection
149. Biologic aspects of radiation
150. Biologic aspects of radiation
151. Minimizing patient exposure
152. Biologic aspects of radiation
153. Radiation exposure and monitoring
154. Personnel protection
155. Personnel protection
156. Biologic aspects of radiation
157. Biologic aspects of radiation
158. Minimizing patient exposure
159. Radiation exposure and monitoring
160. Minimizing patient exposure
161. Radiation exposure and monitoring
162. Biologic aspects of radiation
163. Biologic aspects of radiation
164. Personnel protection
165. Minimizing patient exposure
166. Biologic aspects of radiation

167. Biologic aspects of radiation
168. Minimizing patient exposure
169. Minimizing patient exposure
170. Biologic aspects of radiation
171. Radiation exposure and monitoring
172. Personnel protection
173. Minimizing patient exposure
174. Radiation exposure and monitoring
175. Radiation exposure and monitoring
176. Minimizing patient exposure
177. Personnel protection
178. Personnel protection
179. Personnel protection
180. Radiation exposure and monitoring
181. Radiation exposure and monitoring
182. Personnel protection
183. Radiation exposure and monitoring
184. Personnel protection
185. Biologic aspects of radiation
186. Personnel protection
187. Radiation exposure and monitoring
188. Biologic aspects of radiation
189. Minimizing patient exposure
190. Minimizing patient exposure
191. Radiation exposure and monitoring
192. Minimizing patient exposure
193. Radiation exposure and monitoring
194. Minimizing patient exposure
195. Personnel protection
196. Biologic aspects of radiation
197. Minimizing patient exposure
198. Biologic aspects of radiation
199. Biologic aspects of radiation
200. Biologic aspects of radiation

CHAPTER 4

Image Acquisition and Evaluation
Questions

DIRECTIONS (Questions 1 through 250): Each of the numbered items or incomplete statements in this section is followed by answers or by completions of the statement. Select the *one* lettered answer or completion that is *best* in each case.

1. Geometric blur can be evaluated using all the following devices *except*

    (A) star pattern
    (B) slit camera
    (C) penetrometer
    (D) pinhole camera

2. What pixel size has a 512 × 512 matrix with a 20-cm field of view (FOV)?

    (A) 0.07 mm/pixel
    (B) 0.40 mm/pixel
    (C) 0.04 mm/pixel
    (D) 4.0 mm/pixel

3. In electronic imaging, as digital image matrix size increases

    1. pixel size decreases
    2. resolution decreases
    3. pixel depth decreases

    (A) 1 only
    (B) 2 only
    (C) 1 and 2 only
    (D) 2 and 3 only

4. An increase in added filtration will result in

    1. an increase in maximum energy of the x-ray beam
    2. a decrease in x-ray intensity
    3. an increase in effective energy of the x-ray beam

    (A) 1 only
    (B) 1 and 2 only
    (C) 2 and 3 only
    (D) 1, 2, and 3

5. The chest radiograph shown in Figure 4–1 demonstrates

    (A) part motion
    (B) aliasing artifact
    (C) double exposure
    (D) grid cutoff

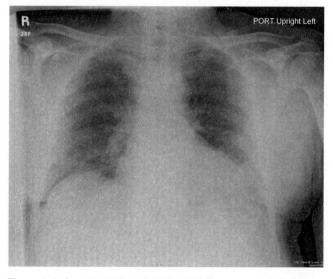

Figure 4–1. Courtesy of Stamford Hospital, Department of Radiology.

6. SID affects recorded detail in which of the following ways?

    (A) Recorded detail is directly related to SID.
    (B) Recorded detail is inversely related to SID.
    (C) As SID increases, recorded detail decreases.
    (D) SID is not a detail factor.

7. Grid interspace material can be made of

    1. carbon fiber
    2. aluminum
    3. plastic fiber

    (A) 1 only
    (B) 1 and 2 only
    (C) 2 and 3 only
    (D) 1, 2, and 3

8. The exposure factors used for a particular nongrid x-ray image were 300 mA, 4 ms, and 90 kV. Another image, using an 8:1 grid, is requested. Which of the following groups of factors is *most appropriate*?

    (A) 400 mA, 3 ms, 110 kV
    (B) 400 mA, 12 ms, 90 kV
    (C) 300 mA, 8 ms, 100 kV
    (D) 200 mA, 240 ms, 90 kV

9. Which of the lines indicated in Figure 4–2 represents the dynamic range offered by computed radiography/digital radiography (CR/DR)?

    (A) Line *A* is representative of CR/DR.
    (B) Line *B* is representative of CR/DR.
    (C) Neither line is representative of CR/DR.
    (D) Both lines are representative of CR/DR.

10. An increase in kilovoltage will have which of the following effects?

    1. More scattered radiation will be produced.
    2. The exposure rate will increase.
    3. Radiographic contrast will increase.

    (A) 1 only
    (B) 1 and 2 only
    (C) 2 and 3 only
    (D) 1, 2, and 3

11. The x-ray tube used in CT must be capable of

    1. high-speed rotation
    2. short pulsed exposures
    3. withstanding millions of heat units

    (A) 1 only
    (B) 1 and 2 only
    (C) 2 and 3 only
    (D) 1, 2, and 3

12. What is the correct critique of the CR image shown in Figure 4–3?

    (A) double exposure
    (B) inverted IP
    (C) incomplete erasure
    (D) image fading

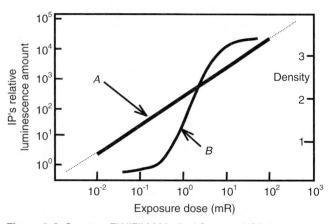

Figure 4–2. Courtesy FUJIFILM Medical Systems USA, Inc.

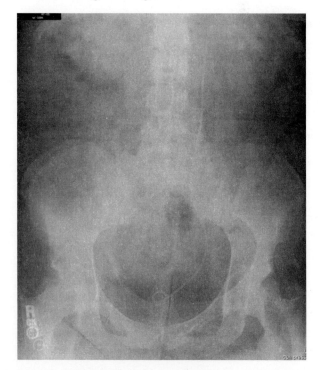

Figure 4–3. Courtesy of Stamford Hospital, Department of Radiology

13. Decreasing field size from 14 × 17 in. to 8 × 10 in., with no other changes, will

    (A) decrease the amount of scattered radiation generated within the part
    (B) increase the amount of scattered radiation generated within the part
    (C) increase x-ray penetration of the part
    (D) decrease x-ray penetration of the part

14. Which of the following groups of exposure factors will produce the most radiographic density?

    (A) 100 mA, 50 ms
    (B) 200 mA, 40 ms
    (C) 400 mA, 70 ms
    (D) 600 mA, 30 ms

15. The component of a CR image plate (IP) that records the radiologic image is the

    (A) emulsion
    (B) helium–neon laser
    (C) photostimulable phosphor
    (D) scanner–reader

16. An x-ray image of the ankle was made at 40-SID, 200 mA, 50 ms, 70 kV, 0.6 mm focal spot, and minimal OID. Which of the following modifications would result in the greatest increase in magnification?

    (A) 1.2 mm focal spot
    (B) 36-in. SID
    (C) 44-in. SID
    (D) 4-in. OID

17. A lateral radiograph of the cervical spine was made at 40 in. using 300 mA and 0.03 second exposure. If it is desired to increase the distance to 72 in., what should be the new milliampere (mA) setting, all other factors remaining constant?

    (A) 100
    (B) 200
    (C) 300
    (D) 400

18. Which of the following statements regarding dual x-ray absorptiometry is (are) true?

    1. Radiation dose is low.
    2. Only low-energy photons are used.
    3. Photon attenuation by bone is calculated.

    (A) 1 only
    (B) 1 and 2 only
    (C) 1 and 3 only
    (D) 1, 2, and 3

19. The luminescent light emitted by the PSP is transformed into the image seen on the CRT by the

    (A) PSP
    (B) scanner–reader
    (C) ADC
    (D) helium–neon laser

20. The lateral coccyx image shown in Figure 4–4 was made using AEC but is overexposed. This is most likely a result of

    (A) incorrect selection of the small focal spot
    (B) insufficient backup time
    (C) selection of the center photocell
    (D) incorrect centering of the part

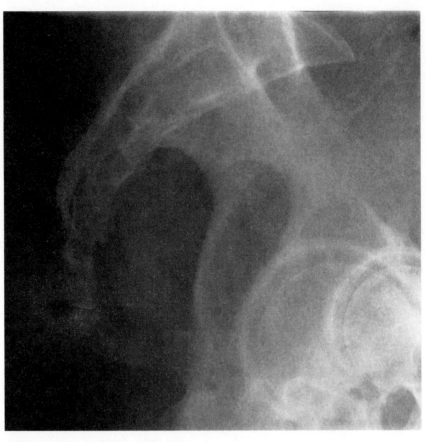

Figure 4–4. Reproduced, with permission, from Shephard CT. *Radiographic Image Production and Manipulation*. New York: McGraw-Hill; 2003.

21. Which of the following is/are true when comparing film-screen imaging to CR imaging?

1. CR DQE is better than film-screen DQE.
2. CR has a wider exposure range than film-screen.
3. CR has better spatial resolution than film-screen.

(A) 1 only
(B) 1 and 2 only
(C) 2 and 3 only
(D) 1, 2, and 3

22. The term *windowing* describes the practice of

(A) varying the automatic brightness control
(B) changing the image brightness and/or contrast scale
(C) varying the FOV
(D) increasing resolution

23. Foreshortening can be caused by

(A) the radiographic object being placed at an angle to the IR
(B) excessive distance between the object and the IR
(C) insufficient distance between the focus and the IR
(D) excessive distance between the focus and the IR

24. Acceptable method(s) of minimizing motion unsharpness is (are)

1. suspended respiration
2. short exposure time
3. patient instruction

(A) 1 only
(B) 1 and 2 only
(C) 1 and 3 only
(D) 1, 2, and 3

25. Using fixed milliampere-seconds and variable kilovoltage technical factors, each centimeter increase in patient thickness requires what adjustment in kilovoltage?

(A) Increase 2 kV
(B) Decrease 2 kV
(C) Increase 4 kV
(D) Decrease 4 kV

26. Unopened boxes of radiographic film should be stored away from radiation and

(A) in the horizontal position
(B) in the vertical position
(C) stacked with the oldest on top
(D) stacked with the newest on top

27. If a duration of 0.05 second was selected for a particular exposure, what milliamperage would be necessary to produce 30 mAs?

(A) 900
(B) 600
(C) 500
(D) 300

28. Factors that contribute to film fog include

1. the age of the film
2. excessive exposure to safelight
3. processor chemistry

(A) 1 only
(B) 1 and 2 only
(C) 1 and 3 only
(D) 1, 2, and 3

29. X-ray photon energy is inversely related to

1. photon wavelength
2. applied milliamperes (mA)
3. applied kilovoltage (kV)

(A) 1 only
(B) 1 and 2 only
(C) 1 and 3 only
(D) 1, 2, and 3

30. Which of the radiographs shown in Figure 4–5 *most likely* required the greater exposure?

(A) Image A
(B) Image B
(C) No difference in exposure was required

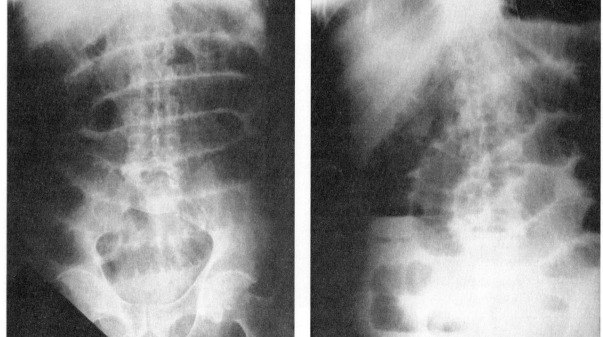

A   B

Figure 4–5. From the American College of Radiology Learning File. Courtesy of the ACR.

31. Characteristics of DR imaging include

    1. solid-state detector receptor plates
    2. a direct-capture imaging system
    3. immediate image display

    (A) 1 only
    (B) 1 and 3 only
    (C) 2 and 3 only
    (D) 1, 2, and 3

32. Compared with a low-ratio grid, a high-ratio grid will

    1. allow more centering latitude
    2. absorb more scattered radiation
    3. absorb more primary radiation

    (A) 1 only
    (B) 1 and 2 only
    (C) 2 and 3 only
    (D) 1, 2, and 3

33. Subject/object unsharpness can result from all of the following *except* when

    (A) object shape does not coincide with the shape of x-ray beam
    (B) object plane is not parallel with x-ray tube and/or IR
    (C) anatomic object(s) of interest is/are in the path of the CR
    (D) anatomic object(s) of interest is/are a distance from the IR

34. What is the correct critique of the CR image shown in Figure 4–6?

    (A) double exposure
    (B) inverted IP
    (C) incomplete erasure
    (D) image fading

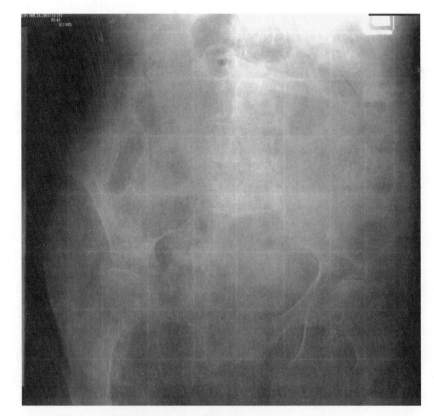

Figure 4–6. Courtesy of Stamford Hospital, Department of Radiology.

35. To be suitable for use in an image intensifier's input screen, a phosphor should have which of the following characteristics?

1. High conversion efficiency
2. High x-ray absorption
3. High atomic number

(A) 1 only
(B) 3 only
(C) 1 and 2 only
(D) 1, 2, and 3

36. Resolution in CR increases as

1. laser beam size decreases
2. monitor matrix size decreases
3. PSP crystal size decreases

(A) 1 only
(B) 1 and 2 only
(C) 1 and 3 only
(D) 1, 2, and 3

37. Pathologic or abnormal conditions that would require an *increase* in exposure factors include all of the following *except*

(A) atelectasis
(B) pneumoperitoneum
(C) Paget disease
(D) congestive heart failure

38. In radiography of a large abdomen, which of the following is (are) effective way(s) to minimize the amount of scattered radiation reaching the image receptor (IR)?

1. Use of close collimation
2. Use of low mAs
3. Use of a low-ratio grid

(A) 1 only
(B) 1 and 2 only
(C) 1 and 3 only
(D) 1, 2, and 3

39. Which of the following factors contribute(s) to the efficient performance of a grid?

1. Grid ratio
2. Number of lead strips per inch
3. Amount of scatter transmitted through the grid

(A) 1 only
(B) 2 only
(C) 1 and 2 only
(D) 1, 2, and 3

40. The changes between the images shown in Figure 4–7 represent changes made to

(A) pixel size
(B) matrix size
(C) window width
(D) window level

41. All the following affect the exposure rate of the primary beam *except*

(A) milliamperage
(B) kilovoltage
(C) distance
(D) field size

42. Factors that determine the production of scattered radiation include

1. field size
2. beam restriction
3. kilovoltage

(A) 1 only
(B) 1 and 2 only
(C) 2 and 3 only
(D) 1, 2, and 3

43. Image contrast is a result of

1. differential tissue absorption
2. atomic number of tissue being traversed
3. proper regulation of milliampere-seconds

(A) 1 only
(B) 1 and 2 only
(C) 1 and 3 only
(D) 1, 2, and 3

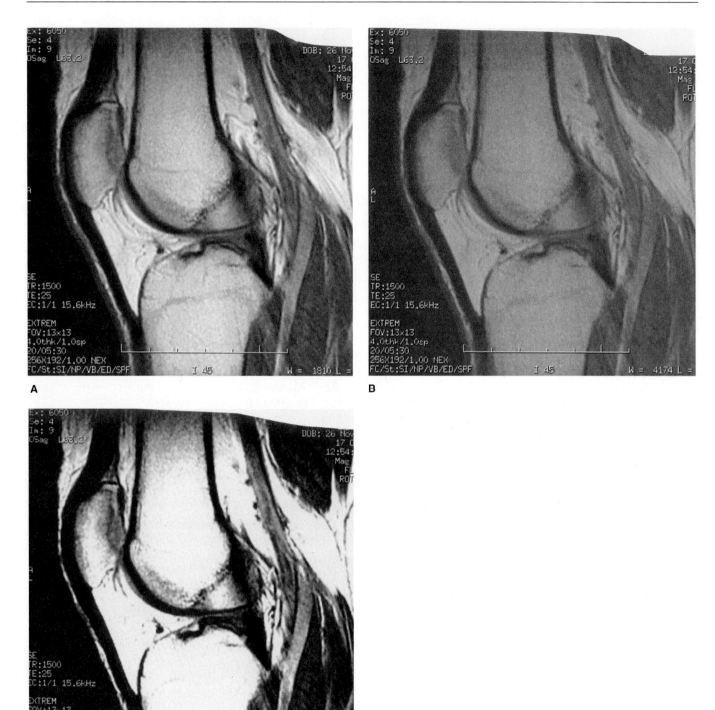

Figure 4–7. Courtesy of Stamford Hospital, Department of Radiology.

44. What grid ratio is represented in Figure 4–8?

(A) 3:1
(B) 5:1
(C) 10:1
(D) 16:1

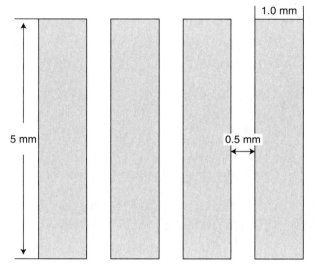

1.0 mm

5 mm

0.5 mm

Figure 4–8.

45. A 5-in. object to be radiographed at a 44-in. SID lies 6 in. from the IR. What will be the image width?

(A) 5.1 in.
(B) 5.7 in.
(C) 6.1 in.
(D) 6.7 in.

46. In comparison with 60 kV, 80 kV will

1. permit greater exposure latitude
2. produce more scattered radiation
3. produce shorter-scale contrast

(A) 1 only
(B) 2 only
(C) 1 and 2 only
(D) 2 and 3 only

47. The term *pixel* is associated with all of the following *except*

(A) two dimensional
(B) picture element
(C) measured in *xy* direction
(D) how much of the part is included in the matrix

48. Misalignment of the tube–part–IR relationship results in

(A) shape distortion
(B) size distortion
(C) magnification
(D) blur

49. Causes of grid cutoff, when using focused reciprocating grids, include the following?

1. Inadequate SID
2. X-ray tube off-center with the long axis of the lead strips
3. Angling the beam in the direction of the lead strips

(A) 1 only
(B) 1 and 2 only
(C) 2 and 3 only
(D) 1, 2, and 3

50. The tiny increased brightness, or minus density, artifacts seen in the more proximal portion of the CR image of the radius shown in Figure 4–9 are representative of

(A) backscatter
(B) skipped scan lines
(C) dust/dirt on the PSP
(D) image fading

51. Using a short (25–30 in.) SID with a large (14 × 17 in.) IR is likely to

(A) increase the scale of contrast
(B) increase the anode heel effect
(C) cause malfunction of the AEC
(D) cause premature termination of the exposure

52. Which of the following groups of factors would produce the least radiographic density?

(A) 400 mA, 0.010 second, 94 kV, 100-speed screens
(B) 500 mA, 0.008 second, 94 kV, 200-speed screens
(C) 200 mA, 0.040 second, 94 kV, 50-speed screens
(D) 100 mA, 0.020 second, 80 kV, 200-speed screens

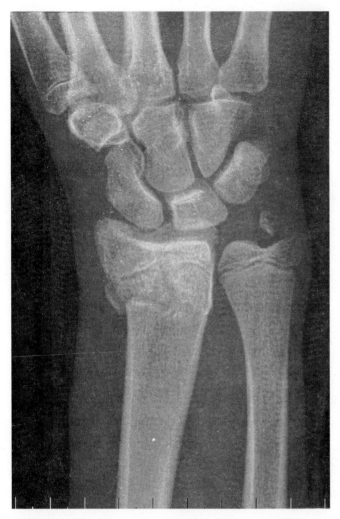

Figure 4–9. Reproduced, with permission, from Shephard CT. *Radiographic Image Production and Manipulation.* New York: McGraw-Hill; 2003.

53. Chemical fog may be attributed to

1. excessive developer temperature
2. oxidized developer
3. excessive replenishment

(A) 1 only
(B) 1 and 2 only
(C) 2 and 3 only
(D) 1, 2, and 3

54. Greater latitude is available to the radiographer in which of the following circumstances?

1. Using high-kV technical factors
2. Using a low-ratio grid
3. Using low-kV technical factors

(A) 1 only
(B) 1 and 2 only
(C) 2 and 3 only
(D) 3 only

55. The differences between CR and DR include

1. CR uses IPs.
2. CR has higher DQE and lower patient dose.
3. CR images are displayed immediately.

(A) 1 only
(B) 1 and 2 only
(C) 2 and 3 only
(D) 1, 2, and 3

56. The term *voxel* is associated with all of the following *except*

(A) bit depth
(B) volume element
(C) measured in Z direction
(D) field of view

57. Using a 48-in. SID, how much OID must be introduced to magnify an object two times?

(A) 8-in. OID
(B) 12-in. OID
(C) 16-in. OID
(D) 24-in. OID

58. A particular radiograph was produced using 12 mAs and 85 kV with a 16:1 ratio grid. The radiograph is to be repeated using an 8:1 ratio grid. What should be the new milliampere-seconds value?

(A) 3
(B) 6
(C) 8
(D) 10

59. The main difference between *direct* capture and *indirect* capture DR is that

    (A) direct capture/conversion has no scintillator
    (B) direct capture/conversion uses a photo-stimulable phosphor
    (C) in direct capture/conversion, light is detected by CCDs
    (D) in direct capture/conversion, light is detected by TFTs

60. The direction of electron travel in the x-ray tube is

    (A) filament to cathode
    (B) cathode to anode
    (C) anode to focus
    (D) anode to cathode

61. Which of the following technical changes would *best* serve to remedy the effect of very dissimilar tissue densities?

    (A) Use of a small focal spot
    (B) Use of a high-ratio grid
    (C) High-kilovoltage exposure factors
    (D) High milliampere-seconds exposure factors

62. For the same FOV, spatial resolution will be improved using

    (A) a smaller matrix
    (B) a larger matrix
    (C) fewer pixels
    (D) shorter SID

63. Which of the following are methods of limiting the production of scattered radiation?

    1. Using moderate ratio grids
    2. Using the prone position for abdominal examinations
    3. Restricting the field size to the smallest practical size

    (A) 1 and 2 only
    (B) 1 and 3 only
    (C) 2 and 3 only
    (D) 1, 2, and 3

64. Two film–screen images of the skull are shown in Figure 4–10. Which of the following best describes their different appearance?

    (A) Image B was made using a grid.
    (B) Image A demonstrates higher contrast.
    (C) Image A demonstrates motion.
    (D) Image B demonstrates shape distortion.

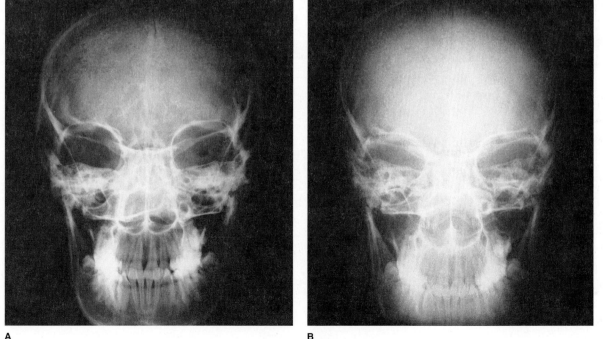

A   B

Figure 4–10A&B. From the American College of Radiology Learning File. Courtesy of the ACR.

65. The absorption of useful radiation by a grid is called

(A) grid selectivity.
(B) grid cleanup.
(C) grid cutoff.
(D) latitude.

66. Which of the images in Figure 4–11 has the largest matrix size?

(A) Image #1
(B) Image #2
(C) Image #3
(D) Image #4

1   2

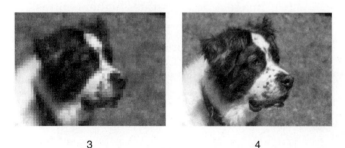

3   4

Figure 4–11.

67. Types of shape distortion include

1. magnification
2. elongation
3. foreshortening

(A) 1 only
(B) 1 and 2 only
(C) 2 and 3 only
(D) 1, 2, and 3

68. For the same FOV, as the matrix size increases

1. spatial resolution increases
2. image quality increases
3. pixel size decreases

(A) 1 only
(B) 1 and 2 only
(C) 2 and 3 only
(D) 1, 2, and 3

69. During CR imaging, the latent image present on the PSP is changed to a computerized image by the

(A) PSP
(B) Scanner–reader
(C) ADC
(D) helium–neon laser

70. All the following are related to recorded detail *except*

(A) milliamperage
(B) focal-spot size
(C) SID
(D) OID

71. A satisfactory radiograph was made using a 36-in. SID, 12 mAs, and a 12:1 grid. If the examination will be repeated at a distance of 42 in. and using a 5:1 grid, what should be the new milliampere-seconds value to maintain the original density?

(A) 5.6
(B) 6.5
(C) 9.7
(D) 13

72. Of the following groups of exposure factors, which will produce the most radiographic density?

(A) 400 mA, 30 ms, 72-in. SID
(B) 200 mA, 30 ms, 36-in. SID
(C) 200 mA, 60 ms, 36-in. SID
(D) 400 mA, 60 ms, 72-in. SID

73. Which of the following groups of exposure factors will produce the *shortest scale of contrast*?

    (A) 200 mA, 0.08 second, 95 kV, 12:1 grid
    (B) 500 mA, 0.03 second, 70 kV, 8:1 grid
    (C) 300 mA, 0.05 second, 95 kV, 8:1 grid
    (D) 600 mA, 1/40 seconds, 70 kV, 6:1 grid

74. Pathologic or abnormal conditions that would require a *decrease* in exposure factors include all of the following *except*

    (A) osteoporosis
    (B) osteomalacia
    (C) emphysema
    (D) pneumonia

75. Which of the following is likely to contribute to the radiographic contrast present on the finished radiograph?

    1. Atomic number of tissues radiographed
    2. Any pathologic processes
    3. Degree of muscle development

    (A) 1 and 2 only
    (B) 1 and 3 only
    (C) 2 and 3 only
    (D) 1, 2, and 3

76. Which of the following factors influence(s) the production of scattered radiation?

    1. Kilovoltage level
    2. Tissue density
    3. Size of field

    (A) 1 only
    (B) 1 and 2 only
    (C) 1 and 3 only
    (D) 1, 2, and 3

77. A 15% decrease in kilovoltage accompanied by a 50% increase in milliampere-seconds will result in a(n)

    (A) shorter scale of contrast
    (B) increase in exposure latitude
    (C) increase in radiographic density
    (D) decrease in recorded detail

78. Which of the following factors impact(s) recorded detail?

    1. Focal-spot size
    2. Subject motion
    3. SOD

    (A) 1 and 2 only
    (B) 1 and 3 only
    (C) 2 and 3 only
    (D) 1, 2, and 3

79. Which of the following is (are) tested as part of a quality assurance (QA) program?

    1. Beam alignment
    2. Reproducibility
    3. Linearity

    (A) 1 only
    (B) 1 and 2 only
    (C) 1 and 3 only
    (D) 1, 2, and 3

80. Focal-spot blur is greatest

    (A) directly along the course of the central ray
    (B) toward the cathode end of the x-ray beam
    (C) toward the anode end of the x-ray beam
    (D) as the SID is increased

81. How are mAs and patient dose related?

    (A) mAs and patient dose are inversely proportional.
    (B) mAs and patient dose are directly proportional.
    (C) mAs and patient dose are unrelated.
    (D) mAs and patient dose are inversely related.

82. Image plate front material can be made of which of the following?

    1. Carbon fiber
    2. Magnesium
    3. Lead

    (A) 1 only
    (B) 1 and 2 only
    (C) 1 and 3 only
    (D) 1, 2, and 3

83. Which of the following pathologic conditions would require a decrease in exposure factors?

    (A) Congestive heart failure
    (B) Pneumonia
    (C) Emphysema
    (D) Pleural effusion

84. If a radiograph exposed using a 12:1 ratio grid exhibits increased brightness/loss of density at its lateral edges, it is probably because the

    (A) SID was too great
    (B) grid failed to move during the exposure
    (C) x-ray tube was angled in the direction of the lead strips
    (D) central ray was off-center

85. Practice(s) that enable the radiographer to reduce the exposure time required for a particular image include

    1. use of a higher milliamperage
    2. use of a higher kilovoltage
    3. use of a higher ratio grid

    (A) 1 only
    (B) 1 and 2 only
    (C) 2 and 3 only
    (D) 1, 2, and 3

86. If 400 mA, 10 ms, and 90 kV were used for a particular exposure using three-phase, 12-pulse equipment, which of the following exposure changes would be *most appropriate* for use on single-phase equipment to produce a similar image?

    (A) Use 200 mA
    (B) Use 20 mAs
    (C) Use 70 kV
    (D) Use 0.02 second

87. Which of the following materials may be used as grid interspace material?

    1. Lead
    2. Plastic
    3. Aluminum

    (A) 1 only
    (B) 1 and 2 only
    (C) 2 and 3 only
    (D) 1, 2, and 3

88. The radiograph shown in Figure 4–12 demonstrates an example of

    (A) motion blur
    (B) underexposure
    (C) scanner/reader artifact
    (D) exposure artifact

89. Which of the following can impact the visibility of the anode heel effect?

    1. SID
    2. IR size
    3. Focal spot size

    (A) 1 only
    (B) 1 and 2 only
    (C) 2 and 3 only
    (D) 1, 2, and 3

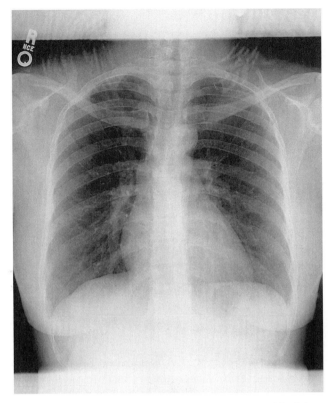

Figure 4–12. Courtesy of Stamford Hospital, Department of Radiology.

90. An increase in the kilovoltage applied to the x-ray tube increases the

    1. x-ray wavelength
    2. exposure rate
    3. patient absorption

    (A) 1 only
    (B) 2 only
    (C) 2 and 3 only
    (D) 1, 2, and 3

91. Which of the following statements about *histograms* is/are true?

    1. A histogram illustrates pixel value distribution.
    2. There is a default histogram for each/different body parts.
    3. A histogram is representative of the image grayscale.

    (A) 1 only
    (B) 1 and 2 only
    (C) 2 and 3 only
    (D) 1, 2, and 3

92. Which of the following is the correct order of radiographic film processing?

    (A) Developer, wash, fixer, dry
    (B) Fixer, wash, developer, dry
    (C) Developer, fixer, wash, dry
    (D) Fixer, developer, wash, dry

93. If the radiographer is unable to achieve a short OID because of the structure of the body part or patient condition, which of the following adjustments can be made to minimize magnification distortion?

    (A) A smaller focal-spot size should be used.
    (B) A longer SID should be used.
    (C) A shorter SID should be used.
    (D) A lower-ratio grid should be used.

94. The reduction in x-ray photon intensity as the photon passes through material is termed

    (A) absorption
    (B) scattering
    (C) attenuation
    (D) divergence

95. The PA chest image shown in Figure 4–13 exhibits which of the following qualities?

    1. Adequate penetration of the heart
    2. Long-scale contrast
    3. Adequate inspiration

    (A) 1 only
    (B) 1 and 2 only
    (C) 2 and 3 only
    (D) 1, 2, and 3

96. Exposure rate will decrease with an increase in

    1. SID
    2. kilovoltage
    3. focal spot size

    (A) 1 only
    (B) 1 and 2 only
    (C) 2 and 3 only
    (D) 1, 2, and 3

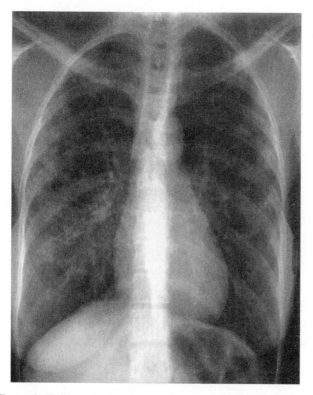

Figure 4–13. Reproduced, with permission, from Slone RM, Guitier-rez FR, Fisher AJ. *Thoracic Imaging*. New York: McGraw-Hill; 1999.

97. Which of the following pathologic conditions probably will require a decrease in exposure factors?

    (A) Osteomyelitis
    (B) Osteoporosis
    (C) Osteosclerosis
    (D) Osteochondritis

98. Diagnostic x-rays are generally associated with

    (A) high frequency and long wavelength
    (B) high frequency and short wavelength
    (C) low frequency and long wavelength
    (D) low frequency and short wavelength

99. A film/screen image exhibiting insufficient density might be attributed to

    1. inadequate kilovoltage
    2. inadequate SID
    3. grid cutoff

    (A) 1 only
    (B) 1 and 2 only
    (C) 1 and 3 only
    (D) 1, 2, and 3

100. If a lateral projection of the chest is being performed on an asthenic patient and the outer photocells are selected, what is likely to be the outcome?

    (A) Decreased density
    (B) Increased density
    (C) Scattered radiation fog
    (D) Motion blur

101. Which of the following devices is used to overcome severe variation in patient anatomy or tissue density, providing more uniform radiographic density?

    (A) Compensating filter
    (B) Grid
    (C) Collimator
    (D) Added filtration

102. What are the effects of scattered radiation on a radiographic image?

    1. It produces fog.
    2. It increases contrast.
    3. It increases grid cutoff.

    (A) 1 only
    (B) 2 only
    (C) 1 and 2 only
    (D) 1, 2, and 3

103. Which of the following groups of exposure factors would be *most appropriate* to control involuntary motion?

    (A) 400 mA, 0.03 second
    (B) 200 mA, 0.06 second
    (C) 600 mA, 0.02 second
    (D) 100 mA, 0.12 second

104. Methods that help to reduce the production of scattered radiation include using

    1. compression
    2. beam restriction
    3. a grid

    (A) 1 and 2 only
    (B) 1 and 3 only
    (C) 2 and 3 only
    (D) 1, 2, and 3

105. The function(s) of the developer in film processing is (are) to

1. remove the unexposed silver bromide crystals
2. change the exposed silver bromide crystals to black metallic silver
3. harden the emulsion

(A) 1 only
(B) 2 only
(C) 1 and 3 only
(D) 2 and 3 only

106. Although the stated focal spot size is measured directly under the actual focal spot, focal spot size actually varies along the length of the x-ray beam. At which portion of the x-ray beam is the effective focal spot the largest?

(A) At its outer edge
(B) Along the path of the central ray
(C) At the cathode end
(D) At the anode end

107. The x-ray image seen in Figure 4–14 is most likely the result of

(A) an off-level grid
(B) pronounced anode heel effect
(C) too low mAs factors
(D) too low kVp factors

108. Which of the following affect(s) both the quantity and the quality of the primary beam?

1. Half-value layer (HVL)
2. Kilovoltage (kV)
3. Milliamperage (mA)

(A) 1 only
(B) 2 only
(C) 1 and 2 only
(D) 1, 2, and 3

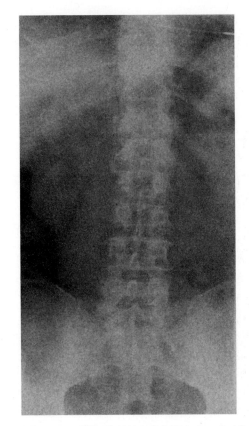

Figure 4–14. Courtesy of Stamford Hospital, Department of Radiology.

109. The intensity of ionizing radiation decreases as

(A) distance from the source of radiation decreases
(B) distance from the source of radiation increases
(C) frequency increases
(D) wavelength decreases

110. Which of the following would be useful for an examination of a patient suffering from Parkinson's disease?

1. Short exposure time
2. Decreased SID
3. Compensating filtration

(A) 1 only
(B) 1 and 2 only
(C) 1 and 3 only
(D) 1, 2, and 3

111. Underexposure of a radiograph can be caused by all the following *except* insufficient

(A) milliamperage (mA)
(B) exposure time
(C) Kilovoltage
(D) SID

112. Potential digital image postprocessing tasks include

1. PACS
2. annotation
3. inversion/reversal

(A) 1 only
(B) 1 and 2 only
(C) 2 and 3 only
(D) 1, 2, and 3

113. An anteroposterior (AP) projection of the femur was made using 300 mA, 0.03 second, 76 kV, 40-in. SID, 1.2-mm focal spot, and a 400-speed film–screen system. With all other factors remaining constant, which of the following exposure times would be required to maintain radiographic density/brightness at a 44-in. SID using 500 mA?

(A) 12 ms
(B) 22 ms
(C) 30 ms
(D) 36 ms

114. An AP radiograph of the femur was made using 300 mA, 30 ms, 76 kV, 40-in. SID, and 1.2-mm focal spot. With all other factors remaining constant, which of the following exposure times would be required to maintain brightness/density using 87 kV and the addition of a 12:1 grid?

(A) 38 ms
(B) 60 ms
(C) 75 ms
(D) 150 ms

115. HVL is affected by the amount of

1. kVp
2. beam filtration
3. tissue density

(A) 1 only
(B) 1 and 2 only
(C) 2 and 3 only
(D) 1, 2, and 3

116. In a posteroanterior (PA) projection of the chest being used for cardiac evaluation, the heart measures 14.7 cm between its widest points. If the magnification factor is known to be 1.2, what is the actual diameter of the heart?

(A) 10.4 cm
(B) 12.25 cm
(C) 13.5 cm
(D) 17.64 cm

117. Bone densitometry is often performed to

1. measure degree of bone (de) mineralization
2. evaluate the results of osteoporosis treatment/therapy
3. evaluate the condition of soft tissue adjacent to bone

(A) 1 only
(B) 1 and 2 only
(C) 2 and 3 only
(D) 1, 2, and 3

118. The differences between CR and DR include

1. DR images are displayed immediately.
2. DR has higher DQE and lower patient dose.
3. DR uses IPs.

(A) 1 only
(B) 1 and 2 only
(C) 2 and 3 only
(D) 1, 2, and 3

119. Which of the following errors is illustrated in Figure 4–15?

(A) Patient not centered to IR
(B) X-ray tube not centered to grid
(C) Inaccurate collimation
(D) Unilateral grid cutoff

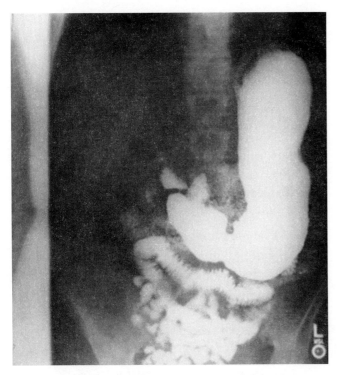

Figure 4–15. Courtesy of Stamford Hospital, Department of Radiology.

120. The process of "windowing" of digital images determines the image

(A) spatial resolution
(B) contrast
(C) pixel size
(D) matrix size

121. What is the purpose of the thin layer of lead that is often located in the rear portion of an IP?

(A) To prevent crossover
(B) To increase speed
(C) To diffuse light photons
(D) To prevent scattered radiation fog

122. The purpose of the electroconductive layer of a CR PSP plate is to

(A) provide support to the PSP layer
(B) provide mechanical strength
(C) facilitate transportation through the scanner/reader
(D) provide better resolution

123. Which of the following combinations is most likely to be associated with quantum mottle?

(A) Decreased milliampere-seconds, decreased SID
(B) Increased milliampere-seconds, decreased kilovoltage
(C) Decreased milliampere-seconds, increased kilovoltage
(D) Increased milliampere-seconds, increased SID

124. What pixel size has a $2,048 \times 2,048$ matrix with a 60-cm FOV?

(A) 0.3 mm
(B) 0.5 mm
(C) 0.15 mm
(D) 0.03 mm

125. Which of the following possesses the widest dynamic range?

(A) Film/screen imaging
(B) Beam restriction
(C) AEC
(D) CR

126. Which of the following matrix sizes is *most likely* to produce the best image resolution?

(A) 128×128
(B) 512×512
(C) $1,024 \times 1,024$
(D) $2,048 \times 2,048$

127. The device shown in Figure 4–16 is used for

(A) CT and MR QA testing
(B) timer and rectifier testing
(C) mammographic QA testing
(D) kilovoltage calibration testing

128. Factors that determine recorded detail in digital imaging include

1. part motion
2. geometric factors
3. spatial resolution

(A) 1 only
(B) 1 and 2 only
(C) 2 and 3 only
(D) 1, 2, and 3

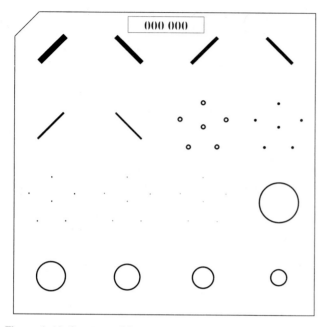

Figure 4–16. Courtesy of Gammex Inc.

129. Examples of health care informatics include

1. HIS
2. RIS
3. PACS

(A) 1 only
(B) 1 and 2 only
(C) 2 and 3 only
(D) 1, 2, and 3

130. The exposure factors of 400 mA, 17 ms, and 82 kV produce a milliampere-seconds value of

(A) 2.35
(B) 6.8
(C) 23.5
(D) 68

131. All the following statements regarding CR IPs are true *except*

(A) IPs do not contain radiographic film.
(B) IPs use no intensifying screens.
(C) IPs must exclude all white light.
(D) IPs function to protect the PSP.

132. The radiographic accessory used to measure the thickness of body parts in order to determine optimal selection of exposure factors is the

(A) fulcrum
(B) caliper
(C) densitometer
(D) ruler

133. The x-ray image seen on the computer display monitor is a (an)

(A) analog image
(B) digital image
(C) phosphor image
(D) emulsion image

134. A focal-spot size of 0.3 mm or smaller is essential for

(A) small-bone radiography
(B) magnification radiography
(C) tomography
(D) fluoroscopy

135. For which of the following examinations can the anode heel effect be an important consideration?

1. Lateral thoracic spine
2. AP femur
3. Right anterior oblique (RAO) sternum

(A) 1 only
(B) 1 and 2 only
(C) 1 and 3 only
(D) 1, 2, and 3

136. All the following have an impact on radiographic contrast *except*

(A) photon energy
(B) grid ratio
(C) OID
(D) focal-spot size

137. A radiograph made with a parallel grid demonstrates decreased density on its lateral edges. This is *most likely* due to

    (A) static electrical discharge
    (B) the grid being off-centered
    (C) improper tube angle
    (D) decreased SID

138. What is the correct critique of the CR image shown in Figure 4–17?

    (A) double exposure
    (B) grid centering error
    (C) incorrect AEC photocell
    (D) inverted focused grid

139. A particular milliampere-seconds value, regardless of the combination of milliamperes and time, will reproduce the same radiographic density. This is a statement of the

    (A) line-focus principle
    (B) inverse-square law
    (C) reciprocity law
    (D) law of conservation of energy

140. OID is related to recorded detail in which of the following ways?

    (A) Radiographic detail is directly related to OID.
    (B) Radiographic detail is inversely related to OID.
    (C) As OID increases, so does radiographic detail.
    (D) OID is unrelated to radiographic detail.

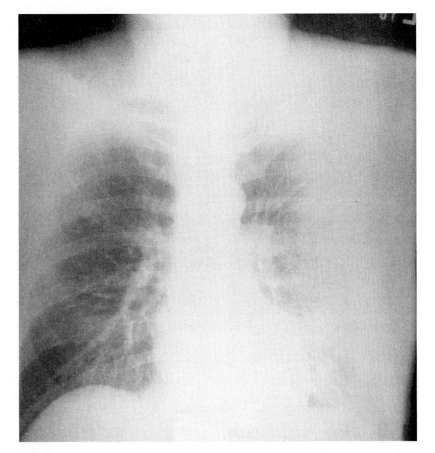

Figure 4–17. From the American College of Radiology Learning File. Courtesy of the ACR.

141. If 300 mA has been selected for a particular exposure, what exposure time would be required to produce 6 mAs?

    (A) 5 ms
    (B) 10 ms
    (C) 15 ms
    (D) 20 ms

142. In digital imaging, as DEL size decreases

    (A) brightness increases
    (B) brightness decreases
    (C) spatial resolution increases
    (D) spatial resolution decreases

143. An increase in kilovoltage will serve to

    (A) produce a longer scale of contrast
    (B) produce a shorter scale of contrast
    (C) decrease the radiographic density
    (D) decrease the production of scattered radiation

144. The functions of automatic beam limitation devices include

    1. reducing the production of scattered radiation
    2. increasing the absorption of scattered radiation
    3. changing the quality of the x-ray beam

    (A) 1 only
    (B) 2 only
    (C) 1 and 2 only
    (D) 1, 2, and 3

145. Recorded detail/resolution is inversely related to

    1. SID
    2. OID
    3. part motion

    (A) 1 only
    (B) 1 and 2 only
    (C) 2 and 3 only
    (D) 1, 2, and 3

146. Of the following groups of exposure factors, which will produce the shortest scale of radiographic contrast?

    (A) 500 mA, 0.040 second, 70 kV
    (B) 100 mA, 0.100 second, 80 kV
    (C) 200 mA, 0.025 second, 92 kV
    (D) 700 mA, 0.014 second, 80 kV

147. The PA chest image shown in Figure 4–18 demonstrates

    1. excessive density
    2. insufficient kilovoltage
    3. underpenetration

    (A) 1 only
    (B) 1 and 2 only
    (C) 2 and 3 only
    (D) 1, 2, and 3

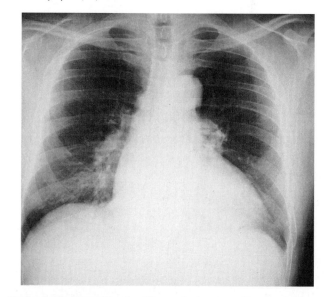

Figure 4–18. Reproduced, with permission, from Shephard CT. *Radiographic Image Production and Manipulation*. New York: McGraw-Hill; 2003.

148. Magnification fluoroscopy is accomplished by

    1. moving the image intensifier focal point further from the output phosphor
    2. selecting a smaller portion of the input phosphor
    3. decreasing the voltage to the electrostatic lenses

    (A) 1 only
    (B) 1 and 2 only
    (C) 2 and 3 only
    (D) 1, 2, and 3

149. Figure 4–19 is representative of

(A) the anode heel effect
(B) the line-focus principle
(C) the inverse-square law
(D) the reciprocity law

A   CR   B
75%   100%   120%

Figure 4–19.

150. Of the following groups of technical factors, which will produce the greatest radiographic density?

(A) 10 mAs, 74 kV, 44-in. SID
(B) 10 mAs, 74 kV, 36-in. SID
(C) 5 mAs, 85 kV, 48-in. SID
(D) 5 mAs, 85 kV, 40-in. SID

151. Which of the following requires two exposures to evaluate focal-spot accuracy?

(A) Pinhole camera
(B) Slit camera
(C) Star pattern
(D) Bar pattern

152. Focusing distance is associated with which of the following?

(A) Computed tomography
(B) Chest radiography
(C) Magnification radiography
(D) Grids

153. The *processing algorithm* represents the

(A) pixel value distribution
(B) anatomical part and projection
(C) image grayscale
(D) screen speed

154. The relationship between the height of a grid's lead strips and the distance between them is referred to as grid

(A) ratio
(B) radius
(C) frequency
(D) focusing distance

155. Because of the anode heel effect, the intensity of the x-ray beam is greatest along the

(A) path of the central ray
(B) anode end of the beam
(C) cathode end of the beam
(D) transverse axis of the IR

156. Characteristics of high-ratio focused grids, compared with lower-ratio grids, include which of the following?

1. They allow more positioning latitude.
2. They are more efficient in collecting SR.
3. They absorb more of the useful beam.

(A) 1 only
(B) 1 and 2 only
(C) 2 and 3 only
(D) 1, 2, and 3

157. Factors that can affect histogram appearance include

1. beam restriction
2. centering errors
3. incorrect SID

(A) 1 only
(B) 1 and 2 only
(C) 2 and 3 only
(D) 1, 2, and 3

158. Figure 4–20 was made using film/screen technique. The area of blurriness seen in the upper part of the radiograph shown is *most likely* due to

   (A) scattered radiation fog
   (B) patient motion
   (C) poor screen–film contact
   (D) grid cutoff

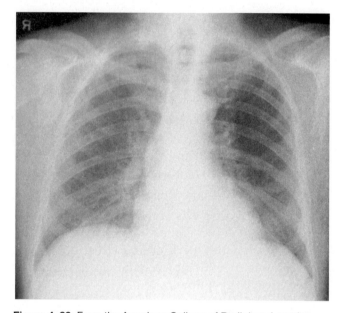

Figure 4–20. From the American College of Radiology Learning File. Courtesy of the ACR.

159. Changes in milliampere-seconds can affect all the following *except*

   (A) quantity of x-ray photons produced
   (B) exposure rate
   (C) optical density
   (D) recorded detail

160. Low-kilovoltage exposure factors usually are indicated for radiographic examinations using

   1. water-soluble, iodinated media
   2. a negative contrast agent
   3. barium sulfate

   (A) 1 only
   (B) 1 and 2 only
   (C) 3 only
   (D) 1 and 3 only

161. Which of the following examinations might require the use of 70 kV?

   1. AP abdomen
   2. Chest radiograph
   3. Barium-filled stomach

   (A) 1 only
   (B) 2 only
   (C) 1 and 2 only
   (D) 2 and 3 only

162. Which of the following is/are associated with magnification fluoroscopy?

   1. Increased mA
   2. Smaller portion of the input phosphor is used.
   3. Image intensifier focal point moves closer to the output phosphor.

   (A) 1 only
   (B) 1 and 2 only
   (C) 2 and 3 only
   (D) 1, 2, and 3

163. A lateral projection of the lumbar spine was made using 200 mA, 1-second exposure, and 90 kV. If the exposure factors were changed to 200 mA, 0.5 second, and 104 kV, there would be an obvious change in which of the following?

   1. Radiographic density
   2. Scale of radiographic contrast
   3. Distortion

   (A) 1 only
   (B) 2 only
   (C) 2 and 3 only
   (D) 1, 2, and 3

164. A decrease in kilovoltage will result in

   (A) a decrease in optical density
   (B) a decrease in contrast
   (C) a decrease in recorded detail
   (D) a decrease in image resolution

165. Brightness and contrast resolution in digital imaging can be influenced by

1. window level (WL)
2. window width (WW)
3. look-up table (LUT)

(A) 1 only
(B) 1 and 2 only
(C) 2 and 3 only
(D) 1, 2, and 3

166. What feature is used to display RIS information on current patients?

(A) HIS
(B) Modality work list
(C) PACS
(D) DICOM

167. A decrease from 200 to 100 mA will result in a decrease in which of the following?

1. Wavelength
2. Exposure rate
3. Beam intensity

(A) 1 only
(B) 1 and 2 only
(C) 2 and 3 only
(D) 1, 2, and 3

168. The radiograph shown in Figure 4–21 illustrates incorrect use of

(A) collimator
(B) grid
(C) AEC
(D) focal spot

169. The effect described as *differential absorption* is

1. responsible for radiographic contrast
2. a result of attenuating characteristics of tissue
3. minimized by the use of a high peak kilovoltage

(A) 1 only
(B) 1 and 2 only
(C) 1 and 3 only
(D) 1, 2, and 3

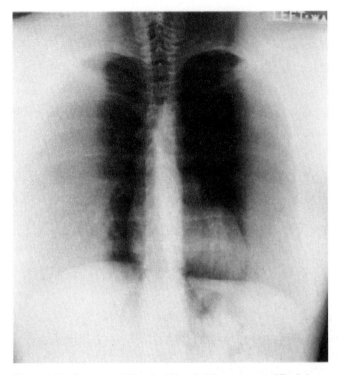

Figure 4–21. Courtesy of Stamford Hospital, Department of Radiology.

170. A satisfactory radiograph of the abdomen was made at a 38-in. SID using 400 mA, 60-ms exposure, and 80 kV. If the distance is changed to 42 in., what new exposure time would be required?

(A) 25 ms
(B) 50 ms
(C) 73 ms
(D) 93 ms

171. Which of the following is (are) associated with subject contrast?

1. Patient thickness
2. Tissue density
3. Kilovoltage

(A) 1 only
(B) 1 and 2 only
(C) 1 and 3 only
(D) 1, 2, and 3

172. Typical patient demographic and examination information include(s)

1. type of examination
2. accession number
3. date and time of examination

(A) 1 only
(B) 1 and 2 only
(C) 2 and 3 only
(D) 1, 2, and 3

173. For which of the following examinations might the use of a grid *not* be necessary in an adult patient?

(A) Hip
(B) Knee
(C) Abdomen
(D) Lumbar spine

174. The quantity of scattered radiation reaching the IR can be reduced through the use of

1. a fast imaging system
2. an air gap
3. a stationary grid

(A) 1 and 2 only
(B) 1 and 3 only
(C) 2 and 3 only
(D) 1, 2, and 3

175. Why is a very short exposure time essential in chest radiography?

(A) To avoid excessive focal-spot blur
(B) To maintain short-scale contrast
(C) To minimize involuntary motion
(D) To minimize patient discomfort

176. The interaction between x-ray photons and matter illustrated in Figure 4–22 is *most likely* to be associated with

1. high kilovoltage
2. high contrast
3. high-atomic-number absorber

(A) 1 only
(B) 1 and 2 only
(C) 2 and 3 only
(D) 1, 2, and 3

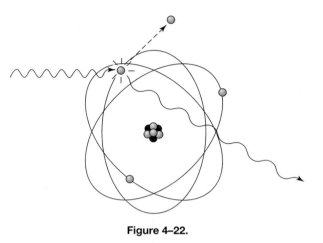

Figure 4–22.

177. Beam attenuation characteristics, or density values, in CT are expressed as

1. Hounsfield units
2. CT numbers
3. heat units

(A) 1 only
(B) 1 and 2 only
(C) 2 and 3 only
(D) 1, 2, and 3

178. An exposure was made at a 36-in. SID using 300 mA, a 30-ms exposure, and 80 kV and an 8:1 grid. It is desired to repeat the radiograph using a 40-in. SID and 70 kV. With all other factors remaining constant, what new exposure time will be required?

(A) 0.03 second
(B) 0.07 second
(C) 0.14 second
(D) 0.36 second

179. Which of the following is (are) characteristic(s) of a 5:1 grid?

1. It allows some positioning latitude.
2. It is used with high-kilovoltage exposures.
3. It absorbs a high percentage of scattered radiation.

(A) 1 only
(B) 1 and 3 only
(C) 2 and 3 only
(D) 1, 2, and 3

180. How is SID related to exposure rate and image density?

(A) As SID increases, exposure rate increases and image density increases.
(B) As SID increases, exposure rate increases and image density decreases.
(C) As SID increases, exposure rate decreases and image density increases.
(D) As SID increases, exposure rate decreases and image density decreases.

181. An x-ray exposure of a particular part is made and restricted to a 14 × 17 in. field size. The same exposure is repeated, but the x-ray beam is restricted to a 4 × 4 in. field. Compared with the first image, the second image will demonstrate

1. more contrast
2. higher contrast
3. more density

(A) 1 only
(B) 1 and 2 only
(C) 3 only
(D) 2 and 3 only

182. In digital imaging, TFT DEL size is related to

(A) contrast
(B) brightness
(C) spatial resolution
(D) plate size

183. Which of the following pathologic conditions would require an increase in exposure factors?

(A) Pneumoperitoneum
(B) Obstructed bowel
(C) Renal colic
(D) Ascites

184. Factors that determine recorded detail in digital imaging include

1. focal spot size
2. SID
3. DEL size

(A) 1 only
(B) 1 and 2 only
(C) 2 and 3 only
(D) 1, 2, and 3

185. The photostimulable phosphor (PSP) plates used in CR are constructed in layers that include

1. light shield layer
2. support layer
3. electroconductive layer

(A) 1 only
(B) 1 and 2 only
(C) 2 and 3 only
(D) 1, 2, and 3

186. A QA program serves to

1. keep patient dose to a minimum
2. keep radiographic quality consistent
3. ensure equipment efficiency

(A) 1 only
(B) 1 and 2 only
(C) 1 and 3 only
(D) 1, 2, and 3

187. The purpose of the electroconductive layer of a CR PSP plate is to

(A) provide support to the PSP layer
(B) provide mechanical strength
(C) facilitate transportation through the scanner/reader
(D) provide better resolution

188. Any images obtained using dual x-ray absorptiometry (DXA) bone densitometry

    1. are used to evaluate accuracy of the region of interest (ROI)
    2. are used as evaluation for various bone/joint disorders
    3. reflect the similar attenuation properties of soft tissue and bone

    (A) 1 only
    (B) 1 and 2 only
    (C) 1 and 3 only
    (D) 1, 2, and 3

189. Foreshortening of an anatomic structure means that

    (A) it is projected on the IR smaller than its actual size
    (B) its image is more lengthened than its actual size
    (C) it is accompanied by geometric blur
    (D) it is significantly magnified

190. To produce a just perceptible increase in radiographic density, the radiographer must increase the

    (A) mAs by 30%
    (B) mAs by 15%
    (C) kV by 15%
    (D) kV by 30%

191. A radiograph made using 300 mA, 0.1 second, and 75 kV exhibits motion unsharpness but otherwise satisfactory technical quality. The radiograph will be repeated using a shorter exposure time. Using 86 kV and 400 mA, what should be the new exposure time?

    (A) 25 ms
    (B) 37 ms
    (C) 50 ms
    (D) 75 ms

192. The radiograph shown in Figure 4–23 was made using screen/film technique and exhibits an artifact caused by

    (A) an inverted focused grid
    (B) poor screen–film contact
    (C) a foreign body in the IR
    (D) static electricity

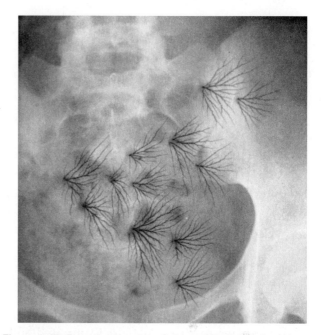

Figure 4–23. From the American College of Radiology Learning File. Courtesy of the ACR.

193. X-ray tubes used in CT differ from those used in x-ray, in that CT x-ray tubes must

    1. have a very high short-exposure rating
    2. be capable of tolerating several million heat units
    3. have a small focal spot for optimal resolution

    (A) 1 only
    (B) 1 and 2 only
    (C) 2 and 3 only
    (D) 1, 2, and 3

194. Figure 4–24 is representative of

    (A) the anode heel effect
    (B) the line-focus principle
    (C) the inverse-square law
    (D) the reciprocity law

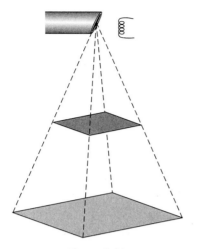

Figure 4–24.

195. Exposure-type artifacts include

1. double exposure
2. motion
3. image fading

(A) 1 only
(B) 1 and 2 only
(C) 2 and 3 only
(D) 1, 2, and 3

196. When involuntary motion must be considered, the exposure time may be cut in half if the kilovoltage is

(A) doubled
(B) increased by 15%
(C) increased by 25%
(D) increased by 35%

197. Which of the following groups of exposure factors would be most effective in eliminating prominent pulmonary vascular markings in the RAO position of the sternum?

(A) 500 mA, ⅟₃₀ s, 70 kV
(B) 200 mA, 0.04 second, 80 kV
(C) 300 mA, ⅟₁₀ s, 80 kV
(D) 25 mA, ⁷⁄₁₀ s, 70 kV

198. An exposure was made of a part using 300 mA and 0.06 second with a 200-speed film–screen combination. An additional radiograph is requested using a 400-speed system to reduce motion unsharpness. Using 400 mA, all other factors remaining constant, what should be the new exposure time?

(A) 5 ms
(B) 11 ms
(C) 22 ms
(D) 44 ms

199. The image seen in Figure 4–25 was made using film/screen technique and the film was processed in a chemical film processor. The artifacts seen on the resulting radiograph are called

(A) pi lines
(B) guide-shoe marks
(C) hesitation marks
(D) reticulation

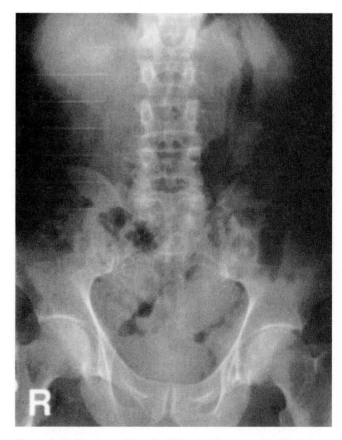

Figure 4–25. Courtesy of Stamford Hospital, Department of Radiology.

200. HVL is affected by the amount of

1. kVp
2. beam filtration
3. tissue density

(A) 1 only
(B) 1 and 2 only
(C) 2 and 3 only
(D) 1, 2, and 3

201. The attenuation of x-ray photons is not influenced by

1. pathology
2. structure atomic number
3. photon quantity

(A) 1 only
(B) 3 only
(C) 2 and 3 only
(D) 1, 2, and 3

202. If, upon QC testing, the HVL of the x-ray beam produced by a particular x-ray tube *increases*, it is an indication of

1. vaporized tungsten deposited on the inner surface of the glass envelope
2. an increase in the kilovoltage being produced by the tube
3. a decrease in the kilovoltage being produced by the tube

(A) 1 only
(B) 1 and 2 only
(C) 2 and 3 only
(D) 1, 2, and 3

203. A compensating filter is used to

(A) absorb the harmful photons that contribute only to patient dose
(B) even out widely differing tissue densities
(C) eliminate much of the scattered radiation
(D) improve fluoroscopy

204. Boxes of film stored in too warm an area may be subject to

(A) static marks
(B) film fog
(C) high contrast
(D) loss of density

205. Which of the following will influence recorded detail?

1. Dynamic range
2. Part motion
3. Focal spot

(A) 1 and 2 only
(B) 1 and 3 only
(C) 2 and 3 only
(D) 1, 2, and 3

206. Which interaction is responsible for producing the most x-ray photons at the x-ray tube target?

(A) Bremsstrahlung
(B) Characteristic
(C) Photoelectric
(D) Compton

207. Which of the following terms is used to describe unsharp edges of tiny radiographic details?

(A) Diffusion
(B) Mottle
(C) Blur
(D) Umbra

208. Which of the following is (are) classified as rare earth phosphors?

1. Lanthanum oxybromide
2. Gadolinium oxysulfide
3. Cesium iodide

(A) 1 only
(B) 1 and 2 only
(C) 2 and 3 only
(D) 1, 2, and 3

209. The mottled appearance of the radiograph shown in Figure 4–26 is *most likely* representative of

(A) Paget disease
(B) osteoporosis
(C) processing artifacts
(D) exposure artifacts

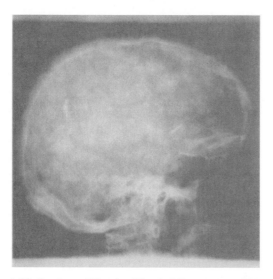

Figure 4–26. Courtesy of Stamford Hospital, Department of Radiology.

210. As grid ratio is decreased,

(A) the scale of contrast becomes longer
(B) the scale of contrast becomes shorter
(C) radiographic density decreases
(D) radiographic distortion decreases

211. X-ray film emulsion is most sensitive to safe-light fog

(A) before exposure and development
(B) after exposure
(C) during development
(D) at low humidity

212. Which of the following focal-spot sizes should be employed for magnification radiography?

(A) 0.2 mm
(B) 0.6 mm
(C) 1.2 mm
(D) 2.0 mm

213. If a 6-in. OID is introduced during a particular radiographic examination, what change in SID will be necessary to overcome objectionable magnification?

(A) The SID must be increased by 6 in..
(B) The SID must be increased by 18 in..
(C) The SID must be decreased by 6 in..
(D) The SID must be increased by 42 in..

214. If a particular grid has lead strips 0.40 mm thick, 4.0 mm high, and 0.25 mm apart, what is its grid ratio?

(A) 8:1
(B) 10:1
(C) 12:1
(D) 16:1

215. The line-focus principle expresses the relationship between

(A) the actual and the effective focal spot
(B) exposure given the IR and resulting density
(C) SID used and resulting density
(D) grid ratio and lines per inch

216. Which of the following has the greatest effect on radiographic density/brightness?

(A) Aluminum filtration
(B) Kilovoltage
(C) SID
(D) Scattered radiation

217. Shape distortion is influenced by the relationship between the

1. x-ray tube and the part to be imaged
2. part to be imaged and the IR
3. IR and the x-ray tube

(A) 1 only
(B) 1 and 2 only
(C) 1 and 3 only
(D) 1, 2, and 3

218. How can the radiograph shown in Figure 4–27 be improved?

1. Decrease milliampere-seconds
2. Eliminate motion
3. Lengthen the scale of contrast

(A) 1 only
(B) 2 only
(C) 1 and 3 only
(D) 1, 2, and 3

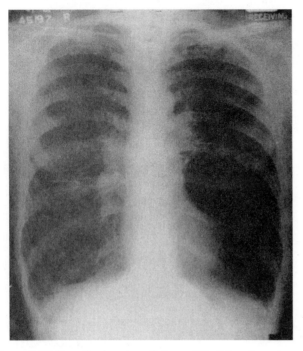

Figure 4–27. From the American College of Radiology Learning File. Courtesy of the ACR.

219. IRs frequently have a rear lead-foil layer that functions to

(A) improve penetration
(B) absorb backscatter
(C) preserve resolution
(D) increase the screen speed

220. The continued emission of light by a phosphor after the activating source has ceased is termed

(A) fluorescence
(B) phosphorescence
(C) image intensification
(D) quantum mottle

221. Which combination of exposure factors *most likely* will contribute to producing the shortest-scale contrast?

	mAs	kV	Film–screen system	Grid ratio	Field size
(A)	10	70	400	5:1	14 × 17 in.
(B)	12	90	200	8:1	14 × 17 in.
(C)	15	90	200	12:1	11 × 14 in.
(D)	20	80	400	10:1	8 × 10 in.

222. How often are radiographic equipment collimators required to be evaluated?

(A) Annually
(B) Biannually
(C) Semiannually
(D) Quarterly

223. In digital imaging, as the size of the image matrix increases,

1. FOV increases
2. pixel size decreases
3. spatial resolution increases

(A) 1 only
(B) 1 and 2 only
(C) 2 and 3 only
(D) 1, 2, and 3

224. Exposed silver halide crystals are changed to black metallic silver by the

(A) preservative
(B) reducers
(C) activators
(D) hardener

225. Grid cutoff due to off-centering would result in

(A) overall loss of density
(B) both sides of the image being underexposed
(C) overexposure under the anode end
(D) underexposure under the anode end

226. The advantage(s) of high-kilovoltage chest radiography is (are) that

1. exposure latitude is increased
2. it produces long-scale contrast
3. it reduces patient dose

(A) 1 only
(B) 1 and 2 only
(C) 2 and 3 only
(D) 1, 2, and 3

227. The exposure factors of 400 mA, 70 ms, and 78 kV were used to produce a particular radiographic density and contrast. A similar radiograph can be produced using 500 mA, 90 kV, and

(A) 14 ms
(B) 28 ms
(C) 56 ms
(D) 70 ms

228. Disadvantages of using low-kilovoltage technical factors include

1. insufficient penetration
2. increased patient dose
3. diminished latitude

(A) 1 only
(B) 1 and 2 only
(C) 1 and 3 only
(D) 1, 2, and 3

229. Which of the following statements is (are) true regarding Figure 4–28?

1. Image A was made using a higher kilovoltage than image B.
2. Image A was made with a higher-ratio grid than image B.
3. Image A demonstrates shorter-scale contrast than image B.

(A) 1 only
(B) 1 and 2 only
(C) 2 and 3 only
(D) 1, 2, and 3

230. Geometric unsharpness is *directly* influenced by

1. OID
2. SOD
3. SID

(A) 1 only
(B) 1 and 2 only
(C) 1 and 3 only
(D) 1, 2, and 3

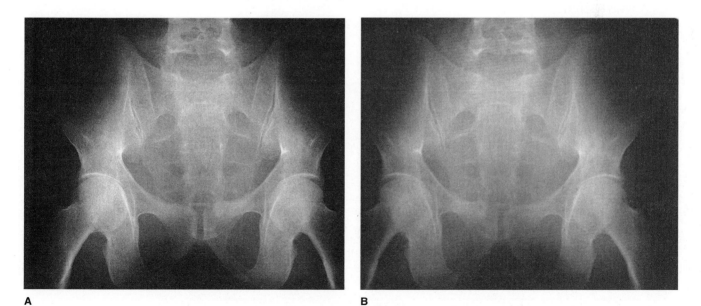

A   B

Figure 4–28A&B. From the American College of Radiology Learning File. Courtesy of the ACR.

231. Which of the following is/are associated with magnification fluoroscopy?

1. Less noise
2. Improved contrast resolution
3. Improved spatial resolution

(A) 1 only
(B) 1 and 2 only
(C) 2 and 3 only
(D) 1, 2, and 3

232. Which of the following may be used to reduce the effect of scattered radiation on a finished radiograph?

1. Grids
2. Collimators
3. Compression bands

(A) 1 only
(B) 1 and 3 only
(C) 2 and 3 only
(D) 1, 2, and 3

233. Which of the following is (are) directly related to photon energy?

1. Kilovoltage
2. Milliamperes
3. Wavelength

(A) 1 only
(B) 1 and 2 only
(C) 1 and 3 only
(D) 1, 2, and 3

234. What information, located on each box of film, is important to note and has a direct relationship to image quality?

(A) Number of films in the box
(B) Manufacturer's name
(C) Expiration date
(D) Emulsion lot

235. If 40 mAs and a 200-speed screen–film system were used for a particular exposure, what new milliampere-seconds value would be required to produce the same density if the screen–film system were changed to 800 speed?

(A) 10
(B) 20
(C) 80
(D) 160

236. An exposure was made using 8 mAs and 60 kV. If the kilovoltage was changed to 70 to obtain longer-scale contrast, what new milliampere-seconds value is required to maintain density?

(A) 2
(B) 4
(C) 16
(D) 32

237. Recorded detail can be improved by decreasing

1. the SID
2. the OID
3. patient/part motion

(A) 1 only
(B) 3 only
(C) 2 and 3 only
(D) 1, 2, and 3

238. Compression of the breast during mammographic imaging improves the technical quality of the image because

1. geometric blurring is decreased
2. less scattered radiation is produced
3. patient motion is reduced

(A) 1 only
(B) 3 only
(C) 2 and 3 only
(D) 1, 2, and 3

239. Distortion can be caused by

1. tube angle
2. the position of the organ or structure within the body
3. the radiographic positioning of the part

(A) 1 only
(B) 1 and 2 only
(C) 2 and 3 only
(D) 1, 2, and 3

240. As window level increases

(A) contrast scale increases
(B) contrast scale decreases
(C) brightness increases
(D) brightness decreases

241. Which of the following statements is (are) true with respect to the radiograph shown in Figure 4–29?

1. The image exhibits long-scale contrast.
2. The image exhibits a clothing artifact.
3. The image demonstrates motion blur.

(A) 1 and 2 only
(B) 1 and 3 only
(C) 2 and 3 only
(D) 1, 2, and 3

242. What is the relationship between tissue attenuation coefficient in CT and its related Hounsfield unit (HU)?

(A) The greater the tissue attenuation coefficient, the lower the HU value.
(B) The greater the tissue attenuation coefficient, the higher the HU value.
(C) Tissue attenuation coefficient and HU value are unrelated.
(D) Tissue attenuation coefficient and HU value are identical.

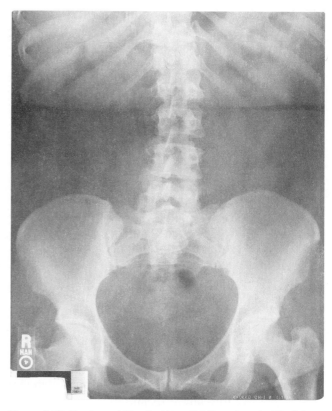

Figure 4–29. Courtesy of Stamford Hospital, Department of Radiology

243. A grid usually is employed in which of the following circumstances?

1. When radiographing a large or dense body part
2. When using high kilovoltage
3. When a lower patient dose is required

(A) 1 only
(B) 3 only
(C) 1 and 2 only
(D) 1, 2, and 3

244. Exposure factors of 90 kV and 3 mAs are used for a particular nongrid exposure. What should be the new milliampere-seconds (mAs) value if a 12:1 grid is added?

(A) 86
(B) 9
(C) 12
(D) 15

245. An exposure was made using 300 mA, 40 ms exposure, and 85 kV. Each of the following changes will decrease the radiographic density by one half *except* a change to

    (A) $^1/_{50}$-s exposure
    (B) 72 kV
    (C) 10 mAs
    (D) 150 mA

246. Which of the following units is (are) used to express resolution?

    1. Line-spread function
    2. Line pairs per millimeter
    3. Line-focus principle

    (A) 1 only
    (B) 1 and 2 only
    (C) 2 and 3 only
    (D) 1, 2, and 3

247. Which of the following is (are) methods used for x-ray film silver reclamation?

    1. Photoelectric method
    2. Metallic replacement method
    3. Electrolytic method

    (A) 1 only
    (B) 1 and 2 only
    (C) 2 and 3 only
    (D) 1, 2, and 3

248. Which of the following groups of technical factors would be *most appropriate* for the radiographic examination shown in Figure 4–30?

    (A) 400 mA, $^1/_{30}$ s, 72 kV
    (B) 300 mA, $^1/_{50}$ s, 82 kV
    (C) 300 mA, $^1/_{120}$ s, 94 kV
    (D) 50 mA, $^1/_4$ s, 72 kV

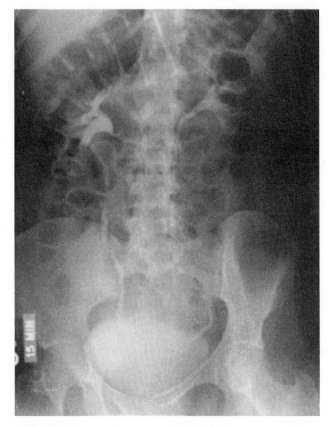

Figure 4–30. Courtesy of Stamford Hospital, Department of Radiology.

249. In which of the following examinations should 70 kV *not* be exceeded?

   (A) Upper GI (UGI)

   (B) Barium enema (BE)

   (C) Intravenous urogram (IVU)

   (D) Chest

250. Which of the following statements is (are) true regarding the artifact seen in the erect PA projection of the chest shown in Figure 4–31?

   (A) The object is located within the patient.

   (B) The object is located within the IP.

   (C) The object is located between the patient and the x-ray tube.

   (D) The object is located between the patient and the IP.

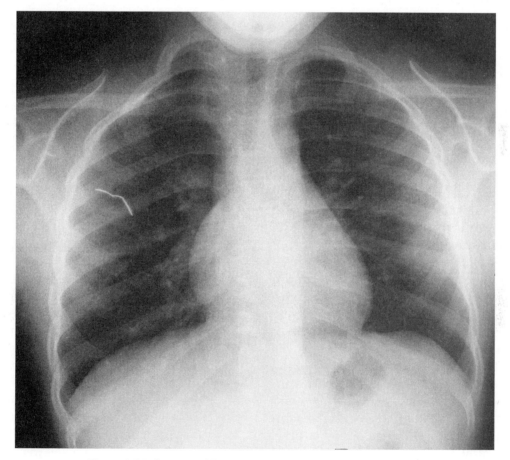

Figure 4–31. Courtesy of Stamford Hospital, Department of Radiology.

Answers and Explanations

1. **(C)** Focal-spot size accuracy is related to the degree of *geometric blur*, that is, edge gradient or penumbra. Manufacturer tolerance for new focal spots is 50%; that is, a 0.3-mm focal spot actually may be 0.45 mm. Additionally, the focal spot can increase in size as the x-ray tube ages—hence the importance of *testing* newly arrived focal spots and periodic testing to monitor focal-spot changes. Focal-spot size can be measured with a *pinhole camera, slit camera,* or *star-pattern-type resolution device.* The pinhole camera is rather difficult to use accurately and requires the use of excessive tube (heat) loading. With a *slit camera*, two exposures are made; one measures the length of the focal spot, and the other measures the width. The *star pattern,* or similar resolution device such as the *bar pattern,* can measure focal-spot size *as a function of geometric blur* and is readily adaptable in a QA program to monitor focal-spot changes over a period of time. It is recommended that focal-spot size be checked on installation of a new x-ray tube and annually thereafter. *(Bushong, 8th ed., p. 462)*

2. **(B)** In digital imaging, pixel size is determined by dividing the field of view (FOV) by the matrix. In this case, the FOV is 20 cm; since the answer is expressed in millimeters, first change 20 cm to 200 mm. Then 200 divided by 512 equals 0.39 mm:

$$20 \text{ cm} = 200 \text{ mm}$$
$$200 \div 512 = 0.39 \text{ mm/pixel}$$

The FOV and matrix size are independent of one another; that is, either can be changed, and the other will remain unaffected. However, pixel size is affected by changes in either the FOV or matrix size. For example, if the matrix size is increased, pixel size decreases. If FOV is increased, pixel size increases. Pixel size is inversely related to resolution. As pixel size increases, resolution decreases. *(Fosbinder and Kelsey, p. 285; Bushong 9th ed., p. 376)*

3. **(A)** Pixel depth is directly related to shades of gray—called *dynamic range*—and is measured in *bits.* The greater the number of bits, the more shades of gray. For example, a 1-bit (2^1) pixel will demonstrate 2 shades of gray, whereas a 6-bit (2^6) pixel can display 64 shades and a 7-bit (2^7) pixel 128 shades. However, pixel depth is unrelated to resolution.

   A digital image is formed by a *matrix of pixels* (picture elements) in rows and columns. A matrix that has 512 pixels in each row and column is a 512 × 512 matrix. The term *field of view* is used to describe how much of the patient (e.g., 150-mm diameter) is included in the matrix. The matrix and the field of view can be changed independently without one affecting the other, but changes in either will change pixel size. As in traditional radiography, *spatial resolution* is measured in line pairs per millimeter (lp/mm). As *matrix size is increased* (e.g., from 512 × 512 to 1,024 × 1,024) there are more and smaller pixels in the matrix and, therefore, *improved resolution.* Fewer and larger pixels result in poor resolution, a "pixelly" image, that is, one in which you can actually see the individual pixel boxes. *(Fosbinder and Kelsey, p. 286; Shephard, p. 336)*

4. **(C)** Added aluminum filtration removes more low-energy photons; therefore there is a decrease in the *number* of photons in the x-ray beam, that is, beam *intensity*. Because low-energy photons are removed, the overall average energy of the x-ray beam is increased. This process can also be referred to as beam *hardening* because its average energy is increased. The maximum energy of the beam is unchanged as long as the kV remains unchanged. *(Bushong, 9th ed., pp. 146–147)*

5. **(B)** The image illustrates *aliasing artifact*, or Moiré effect. Aliasing, or Moiré, has the appearance of somewhat wavy linear lines and can occur in computed radiography when using *stationary grids*. If the grid's lead strip pattern (i.e., frequency) matches the scanning (sampling) pattern of the scanner/reader, the resulting interference can cause aliasing (also called Moiré) artifact. When sampling frequencies are decreased, aliasing/Moiré is less evident. As sampling frequencies increase, aliasing/Moiré is more obvious. *(Seeram, p. 87; Fuji Computed Radiography, p. 70)*

6. **(A)** As the distance from focal spot to IR (SID) increases, so does recorded detail. Because the part is being exposed by more perpendicular (less divergent) rays, less magnification and blur are produced. Although the best recorded detail is obtained using a long SID, the necessary increase in exposure factors and resulting increased patient exposure become a problem. An optimal 40-in. SID is used for most radiography, with the major exception being chest examinations. *(Selman, 9th ed., pp. 206–207; Shephard, pp. 221–222)*

7. **(C)** Grids are composed of alternating strips of lead and radiolucent interspace material. The interspace material is either aluminum or plastic fiber. Aluminum resists moisture, is sturdier, provides a "smoother" appearance with less visible grid lines, but requires a higher mAs and therefore increases patient dose. Plastic fiber interspace material can be

affected by moisture, resulting in warping. Carbon fiber is often used as image plate front material because of its durability and homogeneity. *(Bushong, 9th ed., p. 234)*

8. **(B)** The addition of a grid will help to clean up the scattered radiation produced by higher kilovoltage, but the grid requires an *adjustment of milliampere-seconds*. According to the grid conversion factors listed here, the addition of an 8:1 grid requires that the original milliampere-seconds be multiplied by a factor of 4:

$$
\begin{aligned}
\text{No grid} &= 1 \times \text{original mAs} \\
\text{5:1 grid} &= 2 \times \text{original mAs} \\
\text{6:1 grid} &= 3 \times \text{original mAs} \\
\text{8:1 grid} &= 4 \times \text{original mAs} \\
\text{12:1 (or 10:1)grid} &= 5 \times \text{original mAs} \\
\text{16:1 grid} &= 6 \times \text{original mAs}
\end{aligned}
$$

The original milliampere-seconds value is 1.2. The ideal adjustment, therefore, requires a 4.8 mAs at 90 kV. Although 2.4 mAs with 100 kV (choice C), or 1.2 mAs with 110 kV (choice A), also might seem workable, an increase in kilovoltage would further compromise contrast, nullifying the effect of the grid. Additionally, kilovoltage exceeding 100 should not be used with an 8:1 grid. *(Shephard, pp. 247–248)*

9. **(A)** One of the biggest advantages of CR/DR is the *latitude* it offers. The characteristic curve of typical film emulsion has a "range of correct exposure" limited by the toe and shoulder of the curve. In CR/DR, there is a *linear* relationship between the exposure, given the PSP and its resulting luminescence, as it is scanned by the laser, as illustrated in the figure. This affords much *greater exposure latitude*; technical inaccuracies can be effectively eliminated. Overexposure of up to 500% and underexposure of up to 80% are reported as recoverable, thus eliminating most retakes. *This surely affords increased efficiency; however, this does not mean that images can be exposed arbitrarily.* The professional radiographer has a responsibility to keep dose reduction to a minimum. The same exposure factors as screen–film systems or less generally are recommended for CR/DR. *(Shephard, p. 332)*

10. (B) An increase in kilovoltage (photon energy) will result in a *greater number* (i.e., exposure rate) of scattered photons (Compton interaction). These scattered photons carry no useful information and contribute to radiation *fog*, thus decreasing radiographic contrast. *(Selman, 9th ed., p. 117)*

11. (D) A CT imaging system has three component parts—a gantry, a computer, and an operating console. The gantry component includes an x-ray tube, a detector array, a high-voltage generator, a collimator assembly, and a patient couch with its motorized mechanism. Although the CT x-ray tube is similar to direct-projection x-ray tubes, it has several special requirements. The CT x-ray tube must have a *very high short-exposure rating* and must be capable of *tolerating several million heat units* while still having a *small focal spot* for optimal resolution. To help tolerate the very high production of heat units, the anode must be capable of *high-speed rotation*. The x-ray tube produces a *pulsed x-ray beam (1–5 ms)* using up to about 1,000 mA. *(Bushong, 8th ed., pp. 429–430; Bontrager and Lampignano, 6th ed., p. 731)*

12. (A) The image shown is a double exposure. Note the ilia and lower pelvic structures. Two pelves are clearly identifiable. Particularly noteworthy is how CR will "correct" the exposure values. The image does not appear overexposed, but the superimposed abdominal images are unmistakably evident. An inverted IP would have imaged the rear panel of the IP—a large grid-like appearance. An incomplete erasure or image fading would show only a portion of the image—here we have the entire superimposed abdomen. *(Carlton and Adler, 4th ed., pp. 362–363)*

13. (A) Limiting the size of the radiographic field (irradiated area) serves to limit the amount of scattered radiation produced within the anatomic part. Therefore, as field size *decreases*, scattered radiation production *decreases*, and image quality increases. Limiting the size of the radiographic field is a very effective means of reducing the quantity of non–information-carrying scattered radiation (fog) produced, resulting in improved detail visibility. Limiting the size of the radiographic

field is also the most effective means of patient radiation protection. *(Shephard, p. 203)*

14. (C) Milliampere-seconds (mAs) is the exposure factor that is used to regulate radiographic density. Using the equation milliamperage × time = mAs, determine each mAs: (A) = 5 mAs, (B) = 8 mAs, (C) = 28 mAs, (D) = 18 mAs. Group C will produce the most radiographic density. *(Selman, 9th ed., p. 214)*

15. (C) Inside the IP is the *photostimulable phosphor* (PSP). This PSP (or SPS—Storage Phosphor Screen), with its layer of europium-activated barium fluorohalide, serves as the IR because it is exposed in the traditional manner and receives the latent image. The PSP can *store* the latent image for several hours; after about 8 hours, noticeable image fading will occur. Once the IP is placed into the CR processor (*scanner* or *reader*), the PSP plate is removed automatically. The latent image on the PSP is changed to a manifest image as it is scanned by a narrow, high-intensity *helium–neon laser* to obtain the pixel data. As the PSP is scanned in the reader, it releases a violet light—a process referred to as *photostimulated luminescence* (PSL). *(Carlton and Adler, 4th ed., pp. 357–358; Bushong 9th ed., p. 413)*

16. (D) All the factor changes affect recorded detail, but focal spot size does not affect magnification. An increase in SID would *decrease* magnification. Although a decrease in SID will increase magnification, it does not have as significant an effect as an increase in OID. In general, it requires an increase of 7 in. SID to compensate for every inch of OID. *(Carlton and Adler, 4th ed., pp. 458–460)*

17. (C) When exposure rate decreases (as a result of increased SID), an appropriate increase in milliampere-seconds is required to maintain the original radiographic density. Unless exposure is increased, the resulting radiograph will be underexposed. The formula used to determine the new milliampere-seconds value (*density-maintenance formula*) is substituting known values:

$$\frac{\text{Old mAs}}{\text{New mAs}} = \frac{\text{old } D^2}{\text{new } D^2}$$

Substituting known values:

$$\frac{(Old\ mAs)\ 9}{(New\ mAs)\ x} = \frac{(old\ D^2)\ 1,600}{(new\ D^2)\ 5,184}$$

$$1,600x = 46,656$$

$$\frac{9}{x} = \frac{1,600}{5,184}$$

Thus, $x = 29.16$ mAs at 72 in. SID. To determine the required milliamperes (mA × s = mAs),

$$0.1x = 29.16$$
$$x = 291.6\ mA$$

(Selman, 9th ed., p. 214)

18. **(C)** Dual x-ray absorptiometry (DXA) imaging is used to evaluate bone mineral density (BMD). It is the most widely used method of *bone densitometry*—it is *low-dose*, *precise*, and *uncomplicated* to use/perform. DXA uses *two photon energies*—one for soft tissue and one for bone. Since bone is denser and attenuates x-ray photons more readily, photon *attenuation is calculated* to represent the degree of bone density. Bone densitometry DXA can be used to evaluate bone mineral content of the body, or part of it, to diagnose osteoporosis or to evaluate the effectiveness of treatments for osteoporosis. *(Frank, Long, and Smith, 11th ed., vol. 3, pp. 455–456)*

19. **(C)** The exposed IP is placed into the CR scanner/reader, where the PSP/SPS is removed automatically. The latent image appears as the PSP is scanned by a narrow, high-intensity *helium–neon laser* to obtain the pixel data. As the PSP plate is scanned in the CR reader, it releases a violet light—a process referred to as *photostimulated luminescence* (PSL). The luminescent light is converted to electrical energy representing the *analog* image. The electrical energy is sent to an *analog-to-digital converter* (ADC), where it is digitized and becomes the *digital* image that is displayed eventually (after a short delay) on a high-resolution monitor and/or printed out by a laser printer. The digitized images can also be manipulated in postprocessing, transmitted electronically, and stored/archived. *(Carlton and Adler, 4th ed., pp. 357–358; Bushong 9th ed., p. 421, p. 443)*

20. **(D)** The lateral projection of the coccyx seen in the figure is markedly overexposed. Although a small focal spot would not be a practical selection for a lateral coccyx, focal spot size is unrelated to image density or contrast. If *insufficient* backup time had been selected, the image would be *under*exposed. The center photocell is the *appropriate* photocell to select because the part of interest, the coccyx, should be in the center of the image. Because the *coccyx was not centered* to the IR (but rather the thicker *hip* portion of the body was centered), the AEC correctly exposed the thicker portion—thus overexposing the less dense coccyx area. Accurate positioning/centering is particularly important when using AEC. *(Shephard, p. 281)*

21. **(B)** CR systems convert x-ray photons into useful information much more efficiently than film-screen systems, hence a far better DQE. CR also converts that information over a far wider exposure range (about 10^4 times wider) than screen film. The single negative aspect of CR is its limited spatial resolution (image detail). While film-screen systems resolve about 10–15 lp/mm, CR resolution is about 3–5 lp/mm. *(Seeram, pp. 10–11)*

22. **(B)** In electronic imaging (CR/DR), the radiographer can manipulate the digital image displayed on the CRT through *postprocessing*. One way to alter image contrast and/or brightness is through *windowing*. This refers to some change made to *window width* and/or *window level*. Change in window width changes the number of gray shades, that is, *contrast scale/contrast resolution*. Change in window level changes the image brightness. Windowing and other postprocessing mechanisms permit the radiographer to produce "special effects" such as edge enhancement, image stitching, and image inversion, rotation, and reversal. A digital image is formed by a matrix of pixels in rows and columns. A matrix having 512 pixels in

each row and column is a 512 × 512 matrix. The term *field of view* is used to describe how much of the patient (e.g., 150-mm diameter) is included in the matrix. The matrix or field of view can be changed without affecting the other, but changes in either will change pixel size. Automatic brightness control is associated with image intensification. *(Fosbinder and Kelsey, p. 289; Selman, 9th ed., pp. 190–191)*

23. **(A)** Aligning the x-ray tube, anatomic part, and IR so that they are parallel reduces *shape distortion*. Angulation of the long axis of the part with respect to the IR results in *foreshortening* of the object. Tube angulation causes *elongation* of the part. Size distortion (magnification) is inversely proportional to SID and directly proportional to OID. Decreasing the SID and increasing the OID serve to increase size distortion. *(Shephard, pp. 232–233)*

24. **(D)** *The shortest possible exposure time should be used to minimize motion unsharpness.* Motion causes unsharpness that destroys detail. Careful and accurate patient *instruction* is essential for minimizing voluntary motion. *Suspended respiration* eliminates respiratory motion. Using the shortest possible *exposure time* is essential for decreasing involuntary motion. Immobilization is also very useful in eliminating motion unsharpness. *(Carlton and Adler, 4th ed., p. 451)*

25. **(A)** When the variable-kilovoltage method is used, a particular milliampere-seconds value is assigned to each body part. As part thickness increases, the kilovoltage (i.e., penetration) is also increased. The body part being radiographed must be measured carefully, and *for each centimeter of increase in thickness, 2 kV is added* to the exposure. *(Shephard, pp. 299–300)*

26. **(B)** Boxes of x-ray film, especially the larger sizes, should be stored in the vertical (upright) position. If film boxes are stacked on one another, the sensitive emulsion can be affected by pressure from the boxes above. *Pressure marks* are produced and result in loss of contrast in

that area of the radiographic image. When retrieving x-ray film from storage, the oldest should be used first. *(Shephard, p. 110)*

27. **(B)** The formula for mAs is mA × s = mAs. Substituting known values:

$$0.05x = 30$$
$$x = 600 \text{ mA}$$

(Selman, 9th ed., p. 214)

28. **(D)** Film age is an important consideration when determining the causes of film fog. Outdated film will exhibit loss of contrast in the form of fog and loss of speed. A safelight is "safe" only for practical periods of time required for the necessary handling of film. Films that are left out on the darkroom counter can be fogged by excessive exposure to the safelight. Film emulsion is much more sensitive to safelight fog after exposure. The high temperatures required for automatic processors' rapid processing are a source of film fog. Daily QA ensures that fog levels do not exceed the upper limit of 0.2 density. *(Shephard, pp. 110, 123, 137)*

29. **(A)** As kilovoltage is increased, more high-energy photons are produced, and the overall energy of the primary beam is increased. Photon energy is *inversely* related to wavelength; that is, as photon energy increases, wavelength decreases. An increase in milliamperage serves to increase the *number* of photons produced at the target but is *unrelated* to their energy. *(Selman, 9th ed., p. 118)*

30. **(B)** Of the two radiographs illustrated, image A was made recumbent, and image B was made in the erect position; this may be discerned by the presence of clearly defined air–fluid levels in the lower abdomen. Abdominal viscera move to a lower position in the erect position, making the abdomen "thicker" and requiring an increase in exposure (usually the equivalent of about 10 kV). *(Bontrager and Lampignano, 6th ed., pp. 119, 120)*

31. **(D)** Whereas CR uses traditional x-ray devices to enclose and protect the PSP/SPS, *digital*

radiography (DR) requires the use of somewhat different equipment. DR does not use cassettes or a traditional x-ray table; it is a *direct-capture* system of x-ray imaging. DR uses *solid-state detector* plates as the x-ray IR (instead of a cassette in the Bucky tray) to intercept the collimated x-ray beam and form the latent image. The solid-state detector plates are made of barium fluorohalide compounds similar to that used in CR's PSP/SPSs. DR affords the advantage of *immediate display of the image*, compared with CR's delayed image display. *(Shephard, p. 335)*

32. **(C)** *Grid ratio* is defined as the height of the lead strips to the width of the interspace material (Figure 4–32). The higher the lead strips (or the smaller the distance between the strips), the higher the grid ratio, and the greater the percentage of scattered radiation absorbed. However, a grid does absorb some primary/useful radiation as well. The higher the lead strips, the *more* critical is the need for accurate centering because the lead strips will more readily trap photons whose direction does not parallel them. *(Shephard, pp. 245, 255)*

33. **(C)** A certain amount of object unsharpness is an inherent part of every radiographic image because of the position and shape of anatomic structures within the body. Structures within the three-dimensional human body lie in different *planes*. Additionally, the three-dimensional *shape* of solid anatomic structures rarely coin-

cides with the shape of the divergent beam. Consequently, some structures are imaged with more inherent distortion than others, and shapes of anatomic structures can be entirely misrepresented. Structures *farther* from the IR will be distorted (i.e., *magnified*) more than those *closer* to the IR; structures *closer* to the x-ray source will be distorted (i.e., magnified) more than those *farther* from the x-ray source.

For the *shape* of anatomic structures to be accurately recorded, the structures must be parallel to the x-ray tube and the IR, and aligned with the central ray (CR). *The shape of anatomic structures lying at an angle within the body or placed away from the CR will be misrepresented on the IR.* There are two types of shape distortion. If a linear structure is angled within the body, that is, not parallel with the long axis of the part/body and not parallel to the IR, that anatomic structure will appear *smaller*—it will be *foreshortened*. On the other hand, *elongation* occurs when the x-ray tube is angled.

Image details placed away from the path of the CR will be exposed by more divergent rays, resulting in *rotation distortion*. This is why the CR must be directed to the part of greatest interest.

Unless the edges of a three-dimensional *object* conform to the shape of the x-ray beam, blur or unsharpness will occur at the partially attenuating edge of the object. This can be accompanied by changes in radiographic/image density, according to the thickness of areas traversed by the x-ray beam. *(Bushong, 9th ed., pp. 286–290)*

34. **(B)** **(A)** The image shown is the result of using a CR image plate inadvertently upside down. The rear panel is imaged, showing a large grid-like pattern. A double exposure would have demonstrated superimposed anatomical images (see Figure 4–3). An incomplete erasure or image fading would show only a portion of the anatomical image—here, we see the entire anatomical part. *(PREP, 5th ed., p. 248)*

35. **(D)** Phosphors that have a *high atomic number* are more likely to *absorb* a high percentage of the incident x-ray photons and *convert* x-ray photon energy to fluorescent light energy. How efficiently the phosphors detect and

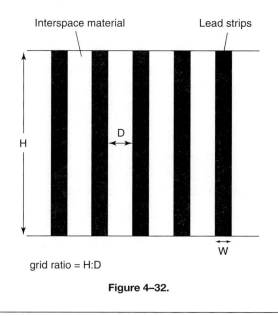

Figure 4–32.

grid ratio = H:D

interact with the x-ray photons is termed *quantum detection efficiency*. How effectively the phosphors make this energy conversion is termed *conversion efficiency*. (*Shephard, p. 65*)

36. **(C)** Spatial resolution in CR is impacted by the size of the PSP, the size of the scanning laser beam, and monitor matrix size. *High-resolution monitors (2–4 MP, megapixels) are required for high-quality, high-resolution image display. The larger the matrix size, the better is the image resolution.* Typical image matrix size (rows and columns) used in chest radiography is 2,048 × 2,048. As in traditional radiography, *spatial resolution* is measured in line pairs per millimeter. As matrix size is increased, there are more and smaller pixels in the matrix and, therefore, improved spatial resolution. Other factors contributing to image resolution are the *size of the laser beam* and the *size of the PSP/SPS phosphors*. Smaller phosphor size improves resolution in ways similar to that of intensifying screens—anything that causes an increase in light diffusion will result in a decrease in resolution. Smaller phosphors in the PSP (SPS) plate allow less light diffusion. Additionally, the scanning laser light must be of the correct intensity and size. A narrow laser beam is required for optimal resolution. (*Shephard, p. 336*)

37. **(B)** Pathologic processes and abnormal conditions that alter tissue composition or thickness can have a significant effect on image density. The radiographer must be aware of these variants and processes to make an appropriate and accurate adjustment of technical factors.

Examples of *additive* pathologic conditions:

- Ascites
- Rheumatoid arthritis
- Paget disease
- Pneumonia
- Atelectasis
- Congestive heart failure
- Edematous tissue

Examples of *destructive* pathologic conditions:

- Osteoporosis
- Osteomalacia
- Pneumoperitoneum
- Emphysema

- Degenerative arthritis
- Atrophic and necrotic conditions

(*Bushong, 9th ed., p. 253*)

38. **(A)** One way to minimize scattered radiation reaching the IR is to use optimal kilovoltage; excessive kilovoltage increases the production of scattered radiation. Close *collimation* is exceedingly important because the smaller the volume of irradiated material, the less scattered radiation will be produced. The mAs selection has no impact on scattered radiation production or cleanup. *Low-ratio* grids allow a greater percentage of scattered radiation to reach the IR. Use of a *high-ratio* grid will clean up a greater amount of scattered radiation before it reaches the IR. Use of a compression band, or the prone position, in a large abdomen has the effect of making the abdomen "thinner"; it will, therefore, generate less scattered radiation. (*Shephard, p. 203*)

39. **(D)** *Grid ratio* is defined as *the ratio of the height of the lead strips to the width of the interspace material;* the higher the lead strips, the more scattered radiation they will trap and the greater is the grid's efficiency. The greater the *number of lead strips per inch*, the thinner and less visible they will be on the finished radiograph. The function of a grid is to absorb scattered radiation in order to improve radiographic contrast. The *selectivity* of a grid is determined by the amount of primary radiation *transmitted* through the grid divided by the amount of scattered radiation *transmitted* through the grid. (*Selman, 9th ed., pp. 236–237*)

40. **(C)** The radiographer can *manipulate* (i.e., change or enhance) digital images displayed on the CRT through *postprocessing*. One way to alter image contrast and/or density is through windowing. The term *windowing* refers to some change made to *window width* and/or *window level*. Change in window width affects change in the number of gray shades, that is, *image contrast*—as demonstrated in the figures shown (Figure 4–7). Change in window level affects change in the image brightness, that is, *optical density*. Windowing and other postprocessing mechanisms permit the radiographer to effect

changes in the image and to produce "special effects" such as edge enhancement, image stitching (useful in scoliosis examinations), image inversion, rotation, and reversal. *(Shephard, p. 346)*

41. **(D)** Exposure rate is regulated by milliamperage. Distance significantly affects the exposure rate according to the inverse-square law of radiation. Kilovoltage also has an effect on exposure rate because an increase in kilovoltage will increase the number of high-energy photons produced at the target. The size of the x-ray field determines the volume of tissue irradiated, and hence the amount of scattered radiation generated, but is unrelated to the exposure rate. *(Selman, 9th ed., p. 117)*

42. **(D)** High kV may be desirable in terms of patient dose, tube life, and making more details visible, but use of excessively high kV will result in production of excessive amounts of *scattered radiation* and fog, resulting in diminished visibility of image details. Much of the scattered radiation produced is highly energetic and exits the patient along with useful image-forming radiation. Scattered radiation carries no useful information but adds *noise* in the form of fog, thereby impairing detail visibility.

Because scattered radiation can have such a devastating effect on image contrast, it is essential that radiographers are knowledgeable about methods of reducing its production. The three factors that have a significant effect on the *production of scattered radiation* are beam restriction (i.e., size of irradiated field), kV, and thickness/volume and density of tissues.

Perhaps the most important way to limit the production of scattered radiation and improve contrast is by *limiting the size of the irradiated field*, that is, through *beam restriction. As the size of the x-ray field is reduced, there is less area and tissue volume for scattered radiation to be generated.*

As the volume and/or density of the irradiated tissues increase(s), so does scattered radiation. Thicker and denser anatomic structures will generate more scattered radiation. *Compression* of certain parts can occasionally be used to minimize the effect of scatter, but close *collimation* can *always* be used effectively. *(Fosbinder and Orth, pp. 165–166)*

43. **(B)** *Radiographic contrast* is defined as the degree of *difference between adjacent densities.* These density differences represent sometimes very subtle differences in the absorbing properties of adjacent body tissues. The *radiographic subject*, the patient, is composed of many different tissue types that have varying densities, resulting in varying degrees of photon attenuation and absorption. The *atomic number* of the tissues under investigation is directly related to their *attenuation coefficient.* This *differential absorption* contributes to the various shades of gray (scale of radiographic contrast) on the finished radiograph. Normal tissue density may be altered significantly in the presence of *pathologic processes.* The technical factor used to regulate contrast is kilovoltage. Radiographic contrast is unrelated to milliampere-seconds. *(Selman, 9th ed., pp. 218–220)*

44. **(C)** *Grid ratio* is defined as the height of the lead strips compared with (divided by) the width of the interspace material. The width of the lead strips has no bearing on the grid ratio. The height of the lead strips is 5 mm; the width of the interspace material (same as the distance between the lead strips) is 0.5 mm. Therefore, the grid ratio is 5/0.5, or a 10:1 grid ratio. *(Bushong, 8th ed., p. 250)*

45. **(B)** Magnification is part of every radiographic image. Anatomic parts within the body are at various distances from the IR and, therefore, have various degrees of magnification. The formula used to determine the amount of image magnification is

$$\frac{\text{Image size}}{\text{Object size}} = \frac{\text{SID}}{\text{SOD}}$$

Substituting known values:

$$\frac{x}{5 \text{ in}} = \frac{44 \text{ in (SID)}}{38 \text{ in (SOD)}}$$

$$(\text{SOD} = \text{SID-OID})$$

$$38x = 220$$

Thus, $x = 5.78$-in. *image width. (Bushong, 8th ed., p. 284)*

46. **(C)** The higher the kilovoltage range, the greater is the exposure latitude (margin of error in exposure). Higher kilovoltage produces more energetic photons, is more penetrating, and produces more grays on the radiographic image, lengthening the scale of contrast. As kilovoltage increases, the percentage of scattered radiation also increases. *(Bushong, 9th ed., pp. 256-257)*

47. **(D)** Digital image storage is located in a *pixel*, which is a *two-dimensional* "*pic*ture *ele*ment," measured in the "XY" direction. The third dimension, "Z" direction, in the matrix of pixels is the *depth* that is referred to as the *voxel* (*vol*ume *ele*ment). The depth of the block is the number of bits required to describe the gray level that each pixel can take on—known as the bit depth.

Bit depth in CT is approximately 2^{12} with a dynamic range of almost 5,000 gray shades, approximately 2^{14} in CR/DR with a dynamic range of more than 16,000 gray shades, and approximately 2^{16} in digital mammography with a dynamic range of more than 65,500 gray shades. The matrix is the number of pixels in the XY direction. As matrix size increases, for a fixed FOV, pixel size is smaller and better spatial resolution results. An electronic/digital image is formed by a matrix of pixels in rows and columns. A matrix having 512 pixels in each row and column is a 512 × 512 matrix (a typical CT image).

The term *FOV* is used to describe how much of the patient is included in the matrix. Either the matrix or the FOV can be changed without one affecting the other, but changes in either will change pixel size. As FOV increases, for a fixed matrix size, the size of each pixel increases and spatial resolution decreases. Fewer and larger pixels result in a poor-resolution "pixelly" or "mosaicked" image, that is, one in which you can actually see the individual pixel boxes.

48. **(A)** Shape distortion (e.g., foreshortening or elongation) is caused by improper alignment of the tube, part, and IR. Size distortion, or magnification, is caused by too great an OID or too short an SID. Focal-spot blur is caused by the use of a large focal spot. *(Fauber, p. 93)*

49. **(A)** If the SID is above or below the recommended focusing distance, the primary beam will not coincide with the angled lead strips at their lateral edges. Consequently, there will be *absorption of the primary beam* termed *grid cutoff*. If the central ray is off-center *longitudinally*, there will be no ill effects. If the central ray is off-center *side to side*, the lead strips are no longer parallel with the divergent x-ray beam, and there will be loss of density owing to grid cutoff. Central ray angulation *in the direction of* the lead strips is appropriate and will not cause grid cutoff. Central ray angulation *against the direction of* the lead strips will cause grid cutoff. *(Selman, 9th ed., pp. 239–242)*

50. **(C)** The tiny minus-density artifacts seen in the more proximal portion of the CR image of the radius shown in the figure are representative of dust/dirt particles that have accumulated on the PSP (SPS). PSPs are susceptible to dust, just as are intensifying screens—and the dust particles are imaged in much the same way—as minus-density artifacts, looking like little pinholes. PSPs are particularly sensitive to scattered radiation fog and backscatter, but these would give the image the typical overall gray appearance of fog. Phantom image artifacts are a result of incomplete erasure of a previous image on that PSP. Image fading occurs if an exposed PSP has been left several hours without processing and usually affects the entire image. *(Shephard, p. 354)*

51. **(B)** Use of a short SID with a large-size IR (and also with anode angles of 10 degrees or less) causes the anode heel effect to be much more apparent. The x-ray beam needs to diverge more to cover a *large-size IR*, and it needs to diverge even more for coverage as the *SID decreases*. The x-ray beam has no problem diverging toward the cathode end of the beam, but as it tries to diverge toward the anode end of the beam, it is eventually stopped by the anode (x-ray photons are absorbed by the anode). This causes a decrease in beam intensity at the anode end of the beam and is characteristic of the *anode heel effect*. *(Carlton and Adler, 4th ed., p. 407)*

52. **(D)** Each milliampere-second setting is determined [(A) = 4; (B) = 4; (C) = 8; (D) = 2] and numbered in order of greatest to least density

[(C) = 1; (A) and (B) = 2; (D) = 3]. Then, the kilovoltages are reviewed and also numbered in order of greatest to least density [(A), (B), and (C) = 1; (D) = 2]. Next, screen speeds are numbered from greatest density-producing to least density-producing [(D) and (B) = 1; (A) = 2; (C) = 3]. Finally, the numbers assigned to the milliampere-seconds, kilovoltage, and screen speed are added up for each of the four groups [(B) = 4; (A) and (C) = 5; (D) = 6]; the *lowest* total (B) indicates the group of factors that will produce the *greatest* radiographic density; the *highest* total (D) indicates the group of factors that will produce the *least* radiographic density. This process is illustrated as follows:

(A) 4 mAs (2) + 94 kV (1) + 100 screens (2) = 5

(B) 4 mAs (2) + 94 kV (1) + 200 screens (1) = 4

(C) 8 mAs (1) + 94 kV (1) + 50 screens (3) = 5

(D) 2 mAs (3) + 80 kV (2) + 200 screens (1) = 6

(Shephard, p. 179)

53. **(D)** If developer *temperature* is too high, some of the less exposed or unexposed silver halide crystals may be reduced, thus creating chemical fog. If the developer solution has become *oxidized* from exposure to air, chemical fog also results. If developer *replenishment* is excessive, and too much new solution is replacing the deteriorated developer, chemical fog is again the result. *(Carlton and Adler, 4th ed., p. 285; Selman, 9th ed., p. 197)*

54. **(B)** In the low-kilovoltage ranges, a difference of just a few kilovolts makes a very noticeable radiographic difference, therefore offering little margin for error/latitude. High-kilovolt technical factors offer much greater margin for error; in the high-kV ranges, an error of a few kV makes little/no difference in the resulting image. Lower-ratio grids offer more tube-centering latitude than high-ratio grids. *(Saia, 4th ed., p. 360)*

55. **(A)** While *CR* utilizes traditional x-ray tables and *IPs* to enclose and protect the flexible PSP screen, *DR* requires the use of significantly different equipment. DR does not use IPs or a traditional x-ray table—it is a direct-capture/conversion, or indirect capture/conversion, system of x-ray imaging. Besides eliminating IPs and their handling, DR affords the advantage of *immediate display* of the image (compared with CR's slightly delayed image display), and DR *exposures can be lower* because of the detector's *higher DQE* (i.e., ability to perceive and interact with x-ray photons). DR, like CR, also offers the advantage of image preview and postprocessing. *(Seeram, pp. 10–11)*

56. **(D)** Digital image storage is located in a *pixel*, which is a *two-dimensional "picture element,"* measured in the "XY" *direction*. The third dimension, "Z" direction, in the matrix of pixels is the *depth* that is referred to as the *voxel (volume element)*. The *depth* of the block is the number of bits required to describe the gray level that each pixel can take on—known as the bit depth.

Bit depth in CT is approximately 2^{12} with a dynamic range of almost 5,000 gray shades, approximately 2^{14} in CR/DR with a dynamic range of more than 16,000 gray shades, and approximately 2^{16} in digital mammography with a dynamic range of more than 65,500 gray shades. The matrix is the number of pixels in the XY direction. As matrix size increases, for a fixed FOV, pixel size is smaller and better spatial resolution results. An electronic/digital image is formed by a matrix of pixels in rows and columns. A matrix having 512 pixels in each row and column is a 512 × 512 matrix (a typical CT image).

The term *FOV* is used to describe how much of the patient is included in the matrix. Either the matrix or the FOV can be changed without one affecting the other, but changes in either will change pixel size. As FOV increases, for a fixed matrix size, the size of each pixel increases and spatial resolution decreases. Fewer and larger pixels result in a poor-resolution "pixelly" or "mosaicked" image, that is, one in which you can actually see the individual pixel boxes.

57. **(D)** Magnification radiography may be used to delineate a suspected hairline fracture or to

enlarge tiny, contrast-filled blood vessels. It also has application in mammography. To magnify an object to twice its actual size, the part must be placed midway between the focal spot and the IR. *(Selman, pp. 223–225; Shephard, pp. 229–231)*

58. **(C)** To change nongrid exposures to grid exposures, or to adjust exposure when changing from one grid ratio to another, you must remember the factor for each grid ratio:

$$No grid = 1 \times original mAs$$
$$5{:}1 grid = 2 \times original mAs$$
$$6{:}1 grid = 3 \times original mAs$$
$$8{:}1 grid = 4 \times original mAs$$
$$12{:}1 grid = 5 \times original mAs$$
$$16{:}1 grid = 6 \times original mAs$$

To adjust exposure factors, you simply compare the old with the new:

$$\frac{12 (\text{old mAs})}{x \, (\text{new mAs})} = \frac{6 \, (\text{old grid factor})}{4 \, (\text{new grid factor})}$$

$$6x = 48$$

$$x = 8 \text{ mAs (using 8:1 grid)}$$

(Shephard, pp. 247–248)

59. **(A)** One type of *indirect*-capture flat-panel detector uses cesium iodide or gadolinium oxysulfide as the *scintillator*, that is, which captures x-ray photons and emits light. That light is then transferred via a photodetector coupling agent—a CCD or TFT. In *direct*-capture flat-panel detector systems, x-ray energy is converted to an electrical signal in a single layer of material such as the semiconductor a-Se. Electric charges are applied to both surfaces of the a-Se, electron–hole pairs are created, and charges are read by TFT arrays located on the surfaces. The electrical signal is transferred directly to the ADC. The number of TFTs is equal to the number of image pixels.

Thus, the direct-capture system *eliminates the scintillator* step required in indirect DR. Since selenium has a relatively low Z number (compared with gadolinium [Z 64] or cesium [Z 55]), a-Se detectors are made thicker to improve detection, thus compensating for the low x-ray absorption of selenium. There is no

diffusion of electrons, so spatial resolution is not affected in this manner. *(Seeram, pp. 107–108, 110)*

60. **(B)** The x-ray tube is a diode tube; that is, it has two electrodes—a negative and a positive. The cathode assembly is the negative terminal of the x-ray tube, and the anode is the positive terminal. Electrons are released by the cathode filament (thermionic emission) as it is heated to incandescence. When kilovoltage is applied, the electrons are driven across to the anode's focal spot. Upon sudden deceleration of electrons at the anode surface, x-rays are produced. Hence, electrons travel from cathode to anode within the x-ray tube. *(Bushong, 9th ed., pp. 122-125)*

61. **(C)** When tissue densities within a part are very dissimilar (e.g., chest x-ray), the radiographic result can be unacceptably high contrast. To "even out" these densities and produce a more appropriate scale of grays, exposure factors using high kilovoltage should be employed. Focal spot size is unrelated to image contrast. The higher the grid ratio, the higher is the contrast. Exposure factors using high milliampere-seconds generally result in unnecessary patient exposure. *(Bushong, 8th ed., p. 273; Shephard, p. 200)*

62. **(B)** *Field of view* (FOV) refers to the area being viewed. The FOV can be increased or decreased. As the FOV is increased, the part being examined is magnified; as the FOV is decreased, the part returns closer to actual size. Pixel size is affected by changes in either the FOV or matrix size. For example, if the matrix size is increased, for example, from 256 × 256 to 512 × 512, pixel size must decrease. If FOV increases, pixel size must increase. Pixel size is inversely related to *resolution*. As pixel size decreases, resolution increases. *(Fosbinder and Kelsey, p. 285)*

63. **(C)** If a fairly large patient is turned *prone*, the abdominal measurement will be significantly different from the AP measurement as a result of the effect of *compression*. Thus, the part is essentially "thinner," and less scattered radiation will be produced. If the patient remains

supine and a compression band is applied, a similar effect will be produced. *Beam restriction* is probably the single most effective means of reducing the production of scattered radiation. *Grid ratio* affects the *cleanup* of scattered radiation; it has no effect on the *production* of scattered radiation. *(Shephard, p. 203)*

64. **(B)** Two film–screen images of the skull are shown and their appearance is quite different. Image A demonstrates higher/shorter scale contrast. Image B is quite gray—demonstrating low/long scale contrast. Image B would have higher contrast if a higher-ratio grid had been used. The positioning of the images is identical; no motion or distortion is apparent. *(Carlton and Adler, 4th ed., p. 432)*

65. **(C)** Grids are used in radiography to *absorb scattered radiation* before it reaches the IR (grid "cleanup"), thus improving radiographic contrast. Contrast obtained with a grid compared with contrast without a grid is termed *contrast-improvement factor.* The greater the percentage of scattered radiation absorbed compared with absorbed primary radiation, the greater is the "selectivity" of the grid. If a grid absorbs an abnormally large amount of useful radiation as a result of improper centering, tube angle, or tube distance, *grid cutoff* occurs. *(Selman, 9th ed., p. 370)*

66. **(D)** Digital image storage is located in a *pixel*, a two-dimensional "*picture element*," measured in the "XY" direction. The third dimension, "Z" direction, in the matrix of pixels is the *depth*—referred to as the *voxel* (volume element). The depth of the block is the number of bits required to describe the *gray level* that each pixel can take on—known as *bit depth*. Bit depth in *CT* is about 2^{12} with a dynamic range of almost 5,000 gray shades, about 2^{14} in *CR/DR* with a dynamic range of more than 16,000 gray shades, and about 2^{16} in digital *mammography* with a dynamic range of more than 65,500 gray shades. The *matrix* is the number of pixels in the XY direction. *As matrix size increases, for a fixed FOV, pixel size is smaller and better image resolution results.* An electronic/digital image is formed by a *matrix* of pixels in *rows* and *columns*. A matrix having

512 pixels in each row and column is a 512 × 512 matrix (a typical CT image). The term FOV is used to describe how much of the patient is included in the matrix. Either the matrix or the FOV can be changed without one affecting the other, but changes in either will change pixel size. *As FOV increases, for a fixed matrix size, the size of each pixel increases and spatial resolution decreases.* Fewer and larger pixels result in a poor-resolution "pixelly" ("*mosaicked*") image, that is, one in which you can actually see the individual pixel boxes. In the figure shown, Image #1 is the most pixelly/mosaicked, having a matrix of 16 × 16, and demonstrates the poorest spatial resolution. The images improve with Image #2 having a matrix of 32 × 32, Image #3 having a matrix 64 × 64, and *Image #4 having a matrix of 128 × 128—and the best spatial resolution.* An image matrix of 256 × 256 would demonstrate even better resolution. *(Seeram, p. 29)*

67. **(C)** *Size* distortion (magnification) is inversely proportional to SID and directly proportional to OID. Increasing the SID and decreasing the OID decreases size distortion. Aligning the tube, part, and IR so that they are parallel reduces *shape* distortion. There are two types of shape distortion—*elongation* and *foreshortening.* Angulation of the part with relation to the IR results in foreshortening of the object. Tube angulation causes elongation of the object. *(Shephard, pp. 228, 231–234)*

68. **(D)** Digital image storage is located in a *pixel*, which is a *two-dimensional "picture element*," measured in the "XY" *direction.* The third dimension, "Z" direction, in the matrix of pixels is the depth that is referred to as the *voxel* (volume element). The depth of the block is the number of bits required to describe the gray level that each pixel can take on—known as the bit depth.

The *matrix* is the number of pixels in the XY direction. As matrix size increases, for a fixed FOV, *pixel size is smaller and better spatial resolution results.* An electronic/digital image is formed by a matrix of pixels in rows and columns. A matrix having 512 pixels in each row and column is a 512 × 512 matrix (a typical CT image).

The term *FOV* is used to describe how much of the patient is included in the matrix. Either the matrix or the FOV can be changed without one affecting the other, but changes in either will change pixel size. As FOV increases, for a fixed matrix size, the size of each pixel increases and spatial resolution decreases. Fewer and larger pixels result in a poor-resolution "pixelly" or "mosaicked" image, that is, one in which you can actually see the individual pixel boxes.

69. **(C)** The exposed CR cassette is placed into the CR scanner/reader, where the PSP (SPS) is removed automatically. The latent image appears as the PSP is scanned by a narrow, high-intensity *helium–neon laser* to obtain the pixel data. As the plate is scanned in the CR reader, it releases a violet light—a process referred to as *photostimulated luminescence* (PSL). The luminescent light is converted to electrical energy representing the *analog* image. The electrical energy is sent to an analog-to-digital converter (ADC), where it is digitized and becomes the *digital image* that is displayed eventually (after a short delay) on a high-resolution monitor and/or printed out by a laser printer. The digitized images can also be manipulated in postprocessing, transmitted electronically, and stored/archived. *(Carlton and Adler, 4th ed., p. 358)*

70. **(A)** The *focal-spot size* selected will determine the amount of focal-spot, or geometric, blur produced in the image. OID and SID are responsible for image magnification and hence recorded detail. The *milliamperage* is unrelated to recorded detail; it affects only the quantity of x-ray photons produced and thus the radiographic density. *(Selman, 9th ed., pp. 206–210)*

71. **(B)** According to the density-maintenance formula, if the SID is changed to 48 in., 16.33 mAs is required to maintain the original radiographic density:

$$\frac{\text{(old mAs) } 12}{\text{(New mAs) } x} = \frac{\text{(old } D^2) \, 36^2}{\text{(new } D^2) \, 42^2}$$

$$\frac{12}{x} = \frac{1,296}{1,764}$$

$$1,296x = 21,168$$

Thus, $x = 16.33$ mAs at 42 in. SID. Then, to compensate for changing from a 12:1 grid to a 5:1 grid, the milliampere-seconds value becomes 6.53 mAs:

$$\frac{\text{(old mAs) } 16.33}{\text{(New mAs) } x} = \frac{\text{(old grid factor) } 5}{\text{(old grid factor) } 2}$$

$$5x = 32.66$$

Thus, x 6.53 mAs with 5:1 grid at 42 in. SID. Hence, 6.53 mAs is required to produce an image density similar to that of the original radiograph. The following are the factors used for milliampere-seconds conversion from non-grid to grid:

$$\text{No grid} = 1 \times \text{original mAs}$$
$$\text{5:1 grid} = 2 \times \text{original mAs}$$
$$\text{6:1 grid} = 3 \times \text{original mAs}$$
$$\text{8:1 grid} = 4 \times \text{original mAs}$$
$$\text{12:1 grid} = 5 \times \text{original mAs}$$
$$\text{16:1 grid} = 6 \times \text{original mAs}$$

(Selman, 9th ed., pp. 214, 243)

72. **(C)** The formula mA $\times$ s = mAs is used to determine each milliampere-second setting (remember to first change milliseconds to seconds). The *greatest* radiographic density will be produced by the combination of highest milliampere-seconds value and shortest SID. The groups in choices (B) and (D) should produce *identical radiographic density*, according to the inverse-square law, because group (D) includes twice the distance and 4 times the milliampere-seconds value of group (B). The group in (A) has twice the distance of the group in (B) but only twice the milliampere-seconds; therefore, it has the *least* density. The group in (C) has the same distance as the group in (B) and twice the milliampere-seconds, making group in (C) the group of technical factors that will produce the *greatest* radiographic density. *(Selman, 9th ed., p. 214)*

73. **(B)** Of the given factors, kilovoltage and grid ratio will have a significant effect on radiographic contrast. Remember that the milliampere-seconds value has no effect on contrast scale. Because a combination of lower kilovoltage and a higher-ratio grid will allow

the least amount of scattered radiation to reach the IR, thereby producing fewer gray tones, (B) is the best answer. (D) also uses low kilovoltage, but the grid ratio is lower—allowing more scatter to reach the IR (therefore, longer-scale contrast). *(Shephard, pp. 305–308)*

74. **(D)** Pathologic processes and abnormal conditions that alter tissue composition or thickness can have a significant effect on image density. The radiographer must be aware of these variants and processes to make an appropriate and accurate adjustment of technical factors.

    Examples of *additive* pathologic conditions:

    - Ascites
    - Rheumatoid arthritis
    - Paget disease
    - Pneumonia
    - Atelectasis
    - Congestive heart failure
    - Edematous tissue

    Examples of *destructive* pathologic conditions:

    - Osteoporosis
    - Osteomalacia
    - Pneumoperitoneum
    - Emphysema
    - Degenerative arthritis
    - Atrophic and necrotic conditions

    (Bushong, 9th ed., p. 253)

75. **(D)** The *radiographic subject*, the patient, is composed of many different tissue types that have varying densities, resulting in varying degrees of photon attenuation and absorption. The *atomic number* of the tissues under investigation is directly related to their *attenuation coefficient*. This *differential absorption* contributes to the various shades of gray (scale of radiographic contrast) on the finished radiograph. Normal tissue density may be altered significantly in the presence of *pathologic processes*. For example, destructive bone disease can cause a dramatic decrease in tissue density (and subsequent increase in radiographic density). Abnormal accumulation of fluid (as in ascites) will cause a significant increase in tissue density. Muscle atrophy or highly developed muscles similarly will decrease or increase tissue density. *(Bushong, 8th ed., pp. 290, 298–299)*

76. **(D)** As *photon energy* (kV) increases, so does the production of scattered radiation. The greater the *density* of the irradiated tissues, the greater is the production of scattered radiation. As the size of the *irradiated field* increases, there is an increase in the volume of tissue irradiated, and the percentage of scatter again increases. Beam restriction is the single most important way to limit the amount of scattered radiation produced. *(Carlton and Adler, 4th ed., p. 228)*

77. **(A)** A 15% decrease in kilovoltage with a 50% increase in milliampere-seconds produces an image *similar* to the original but with some obvious differences. The overall blackness (*radiographic density*) is *doubled* because of the increase in milliampere-seconds. This increase in blackness is compensated for by the loss of gray shades (i.e., *shorter* scale contrast) from the decreased kilovoltage. The decrease in kilovoltage also *decreases exposure latitude*; there is less margin for error in lower-kilovoltage ranges. *Recorded detail* is unaffected by changes in kilovoltage. *(Fauber, pp. 59–60)*

78. **(D)** *Focal-spot size* affects recorded detail by its effect on focal-spot blur: The larger the focal-spot size, the greater is the blur produced. Recorded detail is affected significantly by distance changes because of their effect on magnification. As SID increases and as OID decreases, magnification decreases and recorded detail increases. SOD is determined by subtracting OID from SID. *(Shephard, p. 215)*

79. **(D)** Each of the three is included in a good QA program. *Beam alignment* must be accurate to within 2% of the SID. *Reproducibility* means that repeated exposures at a given technique must provide consistent intensity. *Linearity* means that a given milliampere-second setting, using different milliampere stations with appropriate exposure-time adjustments, will provide consistent intensity. *(Bushong, 8th ed., p. 460)*

80. **(B)** Focal-spot blur, or geometric blur, is caused by photons emerging from a large focal spot. The actual focal spot is always larger than the effective (or projected) focal spot, as illustrated by the line-focus principle. In addition, the effective focal-spot size varies along the longitudinal tube axis, being greatest in size at the cathode end of the beam and smallest at the anode end of the beam. Because the projected focal spot is greatest at the cathode end of the x-ray tube, geometric blur is also greatest at the corresponding part (cathode end) of the radiograph. *(Bushong, 8th ed., pp. 287–288)*

81. **(B)** The milliampere-seconds value regulates the *number* of x-ray photons produced at the target and thus regulates *patient dose*. If the milliampere-seconds is doubled, dose is doubled; therefore, mAs and patient dose are directly proportional. *(Selman, 9th ed., p. 214)*

82. **(B)** The image plate front material must not attenuate the remnant beam yet must be sturdy enough to withstand daily use. Bakelite has long been used as the material for tabletops and IR fronts, but now it has been replaced largely by *magnesium* and *carbon fiber*. Lead would not be a suitable material because it would absorb the remnant beam, and no image would be formed. *(Shephard, p. 41)*

83. **(C)** *Emphysema* is abnormal distension of the pulmonary alveoli (or tissue spaces) with air. The presence of abnormal amounts of air makes a decrease from normal exposure factors necessary to avoid excessive density. *Congestive heart failure, pneumonia*, and *pleural effusion* all involve abnormal amounts of fluid in the chest and, therefore, would require an *increase* in exposure factors. *(Carlton and Adler, 4th ed., p. 251)*

84. **(A)** If the SID is above or below the recommended focusing distance, the primary beam will not coincide with the angled lead strips at the lateral edges. Consequently, there will be absorption of the primary beam, termed *grid cutoff*. If the grid failed to move during the exposure, there would be grid lines throughout. Central ray angulation in the direction of the lead strips is appropriate and will not cause grid cutoff. If the central ray were off-center, there would be uniform loss of density. *(Carlton and Adler, 4th ed., p. 260)*

85. **(B)** If it is desired to reduce the exposure time for a particular radiograph, as it might be when radiographing patients who are unable to cooperate fully, the *milliamperage* must be *increased* sufficiently to maintain the original milliampere-seconds value and thus image density/brightness. A *higher kilovoltage* could be useful because it would allow further reduction of the milliampere-seconds (exposure time) according to the 15% rule. Changing grid ratio is unrelated to desired changes in exposure time. Use of a higher-ratio grid would only necessitate an increase in mAs and not likely a decrease in exposure time. *(Selman, 9th ed., pp. 182, 214)*

86. **(D)** With three-phase equipment, the voltage never drops to zero, and x-ray intensity is significantly greater. When changing *from single-phase to three-phase, six-pulse equipment, two-thirds of the original milliampere-seconds value is required* to produce a radiograph with similar density. When changing *from single-phase to three-phase, 12-pulse equipment, only half the original milliampere-seconds value is required*. In this problem, we are changing from three-phase, 12-pulse to single-phase equipment; therefore, the milliampere-seconds value should be doubled (from 4–8 mAs). *(Carlton and Adler, 4th ed., p. 96)*

87. **(C)** A grid is composed of alternate strips of lead and interspace material. The lead strips serve to trap scattered radiation before it fogs the IR. The interspace material must be radiolucent; plastic or sturdier aluminum usually is used. Cardboard was used in the past as interspace material, but it had the disadvantage of being affected by humidity (moisture). *(Selman, 9th ed., p. 234)*

88. **(D)** The radiograph shown is that of an adult PA erect chest. The image is well positioned and exposed, but observe the *braids of hair* that extend past the neck and superimpose on the

pulmonary apices. Braided hair should be pinned up or otherwise removed from superimposition on thoracic structures. The braided hair was imaged during the exposure of the PA chest and is, therefore, referred to as an *exposure artifact*. Example of a scanner/reader artifact is laser jitter, which results in an image distortion. It is important to inquire about or examine patients for materials that will image radiographically and cast unwanted densities over essential anatomy. *(Bushong, 8th ed., p. 474)*

89. **(B)** Because the focal spot (track) of an x-ray tube is along the anode's beveled edge, photons produced at the target are able to diverge considerably toward the cathode end of the x-ray tube but are absorbed by the heel of the anode at the opposite end of the tube. This results in a greater number of x-ray photons distributed toward the cathode end, which is known as the *anode heel effect*. The effect of this restricting heel is most pronounced when the x-ray photons are required to *diverge* more, as would be the case with *short SID, large-size IRs* and *steeper (smaller) target angles*. *(Carlton and Adler, 4th ed., p. 407; Shephard, p. 192)*

90. **(B)** As the kilovoltage is increased, a *greater number* of electrons are driven across to the anode with *greater force*. Therefore, as energy conversion takes place at the anode, *more high-energy* (short-wavelength) photons are produced. However, because they are higher-energy photons, there will be less patient absorption. *(Selman, 9th ed., pp. 117–118)*

91. **(D)** In digital imaging, as in film/screen radiography, there are numerous *density/brightness values* that represent various *tissue densities* (i.e., x-ray attenuation properties), for example, bone, muscle, fat, blood-filled organs, air/gas, metal, contrast media, and pathologic processes. In CR, the CR scanner/reader recognizes all these values and constructs a representative *grayscale* histogram of them, corresponding to the *anatomic characteristics of the imaged part*. Thus, all PA chest histograms are similar, all lateral chest histograms are similar, all pelvis histograms are similar, etc.

A histogram is a *graphic representation* of *pixel value distribution*. The histogram is an

analysis and graphic representation of all the densities from the PSP screen, demonstrating the quantity of exposure, the number of pixels, and their value. Histograms are *unique to each body part* imaged.

Histogram appearance and *patient dose* can be affected by the radiographer's knowledge and skill using digital imaging, in addition to their degree of accuracy in *positioning* and *centering*. Collimation is exceedingly important to avoid *histogram analysis errors*. Lack of adequate collimation can result in signals outside the anatomic area being included in the exposure data recognition/histogram analysis. This can result in a variety of histogram analysis errors including excessively light, dark, or noisy images. Poor collimation can affect exposure level and exposure latitude; these changes are reflected in the images' informational numbers ("S number," "exposure index," etc.).

Other factors affecting histogram appearance, and therefore these informational numbers, include selection of the *correct processing algorithm* (e.g., chest vs. femur vs. cervical spine), changes in *scatter, source-to-image-receptor distance* (SID), *object-to-image-receptor distance* (OID), and *collimation*—in short, anything that affects scatter and/or dose.

92. **(C)** During automatic processing (Figure 4–33), radiographic film is first immersed in the *developer* solution, which functions to reduce the exposed silver bromide crystals in the film emulsion to black metallic silver (which constitutes the image). Next, the film goes directly into the *fixer*, which functions to remove the *unexposed* silver bromide crystals from the emulsion. The film then is transported to the *wash* tank, where chemicals are removed from the film, and then into the *dryer* section, where it is dried before leaving the processor. *(Fauber, p. 162; Shephard, p. 134)*

93. **(B)** An *increase in SID* will help to decrease the effect of excessive OID. For example, in the lateral projection of the cervical spine, there is normally a significant OID that would result in obvious magnification at a 40-in. SID. This effect is decreased by the use of a 72-in. SID. However, especially with larger body parts, increased SID usually requires a significant

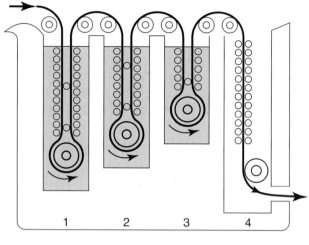

Figure 4–33.

increase in exposure factors. Focal-spot size and grid ratio are unrelated to magnification. (*Selman, 9th ed., p. 224*)

94. **(C)** *Absorption* occurs when an x-ray photon interacts with matter and disappears, as in the photoelectric effect. *Scattering* occurs when there is partial transfer of energy to matter, as in the Compton effect. The reduction in the intensity of an x-ray beam as it passes through matter is called *attenuation*. (*Bushong, 8th ed., p. 185*)

95. **(D)** The PA projection of the chest shown in the figure demonstrates faint visualization of the thoracic vertebrae through the heart—characteristic of adequate penetration. Many shades of gray are seen, illustrating a long scale of contrast. The image is representative of having been exposed at the ideal milliampere-seconds and kilovoltage factors. Ten posterior ribs are seen; this illustrates adequate inspiration. (*Shephard, p. 179*)

96. **(A)** Exposure rate *decreases* with an increase in SID according to the inverse-square law of radiation. The *quantity* of x-ray photons produced at the focal spot is the function of milliampere-seconds. The *quality* (i.e., wavelength, penetration, and energy) of x-ray photons produced at the target is the function of kilovoltage. The kilovoltage also has an effect on exposure rate because an increase in kilovoltage will increase the number of high-

energy x-ray photons produced at the anode. (*Selman, 9th ed., p. 117*)

97. **(B)** *Osteoporosis* is a condition, often seen in the elderly, marked by increased porosity and softening of bone. The bones are much less dense, and thus a decrease in exposure is required. *Osteomyelitis* and *osteochondritis* are inflammatory conditions that usually have no effect on bone density. *Osteosclerosis* is abnormal hardening of the bone, and an increase in exposure factors would be required. (*Carlton and Adler, 4th ed., p. 252*)

98. **(B)** Electromagnetic radiation can be described as wave-like fluctuations of electric and magnetic fields. There are many kinds of electromagnetic radiation; visible light, microwaves, and radio waves, as well as x-ray and gamma rays, are all part of the electromagnetic spectrum. All the electromagnetic radiations have the same velocity, that is, 3×10^8 m/s (1,86,000 miles per second); however, they differ greatly in wavelength and frequency. Wavelength refers to the distance between two consecutive wave crests. Frequency refers to the number of cycles per second; its unit of measurement is hertz (Hz), which is equal to 1 cycle per second. Frequency and wavelength are closely associated with the relative energy of electromagnetic radiations. More energetic radiations have *shorter wavelength and higher frequency*. The relationship among frequency, wavelength, and energy is graphically illustrated in the electromagnetic spectrum.

Some radiations are energetic enough to rearrange atoms in materials through which they pass, and they can therefore be hazardous to living tissue. These radiations are called *ionizing radiation* because they have the energetic potential to break apart electrically neutral atoms, resulting in the production of negative and/or positive ions. (*Fosbinder and Orth, p. 18*)

99. **(C)** As kilovoltage is reduced, the number of high-energy photons produced at the target is reduced; therefore, a decrease in radiographic density occurs. If a grid has been used improperly (off-centered or out of focal range),

the lead strips will absorb excessive amounts of primary radiation, resulting in grid cutoff and loss of radiographic density. If the SID is inadequate (too short), an *increase* in radiographic density will occur. (*Selman, 9th ed., pp. 214, 240–242*)

100. **(A)** If a lateral projection of the chest is being performed on an asthenic patient and the outer photocells are selected incorrectly, the outcome is likely to be an underexposed radiograph. The patient is thin, and the lateral cells have no tissue superimposed on them. Therefore, as soon as the lateral photocells detect radiation (which will be immediately), the exposure will be terminated, giving the lateral chest insufficient exposure. (*Shephard, pp. 280–281*)

101. **(A)** A *compensating filter* is used when the part to be radiographed is of uneven thickness or density (in the chest, mediastinum vs. lungs). The filter (made of aluminum or lead acrylic) is constructed in such a way that it will absorb much of the primary radiation that would expose the low-tissue-density area while allowing the primary radiation to pass unaffected to the high-tissue-density area. A *collimator* is used to decrease the production of scattered radiation by limiting the volume of tissue irradiated. The *grid* functions to trap scattered radiation before it reaches the IR, thus reducing scattered radiation fog. *Added filtration* addresses patient protection, decreasing patient dose. (*Selman, 9th ed., pp. 254–255*)

102. **(A)** Scattered radiation is produced as x-ray photons travel through matter, interact with atoms, and are scattered (change direction). If these scattered rays are energetic enough to exit the body, they will strike the IR from all different angles. They, therefore, do not carry useful information and merely produce a flat, gray (low-contrast) fog over the image. Grid cutoff *increases* contrast and is caused by an improper relationship between the x-ray tube and the grid, resulting in absorption of some of the useful/primary beam. (*Bushong, 8th ed., p. 248*)

103. **(C)** Control of motion, both voluntary and involuntary, is an important part of radiography.

Patients are unable to control certain types of motion, such as heart action, peristalsis, and muscle spasm. In these circumstances, it is essential to use the shortest possible exposure time in order to have a "stop action" effect. (*Carlton and Adler, 4th ed., p. 451*)

104. **(A)** Limiting the *size of the irradiated field* is a most effective method of decreasing the production of scattered radiation. The smaller the *volume of tissue* irradiated, the smaller is the amount of scattered radiation generated; this can be accomplished using *compression* (prone position instead of supine or a compression band). Use of a grid does not affect the *production* of scattered radiation but rather *removes it* once it has been produced. (*Carlton and Adler, 4th ed., p. 228*)

105. **(B)** X-ray film processing consists of four parts: development, fixing, wash, and dry. *Developing* agents change the exposed silver bromide crystals (latent image) to black metallic silver, thus producing a manifest image. The *fixer* solution removes the unexposed silver bromide crystals from the emulsion and hardens the gelatin emulsion, thus ensuring permanence of the radiograph. (*Fauber, p. 167*)

106. **(C)** X-ray tube targets are constructed according to the *line-focus principle*—the focal spot is angled (usually, 12–17 degrees) to the vertical (Figure 4–34). As the actual focal spot is projected downward, it is foreshortened; thus, the effective focal spot is always smaller than the actual focal spot. As it is projected toward the *cathode* end of the x-ray beam, the effective focal spot becomes *larger* and approaches the actual size. As it is projected toward the anode end, it gets smaller because of the anode heel effect. (*Selman, 9th ed., p. 139*)

107. **(C)** Quantum *noise*, or *mottle*, is a grainy appearance; it has a spotted or freckled appearance. It looks very similar to a low-resolution photograph/image that has been enlarged. Low mAs and high kV factors are most likely to be the cause of quantum noise/mottle.

Grid cut-off is absorption of the useful beam by the grid and usually results in increased brightness/loss of density and visibility of

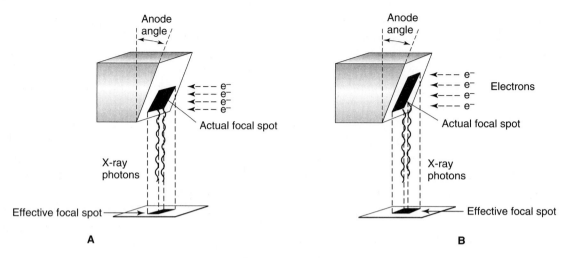

Figure 4–34A&B.

grid lines. The anode heel effect is most pronounced using short SIDs, large IRs, small anode angles, and imaging parts having uneven tissue densities; it is represented by a noticeable brightness/density difference between the anode and cathode ends of the image. *(Selman, 9th ed., p. 211)*

108. **(C)** *Kilovoltage* and the *HVL* affect both the quantity and the quality of the primary beam. The principal qualitative factor for the primary beam is kilovoltage, but an increase in kilovoltage will also create an increase in the *number* of photons produced at the target. *HVL* is defined as the amount of material necessary to decrease the intensity of the beam to one-half its original value, thereby effecting a change in both beam quality and quantity. The milliampere-seconds value is adjusted to regulate the number of x-ray photons produced at the target. X-ray-beam quality is unaffected by changes in milliampere-seconds. *(Carlton and Adler, 4th ed., p. 181)*

109. **(B)** As distance from a light source increases, the light diverges and covers a larger area; the quantity of light available per unit area becomes less and less as distance increases. The intensity (quantity) of light decreases according to the *inverse square law*, that is, the intensity of light at a particular distance from its source is inversely proportional to the square of the distance. For example, if you decreased the distance between a book you were reading

and your illuminating lamp from 6 to 3 feet, you would have four times as much light available.

Similarly, SID has a significant impact on x-ray beam intensity. *As the distance between the x-ray tube and IR increases, exposure rate decreases according to the inverse square law. (Fosbinder and Orth, p. 20)*

110. **(A)** *The shortest possible exposure should be used as a matter of routine.* Parkinson disease is characterized by uncontrollable tremors, and the resulting unsharpness can destroy image resolution/detail. A short exposure time is essential. That can be achieved by increasing the mA or the kV—AEC will react with a shorted exposure time. SID and compensating filtration are unrelated to the problem and are not indicated here. *(Fauber, p. 188)*

111. **(D)** Insufficient milliamperage and/or exposure time will result in lack of radiographic density. Insufficient kilovoltage will result in underpenetration and excessive contrast. Insufficient SID, however, will result in increased exposure rate and radiographic *overexposure. (Selman, 9th ed., pp. 214–215)*

112. **(C)** Digital image postprocessing provides the opportunity for image optimization. Image annotation permits placement of labels, arrow indicators, etc. Windowing allows adjustment of image contrast d/or brightness to diagnostic requirements. Contrast scale enhancement

is the most valuable tool in digital imaging. Image minification, with larger matrix sizes, enables us to see tiny anatomic details and improve spatial resolution. Image inversion, or reversal, provides a different perspective by changing white to black and black to white. Image flip also provides another perspective by enabling us to rotate the image. Edge enhancement is useful for small and high-contrast tissues. Other postprocessing functions include highlighting, zoom, pan, and scroll. The pixel shift feature is important in DSA. Image subtraction is used to enhance contrast. If the part moves during acquisition of serial images, misregistration occurs, making the required exact superimposition impossible. Pixel shift is a function that can correct misregistration. Another emerging postprocessing task used in diagnostic functions is determining numeric pixel value for particular ROI (region of interest). This feature has proved useful in bone densitometry, renal calculus recognition, and calcified lung nodule identification. (*Bushong, 9th ed., p. 473*)

113. **(B)** The original milliampere-seconds value was 9 (300 mA × 0.03 second). Using the *density-maintenance formula*, the new milliampere-seconds value must be determined for the distance change from 40 to 44 in. of the SID:

$$\frac{(\text{old mAs}) \, 9}{(\text{New mAs}) \, x} = \frac{(\text{old } D^2) \, 40^2}{(\text{new } D^2) \, 44^2}$$

$$1{,}600x = 17{,}424$$

Thus, $x = 10.89$ (11) mAs at 44-in. SID. Then, if 500 is the new milliamperage, we must determine what exposure time is required to achieve 8.1 mAs:

$$500 \, x = 11$$

Thus, $x = 0.022$ second (22 ms) at 500 mA and 44-in. SID. (*Selman, 9th ed., pp. 214–215*)

114. **(C)** A 15% increase in kilovoltage was made, increasing the kilovoltage to 87 kV. Because the kilovoltage change effectively doubles the density, the milliampere-seconds value now must

be cut in half (from 9 to 4.5 mAs) to compensate. Grids are used to absorb scattered radiation from the remnant beam before it can contribute to the x-ray image. Because the grid removes scattered radiation (and some useful photons as well) from the beam, an increase in exposure factors is required. The amount of increase depends on the grid ratio; the higher the grid ratio, the higher is the correction factor. The correction factor for a 12:1 grid is 5; therefore, the milliampere-seconds value (4.5) is multiplied by 5 to arrive at the new required milliampere-seconds value (22.5). Using the milliampere-seconds equation mA × s = mAs, it is determined that 0.15 second will be required at 300 mA:

$$300x = 22.5$$
$$x = 0.075 \text{ s} = 75 \text{ ms}$$

(*Fauber, pp. 62, 148*)

115. **(B)** Manufacturers of x-ray equipment must follow guidelines that state maximum x-ray output at specific distances, total quantities of filtration, positive beam limitation, and other guidelines. Radiographers must practice safe principles of operation; preventive maintenance and quality control (QC) checks must be performed at specific intervals to ensure continued safe equipment performance. Radiologic QC involves monitoring and regulating the variables associated with image production and patient care.

HVL testing provides beam quality information that is different from that obtained from kV testing. HVL is defined as the thickness of any absorber that will reduce x-ray beam intensity to one-half its original value. It is determined by measuring the beam intensity without an absorber and then recording the intensity as successive millimeters of aluminum are added to the radiation field. It is *influenced by the type of rectification, total filtration, and kV.* An x-ray tube HVL should remain almost constant. If HVL decreases, it is an indication of a decrease in the actual kV. If the HVL increases, it indicates the deposition of vaporized tungsten on the inner surface of the glass envelope (as a result of tube aging) or an increase in the actual kV. (*Fosbinder and Orth, p. 83*)

116. **(B)** The formula for *magnification factor* (MF) = image size/object size. In the stated problem, the anatomic measurement is 14.7 cm, and the magnification factor is known to be 1.2. Substituting the known factors in the appropriate equation:

$$MF = \frac{\text{image size}}{\text{object size}}$$

$$1.2 = \frac{14.7}{x}$$

$$x = \frac{14.7}{1.2}$$

$$x = 12.25 \text{ cm}$$

(actual anatomic size). *(Fauber, pp. 90–92)*

117. **(B)** DXA imaging is used to evaluate bone mineral density (BMD). Bone densitometry (i.e., DXA) can be used to *evaluate bone mineral content of the body, or part of it, to diagnose osteoporosis* or *to evaluate the effectiveness of treatments for osteoporosis*. It is the most widely used method of *bone densitometry*—it is *low-dose, precise*, and *uncomplicated* to use/perform. DXA uses *two photon energies*—one for soft tissue and one for bone. Since bone is denser and attenuates x-ray photons more readily, their *attenuation is calculated* to represent the degree of bone density. Soft tissue attenuation information is not used to measure bone density. *(Frank, Long, and Smith, 11th ed., vol. 3, pp. 455–456)*

118. **(B)** While *CR* utilizes traditional x-ray tables and *IPs* to enclose and protect the flexible PSP screen, *DR* requires the use of significantly different equipment. DR does not use IPs or a traditional x-ray table—it is a direct-capture/conversion, or indirect-capture/conversion, system of x-ray imaging. Besides eliminating IPs and their handling, DR affords the advantage of *immediate display* of the image (compared with CR's slightly delayed image display), and DR *exposures can be lower* because of the detector's *higher DQE* (i.e., ability to perceive and interact with x-ray photons). DR, like CR, also offers the advantage of image preview and postprocessing. *(Seeram, pp. 10–11)*

119. **(B)** The radiograph shown demonstrates a 1.5-in. unexposed strip along the length of the film. This occurred because, although the patient was centered correctly to the collimator light and x-ray field, the x-ray tube was not centered to the grid. If the patient was off-center, the entire image would be exposed, and the patient's spine would be off-center. Grid cutoff would not appear as such a sharply delineated line but rather as a gradually decreasing density. *(Fauber, p. 125)*

120. **(B)** The digital images' *scale of contrast*, or *contrast resolution*, can be changed electronically through leveling and windowing of the image. The *level control* determines the *central* or *middensity* of the scale of contrast, whereas the *window control* determines the *total number* of densities/grays (to the right and left of the central/middensity). Matrix and pixel sizes are related to (spatial) resolution of digital images. *(Fosbinder and Kelsey, p. 289)*

121. **(D)** The purpose of the thin layer of lead that is often located in the rear portion of an IP is to absorb x-ray photons that strike the rear of the IP and bounce back toward the PSP, resulting in scattered radiation fog. The thin layer of lead absorbs these x-ray photons and thus improves the radiographic image. *(Shephard, pp. 41–42)*

122. **(C)** The PSP plate within the CR cassette/IP has several layers. Its uppermost layer is a *protective* coat for the phosphor layer below. This layer affords durability and must be translucent to allow passage of photostimulable luminescent light. The *phosphor layer* is the "active" layer that responds to the x-ray photons that reach it. Under the phosphor layer is the *electroconductive layer* that serves to facilitate transportation through the scanner/reader and prevent image artifacts resulting from static electricity. Below the electroconductive layer is the plate support layer. Below the *support* layer is a *light-shield layer* that serves to prevent light from erasing image plate data or from approaching through the rear protective layer. Behind the light-shield layer is the rear protective layer of the PSP plate. *(Seeram, p. 53; Fosbinder and Orth, p. 213)*

123. **(C)** Quantum *noise,* or *mottle,* is a grainy appearance; it has a spotted or freckled appearance. It looks very similar to a low-resolution photograph/image that has been enlarged. Low mAs and high kV factors are most likely to be the cause of quantum noise/mottle. SID is unrelated to quantum noise. *(Bushong, 8th ed., p. 273)*

124. **(A)** In digital imaging, pixel size is determined by dividing the FOV by the matrix. In this case, the FOV is 60 cm; since the answer is expressed in millimeters, first change 60 cm to 600 mm. Then 600 divided by 2,048 equals 0.35 mm:

$$60 \text{ cm} = 600 \text{ mm}$$

$$\frac{600}{2,084} = 0.35 \text{ mm}$$

The FOV and matrix size are independent of one another; that is, either can be changed, and the other will remain unaffected. However, pixel size is affected by changes in either the FOV or matrix size. For example, if the matrix size is increased, pixel size decreases. If FOV increases, pixel size increases. Pixel size is inversely related to resolution. As pixel size increases, resolution decreases. *(Fosbinder and Kelsey, p. 285)*

125. **(D)** One of the biggest advantages of CR is the *dynamic range,* or *latitude,* it offers. The characteristic curve of x-ray film emulsion has a certain "range of correct exposure," limited by the toe and shoulder of the curve. In CR, there is a *linear relationship* between the exposure, given the PSP (SPS) and its resulting luminescence as it is scanned by the laser. This affords much greater exposure latitude, and technical inaccuracies can be effectively eliminated. Overexposure of up to 500% and underexposure of up to 80% are reported as recoverable, thus eliminating most retakes. This surely affords increased efficiency; *however, this does not mean that images can be exposed arbitrarily.* The radiographer must keep dose reduction in mind. The same exposure factors as screen–film systems, or less, generally are recommended for CR. Intensifying screens used in screen–film x-ray imaging tend to produce high contrast. The faster the screens, the higher is the contrast; higher contrast often is associated with decreased latitude. AEC refers to automatic exposure control and is unrelated to dynamic range or latitude. *(Shephard, pp. 330–332)*

126. **(D)** The *matrix* is the number of pixels in the *xy* direction. *The larger the matrix size, the better is the image resolution.* Typical image matrix sizes used in radiography are

- Nuclear medicine 128×128
- Digital subtraction $1,024 \times 1,024$
  angiography (DSA)
- CT 512×512
- Chest radiography $2,048 \times 2,048$

A digital image is formed by a *matrix* of pixels in rows and columns. A matrix having 512 pixels in each row and column is a 512×512 matrix. The term *field of view* is used to describe how much of the patient (e.g., 150-mm diameter) is included in the matrix. The matrix or field of view can be changed without affecting the other, but changes in either will change pixel size. As in traditional radiography, *spatial resolution* is measured in line pairs per millimeter (*lp/mm*). As matrix size is increased, there are more and smaller pixels in the matrix and, therefore, improved spatial resolution. Fewer and larger pixels result in a poor-resolution "pixelly" image, that is, one in which you can actually see the individual pixel boxes. *(Fosbinder and Kelsey, p. 286)*

127. **(C)** Quality control in mammography includes scrupulous testing of virtually all component parts of the mammographic imaging system. It includes processor checks, screen maintenance, accurate and consistent viewing conditions, and evaluation of phantom images, to name a few. The device shown constitutes the structures to be imaged within a mammography phantom. A mammographic phantom contains Mylar fibers, simulated masses, and specks of simulated calcifications. The American College of Radiology accreditation criteria state that a minimum of 10 objects (4 fibers, 3 specks, and 3 masses) must be visualized on test images. Changes in any part(s) of the imaging system (e.g., film, screens, image receptors, x-ray equipment, filtration, or viewbox) can result in unsuccessful results. *(Bushong, 8th ed., p. 350)*

128. **(D)** Factors influencing recorded detail in digital imaging are very much the same as those factors affecting recorded detail in analog imaging, that is, *motion, geometric factors* (focal spot size, OID, and SID), and *spatial resolution*. In analog imaging, spatial resolution is related to the speed of the imaging system (intensifying screen speed) and is significantly better than digital imaging resolution. The spatial resolution of direct digital systems, however, is fixed and is related to the detector element (*DEL*) size of the thin film transistor (*TFT*). The smaller the TFT DEL size, the better the spatial resolution. DEL size of 100 microns provides a spatial resolution of about 5 lp/mm (available only in some digital mammography systems). DEL size of 200 microns provides a spatial resolution of about 2.5 lp/mm (general radiography)—lower than that achieved with 400 speed intensifying screen system. A 100 speed intensifying screen system offers a spatial resolution of about 10 lp/mm—significantly greater than, and currently unachievable in, digital imaging. Spatial resolution in digital imaging is fixed, but it is very important that radiographers are alert to the opportunity they have to utilize and control the remaining recorded detail factors (motion and geometric factors). *(Seeram, pp. 97–98)*

129. **(D)** Health care information technology, or health *informatics*, has ever-increasing application and use in the imaging sciences. PACS (Picture Archiving and Communication Systems) is used by health care facilities to economically store, archive, exchange, and transmit digital images from multiple imaging modalities. PACS replaces the need to manually file, retrieve, and transport film and film jackets.

RIS (Radiology Information Systems) and HIS (Hospital Information Systems) can be integrated with PACS for electronic health information storage. The purpose of HIS is to manage health care information and documents electronically, and to ensure data security and

availability. RIS is a system for tracking radiological and imaging procedures. RIS is used for patient registration and scheduling, radiology workflow management, reporting and printout, manipulation and distribution and tracking of patient data, and billing. RIS complements HIS and is critical to competent workflow to radiologic facilities. *(Seeram, p. 9)*

130. **(B)** To calculate milliampere-seconds, multiply milliamperage times exposure time. In this case, 400 mA × 0.017 second (17 ms) = 6.8 mAs. Careful attention to proper decimal placement will help to avoid basic math errors. *(Shephard, p. 170)*

131. **(C)** Externally, IPs (Image Plates) appear very much like traditional film–screen cassettes. However, the main function of an IP is to support and protect the PSP (SPS) that lies within the IP. IPs do not contain intensifying screens or film and, therefore, do not need to be lighttight. The photostimulable PSP is not affected by light. *(Shephard, p. 51)*

132. **(B)** Radiographic technique charts are highly recommended for use with every x-ray unit. A technique chart identifies the standardized factors that should be used with that particular x-ray unit for various examinations/positions of anatomic parts of different sizes. To be used effectively, these technique charts require that the anatomic part in question be measured correctly with a *caliper*. A *fulcrum* is of importance in tomography; a *densitometer* is used in sensitometry and QA. *(Bushong, 8th ed., p. 308)*

133. **(A)** Remnant x-rays emerging from the patient/part are converted to electrical signals. This is an analog image. These electrical signals are sent to the ADC (analog-to-digital converter) to be converted to digital data (in binary digits or bits). Then, the digital image data is transferred to a DAC (digital-to-analog converter) to be converted to a perceptible analog image on the display monitor. The monitor image can be manipulated, postprocessed, stored, or transmitted. *(Seeram, pp. 7–8)*

134. **(B)** A fractional focal spot of 0.3 mm or smaller is essential for reproducing fine detail without

focal-spot blurring in *magnification* radiography. As the object image is magnified, so will be any associated blur unless a fractional focal spot is used. Use of a fractional focal spot on a routine basis is unnecessary; it is not advised because it causes unnecessary wear on the x-ray tube and offers little radiographic advantage. *(Shephard, p. 217)*

135. **(B)** The heel effect is characterized by a variation in beam intensity that *increases gradually from anode to cathode.* This can be effectively put to use when performing radiographic examinations of large body parts with uneven tissue density. For example, the AP thoracic spine is thicker caudally than cranially, so the thicker portion is best placed under the cathode. However, in the lateral projection of the thoracic spine, the upper portion is thicker because of superimposed shoulders, and therefore, that portion is best placed under the cathode end of the beam. The femur is also uneven in density, particularly in the AP position, and can benefit from use of the heel effect. However, the sternum and its surrounding anatomy are fairly uniform in thickness and would not benefit from use of the anode heel effect. *The anode heel effect is most pronounced when using large IRs at short SIDs and with an anode having a steep (small) target angle. (Carlton and Adler, 4th ed., p. 407)*

136. **(D)** As *photon energy* increases, more penetration and greater production of scattered radiation occur, producing a longer scale of contrast. As *grid ratio* increases, more scattered radiation is absorbed, producing a shorter scale of contrast. As OID increases, the distance between the part and the IR acts as a grid, and consequently, less scattered radiation reaches the IR, producing a shorter scale of contrast. Focal-spot size is related only to recorded detail. *(Shephard, p. 203)*

137. **(D)** The lead strips in a parallel grid are *parallel to one another* and, therefore, are *not parallel to the x-ray beam.* The more divergent the x-ray beam, the more likely there is to be cutoff/decreased density at the lateral edges of the radiograph. This problem becomes more pronounced at short SIDs. If there were a centering or tube angle problem, there would be more likely to be a noticeable density loss on one side or the other. *(Carlton and Adler, 4th ed., p. 260)*

138. **(B)** This is an example of *both* off-focus and lateral decentering errors. Note the asymmetric cutoff from right to left. The individual grid errors, as well as the result of both errors together, is summarized below.

- *Off-focus errors:* Grid cutoff will occur if the SID is below the lower limits, or above the upper limits, of the specified focal range. This type of error is also referred to as *focus–grid distance decentering.* Off-focus errors are usually characterized by loss of density at the *periphery* of the image.

- *Off-center errors:* If the x-ray beam is not centered to the grid (i.e., if it is shifted laterally) grid cutoff will occur. This type of error is referred to as lateral decentering and characterized by a *uniform density loss* across the radiographic image.

If the x-ray beam is *both off-center and off-focus below the focusing distance,* the portion of the image below the focus will show *increased* density; if the x-ray beam is *off-center and off-focus above the focusing distance,* the image below the focus will show *decreased* density.

139. **(C)** The *reciprocity law* states that a particular milliampere-seconds value, regardless of the milliamperage and exposure time used, will provide identical radiographic density. This holds true with direct exposure techniques, but it does fail somewhat with the use of intensifying screens. However, the fault is so slight as to be unimportant in most radiographic procedures. *(Shephard, p. 193)*

140. **(B)** As the distance from the object to the IR (OID) increases, so does magnification distortion, thereby decreasing recorded detail. Some magnification is inevitable in radiography because it is not possible to place anatomic structures directly on the IR. However, our understanding of how to minimize magnification distortion is an important part of our everyday work. *(Fauber, pp. 90–91)*

141. **(D)** Milliampere-seconds (mAs) is the exposure factor that regulates radiographic density. The equation used to determine mAs is mA × s = mAs. Substituting the known factors:

$$300x = 6$$
$$x = 0.02 \text{ s (20 ms)}$$

(Fauber, p. 55)

142. **(C)** Factors influencing recorded detail in digital imaging are very much the same as those factors affecting recorded detail in analog imaging, that is, *motion, geometric factors* (focal spot size, OID, and SID), and *spatial resolution*. In analog imaging, spatial resolution is related to the speed of the imaging system (intensifying screen speed) and is significantly better than digital imaging resolution. The spatial resolution of direct digital systems, however, is fixed and is related to the detector element (*DEL*) size of the thin film transistor (*TFT*). The smaller the TFT DEL size, the better the spatial resolution. DEL size of 100 microns provides a spatial resolution of about 5 lp/mm (available only in some digital mammography systems). DEL size of 200 microns provides a spatial resolution of about 2.5 lp/mm (general radiography)—lower than that achieved with 400 speed intensifying screen system. A 100 speed intensifying screen system offers a spatial resolution of about 10 lp/mm—significantly greater than, and currently unachievable in, digital imaging. Spatial resolution in digital imaging is fixed, but it is very important that radiographers are alert to the opportunity they have to utilize and control the remaining recorded detail factors (motion and geometric factors). *(Seeram, pp. 97–98)*

143. **(A)** An increase in kilovoltage increases the overall average energy of the x-ray photons produced at the target, thus giving them greater penetrability. (This can increase the incidence of Compton interaction and, therefore, the production of scattered radiation.) Greater penetration of all tissues serves to lengthen the scale of contrast. However, excessive scattered radiation reaching the IR will cause a fog and carries no useful information. *(Selman, 9th ed., pp. 127–128)*

144. **(A)** Beam restrictors function to limit the size of the irradiated field. In so doing, they limit the volume of tissue irradiated (thereby decreasing the percentage of scattered radiation generated in the part) and help to reduce patient dose. Beam restrictors do not affect the quality (energy) of the x-ray beam—that is, the function of kilovoltage and filtration. Beam restrictors do not absorb scattered radiation—that is a function of grids. *(Shephard, p. 27)*

145. **(C)** SID is *directly* related to recorded detail/resolution because as SID increases, so does recorded detail/resolution (because magnification is decreased). OID is *inversely* related to recorded detail because as OID increases, recorded detail/resolution decreases. Motion is also inversely related to recorded detail/resolution because as motion increases, recorded detail/resolution decreases—as a result of motion blur, the greatest enemy of resolution. Therefore, of the given choices, OID and motion are *inversely* related to recorded detail. SID is *directly* related to recorded detail. *(Shephard, pp. 221–224)*

146. **(A)** The single most important factor regulating radiographic contrast is kilovoltage. The lower the kilovoltage, the shorter is the scale of contrast. All the milliampere-seconds values in this problem have been adjusted for kilovoltage changes to maintain density, but just a glance at each of the kilovoltages is often a good indicator of which will produce the longest scale or shortest scale contrast. *(Shephard, pp. 306, 308)*

147. **(C)** The PA projection of the chest demonstrates high-, or short-scale, contrast. Additionally, faint visualization of the thoracic vertebrae through the heart is not demonstrated—indicating that there is *inadequate penetration*, that is, *insufficient kilovoltage* selected. Density is adequate, but contrast and penetration are unacceptable for diagnostic purposes. *(Shephard, p. 180)*

148. **(B)** The input phosphor of image intensifiers is usually made of cesium iodide. For each x-ray photon absorbed by cesium iodide, approximately 5,000 light photons are emitted. As the light photons strike a photoemissive *photocathode*, a number of electrons are released from the photocathode and focused toward the output side of the image tube by voltage applied to the negatively charged *electrostatic focusing lenses*. The electrons are then accelerated through the neck of the tube where they strike the small (0.5–1 in.) *output phosphor* that is mounted on a flat glass support. The entire assembly is enclosed within a 2–4-mm thick vacuum glass envelope. Remember that the image on the output phosphor is *minified*, *brighter*, and *inverted* (electron focusing causes image inversion).

Input screen diameters of 5–12 in. are available. Although smaller diameter input screens improve resolution, they do not permit a large FOV, that is, viewing of large patient areas.

Dual- and triple-field image intensifiers are available that permit *magnified* viewing of fluoroscopic images. To achieve magnification, the *voltage* to the focusing lenses is increased and a *smaller* portion of the input phosphor is used, thereby resulting in a smaller FOV. Because minification gain is now decreased, the image is not as bright. The mA is automatically increased to compensate for the loss in brightness when the image intensifier is switched to magnification mode. Entrance skin exposure (ESE) can increase dramatically as the FOV decreases (i.e., as magnification increases).

As FOV decreases, *magnification* of the output screen image increases, there is less *noise* because increased mA provides a greater number of x-ray photons, and *contrast* and *resolution* improve. The *focal* point in the magnification mode is *further away from* the output phosphor (as a result of increased voltage applied to the focusing lenses) and therefore the output image is magnified. *(Fosbinder and Orth, pp. 191, 201)*

149. **(A)** The figure represents the *anode heel effect*. Because the anode's focal track is beveled, x-ray photons can freely diverge toward the cathode end of the x-ray tube. However, the "heel" of the focal track prevents x-ray photons from diverging toward the anode end of

the tube. This results in varying intensity with fewer photons at the anode end (A) and more photons at the cathode end (B).

The line-focus principle relates to the anode's focal spot, and x-ray tube targets are constructed according to the line-focus principle—the focal spot is angled to the vertical. As the actual focal spot is projected downward, it is foreshortened; thus, the effective focal spot is always smaller than the actual focal spot.

The inverse-square law deals with the changing x-ray intensity with changes in distance. This principle is important in image formation and in radiation protection.

150. **(B)** If (A) and (B) are reduced to 5 mAs for consistency, the kilovoltage will increase to 85 kV in both cases, thereby balancing radiographic densities. Thus, the greatest density is determined by the shortest SID (greatest exposure rate). *(Shephard, pp. 306–307)*

In electronic imaging (CR, DR), the term *brightness* is used instead of *density*. A film image with little density would be described as a monitor digital image as having greater brightness.

151. **(B)** Focal-spot size accuracy is related to the degree of *geometric blur*, that is, edge gradient or penumbra. Manufacturer tolerance for new focal spots is 50%; that is, a 0.3-mm focal spot actually may be 0.45 mm. Additionally, the focal spot can increase in size as the x-ray tube ages—hence, the importance of *testing* newly arrived focal spots and periodic testing to monitor focal-spot changes. Focal-spot size can be measured with a *pinhole camera*, *slit camera*, or *star-pattern-type resolution device*. The pinhole camera is rather difficult to use accurately and requires the use of excessive tube (heat) loading. With a *slit camera*, two exposures are made; one measures the length of the focal spot, and the other measures the width. The *star pattern*, or similar resolution device, such as the *bar pattern*, can measure focal-spot size *as a function of geometric blur* and is readily adaptable in a QA program to monitor focal-spot changes over a period of time. It is recommended that focal-spot size be checked on installation of a new x-ray tube and annually thereafter. *(Bushong, 8th ed., p. 462)*

152. **(D)** *Focusing distance* is the term used to specify the optimal SID used with a particular focused grid. It is usually expressed as *focal range*, indicating the minimum and maximum SID workable with that grid. Lesser or greater distances can result in grid cutoff. Although proper distance is important in computed tomography and chest and magnification radiography, focusing distance is unrelated to them. (*Selman, 9th ed., pp. 239–240*)

153. **(B)** The radiographer selects a *processing algorithm* by selecting the anatomic part and particular projection on the computer/control panel. The CR unit then matches that information with a particular lookup table (LUT)—a characteristic curve that best matches the anatomic part being imaged. The observer is able to review the image and, if desired, change its appearance (through "windowing"); doing so changes the LUT. Hence, histogram analysis and use of the appropriate LUT together function to produce predictable image quality in CR.

154. **(A)** Grids are used in radiography to trap scattered radiation that otherwise would cause fog on the radiograph. *Grid ratio* is defined as the ratio of the height of the lead strips to the distance between them. *Grid frequency* refers to the number of lead strips per inch. *Focusing distance* and *grid radius* are terms denoting the distance range with which a focused grid may be used. (*Selman, 9th ed., p. 236*)

155. **(C)** Because the anode's focal track is beveled (angled, facing the cathode), x-ray photons can freely diverge toward the cathode end of the x-ray tube. However, the "heel" of the focal track prevents x-ray photons from diverging toward the anode end of the tube. This results in varying intensity from anode to cathode, with fewer photons at the anode end and more photons at the cathode end. *The anode heel effect is most noticeable when using large IRs, short SIDs, and steep target angles. (Carlton and Adler, 4th ed., p. 407)*

156. **(C)** Two of a grid's physical characteristics that determine its degree of efficiency in the removal of scattered radiation are *grid ratio* (the height of the lead strips compared with the distance between them) and the number of *lead strips per inch.* As the lead strips are made taller or the distance between them decreases, scattered radiation is more likely to be trapped before reaching the IR. A 12:1 ratio grid will absorb more scattered radiation than an 8:1 ratio grid. An undesirable but unavoidable characteristic of grids is that they do absorb some primary/useful photons as well as scattered photons. The higher the ratio grid, the more scatter radiation the grid will clean up, but more useful photons will be absorbed as well. The higher the primary to scattered photon transmission ratio, the more desirable is the grid. Higher-ratio grids restrict positioning latitude more severely—grid centering must be more accurate (than with lower-ratio grids) to avoid grid cutoff. (*Shephard, pp. 245–246*)

157. **(D)** In digital imaging, as in film/screen radiography, there are numerous *density/brightness values* that represent various *tissue densities* (i.e., x-ray attenuation properties), for example, bone, muscle, fat, blood-filled organs, air/gas, metal, contrast media, and pathologic processes. In CR, the CR scanner/reader recognizes these values and constructs a representative *grayscale* histogram of them, corresponding to the *anatomic characteristics of the imaged part.* Thus, all PA chest histograms are similar, all lateral chest histograms are similar, all pelvis histograms are similar, etc.

A histogram is a *graphic representation* of *pixel value distribution.* The histogram is an analysis and graphic representation of all the densities from the PSP screen, demonstrating the quantity of exposure, the number of pixels, and their value. Histograms are *unique to each body part* imaged.

Histogram appearance and *patient dose* can be affected by the radiographer's knowledge and skill using digital imaging, in addition to their degree of accuracy in *positioning* and *centering.* Collimation is exceedingly important to avoid *histogram analysis errors.* Lack of adequate collimation can result in signals outside the anatomic area being included in the exposure data recognition/histogram analysis. This can result in a variety of histogram analysis errors including excessively light, dark, or noisy images. Poor *collimation* can affect exposure level and exposure latitude; these changes are reflected in the images' informational numbers ("S number," "exposure index," etc.).

Other factors affecting histogram appearance, and therefore these informational numbers, include selection of the *correct processing algorithm* (e.g., chest vs. femur vs. cervical spine), changes in *scatter, source-to-image-receptor distance* (SID), *object-to-image-receptor distance* (OID), and *collimation*—in short, anything that affects scatter and/or dose.

158. **(C)** The screen/film radiographic image shown is an illustration of poor screen–film contact. Motion and scattered radiation fog can be ruled out because the blurriness is seen only in the apical region. Screen–film contact is evaluated using a wire mesh that is placed on the questionable IR and radiographed (Figure 4–35). Any areas of unsharpness represent poor contact, which can result from warped screens, a foreign body in the IR, or a damaged IR frame. *(Selman, 9th ed., pp. 183–186)*

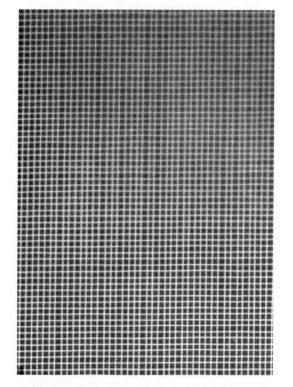

Figure 4–35. From the American College of Radiology Learning File. Courtesy of the ACR.

159. **(D)** Milliampere-seconds (mAs) are the product of milliamperes (mA) and exposure time (seconds). Any combinations of milliamperes and time that will produce a given milliampere-seconds value (i.e., a particular quantity of x-ray photons) will produce identical optical density. This is known as the *reciprocity law*. Density is a quantitative factor because it describes the amount of image blackening. The milliampere-seconds value is also a quantitative factor because it regulates x-ray-beam *intensity, exposure rate, quantity,* or *number* of x-ray photons produced (the milliampere-seconds value is the single most important technical factor associated with image density and is the factor of choice for regulating radiographic/optical density). *The milliampere-seconds value is directly proportional to the intensity* (i.e., exposure rate, number, and quantity) of x-ray photons produced and the resulting radiographic density. If the milliampere-seconds value is doubled, twice the exposure rate and twice the density occur. If the milliampere-seconds value is cut in half, the exposure rate and resulting density are cut in half. The milliampere-seconds value has no effect on recorded detail. *(Shephard, p. 170)*

160. **(B)** Positive contrast medium is *radiopaque;* negative contrast material is *radioparent.* Barium sulfate (radiopaque, positive contrast material) is used most frequently for examinations of the intestinal tract, and high-kilovoltage exposure factors are used to penetrate (to see through and behind) the barium. Water-based iodinated contrast media (Conray, Amipaque) are also positive contrast agents. However, the K-edge binding energy of iodine *prohibits the use of much greater than 70 kV* with these materials. Higher kilovoltage values will obviate the effect of the contrast agent. Air is an example of a negative contrast agent, and high-kilovoltage factors are clearly *not indicated. (Shephard, pp. 200–201)*

161. **(A)** It is appropriate to perform an AP abdomen radiograph with lower kilovoltage because it has such low subject contrast. Abdominal tissue densities are so similar that it takes high- or short-scale contrast (using low kilovoltage) to emphasize the little difference

there is between tissues. However, high-kilovoltage factors are used frequently to even out densities in anatomic parts having high tissue contrast (e.g., the chest). However, since high kilovoltage produces added scattered radiation, it generally must be used with a grid. Barium-filled structures frequently are radiographed using 120 kV or more to penetrate the barium—to see through to posterior structures *(Carlton and Adler, 4th ed., pp. 423–424)*

162. **(B)** The input phosphor of image intensifiers is usually made of cesium iodide. For each x-ray photon absorbed by cesium iodide, approximately 5,000 light photons are emitted. As the light photons strike a photoemissive *photocathode*, a number of electrons are released from the photocathode and focused toward the output side of the image tube by voltage applied to the negatively charged *electrostatic focusing lenses*. The electrons are then accelerated through the neck of the tube where they strike the small (0.5–1 in.) *output phosphor* that is mounted on a flat glass support. The entire assembly is enclosed within a 2–4-mm thick vacuum glass envelope. Remember that the image on the output phosphor is *minified, brighter*, and *inverted* (electron focusing causes image inversion).

Input screen diameters of 5–12 in. are available. Although smaller diameter input screens improve resolution, they do not permit a large FOV, that is, viewing of large patient areas.

Dual- and triple-field image intensifiers are available that permit *magnified* viewing of fluoroscopic images. To achieve magnification, the *voltage* to the focusing lenses is increased and a *smaller* portion of the input phosphor is used, thereby resulting in a smaller FOV. Because minification gain is now decreased, the image is not as bright. The mA is automatically increased to compensate for the loss in brightness when the image intensifier is switched to magnification mode. Entrance skin exposure (ESE) can increase dramatically as the FOV decreases (i.e., as magnification increases).

As FOV decreases, *magnification* of the output screen image increases, there is less *noise* because increased mA provides a greater number of x-ray photons, and *contrast* and *resolution* improve. The *focal point* in the magnification mode is *further away from* the output phosphor (as a result of increased voltage applied to the focusing lenses) and therefore the output image is magnified. *(Fosbinder and Orth, p. 191)*

163. **(B)** The original milliampere-seconds value (regulating radiographic density) was 200. The original kilovoltage (regulating radiographic contrast) was 90. The milliampere-seconds value was cut in half, to 100, causing a decrease in density. The kilovoltage was increased (by 15%) to *compensate for the density loss and thereby increase the scale of contrast. (Shephard, p. 203)*

164. **(A)** As kilovoltage is increased, *more* electrons are driven to the anode with greater speed and energy. More high-energy electrons will result in production of *more high-energy x-rays*. Thus, kilovoltage affects both quantity and quality (energy) of the x-ray beam. However, although kilovoltage and radiographic density are directly *related*, they are not directly proportional; that is, twice the radiographic density does not result from doubling the kilovoltage. With respect to the effect of kilovoltage on image density, if it is desired to double the radiographic density yet impossible to adjust the milliampere-seconds, a similar effect can be achieved by *increasing the kilovoltage by 15%*. Conversely, the density may be cut in half by decreasing the kilovoltage by 15%. Therefore, a decrease in kilovoltage will produce fewer x-ray photons, resulting in decreased density. Additionally, a decrease in kilovoltage will produce fewer shades of gray, that is, a shorter-scale, or higher/increased, contrast. Kilovoltage is unrelated to recorded detail and resolution. *(Shephard, pp. 178, 203–204)*

165. **(D)** The radiographer selects a *processing algorithm* by selecting the anatomic part and particular projection on the computer/control panel. The CR unit then matches that information with a particular lookup table (LUT)—a characteristic curve that best matches the anatomic part being imaged. The observer is

able to review the image and, if desired, change its appearance (through "windowing"); doing so changes the LUT. Histogram analysis and use of the appropriate *LUT* together function to produce predictable image quality in CR. Additionally, the radiographer can manipulate, that is, change and enhance, the digital image displayed on the display monitor through *postprocessing*. One way to alter image contrast and/or brightness is through *windowing*. The term *windowing* refers to some change made to window width and/or window level, that is, a change in the LUT. Change in window *width* affects change in the number of gray shades, that is, *image contrast*. Change in window *level* affects change in the image *brightness*, that is, density. Therefore, windowing and other postprocessing mechanisms permit the radiographer to affect changes in the image and produce "special effects," such as *contrast enhancement, edge enhancement, image stitching. (Seeram, pp. 34–35)*

166. **(B)** Patient demographic and examination information originates from the hospital/facility HIS, where it is obtained when the patient is initially registered. That information is available or retrievable when the patient is scheduled, or arrives, for imaging services. Typical patient information includes name, DOB or age, sex, ID number, accession number, examination being performed, date and time of examination.

Additional information may be available on the examination requisition; more information is usually entered by the technologist at the time of the examination.

A feature that is useful in sorting examinations and decreasing (but not eliminating) errors is the *Modality Work List* (MWL). The MWL "brings up" existing RIS information, that is, the examinations scheduled for each imaging area—for example, x-ray, CT, MR, mammography, ultrasound, etc. The technologist selects the correct patient, which includes that patient's particular demographics, from the particular modality work list.

It is essential that the technologist is attentive to detail and accuracy when entering patient information; errors in patient demographics entry, and entry duplication, must be avoided.

PACS is used by health care facilities to economically store, archive, exchange, transmit digital images from multiple imaging modalities; it replaces the need to manually file, retrieve, and transport film and film jackets.

RIS and HIS can be integrated with PACS for electronic health information storage. The purpose of HIS is to manage health care information and documents electronically, and to ensure data security and availability. RIS is a system for tracking radiological and imaging procedures. RIS is used for patient registration and scheduling, radiology workflow management, reporting and printout, manipulation and distribution and tracking of patient data, and billing. RIS complements HIS and is critical to competent workflow to radiologic facilities. *(Seeram, pp. 222–223, 226)*

167. **(C)** Technical factors can be expressed in terms of milliampere-seconds rather than milliamperes and time. The milliampere-seconds value is a *quantitative* factor because it regulates x-ray-beam *intensity, exposure rate, quantity,* or *number* of x-ray photons produced (the milliampere-seconds value is the single most important technical factor associated with image density and is the factor of choice for regulating radiographic/optical density). *The milliampere-seconds value is directly proportional to the intensity* (i.e., exposure rate, number, and quantity) of x-ray photons produced and the resulting radiographic density. If the milliampere-seconds value is doubled, twice the exposure rate and twice the density occur. If the milliampere-seconds value is cut in half, the exposure rate and resulting density are cut in half. Kilovoltage is the *qualitative* exposure factor—it determines beam quality by regulating photon energy (i.e., wavelength). *(Shephard, p. 120)*

168. **(B)** An *upside-down focused grid* presents its lead strips in the opposite direction to that of the x-ray beam. This results in severe grid cutoff everywhere except in the central portion of the radiographic image. Severe grid cutoff of chest anatomy can be seen outside the central exposed area. A misaligned collimator would not show such symmetrical loss of density, nor would an incorrectly selected AEC photocell. Focal spot is unrelated to image density.

169. **(D)** *Differential absorption* refers to the x-ray absorption characteristics of neighboring anatomic structures. The radiographic representation of these structures is referred to as *radiographic contrast*; it may be enhanced with high-contrast technical factors, especially using low kilovoltage levels. At low-kilovoltage levels, the photoelectric effect predominates. *(Bushong, 8th ed., pp. 181–184)*

170. **(C)** According to the inverse-square law of radiation, as the distance between the radiation source and the IR decreases, the exposure rate increases. Therefore, a decrease in technical factors is indicated. The *density-maintenance formula* is used to determine new milliampere-seconds values when changing distance:

$$\frac{(old\ mAs)\ 24}{(New\ mAs)\ x} = \frac{(old\ mAs\ D^2)\ 38^2}{(new\ D^2)\ 42^2}$$

$$\frac{24}{x} = \frac{1,444}{1,764}$$

$$444x = 42,336$$

Thus, $x = 29.31$ mAs at 42-in. SID. Then, to determine the new exposure time (mA × s = mAs),

$$400x = 29.31$$

Thus, $x = 0.073$ second (73 ms) at 400 mA. *(Selman, 9th ed., p. 214)*

171. **(D)** *Radiographic contrast is the sum of film emulsion contrast and subject contrast.* Subject contrast has by far the greatest influence on radiographic contrast. Several factors influence subject contrast, each as a result of beam-attenuation differences in the irradiated tissues. As patient *thickness* and tissue *density* increase, attenuation increases, and subject contrast is increased. As *kilovoltage* increases, higher-energy photons are produced, beam attenuation is decreased, and *subject contrast decreases. (Carlton and Adler, 4th ed., p. 433)*

172. **(D)** Patient demographic and examination information originates from the hospital/facility HIS, where it is obtained when the patient is initially registered. That information is available or retrievable when the patient is scheduled, or arrives, for imaging services. *Typical patient information includes name, DOB or age, sex, ID number, accession number, examination being performed, date and time of examination.*

Additional information may be available on the examination requisition; more information is usually entered by the technologist at the time of the examination.

A feature that is useful in sorting examinations and decreasing (but not eliminating) errors is the Modality Work List (MWL). The MWL "brings up" existing RIS information, that is, the examinations scheduled for each imaging area—for example, x-ray, CT, MR, mammography, ultrasound, etc. The technologist selects the correct patient, which includes that patient's particular demographics, from the particular modality work list.

It is essential that the technologist is attentive to detail and accuracy when entering patient information; errors in patient demographics entry, and entry duplication, must be avoided. *(Seeram, pp. 222–223, 226)*

173. **(B)** The abdomen is a thick structure that contains many structures of similar density, and thus it requires increased exposure and a grid to absorb scattered radiation. The lumbar spine and hip are also dense structures requiring increased exposure and use of a grid. The knee, however, is frequently small enough to be radiographed without a grid. The general rule is that structures measuring more than 10 cm should be radiographed with a grid. *(Bontrager and Lampignano, 6th ed., p. 45)*

174. **(C)** *Scattered radiation* adds unwanted degrading densities to the x-ray image. The single most important way to reduce the production of scattered radiation is to collimate. Although *collimation*, optimal *kilovoltage*, and *compression* can be used, a large amount of scattered radiation is still generated within the part being imaged, and because it adds unwanted non–information-carrying densities, it can have a severely degrading effect on image quality. A *grid* is a device interposed between the patient and IR that functions to absorb a large percentage of scattered radiation before it reaches the IR. It is constructed of alternating strips of lead foil and *radiolucent* filler material. X-ray photons traveling in the same direction as the primary beam pass between the lead strips. X-ray photons, having undergone interactions within the body and deviated in various directions, are absorbed by the lead strips; this is referred to as *cleanup* of scattered radiation. An *air gap* introduced between the object and IR can have an effect similar to that of a grid. As energetic scattered radiation emerges from the body, it continues to travel in its divergent fashion and much of the time will bypass the IR. It is usually necessary to increase the SID to reduce magnification caused by increased OID. Imaging system speed is unrelated to scattered radiation. (*Shephard, pp. 244, 263*)

175. **(C)** Radiographers usually are able to stop voluntary motion using suspended respiration, careful instruction, and immobilization. However, *involuntary* motion also must be considered. To have a "stop action" effect on the heart when radiographing the chest, it is essential to use a short exposure time. (*Fauber, pp. 87–88*)

176. **(A)** Diagnostic x-ray photons interact with tissue in a number of ways, but mostly they are involved in the production of Compton scatter or the photoelectric effect. *Compton scatter* is pictured; it occurs when a relatively *high-energy* (kV) photon uses *some* of its energy to eject an *outer*-shell electron. In so doing, the photon is deviated in direction and becomes a scattered photon. Compton scatter causes objectionable scattered radiation fog in large structures such as the abdomen and poses a radiation hazard to personnel during procedures such as fluoroscopy. In the *photoelectric effect*, a relatively *low-energy* x-ray photon uses *all* its energy to eject an *inner*-shell electron, leaving a hole in the K shell. An L-shell electron then drops down to fill the K vacancy and in so doing emits a characteristic ray whose energy is equal to the difference between the binding energies of the K and L shells. The photoelectric effect occurs with *high-atomic-number* absorbers such as bone and positive contrast media and is responsi-

ble for the production of radiographic contrast. It is helpful for the production of the radiographic image, but it contributes to the dose received by the patient (because it involves complete absorption of the incident photon). (*Bushong, 8th ed., pp. 174–175*)

177. **(B)** Sir Godfrey Newbold Hounsfield created the first CT unit, describing the reconstruction of data taken from multiple projection angles. Alan MacLeod Cormack worked with the complex mathematical algorithms required for image reconstruction. Their first commercial CT head scanner was available in 1971. In 1979, Hounsfield and Cormack shared the Nobel Prize in Medicine for their historic work with this new imaging science.

To express the beam attenuation characteristics of various tissues, the *Hounsfield unit* (HU) is used. HUs can also be referred to as *CT numbers* or density values. Godfrey Hounsfield assigned a value of 0 to distilled water, a value of +1,000 to dense osseous tissue, and a value of −1,000 to air. There is a direct relationship between the HU and tissue attenuation coefficient. The greater the attenuation coefficient of the particular tissue, the higher the HU value. One HU represents a 0.1% difference between the particular tissue attenuation characteristics and that of distilled water. HU value accuracy can be affected by equipment calibration, volume averaging, and image artifacts. (*Fosbinder and Orth, pp. 262–263*)

178. **(B)** A review of the problem reveals that three changes are being made: an increase in SID, a decrease in kV, and a change in exposure time (to be considered last). The original mAs value was 9. The decrease in kV requires us to double the mAs in order to maintain sufficient exposure. Now, we must deal with the distance change. Using the density-maintenance formula (and remembering that 18 is now the old milliampere-seconds value), we find that the required new milliampere-seconds value at 42 in. is 22.

$$\frac{\text{(old mAs) } 18}{\text{(New mAs) } x} = \frac{\text{(old } D^2) \, 36^2}{\text{(new } D^2) \, 40^2}$$

$$1{,}296x = 28{,}800$$

Thus, $x = 22.22$ mAs at 40-in. SID. Because milliamperage is unchanged, we must determine the exposure time that, when used with 300 mA, will yield 22 mAs.

$$300x = 22$$
$$x = 0.07\text{-s exposure}$$

(Selman, p. 124)

179. **(A)** Low-ratio grids, such as 5:1, 6:1, and 8:1, are used with moderate-kilovolt techniques and are not recommended for use beyond 85 kV. They are not able to clean up the amount of scatter produced at high kilovoltages, but their low ratio permits more positioning latitude than high-ratio grids. High-kilovoltage exposures produce large amounts of scattered radiation, and therefore, high-ratio grids are used in an effort to trap more of this scattered radiation. However, *accurate centering and positioning* become more critical to *avoid grid cutoff. (Selman, 9th ed., p. 243)*

180. **(D)** According to the inverse-square law of radiation, the intensity or exposure rate of radiation is inversely proportional to the square of the distance from its source. Thus, as distance from the source of radiation increases, exposure rate decreases. Because exposure rate and image density are directly proportional, if the exposure rate of a beam directed to an IR is decreased, the resulting image density would be decreased proportionately. *(Selman, 9th ed., p. 117)*

181. **(B)** Less scattered radiation is generated within a part as the kilovoltage is decreased, as the size of the field is decreased, and as the thickness and density of tissue decrease. As the quantity of scattered radiation decreases from any of these sources, the higher/greater will be the contrast and the less is the overall density (greater brightness) of the resulting image. *(Carlton and Adler, 4th ed., p. 256)*

182. **(C)** Factors influencing recorded detail in digital imaging are very much the same as those factors affecting recorded detail in analog imaging, that is, *motion, geometric factors* (focal spot size, OID, and SID), and *spatial resolution.*

The spatial resolution of direct digital systems is *fixed* and is related to the detector element *(DEL)* size of the thin film transistor *(TFT)*. The smaller the TFT DEL size, the better the spatial resolution. DEL size of 100 microns provides a spatial resolution of about 5 lp/mm (available only in some digital mammography systems). DEL size of 200 microns provides a spatial resolution of about 2.5 lp/mm (general radiography)—lower than that achieved with 400 speed intensifying screen system. A 100 speed intensifying screen system offers a spatial resolution of about 10 lp/mm—significantly greater than, and currently unachievable in, digital imaging. Spatial resolution in digital imaging is fixed, but it is very important that radiographers are alert to the opportunity they have to utilize and control the remaining recorded detail factors (motion and geometric factors). *(Seeram, pp. 97–98)*

183. **(D)** Because *pneumoperitoneum* is an abnormal accumulation of *air or gas* in the peritoneal cavity, it would require a *decrease* in exposure factors. *Obstructed bowel* usually involves distended, air- or gas-filled bowel loops, again requiring a *decrease* in exposure factors. With *ascites*, there is an abnormal accumulation of *fluid* in the abdominal cavity, necessitating an *increase* in exposure factors. *Renal colic* is the pain associated with the passage of renal calculi; no change from the normal exposure factors is usually required. *(Carlton and Adler, 4th ed., p. 248)*

184. **(D)** Factors influencing recorded detail in digital imaging are very much the same as those factors affecting recorded detail in analog imaging, that is, *motion, geometric factors* (focal spot size, OID, and SID), and *spatial resolution.* In analog imaging, spatial resolution is related to the speed of the imaging system (intensifying screen speed) and is significantly better than digital imaging resolution. The spatial resolution of direct digital systems, however, is fixed and is related to the detector element *(DEL)* size of the thin film transistor *(TFT)*. The smaller the TFT DEL size, the better the spatial resolution. DEL size of 100 microns provides a spatial resolution of about 5 lp/mm (available

only in some digital mammography systems). DEL size of 200 microns provides a spatial resolution of about 2.5 lp/mm (general radiography)—lower than that achieved with 400 speed intensifying screen system. A 100 speed intensifying screen system offers a spatial resolution of about 10 lp/mm—significantly greater than, and currently unachievable in, digital imaging. Spatial resolution in digital imaging is fixed, but it is very important that radiographers are alert to the opportunity they have to utilize and control the remaining recorded detail factors (motion and geometric factors). *(Seeram, pp. 97–98)*

185. **(D)** The PSP plate within the CR image plate has several layers. Its uppermost layer is a *protective* coat for the phosphor layer below. This layer affords durability and must be translucent to allow passage of photostimulable luminescent light. The *phosphor layer* is the "active" layer that responds to the x-ray photons that reach it. Under the phosphor layer is the *electroconductive layer* that serves to facilitate transportation through the scanner/reader and prevent image artifacts resulting from static electricity. Below the electroconductive layer is the plate *support layer*. Below the support layer is a *light-shield layer* that serves to prevent light from erasing image plate data or from approaching through the rear protective layer. Behind the light-shield layer is the rear *protective* layer of the PSP plate. *(Seeram, p. 53; Fosbinder and Orth, p. 213)*

186. **(D)** A QA program includes regular overseeing of all components of the imaging system—equipment calibration, film and cassettes, processor, x-ray equipment, and so on. With regular maintenance, testing, and repairs, equipment should operate efficiently and consistently. In turn, radiographic quality will be consistent, and repeat exposures will be minimized, thereby reducing patient exposure. *(Carlton and Adler, 4th ed., pp. 480–481)*

187. **(C)** The PSP plate within the CR cassette/IP has several layers. Its uppermost layer is a *protective* coat for the phosphor layer below. This layer affords durability and must be translucent to allow passage of photostimula-

ble luminescent light. The *phosphor layer* is the "active" layer that responds to the x-ray photons that reach it. Under the phosphor layer is the *electroconductive layer* that serves to facilitate transportation through the scanner/reader and prevent image artifacts resulting from static electricity. Below the electroconductive layer is the plate *support* layer. Below the support layer is a *light-shield layer* that serves to prevent light from erasing image plate data or from approaching through the rear protective layer. Behind the light-shield layer is the rear *protective* layer of the PSP plate. *(Seeram, p. 53; Fosbinder and Orth, p. 213)*

188. **(A)** DXA imaging is used to evaluate BMD. It is the most widely used method of *bone densitometry*—it is *low-dose*, *precise*, and *uncomplicated* to use/perform. DXA uses *two photon energies*—one for soft tissue and one for bone. Since bone is denser and attenuates x-ray photons more readily, their *attenuation is calculated* to represent the degree of bone density. Soft tissue attenuation information is not used to measure bone density. Any images obtained in DXA/bone densitometry are strictly to evaluate the *accuracy of the region of interest* (ROI); they are not used for further diagnostic purposes—additional diagnostic examinations are done for any required further evaluation. Bone densitometry/DXA can be used to evaluate bone mineral content of the body or part of it, to diagnose osteoporosis, or to evaluate the effectiveness of treatments for osteoporosis. *(Frank, Long, and Smith, 11th ed., vol. 3, pp. 455–456)*

189. **(A)** If a structure of a given length is not positioned parallel to the recording medium (PSP or film), it will be projected smaller than its actual size (foreshortened). An example of this can be a lateral projection of the third digit. If the finger is positioned so as to be parallel to the IR, no distortion will occur. If, however, the finger is positioned so that its distal portion rests on the cassette while its proximal portion remains a distance from the IR, foreshortening will occur. *(Shephard, pp. 232–233)*

190. **(A)** If a radiograph lacks sufficient blackening, an increase in milliampere-seconds is

required. The milliampere-seconds value regulates the *number* of x-ray photons produced at the target. An increase or decrease in milliampere-seconds of *at least 30%* is necessary to produce a perceptible effect. Increasing the kilovoltage by 15% will have about the same effect as *doubling* the milliampere-seconds. *(Shephard, p. 173)*

191.   **(B)** The milliampere-seconds (mAs) formula is milliamperage × time = mAs. With two of the factors known, the third can be determined. To find the milliampere-seconds value that was used originally, substitute the known values:

$$300 \times 0.1 = 30$$

We have increased the kilovoltage to 86 kV, an increase of 15%, which has an effect similar to that of doubling the milliampere-seconds. Therefore, only 15 mAs is now required as a result of the kilovoltage increase:

$$mA \times s = mAs$$
$$400x = 15$$

Thus, $x = 0.0375$-s exposure = 37.5 ms. *(Selman, 9th ed., p. 214)*

192.   **(D)** *Static electricity* can be a problem in screen/film imaging, especially in cool, dry weather. *Sliding* the film in and out of the cassette/IR can be the cause of a static electrical buildup and subsequent discharge. Removing one's sweater in the darkroom on a dry winter day can cause static electrical sparking. The film exposed by a large static discharge *(tree static)* frequently exhibits black, branching artifacts such as those illustrated. *Poor screen–film contact* results in very blurry areas of the finished radiograph. A *foreign body* in the IR will be sharply imaged on the finished radiograph. An *inverted focused grid* will result in an area of exposure down the middle of the image and grid cutoff everywhere else. *(Shephard, p. 160)*

193.   **(D)** A CT imaging system has *three component parts*—a gantry, a computer, and an operating console. The gantry component includes an x-ray tube, a detector array, a high-voltage generator, a collimator assembly, and a patient couch with its motorized mechanism. While the CT x-ray tube is similar to direct-projection x-ray tubes, it has several special requirements. The CT x-ray tube must have a *very high short-exposure rating* and must be capable of *tolerating several million heat units* while still having a *small focal spot* for optimal resolution. To help tolerate the very high production of heat units, the anode must be capable of *high-speed rotation*. The x-ray tube produces a *pulsed x-ray beam (1–5 ms)* using up to about 1,000 mA. *(Bushong, 8th ed., pp. 429–430; Bontrager and Lampignano, 6th ed., p. 731)*

194.   **(C)** The figure illustrates that as distance from a light/x-ray source increases, the light/x-rays diverge and cover a larger area; the quantity of light/x-ray available per unit area becomes less and less as distance increases. The intensity (quantity) of light/x-ray decreases according to the *inverse-square law*; that is, the intensity at a particular distance from its source is inversely proportional to the square of the distance. *As the distance between the x-ray tube and image receptor increases, exposure rate (and, therefore, radiographic density/brightness) decreases according to the inverse-square law.*

Because the anode's focal track is beveled, x-ray photons can freely diverge toward the cathode end of the x-ray tube. However, the "heel" of the focal track prevents x-ray photons from diverging toward the anode end of the tube. This results in varying intensity with fewer photons at the anode end and more photons at the cathode end

X-ray tube targets are constructed according to the line-focus principle—the focal spot is angled to the vertical. As the actual focal spot is projected downward, it is foreshortened; thus, the effective focal spot is always smaller than the actual focal spot.

195.   **(B)** Artifacts can be a result of *exposure, handling, and storage*, or *processing*. Exposure artifacts include *motion, double exposure*, and *patient clothing/jewelry*—the effects of these are seen as a result of the exposure. Handling and storage artifacts include fogged PSP,

image fading, upside down IP, damaged PSP—all these occur as a result of improper use or storage. Processing artifacts occur while the PSP is in the scanner/reader and include skipped scan lines, laser jitter, etc. *(Bushong, 8th ed., p. 473)*

196. (B) If the exposure time is cut in half, one normally would double the milliamperage to maintain the same milliampere-seconds value and, consequently, the same radiographic density. However, increasing the kilovoltage by 15% has a similar effect. For example, if the original kilovoltage were 85 kV, 15% of this is 13, and therefore, the new kilovoltage would be 98 kV. The same percentage value would be used to cut the radiographic density in half (reduce kilovoltage by 15%). *(Shephard, pp. 178–181)*

197. (D) In the RAO position, the sternum must be visualized through the thorax and heart. Prominent pulmonary vascular markings can hinder good visualization. A method frequently used to overcome this problem is to use a milliampere-seconds value with a long exposure time. The patient is permitted to breathe normally during the (extended) exposure and by so doing blurs out the prominent vascularities. *(Frank, Long, and Smith, 11th ed., vol. 1, p. 470)*

198. (A) High-speed imaging systems are valuable for reducing patient exposure and patient motion. However, some detail will be sacrificed, and quantum mottle can cause further image impairment. In general, *doubling the film–screen speed doubles the radiographic density*, thereby requiring that the milliampere-seconds value be halved to maintain the original radiographic density. Changing from 200 to 400 screens requires halving the milliampere-seconds value to 9 mAs. The new exposure time, using 400 mA, is $400x = 9$. Thus, $x = 0.0225$-s exposure using 400 mA and 400-speed screens ($0.0225 = 22.5$ ms). *(Selman, 9th ed., p. 181)*

199. (B) The automatic film processor has a number of component systems. The *transport* system moves film from solution to solution

between rollers, changing the direction of the film around critical turns. The circulation system functions to agitate, mix, and filter solutions. The *temperature control* system functions to monitor and control solution temperature. The *replenishment* system serves to monitor the solution and replace it as needed. Guide shoes are found at crossover and turnaround assemblies and function to direct the film around corners as it changes direction. If a guide shoe becomes misaligned, it will scratch the emulsion and leave the characteristic *guide-shoe marks* running in the direction of film travel, as seen in the radiograph shown. *Pi lines* appear as plus-density lines running perpendicular to the direction of film travel; they are sometimes seen in new processors or after a complete maintenance/ overhaul. *Hesitation marks* are plus-density lines occurring as a result of pauses, or hesitations, in a faulty roller transport system. *(Bushong, 8th ed., p. 212; Shephard, pp. 154, 156)*

200. (B) Manufacturers of x-ray equipment must follow guidelines that state maximum x-ray output at specific distances, total quantities of filtration, positive beam limitation, and other guidelines. Radiographers must practice safe principles of operation; preventive maintenance and quality control (QC) checks must be performed at specific intervals to ensure continued safe equipment performance. Radiologic QC involves monitoring and regulating the variables associated with image production and patient care.

HVL testing provides beam quality information that is different from that obtained from kV testing. HVL is defined as the thickness of any absorber that will reduce x-ray beam intensity to one-half its original value. It is determined by measuring the beam intensity without an absorber and then recording the intensity as successive millimeters of aluminum are added to the radiation field. It is *influenced by the type of rectification, total filtration, and kV*. An x-ray tube HVL should remain almost constant. If HVL decreases, it is an indication of a decrease in the actual kV. If the HVL increases, it indicates the deposition of vaporized tungsten on the inner surface of the glass envelope (as a result of tube aging) or an increase in the actual kV. *(Fosbinder and Orth, p. 83)*

201. **(B)** *Attenuation* (decreased intensity through scattering or absorption) of the x-ray beam is a result of its *original energy and its interactions with different types and thicknesses of tissue.* The greater the original energy/quality (the higher the kilovoltage) of the incident beam, the less is the attenuation. The greater the effective *atomic number* of the tissues (tissue type and pathology determine absorbing properties), the greater is the beam attenuation. The greater the *volume of tissue* (subject density and thickness), the greater is the beam attenuation. *(Bushong, 8th ed., p. 185)*

202. **(B)** Manufacturers of x-ray equipment must follow guidelines that state maximum x-ray output at specific distances, total quantities of filtration, positive beam limitation, and other guidelines. Radiographers must practice safe principles of operation; preventive maintenance and quality control (QC) checks must be performed at specific intervals to ensure continued safe equipment performance. Radiologic QC involves monitoring and regulating the variables associated with image production and patient care.

HVL testing provides beam quality information that is different from that obtained from kV testing. HVL is defined as the thickness of any absorber that will reduce x-ray beam intensity to one-half its original value. It is determined by measuring the beam intensity without an absorber and then recording the intensity as successive millimeters of aluminum are added to the radiation field. It is influenced by the type of rectification, total filtration, and kV. An x-ray tube HVL should remain almost constant. If HVL decreases, it is an indication of a decrease in the actual kV. If the HVL *increases,* it indicates the *deposition of vaporized tungsten on the inner surface of the glass envelope* (as a result of tube aging) or *an increase in the actual kV.*

203. **(B)** A compensating filter is used to make up for widely differing tissue densities. For example, it is difficult to obtain a satisfactory image of the mediastinum and lungs simulta-

neously without the use of a compensating filter to "even out" the densities. With this device, the chest is radiographed using mediastinal factors, and a trough-shaped filter (thicker laterally) is used to absorb excess photons that would overexpose the lungs. The middle portion of the filter lets the photons pass to the mediastinum almost unimpeded. Filters that absorb the photons contributing to skin dose are inherent and added filters. Compensating filtration is unrelated to elimination of scattered radiation or fluoroscopy. *(Selman, 9th ed., p. 254)*

204. **(B)** X-ray film emulsion is sensitive and requires proper handling and storage. It should be stored in a cool (40–60°F), dry (40–60% humidity) place. Exposure to excessive temperatures or humidity can lead to film fog and loss of contrast. Static marks are a result of low humidity. *(Fauber, p. 182)*

205. **(C)** *Motion* is the greatest enemy of resolution. While everything else may be perfect, if motion is introduced, resolution is lost. *Focal spot blur* is related to focal spot size; smaller focal spots produce less blur and thus better recorded detail/resolution. Pixel depth is directly related to shades of gray—called *dynamic range*—and is measured in *bits.* The greater the number of bits, the more shades of gray. Dynamic range is not related to resolution.

206. **(A)** Diagnostic x-rays are produced within the x-ray tube when high-speed electrons are rapidly decelerated upon encountering the tungsten atoms of the anode/target. The *source of electrons* is the heated cathode filament; they are driven across to the anode focal spot when thousands of volts (kV) are applied. When the high-speed electrons are suddenly stopped at the focal spot, their kinetic energy is converted to x-ray photon energy. This happens in two ways:

Bremsstrahlung ("Brems") or "braking" *radiation*: A high-speed electron, passing near or through a tungsten atom, is attracted and "braked" (i.e., slowed down) by the positively charged nucleus and deflected from its course with a loss of energy. *This energy loss is given up in the form of an x-ray photon.* The electron might not give up all its kinetic energy in one interaction; it can go on to have several more interactions deeper in the anode, each time producing an x-ray photon having less and less energy. This is one reason the x-ray beam is *polyenergetic*, that is, has a spectrum of energies. *Brems radiation comprises 70–90% of the x-ray beam.*

Characteristic radiation: In this case, a high-speed electron encounters a tungsten atom within the anode and *ejects* a K shell electron, leaving a vacancy in that shell. An electron from the adjacent L shell moves to the K shell to fill its vacancy and in doing so *emits a K characteristic ray.* The energy of the characteristic ray is equal to the difference in energy between the K and L shell energy levels. *Characteristic radiation comprises 10–30% of the x-ray beam.*

Photoelectric effect and Compton scatter are interactions that occur between x-ray photons and matter. *(Fosbinder and Orth, p. 74)*

207. **(C)** Recorded detail is evaluated by how sharply tiny anatomic details are imaged on the radiograph. The area of blurriness that may be associated with small image details is termed *geometric blur.* The blurriness can be produced by using a large focal spot or by diffused fluorescent light from intensifying screens. The image proper (i.e., without blur) is termed the *umbra. Mottle* is a grainy appearance caused by fast imaging systems. *(Selman, 9th ed., pp. 206–207)*

208. **(B)** Rare earth phosphors have a greater *conversion efficiency* than do other phosphors. Lanthanum oxybromide is a blue-emitting rare earth phosphor, and gadolinium oxysulfide is a green-emitting rare earth phosphor. Cesium iodide is the phosphor used on the input screen of image intensifiers; it is not a rare earth phosphor. *(Shephard, p. 68)*

209. **(D)** The lateral skull radiograph shown illustrates the result of great care taken by the radiographer to secure patient comfort. A skull examination was requested for this patient of advanced years. The radiographer positioned the patient, taking care to position and collimate accurately, all the while trying to ensure

the patient's comfort by letting her keep her pillow. The foam stuffing of the pillow is nicely imaged. Although the artifacts somewhat resemble Paget disease or osteoporosis, note that they extend outside the anatomic part. Examples of processing artifacts include skipped scan lines, laser jitter, etc. *(Bushong, 8th ed., pp. 473, 474)*

210. **(A)** Because lead content decreases when grid ratio decreases, a smaller amount of scattered radiation is trapped before reaching the IR. More grays, therefore, are recorded, and a longer scale of contrast results. *Radiographic density* would *increase* with a decrease in grid ratio. Grid ratio is unrelated to distortion. *(Carlton and Adler, 4th ed., p. 432)*

211. **(B)** X-ray film emulsion becomes more sensitive to safelight fog *following exposure* to fluorescent light from intensifying screens. Care must be taken not to leave exposed film on the darkroom workbench for any length of time because its sensitivity to safelight fog is now greatly heightened. *(Shephard, p. 123)*

212. **(A)** Proper use of focal spot size is of paramount importance in magnification radiography. A magnified image that is diagnostic can be obtained only by using a *fractional focal spot* of *0.3 mm or smaller.* The amount of blur or geometric unsharpness produced by focal spots that are larger in size render the radiograph undiagnostic. *(Selman, 9th ed., p. 226)*

213. **(D)** As OID is increased, recorded detail is diminished as a result of magnification distortion. If the OID cannot be minimized, an increase in SID is required to reduce the effect of magnification distortion. However, the relationship between OID and SID is not an equal relationship. In fact, to compensate for every 1 in. of OID, an increase of 7 in. of SID is required. Therefore, an OID of 6 in. requires an SID increase of 42 in.. This is why a chest radiograph with a 6-in. air gap usually is performed at a 10-ft SID. *(Saia, 4th ed., p. 290)*

214. **(D)** *Grid ratio* is defined as the ratio between the height of the lead strips and the width of the distance between them (i.e., their height

divided by the distance between them). If the height of the lead strips is 4.0 mm and the lead strips are 0.25 mm apart, the grid ratio must be 16:1 (4.0 divided by 0.25). The thickness of the lead strip is unrelated to grid ratio. *(Selman, 9th ed., p. 236)*

215. **(A)** The line-focus principle is a geometric principle illustrating that the *actual focal spot is larger than the effective (projected) focal spot.* The actual focal spot (target) is larger, to accommodate heat over a larger area, and is angled so as to *project* a smaller focal spot, thus maintaining recorded detail by reducing blur. The relationship between the exposure given the IR and the resulting density is expressed in the reciprocity law; the relationship between the SID and resulting density is expressed by the inverse-square law. Grid ratio and lines per inch are unrelated to the line-focus principle. *(Selman, p. 138; Shephard, pp. 218–219).*

216. **(C)** Radiographic density is greatly affected by changes in the SID, as expressed by the inverse-square law of radiation. As distance from the radiation source increases, exposure rate decreases, and radiographic density decreases. Exposure rate is inversely proportional to the square of the SID. *Aluminum filtration, kilovoltage,* and *scattered radiation* all have a significant effect on density, but they are not the primary controlling factors. *(Selman, 9th ed., p. 214)*

217. **(D)** Shape distortion is caused by *misalignment of the x-ray tube, the part to be radiographed, and the IR/film.* An object can be falsely imaged (*foreshortened* or *elongated*) by incorrect placement of the tube, the body part, or the IR. Only one of the three need be misaligned for distortion to occur. *(Shephard, pp. 231–234)*

218. **(C)** The radiograph shown in the figure demonstrates adequate positioning, inspiration, and beam restriction. However, it has *too much background density* (too much milliampere-seconds), *excessively high contrast* (too low kilovoltage, too short a scale of contrast), and areas of *inadequate penetration.* This radiograph should be repeated at a lower milliampere-seconds and appropriately higher kilovoltage. *(Carlton and Adler, 4th ed., pp. 423–424)*

219. **(B)** Many IR have a thin lead-foil layer behind their rear section to absorb backscattered radiation that is energetic enough to exit the rear, strike the metal back, and bounce back to fog the image.

The lead foil absorbs the backscatter before it can fog the PSP. *(Shephard, pp. 41–42)*

220. **(B)** *Fluorescence* occurs when an intensifying screen absorbs x-ray photon energy, emits light, and then *ceases* to emit light as soon as the energizing source ceases. *Phosphorescence* occurs when an intensifying screen absorbs x-ray photon energy, emits light, and *continues* to emit light for a short time after the energizing source ceases. *Quantum mottle* is the freckle-like appearance on some radiographs made using a very fast imaging system. The brightness of a fluoroscopic image is amplified through *image intensification. (Bushong, 8th ed., p. 221)*

221. **(D)** Review the groups of factors. First, because the milliampere-seconds value has no effect on the scale of contrast produced, eliminate milliampere-seconds from consideration by drawing a line through the column. Then, check the two entries in each column that are likely to produce shorter-scale contrast. For example, in the kilovoltage column, because lower kilovoltage will produce shorter-scale contrast, place checkmarks next to the 70 and 80 kV. In the film–screen column, the faster screens (400) will produce higher (shorter-scale) contrast than the slower screens; place a checkmark next to each. Because higher-ratio grids permit less scattered radiation to reach the IR, the 10:1 and 12:1 grids will produce a shorter scale of contrast than the lower-ratio grids; check them. As the volume of irradiated tissue decreases, so does the amount of scattered radiation produced, and consequently, the shorter is the scale of radiographic contrast; therefore, check the 11 × 14 and 8 × 10 in. field sizes. An overview shows that the factors in groups (A) and (C) have two checkmarks, whereas the factors in group (D) have

four checkmarks, indicating that group (D) will produce the shortest-scale contrast. *(Shephard, pp. 306–308)*

222. **(C)** Quality Control refers to our equipment and its safe and accurate operation. Various components must be tested at specified intervals, and test results must be within specified parameters. Any deviation from those parameters must be corrected. Examples of equipment components that are tested annually are the focal spot size, linearity, reproducibility, filtration, kV, and exposure time. Congruence is a term used to describe the relationship between the collimator light field and the actual x-ray field—they must be congruent (i.e., match) to within 2% of the SID. Radiographic equipment collimators should be inspected and verified as accurate semiannually, that is, twice a year. Kilovoltage settings can most effectively be tested using an electronic kV meter; to meet required standards, the kV should be accurate to within +/− 4 kV. Reproducibility testing should specify that radiation output be consistent to within +/− 5%. *(Fosbinder and Orth, pp. 223–225; NCRP Report No. 99, p. 64)*

223. **(C)** The FOV and matrix size are independent of one another; that is, either can be changed, and the other will remain unaffected. However, *pixel size is affected by changes in either the FOV or matrix size*. For example, if the matrix size is increased, pixel size decreases. If FOV increases, pixel size increases. Pixel size is inversely related to resolution. As pixel size decreases, resolution increases. *(Fosbinder and Kelsey, p. 285)*.

224. **(B)** As the film emulsion is exposed to light or x-rays, latent image formation takes place. The exposed silver halide crystals are *reduced* to black metallic silver by the developer/reducing agents in the automatic processor's developer solution. The *preservative* helps to prevent oxidation of the developer solution. The *activator* provides the necessary alkalinity for the developer solution, and *hardener* is added to the developer in automatic processing to keep emulsion swelling to a minimum. *(Fauber, p. 164)*

225. **(A)** Grids are composed of alternate strips of lead and interspace material and are used to trap scattered radiation after it emerges from the patient and before it reaches the IR. Accurate centering of the x-ray tube is required. If the x-ray tube is off-center but within the recommended focusing distance, there usually will be an overall loss of density. Over- or under-exposure under the anode is usually the result of exceeding the focusing distance limits in addition to being off-center. *(Carlton and Adler, 4th ed., p. 257)*

226. **(D)** The chest is composed of tissues with widely differing densities (bone and air). In an effort to "even out" these tissue densities and better visualize pulmonary vascular markings, high kilovoltage generally is used. This produces more uniform penetration and results in a *longer scale of contrast* with visualization of the pulmonary vascular markings as well as bone (which is better penetrated) and air densities. The increased kilovoltage also affords the advantage of greater exposure latitude (an error of a few kilovolts will make little, if any, difference). The fact that the kilovoltage is increased means that the milliampere-seconds value is reduced accordingly, and thus *patient dose is reduced as well*. A grid usually is used whenever high kilovoltage is required. *(Carlton and Adler, 4th ed., pp. 423–424)*

227. **(B)** First, evaluate the change(s): The kilovoltage was increased by 15% (78 + 15% = 90). A 15% increase in kilovoltage will double the radiographic density; therefore, it is necessary to use *half* the original milliampere-seconds value to maintain the original density. The original milliampere-seconds value was 28 mAs (300 mA × 0.07 second [70 ms] 28 mAs), so we now need 14 mAs, using 500 mA. Because mA × s mAs:

$$500x = 14$$
$$x = 0.028 \text{ s (28 ms)}$$

(Fauber, pp. 55, 59–60)

228. **(D)** As the kilovoltage is decreased, x-ray-beam energy (i.e., penetration) is also decreased.

Consequently, a *shorter scale of contrast* is obtained, and at lower kilovoltage levels, there is less *exposure latitude* (less margin for error in exposure). As kilovoltage is reduced, the milliampere-seconds value must be increased accordingly to maintain adequate density. This increase in milliampere-seconds results in greater *patient dose.* *(Shephard, p. 204)*

229. **(C)** *Image A* was made using 80 kV at 75 mAs; *image B* was made using 100 kV at 18 mAs; all other exposure factors remained the same. As kilovoltage is increased, the percentage of scattered radiation relative to primary radiation increases—hence, the grayer appearance of image B. Use of optimal kilovoltage for each anatomic part is helpful in keeping scatter to a minimum. The production of scattered radiation also will be limited if the field size is as small as possible. A grid is the most effective way to remove scattered photons from those exiting the patient. Grids are designed to selectively absorb scattered radiation while absorbing as little of the primary radiation as possible. Images produced with higher-ratio grids will possess fewer grays than those made with lower-ratio grids. *(Shephard, pp. 204, 244)*

230. **(A)** Geometric unsharpness is affected by all three factors listed. As OID increases, so does magnification—therefore, OID is *directly* related to magnification. As SOD and SID *decrease*, magnification increases—therefore, SOD and SID are *inversely* related to magnification. *(Carlton and Adler, 4th ed., pp. 444–445)*

231. **(D)** The input phosphor of image intensifiers is usually made of cesium iodide. For each x-ray photon absorbed by cesium iodide, approximately 5,000 light photons are emitted. As the light photons strike a photoemissive *photocathode*, a number of electrons are released from the photocathode and focused toward the output side of the image tube by voltage applied to the negatively charged *electrostatic focusing lenses*. The electrons are then accelerated through the neck of the tube where they strike the small (0.5–1 in.) *output*

phosphor that is mounted on a flat glass support. The entire assembly is enclosed within a 2–4-mm thick vacuum glass envelope. Remember that the image on the output phosphor is *minified, brighter,* and *inverted* (electron focusing causes image inversion).

Input screen diameters of 5–12 in. are available. Although smaller diameter input screens improve resolution, they do not permit a large FOV, that is, viewing of large patient areas.

Dual- and triple-field image intensifiers are available that permit *magnified* viewing of fluoroscopic images. To achieve magnification, the *voltage* to the focusing lenses is increased and a *smaller* portion of the input phosphor is used, thereby resulting in a smaller FOV. Because minification gain is now decreased, the image is not as bright. The mA is automatically increased to compensate for the loss in brightness when the image intensifier is switched to magnification mode. Entrance skin exposure (ESE) can increase dramatically as the FOV decreases (i.e., as magnification increases).

As FOV decreases, *magnification* of the output screen image increases, there is *less noise* because increased mA provides a greater number of x-ray photons, and *contrast* and *spatial resolution* improve. The *focal point* in the magnification mode is *further away from* the output phosphor (as a result of increased voltage applied to the focusing lenses) and therefore the output image is magnified. *(Fosbinder and Orth, pp. 191–192)*

232. **(D)** *Collimators* restrict the size of the irradiated field, thereby limiting the volume of irradiated tissue, and hence less scattered radiation is produced. Once radiation has scattered and emerged from the body, it can be trapped by the grid's lead strips. *Grids* effectively remove much of the scattered radiation in the remnant beam before it reaches the IR. *Compression* can be applied to reduce the effect of excessive fatty tissue (e.g., in the abdomen); in effect, reducing the thickness of the part to be radiographed. *(Selman, 9th ed., pp. 234, 247, 289)*

233. **(A)** Kilovoltage is the qualitative regulating factor; it has a *direct* effect on photon energy.

That is, as kilovoltage is *increased*, photon energy *increases*. Photon energy is *inversely* related to wavelength. That is, as photon energy *increases*, wavelength *decreases*. Photon energy is unrelated to milliamperage. (*Shephard, pp. 173, 178*)

234. **(C)** Every box of film comes with the *expiration date* noted. Film used after its expiration date usually will suffer a *loss of speed and contrast* and will exhibit fog. Film should be ordered in quantities that will ensure that it is used before it becomes outdated, and it should be rotated in storage so that the oldest is used first. (*Fauber, p. 182*)

235. **(A)** The screen–film system and radiographic density are directly proportional; that is, if the system speed is doubled, the radiographic density is doubled. In this case, we started at 40 mAs with a 200-speed system. If the system speed is doubled to 400, we should decrease the milliampere-seconds to 20 mAs. If the speed is again doubled to 800, we use half the 20 mAs, or 10 mAs. Or milliampere-seconds conversion factors and the following formula may be used:

$$\frac{\text{Screen speed factor 1}}{\text{Screen speed factor 2}} = \frac{\text{mAs 1}}{\text{mAs 2}}$$

$$\frac{2}{0.5} = \frac{40}{x}$$

$$2x = 20$$

Thus, $x = 10$ mAs with a 800-speed screen–film system. (*Shephard, p. 184*)

236. **(B)** According to the *15% rule*, if the kilovoltage is increased by 15%, radiographic density will be doubled. Therefore, to compensate for this change and to maintain radiographic density, the milliampere-seconds value should be reduced to 4 mAs. (*Shephard, p. 178*)

237. **(C)** *Motion*, voluntary or involuntary, is most detrimental to good recorded detail. Even if all other factors are adjusted to maximize detail, if motion occurs during exposure, detail is lost. The most important ways to reduce the possibility of motion are using the shortest possible exposure time, careful patient instruction (for

suspended respiration), and adequate immobilization when necessary. Minimizing magnification through the use of *increased* SID and *decreased* OID functions to improve recorded detail. (*Carlton and Adler, 4th ed., p. 451*)

238. **(D)** Compression of the breast tissue during mammographic imaging improves the technical quality of the image for several reasons. Compression brings breast structures into *closer contact* with the IR, thus reducing geometric blur and improving detail. As the breast tissue is compressed and essentially becomes thinner, less *scattered radiation* is produced. Compression serves as excellent *immobilization* as well. (*Peart, p. 49*)

239. **(D)** Distortion is caused by *improper alignment of the tube, body part, and IR*. Anatomic structures within the body are rarely parallel to the IR in a simple recumbent position. In an attempt to overcome this distortion, we position the part to be parallel with the IR or angle the central ray to "open up" the part. Examples of this technique are obliquing the pelvis to place the ilium parallel to the IR or angling the central ray cephalad to "open up" the sigmoid colon. (*Shephard, pp. 228–234*)

240. **(C)** In electronic/digital imaging, changes in window width affect changes in contrast scale, while changes in window level affect changes in brightness (in analog terms, density). As window width increases, the scale of contrast increases (i.e., contrast decreases). As window level increases, brightness increases. It should be noted that, to describe an increase in brightness, our old analog terminology would say that density decreases. This can be easily illustrated as you postprocess/window your own digital photographs or scanned documents. As you slide the brightness scale to increase brightness, the photo/image gets darker, that is, increased density. (*Fosbinder and Orth, p. 208*)

241. **(D)** The abdomen radiograph shown in the figure demonstrates *motion* blur. This can be seen particularly in the upper abdomen and in the bowel gas patterns. Motion obliterates detail. Patients who are in pain often are unable to cooperate as fully as patients who are not in pain. Careful positioning and patient instruction are helpful, but it remains useful to use the shortest exposure time possible. The radiograph also demonstrates good long-scale contrast that enables visualization of many tissue densities. The dark horizontal line across the abdomen is a clothing artifact resulting from a taut elastic underwear waistband. *(Fauber, p. 87; Shephard, p. 197)*

242.   **(B)** Sir Godfrey Newbold Hounsfield created the first CT unit, describing the reconstruction of data taken from multiple projection angles. Alan MacLeod Cormack worked with the complex mathematical algorithms required for image reconstruction. Their first commercial CT head scanner was available in 1971. In 1979, Hounsfield and Cormack shared the Nobel Prize in Medicine for their historic work with this new imaging science.

To express the beam attenuation characteristics of various tissues, the *Hounsfield unit* (HU) is used. HUs can also be referred to as *CT numbers* or density values. Godfrey Hounsfield assigned a value of 0 to distilled water, a value of +1,000 to dense osseous tissue, and a value of −1,000 to air. There is a direct relationship between the HU and tissue attenuation coefficient. The greater the attenuation coefficient of the particular tissue, the higher the HU value. One HU represents a 0.1% difference between the particular tissue attenuation characteristics and that of distilled water. HU value accuracy can be affected by equipment calibration, volume averaging, and image artifacts. *(Fosbinder and Orth, pp. 262–263)*

243.   **(C)** Significant scattered radiation is generated within the part when imaging large or dense body parts and when using high kilovoltage. A radiographic grid is made of alternating lead strips and interspace material; it is placed between the patient and the IR to absorb energetic scatter emerging from the patient. Although a grid prevents much of the scattered radiation from reaching the radiograph, its use does necessitate a significant *increase* in patient exposure. *(Bushong, 8th ed., p. 248)*

244.   **(D)** To change nongrid to grid exposure or to adjust exposure when changing from one grid ratio to another, it is necessary to recall the factor for each grid ratio:

No grid = 1 × original mAs
5:1 grid = 2 × original mAs
6:1 grid = 3 × original mAs
8:1 grid = 4 × original mAs
12:1 (or 10:1) grid = 5 × original mAs
16:1 grid = 6 × original mAs

Therefore, to change from nongrid to a 12:1 grid, multiply the original milliampere-seconds value by a factor of 5. A new milliampere-seconds value of 15 is required. *(Shephard, pp. 247–248)*

245.   **(C)** Radiographic density is directly proportional to milliampere-seconds. If exposure time is *halved* from 40 ms (0.04 or $\frac{1}{25}$ s) to 0.02 ($\frac{1}{50}$) s, radiographic density will be cut in half. Changing to 150 mA also will halve the milliampere-seconds, effectively halving the radiographic density. If the kilovoltage is decreased by 15%, from 85 to 72 kV, radiographic density will be halved according to the *15% rule*. To cut the density in half, the milliampere-seconds value must be reduced to 6 mAs (rather than 10 mAs). *(Selman, 9th ed., pp. 213–214)*

246.   **(B)** *Resolution* describes how closely fine details may be associated and still be recognized as separate details before seeming to blend into each other and appear "as one." The degree of resolution transferred to the IR is a function of the resolving power of each of the system components and can be expressed in *line pairs per millimeter* (lp/mm), *line-spread function* (LSP), or *modulation transfer function* (MTF). Lp/mm can be measured using a resolution test pattern; a number of resolution test tools are available. LSP is measured using a 10-μm x-ray beam; MTF measures the amount of information lost between the object and the IR. The effective focal spot is the foreshortened size of the actual focal spot as it is projected down toward the IR, that is, as it would be seen looking up into the emerging x-ray beam. This is called the *line-focus principle*

and is not a unit used to express resolution. *(Carlton and Adler, 4th ed., p. 334)*

247. **(C)** About half the silver in a film emulsion remains to form the image. The other half is removed from the film during the fixing process. Therefore, fixer solution has a high silver content. Silver is a *toxic metal* and cannot simply be disposed of into the public sewer system. Since silver is also a precious metal, it becomes financially wise to recycle the silver removed from x-ray film. The three most commonly used silver recovery systems are the *electrolytic, metallic replacement,* and *chemical precipitation methods.* In *electrolytic* units, an electric current is passed through the fixer solution. Silver ions are attracted to and become plated onto the negative electrode of the unit. The plated silver is periodically scraped from the cathode and accurately measured so that the hospital can be reimbursed appropriately. The electrolytic method is a practical recovery system for moderate- and high-use processors. The *metallic replacement* (or *displacement*) *method* of silver recovery uses a steel mesh/steel wool type of cartridge that traps silver as fixer is run through it. This system is useful for low-volume processors and is often also used as a backup to the electrolytic unit. *Chemical precipitation* adds chemicals that release electrons into the fixer solution. This causes the metallic silver to precipitate out, fall to the bottom of the tank, and form a recoverable sludge. This method is used principally by commercial silver dealers. *(Carlton and Adler, 4th ed., pp. 298–299)*

248. **(A)** A 15-minute oblique image of an IVU is pictured. IVU requires the use of iodinated contrast medium. *Low kilovoltage* (about 70 kV) usually is employed to enhance the photoelectric effect and, in turn, better visualize the renal collecting system. *High kilovoltage* will produce excessive scattered radiation and obviate the effect of the contrast agent. A higher milliamperage with a shorter exposure time is preferred to decrease the possibility of motion. *(Bontrager and Lampignano, 6th ed., p. 574)*

249. **(C)** The iodine-based contrast material used in IVU gives optimal opacification at 60 to 70 kV. Use of higher kilovoltage will negate the effect of the contrast medium; a lower contrast will be produced, and poor visualization of the renal collecting system will result. GI and BE examinations employ high-kilovoltage exposure factors (about 120 kV) to penetrate *through* the barium. In chest radiography, high-kilovoltage technical factors are preferred for maximum visualization of pulmonary vascular markings made visible with long-scale contrast. *(Saia, 4th ed., p. 347)*

250. **(B)** The artifact shown in the figure has *sharply delineated edges*, indicating that it is located adjacent to the PSP within the IP. The *farther* the object is from the IR, the more *blurred* its edges will be as a result of magnification distortion. *(Saia, 4th ed., p. 378)*

Subspecialty List

65. Selection of technical factors
66. Image processing and quality assurance
67. Selection of technical factors
68. Image processing and quality assurance
69. Computed/digital imaging
70. Selection of technical factors
71. Selection of technical factors
72. Selection of technical factors
73. Selection of technical factors
74. Criteria for image evaluation
75. Selection of technical factors
76. Criteria for image evaluation
77. Criteria for image evaluation
78. Selection of technical factors
79. Image processing and quality assurance
80. Selection of technical factors
81. Selection of technical factors
82. Selection of technical factors
83. Criteria for image evaluation
84. Selection of technical factors
85. Selection of technical factors
86. Selection of technical factors
87. Image processing and quality assurance
88. Criteria for image evaluation
89. Criteria for image evaluation
90. Selection of technical factors
91. Image processing and quality assurance
92. Image processing and quality assurance
93. Criteria for image evaluation
94. Selection of technical factors
95. Criteria for image evaluation
96. Selection of technical factors
97. Criteria for image evaluation
98. Image processing and quality assurance
99. Criteria for image evaluation
100. Criteria for image evaluation
101. Selection of technical factors
102. Criteria for image evaluation
103. Selection of technical factors
104. Selection of technical factors
105. Image processing and quality assurance
106. Criteria for image evaluation
107. Criteria for image evaluation
108. Selection of technical factors
109. Selection of technical factors
110. Criteria for image evaluation
111. Selection of technical factors
112. Selection of technical factors
113. Selection of technical factors
114. Selection of technical factors
115. Selection of technical factors
116. Criteria for image evaluation
117. Computed/digital imaging
118. Selection of technical factors
119. Criteria for image evaluation
120. Computed/digital imaging
121. Image processing and quality assurance
122. Selection of technical factors
123. Selection of technical factors
124. Computed/digital imaging
125. Computed/digital imaging
126. Computed/digital imaging
127. Image processing and quality assurance
128. Criteria for image evaluation
129. Image processing and quality assurance
130. Selection of technical factors
131. Computed/digital imaging
132. Selection of technical factors
133. Image processing and quality assurance
134. Selection of technical factors
135. Criteria for image evaluation
136. Selection of technical factors
137. Criteria for image evaluation
138. Criteria for image evaluation
139. Selection of technical factors
140. Selection of technical factors
141. Selection of technical factors
142. Selection of technical factors
143. Selection of technical factors
144. Selection of technical factors
145. Criteria for image evaluation
146. Selection of technical factors
147. Criteria for image evaluation
148. Image processing and quality assurance
149. Selection of technical factors
150. Selection of technical factors
151. Image processing and quality assurance
152. Selection of technical factors
153. Selection of technical factors
154. Selection of technical factors
155. Selection of technical factors
156. Selection of technical factors
157. Image processing and quality assurance
158. Criteria for image evaluation
159. Selection of technical factors
160. Selection of technical factors
161. Selection of technical factors
162. Image processing and quality assurance
163. Selection of technical factors
164. Selection of technical factors
165. Image processing and quality assurance
166. Selection of technical factors

167. Selection of technical factors
168. Criteria for image evaluation
169. Selection of technical factors
170. Selection of technical factors
171. Selection of technical factors
172. Image processing and quality assurance
173. Selection of technical factors
174. Selection of technical factors
175. Selection of technical factors
176. Selection of technical factors
177. Selection of technical factors
178. Selection of technical factors
179. Selection of technical factors
180. Selection of technical factors
181. Selection of technical factors
182. Image processing and quality assurance
183. Selection of technical factors
184. Selection of technical factors
185. Image processing and quality assurance
186. Image processing and quality assurance
187. Image processing and quality assurance
188. Computed/digital imaging
189. Criteria for image evaluation
190. Selection of technical factors
191. Selection of technical factors
192. Criteria for image evaluation
193. Computed/digital imaging
194. Image processing and quality assurance
195. Image processing and quality assurance
196. Selection of technical factors
197. Selection of technical factors
198. Selection of technical factors
199. Image processing and quality assurance
200. Selection of technical factors
201. Selection of technical factors
202. Image processing and quality assurance
203. Selection of technical factors
204. Image processing and quality assurance
205. Selection of technical factors
206. Selection of technical factors
207. Selection of technical factors
208. Selection of technical factors
209. Criteria for image evaluation
210. Selection of technical factors
211. Image processing and quality assurance
212. Selection of technical factors
213. Selection of technical factors
214. Selection of technical factors
215. Selection of technical factors
216. Selection of technical factors
217. Selection of technical factors
218. Criteria for image evaluation
219. Image processing and quality assurance
220. Criteria for image evaluation
221. Selection of technical factors
222. Image processing and quality assurance
223. Computed/digital imaging
224. Image processing and quality assurance
225. Criteria for image evaluation
226. Selection of technical factors
227. Selection of technical factors
228. Selection of technical factors
229. Criteria for image evaluation
230. Selection of technical factors
231. Image processing and quality assurance
232. Selection of technical factors
233. Selection of technical factors
234. Image processing and quality assurance
235. Selection of technical factors
236. Selection of technical factors
237. Selection of technical factors
238. Selection of technical factors
239. Selection of technical factors
240. Selection of technical factors
241. Criteria for image evaluation
242. Selection of technical factors
243. Selection of technical factors
244. Selection of technical factors
245. Selection of technical factors
246. Selection of technical factors
247. Image processing and quality assurance
248. Selection of technical factors
249. Selection of technical factors
250. Criteria for image evaluation

CHAPTER 5

Equipment Operation and Quality Control
Questions

DIRECTIONS (Questions 1 through 120): Each of the numbered items or incomplete statements in this section is followed by answers or by completions of the statement. Select the *one* lettered answer or completion that is *best* in each case.

1. All the following are associated with the anode *except*

   (A) the line-focus principle
   (B) the heel effect
   (C) the focal track
   (D) thermionic emission

2. The type of x-ray tube designed to turn on and off rapidly, providing multiple short, precise exposures, is

   (A) high speed
   (B) grid-controlled
   (C) diode
   (D) electrode

3. Typical examples of digital imaging include

   1. MRI
   2. CT
   3. CR

   (A) 1 only
   (B) 1 and 2 only
   (C) 1 and 3 only
   (D) 1, 2, and 3

4. Component parts of a CT gantry include

   1. high-voltage generator
   2. multidetector array
   3. x-ray tube

   (A) 1 only
   (B) 1 and 2 only
   (C) 2 and 3 only
   (D) 1, 2, and 3

5. Which of the following circuit devices operate(s) on the principle of self-induction?

   1. Autotransformer
   2. Choke coil
   3. High-voltage transformer

   (A) 1 only
   (B) 1 and 2 only
   (C) 2 and 3 only
   (D) 1, 2, and 3

6. If exposure factors of 85 kV, 400 mA, and 12 ms yield an output exposure of 150 mR, what is the milliroentgens per milliampere-seconds (mR/mAs)?

   (A) 0.32
   (B) 3.1
   (C) 17.6
   (D) 31

7. If a high-voltage transformer has 100 primary turns and 50,000 secondary turns and is supplied by 220 V and 100 A, what are the secondary voltage and current?

(A) 200 A and 110 V
(B) 200 mA and 110 kV
(C) 20 A and 100 V
(D) 20 mA and 100 kV

8. Waveform C shown in Figure 5–1 represents

(A) half-wave rectification
(B) direct current
(C) full-wave rectification
(D) alternating current

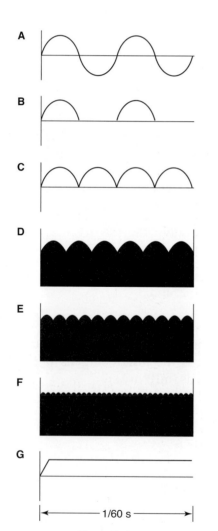

A

B

C

D

E

F

G

|← 1/60 s →|

Figure 5–1.

9. When using the smaller field in a dual-field image intensifier,

1. the image is magnified
2. the image is brighter
3. a larger anatomic area is viewed

(A) 1 only
(B) 1 and 3 only
(C) 2 and 3 only
(D) 1, 2, and 3

10. The minimum response time of an automatic exposure control (AEC)

(A) is the time required to energize the intensifying phosphors
(B) is its shortest possible exposure time
(C) functions to protect the patient from overexposure
(D) functions to protect the tube from excessive heat

11. The electron cloud within the x-ray tube is the product of a process called

(A) electrolysis
(B) thermionic emission
(C) rectification
(D) induction

12. Which of the following causes pitting, or many small surface melts, of the anode's focal track?

(A) Vaporized tungsten on the glass envelope
(B) Loss of anode rotation
(C) A large amount of heat to a cold anode
(D) Repeated, frequent overloading

13. Which of the following is (are) characteristics of the x-ray tube?

1. The target material should have a high atomic number and a high melting point.
2. The useful beam emerges from the port window.
3. The cathode assembly receives both low and high voltages.

(A) 1 only
(B) 2 only
(C) 1 and 2 only
(D) 1, 2, and 3

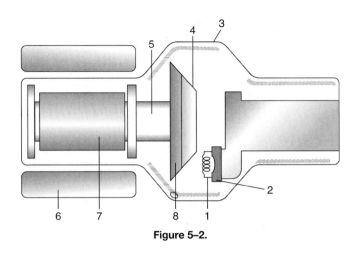

Figure 5–2.

14. A parallel-plate ionization chamber receives a particular charge as x-ray photons travel through it. This is the operating principle of which of the following devices?

(A) AEC
(B) Image intensifier
(C) Cine-film camera
(D) Spot-film camera

15. Which of the following will serve to increase the effective energy of the x-ray beam?

1. Increase in added filtration
2. Increase in kilovoltage
3. Increase in milliamperage

(A) 1 only
(B) 2 only
(C) 1 and 2 only
(D) 1, 2, and 3

16. Which of the following combinations would pose the *least* hazard to a particular anode?

(A) 1.2-mm focal spot, 92 kV, 1.5 mAs
(B) 0.6-mm focal spot, 80 kV, 3 mAs
(C) 1.2-mm focal spot, 70 kV, 6 mAs
(D) 0.6-mm focal spot, 60 kV, 12 mAs

17. The number 2 in Figure 5–2 indicates the

(A) molybdenum focusing cup
(B) actual focal spot
(C) actual focal spot
(D) anode stem

18. Congruence of the x-ray beam with the light field is tested using

(A) a pinhole camera
(B) a star pattern
(C) radiopaque objects
(D) a slit camera

19. Delivery of large exposures to a cold anode or the use of exposures exceeding tube limitation can result in

1. increased tube output
2. cracking of the anode
3. rotor-bearing damage

(A) 1 only
(B) 1 and 2 only
(C) 2 and 3 only
(D) 1, 2, and 3

20. If the primary coil of a high-voltage transformer is supplied by 220 V and has 400 turns and the secondary coil has 100,000 turns, what is the voltage induced in the secondary coil?

(A) 80 kV
(B) 55 kV
(C) 80 V
(D) 55 V

21. What is the relationship between kV and HVL?

(A) As kV increases, the HVL increases.
(B) As kV decreases, the HVL decreases.
(C) If the kV is doubled, the HVL doubles.
(D) If the kV is doubled, the HVL is squared.

22. As window level increases

(A) contrast scale increases
(B) contrast scale decreases
(C) brightness increases
(D) brightness decreases

23. Which of the following is/are components of the secondary, or high voltage, side of the x-ray circuit?

1. Rectification system
2. Autotransformer
3. kV meter

(A) 1 only
(B) 1 and 2 only
(C) 2 and 3 only
(D) 1, 2, and 3

24. Patient dose during fluoroscopy is affected by the

1. distance between the patient and the input phosphor
2. amount of magnification
3. tissue density

(A) 1 only
(B) 3 only
(C) 2 and 3 only
(D) 1, 2, and 3

25. A backup timer for the AEC serves to

1. protect the patient from overexposure
2. protect the x-ray tube from excessive heat
3. increase or decrease master density

(A) 1 only
(B) 1 and 2 only
(C) 2 and 3 only
(D) 1, 2, and 3

26. Which of the following devices converts electrical energy to mechanical energy?

(A) Motor
(B) Generator
(C) Stator
(D) Rotor

27. The essential function of a phototimer is to

(A) provide a brighter fluoroscopic image
(B) automatically restrict the field size
(C) terminate the x-ray exposure once the IR is correctly exposed
(D) automatically increase or decrease incoming line voltages

28. A slit camera is used to measure

1. focal-spot size
2. spatial resolution
3. intensifying-screen resolution

(A) 1 only
(B) 1 and 2 only
(C) 1 and 3 only
(D) 1, 2, and 3

29. In which of the following examinations would an IP front with very low absorption properties be especially important?

(A) Abdominal radiography
(B) Extremity radiography
(C) Angiography
(D) Mammography

30. Which of the following will improve the spatial resolution of image-intensified images?

    1. A very thin coating of cesium iodide on the input phosphor
    2. A smaller-diameter input screen
    3. Increased total brightness gain

    (A) 1 only
    (B) 1 and 2 only
    (C) 1 and 3 only
    (D) 1, 2, and 3

31. The advantages of collimators over aperture diaphragms and flare cones include

    1. the variety of field sizes available
    2. more efficient beam restriction
    3. better cleanup of scattered radiation

    (A) 1 only
    (B) 1 and 2 only
    (C) 1 and 3 only
    (D) 2 and 3 only

32. Which of the following occurs during Bremsstrahlung (Brems) radiation production?

    (A) An electron makes a transition from an outer to an inner electron shell.
    (B) An electron approaching a positive nuclear charge changes direction and loses energy.
    (C) A high-energy photon ejects an outer-shell electron.
    (D) A low-energy photon ejects an inner-shell electron.

33. Characteristics of the metallic element tungsten include

    1. ready dissipation of heat
    2. high melting point
    3. high atomic number

    (A) 1 only
    (B) 1 and 2 only
    (C) 2 and 3 only
    (D) 1, 2, and 3

34. Which of the illustrations in Figure 5–3 depicts the ion-chamber-type automatic exposure control (AEC)?

    (A) Image A
    (B) Image B
    (C) Both illustrate a phototimer-type AEC
    (D) Neither illustrates a phototimer-type AEC

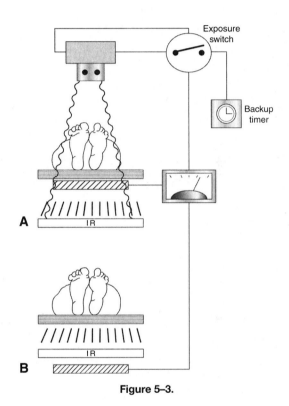

Figure 5–3.

35. The voltage ripple associated with a three-phase, six-pulse rectified generator is about

    (A) 100%
    (B) 32%
    (C) 13%
    (D) 3%

36. The device that receives the remnant beam, converts it into light, and then increases the brightness of that light is the

    (A) charge-coupled device (CCD)
    (B) spot-film camera
    (C) image intensifier
    (D) television monitor

37. A high-speed electron entering the tungsten target is attracted to the positive nucleus of a tungsten atom and, in the process, is decelerated. This results in

   (A) characteristic radiation
   (B) Bremsstrahlung radiation
   (C) Compton scatter
   (D) a photoelectric effect

38. All the following are components of the image intensifier *except*

   (A) the photocathode
   (B) the focusing lenses
   (C) the TV monitor
   (D) the accelerating anode

39. Components of digital imaging include

   1. computer manipulation of the image
   2. formation of an electronic image on the radiation detector
   3. formation of an x-ray image directly on the IR

   (A) 1 only
   (B) 1 and 2 only
   (C) 2 and 3 only
   (D) 1, 2, and 3

40. Which of the following is used in digital fluoroscopy, replacing the image intensifier's television camera tube?

   (A) Solid-state diode
   (B) Charge-coupled device
   (C) Photostimulable phosphor
   (D) Vidicon

41. A three-phase timer can be tested for accuracy using a synchronous spinning top. The resulting image looks like a

   (A) series of dots or dashes, each representative of a radiation pulse
   (B) solid arc, with the angle (in degrees) representative of the exposure time
   (C) series of gray tones, from white to black
   (D) multitude of small, mesh-like squares of uniform sharpness

42. The regular measurement and evaluation of radiographic equipment components and their performance is most accurately termed as

   (A) postprocessing
   (B) quality assurance
   (C) quality control
   (D) quality congruence

43. The procedure whose basic operation involves reciprocal motion of the x-ray tube and film is

   (A) cinefluorography
   (B) spot filming
   (C) tomography
   (D) image intensification

44. In fluoroscopy, the automatic brightness control is used to adjust the

   (A) kilovoltage (kV) and milliamperage (mA)
   (B) backup timer
   (C) milliamperage (mA) and time
   (D) kilovoltage (kV) and time

45. When the radiographer selects kilovoltage on the control panel, which device is adjusted?

   (A) Step-up transformer
   (B) Autotransformer
   (C) Filament circuit
   (D) Rectifier circuit

46. Star and wye configurations are related to

   (A) autotransformers
   (B) three-phase transformers
   (C) rectification systems
   (D) AECs

47. What is the device that directs the light emitted from the image intensifier to various viewing and imaging apparatus?

(A) Output phosphor
(B) Beam splitter
(C) Spot-film changer
(D) Automatic brightness control

48. As electrons impinge on the anode surface, less than 1% of their kinetic energy is changed to

(A) x-rays
(B) heat
(C) gamma rays
(D) recoil electrons

49. Which of the following contribute(s) to inherent filtration?

1. X-ray tube glass envelope
2. X-ray tube port window
3. Aluminum between the tube housing and the collimator

(A) 1 only
(B) 1 and 2 only
(C) 1 and 3 only
(D) 1, 2, and 3

50. A quality-control (QC) program includes checks on which of the following radiographic equipment conditions?

1. Reproducibility
2. Linearity
3. Positive beam limitation/automatic collimation

(A) 1 only
(B) 1 and 2 only
(C) 1 and 3 only
(D) 1, 2, and 3

51. What x-ray tube component does the number 6 in Figure 5–4 indicate?

(A) Anode stem
(B) Rotor
(C) Stator
(D) Focal track

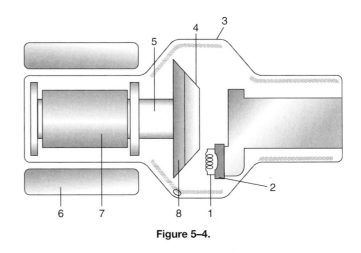

Figure 5–4.

52. Characteristics of x-ray photons include

1. a penetrating effect on all matter
2. an ionizing effect on air
3. travelling at the speed of sound

(A) 1 only
(B) 1 and 2 only
(C) 2 and 3 only
(D) 1, 2, and 3

53. All the following x-ray circuit devices are located between the incoming power supply and the primary coil of the high-voltage transformer *except*

(A) the timer
(B) the kilovoltage meter
(C) the milliamperage meter
(D) the autotransformer

54. Which of the following systems function(s) to compensate for changing patient/part thicknesses during fluoroscopic procedures?

(A) Automatic brightness control
(B) Minification gain
(C) Automatic resolution control
(D) Flux gain

55. Disadvantages of moving grids over stationary grids include which of the following?

1. They can prohibit the use of very short exposure times.
2. They increase patient radiation dose.
3. They can cause phantom images when anatomic parts parallel their motion.

(A) 1 only
(B) 1 and 2 only
(C) 2 and 3 only
(D) 1, 2, and 3

56. The functions of a picture archiving and communication system (PACS) include

1. storage of analog images
2. acquisition of digital images
3. storage of digital images

(A) 1 only
(B) 1 and 2 only
(C) 2 and 3 only
(D) 1, 2, and 3

57. How many half-value layers will it take to reduce an x-ray beam whose intensity is 78 R/min to an intensity of less than 10 R/min?

(A) 2
(B) 3
(C) 4
(D) 8

58. The kV settings on radiographic equipment must be tested annually and must be accurate to within

(A) +/−2 kV
(B) +/−4 kV
(C) +/−6 kV
(D) +/−8 kV

59. An incorrect relationship between the primary beam and the center of a focused grid results in

1. an increase in scattered radiation production
2. grid cutoff
3. insufficient radiographic density

(A) 1 only
(B) 1 and 2 only
(C) 2 and 3 only
(D) 1, 2, and 3

60. The x-ray tube in a CT imaging system is *most likely* to be associated with

(A) low-energy photons
(B) an unrestricted x-ray beam
(C) a pulsed x-ray beam
(D) a large focal spot

61. The radiograph shown in Figure 5–5 was made using a

(A) three-phase, 6-pulse rectified unit
(B) three-phase, 12-pulse rectified unit
(C) single-phase, full-wave rectified unit
(D) high-frequency rectified unit

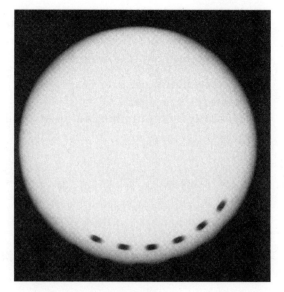

Figure 5–5.

62. Conditions that contribute to x-ray tube damage include

    1. lengthy anode rotation
    2. exposures to a cold anode
    3. low-milliampere-seconds/high-kilovoltage exposure factors

    (A) 1 only
    (B) 1 and 2 only
    (C) 1 and 3 only
    (D) 1, 2, and 3

63. The total brightness gain of an image intensifier is the product of

    1. flux gain
    2. minification gain
    3. focusing gain

    (A) 1 only
    (B) 2 only
    (C) 1 and 2 only
    (D) 1 and 3 only

64. Which of the following information is necessary to determine the maximum safe kilovoltage using the appropriate x-ray tube rating chart?

    1. Milliamperage and exposure time
    2. Focal-spot size
    3. Imaging-system speed

    (A) 1 only
    (B) 1 and 2 only
    (C) 2 and 3 only
    (D) 1, 2, and 3

65. A spinning-top device can be used to evaluate

    1. timer accuracy
    2. rectifier failure
    3. the effect of kilovoltage on contrast

    (A) 1 only
    (B) 2 only
    (C) 1 and 2 only
    (D) 1, 2, and 3

66. A device used to ensure reproducible radiographs, regardless of tissue-density variations, is the

    (A) automatic exposure control
    (B) penetrometer
    (C) grid device
    (D) induction motor

67. The device used to change alternating current to unidirectional current is

    (A) a capacitor
    (B) a solid-state diode
    (C) a transformer
    (D) a generator

68. If the distance from the focal spot to the center of the collimator's mirror is 6 in., what distance should the illuminator's light bulb be from the center of the mirror?

    (A) 3 in.
    (B) 6 in.
    (C) 9 in.
    (D) 12 in.

69. To maintain image clarity in an image-intensifier system, the path of electron flow from the photocathode to the output phosphor is controlled by

    (A) the accelerating anode
    (B) electrostatic lenses
    (C) the vacuum glass envelope
    (D) the input phosphor

70. The image-intensifier tube's input phosphor functions to convert

    (A) kinetic energy to light
    (B) x-rays to light
    (C) electrons to light
    (D) fluorescent light to electrons

71. Which of the following equipment is mandatory for performance of a myelogram?

(A) Cine camera
(B) 105-mm spot film
(C) Tilting x-ray table
(D) Tomography

72. Deposition of vaporized tungsten on the inner surface of the x-ray tube glass window

1. acts as additional filtration
2. results in increased tube output
3. results in anode pitting

(A) 1 only
(B) 1 and 2 only
(C) 2 and 3 only
(D) 1, 2, and 3

73. Design characteristics of x-ray tube targets that determine heat capacity include the

1. rotation of the anode
2. diameter of the anode
3. size of the focal spot

(A) 1 only
(B) 1 and 2 only
(C) 1 and 3 only
(D) 1, 2, and 3

74. Which of the following terms describes the amount of electric charge flowing per second?

(A) Voltage
(B) Current
(C) Resistance
(D) Capacitance

75. The brightness level of the fluoroscopic image can vary with

1. milliamperage
2. kilovoltage
3. patient thickness

(A) 1 only
(B) 1 and 2 only
(C) 1 and 3 only
(D) 1, 2, and 3

76. Which of the following does Figure 5–6 represent?

(A) Compton scatter
(B) Bremsstrahlung radiation
(C) Photoelectric effect
(D) Characteristic radiation

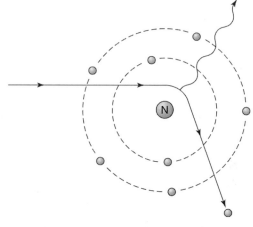

Figure 5–6.

77. Which of the following is the correct formula for determining heat units for a three-phase, 12-pulse x-ray machine?

(A) kV × mA × time
(B) mA × kV × mAs
(C) kV × mAs × 1.35
(D) mA × time × kV × 1.41

78. Component parts of a CT imaging system include a(n)

1. high-frequency generator
2. x-ray tube
3. operator console

(A) 1 only
(B) 1 and 2 only
(C) 1 and 3 only
(D) 1, 2, and 3

79. With what frequency must radiographic equipment be checked for linearity and reproducibility?

   (A) Annually
   (B) Biannually
   (C) Semiannually
   (D) Quarterly

80. Which part of an induction motor is located within the x-ray tube glass envelope?

   (A) Filament
   (B) Focusing cup
   (C) Stator
   (D) Rotor

81. A technique chart should be prepared for each AEC x-ray unit and should contain which of the following information for each type of examination?

   1. Photocell(s) used
   2. Optimum kilovoltage
   3. Backup time

   (A) 1 only
   (B) 1 and 2 only
   (C) 2 and 3 only
   (D) 1, 2, and 3

82. Which part of an induction motor is located outside the x-ray tube glass envelope?

   (A) Filament
   (B) Focusing cup
   (C) Stator
   (D) Rotor

83. Moving the image intensifier closer to the patient during fluoroscopy

   1. decreases the SID
   2. decreases patient dose
   3. improves image quality

   (A) 1 only
   (B) 1 and 2 only
   (C) 1 and 3 only
   (D) 1, 2, and 3

84. Figure 5–7 illustrates the

   (A) inverse-square law
   (B) line-focus principle
   (C) reciprocity law
   (D) anode heel effect

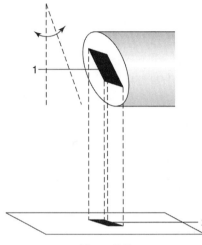

Figure 5–7.

85. If a radiograph exposed using an AEC is overexposed because an exposure shorter than the minimum response time was required, the radiographer generally should

   (A) decrease the milliamperage
   (B) use the minus density
   (C) use the plus density
   (D) decrease the kilovoltage

86. Exposures less than the minimum response time of an AEC may be required when

   1. using high milliamperage
   2. using fast film–screen combinations
   3. examining large patients or body parts

   (A) 1 only
   (B) 1 and 2 only
   (C) 2 and 3 only
   (D) 1, 2, and 3

87. Which of the following is/are associated with magnification fluoroscopy?

    1. Higher patient dose than nonmagnification fluoroscopy
    2. Higher voltage to the focusing lenses
    3. Image intensifier focal point closer to the input phosphor

    (A) 1 only
    (B) 1 and 2 only
    (C) 2 and 3 only
    (D) 1, 2, and 3

88. Advantages of battery-powered mobile x-ray units include their

    1. ability to store a large quantity of energy
    2. ability to store energy for extended periods of time
    3. lightness and ease of maneuverability

    (A) 1 only
    (B) 1 and 2 only
    (C) 2 and 3 only
    (D) 1, 2, and 3

89. Which of the following modes of a trifield image intensifier will result in the highest patient dose?

    (A) Its 25-in. mode
    (B) Its 17-in. mode
    (C) Its 12-in. mode
    (D) Diameter does not affect patient dose

90. Off-focus, or extrafocal, radiation is minimized by

    (A) avoiding the use of very high kilovoltages
    (B) restricting the x-ray beam as close to its source as possible
    (C) using compression devices to reduce tissue thickness
    (D) avoiding extreme collimation

91. Circuit devices that permit electrons to flow in only one direction are

    (A) solid-state diodes
    (B) resistors
    (C) transformers
    (D) autotransformers

92. An AEC device can operate on which of the following principles?

    1. A photomultiplier tube charged by a fluorescent screen
    2. A parallel-plate ionization chamber charged by x-ray photons
    3. Motion of magnetic fields inducing current in a conductor

    (A) 1 only
    (B) 2 only
    (C) 1 and 2 only
    (D) 1, 2, and 3

93. Which of the following functions to increase the milliamperage?

    (A) Increase in charge of anode
    (B) Increase in heat of the filament
    (C) Increase in kilovoltage
    (D) Increase in focal spot size

94. If 92 kV and 15 mAs were used for a particular abdominal exposure with single-phase equipment, what milliampere-seconds value would be required to produce a similar radiograph with three-phase, 12-pulse equipment?

    (A) 36
    (B) 24
    (C) 10
    (D) 7.5

95. Fractional-focus tubes, with a 0.3-mm focal spot or smaller, have special application in

    (A) magnification radiography
    (B) fluoroscopy
    (C) tomography
    (D) image intensification

96. In the radiographic rating charts shown in Figure 5–8, what is the maximum safe kilovoltage that may be used with the 1.0-mm focal-spot, single-phase x-ray tube using 400 mA and a 0.02-s exposure?

    (A) 70 kV
    (B) 75 kV
    (C) 80 kV
    (D) 85 kV

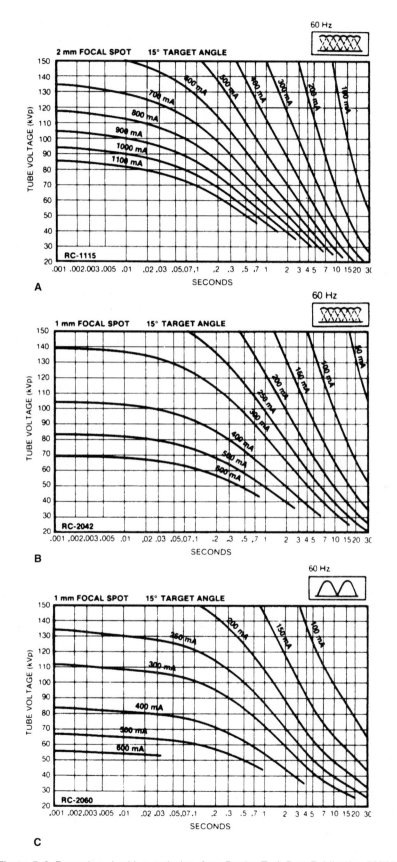

Figure 5–8. Reproduced, with permission, from Dunlee Tech Data Publication 50014.

97. In Figure 5–8, which of the illustrated x-ray tubes permit(s) an exposure of 400 mA, 0.1 s, and 80 kV?

    1. Tube A
    2. Tube B
    3. Tube C

    (A) 1 only
    (B) 1 and 2 only
    (C) 2 and 3 only
    (D) 1, 2, and 3

98. In Figure 5–8, what is the maximum safe milliamperage that may be used with a 0.10-s exposure and 120 kV, using the 3-phase, 1.0-mm focal-spot x-ray tube?

    (A) 300 mA
    (B) 400 mA
    (C) 500 mA
    (D) 600 mA

99. Referring to the anode cooling chart in Figure 5–9, if the anode is saturated with 300,000 heat units (HU), how long will the anode need to cool before another 160,000 HU can be safely applied?

    (A) 3 minutes
    (B) 4 minutes
    (C) 5 minutes
    (D) 7 minutes

100. Which of the following devices is used to control voltage by varying resistance?

    (A) Autotransformer
    (B) High-voltage transformer
    (C) Rheostat
    (D) Fuse

101. Anode angle will have an effect on the

    1. severity of the heel effect
    2. focal-spot size
    3. heat-load capacity

    (A) 1 only
    (B) 2 only
    (C) 1 and 2 only
    (D) 1, 2, and 3

102. Light-sensitive AEC devices are known as

    (A) phototimers
    (B) ionization chambers
    (C) sensors
    (D) backup timers

103. Which of the following devices is (are) component(s) of a typical fluoroscopic video display system?

    1. Videotape recorder
    2. TV camera
    3. TV monitor

    (A) 1 only
    (B) 1 and 3 only
    (C) 2 and 3 only
    (D) 1, 2, and 3

104. Which of the following is most closely related to Figure 5–10?

    (A) low kV
    (B) high kV
    (C) low mA
    (D) high mA

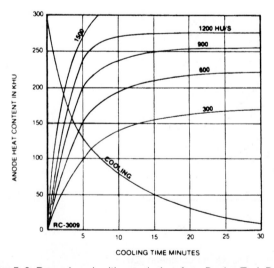

Figure 5–9. Reproduced, with permission, from Dunlee Tech Data Publication 50014.

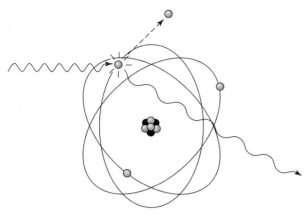

Figure 5–10.

105. Which of the following formulas would the radiographer use to determine the total number of heat units produced with a given exposure using three-phase, six-pulse equipment?

(A) mA × time × kV

(B) mA × time × kV × 3.0

(C) mA × time × kV × 1.35

(D) mA × time × kV × 1.41

106. With three-phase equipment, the voltage across the x-ray tube

1. drops to zero every 180 degrees
2. is 87% to 96% of the maximum value
3. is at nearly constant potential

(A) 1 only

(B) 2 only

(C) 1 and 2 only

(D) 2 and 3 only

107. Radiographs from a particular single-phase, full-wave-rectified x-ray unit were overexposed, using known correct exposures. A spinning-top test was performed at 200 mA, 0.05 s, and 70 kV, and 8 dots were visualized on the finished film. Which of the following is indicated?

(A) The 0.05-s time station is inaccurate.

(B) The 200-mA station is inaccurate.

(C) A rectifier is not functioning.

(D) The processor needs servicing.

108. Which of the following combinations will offer the greatest heat-loading capability?

(A) 17-degree target angle, 1.2-mm actual focal spot

(B) 10-degree target angle, 1.2-mm actual focal spot

(C) 17-degree target angle, 0.6-mm actual focal spot

(D) 10-degree target angle, 0.6-mm actual focal spot

109. Which of the following would be appropriate IP front material(s)?

1. Tungsten
2. Magnesium
3. Bakelite

(A) 1 only

(B) 1 and 2 only

(C) 2 and 3 only

(D) 1, 2, and 3

110. How often are radiographic equipment kV settings required to be evaluated?

(A) Annually

(B) Biannually

(C) Semiannually

(D) Quarterly

111. What x-ray tube component does the number 8 in Figure 5–11 indicate?

(A) Anode stem

(B) Rotor

(C) Stator

(D) Focal track

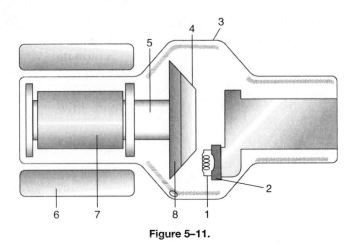

Figure 5–11.

112. The filtering effect of the x-ray tube's glass envelope and its oil coolant are referred to collectively as

   (A) inherent filtration
   (B) added filtration
   (C) compensating filtration
   (D) port filtration

113. Accurate operation of the AEC device depends on

   1. the thickness and density of the object
   2. positioning of the object with respect to the photocell
   3. beam restriction

   (A) 1 only
   (B) 1 and 2 only
   (C) 2 and 3 only
   (D) 1, 2, and 3

114. The image intensifier's input phosphor generally is composed of

   (A) cesium iodide
   (B) zinc cadmium sulfide
   (C) gadolinium oxysulfide
   (D) calcium tungstate

115. The total number of x-ray photons produced at the target is contingent on the

   1. tube current
   2. target material
   3. square of the kilovoltage

   (A) 1 only
   (B) 1 and 2 only
   (C) 2 and 3 only
   (D) 1, 2, and 3

116. A photostimulable phosphor plate is used with

   (A) CR
   (B) radiographic intensifying screens
   (C) fluoroscopic intensifying screens
   (D) image-intensified fluoroscopy

117. X-ray tubes used in CT imaging systems must be capable of

   1. high short-exposure rating
   2. tolerating millions of heat units
   3. high-speed anode rotation

   (A) 1 only
   (B) 1 and 2 only
   (C) 1 and 3 only
   (D) 1, 2, and 3

118. The device used to test the accuracy of the x-ray timer is the

   (A) densitometer
   (B) sensitometer
   (C) penetrometer
   (D) spinning top

119. QA was being performed on a three-phase, full-wave-rectified x-ray unit. A synchronous spinning-top test was performed using 300 mA, 60 ms, and 70 kV, and a 22-degree arc is observed on the test film. Which of the following statements regarding these results is *most* correct?

(A) The timer is inaccurate.

(B) The milliamperage station is inaccurate.

(C) One rectifier is malfunctioning.

(D) The test results are satisfactory.

120. Which of the following statements regarding dual x-ray absorptiometry is (are) true?

1. It is a low-dose procedure.
2. Two x-ray photon energies are used.
3. Photon attenuation by bone is calculated.

(A) 1 only

(B) 1 and 2 only

(C) 1 and 3 only

(D) 1, 2, and 3

Answers and Explanations

1. **(D)** The rotating *anode* has a target (or focal spot) on its beveled edge that forms the target angle. As the anode rotates, it constantly turns a new face to the incoming electrons; this is the *focal track.* The portion of the focal track that is bombarded by electrons is the actual focal spot, and because of the target's angle, the effective or projected focal spot is always smaller (line-focus principle). The *anode heel effect* refers to decreased beam intensity at the anode end of the x-ray beam. The electrons impinging on the target have "boiled off" the cathode filament as a result of thermionic emission. *(Selman, 9th ed., pp. 138–139)*

2. **(B)** X-ray tubes are diode tubes; that is, they have two electrodes—a positive electrode called the *anode* and a negative electrode called the *cathode.* The cathode filament is heated to incandescence and releases electrons—a process called *thermionic emission.* During the exposure, these electrons are driven by thousands of volts toward the anode, where they are suddenly decelerated. That deceleration is what produces x-rays. Some x-ray tubes, such as those used in fluoroscopy, digital radiography, and DSA, are required to make short, precise—sometimes multiple—exposures. This need is met by using a grid-controlled tube. A grid-controlled tube uses the molybdenum focusing cup as the switch, permitting very precise control of the tube current (flow of electrons between cathode and anode). *(Bushong, 9th ed., p. 123)*

3. **(D)** CT (Computed Tomography), MRI (Magnetic Resonance Imaging), and CR (Computed Radiography) are three common examples of *digital imaging.* Special equipment is also available for direct digital radiography (DR)—images produced by either a fan-shaped x-ray beam received by linearly arrayed radiation detectors or a traditional fan-shaped x-ray beam received by a light-stimulated phosphor plate. Digital images can also be obtained in digital subtraction angiography (DSA), nuclear medicine, and diagnostic sonography. *Analog* images are conventional images; they can be converted to digital images with a device called a *digitizer.* *(Shephard, p. 367)*

4. **(D)** A CT imaging system has three component parts—a gantry, a computer, and an operating console. The gantry component includes an x-ray tube, a detector array, a high-voltage generator, a collimator assembly, and a patient couch with its motorized mechanism. Although the CT x-ray tube is similar to direct-projection x-ray tubes, it has several special requirements. The CT x-ray tube must have a very high short-exposure rating and must be capable of tolerating several million heat units while still having a small focal spot for optimal resolution. To help tolerate the very high production of heat units, the anode must be capable of high-speed rotation. The x-ray tube produces a pulsed x-ray beam (1–5 ms) using up to about 1,000 mA. The scintillation detector

array is made of thousands of solid-state photodiodes. These scintillation crystal photodiode assemblies (cadmium tungstate or rare earth oxide ceramic crystals) convert the transmitted x-ray energy into light. The light then is converted into electrical energy and finally into an electronic/digital signal. If the scintillation crystals are packed tightly together so that there is virtually no distance between them, efficiency of x-ray absorption is increased, and patient dose is decreased. Detection efficiency is extremely high—approximately 90%. The high-voltage generator provides high-frequency power to the CT x-ray tube, enabling the high-speed anode rotation and the production of high-energy pulsed x-ray photons. Similar to the high-frequency x-ray tubes used in projection radiography, conventional 60-Hz full-wave-rectified power is converted to a higher frequency of 500 to 25,000 Hz. The high-frequency generator is small in size, in addition to producing an almost constant potential waveform. The CT high-frequency generator is often mounted in the gantry's rotating wheel. The collimator assembly has two parts: The prepatient, or predetector, collimator is at the x-ray tube and consists of multiple beam restrictions so that the x-ray beam diverges little. This reduces patient dose and reduces the production of scattered radiation, thereby improving the CT image. The postpatient collimator, or predetector collimator, confines the exit photons before they reach the detector array and determines slice thickness. The patient table, or couch, provides positioning support for the patient. Its motorized movement should be smooth and accurate. Inaccurate indexing can result in missed anatomy and/or double-exposed anatomy. (*Bushong, 8th ed., pp. 429–430; Bontrager and Lampignano, 6th ed., p. 731*)

5. **(B)** The principle of self-induction is an example of the second law of electromagnetics (Lenz's law), which states that an induced current within a conductive coil will oppose the direction of the current that induced it. It is important to note that self-induction is a characteristic of AC only. The fact that AC is constantly changing direction accounts for the opposing current set up in the coil. Two x-ray circuit devices operate on the principle of self-induction. The autotransformer operates on the principle of self-induction and enables the radiographer to vary the kilovoltage. The choke coil also operates on the principle of self-induction; it is a type of variable resistor that may be used to regulate filament current. The high-voltage transformer operates on the principle of mutual induction. (*Selman, 9th ed., p. 89*)

6. **(D)** Determining milliroentgens per milliampere-seconds output is often done to determine linearity among x-ray machines. However, all the equipment being compared must be of the same type (e.g., all single-phase or all three-phase, six-pulse). If there is linearity among these machines, then identical technique charts can be used. In the example given, 400 mA and 12 ms were used, equaling 4.8 mAs. If the output for 4.8 mAs was 150 mR, then 1 mAs is equal to 31.25 mR (150 mR ÷ 4.8 mAs = 31.25 mR/mAs). (*Bushong, 8th ed., pp. 248–249*)

7. **(B)** The high-voltage, or step-up, transformer functions to increase voltage to the necessary kilovoltage. It decreases the amperage to milliamperage. The amount of increase or decrease depends on the transformer ratio—the ratio of the number of turns in the primary coil to the number of turns in the secondary coil. The transformer law is as follows: To determine secondary V,

$$\frac{V_s}{V_p} = \frac{N_s}{N_p}$$

To determine secondary I,

$$\frac{N_s}{N_p} = \frac{I_p}{I_s}$$

Substituting known factors:

$$\frac{x}{220} = \frac{50,000}{100}$$

$$100x = 11,000,000$$

$$x = 110,000 \text{ V (110 kV)}$$

$$\frac{50,000}{100} = \frac{100}{x}$$

$$50,000x = 10,000$$

$$x = 0.2 \text{ A (200 mA)}$$

(Selman, 9th ed., pp. 84–85)

8. **(C)** Seven waveforms are illustrated. Waveform *A* represents alternating current. Waveform *B* illustrates half-wave rectification; each useful pulse (of x-ray) is followed by a pause of equal length. Figure C illustrates full-wave rectification. Note the 100% voltage ripple as each pulse starts at 0 potential, makes its way to 100%, and returns to 0 potential. Waveform *D* represents three-phase, six-pulse current exhibiting a 13% voltage drop between peak potentials. Waveform *E* represents three-phase, 12-pulse current having only about a 4% voltage drop between peak potentials. A big advantage of three-phase current is the very small drop in voltage between pulses. Waveform *F* illustrates high-frequency current, which is most efficient and produces less than 1% voltage ripple. Here, 60 Hz full-wave-rectified current is converted to higher frequency (500–25,000 Hz). Mobile x-ray units first used this technology, because one of its greatest advantages is its small size. High-frequency generators are also used in mammography units and helical CT. More and more traditional x-ray equipment is using high-frequency technology because of its compact size, lower cost, and greater efficiency. *(Kelsey and Fosbinder, pp. 74–75, 83–85; Bushong, 9th ed., p. 114)*

9. **(A)** When a dual-field image intensifier is switched to the smaller field, the electrostatic focusing lenses are given a greater charge to focus the electron image more tightly. The focal point, then, moves further from the output phosphor (the diameter of the electron image is, therefore, smaller as it reaches the output phosphor), and the brightness gain is somewhat diminished. Hence, the patient area viewed is somewhat *smaller* and is *magnified*. However, the minification gain has been reduced, and the image is somewhat *less bright*. *(Bushong, 8th ed., p. 363)*

10. **(B)** The *minimum response time*, or *minimum reaction time*, is the length of the shortest exposure possible with a particular AEC. If less than the minimum response time is required for a particular exposure, the radiograph will exhibit excessive density. The problem may become apparent when using fast film–screen combinations or high milliamperage or when imaging small or easily penetrated body parts. The backup timer functions to protect the patient from overexposure and the x-ray tube from overload. *(Carlton and Adler, 4th ed., pp. 102–103)*

11. **(B)** The thoriated tungsten filament of the cathode is heated by its own filament circuit. The x-ray tube filament is made of thoriated tungsten and is part of the cathode assembly. Its circuit provides current and voltage to heat it to incandescence, at which time it undergoes *thermionic emission*—the liberation of valence electrons from the filament atoms. *Electrolysis* describes the chemical ionization effects of an electric current. *Rectification* is the process of changing alternating current to unidirectional current. *(Bushong, 8th ed., p. 118)*

12. **(D)** As the filament ages, vaporized tungsten may be deposited on the port window and act as an additional filter. Tungsten may also vaporize as a result of anode abuse. Exposures in excess of safe values deliver sufficient heat to cause surface melts, or pits, on the focal track. This results in roughening of the anode surface and decreased tube output. Delivery of a large amount of heat to a cold anode can cause cracking if the anode does not have sufficient time to disperse the heat. Loss of anode rotation would cause one large melt on the focal track because the electrons would bombard only one small area. If the anode is not heard to be rotating, the radiographer should not make an exposure. *(Selman, 9th ed., pp. 137–138)*

13. **(D)** Anode target material with a *high atomic number* produces higher-energy x-rays more efficiently. Because a great deal of heat is produced at the target, the material should have a *high melting point* so as to avoid damage to the target surface. Most of the x-rays generated at

the focal spot are directed downward and pass through the x-ray tube's *port window*. The cathode filament receives *low-voltage* current to heat it to the point of thermionic emission. Then, *high voltage* is applied to drive the electrons across to the focal track. *(Selman, 9th ed., p. 111)*

14. **(A)** A parallel-plate ionization chamber is a type of AEC. A radiolucent chamber is beneath the patient (between the patient and the film). As photons emerge from the patient, they enter the chamber and ionize the air within it. Once a predetermined charge has been reached, the exposure is terminated automatically. *(Carlton and Adler, 4th ed., p. 102)*

15. **(C)** As *filtration* is added to the x-ray beam, the lower-energy photons are removed, and the overall energy or wavelength of the beam is greater. As *kilovoltage* is increased, more high-energy photons are produced, and again, the overall, or average, energy of the beam is greater. An increase in *milliamperage* serves to increase the number of photons produced at the target but is unrelated to their energy. *(Selman, 9th ed., p. 171)*

16. **(A)** Radiographic rating charts enable the operator to determine the maximum safe milliamperage, exposure time, and kilovoltage for a particular exposure using a particular x-ray tube. An exposure that can be made safely with the large focal spot may not be safe for use with the small focal spot of the same x-ray tube. The total number of heat units that an exposure generates also influences the amount of stress (in the form of heat) imparted to the anode. The product of milliampere-seconds and kilovoltage determines heat units. Group (A) produces 138 HU, group (B) produces 240 HU, group (C) produces 420 HU, and group (D) produces 720 HU. The *least hazardous* group of technical factors is, therefore, group (A). Group (A) is also delivering its heat to the *large focal spot*, thereby decreasing the heat load to the anode. *(Selman, 9th ed., pp. 144–145)*

17. **(A)** The figure illustrates the component parts of a rotating-anode x-ray tube enclosed within a glass envelope (number 3) to preserve the *vacuum* necessary for x-ray production. Number 4 is the *rotating anode* with its beveled focal track at the periphery (number 8) and its *stem* (at number 5). Numbers 6 and 7 are the *stator* and *rotor*, respectively—the two components of an induction motor—whose function it is to rotate the anode. Number 1 is the filament of the cathode assembly, which is made of thoriated tungsten and functions to liberate electrons (thermionic emission) when heated to white hot (incandescence). Number 2 is the molybdenum focusing cup, which functions to direct the liberated filament electrons to the focal spot. *(Shephard, pp. 5–6; Bushong, 9th ed., pp. 126-127)*

18. **(C)** Radiographic results should be consistent and predictable with respect to positioning accuracy, exposure factors, and equipment operation. X-ray equipment should be tested and calibrated periodically as part of an ongoing quality assurance (QA) program. The focal spot should be tested periodically to evaluate its size and its impact on recorded detail; this is accomplished using a slit camera, a pinhole camera, or a star pattern. To test the congruence of the light and x-ray fields, a radiopaque object such as a paper clip or a penny is placed at each corner of the light field before the test exposure is made. After processing, the corners of the x-ray field should be exactly delineated by the radioopaque objects. *(Carlton and Adler, 4th ed., p. 484)*

19. **(C)** A large quantity of heat applied to a cold anode can cause enough surface heat to crack the anode. Excessive heat to the target can cause pitting or localized melting of the focal track. Localized melts can result in vaporized tungsten deposits on the glass envelope, which can cause a filtering effect, decreasing tube output. Excessive heat also can be conducted to the rotor bearings, causing increased friction and tube failure. *(Selman, 9th ed., p. 146)*

20. **(B)** The high-voltage, or step-up, transformer functions to *increase voltage* to the necessary kilovoltage. It *decreases the amperage* to

milliamperage. The amount of increase or decrease *depends on the transformer ratio*, that is, the ratio of the number of turns in the primary coil to the number of turns in the secondary coil. The transformer law is as follows: To determine secondary V,

$$\frac{V_s}{V_p} = \frac{N_s}{N_p}$$

To determine secondary I,

$$\frac{N_s}{N_p} = \frac{I_p}{I_s}$$

Substituting known values:

$$\frac{x}{220} = \frac{100,000}{400}$$

$$400x = 22,000,000$$

Thus, $x = 55,000$ V (55 kV). *(Selman, 9th ed., pp. 84–85)*

21. **(A)** The HVL of a particular beam is defined as that thickness of a material that will reduce the exposure rate to one-half of its original value. The more energetic the beam (the higher the kilovoltage), the greater is the HVL thickness required to cut its intensity in half. *Therefore, it may be stated that kilovoltage and HVL have a direct relationship: As kilovoltage increases, HVL increases. (Selman, 9th ed., pp. 122–123)*

22. **(C)** In electronic/digital imaging, changes in window width affect changes in contrast scale, while changes in window level affect changes in brightness (in analog terms, density). As window width increases, the scale of contrast increases (i.e., contrast decreases). As window level increases, brightness increases. It should be noted that, to describe an increase in brightness, our old analog terminology would say that density decreases. This can be easily illustrated as you postprocess/window your personal digital photographs or scanned documents. As you slide the brightness scale to increase brightness, the photo/image gets darker, that is, density increases. *(Fosbinder and Orth, p. 208)*

23. **(A)** All circuit devices located *before* the primary coil of the high-voltage transformer are said to be on the *primary or low-voltage* side of the x-ray circuit. The timer, autotransformer, and (prereading) kilovoltage meter are all located in the *low*-voltage circuit.

The *secondary/high-voltage* side of the circuit begins with the *secondary coil* of the high-voltage transformer. The *mA meter* is connected at the midpoint of the secondary coil of the high-voltage transformer. Following the secondary coil is the *rectification system*, and the *x-ray tube. (Selman, 9th ed., pp. 150–151)*

Transformers are used to change the value of alternating current (AC). They operate on the principle of mutual induction. The secondary coil of the step-up transformer is located in the high-voltage (secondary) side of the x-ray circuit. The step-down transformer, or filament transformer, is located in the filament circuit and serves to regulate the voltage and current provided to heat the x-ray tube filament. The rectification system is also located on the high-voltage, or secondary, side of the x-ray circuit. *(Selman, 9th ed., pp. 155–156)*

24. **(D)** Moving the image intensifier closer to the patient during fluoroscopy decreases the SID and patient dose (as SID is reduced, the intensity of the x-ray photons at the image intensifier's input phosphor increases; the automatic brightness control then automatically decreases the milliamperage and, therefore, patient dose). Moving the image intensifier closer to the patient during fluoroscopy also decreases the OID and, therefore, magnification. As tissue density increases, a greater exposure dose is required. *(Fosbinder and Kelsey, pp. 265–267)*

25. **(B)** When an AEC is installed in an x-ray circuit, it is calibrated to produce radiographic densities as required by the radiologist. Once the part being radiographed has been exposed to produce the correct film density, the AEC automatically terminates the exposure. The manual timer should be used as a backup timer; in case the AEC fails to terminate the exposure, the backup timer would protect the patient from overexposure and the x-ray

tube from excessive heat load. The master density generally is set on normal to produce the required densities. In special cases, when this produces excessive or insufficient density, the master density may be adjusted to plus or minus density. *(Selman, 9th ed., p. 154)*

26. **(A)** A *motor* is a device used to convert electrical energy to mechanical energy. The *stator* and *rotor* are the two principal parts of an *induction motor*. A *generator* converts mechanical energy into electrical energy. *(Selman, 9th ed., p. 78)*

27. **(C)** A *phototimer* is a type of AEC that is used to automatically terminate the x-ray exposure once the film is correctly exposed. Another type of AEC is the *ionization chamber*. An image intensifier functions to provide a brighter fluoroscopic image, and positive beam limitation (PBL), or automatic collimation, serves to restrict the field size to the size of the cassette/IR used in the Bucky tray. The line-voltage compensator automatically adjusts the incoming line voltage to the x-ray machine to correct for any voltage drops or surges. *(Selman, 9th ed., pp. 153–154)*

28. **(B)** A quality-control (QC) program requires the use of a number of devices to test the efficiency of various parts of the imaging system. Spatial resolution is most significantly affected by the focal spot size. A *slit camera*, as well as a *star pattern* (Figure 5–12), or pinhole camera, is used to test focal-spot size. The slit camera is considered the standard for (annual) measurement of the effective focal spot size. A parallel line–type resolution test pattern (Figure 5–12) can be used to test the resolution capability of intensifying screens. *(Bushong, 9th ed., pp. 307–308)*

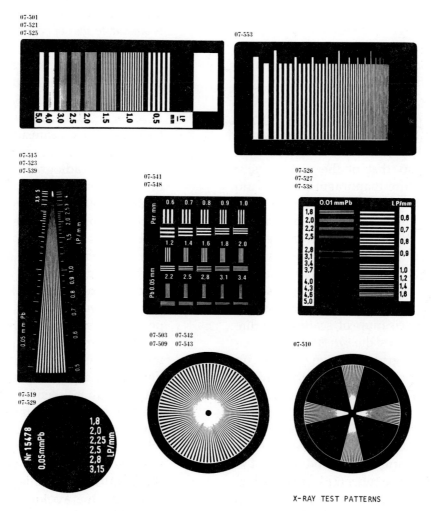

Figure 5–12. Courtesy of Nuclear Associates

29. **(D)** Because mammography uses such low-kilovoltage levels, IR front material becomes especially important. Any attenuation of the beam by the IR front would be most undesirable. Low-attenuating carbon fibers or special plastics that resist impact and heat softening (e.g., polystyrene and polycarbonate) are used frequently as IR front material. *(Carlton and Adler, 4th ed., p. 619)*

30. **(B)** An image's *spatial resolution* refers to its recorded detail. The effect of the input screen's phosphor layer is similar to the effect of the phosphor layer thickness in intensifying screens; that is, as the phosphor layer is made thinner, recorded detail increases. Also, the smaller the input phosphor diameter, the greater is the spatial resolution. A brighter image is easier to see but does not affect resolution. *(Bushong, 8th ed., pp. 360–363)*

31. **(B)** There are three types of beam restrictors—aperture diaphragms, cones and cylinders, and collimators. The most practical and efficient type is the collimator. Its design makes available an infinite number of field-size variations that are not available with the other types of beam restrictors. Because aperture diaphragms and flare cones have a fixed aperture size and shape, their beam restriction is not as efficient as that of the variable size collimator. Aperture diaphragms, cones, and cylinders may be placed on a collimator track so that the illuminated crosshairs are visualized. Although the collimator assembly contributes approximately 1.0 mm Al equivalent to the added filtration of the x-ray tube (because of the plastic exit portal and silver-coated reflective mirror), its functions are unrelated to the cleanup of scattered radiation. This is so because the *patient* is the principal scatterer, and grids function to clean up scattered radiation generated by the patient. *(Bushong, 8th ed., pp. 241–243)*

32. **(B)** Two types of interactions between high-speed incident electrons and the tungsten-target atoms account for the production of x-rays within the x-ray tube. (1) In the production of Brems ("braking") radiation, a high-speed electron is attracted to the positive nuclear charge of a tungsten atom. In so doing, it is "braked" and gives up energy in the form of an x-ray photon. Most of the primary beam is made up of Brems radiation. (2) If the incident electron were to eject a K-shell electron, an L-shell electron would move in to fill the vacancy. It releases a photon (K-characteristic ray) whose energy equals the difference between the K- and L-shell energy levels. This is characteristic radiation; it is responsible for only a small portion of the primary beam. *(Bushong, 8th ed., pp. 149–152)*

33. **(D)** The x-ray anode may be a molybdenum disk coated with a tungsten–rhenium alloy. Because tungsten has a *high atomic number* (74), it produces high-energy x-rays more efficiently. Since a great deal of heat is produced at the target, tungsten's *high melting point* (3,410°C) helps to avoid damage to the target surface. Heat produced at the target should be dissipated readily, and tungsten's *conductivity is similar to that of copper.* Therefore, as heat is applied to the focus, it can be conducted throughout the disk to equalize the temperature and thus avoid pitting, or localized melting, of the focal track. *(Selman, 9th ed., p. 138)*

34. **(A)** AEC devices are used in today's equipment and serve to produce consistent and comparable radiographic results. In one type of AEC, there is an *ionization chamber* just beneath the tabletop above the IR (A). The part to be examined is centered to it (the sensor) and radiographed. When a predetermined quantity of ionization has occurred (equal to the correct density), the x-ray exposure terminates automatically. In the other type of AEC, the *phototimer*, a small fluorescent screen is positioned beneath the IR (B). When remnant radiation emerging from the patient exposes and exits the IR, the fluorescent screen emits light. Once a predetermined amount of fluorescent light is "seen" by the photocell sensor, the exposure is terminated. A special IR, one without lead foil backing, is often required with this type of AEC. *In either case, the manual timer should be used as a backup timer.* In case of AEC malfunction, this would terminate the exposure, thus avoiding patient overexposure and tube overload. *(Shephard, pp. 275–276)*

35. **(C)** *Voltage ripple* refers to the percentage drop from maximum voltage each pulse of current experiences. In single-phase rectified equipment, the entire pulse (half-cycle) is used; therefore, there is first an increase to the maximum (peak) voltage value and then a decrease to zero potential (90-degree past-peak potential). The entire waveform is used; if 100 kV were selected, the actual average kilovoltage output would be approximately 70 kV. Three-phase rectification produces almost constant potential, with just small ripples (drops) in maximum potential between pulses. Approximately a 13% voltage ripple (drop from maximum value) characterizes the operation of three-phase, six-pulse generators. Three-phase, 12-pulse generators have about a 3.5% voltage ripple. *(Selman, 9th ed., p. 162)*

36. **(C)** The visual apparatus that is responsible for visual acuity and contrast perception is the *cones* within the retina. Cones are also used for daylight vision. Therefore, the most desirable condition for fluoroscopic viewing is to have a bright enough image to permit cone (daylight) vision for better detail perception. The image intensifier accomplishes this. The intensified image is then transferred to a TV monitor for viewing. Cine- and spot-film cameras record fluoroscopic events. *(Selman, 9th ed., pp. 259–260)*

37. **(B)** The incident electron has a certain amount of energy as it approaches the tungsten target. If the positive nucleus of a tungsten atom attracts the electron, changing its course, a certain amount of energy is released during the "braking" action. This energy is given up in the form of an x-ray photon called *Bremsstrahlung* ("braking") *radiation. Characteristic radiation* is also produced at the target (less frequently) when an incident electron ejects a K-shell electron, and an L-shell electron drops into its place. Energy is liberated in the form of a characteristic ray, and its energy is representative of the difference in energy levels. *Compton scatter* and the *photoelectric effect* are interactions between x-ray photons and tissue atoms. *(Selman, 9th ed., p. 113)*

38. **(C)** The *input phosphor* of an image intensifier receives remnant radiation emerging from the patient and converts it to a fluorescent light image. Directly adjacent to the input phosphor is the *photocathode*, which is made of a photoemissive alloy (usually, a cesium and antimony compound). The fluorescent light image strikes the photocathode and is converted to an electron image. The electrons are focused carefully, to maintain image resolution, by the *electrostatic focusing lenses*, through the *accelerating anode* and to the *output phosphor* for conversion back to light. The *TV monitor* is not part of the image intensifier but serves to display the image that is transmitted to it from the output phosphor. *(Bushong, 8th ed., pp. 360–363)*

39. **(B)** Traditional x-ray imaging involves formation of the x-ray image directly on the IR (film). In digital imaging, x-rays form an electronic image on a special radiation detector. This electronic image can be manipulated by a computer and stored in the computer memory or displayed as a matrix of intensities. This final digital image is often viewed on a computer monitor and looks just like a traditional x-ray image, but the computer often has the capability of postprocessing image enhancement. *(Bushong, 8th ed., p. 402)*

40. **(B)** In digital fluoroscopy (DF), the image-intensifier output screen image is coupled via a *charge-coupled device* (CCD) for viewing on a display monitor. A CCD converts visible light to an electrical charge that is then sent to the analog-to-digital converter (ADC) for processing. When output screen light strikes the CCD cathode, a proportional number of electrons are released by the cathode and stored as digital values by the CCD. The CCD's rapid discharge time virtually eliminates image lag and is particularly useful in high-speed imaging procedures such as cardiac catheterizations. CCD cameras have replaced analog cameras (such as the Vidicon and Plumbicon) in new fluoroscopic equipment. CCDs are more sensitive to the light emitted by the output phosphor (than the analog cameras) and are associated with less "noise." DF eliminates the need for cassette-loaded spot

films and/or 100-mm spot films. DF photo-spot images, which are simply still-frame images, need no chemical processing, require less patient dose, and offer postprocessing capability. DF also offers "road-mapping" capability. "Road-mapping" is a technique useful in procedures involving guidewire/catheter placement. During the fluoroscopic examination, the most recent fluoroscopic image is stored on the monitor, thereby reducing the need for continuous x-ray exposure. This technique can offer significant reductions in patient and personnel radiation exposure. (Bushong, 8th ed., p. 410)

41. **(B)** When a spinning top is used to test the efficiency of a single-phase timer, the result is a series of dots or dashes, with each representing a pulse of radiation. With full-wave-rectified current and a possible 120 dots (pulses) available per second, one should visualize 12 dots at 1/10 s, 24 dots at 1/5 s, 6 dots at 1/20 s, and so on.

However, because three-phase equipment is at almost constant potential, a *synchronous* spinning top must be used, and the result is a *solid arc* (rather than dots). The number of degrees formed by the arc is measured and equated to a particular exposure time.

A multitude of small, mesh-like squares describes a screen contact test. An aluminum step wedge (penetrometer) may be used to demonstrate the effect of kilovoltage on contrast (demonstrating a series of gray tones from white to black), with a greater number of grays demonstrated at higher kilovoltage levels. (Selman, 9th ed., p. 106)

42. **(C)** Quality Control refers to our equipment and its safe and accurate operation. Various components must be tested at specified intervals and test results must be within specified parameters. Any deviation from those parameters must be corrected. Examples of equipment components that are tested annually are the focal spot size, linearity, reproducibility, collimation, filtration, kV, and exposure time. Quality Assurance is associated with patients and staff, and their interactions and relationships. Congruence is a term used to describe the relationship between the

collimator light field and the actual x-ray field—they must be congruent (i.e., match) to within 2% of the SID. Postprocessing refers to the windowing or other manipulation of a digital image. (Fosbinder and Orth, pp. 222–223)

43. **(C)** Structures that we wish to visualize frequently are superimposed on other structures of lesser interest. Tomography uses reciprocal motion between the x-ray tube and the film to image structures at a particular level in the body while blurring everything above and below that level. The thickness of the level visualized can be changed by changing the tube angle (amplitude). The greater the tube angle, the thinner is the section imaged. (Selman, 9th ed., pp. 276–277)

44. **(A)** As body areas of different thicknesses and densities are scanned with the image intensifier, image brightness and contrast require adjustment. The ABC functions to maintain constant brightness and contrast of the output screen image, correcting for fluctuations in x-ray beam attenuation with adjustments in kilovoltage and/or milliamperage. There are also brightness and contrast controls on the monitor that the radiographer can regulate. (Bushong, 8th ed., p. 358)

45. **(B)** Because the high-voltage transformer has a fixed ratio, there must be a means of changing the voltage sent to its primary coil; otherwise, there would be a fixed kilovoltage. The autotransformer makes these changes possible. When kilovoltage is selected on the control panel, the radiographer actually is adjusting the autotransformer and selecting the amount of voltage to send to the high-voltage transformer to be stepped up (to kilovoltage). The filament circuit supplies the proper current and voltage to the x-ray tube filament for proper thermionic emission. The rectifier circuit is responsible for changing AC to unidirectional current. (Selman, 9th ed., pp. 88–89)

46. **(B)** The terms *star* and *wye* (or *delta*) refer to the configuration of transformer windings in three-phase equipment. Instead of having a

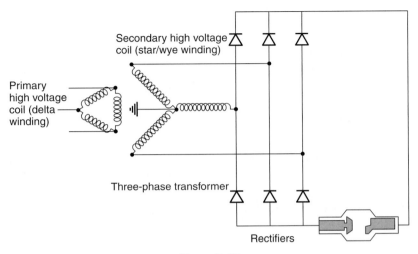

Secondary high voltage
coil (star/wye winding)

Primary
high voltage
coil (delta
winding)

Three-phase transformer

Rectifiers

Figure 5–13.

single primary coil and a single secondary coil, the high-voltage transformer has three primary and three secondary windings—one winding for each phase (Figure 5–13). Autotransformers operate on the principle of self-induction and have only one winding. Three-phase x-ray equipment often has three autotransformers. *(Selman, 9th ed., p. 163)*

47. **(B)** The light image emitted from the output phosphor of the image intensifier is directed to the TV monitor for viewing and sometimes to recording devices such as a spot-film camera or cine film. The light is directed to these places by a *beam splitter* or objective lens located between the output phosphor and the TV camera tube (or CCD). The majority of the light will go to the recording device, whereas a small portion goes to the TV so that the procedure may continue to be monitored during filming. *(Selman, 9th ed., p. 262)*

48. **(A)** The vast majority of target interactions involve the incident electrons and outer-shell tungsten electrons. No ionization occurs, and the energy loss is reflected in heat generation. The production of x-rays is an amazingly inefficient process: *More than 99% of the electrons' kinetic energy is changed to heat energy and less than 1% into x-ray photon energy.* This presents a serious heat-buildup problem in the anode because heat production is directly proportional to tube current. *(Selman, 9th ed., p. 115)*

49. **(B)** *Inherent* filtration is that which is "built into" the construction of the x-ray tube. Before exiting the x-ray tube, x-ray photons must pass through the tube's glass envelope and port window; the photons are filtered somewhat as they do so. This inherent filtration is usually the equivalent of 0.5 mm Al. Aluminum filtration *placed* between the x-ray tube housing and the collimator is added to contribute to the total necessary requirement of 2.5 mm Al equivalent. The collimator itself is considered part of the *added filtration* (1.0 mm Al equivalent) because of the silver surface of the mirror within. It is important to remember that as aluminum filtration is added to the x-ray tube, the HVL increases. *(Selman, 9th ed., p. 132)*

50. **(D)** The accuracy of all three is important to ensure adequate patient protection. *Reproducibility* means that repeated exposures at a given technique must provide consistent intensity. *Linearity* means that a given milliampere-seconds value, using different milliamperage stations with appropriate exposure time adjustments, will provide consistent intensity. PBL is automatic collimation and must be accurate to 2% of the SID. Light-localized collimators must be available and must be accurate to within 2%. *(Bushong, 8th ed., p. 462)*

51. **(C)** The figure illustrates the component parts of a rotating-anode x-ray tube enclosed

within a glass envelope (number 3) to preserve the *vacuum* necessary for x-ray production. Number 4 is the *rotating anode* with its beveled focal track at the periphery (number 8) and its *stem* (at number 5). Numbers 6 and 7 are the *stator* and *rotor*, respectively—the two components of an induction motor—whose function it is to rotate the anode. Number 1 is the filament of the cathode assembly, which is made of thoriated tungsten and functions to liberate electrons (thermionic emission) when heated to white hot (incandescence). Number 2 is the molybdenum focusing cup, which functions to direct the liberated filament electrons to the focal spot. *(Shephard, pp. 5–6; Bushong 9th ed., pp. 126–127)*

52. **(B)** X-rays are energetic enough to rearrange atoms in materials through which they pass, and they can, therefore, be hazardous to living tissue. X-rays are called *ionizing* radiation because they have the energetic potential to break apart electrically neutral atoms, resulting in the production of negative and/or positive *ions*. X-rays are infinitesimal bundles of energy called *photons* that deposit some of their energy into matter as they travel through it. This deposition of energy and subsequent *ionization* has the potential to cause chemical and biologic damage. Several of the outstanding properties of x-ray photons are:

- X-rays are not perceptible by the senses.
- X-rays travel in straight lines.
- X-rays travel at the speed of light.
- X-rays are electrically neutral.
- X-rays have a penetrating effect on all matter.
- X-rays have a physiological effect on living tissue.
- X-rays have an ionizing effect on air.
- X-rays have a photographic effect on film emulsion.
- X-rays produce fluorescence in certain phosphors.
- X-rays cannot be focused.
- X-rays have a spectrum of energies.
- X-rays are unaffected by a magnetic field.

53. **(C)** All circuit devices located before the primary coil of the high-voltage transformer are said to be on the primary or low-voltage side of the x-ray circuit. The timer, autotransformer, and (prereading) kilovoltage meter are all located in the low-voltage circuit. The milliampere meter, however, is connected at the midpoint of the secondary coil of the high-voltage transformer. When studying a diagram of the x-ray circuit, it will be noted that the milliampere meter is grounded at the midpoint of the secondary coil (where it is at zero potential). Therefore, it may be placed in the control panel safely. *(Selman, 9th ed., pp. 150–151)*

54. **(A)** Parts being examined during fluoroscopic procedures change in thickness and density as the patient is required to change positions and as the fluoroscope is moved to examine different regions of the body that have varying thickness and tissue densities. The *automatic brightness control* functions to vary the required milliampere-seconds and/or kilovoltage as necessary. With this method, patient dose varies, and image quality is maintained. Minification and flux gain contribute to total brightness gain. *(Bushong, 8th ed., p. 360)*

55. **(B)** One generally thinks in terms of moving grids being totally superior to stationary grids because moving grids function to blur the images of the lead strips on the radiographic image. Moving grids do, however, have several disadvantages. First, their complex mechanism is expensive and subject to malfunction. Second, today's sophisticated x-ray equipment makes possible the use of extremely short exposures, a valuable feature whenever motion may be a problem (as in pediatric radiography). However, grid mechanisms frequently are not able to oscillate rapidly enough for the short exposure times, and as a result, the grid motion is "stopped," and the lead strips are imaged. Third, patient dose is increased with moving grids. Since the central ray is not always centered to the grid because it is in motion, lateral decentering occurs (resulting in diminished density), and consequently, an increase in exposure is needed to compensate (either manually or via AEC). *(Shephard, p. 249)*

56. **(C)** PACS refers to a picture archiving and communication system. *Analog* images (conventional images) can be digitized with a digitizer. PACS systems receive *digital* images and display them on monitors for interpretation. These systems also store images and allow their retrieval at a later time. PACS systems provide us with the option of a completely filmless radiology department. *(Shephard, pp. 365–367)*

57. **(B)** HVL may be used to express the quality of an x-ray beam. *The HVL of a particular beam is that thickness of an absorber that will decrease the intensity of the beam to one-half its original value.* If the original intensity of the beam was 78 R/min, the first HVL will reduce the intensity to 39 R/min, the second HVL will reduce it to 19.5 R/min, and the third HVL will reduce it to 9.75 R/min. *(Bushong, 8th ed., p. 52)*

58. **(B)** Quality Control refers to our equipment and its safe and accurate operation. Various components must be tested at specified intervals and test results must be within specified parameters. Any deviation from those parameters must be corrected. Examples of equipment components that are tested annually are the focal spot size, linearity, reproducibility, filtration, kV, and exposure time. Kilovoltage settings can most effectively be tested using an electronic kV meter; to meet required standards, the kV should be accurate to within +/−4 kV.

Congruence is a term used to describe the relationship between the collimator light field and the actual x-ray field—they must be congruent (i.e., match) to within 2% of the SID. Collimators should be inspected and verified as accurate semiannually, that is, twice a year. Reproducibility testing should specify that radiation output be consistent to within +/−5%. *(Fosbinder and Orth, pp. 223–225; NCRP Report No. 99, pp. 69–70)*

59. **(C)** The lead strips of a focused grid are angled to correspond to the configuration of the divergent x-ray beam. Thus, any radiation that is changing direction, as is typical of scattered radiation, will be trapped by the lead foil strips. However, if the central ray and the grid center do not correspond, the lead strips will absorb primary radiation. The absorption of primary radiation is termed *cutoff* and results in diminished radiographic density. *(Carlton and Adler, 4th ed., p. 260)*

60. **(C)** Although the CT x-ray tube is similar to direct-projection x-ray tubes, it has several special requirements. The CT x-ray tube must have a very high short-exposure rating and must be capable of tolerating several million heat units while still having a small focal spot for optimal resolution. To help tolerate the very high production of heat units, the anode must be capable of high-speed rotation. The x-ray tube produces a pulsed x-ray beam (1–5 ms) using up to about 1,000 mA. The collimator assembly has two parts: The prepatient, or predetector, collimator is at the x-ray tube and consists of multiple beam restrictions so that the x-ray beam diverges little. This reduces patient dose and reduces the production of scattered radiation, thereby improving the CT image. The postpatient collimator, or predetector collimator, confines the exit photons before they reach the detector array and determines slice thickness. *(Bushong, 8th ed., pp. 429–430)*

61. **(C)** A spinning top is used to test the timer efficiency of full-wave-rectified single-phase equipment. The result should be a *series of dots* or dashes, with each dot representing a pulse of x-radiation. With full-wave-rectified current there should be 120 dots/pulses seen per second. One should visualize 12 dots/pulses at 1/10 s, 6 dots at 0.05 s, 10 dots at 1/12 s, and 3 dots at 0.025 s. If an incorrect number of dots/pulses is obtained, it is an indication of either timer malfunction or rectifier failure. Because three-phase equipment is at almost constant potential, a *synchronous* spinning top must be used for timer testing, and the result is a *solid arc* (rather than dots). The number of degrees covered by the arc is measured and equated to a particular exposure time; one second exposure should demonstrate 360 degrees. *(Selman, 9th ed., p. 106)*

62. **(B)** X-ray tube life may be extended by using exposure factors that produce a *minimum of* *heat*, that is, a lower milliampere-seconds and higher kilovoltage combination, whenever possible. When the rotor is activated, the filament current is increased to produce the required electron source (thermionic emission). *Prolonged rotor time*, then, can lead to shortened filament life as a result of early vaporization. Large exposures to a cold anode will heat the anode surface, and the big temperature difference can cause cracking of the anode. This can be avoided by proper warming of the anode prior to use, thereby allowing sufficient dispersion of heat through the anode. *(Selman, 9th ed., pp. 143–145)*

63. **(C)** The brightness gain of image intensifiers is 5,000 to 20,000. This increase is accounted for in two ways. As the electron image is focused to the output phosphor, it is accelerated by high voltage (about 25 kV). The output phosphor is only a fraction of the size of the input phosphor, and this decrease in image size represents brightness gain, termed *minification gain*. The *ratio* of the number of x-ray photons at the input phosphor compared to the number light photons at the output phosphor is termed *flux gain*. *Total brightness gain is equal to the product of minification gain and flux gain. (Bushong, 9th ed., p. 351)*

64. **(B)** Given the milliamperage and exposure time, a radiographic rating chart enables the radiographer to determine the maximum safe kilovoltage for a particular exposure. Because the heat load an anode will safely accept varies with the size of the focal spot and the type of rectification, these variables must be identified. Each x-ray tube has its own radiographic rating chart. The speed of the imaging system has no impact on the use of a radiographic rating chart. *(Selman, 9th ed., p. 145)*

65. **(C)** The spinning-top test is used to evaluate *timer accuracy* or *rectifier failure*. With single-phase, full-wave-rectified equipment (120 pulses/s), for example, 12 dots should be visualized when using the 1/10-s time station. A few dots more or less indicate timer inaccuracy. If the test demonstrated exactly six dots, rectifier failure is strongly suspected. With three-phase equipment, a special synchro-

nous spinning top (or oscilloscope) is used, and a solid black arc is obtained rather than dots. The length of this arc is measured and compared with the known correct arc. *(Selman, 9th ed., pp. 105–106)*

66. **(A)** Radiographic reproducibility is an important concept in producing high-quality diagnostic films. Radiographic results should be consistent and predictable not only in terms of positioning accuracy but also with respect to exposure factors. AEC devices (phototimers and ionization chambers) automatically terminate the x-ray exposure once a predetermined quantity of x-rays has penetrated the patient, thus ensuring consistent results. A penetrometer can be used to demonstrate effects of kV on contrast. An induction motor has two parts, a stator and a rotor, and is used to rotate the anode. *(Shephard, p. 274)*

67. **(B)** Some x-ray circuit devices, such as the transformer and autotransformer, will operate only on AC. The efficient operation of the x-ray tube, however, requires the use of unidirectional current, so current must be *rectified* before it gets to the x-ray tube. The process of full-wave *rectification* changes the negative half-cycle to a useful positive half-cycle. An x-ray circuit rectification system is located between the secondary coil of the high-voltage transformer and the x-ray tube. Rectifiers are solid-state diodes made of *semiconductive materials* such as silicon, selenium, or germanium that conduct electricity *in only one direction*. Thus, a series of rectifiers placed between the transformer and x-ray tube function to change AC to a more useful unidirectional current. *(Bushong, 8th ed., p. 119)*

68. **(B)** The collimator assembly includes a series of lead shutters, a mirror, and a light bulb (Figure 5–14). The mirror and light bulb function to project the size, location, and center of the irradiated field. The bulb's emitted beam of light is deflected by a mirror placed at an angle of 45 degrees in the path of the light beam. *In order for the projected light beam to be the same size as the x-ray beam, the focal spot and the light bulb must be exactly the same distance from the center of the mirror. (Carlton and Adler, 4th ed., p. 232)*

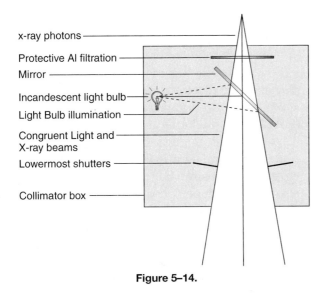

x-ray photons

Protective Al filtration

Mirror

Incandescent light bulb

Light Bulb illumination

Congruent Light and
X-ray beams

Lowermost shutters

Collimator box

Figure 5–14.

69. **(B)** The *input phosphor* of an image intensifier receives remnant radiation emerging from the patient and converts it to a fluorescent light image. Directly adjacent to the input phosphor is the *photocathode*, which is made of a photoemissive alloy (usually, a cesium and antimony compound). The fluorescent light image strikes the photocathode and is converted to an electron image. The electrons are carefully focused to maintain image resolution by the *electrostatic focusing lenses* through the *accelerating anode* and to the *output phosphor* for conversion back to light. *(Carlton and Adler, 4th ed., pp. 569–570)*

70. **(B)** The image intensifier's input phosphor receives the remnant radiation emerging from the patient and converts it into a fluorescent light image. Very close to the input phosphor, separated by a thin, transparent layer, is the photocathode. The photocathode is made of a photoemissive alloy, usually an antimony and cesium compound. The fluorescent light image strikes the photocathode and is converted to an electron image that is focused by the electrostatic lenses to the output phosphor. *(Bushong, 8th ed., p. 360)*

71. **(C)** Myelography requires that contrast medium be instilled into the lumbar subarachnoid space and distributed via gravity to various levels of the subarachnoid space.

This gravitational distribution is accomplished through the use of an x-ray table that is capable of angling or tilting during the procedure. *(Bontrager and Lampignano, 6th ed., pp. 762–763)*

72. **(A)** Through the action of thermionic emission, as the tungsten filament continually gives up electrons, it gradually becomes thinner with age. This evaporated tungsten frequently is deposited on the inner surface of the glass envelope at the tube window. When this happens, *it acts as an additional filter* of the x-ray beam, thereby *reducing tube output*. Also, the tungsten deposit actually may attract electrons from the filament, creating a tube current and causing *puncture of the glass envelope*. *(Selman, 9th ed., pp. 137–138)*

73. **(D)** Each time an x-ray exposure is made, less than 1% of the total energy is converted to x-rays, and the remainder (more than 99%) of the energy is converted to heat. Thus, it is important to use target material with a high atomic number and high melting point. The larger the actual focal-spot size, the larger is the area over which the generated heat is spread, and the more tolerant the x-ray tube is. Heat is particularly damaging to the target if it is concentrated or limited to a small area. A target that rotates during the exposure is spreading the heat over a large area, the entire surface of the focal track. If the diameter of the anode is greater, the focal track will be longer, and heat will be spread over an even larger area. *(Bushong, 8th ed., pp. 135–136)*

74. **(B)** *Current* is defined as the amount of electric charge flowing per second. *Voltage* is the potential difference existing between two points. *Resistance* is the property of a circuit that opposes current flow. *Capacitance* describes a quantity of stored electricity. *(Selman, 9th ed., pp. 46–47)*

75. **(D)** The thicker and more dense the anatomic part being studied, the less bright will be the fluoroscopic image. Both milliamperage and kilovoltage affect the fluoroscopic image in a way similar to the way in which they affect the radiographic image. For optimal contrast, especially taking patient dose into consideration, higher kilovoltage and lower milliamperage are generally preferred. *(Bushong, 8th ed., p. 363)*

76. (B) In Bremsstrahlung (Brems) or "braking" x-ray production, a high-speed electron, accelerated toward a tungsten atom, is attracted (and "braked," that is, slowed down) by the positively charged nucleus and therefore is deflected from its original course with a resulting loss of energy. This energy loss is given up in the form of an x-ray photon. The electron might not give up all its kinetic energy in one such interaction; it might go on to have several more interactions deeper in the target, each time giving up an x-ray photon having less and less energy. This is one reason the x-ray beam is heterogeneous (i.e., has a spectrum of energies). *Brems radiation comprises 70% to 90% of the x-ray beam.* The other type of x-ray production that occurs in the tungsten anode is *characteristic* radiation. In this case, a high-speed electron encounters the tungsten atom and ejects a K-shell electron, leaving a vacancy in the K shell. An electron from a shell above (e.g., the L shell) fills the vacancy and in so doing emits a K-characteristic ray. The energy of the characteristic ray is equal to the difference in energy between the K and L shells. K-characteristic x-rays from a tungsten-target x-ray tube have 69 keV of energy. Characteristic radiation comprises very little of the x-ray beam (10%–30%). *(Bushong, 8th ed., p. 151)*

77. (D) Each time an x-ray exposure is made, heat is produced in the x-ray tube. Actually, of all the energy used to make an exposure, *99.8% is converted to heat*, and only 0.2% is converted to x-ray photon energy. Since greater heat production leads to increased wear and tear on the x-ray tube, thereby decreasing its useful life, it behooves the radiographer to be able to calculate heat units and to understand the means of keeping heat production to a minimum. Heat units (HU) for a *single-phase* x-ray unit are determined by using the formula HU = mA × kV × time. Heat units for a three-phase, six-pulse x-ray unit are determined by using the formula HU = mA × kV × time × 1.35. Heat units for a three-phase, 12-pulse x-ray unit are determined by using the formula HU = mA × kV × time × 1.41. High milliampere-seconds technical factors produce far more heat units than low milliampere-seconds technical factors. *(Carlton and Adler, 4th ed., p. 121)*

78. (D) A computed tomographic (CT) imaging system has three component parts: a *gantry*, a *computer*, and an *operator console*. The gantry component includes an x-ray tube, a detector array, a high-voltage generator, a collimator assembly, and a patient couch with its motorized mechanism. The computer is exceedingly sophisticated, performing thousands of calculations simultaneously per second. It is responsible for image reconstruction and postprocessing functions. At the operator console, somewhat similar to a control panel used in projection radiography, are the controls for equipment operation and image manipulation. Technical factors are selected and monitored here, adjustments can be made, and the patient couch is operated from here. *(Bushong, pp. 429–430; Bontrager and Lampignano, 6th ed., p. 731)*

79. (A) Quality Control refers to our equipment and its safe and accurate operation. Various components must be tested at specified intervals and test results must be within specified parameters. Any deviation from those parameters must be corrected. Examples of equipment components that are tested annually are the focal spot size, linearity, reproducibility, filtration, kV, and exposure time. Reproducibility specifies that radiation output must be consistent to within +/−5%. Linearity tests x-ray output with increasing mAs; mR/mAs should be accurate to within 10%. Kilovoltage settings can most effectively be tested using an electronic kV meter; to meet required standards, the kV should be accurate to within +/−4 kV. Congruence is a term used to describe the relationship between the collimator light field and the actual x-ray field—they must be congruent to within 2% of the SID. Radiographic equipment collimators should be inspected and verified as accurate semiannually. *(Fosbinder and Orth, pp. 223–225; NCRP Report No. 99, pp. 72–74)*

80. (D) The anode is made to rotate through the use of an *induction motor*. An induction motor has two main parts, a *stator* and a *rotor*. The stator is the part located *outside the glass envelope* and consists of a series of electromagnets occupying positions around the stem of the anode. The stator's electromagnets are supplied with current, and the associated magnetic fields function to exert a drag or pull on the *rotor within the glass envelope.* The anode is a 2- to 5-in.-diameter molybdenum or graphite disk with a beveled edge. The beveled surface has a *focal track* of tungsten and rhenium alloy. The anode rotates at about 3,600 rpm (high-speed anode rotation is about 10,000 rpm) so that heat generated during x-ray production is distributed evenly over the entire track. *Rotating anodes* can withstand delivery of a greater amount of heat for a longer period of time than *stationary anodes. (Carlton and Adler, 4th ed., p. 73)*

81. **(D)** The AEC automatically adjusts the exposure required for body parts that have different *thicknesses and densities.* Proper functioning of the phototimer depends on accurate positioning by the radiographer. The correct *photocell*(s) must be selected, and the anatomic part of interest must completely cover the photocell to achieve the desired density. If *collimation* is inadequate and a field size larger than the part is used, excessive scattered radiation from the body or tabletop can cause the AEC to terminate the exposure prematurely, resulting in an underexposed radiograph. Backup time always should be selected on the manual timer to prevent patient overexposure and to protect the x-ray tube from excessive heat production should the AEC malfunction. Selection of the optimal kilovoltage for the part being radiographed is essential—no practical amount of milliampere-seconds can make up for inadequate penetration (kilovoltage), and excessive kilovoltage can cause the AEC to terminate the exposure prematurely. *A technique chart, therefore, is strongly recommended for use with AEC; it should indicate the optimal kilovoltage for the part, the photocells that should be selected, and the backup time that should be set. (Carlton and Adler, 4th ed., p. 540)*

82. **(C)** The anode is made to rotate through the use of an *induction motor.* An induction motor has two main parts, a *stator* and a *rotor.* The stator is the part located *outside the glass*

envelope and consists of a series of electromagnets occupying positions around the stem of the anode. The stator's electromagnets are supplied with current and the associated magnetic fields function to exert a drag or pull on the *rotor within the glass envelope.* The anode is a 2- to 5-in. diameter molybdenum or graphite disc with a beveled edge. The beveled surface has a *focal track* of tungsten and rhenium alloy. The anode rotates at about 3,600 rpm (high-speed anode rotation is about 10,000 rpm), so that heat generated during x-ray production is evenly distributed over the entire track. *Rotating anodes* can withstand delivery of a greater amount of heat for a longer period of time than *stationary anodes. (Carlton and Adler, 4th ed., p. 73)*

83. **(D)** Moving the image intensifier *closer to the patient* during fluoroscopy *reduces* the distance between the x-ray tube (source) and the image intensifier (IR), that is, the SID. It follows that the distance between the part being imaged (object) and the image intensifier (IR), that is, the object-to-image distance (OID), is also reduced. The shorter OID produces *less magnification* and *better image quality.* As the SID is reduced, the intensity of the x-ray photons at the image intensifier's input phosphor increases, stimulating the automatic brightness control (ABC) to decrease the milliamperage and thereby *decreasing patient dose* (Figure 5–15). *(Fosbinder and Kelsey, pp. 265–267)*

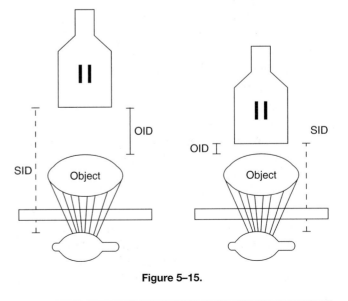

Figure 5–15.

84. **(B)** The figure illustrates the component parts of a rotating-anode x-ray tube enclosed within a glass envelope (number 3) to preserve the *vacuum* necessary for x-ray production. Number 4 is the *rotating anode* with its beveled focal track at the periphery (number 8) and its *stem* (at number 5). Numbers 6 and 7 are the *stator* and *rotor* respectively—the two components of an induction motor—whose function it is to rotate the anode. Number 1 is the filament of the cathode assembly, which is made of thoriated tungsten and functions to liberate electrons (thermionic emission) when heated to white hot (incandescence). Number 2 is the molybdenum focusing cup, which functions to direct the liberated filament electrons to the focal spot. *(Shephard, pp. 5–6; Bushong 9th ed., pp. 126–127)*

85. **(A)** Because using the master control's minus-density adjustment involves decreasing the exposure time (and this is not possible), this adjustment will be ineffective. Decreasing the kilovoltage will produce a change in radiographic contrast. Because too long an exposure time results in excessive density, the best way to compensate is to decrease the milliamperage. *(Carlton and Adler, 4th ed., p. 541; Shephard, p. 286)*

86. **(B)** The *minimum response time*, or *minimum reaction time*, is the length of the shortest exposure possible with a particular AEC. If less than the minimum response time is required for a particular exposure, the radiograph will exhibit excessive density. This problem becomes apparent when making exposures that require very short exposure times, such as when using high-milliamperage and fast film–screen combinations. To resolve this problem, the radiographer should decrease the milliamperage rather than the kilovoltage in order to leave contrast unaffected. *(Carlton and Adler, 4th ed., p. 102)*

87. **(D)** The input phosphor of image intensifiers is usually made of cesium iodide. For each x-ray photon absorbed by cesium iodide, approximately 5,000 light photons are emitted. As the light photons strike a photoemissive *photocathode*, a number of electrons are released from the photocathode and focused toward the output side of the image tube by voltage applied to the negatively charged *electrostatic focusing lenses*. The electrons are then accelerated through the neck of the tube, where they strike the small (0.5–1 in.) *output phosphor* that is mounted on a flat glass support. The entire assembly is enclosed within a 2–4-mm thick vacuum glass envelope. Remember that the image on the output phosphor is *minified, brighter,* and *inverted* (electron focusing causes image inversion).

Input screen diameters of 5–12 in. are available. Although smaller diameter input screens improve resolution, they do not permit a large FOV, that is, viewing of large patient areas.

Dual- and triple-field image intensifiers are available that permit *magnified* viewing of fluoroscopic images. To achieve magnification, the *voltage* to the focusing lenses is increased and a *smaller* portion of the input phosphor is used, thereby resulting in a smaller FOV. Because minification gain is now decreased, the image is not as bright. The mA is automatically increased to compensate for the loss in brightness when the image intensifier is switched to magnification mode. Entrance skin exposure (ESE) can increase dramatically as the FOV decreases (i.e., as magnification increases).

As FOV decreases, *magnification* of the output screen image increases, there is less *noise* because increased mA provides a greater number of x-ray photons, and *contrast* and *resolution* improve. The *focal point* in the magnification mode is *further away from* the output phosphor (as a result of increased voltage applied to the focusing lenses) and therefore the output image is magnified. *(Fosbinder and Orth, p. 191)*

88. **(B)** There are two main types of mobile x-ray equipment—capacitor-discharge and battery-powered. Although capacitor-discharge units are light, and therefore fairly easy to maneuver, the battery-powered mobile unit is very heavy (largely because it carries its heavy-duty power source). It is, however, capable of storing a large milliampere-seconds capacity for extended periods of time. These units frequently have a capacity of 10,000 mAs, with 12 hours required for a full charge. *(Carlton and Adler, 4th ed., pp. 558–561)*

89. **(C)** Most image-intensifier tubes are either dual-field or trifield, indicating the diameter of the input phosphor. When a change to a smaller-diameter mode is made, the voltage on the electrostatic focusing lenses is increased, and the result is a *magnified but dimmer* image. The milliamperage will be increased automatically to compensate for the loss in brightness with a magnified image, resulting in *higher patient dose in the smaller-diameter modes.* (*Bushong, 8th ed., p. 363*)

90. **(B)** Off-focus, or extrafocal, radiation is produced as electrons strike metal surfaces other than the focal track and produce x-rays that emerge with the primary beam at a variety of angles. This radiation is responsible for indistinct images outside the collimated field. Mounting a pair of shutters as close to the source as possible minimizes off-focus radiation. (*Bushong, 8th ed., p. 140*)

91. **(A)** *Rectifiers change AC into unidirectional current by allowing current to flow through them in only one direction.* Valve tubes are vacuum rectifier tubes found in older equipment. *Solid-state diodes* are the types of rectifiers used in today's x-ray equipment. Rectification systems are found between the secondary coil of the high-voltage transformer and the x-ray tube. *Resistors,* such as rheostats or choke coils, are circuit devices used to vary voltage or current. *Transformers,* operating on the principle of mutual induction, change the voltage (and current) to useful levels. *Autotransformers,* operating on the principle of self-induction, enable us to select the required kilovoltage. (*Selman, 9th ed., p. 101*)

92. **(C)** A *phototimer* is one type of AEC that actually measures light. As x-ray photons penetrate and emerge from a part, a fluorescent screen beneath the IR glows, and the fluorescent light charges a photomultiplier tube. Once a predetermined charge has been reached, the exposure terminates automatically. A parallel-plate *ionization chamber* is another type of AEC. A radiolucent chamber is located beneath the patient (between the patient and the film). As photons emerge from the patient, they enter the chamber and ionize the air within it. Once a predetermined charge has been reached, the

exposure is terminated automatically. Motion of magnetic fields inducing current in a conductor refers to the *principle of mutual induction.* (*Selman, 9th ed., pp. 153–154*)

93. **(B)** The x-ray tube filament is made of thoriated tungsten. When heated to incandescence (white hot), the filament liberates electrons—a process called *thermionic emission.* It is these electrons that will become the tube current (mA). As heat is increased, more electrons are released, and milliamperage increases. (*Bushong, 8th ed., p. 132*)

94. **(D)** Single-phase radiographic equipment is less efficient than three-phase equipment because it has a 100% voltage ripple. *With three-phase equipment, voltage never drops to zero,* and x-ray intensity is significantly greater. To produce similar density, only *two-thirds* of the original milliampere-seconds would be used for three-phase, six-pulse equipment. With three-phase, 12-pulse equipment, the original milliampere-seconds would be cut in *half* (one-half of 15 mAs = 7.5). (*Carlton and Adler, 4th ed., p. 96*)

95. **(A)** *Magnification radiography* may be used to demonstrate small, delicate structures that are difficult to image with conventional radiography. Because OID is an integral part of magnification radiography, the problem of magnification unsharpness arises. The use of a *fractional focal spot* (0.3 mm or smaller) is essential to the maintenance of image sharpness in magnification films. *Radiographic rating charts* should be consulted because the heat load to the anode may be critical in magnification radiography. The long exposures typical of *image-intensified fluoroscopy* and *tomography* make the use of a fractional focal spot generally impractical and hazardous to the anode. (*Selman, 9th ed., p. 226*)

96. **(C)** A radiographic rating chart enables the radiographer to determine the maximum safe milliamperage, exposure time, and kilovoltage for a given exposure using a particular x-ray tube. Because the heat load that an anode will safely accept varies with the size of the focal spot, type of rectification, and anode rotation, these variables must also be identified.

Each x-ray tube has its own characteristics and its own rating chart. First, find the chart with the identifying single-phase sine wave in the upper right corner and the correct focal-spot size in the upper left corner (chart C). Once the correct chart has been identified, locate 0.02 s on the horizontal axis, and follow its line up to where it intersects with the 400-mA curve. Then, draw a line to where this point meets the vertical (kV) axis; it intersects at exactly 80 kV. This is the maximum permissible kilovoltage exposure at the given milliampere-seconds for this x-ray tube. The radiographer should always use somewhat less than the maximum exposure. *(Selman, 9th ed., p. 145)*

97. **(B)** A radiographic rating chart enables the radiographer to determine the maximum safe milliamperage, exposure time, and kilovoltage for a given exposure using a particular x-ray tube. Because the heat load that an anode will accept safely varies with the size of the focal spot, type of rectification, and anode rotation, these variables must also be identified. Each x-ray tube has its own characteristics and its own rating chart. Only x-ray tubes A and B, the three-phase rectified x-ray tubes, will safely permit this exposure. Locate 0.1 s on the horizontal axis and follow it up to where it intersects with the 400-mA curve. X-ray tube A will permit over 150 kV safely, whereas x-ray tube B will permit only about 92 kV safely. Notice the significant difference between the two, which is solely due to the difference in focal-spot size. X-ray tube C will permit only about 75 kV at the given mAs. *(Selman, 9th ed., p. 145)*

98. **(A)** A radiographic rating chart enables the radiographer to determine the maximum safe milliamperage, exposure time, and kilovoltage for a given exposure using a particular x-ray tube. Because the heat load that an anode will safely accept varies with the size of the focal spot, type of rectification, and anode rotation, these variables must also be identified. Each x-ray tube has its own characteristics and its own rating chart. Find the correct chart for the three-phase, 1.0-mm focal-spot x-ray tube. Locate 0.1 s on the horizontal (seconds) axis and follow it up to where it intersects with the 120-kV line on the vertical (kV) axis. They

intersect just below the 300-mA curve, at approximately 310 mA. Thus, 300 mA is the maximum safe milliamperage for this particular group of exposure factors and x-ray tube. *(Selman, 9th ed., p. 145)*

99. **(B)** Each x-ray exposure made by the radiographer produces hundreds or thousands of heat units at the target. If the examination requires several consecutive exposures, the potential for extreme heat load is increased. Just as each x-ray tube has its own radiographic rating chart, each tube also has its own anode cooling curve to describe its unique heating and cooling characteristics. An x-ray tube generally cools most rapidly during the first 2 minutes of nonuse. First, note that the tube is saturated with heat at 300,000 HU. In order for another 160,000 HU to be safely applied, the x-ray tube must first release 160,000 HU, which means that it has to cool down at least to 140,000 HU. Find the 140,000 HU point on the vertical axis and follow across to where it intersects with the cooling curve. It intersects at about the 4-minute point. *(Selman, 9th ed., p. 147)*

100. **(C)** The *autotransformer* operates on the principle of *self-induction* and functions to select the correct voltage to be sent to the *high-voltage transformer* to be "stepped up" to kilovoltage. The high-voltage transformer increases the voltage and decreases the current. The *rheostat* is a type of *variable resistor* that is used to change voltage or current values. It is found frequently in the filament circuit. A *fuse* is a device used to protect the circuit elements from overload by opening the circuit in the event of a power surge. *(Selman, 9th ed., pp. 90–91)*

101. **(D)** As the anode angle is decreased (made steeper), a larger actual focal spot may be used while still maintaining the same small effective focal spot. Because the actual focal spot is larger, it can accommodate a greater heat load. However, with steeper (smaller) anode angles, the anode heel effect is accentuated and can compromise film coverage. *(Selman, 9th ed., pp. 138–139)*

102. **(A)** AECs are used in today's equipment and serve to produce consistent and comparable

results. In one type of AEC, there is an ionization chamber beneath the tabletop above the IR. The part to be examined is centered to it (the sensor) and radiographed. When a predetermined quantity of ionization has occurred (equal to the correct density), the exposure terminates automatically. With the second type of AEC, the phototimer, a small fluorescent screen, is positioned *beneath* the cassette. When remnant radiation emerging from the patient exposes the film and exits the cassette, the fluorescent screen emits light. Once a predetermined amount of fluorescent light has been "seen" by the photocell sensor, the exposure is terminated automatically. In either case, the manual timer should be used as a *backup timer*; in case of AEC malfunction, the exposure would terminate, thus avoiding patient overexposure and tube overload. (*Shephard, pp. 275–276*)

103. **(C)** The image on the image intensifier's output phosphor may be displayed for viewing through the use of either a series of lenses or a fiberoptic link. The two devices needed to view the image are a TV camera tube and a TV monitor. The TV camera tube (usually, a Plumbicon or Vidicon) converts the output phosphor image into an electrical signal. The TV monitor (a cathode-ray tube) then converts the electrical signal into a visible light image. (*Thompson et al., p. 370*)

104. **(B)** In *Compton scatter*, a *high-energy* (high kilovoltage) x-ray photon ejects an *outer-shell* electron in tissue or other absorber. The ejected electron is called a *recoil electron*. Although the x-ray photon is deflected with somewhat reduced energy (modified *scatter*), it *retains most* of its original energy and exits the body as an energetic scattered photon. Because the scattered photon exits the body, it does not pose a radiation hazard to the patient. It can, however, contribute to *image fog* and pose a *radiation hazard to personnel* (as in fluoroscopic procedures). In the *photoelectric effect*, a relatively *low-energy* (low kilovoltage) x-ray photon uses *all* its energy (true/total absorption) to eject an *inner-shell* electron, leaving an orbital vacancy. An electron from the shell above drops down to fill the vacancy and in so doing gives up energy in the form of a *char-*

acteristic ray. The photoelectric effect is more likely to occur in absorbers having *high atomic number* (e.g., bone or positive contrast media) and contributes significantly to patient dose because all the photon energy is absorbed by the patient (and, therefore, is responsible for the production of short-scale contrast). Brems and characteristic x-rays are produced at the focal spot as high-speed electrons are rapidly decelerated. (*Bushong, 8th ed., p. 174*)

105. **(C)** The number of heat units (HU) produced during a given exposure with single-phase equipment is determined by multiplying mA × time × kV. Correction factors are required with three-phase equipment. Unless the equipment manufacturer specifies otherwise, heat units for three-phase, six-pulse equipment are determined by multiplying mA × time × kV × 1.35. Heat units for three-phase, 12-pulse equipment are determined by multiplying mA × time × kV × 1.41. (*Selman, 9th ed., pp. 145–146*)

106. **(D)** With *single-phase*, full-wave-rectified equipment, the voltage is constantly changing from 0% to 100% of its maximum value. It drops to 0 every 180 degrees (of the AC waveform); that is, there is 100% voltage ripple. With *three-phase* equipment, the voltage ripple is significantly smaller. Three-phase, six-pulse equipment has a 13% voltage ripple, and three-phase, 12-pulse equipment has a 3.5% ripple. Therefore, *the voltage never falls below 87% to 96.5% of its maximum value with three-phase equipment*, and it closely approaches constant potential [direct current (DC)]. (*Carlton and Adler, 4th ed., pp. 91–93*)

107. **(A)** The spinning-top test is used to test timer accuracy or rectifier operation. Because single-phase, full-wave-rectified current has 120 useful impulses per second, a 1-s exposure of the spinning top should demonstrate 120 dots. Therefore, a 0.05-s exposure should demonstrate six dots. Anything more or less than this indicates that the time station needs calibration. If exactly one-half the expected number of dots appears, one should suspect rectifier failure. (*Selman, 9th ed., p. 106*)

108. **(B)** The smaller the focal spot, the more limited the anode is with respect to the quantity of heat it can safely accept. As the target angle decreases, the actual focal spot can be increased while still maintaining a small effective focal spot. Therefore, group (B) offers the greatest heat-loading potential, with a steep target angle and a large actual focal spot. It must be remembered, however, *that a steep target angle increases the heel effect,* and IR coverage may be compromised. *(Selman, 9th ed., pp. 145–146)*

109. **(C)** The IP is used to house, support, and protect the PSP. The IP front should be made of a sturdy material with a low atomic number because attenuation of the remnant beam is undesirable. Bakelite (the forerunner of today's plastics) and magnesium (the lightest structural metal) are the materials used most commonly for cassette fronts. The high atomic number of tungsten makes it inappropriate as an IP front material. *(Shephard, p. 41)*

110. **(A)** Quality Control refers to our equipment and its safe and accurate operation. Various components must be tested at specified intervals and test results must be within specified parameters. Any deviation from those parameters must be corrected. Examples of equipment components that are tested annually are the focal spot size, linearity, reproducibility, filtration, kV, and exposure time. Kilovoltage settings can most effectively be tested using an electronic kV meter; to meet required standards, the kV should be accurate to within $+/-4$ kV. Congruence is a term used to describe the relationship between the collimator light field and the actual x-ray field—they must be congruent (i.e., match) to within 2% of the SID. Collimators should be inspected and verified as accurate semiannually. Reproducibility testing should specify that radiation output be consistent to within $+/-5\%$. *(Fosbinder and Orth, pp. 223–225; NCRP Report No. 99, p. 69)*

111. **(D)** The figure illustrates the component parts of a rotating-anode x-ray tube enclosed within a glass envelope (number 3) to preserve the *vacuum* necessary for x-ray production. Number 4 is the *rotating anode* with its beveled focal track at the periphery (number 8) and its *stem* (at

number 5). Numbers 6 and 7 are the *stator* and *rotor*, respectively—the two components of an induction motor—whose function it is to rotate the anode. Number 1 is the filament of the cathode assembly, which is made of thoriated tungsten and functions to liberate electrons (thermionic emission) when heated to white hot (incandescence). Number 2 is the molybdenum focusing cup, which functions to direct the liberated filament electrons to the focal spot. *(Shephard, pp. 5–6; Bushong 9th ed., pp. 126–127)*

112. **(A)** The x-ray photons emitted from the anode focus are heterogeneous in nature. The low-energy photons must be removed because they are not penetrating enough to contribute to the image and because they *do* contribute to the patient's skin dose. The glass envelope and oil coolant provide approximately 0.5- to 1.0-mm Al equivalent filtration, which is referred to as *inherent* because it is a built-in, permanent part of the tube head. *(Selman, 9th ed., p. 132)*

113. **(C)** The AEC automatically terminates the exposure when the proper density has been recorded on the film. The important advantage of the phototimer, then, is that it can accurately duplicate radiographic densities. It is very useful in providing accurate comparison in follow-up examinations and in decreasing patient exposure dose by reducing the number of "retakes" needed because of improper exposure. The AEC automatically adjusts the exposure required for body parts with different thicknesses and densities. However, proper functioning of the phototimer depends on accurate positioning by the radiographer. The correct photocell(s) must be selected, and the anatomic part of interest must completely cover the photocell to achieve the desired density. If collimation is inadequate and a field size larger than the part is used, excessive scattered radiation from the body or tabletop can cause the AEC to terminate the exposure prematurely, resulting in an underexposed radiograph. *(Carlton and Adler, 4th ed., pp. 540–541)*

114. **(A)** The image intensifier's input phosphor receives the remnant beam from the patient and converts it to a fluorescent light image. To

maintain resolution, the input phosphor is made of cesium iodide crystals. Cesium iodide is much more efficient in this conversion process than was the phosphor used previously, zinc cadmium sulfide. Calcium tungstate was the phosphor used in cassette intensifying screens for many years prior to the development of rare earth phosphors such as gadolinium oxysulfide. (*Bushong, 8th ed., p. 360*)

115. **(D)** The greater the number of electrons making up the electron stream and bombarding the target, the greater is the number of x-ray photons produced. Although kilovoltage usually is associated with the energy of the x-ray photons, because a greater number of more energetic electrons will produce more x-ray photons, an increase in kilovoltage also will increase the number of photons produced. Specifically, the quantity of radiation produced increases as the square of the kilovoltage. The material composition of the tube target also plays an important role in the number of x-ray photons produced. The higher the atomic number of this material, the denser and more closely packed are the atoms making up the material, and therefore, the greater is the chance of an interaction between a high-speed electron and the target material. (*Bushong, 8th ed., p. 132*)

116. **(A)** A *photostimulable* (light-stimulated) *phosphor plate*, or simply *image plate* (IP), is used in CR. CR does not use traditional intensifying screens or film. Rather, the CR cassette contains a photostimulable IP that functions as the IR (rather than as film emulsion). On exposure, the IP stores information. The cassette is placed into a special scanner/processor where the IP is scanned with a laser light and the stored image is displayed on the computer monitor. (*Shephard, pp. 321–329*)

117. **(D)** Although the CT x-ray tube is similar to direct-projection x-ray tubes, it has several special requirements. The CT x-ray tube must have a very high short-exposure rating and must be capable of tolerating several million heat units while still having a small focal spot for optimal resolution. To help tolerate the very high production of heat units, the anode must be capable of high-speed rotation. The x-ray tube produces a pulsed x-ray beam (1–5 ms) using up to about 1,000 mA. (*Bushong, 8th ed., pp. 429–430*)

118. **(D)** The spinning-top test may be used to test timer accuracy in single-phase equipment. A spinning top is a metal disk with a small hole in its outer edge that is placed on a pedestal about 6 in. high. An exposure is made (e.g., 0.1 s) while the top spins. Because a full-wave-rectified unit produces 120 x-ray photon impulses per second, in 0.1 s the film should record 12 dots (if the timer is accurate). Because three-phase equipment produces almost constant potential rather than pulsed radiation, the standard spinning top cannot be used. An oscilloscope or synchronous spinning top must be employed to test the timers of three-phase equipment. (*Selman, 9th ed., p. 106*)

119. **(D)** A synchronous spinning-top test is used to test timer accuracy or rectifier function in three-phase equipment. Because three-phase, full-wave-rectified current would expose a 360-degree arc each second, a 60-ms (0.06-s) exposure should expose a 21.6-degree arc (360 degrees × 0.06 = 21.6 degrees). Anything more or less indicates timer inaccuracy. If exactly one-half the expected arc appears, rectifier failure should be suspected. (*Selman, 9th ed., p. 106*)

120. **(D)** DXA imaging is used to evaluate bone mineral density (BMD). It is the most widely used method of *bone densitometry*—it is *low-dose, precise,* and *uncomplicated* to use/perform. DXA uses *two photon energies*—one for soft tissue and one for bone. Since bone is denser and attenuates x-ray photons more readily, their *attenuation is calculated* to represent the degree of bone density. Bone densitometry/DXA can be used to evaluate bone mineral content of the body or part of it, to diagnosis osteoporosis, or to evaluate the effectiveness of treatments for osteoporosis. (*Frank, Long, and Smith, 11th ed., vol. 3, pp. 454–455*)

Subspecialty List

51. Imaging equipment
52. Principles of radiation physics
53. Imaging equipment
54. Imaging equipment
55. Imaging equipment
56. Imaging equipment
57. Principles of radiation physics
58. Quality control of imaging equipment and accessories
59. Quality control of imaging equipment and accessories
60. Imaging equipment
61. Quality control of imaging equipment and accessories
62. Imaging equipment
63. Imaging equipment
64. Imaging equipment
65. Quality control of imaging equipment and accessories
66. Quality control of imaging equipment and accessories
67. Imaging equipment
68. Quality control of imaging equipment and accessories
69. Imaging equipment
70. Imaging equipment
71. Imaging equipment
72. Quality control of imaging equipment and accessories
73. Imaging equipment
74. Principles of radiation physics
75. Imaging equipment
76. Principles of radiation physics
77. Imaging equipment
78. Imaging equipment
79. Quality control of imaging equipment and accessories
80. Imaging equipment
81. Imaging equipment
82. Imaging equipment
83. Imaging equipment
84. Imaging equipment
85. Quality control of imaging equipment and accessories
86. Imaging equipment
87. Imaging equipment
88. Imaging equipment
89. Imaging equipment
90. Quality control of imaging equipment and accessories
91. Imaging equipment
92. Imaging equipment
93. Imaging equipment
94. Imaging equipment
95. Imaging equipment
96. Quality control of imaging equipment and accessories
97. Quality control of imaging equipment and accessories
98. Quality control of imaging equipment and accessories
99. Quality control of imaging equipment and accessories
100. Imaging equipment
101. Imaging equipment
102. Imaging equipment
103. Imaging equipment
104. Principles of radiation physics
105. Imaging equipment
106. Principles of radiation physics
107. Quality control of imaging equipment and accessories
108. Imaging equipment
109. Imaging equipment
110. Quality control of imaging equipment and accessories
111. Imaging equipment
112. Imaging equipment
113. Imaging equipment
114. Imaging equipment
115. Principles of radiation physics
116. Imaging equipment
117. Imaging equipment
118. Quality control of imaging equipment and accessories
119. Quality control of imaging equipment and accessories
120. Imaging equipment

CHAPTER 6

Practice Test 1
Questions

DIRECTIONS (Questions 1 through 200): Each of the numbered items or incomplete statements in this section is followed by answers or by completions of the statement. Select the *one* lettered answer or completion that is *best* in each case.

1. The drug acetaminophen is classified as a(n)

    (A) diuretic
    (B) antipyretic
    (C) antihistamine
    (D) emetic

2. A graphic diagram of signal values representing various densities within the part being imaged is called a

    (A) processing algorithm
    (B) DICOM
    (C) histogram
    (D) window

3. Which of the following is (are) characteristic(s) of anemia?

    1. Decreased number of circulating red blood cells
    2. Decreased hemoglobin
    3. Hematuria

    (A) 1 only
    (B) 1 and 2 only
    (C) 1 and 3 only
    (D) 1, 2, and 3

4. A positive contrast agent

    1. absorbs x-ray photons
    2. results in a dark area on the radiograph
    3. is composed of elements having low atomic number

    (A) 1 only
    (B) 1 and 2 only
    (C) 2 and 3 only
    (D) 1, 2, and 3

5. An exposure was made using 300 mA and 50 ms. If the exposure time is changed to 22 ms, which of the following milliamperage selections would *most* closely approximate the original radiographic density?

    (A) 300 mA
    (B) 400 mA
    (C) 600 mA
    (D) 700 mA

6. It is recommended that a thermoluminescent dosimeter (TLD) or film badge be worn

    (A) under the lead apron at waist level
    (B) outside the lead apron at waist level
    (C) under the lead apron at collar level
    (D) outside the lead apron at collar level

7. The mediolateral projection of the knee shown in Figure 6–1 could *best* be improved by

   (A) rotating the patient forward
   (B) rotating the patient backward
   (C) angling the central ray (CR) about 5 degrees caudad
   (D) angling the CR about 5 degrees cephalad

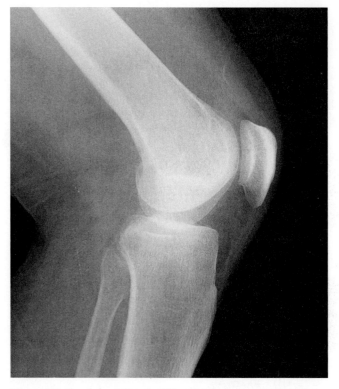

Figure 6–1. Courtesy of Stamford Hospital, Department of Radiology.

8. Which of the following types of adult tissue is (are) comparatively insensitive to effects of ionizing radiation?

   1. Epithelial tissue
   2. Nerve tissue
   3. Muscle tissue

   (A) 1 only
   (B) 1 and 2 only
   (C) 2 and 3 only
   (D) 1, 2, and 3

9. Which of the following exposures would most likely deliver the greatest dose to the thyroid?

   (A) AP skull
   (B) PA skull
   (C) PA esophagus
   (D) PA chest

10. Which of the dose–response curves shown in Figure 6–2 illustrate(s) a direct relationship between dose and response?

   1. Curve number 1
   2. Curve number 2
   3. Curve number 3

   (A) 1 only
   (B) 2 only
   (C) 1 and 3 only
   (D) 1, 2, and 3

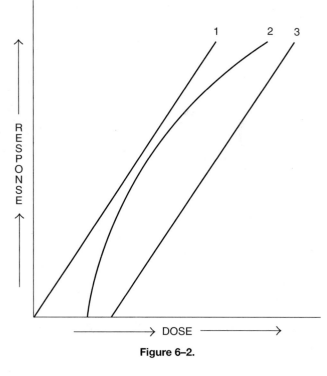

Figure 6–2.

11. The carpal scaphoid can be demonstrated in which of the following projection(s) of the wrist?

1. PA oblique
2. PA with radial flexion
3. PA with elbow elevated 20 degrees

(A) 1 only
(B) 1 and 2 only
(C) 1 and 3 only
(D) 1, 2, and 3

12. A patient who has been recumbent for some time and gets up quickly may suffer from light-headedness or feel faint. This is referred to as

(A) dyspnea
(B) orthopnea
(C) hypertension
(D) orthostatic hypotension

13. Dorsal decubitus projections of the chest are used to evaluate small amounts of

1. fluid in the posterior chest
2. air in the posterior chest
3. fluid in the anterior chest

(A) 1 only
(B) 1 and 2 only
(C) 2 and 3 only
(D) 1, 2, and 3

14. Which of the following is (are) evaluation criteria for a PA chest radiograph of the heart and lungs?

1. Ten posterior ribs should be seen above the diaphragm.
2. The medial ends of the clavicles should be equidistant from the vertebral column.
3. The scapulae should be seen through the upper lung fields.

(A) 1 only
(B) 1 and 2 only
(C) 2 and 3 only
(D) 1, 2, and 3

15. The housing surrounding an x-ray tube functions to

1. retain heat within the glass envelope
2. protect from electric shock
3. keep leakage radiation to a minimum

(A) 1 and 2 only
(B) 1 and 3 only
(C) 2 and 3 only
(D) 1, 2, and 3

16. When interviewing a patient, what is it that the health care professional can observe?

(A) Symptoms
(B) History
(C) Objective signs
(D) Chief complaint

17. The effective energy of an x-ray beam is increased by increasing the

1. added filtration
2. kilovoltage
3. milliamperage

(A) 1 only
(B) 2 only
(C) 1 and 2 only
(D) 1, 2, and 3

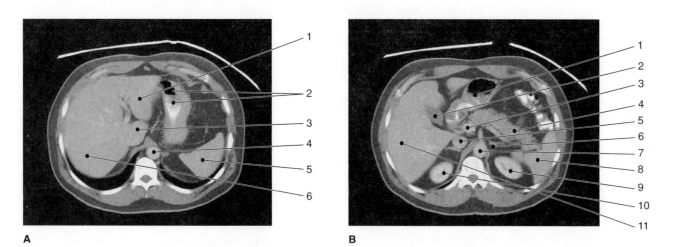

Figure 6–3A&B. Courtesy of Stamford Hospital, Department of Radiology.

18. Which of the following statements is *true* with regard to the two CT images seen in Figure 6–3?

    1. Image A illustrates more superior structures.
    2. The images are sagittal reconstructions.
    3. The examination was performed without artificial contrast.

    (A) 1 only
    (B) 1 and 3 only
    (C) 2 and 3 only
    (D) 1, 2, and 3

19. The structure labeled number 2 in Figure 6–3, image B is the

    (A) caudate lobe of liver
    (B) duodenum
    (C) colon
    (D) gallbladder

20. Drugs that may be used to prolong blood clotting time include

    1. heparin
    2. diphenhydramine (Benadryl)
    3. lidocaine

    (A) 1 only
    (B) 1 and 2 only
    (C) 1 and 3 only
    (D) 1, 2, and 3

21. Characteristics of a patient with pulmonary emphysema include

    1. shoulder girdle elevation
    2. increased AP diameter of the chest
    3. hyperventilation

    (A) 1 only
    (B) 1 and 2 only
    (C) 2 and 3 only
    (D) 1, 2, and 3

22. Which among the following components is (are) part of the gantry of a CT imaging system?

    1. X-ray tube
    2. Detector array
    3. Control panel

    (A) 1 only
    (B) 1 and 2 only
    (C) 2 and 3 only
    (D) 1, 2, and 3

23. Which of the following is (are) included in whole-body dose equivalents?

    1. Gonads
    2. Lens
    3. Extremities

    (A) 1 only
    (B) 1 and 2 only
    (C) 2 and 3 only
    (D) 1, 2, and 3

24. Which of the following is the approximate skin dose for 5 minutes of fluoroscopy performed at 1.5 mA?

    (A) 3.7 rad
    (B) 7.5 rad
    (C) 15 rad
    (D) 21 rad

25. To radiograph an infant for suspected free air within the abdominal cavity, which of the following projections of the abdomen will demonstrate the condition with the *least* patient exposure?

    (A) PA erect with grid
    (B) Right lateral decubitus with grid
    (C) Right lateral decubitus without grid
    (D) Recumbent AP without grid

26. Which of the following is an AP oblique projection (lateral rotation) of the elbow demonstrates?

    1. Radial head free of superimposition
    2. Capitulum of the humerus
    3. Olecranon process within the olecranon fossa

    (A) 1 only
    (B) 1 and 2 only
    (C) 2 and 3 only
    (D) 1, 2, and 3

27. Which of the following x-ray circuit devices operate(s) on the principle of mutual induction?

    1. High-voltage transformer
    2. Filament transformer
    3. Autotransformer

    (A) 1 only
    (B) 1 and 2 only
    (C) 1 and 3 only
    (D) 1, 2, and 3

28. Pathologic or abnormal conditions that would require an *increase* in exposure factors include all of the following *except*

    (A) atelectasis
    (B) pneumoperitoneum
    (C) Paget disease
    (D) congestive heart failure

29. The risk of inoculation with HIV is considered high for which of the following entry sites?

    1. Broken skin
    2. Perinatal exposure
    3. Accidental needle stick

    (A) 1 only
    (B) 1 and 2 only
    (C) 2 and 3 only
    (D) 1, 2, and 3

30. Which of the following medication routes refers to the term *parenteral*?

1. Subcutaneous
2. Intramuscular
3. Oral

   (A) 1 only
   (B) 1 and 2 only
   (C) 2 and 3 only
   (D) 1, 2, and 3

31. The position illustrated in Figure 6–4 can be used successfully to demonstrate the

1. PA oblique sternum
2. barium-filled pylorus and duodenum
3. left anterior ribs

   (A) 1 only
   (B) 1 and 2 only
   (C) 2 and 3 only
   (D) 1, 2, and 3

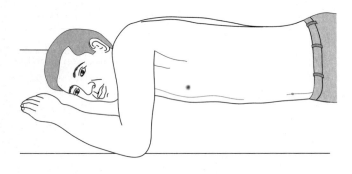

Figure 6–4.

32. The AP axial projection of the pulmonary apices requires the CR to be directed

   (A) 15 degrees cephalad
   (B) 15 degrees caudad
   (C) 30 degrees cephalad
   (D) 30 degrees caudad

33. Which of the following is an acceptable approximate entrance skin exposure (ESE) for a PA chest radiograph?

   (A) 6 mR
   (B) 20 mR
   (C) 38 mR
   (D) 0.6 R

34. Typical patient demographic and examination information include(s)

1. type of examination
2. accession number
3. date and time of examination

   (A) 1 only
   (B) 1 and 2 only
   (C) 2 and 3 only
   (D) 1, 2, and 3

35. Differences between body habitus types are likely to affect all the following *except*

   (A) the size and shape of an organ
   (B) the position of an organ
   (C) the position of the diaphragm
   (D) the degree of bone porosity

36. The fact that x-ray intensity across the primary beam can vary as much as 45% describes the

   (A) line-focus principle
   (B) transformer law
   (C) anode heel effect
   (D) inverse-square law

37. Which of the x-ray circuit devices shown in Figure 6–5 operates on the principle of self-induction?

(A) Number 1
(B) Number 3
(C) Number 5
(D) Number 7

38. Referring to the simplified x-ray circuit shown in Figure 6–5, what is indicated by the number 3?

(A) Step-up transformer
(B) Autotransformer
(C) Filament circuit
(D) Rectification system

39. Another name for Hirschsprung's disease, the most common cause of lower GI obstruction in neonates, is

(A) intussusception
(B) volvulus
(C) congenital megacolon
(D) pyloric stenosis

40. Which of the following terms/units is used to express the resolution of a diagnostic image?

(A) Line pairs per millimeter (lp/mm)
(B) Speed
(C) Latitude
(D) Kiloelectronvolts (keV)

41. The advantages of high-frequency generators over earlier types of generators include

1. smaller size
2. nearly constant potential
3. lower patient dose

(A) 1 only
(B) 1 and 2 only
(C) 1 and 3 only
(D) 1, 2 and 3

42. A radiograph exposed using a 12:1 ratio grid may exhibit a loss of density at its lateral edges because the

(A) SID was too great
(B) grid failed to move during the exposure
(C) x-ray tube was angled in the direction of the lead strips
(D) CR was off-center

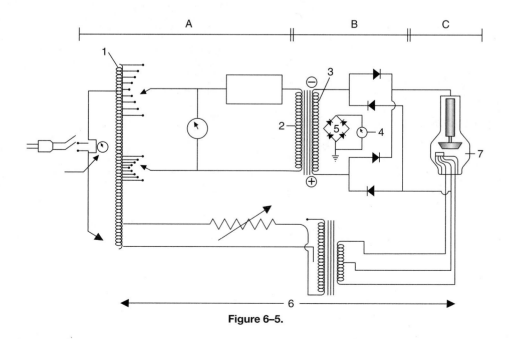

Figure 6–5.

43. In what order should the following examinations be scheduled?

1. Upper GI
2. Intravenous pyelogram (IVP)
3. Barium enema (BE)

(A) 3, 1, 2
(B) 1, 3, 2
(C) 2, 1, 3
(D) 2, 3, 1

44. The *best* projection to demonstrate the articular surfaces of the femoropatellar articulation is the

(A) AP knee
(B) PA knee
(C) tangential ("sunrise") projection
(D) tunnel view

45. Which of the following is (are) valid evaluation criteria for a lateral projection of the forearm?

1. The radius and the ulna should be superimposed distally.
2. The coronoid process and the radial head should be partially superimposed.
3. The humeral epicondyles should be superimposed.

(A) 1 only
(B) 1 and 2 only
(C) 2 and 3 only
(D) 1, 2, and 3

46. In amorphous selenium flat-panel detectors, the term *amorphous* refers to a

(A) crystalline material having typical crystalline structure
(B) crystalline material lacking typical crystalline structure
(C) toxic crystalline material
(D) homogeneous crystalline material

47. The National Council on Radiation Protection and Measurements (NCRP) recommends an annual occupational effective (stochastic) dose equivalent limit of

(A) 50 mSv (5 rem)
(B) 100 mSv (10 rem)
(C) 25 mSv (2.5 rem)
(D) 200 mSv (20 rem)

48. The image in Figure 6–6 was obtained while testing

(A) rectifier operation in a single-phase x-ray machine
(B) rectifier operation in a three-phase x-ray machine
(C) timer accuracy in a single-phase x-ray machine
(D) timer accuracy in a three-phase x-ray machine

49. All the following procedures demonstrate renal function *except*

(A) IVP
(B) descending urography
(C) retrograde urography
(D) infusion nephrotomography

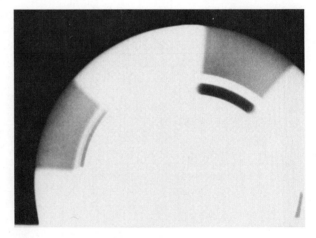

Figure 6–6.

50. To eject a K-shell electron from a tungsten atom, the incoming electron must have an energy of *at least*

(A) 60 keV

(B) 70 keV

(C) 80 keV

(D) 90 keV

51. The sternoclavicular joints will be *best* demonstrated in which of the following positions?

(A) Apical lordotic

(B) Anterior oblique

(C) Lateral

(D) Weight-bearing

52. The output phosphor can be coupled with the Vidicon TV camera or charge-coupled device (CCD) via

1. fiber optics
2. an image distributor or lens
3. closed-circuit TV

(A) 1 only

(B) 1 and 2 only

(C) 2 and 3 only

(D) 1, 2, and 3

53. The *most frequent* site of hospital-acquired infection is the

(A) urinary tract

(B) blood

(C) respiratory tract

(D) digestive tract

54. Which of the following statements is (are) *true* regarding the control dosimeter that accompanies each shipment of personal radiation monitors?

1. It should be stored away from all radiation sources.
2. It should be stored in the main work area.
3. It should be used to replace an employee's lost monitor.

(A) 1 only

(B) 2 only

(C) 1 and 3 only

(D) 2 and 3 only

55. Continuous rotation of the CT x-ray tube and detector array, with simultaneous movement of the CT couch, has been accomplished through implementation of

(A) additional cables

(B) slip rings

(C) multiple rows of detectors

(D) electron beam CT

56. The late effects of radiation are considered to

1. have no threshold dose
2. be directly related to dose
3. occur within hours of exposure

(A) 1 only

(B) 1 and 2 only

(C) 2 and 3 only

(D) 1, 2, and 3

57. A satisfactory radiograph was made without a grid using a 72-in. SID and 8 mAs. If the distance is changed to 40 in. and an 12:1 ratio grid is added, what should be the new milliampere-seconds value?

(A) 9.5 mAs

(B) 12 mAs

(C) 21 mAs

(D) 26 mAs

58. Which of the following involve(s) intentional misconduct?

    1. Invasion of privacy
    2. False imprisonment
    3. Patient sustaining injury from a fall while left unattended

    (A) 1 only
    (B) 3 only
    (C) 1 and 2 only
    (D) 2 and 3 only

59. The brightness level of the fluoroscopic image depends on

    1. milliamperage
    2. kilovoltage
    3. patient thickness

    (A) 1 only
    (B) 1 and 2 only
    (C) 1 and 3 only
    (D) 1, 2, and 3

60. Which of the following contribute to the radiographic contrast present in a film/screen radiograph?

    1. Tissue density
    2. Pathology
    3. Muscle development

    (A) 1 and 2 only
    (B) 1 and 3 only
    (C) 2 and 3 only
    (D) 1, 2, and 3

61. In 1906, Bergonié and Tribondeau theorized that undifferentiated cells are highly radiosensitive. Which of the following is (are) characteristic(s) of undifferentiated cells?

    1. Young cells
    2. Highly mitotic cells
    3. Precursor cells

    (A) 1 only
    (B) 1 and 2 only
    (C) 1 and 3 only
    (D) 1, 2, and 3

62. The submentovertical (SMV) oblique axial projection of the zygomatic arches requires that the skull be rotated

    (A) 15 degrees toward the affected side
    (B) 15 degrees away from the affected side
    (C) 45 degrees toward the affected side
    (D) 45 degrees away from the affected side

63. The radiograph of the pelvis shown in Figure 6–7 is unacceptable because of

    (A) motion
    (B) inadequate penetration
    (C) scattered radiation fog
    (D) excessive density

64. The effect that differential absorption has on radiographic contrast of a high-subject-contrast part can be minimized by

    1. using a compensating filter
    2. using high-kilovoltage exposure factors
    3. increased collimation

    (A) 1 only
    (B) 1 and 2 only
    (C) 2 and 3 only
    (D) 1, 2, and 3

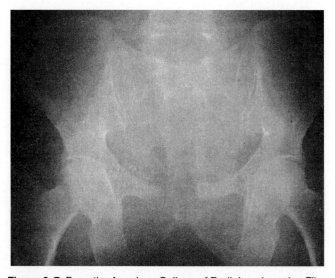

Figure 6–7. From the American College of Radiology Learning File. Courtesy of the ACR.

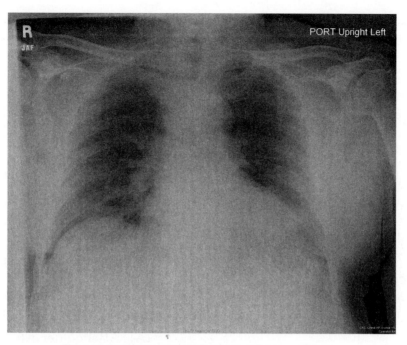

Figure 6–8. Courtesy FUJIFILM Medical Systems USA, Inc.

65. The chest radiograph shown in Figure 6–8 demonstrates

(A) breathing motion
(B) aliasing artifact
(C) double exposure
(D) off-level grid cutoff

66. Which of the following is *most likely* to occur as a result of using a 30-in. SID with a 14 × 17 in. IR to radiograph a fairly homogeneous structure?

(A) Production of quantum mottle
(B) Density variation between opposite ends of the IR
(C) Production of scatter radiation fog
(D) Excessively short-scale contrast

67. Which of the following is (are) correct regarding care of protective leaded apparel?

1. Lead aprons should be fluoroscoped yearly to check for cracks.
2. Lead gloves should be fluoroscoped yearly to check for cracks.
3. Lead aprons should be hung on appropriate racks when not in use.

(A) 1 only
(B) 1 and 2 only
(C) 1 and 3 only
(D) 1, 2, and 3

68. The primary function of filtration is to reduce

(A) patient skin dose
(B) operator dose
(C) image noise
(D) scattered radiation

69. Which of the following is (are) considered long-term somatic effect(s) of exposure to ionizing radiation?

    1. Life-span shortening
    2. Carcinogenesis
    3. Cataractogenesis

    (A) 1 only
    (B) 1 and 2 only
    (C) 2 and 3 only
    (D) 1, 2, and 3

70. Advantages of digital radiography (DR) over computed radiography (CR) include

    1. DR is less expensive
    2. DR has immediate readout
    3. Cassettes are not needed for DR

    (A) 1 only
    (B) 1 and 2 only
    (C) 2 and 3 only
    (D) 1, 2, and 3

71. The collimator light and actual irradiated area must be accurate to within

    (A) 2% of the SID
    (B) 5% of the SID
    (C) 10% of the SID
    (D) 15% of the SID

72. All the following statements regarding the bony thorax are true *except*

    (A) the first seven pairs of ribs are referred to as vertebrosternal, or true, ribs
    (B) the only articulation between the thorax and the upper extremity is the sternoclavicular joint
    (C) the gladiolus is the upper part of the sternum and is quadrilateral in shape
    (D) the anterior ends of the ribs are about 4 in. below the level of the vertebral ends

73. Several types of exposure timers may be found on x-ray equipment. Which of the following types of timers is the most accurate?

    (A) Synchronous
    (B) Impulse
    (C) Electronic
    (D) Transformer

74. The two types of cells in the body are

    (A) connective and nerve
    (B) genetic and connective
    (C) somatic and nerve
    (D) somatic and genetic

75. The lesser tubercle of the humerus will be visualized in profile in the

    (A) AP shoulder external rotation radiograph
    (B) AP shoulder internal rotation radiograph
    (C) AP elbow radiograph
    (D) Lateral elbow radiograph

76. Which one of the following is (are) used to control the production of scattered radiation?

    1. Collimators
    2. Optimal kV
    3. Use of grids

    (A) 1 only
    (B) 1 and 2 only
    (C) 2 and 3 only
    (D) 1, 2, and 3

77. With the patient in an erect 45-degree LPO and the CR directed 2 in. medial and 2 in. lateral to the upper outer border of the shoulder, which of the following will be visualized to best advantage?

    (A) Coronoid process free of superimposition
    (B) Coracoid process free of superimposition
    (C) Glenoid cavity in profile
    (D) Greater tubercle in profile

78. Which of the following groups of exposure factors would deliver the *lowest* patient dose?

(A) 2.5 mAs, 100 kVp
(B) 5 mAs, 90 kVp
(C) 5 mAs, 70 kVp
(D) 10 mAs, 80 kVp

79. Brightness and contrast resolution in digital imaging can be influenced by

1. window level (WL)
2. window width (WW)
3. look-up table (LUT)

(A) 1 only
(B) 1 and 2 only
(C) 2 and 3 only
(D) 1, 2, and 3

80. Acceptable method(s) of minimizing motion unsharpness is (are)

1. suspended respiration
2. short exposure time
3. patient instruction

(A) 1 only
(B) 1 and 2 only
(C) 1 and 3 only
(D) 1, 2, and 3

81. If a quantity of radiation is delivered to a body over a short period of time, its effect

(A) will be greater than if it were delivered over a long period of time
(B) depends solely on the distance factor
(C) has no relation to how it is delivered in time
(D) depends solely on the radiation quantity

82. According to the line-focus principle, an anode with a small angle provides

1. improved recorded detail
2. improved heat capacity
3. less heel effect

(A) 1 and 2 only
(B) 1 and 3 only
(C) 2 and 3 only
(D) 1, 2, and 3

83. Which section of the automatic processor shown in Figure 6–9 acts upon unexposed silver grains?

(A) Section 1
(B) Section 2
(C) Section 3
(D) Section 4

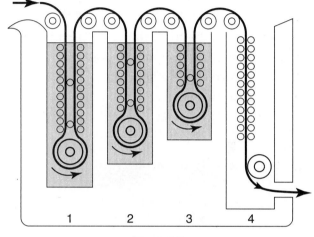

Figure 6–9.

84. Which of the following expresses the *gonadal dose* that, if received by every member of the population, would be expected to produce the same total genetic effect on that population as the actual doses received by each of the individuals?

(A) Genetically significant dose
(B) Somatically significant dose
(C) Maximum permissible dose
(D) Lethal dose

85. A patient with an upper respiratory tract infection is transported to the radiology department for a chest examination. Who should be masked?

1. Technologist
2. Transporter
3. Patient

(A) 1 only
(B) 1 and 2 only
(C) 3 only
(D) 1, 2, and 3

86. The kV settings on radiographic equipment must be tested annually and must be accurate to within

    (A) +/− 2 kV
    (B) +/− 4 kV
    (C) +/− 6 kV
    (D) +/− 8 kV

87. The radiograph shown in Figure 6–10 exhibits a loss of radiographic density as a result of

    (A) x-ray tube angulation across grid lines
    (B) exceeding the focusing distance
    (C) incorrect grid placement
    (D) insufficient SID

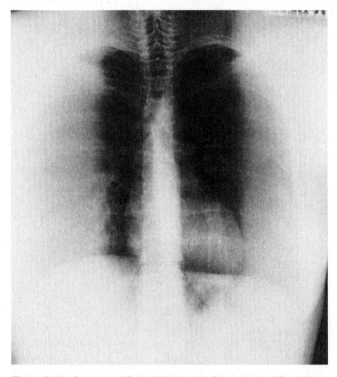

Figure 6–10. Courtesy of Stamford Hospital, Department of Radiology.

88. Which of the following waveforms has the lowest percentage voltage ripple?

    (A) Single-phase
    (B) Three-phase, six-pulse
    (C) Three-phase, 12-pulse
    (D) High-frequency

89. The reduction in x-ray photon intensity as the photon passes through a material is termed

    (A) anode heel effect
    (B) grid cut-off
    (C) attenuation
    (D) divergence

90. To demonstrate the glenoid fossa in profile, the patient is positioned

    (A) 45 degrees oblique, affected side up
    (B) 45 degrees oblique, affected side down
    (C) 25 degrees oblique, affected side up
    (D) 25 degrees oblique, affected side down

91. Which of the following groups of exposure factors will produce the shortest scale of contrast?

    (A) 200 mA, 0.25 s, 70 kVp, 12:1 grid
    (B) 500 mA, 0.10 s, 90 kVp, 8:1 grid
    (C) 400 mA, 0.125 s, 80 kVp, 12:1 grid
    (D) 300 mA, 0.16 s, 70 kVp, 8:1 grid

92. Which of the following is the most likely site for a lumbar puncture?

    (A) S1–2
    (B) L3–4
    (C) L1–2
    (D) C6–7

93. How are LET and biologic response related?

    (A) They are inversely related.
    (B) They are directly related.
    (C) They are related in a reciprocal fashion.
    (D) They are unrelated.

94. An increase in the kilovoltage applied to the x-ray tube increases the

    1. percentage of high-energy photons produced
    2. exposure rate
    3. patient absorption

    (A) 1 only
    (B) 1 and 2 only
    (C) 2 and 3 only
    (D) 1, 2, and 3

95. Which of the following is/are associated with magnification fluoroscopy?

    1. Higher patient dose than nonmagnification fluoroscopy
    2. Higher voltage to the focusing lenses
    3. Image intensifier focal point closer to the input phosphor

    (A) 1 only
    (B) 1 and 2 only
    (C) 2 and 3 only
    (D) 1, 2, and 3

96. Replacing 200-speed intensifying screens with 400-speed screens will

    1. require the exposure to be cut in half
    2. enable the radiographer to decrease the exposure time
    3. increase the production of scattered radiation

    (A) 1 only
    (B) 1 and 2 only
    (C) 1 and 3 only
    (D) 1, 2, and 3

97. The structure indicated by the number 2 in Figure 6–11 is the

    (A) ascending colon
    (B) descending colon
    (C) transverse colon
    (D) sigmoid colon

98. The structure indicated by the number 5 in Figure 6–11 is the

    (A) sigmoid
    (B) ileum
    (C) cecum
    (D) ascending colon

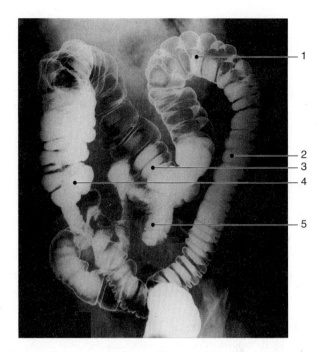

Figure 6–11. Courtesy of Stamford Hospital, Department of Radiology

99. Geometric unsharpness will be *least obvious*

    1. at long SIDs
    2. with small focal spots
    3. at the anode end of the image

    (A) 1 only
    (B) 1 and 2 only
    (C) 2 and 3 only
    (D) 1, 2, and 3

100. Which of the following conditions require(s) a decrease in technical factors?

    1. Emphysema
    2. Osteomalacia
    3. Atelectasis

    (A) 1 only
    (B) 1 and 2 only
    (C) 2 and 3 only
    (D) 1, 2, and 3

101. Which of the following cells is the *least* radiosensitive?

    (A) Myelocytes
    (B) Myocytes
    (C) Megakaryocytes
    (D) Erythroblasts

102. Which of the following is (are) characteristic(s) of a 16:1 grid?

    1. It absorbs more useful radiation than an 8:1 grid.
    2. It has more centering latitude than an 8:1 grid.
    3. It is used with higher-kilovoltage exposures than an 8:1 grid.

    (A) 1 only
    (B) 1 and 3 only
    (C) 2 and 3 only
    (D) 1, 2, and 3

103. An exposure was made at 40-in. SID using 5 mAs and 105 kVp with an 8:1 grid. In an effort to improve radiographic contrast, the image is repeated using a 12:1 grid and 90 kVp. Which of the following exposure times will be *most appropriate*, using 400 mA, to maintain the original density?

    (A) 0.01 s
    (B) 0.03 s
    (C) 0.1 s
    (D) 0.3 s

104. All the following statements regarding three-phase current are true *except*

    (A) three-phase current is constant-potential direct current
    (B) three-phase equipment produces more x-rays per milliampere-second
    (C) three-phase equipment produces higher-average-energy x-rays than single-phase equipment
    (D) the three-phase waveform has less ripple than the single-phase waveform

105. The pyloric canal and duodenal bulb are *best* demonstrated during an upper GI series in which of the following positions?

    (A) RAO
    (B) Left lateral
    (C) Recumbent PA
    (D) Recumbent AP

106. The most common cause of x-ray tube failure is

    (A) a cracked anode
    (B) a pitted anode
    (C) vaporized tungsten on glass envelope
    (D) insufficient heat production

107. If a radiograph were made of an average-size knee using automatic exposure control (AEC) and all three photocells were selected, the resulting radiograph would demonstrate

    (A) excessive density
    (B) insufficient density
    (C) poor detail
    (D) adequate exposure

108. With milliamperage adjusted to produce equal exposures, all the following statements are true *except*

    (A) A single-phase examination done at 10 mAs can be duplicated with three-phase, 12-pulse at 5 mAs.
    (B) There is greater patient dose with three-phase equipment than with single-phase equipment.
    (C) Three-phase equipment can produce comparable radiographs with less heat unit (HU) buildup.
    (D) Three-phase equipment produces lower-contrast radiographs than single-phase equipment.

109. In which of the following examinations would a cassette front with very low absorption properties be especially desirable?

    (A) Extremity radiography
    (B) Abdominal radiography
    (C) Mammography
    (D) Angiography

110. The regular measurement and evaluation of radiographic equipment components and their performance is most accurately termed

    (A) postprocessing
    (B) quality assurance
    (C) quality control
    (D) quality congruence

111. The radiograph in Figure 6–12 could be improved in which of the following ways?

    (A) The MSP should be 45 degrees to the plane of the IR.

    (B) The MSP should be 90 degrees to the plane of the cassette.

    (C) The chin should be elevated slightly.

    (D) The head should be flexed slightly.

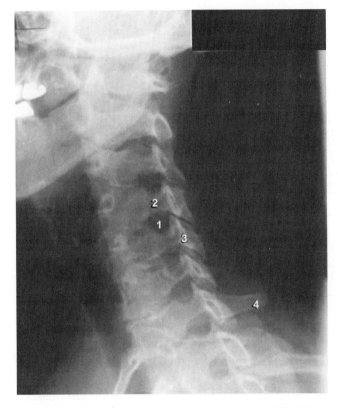

Figure 6–12. Courtesy of Stamford Hospital, Department of Radiology.

112. What is the anatomic structure indicated by the number 3 in the radiograph in Figure 6–12?

    (A) Spinous process

    (B) Transverse process

    (C) Pedicle

    (D) Intervertebral foramen

113. With the patient positioned as shown in Figure 6–13, how should the CR be directed to *best* demonstrate the intercondyloid fossa?

    (A) Perpendicular to the popliteal depression

    (B) 40 degrees caudad to the popliteal depression

    (C) Perpendicular to the long axis of the femur

    (D) 40 degrees cephalad to the popliteal depression

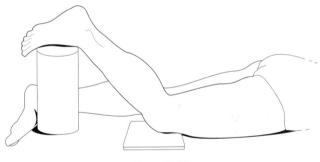

Figure 6–13.

114. The cardiopulmonary resuscitation (CPR) procedure for infants differs from that of adults with respect to

    1. hand placement
    2. number of compressions
    3. volume of air delivered

    (A) 1 and 2 only

    (B) 1 and 3 only

    (C) 2 and 3 only

    (D) 1, 2, and 3

115. The decision as to whether to deliver ionic or nonionic contrast medium should include a preliminary patient history including, but not limited to

1. patient age
2. history of respiratory disease
3. history of cardiac disease

(A) 1 and 2
(B) 1 and 3
(C) 2 and 3
(D) 1, 2, and 3

116. Which of the following is a functional study used to demonstrate the degree of AP motion present in the cervical spine?

(A) Moving mandible position
(B) AP open-mouth projection
(C) Flexion and extension laterals
(D) AP right and left bending

117. At what frequency must the radiographic equipment be checked for linearity and reproducibility?

(A) Annually
(B) Biannually
(C) Semiannually
(D) Quarterly

118. Which of the labeled bones in Figure 6–14 identifies the tarsal navicular?

(A) Number 2
(B) Number 3
(C) Number 6
(D) Number 7

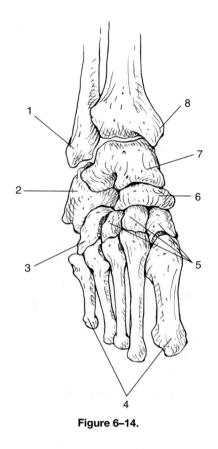

Figure 6–14.

119. What does the number 8 in Figure 6–14 identify?

(A) Medial malleolus
(B) Lateral malleolus
(C) Medial cuneiform
(D) Talus

120. Routine excretory urography usually includes a postmicturition radiograph of the bladder. This is done to demonstrate

1. tumor masses
2. residual urine
3. prostatic enlargement

(A) 2 only
(B) 1 and 3 only
(C) 2 and 3 only
(D) 1, 2, and 3

121. TV camera tubes used in image intensification, such as the Plumbicon and Vidicon, function to

     (A) increase the brightness of the input-phosphor image

     (B) transfer the output-phosphor image to the TV monitor

     (C) focus and accelerate electrons toward the output phosphor

     (D) record the output-phosphor image on 16- or 35-mm film

122. Sterile technique is required when contrast agents are administered

     (A) through a nasogastric tube

     (B) intrathecally

     (C) rectally

     (D) orally

123. Which of the following groups of exposure factors would be *most appropriate* for a sthenic adult IVU?

     (A) 300 mA, 0.02 s, 72 kVp

     (B) 300 mA, 0.01 s, 82 kVp

     (C) 150 mA, 0.01 s, 94 kVp

     (D) 100 mA, 0.03 s, 82 kVp

124. Which of the four baselines illustrated in Figure 6–15 should be used for a lateral projection of facial bones?

     (A) Baseline 1

     (B) Baseline 2

     (C) Baseline 3

     (D) Baseline 4

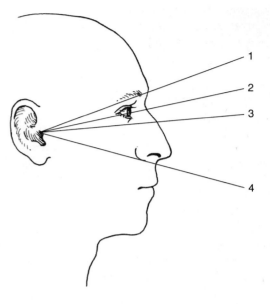

Figure 6–15.

125. Which of the following statements is (are) true regarding the radiograph shown in Figure 6–16?

     1. The part is rotated.
     2. The patient is not shielded correctly.
     3. There is excessive density.

     (A) 1 only

     (B) 2 only

     (C) 1 and 2 only

     (D) 1, 2, and 3

126. The radiation dose to an individual depends on which of the following?

     1. Type of tissue interaction(s)
     2. Quantity of radiation
     3. Biologic differences

     (A) 1 only

     (B) 1 and 2 only

     (C) 1 and 3 only

     (D) 1, 2, and 3

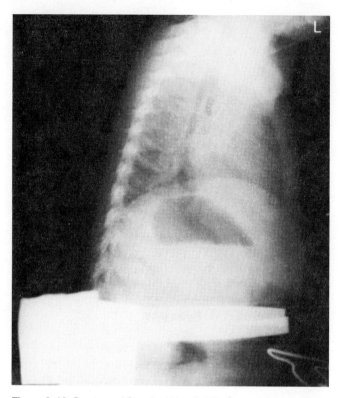

Figure 6–16. Courtesy of Stamford Hospital, Department of Radiology.

127. While measuring blood pressure, the first pulse that is heard is recorded as the

    (A) diastolic pressure
    (B) systolic pressure
    (C) venous pressure
    (D) valvular pressure

128. The AP oblique projection (Grashey method) of the glenoid fossa requires that the body is rotated

    (A) 35 to 45 degrees toward the unaffected side
    (B) 35 to 45 degrees toward the affected side
    (C) 15 to 20 degrees toward the affected side
    (D) 15 to 20 degrees toward the unaffected side

129. When the collimated field must extend past the edge of the body, allowing primary radiation to strike the tabletop, as in a lateral lumbar spine radiograph, what may be done to prevent excessive radiographic density owing to undercutting?

    (A) Reduce the milliampere-seconds.
    (B) Reduce the kilovoltage.
    (C) Use a shorter SID.
    (D) Use lead rubber to absorb tabletop primary radiation.

130. What is the name of the plane indicated by the number 1 in Figure 6–17?

    (A) Midcoronal plane
    (B) Midsagittal plane
    (C) Transverse plane
    (D) Horizontal plane

131. In which of the following procedures is quiet, shallow breathing recommended during the exposure to obliterate prominent pulmonary vascular markings?

    1. RAO sternum
    2. Lateral thoracic spine
    3. AP scapula

    (A) 1 only
    (B) 1 and 2 only
    (C) 2 and 3 only
    (D) 1, 2, and 3

132. The infection streptococcal pharyngitis ("strep throat") is caused by a

    (A) virus
    (B) fungus
    (C) protozoon
    (D) bacterium

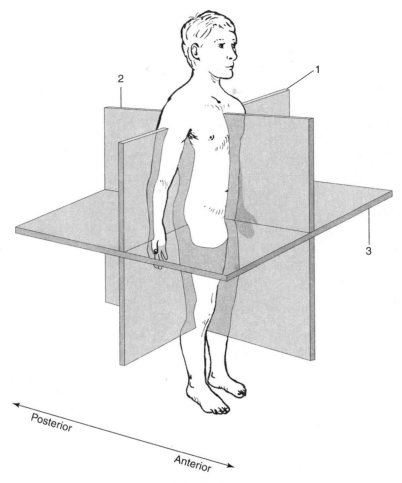

Posterior

Anterior

Figure 6–17.

133. Abdominal viscera located in the retroperitoneum include the

1. kidneys
2. duodenum
3. ascending and descending colon

(A) 1 only
(B) 1 and 2 only
(C) 2 and 3 only
(D) 1, 2, and 3

134. Exposure factors of 80 kVp and 8 mAs are used for a particular nongrid exposure. What should be the new milliampere-seconds value if an 8:1 grid is added?

(A) 16 mAs
(B) 24 mAs
(C) 32 mAs
(D) 40 mAs

135. The radiographic position illustrated in Figure 6–18 is used to demonstrate

(A) ethmoidal and frontal sinuses
(B) maxillary sinuses
(C) sphenoidal sinuses through the open mouth
(D) mastoid sinuses

136. Which of the following functions to protect the x-ray tube and the patient from overexposure in the event that the phototimer fails to terminate an exposure?

(A) Circuit breaker
(B) Fuse
(C) Backup timer
(D) Rheostat

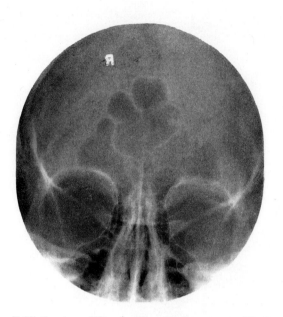

Figure 6–18. Courtesy of Stamford Hospital, Department of Radiology.

137. Which of the following positions can be used to effectively demonstrate the left colic flexure during radiographic examination of the large bowel?

   1. RAO
   2. LAO
   3. RPO

   (A) 1 only
   (B) 1 and 2 only
   (C) 1 and 3 only
   (D) 2 and 3 only

138. Which cholangiographic procedure uses an indwelling drainage tube for contrast medium administration?

   (A) Endoscopic retrograde cholangiographic pancreatography (ERCP)
   (B) Operative cholangiography
   (C) T-tube cholangiography
   (D) Percutaneous transhepatic cholangiography

139. Maslow's hierarchy of basic human needs includes which of the following?

   1. Self-esteem
   2. Love and belongingness
   3. Death with dignity

   (A) 1 only
   (B) 1 and 2 only
   (C) 2 and 3 only
   (D) 1, 2, and 3

140. Which of the following combinations would deliver the least amount of heat to the anode of a three-phase, 12-pulse x-ray unit?

   (A) 400 mA, 0.12 s, 90 kVp
   (B) 300 mA, ½ s, 70 kVp
   (C) 500 mA, 1/30 s, 85 kVp
   (D) 700 mA, 0.06 s, 120 kVp

141. Which of the following is *most likely* to permit the greatest decrease in patient exposure?

   (A) Increasing the mAs by half and decreasing the kVp by 15%
   (B) Increasing kilovoltage by 15% and cutting the milliampere-seconds value in half
   (C) Changing collimation from 10 × 12 to 14 × 17
   (D) Changing from an 8:1 grid technique to nongrid

142. Which of the following statements is (are) correct regarding the chest radiograph in Figure 6–19?

   1. Rotation of the chest is demonstrated.
   2. The pulmonary apices are not visualized.
   3. The costophrenic angles are demonstrated.

   (A) 1 only
   (B) 1 and 3 only
   (C) 2 and 3 only
   (D) 1, 2, and 3

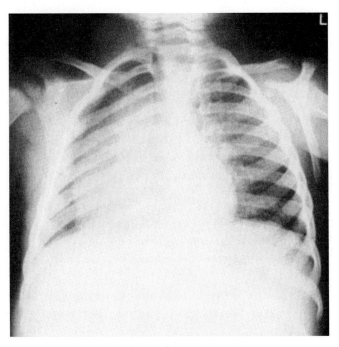

Figure 6–19. Courtesy of Stamford Hospital, Department of Radiology.

143. The major difference between excretory and retrograde urography is that

(A) they each require a different type of contrast agent

(B) intravenous studies require more images

(C) retrograde studies do not demonstrate function

(D) more contrast medium–induced adverse reactions occur in retrograde studies

144. In myelography, the contrast medium generally is injected into the

(A) cisterna magna

(B) individual intervertebral disks

(C) subarachnoid space between the first and second vertebrae

(D) subarachnoid space between the third and fourth lumbar vertebrae

145. Body substances and fluids that are considered infectious or potentially infectious include

1. feces
2. breast milk
3. wound drainage

(A) 1 only

(B) 1 and 2 only

(C) 2 and 3 only

(D) 1, 2, and 3

146. Which of the following is (are) demonstrated in the lateral projection of the cervical spine?

1. Intervertebral joints
2. Apophyseal joints
3. Intervertebral foramina

(A) 1 only

(B) 1 and 2 only

(C) 2 and 3 only

(D) 1, 2, and 3

147. Which of the following statements is (are) correct with respect to postoperative cholangiography?

1. A T-tube is in place in the common bile duct.
2. Water-soluble contrast material is injected.
3. The patency of biliary ducts is evaluated.

(A) 1 only

(B) 1 and 2 only

(C) 2 and 3 only

(D) 1, 2, and 3

148. If the entrance dose for a particular radiograph is 320 mR, the radiation exposure at 1 m from the patient will be approximately

(A) 32 mR

(B) 3.2 mR

(C) 0.32 mR

(D) 0.032 mR

149. What feature is used to display RIS information on current patients?

   (A) HIS
   (B) Modality work list
   (C) PACS
   (D) DICOM

150. Which of the following would be the safest interval of time for a fertile woman to undergo abdominal radiography without significant concern for irradiating a recently fertilized ovum?

   (A) The first 10 days following the cessation of menstruation
   (B) The first 10 days following the onset of menstruation
   (C) The 10 days preceding the onset of menstruation
   (D) About 14 days before menstruation

151. What is the anatomic structure indicated by number 1 in the radiograph shown in Figure 6–20?

   (A) Mandibular angle
   (B) Coronoid process
   (C) Zygomatic arch
   (D) Maxillary sinus

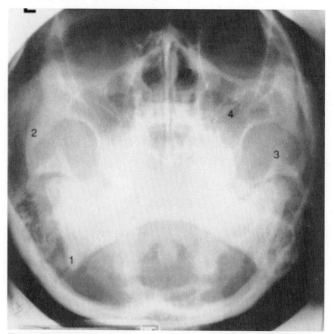

Figure 6–20. Courtesy of Stamford Hospital, Department of Radiology.

152. What is the anatomic structure indicated by number 3 in the radiograph in Figure 6–20?

   (A) Mandibular angle
   (B) Coronoid process
   (C) Zygomatic arch
   (D) Maxillary sinus

153. Esophageal varices are best demonstrated in which of the following positions?

   (A) Erect
   (B) Recumbent
   (C) Fowler
   (D) Sims

154. Greater latitude is available to the radiographer in film/screen imaging when using

   1. high-kilovoltage factors
   2. a small focal spot
   3. a high-ratio grid

   (A) 1 only
   (B) 1 and 2 only
   (C) 2 and 3 only
   (D) 1, 2, and 3

155. Recorded detail is directly related to

   1. SID
   2. tube current
   3. focal-spot size

   (A) 1 only
   (B) 1 and 2 only
   (C) 2 and 3 only
   (D) 1, 2, and 3

156. With the patient supine, the left side of the pelvis elevated 25 degrees, and the CR entering 1 in. medial to the left anterosuperior iliac spine (ASIS), which of the following is demonstrated?

   (A) Left sacroiliac joint
   (B) Left ilium
   (C) Right sacroiliac joint
   (D) Right ilium

157. Double-focus x-ray tubes have two

1. focal spots
2. filaments
3. anodes

(A) 1 only
(B) 1 and 2 only
(C) 1 and 3 only
(D) 2 and 3 only

158. What is the anatomic structure indicated by number 1 in the radiograph shown in Figure 6–21?

(A) Superior articular process
(B) Inferior articular process
(C) Transverse process
(D) Lamina

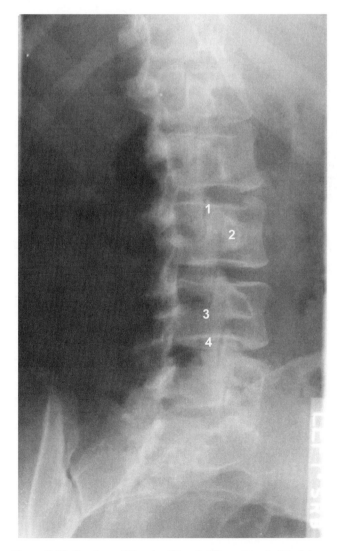

Figure 6–21. Courtesy of Stamford Hospital, Department of Radiology.

159. What is the anatomic structure indicated by number 3 in the radiograph in Figure 6–21?

(A) Superior articular process
(B) Inferior articular process
(C) Pedicle
(D) Lamina

160. Which of the following statements is (are) true regarding the lateral projection of the lumbar spine?

1. The MSP is parallel to the tabletop.
2. The vertebral foramina are well visualized.
3. The pedicles are well visualized.

(A) 1 only
(B) 1 and 2 only
(C) 1 and 3 only
(D) 1, 2, and 3

161. If a patient received 4,500 mrad during a 6-minute fluoroscopic examination, what was the dose rate?

(A) 0.75 rad/min
(B) 2.7 rad/min
(C) 7.5 rad/min
(D) 27 rad/hr

162. Which of the following is (are) essential to high-quality mammographic examinations?

1. Small focal spot x-ray tube
2. Short scale contrast
3. Use of a compression device

(A) 1 only
(B) 1 and 2 only
(C) 1 and 3 only
(D) 1, 2, and 3

163. An exposure was made at a 36-in. SID using 12 mAs and 75 kVp with a 400-speed imaging system and an 8:1 grid. A second radiograph is requested with improved recorded detail. Which of the following groups of technical factors will *best* accomplish this task?

(A) 15 mAs, 12:1 grid, 75 kVp, 400-speed system, 36-in. SID
(B) 15 mAs, 12:1 grid, 75 kVp, 400-speed system, 40-in. SID
(C) 30 mAs, 12:1 grid, 75 kVp, 200-speed system, 40-in. SID
(D) 12 mAs, 8:1 grid, 86 kVp, 200-speed system, 36-in. SID

164. What is the anatomic structure indicated by the number 7 in Figure 6–22?

(A) Coracoid process
(B) Coronoid process
(C) Trochlear notch
(D) Radial notch

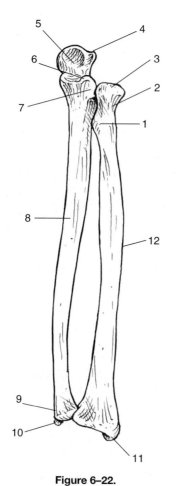

Figure 6–22.

165. Which of the following *correctly* identifies the head of the ulna in the illustration in Figure 6–22?

(A) Number 3
(B) Number 4
(C) Number 5
(D) Number 9

166. Which of the following statements is (are) *true* regarding the PA axial projection of the paranasal sinuses?

1. The CR is directed caudally to the orbito-meatal line (OML).
2. The petrous pyramids are projected into the lower third of the orbits.
3. The frontal sinuses are visualized.

(A) 1 only
(B) 1 and 2 only
(C) 1 and 3 only
(D) 1, 2, and 3

167. What percentage of x-ray attenuation does a 0.5-mm lead-equivalent apron at 75 kVp provide?

(A) 51%
(B) 66%
(C) 75%
(D) 88%

168. Shape distortion is influenced by the relationship between the

1. x-ray tube and the part to be imaged
2. body part to be imaged and the IR
3. IR and the x-ray tube

(A) 1 and 2 only
(B) 1 and 3 only
(C) 2 and 3 only
(D) 1, 2, and 3

169. To better demonstrate the interphalangeal joints of the toes, which of the following procedures may be employed?

1. Angle the CR 15 degrees caudad.
2. Angle the CR 15 degrees cephalad.
3. Place a sponge wedge under the foot with the toes elevated 15 degrees.

(A) 1 only
(B) 1 and 2 only
(C) 1 and 3 only
(D) 2 and 3 only

170. The *most commonly used* method of low-flow oxygen delivery is the

(A) oxygen mask
(B) nasal cannula
(C) respirator
(D) oxyhood

171. The femoral neck can be located

(A) parallel to the femoral shaft
(B) perpendicular to the femoral shaft
(C) perpendicular to a line drawn from the ASIS to the pubic symphysis
(D) perpendicular to a line from the iliac crest to the pubic symphysis

172. A signed consent form is necessary prior to performing all the following procedures *except*

(A) myelogram
(B) cardiac catheterization
(C) upper GI series
(D) interventional vascular procedure

173. Improper support of a patient's fractured lower leg (tibia/fibula) while performing radiography could result in

1. movement of fracture fragments
2. tearing of soft tissue, nerves, and blood vessels
3. initiation of muscle spasm

(A) 1 and 2 only
(B) 1 and 3 only
(C) 2 and 3 only
(D) 1, 2, and 3

174. Personal radiation monitor reports must include which of the following information?

1. Dose equivalents for report period
2. Dosimeter type
3. Radiation quality

(A) 1 only
(B) 1 and 2 only
(C) 2 and 3 only
(D) 1, 2, and 3

175. The intertrochanteric crest is located on the

(A) proximal posterior femur
(B) proximal anterior femur
(C) distal posterior femur
(D) distal anterior femur

176. The ethical principle that aspires never to, above all, do harm describes

(A) fidelity.
(B) veracity.
(C) nonmalficence.
(D) beneficence.

177. A radiographer would be in violation of the American Registry of Radiologic Technologists (ARRT) *Code of Ethics for the Profession of Radiologic Technology* for all of the following *except*

(A) failing to wear a lead apron when performing mobile radiography
(B) failing to participate in continuing education
(C) communicating information regarding suspected child abuse to the referring physician
(D) refusing to participate in new and innovative technical procedures

178. Hospitals and other health care providers must ensure patient confidentiality in compliance with which of the following legislation?

(A) MQSA
(B) MRSA
(C) HIPAA
(D) HIPPA

179. The term *dysplasia* refers to

    (A) difficulty speaking
    (B) abnormal development of tissue
    (C) malposition
    (D) difficult or painful breathing

180. The ethical principle that refers to bringing about good, or benefiting others, is called

    (A) fidelity
    (B) veracity
    (C) nonmalficence
    (D) beneficence

181. Which of the following radiographic examinations require(s) the patient to be NPO 8–10 hours prior to examination for proper patient preparation?

    1. Abdominal survey
    2. Upper GI series
    3. BE

    (A) 1 and 2 only
    (B) 1 and 3 only
    (C) 2 and 3 only
    (D) 1, 2, and 3

182. What is the established fetal dose-limit guideline for pregnant radiographers during the entire gestation period?

    (A) 0.1 rem
    (B) 0.5 rem
    (C) 5.0 rem
    (D) 10 rem

183. The acquired immune deficiency syndrome (AIDS) virus may be transmitted

    1. by sharing contaminated needles
    2. from mother to child during birth
    3. by intimate contact with body fluids

    (A) 1 only
    (B) 1 and 2 only
    (C) 1 and 3 only
    (D) 1, 2, and 3

184. Which of the following vessels does *not* carry oxygenated blood?

    (A) Pulmonary vein
    (B) Pulmonary artery
    (C) Coronary artery
    (D) Chordae tendineae

185. Which of the following are considered *most* radiosensitive?

    (A) Lymphocytes
    (B) Ova
    (C) Neurons
    (D) Myocytes

186. Proper body mechanics includes a wide base of support. The base of support is the portion of the body

    (A) in contact with the floor or other horizontal surface
    (B) in the midportion of the pelvis or lower abdomen
    (C) passing through the center of gravity
    (D) None of the above

187. Which of the following is/are associated with magnification fluoroscopy?

    1. Increased mA.
    2. Smaller portion of the input phosphor is used.
    3. Image intensifier focal point moves closer to the output phosphor.

    (A) 1 only
    (B) 1 and 2 only
    (C) 2 and 3 only
    (D) 1, 2, and 3

188. An illness of unknown or obscure cause is said to be

    (A) systemic
    (B) epidemic
    (C) idiopathic
    (D) pathogenic

189. Linear energy transfer (LET) may be *best* described as

 (A) the amount of energy delivered per distance traveled in tissue
 (B) the unit of absorbed dose
 (C) radiation equivalent man
 (D) radiation absorbed dose

190. Contaminated needles are disposed of in special containers in which of the following ways?

 (A) Recap the needle, remove syringe, dispose of.
 (B) Do not recap needle, remove from syringe, dispose of.
 (C) Recap the needle, dispose of entire syringe.
 (D) Do not recap needle, dispose of entire syringe.

191. Which of the following is a fast-acting vasodilator used to lower blood pressure and relieve the pain of angina pectoris?

 (A) Digitalis
 (B) Dilantin
 (C) Nitroglycerin
 (D) Cimetidine (Tagamet)

192. In film/screen imaging, an increase in kilovoltage with appropriate compensation of milliampere-seconds will result in

 1. increased exposure latitude
 2. higher contrast
 3. increased density

 (A) 1 only
 (B) 1 and 2 only
 (C) 2 and 3 only
 (D) 1 and 3 only

193. The annual dose limit for occupationally exposed individuals is valid for

 (A) alpha, beta, and x-radiations
 (B) x- and gamma radiations only
 (C) beta, x-, and gamma radiations
 (D) all ionizing radiations

194. If 85 kVp, 400 mA, and ⅛ s were used for a particular exposure using single-phase equipment, which of the following milliamperage or time values would be required, all other factors being constant, to produce a similar density using three-phase, 12-pulse equipment?

 (A) 200 mA
 (B) 600 mA
 (C) 0.125 s
 (D) 0.25 s

195. When examining a patient whose elbow is in partial flexion,

 (A) the AP projection requires two separate positions and exposures
 (B) the AP projection is made through the partially flexed elbow, resting on the olecranon process, CR perpendicular to IR
 (C) the AP projection is made through the partially flexed elbow, resting on the olecranon process, CR parallel to the humerus
 (D) the AP projection is eliminated from the routine

196. With which of the following does the lateral extremity of the clavicle articulate?

 (A) Manubrium
 (B) Coracoid process
 (C) Coronoid process
 (D) Acromion process

197. The Centers for Disease Control and Prevention (CDC) suggests that health care workers protect themselves and their patients from blood and body fluid contamination by using

 (A) strict isolation precautions
 (B) standard precautions
 (C) respiratory precautions
 (D) sterilization

198. X-ray tube life may be extended by

1. using high-milliampere-second, low-kilo-voltage exposure factors
2. avoiding lengthy anode rotation
3. avoiding exposures to a cold anode

(A) 1 only

(B) 1 and 2 only

(C) 2 and 3 only

(D) 1, 2, and 3

199. Which of the following functions to increase the milliamperage?

(A) Increasing the speed of anode rotation

(B) Increasing the transformer turns ratio

(C) Using three-phase rectification

(D) Increasing the heat of the filament

200. A technique chart should include which of the following information?

1. Recommended SID
2. Grid ratio
3. CR angulation

(A) 1 only

(B) 1 and 2 only

(C) 1 and 3 only

(D) 1, 2, and 3

Answers and Explanations

1. **(B)** An *antipyretic* is used to reduce fever. Tylenol (acetaminophen) is an example of an antipyretic. An *antihistamine* is used to relieve allergic effects. Benadryl (diphenhydramine hydrochloride) is an example of an antihistamine that is often on hand in radiology departments in the event of a minor reaction to contrast media. Ipecac is a medication used to induce vomiting and is classified as an *emetic*. This is easy to remember if you think of what an emesis basin is for. A *diuretic* is a medication that stimulates the *production of urine*. Lasix (furosemide) is an example of a diuretic. *(Adler and Carlton, 4th ed., p. 265)*

2. **(C)** A *histogram* is a graph usually having several peaks and valleys representing the pixel values/absorbing properties of the various tissues, and so on that make up the imaged part. These various attenuators include such things as bone, muscle, air, contrast agents, foreign bodies, and pathology. The various pixel values, then, represent image contrast. If the histogram has a rather flat "tail," this represents underexposed areas at the periphery of the image, which can skew the overall histogram analysis. The radiographer selects the particular processing algorithm on the computer/control panel that corresponds to the anatomic part and projection being performed. DICOM (Digital Imaging and Communications in Medicine) refers to the standard for communication between PACS and HIS/RIS systems. *Windowing* refers to the radiographer's postprocessing adjustment of

contrast and density (at the workstation). *(Shephard, pp. 341, 345)*

3. **(B)** *Anemia* is a blood condition characterized by a decreased number of circulating red blood cells and decreased hemoglobin; it has many causes. Adequate hemoglobin is required to provide oxygen to the body. Anemia is treated according to its cause. *Hematuria* is the term used to describe blood in the urine and is unrelated to anemia. *(Tortora and Derrickson, 11th ed., p. 689)*

4. **(A)** *Radiopaque* contrast agents appear white on the finished image because many x-ray photons are *absorbed*. These are referred to *positive* contrast agents—composed of dense (i.e., *high atomic number*) material through which x-rays will not pass easily. Radiolucent contrast agents appear black on the finished image because x-ray photons pass through easily. An example of a radiolucent contrast agent is air. *(Shephard, pp. 200–202)*

5. **(D)** Since 50 ms is equal to 0.050 s, and since mA × time mAs, the original milliampere-seconds value was 15 mAs. Now, it is only necessary to determine what milliamperage must be used with 22 ms to provide the same 15 mAs (and thus the same radiographic density). Because mA × time = mAs,

$$0.022x = 15$$
$$x = 682 \ (700 \ \text{mA})$$

(Selman, 9th ed., p. 214)

6. **(D)** Most of the occupational exposure received by radiographers is received during fluoroscopy and mobile radiography, and the use of lead aprons is required during both these procedures. The position of the personal monitor relative to the lead apron, therefore, becomes important. It is recommended that the badge be worn outside the lead apron at collar level. In this position, the badge will record the maximum possible exposure received by the radiographer and will provide a realistic estimate of thyroid and lens exposure. *(Bushong, 8th ed., p. 594)*

7. **(D)** The knee is formed by the proximal tibia, the patella, and the distal femur, which articulate to form the femorotibial and femoropatellar joints. The distal posterior femur presents two large *medial* and *lateral condyles* separated by the deep intercondyloid fossa. Because the medial femoral condyle is further from the IR, it is magnified and will obscure the femorotibial joint space, as seen in the figure. If the CR is angled about 5 degrees cephalad, the medial femoral condyle will be projected superiorly and superimposed on the lateral femoral condyle, thus opening the joint space. The patient should lie on the affected side with the patella perpendicular to the tabletop and the knee flexed 20 to 30 degrees. Rotating the part forward or backward will affect visualization of the *femoropatellar* joint. *(Bontrager and Lampignano, 6th ed., p. 248)*

8. **(C)** Because *muscle* and *nerve* tissues perform specific functions and do not divide, they are relatively *insensitive* to ionizing radiation exposure. *Epithelial* cells cover the outer surface of the body; they also line body cavities and tubes and passageways leading to the exterior. They contain very little intercellular substance and are devoid of blood vessels. Because epithelial cells constantly regenerate through mitosis they are very *radiosensitive*. *(Dowd and Tilson, 2nd ed., pp. 121–122)*

9. **(A)** Remember that the x-ray beam is polyenergetic/heterogeneous—made up of many energies of x-ray photons. The use of aluminum filtration to decrease the number of low-energy photons entering the body does not solve the problem completely. Remaining low-energy photons will be absorbed by the tissue structures closest to the entering x-ray beam. If the patient is positioned for an AP projection, anterior structures will receive a higher (entry) dose than posterior structures; that is, the exit dose is less. If the patient is positioned for a PA projection, posterior structures will receive the higher entry dose. Abdomen imaging performed in the PA projection, whenever possible, will reduce exposure to the gonads. Skull and cervical spine projections performed PA will reduce exposure to the lens and to the thyroid.

A PA chest radiograph delivers about 1 mrad to the thyroid; a PA skull radiograph, about 8 mrad; and a PA esophagram, about 9 mrad. An AP skull radiograph delivers about 92 mrad to the thyroid. As can be seen from these figures, giving some thought to projection/position selection can decrease critical organ dose significantly. *(Bontrager and Lampignano, 6th ed., p. 67)*

10. **(C)** Three dose–response (dose–effect) curves are illustrated, representing the body's response to ionizing radiation exposure. *Dose* is indicated by the horizontal axis (increasing to the right); *response* is indicated by the vertical axis (increasing upward). Two of the curves (numbers 1 and 3) are *linear*; that is, *response is directly related to dose.* Curve 2 is not a straight line and is, therefore, *nonlinear.* Curves 2 and 3 show that a particular dose (*threshold* quantity) of radiation is required before any effect will occur; therefore, curve 2 is *nonlinear threshold,* and curve 3 is *linear threshold.* Curve 1, however, shows that any dose of radiation (theoretically, even a single x-ray photon; that is, there is no threshold) can result in a particular biologic effect; therefore, it is *linear nonthreshold.* *(Bushong, 8th ed., p. 498)*

11. **(A)** The scaphoid can be difficult to image because its curved shape lends itself to foreshortening and self-superimposition. The lateral carpals, especially the scaphoid, are well demonstrated in the PA oblique projection. The *ulnar* flexion maneuver helps to overcome the scaphoid's self-superimposition. The scaphoid may also be demonstrated with less

foreshortening with the *wrist* PA and elevated 20 degrees. The CR is directed perpendicular to the carpal scaphoid.

The medial carpals, especially the pisiform, are well demonstrated in the AP oblique projection with the radial flexion maneuver. *(Bontrager and Lampignano, 6th ed., pp. 161–162)*

12. **(D)** A patient who has been recumbent for some period of time and gets up quickly may suffer from light-headedness or feel faint. This is referred to as *orthostatic hypertension.* It is best to have patients sit up and dangle their feet from the table for a moment while being supported and then assist them off the table. Patients also will feel better emotionally if they are not rushed or treated like they are on an assembly line. Always assist patients on and off of the radiographic table. Even healthy, young outpatients can injure themselves. Patients with dyspnea or orthopnea are unable to lie supine. *Dyspnea* and *orthopnea* refer to difficulty breathing; this may be due to a heart condition, asthma, strenuous exercise, or excessive anxiety. *Hypertension* refers to the condition of elevated blood pressure. *(Adler and Carlton, 4th ed., p. 168)*

13. **(A)** The *dorsal decubitus* position is obtained with the patient supine and the x-ray beam directed horizontally. The finished image looks similar to a lateral projection of the chest. However, small amounts of fluid will gravitate to the posterior chest, and small amounts of air will rise to the anterior chest. The *ventral decubitus* position is obtained with the patient prone and the x-ray beam directed horizontally. The finished image can demonstrate small amounts of fluid anteriorly and small amounts of air posteriorly. *(Frank, Long, and Smith, 11th ed., vol. 1, p. 540)*

14. **(B)** Sufficient inspiration is demonstrated by the visualization of 10 posterior ribs projected above the diaphragm. Rotation of the chest is detected by asymmetry in the distance between the medial ends of the clavicles and the vertebral column. The scapulae should be free of superimposition with the lung fields; this is accomplished by rolling the shoulders forward while positioning for

the PA projection. *(Frank, Long, and Smith, 11th ed., vol. 1, p. 521)*

15. **(C)** When high-speed electrons strike surfaces other than the tungsten target, x-rays may be produced and emitted in all directions. X-ray tubes, therefore, have a lead-lined metal protective housing to absorb much of this "leakage radiation." Leakage radiation must not exceed 100 mR/h at a distance of 1 m from the tube. Because the production of x-radiation requires the use of exceedingly high voltage, the tube housing also serves to protect from electric shock. The production of x-rays involves the production of large quantities of heat, which can be damaging to the x-ray tube. Therefore, an oil coolant surrounds the x-ray tube to further insulate it and to absorb heat from the x-ray tube structures. *(Bushong, 8th ed., p. 131)*

16. **(C)** Interviewing skills and the collection of valuable, objective, and subjective patient data (clinical history) are an important function of the health care professional. Objective data are those that are discernible to the senses of the interviewer—objective signs that can be heard, seen, or felt. Subjective data are those that can be discerned only by the patient—pain, emotions, and so on. Chief complaint is the principal medical problem as stated by the patient. *(Adler and Carlton, 4th ed., p. 159)*

17. **(C)** As filtration is added to the x-ray beam, the lower-energy photons are removed, and the overall energy or wavelength of the beam is greater. As kilovoltage is increased, more high-energy photons are produced, and again, the overall or average energy of the beam is greater. *An increase in milliamperage serves to increase the number of photons produced at the target but is unrelated to their energy.* *(Bushong, 8th ed., pp. 165, 166)*

18. **(A)** The figures are *axial* CT images of the abdomen *with contrast.* In Figure A, the liver (number 1 left lobe; number 6 right lobe; number 3 caudate lobe), barium-filled stomach (number 2), spleen (number 5), and aorta (number 4) are seen in image A. More *inferior* structures such

as the inferior vena cava (number 5) and kidneys (number 9 and number 10) are seen in image B.

19. **(D)** Image B is an axial CT section of the abdomen with contrast. Structures demonstrated include the barium-filled stomach (number 1), the gallbladder (number 2), duodenum (number 3), pancreas (number 4), IVC (number 5), left adrenal gland (number 6), aorta (number 7), spleen (number 8), left kidney (number 9), right kidney (number 10), and liver (number 11).

20. **(A)** *Heparin* is produced by the body (especially in the liver) and functions to prevent intravascular clotting. Heparin is also produced artificially and used to treat thromboembolic disorders. Lidocaine and Benadryl are drugs that are usually available on crash carts for emergency use. *Lidocaine* is used to treat ventricular arrhythmias, and *Benadryl* is used to treat allergic reactions and acute anaphylaxis. *(Torres et al., 6th ed., p. 284)*

21. **(B)** Emphysema is a chronic obstructive pulmonary disease (COPD) characterized by pathologic distension of the pulmonary alveoli with (destructive) changes in their walls, resulting in a loss of elasticity. Emphysema is seen occasionally following asthma or tuberculosis, but it is caused most frequently by cigarette smoking. Because the emphysematous patient's greatest difficulty is exhalation, it becomes a conscious, forced effort. Breathing is shallow and rapid. Forced and ineffective breathing results in expansion of the AP diameter of the chest and elevated shoulder girdle in established emphysema. Hyperventilation results from too frequent deep breaths in the anxious or tense individual. This results in a feeling of dizziness and tingling of the extremities. *(Tortora and Derrickson, 11th ed., p. 887)*

22. **(B)** A computed tomographic (CT) imaging system has three component parts—a gantry, a computer, and an operator console. The *gantry* component includes an x-ray tube, a detector array, a high-voltage generator, a collimator assembly, and a patient couch with its motorized mechanism. The *computer* is exceedingly sophisticated, performing thousands of calculations simultaneously per second. It is responsible for image reconstruction and postprocessing functions. At the *operator console*, somewhat similar to a control panel used in projection radiography, has the controls for equipment operation and image manipulation. Technical factors are selected and monitored here, adjustments can be made, and the patient couch is operated. *(Bushong, 8th ed., pp. 429–430; Bontrager and Lampignano, 6th ed., p. 731)*

23. **(B)** Whole-body dose is calculated to include all the especially radiosensitive organs. The *gonads*, the *lens* of the eye, and the *blood-forming organs* are particularly radiosensitive. The annual dose limit to the less sensitive skin, hands, and feet (extremities) is 50 rem/year. *(Bushong, 8th ed., p. 557)*

24. **(C)** Fluoroscopic skin dose is greater than radiographic skin dose because the x-ray source is much closer to the patient. The generally accepted rule is that the skin receives 2 rad/min/mA. Therefore, 2 rad/min for 5 minutes equals 10 rad/mA. At 1.5 mA, the patient dose is 15 rad (2 rad/5 min/1.5 mA). *(Bushong, 8th ed., p. 584)*

25. **(C)** *Air–fluid levels* are demonstrated in the erect or decubitus position. Grid radiography requires about a 3 to 4 times greater dose than nongrid radiography. A right lateral decubitus projection without a grid, then, would demonstrate fluid levels with a considerably smaller dose to the infant. A recumbent AP projection would not demonstrate air–fluid levels. *(Bontrager and Lampignano, 6th ed., p. 676)*

26. **(B)** The radial head and neck are projected free of superimposition in the AP oblique projection (lateral rotation) of the elbow. The humeral capitulum is also well demonstrated in this external oblique position. The AP oblique projection (medial rotation) of the elbow superimposes the radial head and neck on the proximal ulna. It demonstrates the olecranon process within the olecranon fossa, and it projects the coronoid process free of superimposition. *(Bontrager and Lampignano, 6th ed., p. 171)*

27. **(B)** In mutual induction, two coils are in close proximity, and a current is supplied to one of the coils. As the magnetic field associated with every electric current expands and "grows up" around the first coil, it interacts with and "cuts" the turns of the second coil. This interaction, motion between magnetic field and coil (conductor), induces an electromotive force (emf) in the second coil. This is *mutual induction*, the production of a current in a neighboring circuit. Transformers, such as the high-voltage transformer and the filament (step-down) transformer, operate on the principle of mutual induction. The autotransformer operates on the principle of self-induction. Both the transformer and the autotransformer require the use of alternating current. *(Bushong, 8th ed., p. 99)*

28. **(B)** Pathologic processes and abnormal conditions that alter tissue composition or thickness can have a significant effect on image density. The radiographer must be aware of these variants and processes to make an appropriate and accurate adjustment of technical factors.

Examples of *additive* pathologic conditions:

- Ascites
- Rheumatoid arthritis
- Paget disease
- Pneumonia
- Atelectasis
- Congestive heart failure
- Edematous tissue

Examples of *destructive* pathologic conditions:

- Osteoporosis
- Osteomalacia
- Pneumoperitoneum
- Emphysema
- Degenerative arthritis
- Atrophic and necrotic conditions

(Bushong, 9th ed., p. 253)

29. **(B)** The overall chance that a person will become infected with HIV is high with entry sites such as the anus, broken skin, shared needles, infected blood products, and perinatal exposure. Low-risk entry methods include oral and nasal, conjunctiva, and accidental needle stick. *(Ehrlich et al., 6th ed., p. 150)*

30. **(B)** The term *parenteral* denotes any medication route other than the alimentary canal (by mouth). Examples of parenteral routes are subcutaneous, intravenous, intramuscular, and intracardiac. The speed of absorption varies with the route used. *(Torres et al., 6th ed., p. 270)*

31. **(D)** The RAO position is shown. The barium-filled pylorus and duodenum are well demonstrated in this position, and the esophagus can be projected between the vertebrae and heart in this position. This RAO position is also used to superimpose the sternum onto the heart shadow to provide uniform density throughout the sternum. The degree of obliquity depends on the patient's body habitus—greater obliquity is required for thinner chests. The RAO position is also used to see axillary portions of left anterior ribs; in the anterior oblique positions, the affected side is away from the IR. *(Frank, Long, and Smith, 11th ed., vol. 1, p. 470)*

32. **(A)** It is occasionally necessary to view the lung apices free of superimposition with the clavicles. This objective can be achieved in an AP axial projection. The patient is positioned AP erect with the CR directed 15 degrees cephalad, entering the manubrium. An AP axial projection can also be obtained with the patient in the lordotic position. If sufficient lordosis can be assumed, the CR is directed perpendicular to the IR. *(Frank, Long, and Smith, 11th ed., vol. 1, p. 537)*

33. **(B)** If it is desired to determine entrance skin exposure (ESE), a small ionization chamber (pocket dosimeter) can be placed on the skin, and the approximate ESE can be read immediately. These devices are readily imaged, however, and are awkward to position. For these reasons, thermoluminescent dosimeters (TLDs) or optically stimulated luminescence (OSL) dosimeters are more easily used; they are precise and will not interfere with the radiographic image. The acceptable ESE for a PA chest is approximately 20 mR (12–26 mR is the acceptable range). An image taken with an ESE of 6 mR would be underexposed and require repeating. Similarly, ESEs of 38 mR and 0.6 R (600 mR) would lead to overexposed images that would need to be repeated. *(Bushong, 8th ed., p. 586)*

34. **(D)** Patient demographic and examination information originates from the hospital/facility HIS, where it is obtained when the patient is initially registered. That information is available or retrievable when the patient is scheduled, or arrives, for imaging services. *Typical patient information includes name, DOB or age, sex, ID number, accession number, examination being performed, date and time of examination.*

Additional information may be available on the examination requisition; more information is usually entered by the technologist at the time of the examination.

A feature that is useful in sorting examinations and decreasing (but not eliminating) errors is the Modality Work List (MWL). The MWL "brings up" existing RIS information, that is, the examinations scheduled for each imaging area—for example, x-ray, CT, MR, mammography, ultrasound, etc. The technologist selects the correct patient, which includes that patient's particular demographics, from the particular modality work list.

It is essential that the technologist is attentive to detail and accuracy when entering patient information; errors in patient demographics entry, and entry duplication, must be avoided. *(Seeram, pp. 222–223, 226)*

35. **(D)** The four types of body habitus are (from upper extreme to lower extreme) hypersthenic, sthenic, hyposthenic, and asthenic. The gallbladder and stomach are higher and more lateral and the large bowel more peripheral in the hypersthenic individual. The diaphragm is in a higher position in the hypersthenic individual. Recognition of a patient's body habitus and its characteristics is an important part of accurate radiography. Bone porosity generally is unrelated to body habitus. *(Frank, Long, and Smith, 11th ed., vol. 1, p. 65)*

36. **(C)** A beveled focal track extends around the periphery of the anode disk; when a small angle is used, the beveled edge allows for a smaller effective focal spot and better detail. The disadvantage, however, is that photons are noticeably absorbed by the "heel" of the anode, resulting in a smaller percentage of x-ray photons at the anode end of the x-ray beam and a concentration of x-ray photons at the cathode end of the beam. This is known as the *anode heel effect* and can cause a primary beam variation of up to 45%. The anode heel effect becomes more pronounced as the SID decreases, as IR size increases, and as target angle decreases. *(Bushong, 8th ed., pp. 138–140)*

37. **(A)** Transformers and autotransformers require alternating current (AC) to operate. Number 1 is the autotransformer, which operates on the principle of *self-induction*. It is from here that actual kilovolt selection takes place. Numbers 2 and 3 are the primary and secondary coils of the step-up/high-voltage transformer, which operates on the principle of *mutual induction*. Number 5 is the rectification system, which serves to change AC to unidirectional current. The rectification system is needed because the x-ray tube (number 7) operates most efficiently on *unidirectional current*. (Selman, 9th ed., pp. 88, 159)

38. **(A)** The autotransformer is labeled 1, the primary coil of the high-voltage transformer is labeled 2, the grounded milliampere meter is labeled 4, and the filament circuit is labeled 6. The rectification system, which is used to change alternating current to unidirectional current, is indicated by number 5. The rectification system is located between the secondary coil of the high-voltage (step-up) transformer (number 3) and the x-ray tube (number 7). *(Selman, 9th ed., pp. 98, 159)*

39. **(C)** Hirschsprung disease, or congenital megacolon, is caused by the absence of some or all of the bowel ganglion cells—usually in the rectosigmoid area but occasionally more extensively. Hirschsprung disease is the most common cause of lower GI obstruction in neonates and is treated surgically by excision of the affected area followed by reanastomosis with the normal, healthy bowel. Hirschsprung disease is diagnosed by BE or, in mild cares, by rectal biopsy. Intussusception is "telescoping" of the bowel, causing (mechanical) obstruction. Volvulus is twisting of the bowel on itself causing (mechanical) obstruction. Pyloric stenosis is a condition of the upper GI tract. *(Bontrager and Lampignano, 6th ed., p. 659)*

40. **(A)** *Resolution* describes how closely fine details may be associated and still be recognized as separate details before seeming to blend into each other and appear "as one." The degree of resolution transferred to the IR is a function of the resolving power of each of the system components and can be expressed in line pairs per millimeter (lp/mm). It can be measured using a resolution test pattern; a variety of resolution test tools are available. The star pattern generally is used for focal-spot-size evaluation, whereas the parallel-line type is used for evaluating intensifying screens. Resolution can also be expressed in terms of line-spread function (LSP) or modulation transfer function (MTF). LSP is measured using a 10-×m x-ray beam; MTF measures the amount of information lost between the object and the IR. (*Carlton and Adler, 4th ed., p. 334*)

41. **(D)** High-frequency generators first appeared in mobile x-ray units and were then adopted by mammography and CT equipment. Today, more and more radiographic equipment uses high-frequency generators. Their compact size makes them popular, and the fact that they produce nearly constant potential voltage helps to improve image quality and decrease patient dose (fewer low-energy photons to contribute to skin dose). (*Bushong, 8th ed., p. 122*)

42. **(A)** If the SID is above or below the recommended focusing distance, the primary beam at the lateral edges will not coincide with the angled lead strips. Consequently, there will be absorption of the primary beam, termed *grid cutoff*. If the grid failed to move during the exposure, there would be grid lines throughout. CR angulation in the direction of the lead strips is appropriate and will not cause grid cutoff. If the CR were off-center, there would be uniform loss of density. (*Selman, 9th ed., p. 240*)

43. **(D)** When scheduling patient examinations, it is important to avoid the possibility of residual contrast medium covering areas of interest on later examinations. The IVP should be scheduled first because the contrast medium used is excreted rapidly. The BE should be scheduled next. Finally, the upper GI series is scheduled. Any barium remaining from the previous BE should not be enough to interfere with the stomach or duodenum (a preliminary scout image should be taken in each case). (*Torres et al., 6th ed., pp. 233–234*)

44. **(C)** The tangential ("sunrise") projection is used to demonstrate the articular surfaces of the femur and patella. It is also used to demonstrate vertical fractures of the patella. The AP, PA, and oblique projections of the knee are used primarily to evaluate the joint space and articulating structures. The tunnel view is used to demonstrate the intercondyloid fossa. (*Bontrager and Lampignano, 6th ed., p. 255*)

45. **(D)** To accurately position a lateral forearm, the elbow must form a 90-degree angle with the humeral epicondyles superimposed. The radius and ulna are superimposed distally. Proximally, the coronoid process and radial head are partially superimposed. Failure of the elbow to form a 90-degree angle or the hand to be lateral results in a less than satisfactory lateral projection of the forearm. (*Frank, Long, and Smith, 11th ed., vol. 1, p. 142*)

46. **(B)** Flat-panel detectors used in DR are often made of an amorphous selenium (a-Se)–coated thin-film transistor (TFT) array. They function to convert the x-ray energy (emerging from the radiographed part) into an electrical signal. The TFT capacitors send the electrical signal to the analog-to-digital converter (ADC) to be changed to a digital signal. *Amorphous selenium* refers to a crystalline material (selenium) that lacks its crystalline structure. Amorphous selenium or silicon is used to produce the direct-conversion flat-panel detectors used in DR. (*Bushong, 8th ed., p. 404*)

47. **(A)** A 1984 review of radiation exposure data revealed that the average annual dose equivalent for monitored radiation workers was approximately 0.23 rem (2.3 mSv). The fact that this is approximately one-tenth the recommended limit indicates that the limit is adequate for radiation protection purposes. Therefore, the NCRP reiterates its 1971 recommended annual limit of 5 rem (50 mSv). (*Bushong, 8th ed., p. 557*)

48. **(D)** A spinning-top test may be performed to evaluate timer accuracy or rectifier efficiency in single-phase equipment. The number of dots or dashes imaged on the IR is counted and should equal the number of radiation "pulses" occurring during that exposure time. Because three-phase equipment does not emit pulsed radiation but rather almost constant potential, a synchronous spinning top must be used to evaluate timer accuracy. The resulting image is a solid black arc. The angle of the arc is measured and should correspond to the known correct angle. *(Selman, 9th ed., pp. 105–106)*

49. **(C)** Retrograde urography is not considered a functional study of the urinary system. IVP, descending urography, and infusion nephrotomography are all considered functional urinary tract studies because the contrast medium is introduced intravenously and excreted by the kidneys. Retrograde urography involves introduction of contrast medium into the kidneys via catheter, thereby demonstrating their structure but not their function. *(Frank, Long, and Smith, 11th ed., vol. 2, p. 207)*

50. **(B)** X-ray photons are produced in two ways as high-speed electrons interact with target tungsten atoms. First, if the high-speed electron is attracted by the nucleus of a tungsten atom and changes its course, as the electron is "braked," energy is given up in the form of an x-ray photon. This is called *Bremsstrahlung* ("braking") *radiation*, and it is responsible for most of the x-ray photons produced at the conventional tungsten target. Second, a high-speed electron having an energy of at least 70 keV may eject a tungsten K-shell electron, leaving a vacancy in the shell. An electron from the next energy level, the L shell, drops down to fill the vacancy, emitting the difference in energy as a K-characteristic ray. Characteristic radiation makes up only about 15% of the primary beam. *(Bushong, 8th ed., p. 176)*

51. **(B)** The (diarthrotic) sternoclavicular joints are formed by the medial (sternal) extremities of the clavicles and the clavicular notches of the manubrium (of the sternum). They can be demonstrated in the LAO and RAO positions. The LAO projection demonstrates the left sternoclavicular joint, whereas the RAO projection demonstrates the joint on the right. The patient is obliqued about 15 degrees with the side of interest adjacent to the IR. *(Frank, Long, and Smith, 11th ed., vol. 1, p. 481)*

52. **(B)** The output phosphor of the image intensifier displays the brighter, minified, and inverted image. From the output phosphor, the light image is conveyed to its destination by some kind of image distributor—either a series of lenses and a mirror or via fiber optics. Fiber optics is often the method of choice where equipment size is of concern (e.g., mobile equipment). The image distributor, that is, the lens or fiber optics, then sends the majority of light to the TV monitor for direct viewing and the remaining light (about 10%) to the IR (e.g., photospot camera). *(Bushong, 8th ed., p. 366)*

53. **(A)** Hospital-acquired infections (HAIs) are also referred to as *nosocomial*. Despite the efforts of infectious disease departments, HAIs continue to be a problem in hospitals today. This is at least partly due to there being a greater number of older, more vulnerable patients and an increase in the number of invasive procedures performed today (i.e., needles and catheters). The most frequent site of HAI is the urinary tract, followed by wounds, the respiratory tract, and blood. *(Torres et al., 6th ed., p. 47)*

54. **(A)** The control badge is an important part of the monitoring system. It should be stored somewhere away from radiation sources. At the end of the monitoring period, when the badges are returned to the dosimetry service, the exposure to the control badge (which should be zero) is compared with the exposure received by the rest of the personal monitors. If the control badge is stored near radiation or used to replace someone's lost badge, there is no standard for comparison for the rest of the group of monitors. *(Bushong, 8th ed., p. 596)*

55. **(B)** In the 1990s, the implementation of *slip ring technology* allowed *continuous* rotation of the x-ray tube (through elimination of cables) and *simultaneous* couch movement. Sixth-generation CT scanning is termed *helical*

(or spiral) CT—permitting acquisition of volume multislice scanning. Today's helical multislice scanners, employing thousands of detectors (up to 60+ rows), can obtain uninterrupted data acquisition of 128 "slices" per tube rotation and can perform *3D multiplanar reformation* (MPR). Fifth-generation CT is electron beam; ultra high-speed CT is used specifically for cardiac imaging. *(Bushong, 9th ed., p. 375; Romans, pp. 50–51)*

56. **(B)** Exposure to high doses of radiation results in *early* effects. Examples of early effects are blood changes and erythema. If the exposed individual survives, then *late*, or long-term, effects must be considered. Individuals who receive small amounts of low-level radiation (such as those who are occupationally exposed) are concerned with the late effects of radiation exposure—effects that can occur many years after the initial exposure. *Late* effects of radiation exposure, such as carcinogenesis, are considered to be related to the linear nonthreshold dose–response curve. That is, there is *no safe dose;* theoretically, even one x-ray photon can induce a later response. *(Bushong, 8th ed., pp. 532, 537)*

57. **(B)** According to the inverse-square law of radiation, as the distance between the radiation source and the IR decreases, the exposure rate increases. Therefore, a decrease in technical factors is first indicated to compensate for the distance change. The following formula (density-maintenance formula) is used to determine new milliampere-seconds values when changing distance:

$$\frac{mAs_1}{mAs_2} = \frac{D_1^2}{D_2^2}$$

Substituting known values:

$$\frac{8}{x} = \frac{5,184}{1,600}$$

$$5,184x = 12,800$$

Thus, $x = 2.47$ mAs at 40-in. SID. To then compensate for adding a 12:1 grid, you must multiply the 2.47 mAs by a factor of 5. Thus, 12 mAs is required to produce an image density similar to the original radiograph. The following are the factors used for milliampere-seconds conversion from nongrid to grid:

No grid = 1 × original mAs
5:1 = grid 2 × original mAs
6:1 = grid 3 × original mAs
8:1 = grid 4 × original mAs
12:1 = grid 5 × original mAs
16:1 = grid 6 × original mAs

(Bushong, 8th ed., pp. 69, 252)

58. **(C)** Invasion of privacy—that is, public discussion of privileged and confidential information—is intentional misconduct. False imprisonment, such as unnecessarily restraining a patient, is also intentional misconduct. However, if a radiographer left a weak patient standing while leaving the room to check images or get supplies and the patient fell and sustained an injury, that would be considered unintentional misconduct or negligence. *(Gurley and Callaway, 6th ed., p. 193)*

59. **(D)** The thicker and denser the anatomic part being studied, the less bright will be the fluoroscopic image. Both milliamperage and kilovoltage affect the fluoroscopic image in a way similar to the way they affect the radiographic image. For optimal contrast, especially taking into consideration the patient dose, higher kilovoltage and lower milliamperage generally are preferred. *(Carlton and Adler, 4th ed., p. 572)*

60. **(D)** The radiographic subject (the patient) is composed of many different tissue types of varying densities, resulting in varying degrees of photon attenuation and absorption. This *differential absorption* contributes to the various shades of gray (scale of radiographic contrast) on the finished radiograph. Normal tissue density may be significantly altered in the presence of pathology. For example, destructive bone disease can cause a dramatic decrease in tissue density. Abnormal accumulation of fluid (as in ascites) will cause a significant increase in tissue density. Muscle atrophy or highly developed muscles similarly will decrease or increase tissue density. *(Shephard, p. 203)*

61. **(D)** Cells that are termed *undifferentiated* are immature or young. They have no specific function and/or structure. They are usually precursor cells; their most important function is to divide. Mitosis is the most radiosensitive part of the cell cycle. *(Bushong, 8th ed., p. 495)*

62. **(A)** The oblique axial projection is valuable when the zygomatic arches cannot be demonstrated bilaterally with the submentovertical projection because they are not prominent enough or because of a depressed fracture. The patient still may be positioned as for an SMV projection, but the head is obliqued 15 degrees toward the side being examined. This serves to move the zygomatic arch away from superimposed structures and provides a slightly oblique axial projection of the arch. *(Bontrager and Lampignano, 6th ed., p. 426)*

63. **(C)** Radiographic contrast is greatly affected by changes in kilovoltage (Figure 6–23). As kilovoltage increases, a greater number of high-energy photons are produced at the target. These photons are more penetrating, but they also produce more scattered radiation, contributing to lower radiographic contrast as a result of scattered *radiation fog*. *Radiograph B* was made using 100 kVp and 18 mAs. *Radiograph A* was made of the same part using 80 kVp and 75 mAs, all other factors constant. The image details in *radiograph A* are far more perceptible as

a result of the production of less scattered radiation. *(Carlton and Adler, 4th ed., p. 423)*

64. **(B)** *Differential absorption* refers to the different attenuation, or absorption, properties of adjacent body tissues. Two parts with widely differing absorption characteristics will produce a high radiographic contrast. Frequently, exposure factors that would properly expose one part will severely overexpose or underexpose the neighboring part (as with lungs vs. the thoracic spine). This effect can be minimized by the use of a *compensating filter* or by the use of high kilovoltage (for more uniform penetration). Increased collimation is important in the control of patient dose and scattered radiation, not differential absorption. *(Bushong, 8th ed., pp. 169, 170)*

65. **(B)** The image illustrates *aliasing artifact*, or Moiré effect. Aliasing, or Moiré, has the appearance of somewhat wavy linear lines and can occur in computed radiography when using *stationary grids*. If the grid's lead strip pattern (i.e., frequency) matches the scanning (sampling) pattern of the scanner/reader, the resulting interference can cause aliasing (also called Moiré) artifact. When sampling frequencies are decreased, aliasing/Moiré is less evident. As sampling frequencies increase, aliasing/Moiré is more obvious. *(Seeram, p. 87; Fuji Computed Radiography, p. 70)*

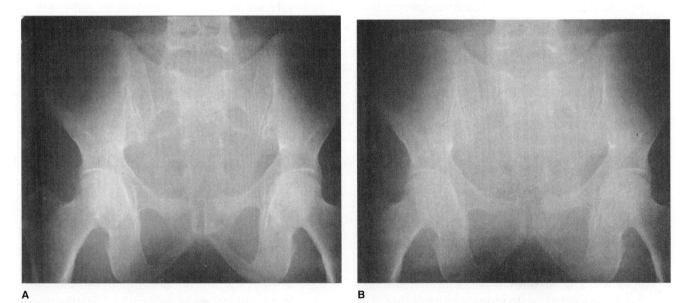

A   B

Figure 6–23A&B. From the American College of Radiology Learning File. Courtesy of the ACR.

66. **(B)** Since x-ray photons are produced at the tungsten target, they more readily diverge toward the cathode end of the x-ray tube. As they try to diverge toward the anode, they interact with and are absorbed by the anode "heel." Consequently, there is a greater intensity of x-ray photons at the cathode end of the x-ray beam. This phenomenon is known as the *anode heel effect*. Because shorter SIDs and larger IR sizes require greater divergence of the x-ray beam to provide coverage, the anode heel effect will be accentuated. *(Bushong, 8th ed., pp. 138–140)*

67. **(D)** Proper care of leaded protective apparel is required to ensure its continued usefulness. If lead aprons and gloves are folded, cracks will develop, and this will decrease their effectiveness. Both items should be fluoroscoped annually to check for the formation of cracks. *(Bushong, 8th ed., pp. 596, 597)*

68. **(A)** It is our ethical responsibility to minimize radiation dose to patients. X-rays produced at the target make up a heterogeneous primary beam. There are many "soft" (low-energy) photons that, if not removed, would contribute only to greater patient dose. They are too weak to penetrate the patient and expose the IR. These soft x-rays penetrate only a small thickness of tissue before being absorbed. *(Fauber, 2nd ed., pp. 32–33)*

69. **(D)** Follow-up studies have been done on individuals receiving accidental exposure to radiation (e.g., medical personnel, uranium miners, and children irradiated in vivo). Pioneer radiation workers developed leukemia and other cancers, their vision was clouded by the formation of cataracts, and their lives were shorter than those of their colleagues. With today's sophisticated equipment and knowledge of radiation protection, none of these situations should occur. *(Bushong, 8th ed., pp. 537–540)*

70. **(C)** Computed radiography (CR) is less expensive primarily because it is compatible with existing equipment. Digital radiography (DR) requires existing equipment to be modified or new equipment purchased. Because there is an image plate (IP), CR can be used for mobile studies; DR cannot—because no cassettes are used. After image processing, the IP is erased and reused. DR offers the advantage of immediate visualization of the x-ray image; in CR, there is a short delay. *(Shephard, p. 335)*

71. **(A)** Restriction of field size is one important method of patient protection. However, the accuracy of the light field must be evaluated periodically as part of a quality assurance (QA) program. Guidelines set forth for patient protection state that the collimator light and actual irradiated area must be accurate to within 2% of the SID employed. *(Bushong, 8th ed., p. 568)*

72. **(C)** The sternum has three parts: The uppermost portion is the *manubrium* (and is quadrilateral in shape), the midportion is the *body* or *gladiolus*, and the distal portion is the *ensiform* or *xiphoid process*. The sternum supports the clavicles superiorly and provides attachment for the ribs laterally. The first seven pairs of ribs are true, or *vertebrosternal*, ribs because they attach directly to the sternum. The ribs angle obliquely anteriorly and inferiorly so that their anterior portions are 3 to 5 in. inferior to their posterior attachment. The *sternoclavicular joints* afford the only bony attachment between the thorax and the upper extremity. *(Bontrager and Lampignano, 6th ed., p. 350)*

73. **(C)** The *synchronous timer* is an older type of x-ray timer that does not permit very precise, short exposures. The *impulse timer* permits a shorter, more precise exposure, and the *electronic timer* may be used for exposures as short as 0.001 s. The electronic timer is very precise and accurate; it is widely used for rapid serial fluoroscopic exposures. *(Bushong, 9th ed., p. 108)*

74. **(D)** The human body is composed of approximately 80% water; the remaining 20% is a combination of substances such as proteins, carbohydrates, and lipids. The smallest functional unit of the body is the *cell*; the structure/content of which often determines its function. Cells form tissues and organs that

also have functional characteristics. The two basic types of cells are *somatic* and *genetic*. Somatic cells are all the body's cells (bone, muscle, nerve, etc.) except those concerned with reproduction—those cells are termed genetic.

DNA is located in the nucleus of each cell, packaged into thread-like structures called *chromosomes*. Each chromosome is made up of DNA tightly coiled many times around proteins called histones that support its structure. Passed from parents to offspring, DNA contains the specific instructions that make each individual unique.

Chromosomes are visible, under microscope, in the cell's nucleus only when the cell is dividing (*mitosis*). Most of what researchers know about chromosomes has been learned by observing chromosomes during mitotic activity. Division of *somatic* cells is *mitosis*, while (reduction) division of *genetic* cells is *meiosis*.

Every chromosome has a constricted portion called its *centromere*, which divides the chromosome into two sections, or "arms." The chromosome's short arm is referred to as its "p arm." The chromosome's long arm is referred to as its "q arm." The location of the centromere on each chromosome is often used to assist description of the location of specific genes. *(Fosbinder and Orth, p. 287)*

75. **(B)** The greater and lesser tubercles are prominences on the proximal humerus, separated by the bicipital groove. The AP projection of the humerus in external rotation demonstrates the greater tubercle in profile. With the arm placed in internal rotation, the humerus is placed in a true lateral position, and the lesser tubercle is demonstrated. *(Bontrager and Lampignano, 6th ed., p. 176)*

76. **(B)** As kilovoltage is increased, x-ray photons begin to interact with atoms of tissue via the Compton scattered interaction. Scattered x-ray photons result, which serve only to add unwanted, undiagnostic densities (scattered radiation fog) to the radiologic image. (While Compton scatter reduces patient dose compared with photoelectric interactions, it can pose a significant radiation hazard to person-

nel during fluoroscopic procedures.) Therefore, the use of *optimal kilovoltage* is recommended to reduce the production of scattered radiation. Scattered radiation is also a function of the size and content of the irradiated field. The greater the volume and atomic number of the tissue, the greater is the production of scattered radiation. Although there is little that can be done about the atomic number of the structure to be radiographed, every effort can be made to keep the field size restricted to the essential area of interest in an effort to decrease production of scattered radiation. Grids have no effect on the production of scattered radiation, but they are very effective in removing scattered radiation from the beam before it strikes the IR. *(Fauber, 2nd ed., pp. 71, 103)*

77. **(C)** The AP oblique projection (LPO, RPO position/Grashey method) is used to demonstrate the glenoid fossa in profile. The position is most comfortably performed in the erect position. The body is rotated 35 to 45 degrees toward the affected side. The CR is directed 2 in. medial and 2 in. lateral to the upper outer border of the shoulder. The glenohumeral joint space is open and the glenoid cavity is demonstrated in profile. *(Frank, Long, and Smith, 11th ed., vol. 1, p. 192)*

78. **(A)** Because patient dose is regulated by the quantity of x-ray photons delivered to the patient, the milliampere-seconds value regulates patient dose. Highly energetic x-ray photons (high kilovoltage) are more likely to penetrate the patient rather than be absorbed by biologic tissue. Consequently, the use of high-kilovoltage and low-milliampere-seconds exposure factors is preferred in an effort to reduce patient dose. *(Bushong, 8th ed., p. 162)*

79. **(C)** The radiographer selects a *processing algorithm* by selecting the anatomic part and particular projection on the computer/control panel. The CR unit then matches that information with a particular *lookup table* (LUT)—a characteristic curve that best matches the anatomic part being imaged. The observer is able to review the image and, if desired, change its appearance (through "windowing"); doing so

changes the LUT. Histogram analysis and use of the appropriate *LUT* together function to produce predictable image quality in CR. Additionally, the radiographer can manipulate, that is, change and enhance, the digital image displayed on the display monitor through *postprocessing*. One way to alter image contrast and/or brightness is through *windowing*. The term *windowing* refers to some change made to window width and/or window level, that is, a change in the LUT. Change in window width affects change in the number of gray shades, that is, *image contrast*. Change in window *level* affects change in the image *brightness,* that is, density. Therefore, windowing and other postprocessing mechanisms permit the radiographer to affect changes in the image and produce "special effects," such as *contrast enhancement, edge enhancement,* and *image stitching. (Seeram, pp. 34–35)*

80. **(D)** Motion causes unsharpness that destroys detail. Careful and accurate patient instruction is essential for minimizing voluntary motion. Suspended respiration eliminates respiratory motion. Using the shortest possible exposure time is essential to decrease involuntary motion. Immobilization can also be very useful in eliminating motion unsharpness. *(Fauber, 2nd ed., pp. 87–88)*

81. **(A)** The effects of a quantity of radiation delivered to a body depend on several factors—the amount of radiation received, the size of the irradiated area, and how the radiation is delivered in time. If the radiation is delivered in portions over a period of time, it is said to be *fractionated* and has a *less harmful* effect than if the radiation were delivered all at once. With fractionation, cells have an opportunity to repair, and so some recovery occurs between doses. *(Bushong, 8th ed., p. 496)*

82. **(A)** The line-focus principle illustrates that as the target angle decreases, the effective focal spot decreases (providing improved recorded detail), but the actual area of electron interaction remains much larger (allowing for greater heat capacity). *It must be remembered, however, that a steep (small) target angle increases*

the heel effect, and part coverage may be compromised. (Shephard, p. 219)

83. **(B)** As the exposed film enters the processor from the feed tray, it first enters the *developer* section (number 1), where *exposed* silver bromide crystals are reduced to black metallic silver. The film then enters the *fixer* (number 2), where the *unexposed* silver grains are removed from the film by the clearing agent. The film then enters the wash section (number 3), where chemicals are removed from the film to preserve the image, improving archival quality. From the wash, the film enters the dryer section (number 4). *(Selman, 9th ed., p. 194)*

84. **(A)** The *genetically significant dose* (GSD) illustrates that large exposures to a few people are cause for little concern when diluted by the total population. On the other hand, we all share the burden of the radiation that is received by the total population, and especially as the use of medical radiation increases, each individual's share of the total exposure increases. *(Bushong, 8th ed., p. 589)*

85. **(C)** A patient with a respiratory disease can transmit infectious organisms via airborne contamination (if the patient sneezes or coughs). Therefore, patients with upper respiratory tract infection should be transported wearing a mask to prevent the possibility of airborne contamination. It is not necessary for the radiographer to be masked. *(Torres et al., 6th ed., p. 69)*

86. **(B)** Quality Control refers to our equipment and its safe and accurate operation. Various components must be tested at specified intervals and test results must be within specified parameters. Any deviation from those parameters must be corrected. Examples of equipment components that are tested annually are the focal spot size, linearity, reproducibility, filtration, kV, and exposure time. Kilovoltage settings can most effectively be tested using an electronic kV meter; to meet required standards, the kV should be accurate to within +/− 4 kV.

Congruence is a term used to describe the relationship between the collimator light field and the actual x-ray field—they must be congruent (i.e., match) to within 2% of the SID. Collimators should be inspected and verified as accurate semiannually, that is, twice a year. Reproducibility testing should specify that radiation output be consistent to within +/− 5%. (*Fosbinder and Orth, pp. 223–225; NCRP Report No. 99, pp. 69–70*)

87. **(C)** If the x-ray tube is angled significantly *across the lead strips* of a focused grid, there is uniform loss of density (grid cutoff). Insufficient or excessive *distance* with focused grids causes loss of density (grid cutoff) along the periphery of the image. Figure 6–10 demonstrates grid cutoff everywhere except along a central vertical strip of the image. This density loss is due to the focused grid's being placed *upside down.* Thus, the middle vertical lead strips allow x-rays to pass, but because the lead strips cant laterally, they are directly opposite to the direction of the x-ray photons (rather than parallel to them), and severe grid cutoff results. (*Fauber, 2nd ed., pp. 123–124*)

88. **(D)** Single-phase current has a 100% voltage drop between peak voltages. Three-phase current decreases this voltage drop considerably. Three-phase, six-pulse current has about a 13% voltage drop between peak voltages, and three-phase, 12-pulse current has only about a 4% drop between peak voltages. However, high-frequency current is almost constant potential, having less than 1% voltage ripple. (*Bushong, 8th ed., pp. 122, 123*)

89. **(C)** The reduction in x-ray beam intensity that results from scattering (Compton) and absorption (photoelectric) processes is termed *attenuation.* The anode heel effect is related to the variation in x-ray beam intensity as it emerges in a divergent cone-shaped fashion from the x-ray tube, with greater intensity being at the cathode end of the beam. Grid cutoff is absorption of the useful remnant beam as a result of misalignment or miscentering with the grid. (*Bushong, 9th ed., pp. 155, 175*)

90. **(B)** When viewing the glenoid fossa from the anterior, it is seen to angle posteriorly and approximately 45 degrees. To view it in profile, then, it must be placed so that its surface is perpendicular to the IR. The patient is positioned in a 45-degree oblique, affected-side-down position, which places the glenoid fossa approximately perpendicular to the IR. The arm is abducted slightly, the elbow is flexed, and the hand and forearm are placed over the abdomen. The CR is directed perpendicular to the glenohumeral joint. (*Frank, Long, and Smith, 11th ed., vol. 1, pp. 192–193*)

91. **(A)** Of the given factors, kilovoltage and grid ratio will have a significant effect on the scale of radiographic contrast. The milliampere-seconds values are almost identical. Because decreased kilovoltage and high-ratio grid combination would allow the least amount of scattered radiation to reach the IR, thereby producing *fewer* gray tones, (A) is the best answer. Group (D) also uses low kilovoltage, but the grid ratio is lower, thereby allowing more scatter to reach the IR and producing *more* gray tones. (*Shephard, p. 308*)

92. **(B)** The spinal cord is a column of nervous tissue about 17 in. (44 cm) in length. It is somewhat flattened anteroposteriorly and extends from the medulla oblongata of the brain to the level of L2 within the spinal canal. Because the adult spinal cord ends at the level of L2, a lumbar puncture usually is performed below that level—generally, at the level of L3 to L4. A lumbar puncture may be performed for the removal of spinal fluid for diagnostic purposes or for the injection of medications. (*Tortora and Derrickson, 11th ed., p. 440*)

93. **(B)** LET expresses the rate at which photon or particulate energy is transferred to (absorbed by) biologic material (through ionization processes); it depends on the type of radiation and absorber characteristics. *Relative biologic effectiveness* (RBE) describes the degree of response or amount of biologic change that one can expect of the irradiated material. As the amount of transferred energy (LET) increases (from interactions occurring between radiation and biologic material), the amount of biologic effect/damage also will increase; that is, the two are directly related. (*Bushong, 8th ed., p. 495*)

94. (B) As the kilovoltage is increased, a greater number of electrons are driven across to the anode with greater force. Therefore, as energy conversion takes place at the anode, *more* high-energy photons are produced. However, because they are *higher-energy* photons, there will be less patient absorption. *(Fauber, 2nd ed., p. 58)*

95. (D) The input phosphor of image intensifiers is usually made of cesium iodide. For each x-ray photon absorbed by cesium iodide, approximately 5,000 light photons are emitted. As the light photons strike a photoemissive *photocathode*, a number of electrons are released from the photocathode and focused toward the output side of the image tube by voltage applied to the negatively charged *electrostatic focusing lenses*. The electrons are then accelerated through the neck of the tube where they strike the small (0.5–1 in.) *output phosphor* that is mounted on a flat glass support. The entire assembly is enclosed within a 2–4-mm thick vacuum glass envelope. Remember that the image on the output phosphor is *minified, brighter,* and *inverted* (electron focusing causes image inversion).

Input screen diameters of 5–12 in. are available. Although smaller diameter input screens improve resolution, they do not permit a large FOV, that is, viewing of large patient areas.

Dual- and triple-field image intensifiers are available that permit *magnified* viewing of fluoroscopic images. To achieve magnification, the *voltage* to the focusing lenses is increased and a *smaller* portion of the input phosphor is used, thereby resulting in a smaller FOV. Because minification gain is now decreased, the image is not as bright. The mA is automatically increased to compensate for the loss in brightness when the image intensifier is switched to magnification mode. Entrance skin exposure (ESE) can increase dramatically as the FOV decreases (i.e., as magnification increases).

As FOV decreases, *magnification* of the output screen image increases, there is less *noise* because increased mA provides a greater number of x-ray photons, and *contrast* and *resolution* improve. The *focal point* in the magnification mode is *further away from the* output phosphor (as a result of increased voltage

applied to the focusing lenses) and therefore the output image is magnified. *(Fosbinder and Orth, p. 191)*

96. (B) At a given exposure, higher-speed intensifying screens (400) will emit more fluorescent light, thereby increasing radiographic density. Faster intensifying screens, therefore, allow a considerable reduction in milliampere-seconds and, therefore, in patient dose and motion unsharpness. Intensifying-screen speed is unrelated to scattered radiation. *(Shephard, p. 68)*

97. (B) 98. (B) The figure shown is a double-contrast BE, oblique position. Since the left colic/splenic flexure (number 1) is "open," this is either a RPO or LAO position. Also demonstrated are the descending colon (number 2), and transverse colon (number 3). Barium has refluxed into the ileum (number 5).

99. (D) The x-ray tube anode is designed according to the line-focus principle, that is, with the focal track beveled (Figure 6–24). This allows a larger actual focal spot to project a smaller effective focal spot, resulting in improved recorded detail with less blur. However, because of the target angle, penumbral blur varies along the longitudinal tube axis, being greater at the cathode end of the image and less at the anode end of the image. Therefore, better detail will be appreciated using small focal spots at the anode end of the x-ray beam and at longer SIDs. *(Bushong, 8th ed., p. 287)*

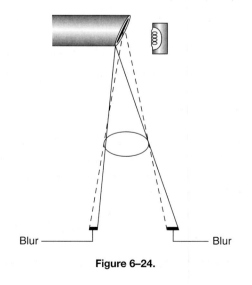

Figure 6–24.

100. (B) *Subcutaneous emphysema* is a pathologic distension of tissues with air; *pulmonary emphysema* is a chronic disease characterized by overdistension of the alveoli with air. *Osteomalacia* is a softening of bone so that it becomes flexible, brittle, and deformed. All three of these conditions involve a decrease in tissue density and, therefore, require a decrease in exposure factors. *Atelectasis* is a collapsed or airless lung; it requires an increase in exposure factors. *(Carlton and Adler, 4th ed., p. 248)*

101. (B) Bergonié and Tribondeau theorized in 1906 that all precursor cells are particularly radiosensitive (e.g., stem cells found in bone marrow). There are several types of stem cells in bone marrow, and the different types differ in degree of radiosensitivity. Of these, red blood cell precursors, or *erythroblasts*, are the most radiosensitive. White blood cell precursors, or *myelocytes*, follow. Platelet precursor cells, or *megakaryocytes*, are even less radiosensitive. *Myocytes* are mature muscle cells and are fairly radioresistant. *(Bushong, 8th ed., p. 495)*

102. (B) High-kilovoltage exposures produce large amounts of scattered radiation, and high-ratio grids are used often with high-kilovoltage techniques in an effort to absorb more of this scattered radiation. However, as more scattered radiation is absorbed, more primary radiation is absorbed as well. This accounts for the increase in milliampere-seconds required when changing from an 8:1 to a 16:1 grid. In addition, precise centering and positioning become more critical; a small degree of inaccuracy is more likely to cause grid cutoff in a high-ratio grid. *(Bushong, 8th ed., pp. 252–255)*

103. (B) The use of high kilovoltage with a fairly low-ratio grid will be ineffective in ridding the remnant beam of scattered radiation. To improve contrast in this example, it has been decided to decrease the kilovoltage by 15%, thus making it necessary to increase the milliampere-seconds from 5 mAs to 10 mAs. Because an increase in the grid ratio to 12:1 is also desired, another change in milliampere-seconds will be required (remember, 10 mAs

is now the *old* mAs):

$$\frac{10 \ (\text{old mAs})}{x \ (\text{new mAs})} = \frac{4 \ (8{:}1 \ \text{grid factor})}{5 \ (12{:}1 \ \text{grid factor})}$$

$$4x = 50$$

Thus, $x = 12.5$ mAs at 90 kVp. Now, determine the *exposure time* required with 400 mA to produce 12.5 mAs:

$$400x = 12.5$$
$$x = 0.03\text{-s exposure}$$

(Selman, 9th ed., p. 214)

104. (A) Three-phase current is obtained from three individual alternating currents superimposed on, but out of step with, one another by 120 degrees. The result is an *almost* constant potential current, with only a very small voltage ripple (4%–13%), producing more x-rays per milliampere-second. *(Carlton and Adler, 4th ed., p. 96)*

105. (A) The RAO position affords a good view of the pyloric canal and duodenal bulb. It is also a good position for the barium-filled esophagus, projecting it between the vertebrae and the heart. The left lateral projection of the stomach demonstrates the left retrogastric space, the recumbent PA projection is used as a general survey of the gastric surfaces, and the recumbent AP projection with slight left oblique affords a double contrast of the pylorus and duodenum. *(Bontrager and Lampignano, 6th ed., p. 479)*

106. (C) Excessive heat production is a major problem in x-ray production. Of the energy required to produce x-rays, 0.2% is transformed to x-rays, and 99.8% is transformed to heat. The copper anode stem and the oil surrounding the x-ray tube help to move heat away from the face of the anode. Excessive heat can cause pitting of the anode (resulting in decreased output) or actual cracking of the anode or damage to the rotor bearings (resulting in tube failure). As the cathode filament is heated for exposure after exposure, some of its tungsten is vaporized and deposited on the inner surface of the glass envelope near the tube window. After a time, this can cause electric arcing and tube failure. This is the most common cause of tube failure because it can occur even with normal use. (*Bushong, 8th ed., pp. 142–143*)

107. **(B)** Proper functioning of the photo timer depends on accurate positioning by the radiographer. The correct photocell(s) must be selected, and the anatomic part of interest must completely cover the photocell(s) to achieve the desired density. If a photocell is left uncovered, scattered radiation from the part being examined will cause premature termination of exposure and an underexposed radiograph. (*Carlton and Adler, 4th ed., p. 102*)

108. **(B)** If the same kilovoltage is used with single-phase and three-phase equipment, the three-phase unit will require about 50% fewer milliampere-seconds to produce similar radiographs. Because three-phase equipment has much higher effective voltage than single-phase equipment, the three-phase radiograph will have lower contrast. A lower milliampere-seconds value can be used with three-phase equipment, so heat units are not built up as quickly. *When technical factors are adjusted to obtain the same density and contrast, there is no difference in patient dose.* (*Selman, 9th ed., pp. 162–164*)

109. **(C)** Because mammographic techniques operate at very low kilovoltage levels, the cassette front material becomes especially important. The use of soft, low-energy x-ray photons is the underlying principle of mammography; any attenuation of the beam would be most undesirable. Special plastics that resist impact and heat softening, such as polystyrene and polycarbonate, are used frequently as cassette front material. (*Shephard, p. 49*)

110. **(C)** Quality Control refers to our equipment and its safe and accurate operation. Various components must be tested at specified intervals and test results must be within specified parameters. Any deviation from those parameters must be corrected. Examples of equipment components that are tested annually are the focal spot size, linearity, re-

producibility, collimation, filtration, kV, and exposure time. Quality Assurance is associated with patients and staff and their interactions and relationships. Congruence is a term used to describe the relationship between the collimator light field and the actual x-ray field—they must be congruent (i.e., match) to within 2% of the SID. Postprocessing refers to the windowing or other manipulation of a digital image. (*Fosbinder and Orth, pp. 222–223*)

111. **(C)** An oblique projection of the cervical spine is shown. The first two cervical vertebrae are poorly visualized because of superimposition with the mandible; the chin should be elevated to correct this problem. Otherwise, the positioning is satisfactory, with good demonstration of the remainder of the cervical intervertebral foramina. The patient has been accurately rotated 45 degrees, and a 15- to 20-degree tube angle was used. (*Bontrager and Lampignano, 6th ed., p. 308*)

112. **(B)** An oblique projection of the cervical spine is shown. The patient has been accurately positioned RAO with the MSP 45 degrees to the IR and the CR angled 15 to 20 degrees caudad, but the chin should be elevated to avoid superimposition on the first two cervical vertebrae. This position offers excellent delineation of the intervertebral foramina (number 1) formed by the adjacent vertebral notches of pedicles (number 2). This projection gives an "on end" view of the transverse processes (number 3). A portion of the spinous processes (number 4) may be seen, especially in the lower cervical vertebrae. (*Frank, Long, and Smith, 11th ed., vol. 1, p. 401*)

113. **(B)** To demonstrate the intercondyloid fossa, the CR must be directed perpendicular to the long axis of the tibia (Figure 6–25). Because the knee is flexed so that the tibia forms a 40-degree angle with the IR, the CR must be directed 40 degrees caudad to place the CR perpendicular to the long axis of the tibia. Directing the CR to the popliteal depression aligns the CR parallel with the knee joint space. (*Bontrager and Lampignano, 6th ed., p. 250*)

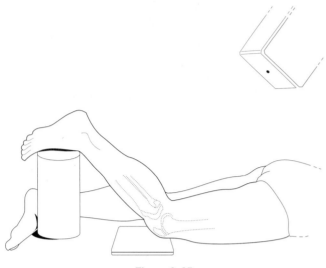

Figure 6–25.

114. (D) In CPR for infants, the rescuer places his or her index finger on the sternum just below the level of the intermammary line. The second and third fingers are used to compress the sternum 1/2 to 1 in. during compressions. The recommended rate is 100 compressions per minute. The volume of air delivered during ventilation should be just enough to make the infants chest rise and fall. (*Adler and Carlton, 4th ed., p. 285*)

115. (D) All the choices listed in the question should be part of a preliminary patient history before deciding to inject ionic or nonionic contrast media. As patients age, their general health decreases, and they are, therefore, more likely to suffer from adverse reactions. Patients with a history of respiratory disease, such as asthma or emphysema and COPD, are more likely to have a reaction and to suffer greater distress in the event of a reaction. Patients with cardiac disease run an increased risk of changes in heart rate and myocardial infarction. Patients also should be screened for decreased renal or hepatic function, sickle-cell disease, diabetes, and pregnancy. (*Adler and Carlton, 4th ed., pp. 360–361*)

116. (C) The degree of anterior and posterior motion is occasionally diminished with a whiplash-type injury. Anterior (forward, flexion) and posterior (backward, extension) motion is evaluated in the lateral position with the patient assuming flexion and extension as best as he or she can. Left and right bending images of the thoracic and lumbar vertebrae are obtained frequently when evaluating scoliosis. The AP open-mouth projection is used to evaluate the first two cervical vertebrae. The moving mandible AP projection is used to demonstrate the entire cervical spine while blurring out the superimposed mandible. (*Frank, Long, and Smith, 11th ed., vol. 1, p. 402*)

117. (A) Quality Control refers to our equipment and its safe and accurate operation. Various components must be tested at specified intervals and test results must be within specified parameters. Any deviation from those parameters must be corrected. Examples of equipment components that are tested annually are the focal spot size, linearity, reproducibility, filtration, kV, and exposure time. Reproducibility specifies that radiation output must be consistent to within +/−5%. Linearity tests x-ray output with increasing mAs; mR/mAs should be accurate to within 10%. Kilovoltage settings can most effectively be tested using an electronic kV meter; to meet required standards, the kV should be accurate to within +/−4 kV. Congruence is a term used to describe the relationship between the collimator light field and the actual x-ray field—they must be congruent to within 2% of the SID. Radiographic equipment collimators should be inspected and verified as accurate semiannually. (*Fosbinder and Orth, pp. 223–225; NCRP Report No. 99, pp. 72–74*)

118 and 119. (118, C; 119, A) An anterior view of the foot and ankle bones is shown. The ankle joint is formed by the articulation of the tibia, fibula, and talus (number 7). The tibial (medial) malleolus is labeled 8; the fibular (lateral) malleolus is labeled 1. The talus articulates with the calcaneus (number 2) inferiorly and with the navicular (number 6) anteriorly. The cuboid (number 3) is seen anterior to the calcaneus, and the three cuneiforms (number 5) are anterior to the navicular. (*Tortora and Derrickson, 11th ed., p. 250*)

120. (D) Variance from the normal bladder contour will be noted while the bladder is full of contrast medium. However, a postmicturition (postvoiding) radiograph is also an essential part of an IVU/IVP. The presence of residual urine may be an indication of small tumor masses or, in male patients, enlargement of the prostate gland. *(Frank, Long, and Smith, 11th ed., vol. 2, p. 217)*

121. **(B)** Image intensification is a process that converts the dim fluoroscopic image into a much brighter image, much like normal daylight. As x-ray photons emerge from the patient and enter the image intensifier, they first encounter the input phosphor, which is generally composed of cesium iodide phosphors. At the input phosphor, x-ray photons are converted to light photons, which, in turn, strike the photocathode. The photocathode is a photoemissive metal (usually, antimony and cesium compounds); when struck by light, it emits electrons in proportion to the intensity of the light striking it. The electrons then are directed to the output phosphor via the electrostatic focusing lenses, speeded up in the neck of the tube by the accelerating anode and directed to the output phosphor for further amplification. Most image intensifiers offer brightness gains of 5,000–20,000. *From the output phosphor, the image is taken by the TV camera, most often a Plumbicon or Vidicon tube, and transferred to the TV monitor. A cine camera is required to record images on 16- or 35-mm film. (Thompson et al., p. 370)*

122. **(B)** Sterile technique is required for administration of contrast media by the intravenous and intrathecal (intraspinal) methods. Aseptic technique is used for administration of contrast media by the oral and rectal routes as well as through the nasogastric tube. *(Torres et al., 6th ed., pp. 270–271)*

123. **(A)** IVU requires the use of iodinated contrast media. Low kilovoltage (about 70 kVp) is usually used to enhance the photoelectric effect and, in turn, to better visualize the renal collecting system. High kilovoltage will produce excessive scattered radiation and obviate the effect of the contrast agent. A higher milliamperage with a short exposure time generally is preferable. *(Fauber, 2nd ed., p. 264)*

124. **(C)** The infraorbitomeatal line (IOML) is an imaginary line extending from the infraorbital margin to the external auditory meatus and is represented by number 3. The IOML is used for most lateral skull projections, including lateral projections of facial bones. The skull is positioned so that the MSP is parallel to the cassette, the interpupillary line is perpendicular to the cassette, and the IOML is parallel to the long (transverse) axis of the cassette. Number 1 is the glabellomeatal line, number 2 is the OML (orbitomeatal line), and number 4 is the acanthomeatal line. These baselines are used to obtain accurate positioning in skull radiography. *(Frank, Long, and Smith, 11th ed., vol. 2, p. 300)*

125. **(B)** The patient is well positioned; the spinous processes and sternum are seen clearly without superimposition. Adequate penetration and long-scale contrast are present without excessive radiographic density. The patient had been shielded properly for the PA projection, but the shield was not moved to the correct location prior to the lateral exposure. *(Bontrager and Lampignano, 6th ed., p. 98)*

126. **(D)** Photoelectric interaction in tissue involves complete absorption of the incident photon, whereas Compton interactions involve only partial transfer of energy. The larger the quantity of radiation and the greater the number of photoelectric interactions, the greater is the patient dose. Radiation dose to more radiosensitive tissues, such as gonadal tissue or blood-forming organs, is more harmful than the same dose to muscle tissue. *(Bushong, 8th ed., p. 197)*

127. **(B)** With the blood pressure cuff wrapped snugly around the patient's brachial artery and the pump inflated to approximately 180 mm Hg, the valve is opened only slightly to release pressure very slowly. With the stethoscope over the brachial artery, listen for the pulse while watching the mercury column (gauge). Note the point at which the first pulse is heard as the systolic pressure. As the valve is opened further, the sound is louder; the point at which it suddenly becomes softer is recorded as the diastolic pressure. *(Torres et al., 6th ed., p. 149)*

128. **(B)** The AP oblique projection (LPO, RPO position/Grashey method) is used to demonstrate the glenoid fossa in profile. The position is most comfortably performed in the erect position. The body is rotated 35 to 45 degrees toward the affected side. The CR is directed 2 in. medial and 2 in. lateral to the upper outer border of the shoulder. The glenohumeral joint space is open and the glenoid cavity is demonstrated in profile. *(Frank, Long, and Smith, 11th ed., vol. 1, p. 192)*

129. **(D)** When the primary beam is restricted to an area near the periphery of the body, sometimes part of the illuminated area overhangs the edge of the body. If the exposure is then made, scattered radiation from the tabletop (where there is no absorber) will undercut the part, causing excessive image density. If, however, a *lead rubber mat* is placed on the overhanging illuminated area, most of this scatter will be absorbed. This is frequently helpful in lateral lumbar spine and AP shoulder radiographs. *(Carlton and Adler, 4th ed., pp. 233–234)*

130. **(A)** The midcoronal plane (number 1) divides the body into anterior and posterior halves. A coronal plane is any plane parallel to the midcoronal plane. The midsagittal plane (number 2) divides the body into left and right halves. A sagittal plane is any plane parallel to the midsagittal plane. A transverse or horizontal plane (number 3) is perpendicular to the midsagittal plane and midcoronal plane, dividing the body into superior and inferior portions. *(Frank, Long, and Smith, 11th ed., vol. 1, p. 58)*

131. **(D)** Pulmonary vascular markings often are prominent in the elderly and in smokers. Quiet, shallow breathing may be used during a long exposure (with a compensating low milliamperage) to blur them out. Oblique sternum, AP scapula, and lateral thoracic spine projections are examinations in which this technique is useful. *(Frank, Long, and Smith, 11th ed., vol. 1, pp. 213, 418, 470)*

132. **(D)** Streptococcal pharyngitis ("strep throat") is caused by bacteria. To know this, you have to remember that bacteria are classified according to their morphology (i.e., size and shape). The three classifications are spirals, rods (bacilli), and spheres (cocci). Viruses, unlike bacteria, cannot live outside a human cell. Viruses attach themselves to a host cell and invade the cell with their genetic information. Various fungal infections may grow on the skin (cutaneously), or they may enter the skin. Fungal infections that enter the circulatory or lymphatic system can be deadly. Protozoa are one-celled organisms classified by their motility. Ameboids move by locomotion, flagella use their protein tail, cilia possess numerous short protein tails, and sporozoans actually are not mobile. *(Adler and Carlton, 4th ed., pp. 221–223)*

133. **(D)** Structures located behind the parietal peritoneum are referred to as *retroperitoneal*. Retroperitoneal structures include the kidneys, adrenal glands, pancreas, duodenum, ascending and descending colon, portions of the aorta, and the inferior vena cava. *(Tortora and Derrickson, 11th ed., p. 19)*

134. **(C)** To change nongrid to grid exposure, or to adjust exposure when changing from one grid ratio to another, remember the factor for each grid ratio:

   No grid = 1 × original mAs
   5:1 grid = 2 × original mAs
   6:1 grid = 3 × original mAs
   8:1 grid = 4 × original mAs
   12:1 grid = 5 × original mAs
   16:1 grid = 6 × original mAs

   Therefore, to change from nongrid exposure to an 8:1 grid, multiply the original milliampere-seconds value by a factor of 4. Thus, a new setting of 32 mAs is required. *(Shephard, p. 248)*

135. **(A)** A PA axial Caldwell position is shown, demonstrating the frontal and ethmoidal sinuses. The Caldwell position requires an angle of 15 degrees caudad, exiting the nasion. The petrous ridges should be projected in the lower third of the orbits. The radiograph shown demonstrates somewhat excessive angulation because the petrous pyramids are projected at the bottom of the orbits. The

maxillary sinuses are demonstrated in the parietoacanthal projection (Waters position), and the sphenoidal sinuses are demonstrated through the open mouth in a modified Waters position. The mastoid sinuses/ air cells are part of the temporal bone and are radiographically unrelated to the paranasal sinuses. (*Bontrager and Lampignano, 6th ed., p. 439*)

136. **(C)** A photo timer is one type of automatic exposure device. When it is installed in an x-ray unit, it is calibrated to produce radiographic densities as required by the radiologist. Once the part being radiographed has been exposed to produce the proper image density, the photo timer automatically terminates the exposure. *The manual timer should be used as a backup timer should the photo timer fail to terminate the exposure, thus protecting the patient from overexposure and the x-ray tube from excessive heat load.* Circuit breakers and fuses are circuit devices used to protect circuit elements from overload. In case of current surge, the circuit will be broken, thus preventing equipment damage. A rheostat is a type of variable resistor. (*Shephard, p. 274*)

137. **(D)** The hepatic (right colic) and splenic (left colic) flexures are not generally well demonstrated in the AP and PA projections. To "open" the flexures, oblique projections are required. The left anterior oblique (LAO, left PA oblique) and right posterior oblique (RPO, right PA oblique) positions are used to demonstrate the splenic flexure. The hepatic flexure is usually well demonstrated in the RAO and LPO positions. (*Bontrager and Lampignano, 6th ed., pp. 515–517*)

138. **(C)** Contrast media may be administered in a variety of manners in cholangiography, including (1) an endoscope with a cannula placed in the hepatopancreatic ampulla (of Vater) for an ERCP, (2) a needle or small catheter placed directly in the common bile duct for an operative cholangiogram, (3) a very fine needle through the patient's side and into the liver for a percutaneous transhepatic cholangiogram, and (4) via an indwelling T-tube for a postoperative or T-tube

cholangiogram. (*Frank, Long, and Smith, 11th ed., vol. 2, pp. 111–116*)

139. **(B)** Psychologist Abraham Maslow described a hierarchy, or pyramid, of needs with primary (physiologic) needs at the base and secondary (nonphysiologic) needs at higher levels. Maslow postulated that as the most basic survival needs are met, new needs emerge. At the bottom of the hierarchy are physiologic needs such as food, water, air, rest, and so on. One step up in the hierarchy is safety and security. Next is love and belongingness, followed by self-esteem and the esteem of others. Last is self-actualization, which is a kind of spiritual growth, satisfaction from life achievement, the feeling of leaving one's mark. (*Adler and Carlton, 4th ed., p. 143*)

140. **(C)** Radiographic rating charts enable the operator to determine the maximum safe milliamperage, exposure time, and kilovoltage for a particular exposure using a particular x-ray tube. An exposure that can be made using the large focal spot may not be safe when the small focal spot of the same x-ray tube is used. The total number of heat units an exposure generates also influences the amount of stress (in the form of heat) imparted to the anode. Single-phase heat units are determined by the product of milliampere-seconds and kilovoltage. Three-phase, six-pulse heat units are determined from the product of milliamperage × time × kilovoltage × 1.35. Three-phase, 12-pulse heat units are determined from the product of milliamperage × time × kilovoltage × 1.41. In the examples given, then, group (A) produces 6,091 HU, group (B) produces 14,805 HU, group (C) produces 1,997 HU, and group (D) produces 7,106 HU. Therefore, group (A) exposure factors will deliver the *least amount of heat* to the anode. (*Fauber, 2nd ed., pp. 36–37*)

141. **(D)** Converting from an 8:1 grid to nongrid requires about a fourfold decrease in milliampere-seconds. Increasing the kilovoltage by 15% and cutting the milliampere-seconds in half would reduce patient dose by half. Increasing mAs will always increase exposure dose. Therefore, the largest decrease

will occur with removal of a grid. *(Bushong, 8th ed., p. 252)*

142.   **(B)** Rotation of the chest is evidenced in the following ways: The distance between the medial aspect of the clavicles and the lateral portion of the vertebral column is asymmetric, the air-filled trachea is off midline, and the scapulae and air-filled lungs are asymmetric. The exposure was made during reasonably good inspiration, as evidenced by visualization of eight ribs above the diaphragm. The upper and lateral aspects of the lungs, including the pulmonary apices and costophrenic angles, are demonstrated. Even minimal rotation of the chest introduces significant distortion of the heart. *(Frank, Long, and Smith, 11th ed., vol. 1, p. 521)*

143.   **(C)** Retrograde urography requires ureteral catheterization so that a contrast medium can be introduced directly into the pelvicalyceal system. This procedure provides excellent opacification and structural information but does not demonstrate the function of these structures. Intravenous studies such as the IVU demonstrate function. *(Frank, Long, and Smith, vol. 2, 11th ed., p. 207)*

144.   **(D)** Generally, contrast medium is injected into the subarachnoid space between the third and fourth lumbar vertebrae. Because the spinal cord ends at the level of the first or second lumbar vertebra, this is considered to be a relatively safe injection site. The cisterna magna can be used, but the risk of contrast medium entering the ventricles and causing side effects increases. Diskography requires injection of contrast medium into the individual intervertebral disks. *(Frank, Long, and Smith, 11th ed., vol. 3, p. 6)*

145.   **(D)** Body substance precaution procedures identify various body fluids as infectious or potentially infectious. These body substances include pleural, pericardial, peritoneal, and amniotic fluids; synovial fluid; cerebrospinal fluid (CSF); breast milk; and vaginal secretions, as well as nasal secretions, tears, saliva, sputum, feces, urine, and wound drainage. *(Torres et al., 6th ed., p. 63)*

146.   **(B)** Intervertebral joints are well visualized in the lateral projection of all the vertebral groups. Cervical articular facets (forming apophyseal joints) are 90 degrees to the MSP and, therefore, are well demonstrated in the lateral projection. The cervical intervertebral foramina lie 45 degrees to the MSP (and 15–20 degrees to a transverse plane) and, therefore, are demonstrated in the oblique position. *(Bontrager and Lampignano, 6th ed., p. 296)*

147.   **(D)** Postoperative, or T-tube, cholangiography frequently is performed to evaluate the patency of the biliary ducts and to identify any previously undetected stones. Following surgery, a T-tube is left in place within the common bile duct, with the vertical portion of the T extending outside the body. Water-soluble iodinated contrast medium is injected, and fluoroscopic examination is carried out. *(Frank, Long, and Smith, 11th ed., vol. 2, p. 114)*

148.   **(C)** During radiography and fluoroscopy, radiation scatters from the patient in all directions. In fact, the patient is the single most important scattering object in both radiographic and fluoroscopic procedures. The approximate intensity (quantity) of scattered radiation at 1 m from the patient is 0.1% of the entrance dose. Therefore, if the entrance dose for this image is 320 mR, the intensity of radiation at 1 m from the patient is 0.1% of that, or 0.32 mR (0.001 × 320 = 0.32). *(Bushong, 8th ed., p. 572)*

149.   **(B)** Patient demographic and examination information originates from the hospital/facility HIS, where it is obtained when the patient is initially registered. That information is available or retrievable when the patient is scheduled, or arrives, for imaging services. Typical patient information includes name, DOB or age, sex, ID number, accession number, examination being performed, date and time of examination.

Additional information may be available on the examination requisition; more information is usually entered by the technologist at the time of the examination.

A feature that is useful in sorting examinations and decreasing (but not eliminating) errors is the *Modality Work List* (MWL). The MWL "brings up" existing RIS information, that is, the examinations scheduled for each imaging area—for example, x-ray, CT, MR, mammography, ultrasound, etc. The technologist selects the correct patient, which includes that patient's particular demographics, from the particular modality work list.

It is essential that the technologist is attentive to detail and accuracy when entering patient information; errors in patient demographics entry, and entry duplication, must be avoided.

PACS is used by health care facilities to economically store, archive, exchange, and transmit digital images from multiple imaging modalities; it replaces the need to manually file, retrieve, and transport film and film jackets.

RIS and HIS can be integrated with PACS for electronic health information storage. The purpose of HIS is to manage health care information and documents electronically, and to ensure data security and availability. RIS is a system for tracking radiological and imaging procedures. RIS is used for patient registration and scheduling, radiology workflow management, reporting and printout, manipulation and distribution and tracking of patient data, and billing. RIS complements HIS and is critical to competent workflow to radiologic facilities. *(Seeram, p. 222–223, 226)*

150. **(B)** The most hazardous time for abdominal irradiation is in the earliest stages of pregnancy, when many women are unaware that they are pregnant. For this reason, *it is recommended that elective radiologic procedures be performed within the first 10 days following the onset of the menses.* It is during this time that the danger of irradiating a recently fertilized ovum is most unlikely. About 14 days before the onset of menses is when the ovarian follicle ruptures and liberates an ovum. *(Bushong, 8th ed., pp. 563–564)*

151–152. **(151, A; 152, B)** A parietoacanthal projection (Waters position) of the skull is shown. The chin is elevated sufficiently to project the petrous ridges below the *maxillary sinuses* (number 4). Note that the foramen rotundum

is seen near the upper margin of the maxillary sinuses. Other paranasal sinus groups are not well visualized in this position, although a modification with the mouth open may be taken to demonstrate the sphenoidal sinuses. This is also the single best projection to demonstrate the facial bones. The *zygomatic arch* (number 2) is well demonstrated; the mandible, its *angle* (number 1), and the *coronoid process* (number 3) are also well demonstrated. The odontoid process is seen projected through the foramen magnum. The *mastoid* air cells are seen adjacent to the mandibular angle as multiple small, air-filled, bony spaces. *(Frank, Long, and Smith, 11th ed., vol. 2, pp. 333, 399)*

153. **(B)** Esophageal varices are best demonstrated when there is increased venous pressure and when blood is flowing against gravity. Therefore, to demonstrate the twisted, dilated condition of venous varicosities, esophagograms must be performed in the recumbent position. In the erect position, the veins appear more smooth and normal. The Fowler position describes a position in which the patient's head is higher than the feet, and the Sims position is preferred for insertion of the enema tip. *(Frank, Long, and Smith, 11th ed., vol. 2, p. 138)*

154. **(A)** With reference to film/screen imaging, in the low kilovoltage ranges a difference of just a few kilovolts makes a very noticeable radiographic difference, that is, there is little latitude. High-kilovoltage techniques offer a much greater margin for error. Grid ratio is unrelated to exposure latitude, but higher-ratio grids offer less tube-centering latitude (i.e., leeway, margin for error) than low-ratio grids. *(Carlton and Adler, 4th ed., p. 185)*

155. **(A)** As SID increases, so does recorded detail because magnification is decreased. Therefore, SID is directly related to recorded detail. As focal spot size increases, recorded detail decreases because more penumbra is produced. Focal spot size is thus inversely related to radiographic sharpness or recorded detail. Tube current affects radiographic density and is unrelated to recorded detail. *(Fauber, 2nd ed., pp. 79, 81)*

156. **(A)** The sacroiliac joints angle posteriorly and medially 25 degrees to the MSP. Therefore, to demonstrate them with an AP oblique projection, the affected side must be elevated 25 degrees. This places the joint space perpendicular to the IR and parallel to the CR. When the PA oblique projection is used, the unaffected side will be elevated 25 degrees. *(Frank, Long, and Smith, 11th ed., vol. 1, pp. 438–441)*

157. **(B)** A double-focus tube has two focal-spot sizes available. These focal spots actually are two available paths on the focal track. There are also two filaments. When the small focal spot is selected, the small filament is heated, and electrons are driven across to the smaller portion of the focal track. When the large focal spot is selected, the large filament is heated, and electrons are driven across to the larger portion of the focal track. *(Bushong, 8th ed., pp. 132–134)*

158–159. **(158, A; 159, D)** An LPO projection of the lumbar spine is shown. The patient is positioned so that the lumbar spine forms a 45-degree angle with the IR. The apophyseal joints (those closest to the IR) are well demonstrated in this position. The typical "Scotty dog" image is depicted. The "ear" of the Scotty is the superior articular process (number 1), and the front foot is the inferior articular process (number 4). The Scotty's eye is the pedicle, its body is the lamina (number 3), and its nose is the transverse process (number 2). *(Bontrager and Lampignano, 7th ed., p. 326)*

160. **(C)** With the patient in the lateral position, the MSP is parallel to the x-ray tabletop. Because the *inter*vertebral foramina, which are formed by the pedicles, are 90 degrees to the MSP, they are well demonstrated in the lateral projection. The intervertebral joints (i.e., disk spaces) are also well demonstrated. The spinal cord passes through the vertebral foramina, which would not be visualized in conventional radiography of the lumbar spine. *(Frank, Long, and Smith, 11th ed., vol. 1, p. 428)*

161. **(A)** Since 4,500 mrad is equal to 4.5 rad, if 4.5 rad were delivered in 6 minutes, then the dose rate must be 0.75 rad/min:

$$\frac{4.5 \text{ rad}}{6 \text{ min}} = \frac{x \text{ rad}}{1 \text{ min}}$$

$$6x = 4.5$$

Thus, $x = 0.75$ rad/min. *(Selman, 9th ed., p. 528)*

162. **(D)** Breast tissue has very low subject contrast, but it is imperative to visualize microcalcifications and subtle density differences. Fine detail is necessary to visualize any microcalcifications; therefore, a small focal spot tube is essential. Short scale (high) contrast (and, therefore, low kilovoltage) is needed to accentuate any differences in tissue density. A compression device serves to even out differences in tissue thickness (thicker at the chest wall, thinner at the nipple) and decrease OID and helps to decrease the production of scattered radiation. *(Peart, pp. 49–50)*

163. **(C)** Look over the choices again, keeping in mind the factors that affect recorded detail. Looking first at SID, the options may be reduced to (B) and (C) because the increase to a 40-in. SID certainly will improve recorded detail. There is one other factor that will affect detail—the speed of the system (intensifying screens). Because a slower system will render better recorded detail, the best answer is (C). The technical factors such as milliampere-seconds, kilovoltage, and grid ratio have no effect on recorded detail. *(Shephard, pp. 247, 310)*

164–165. **(164, D; 165, D)** An anterior view of the forearm is shown. The proximal anterior surface of the ulna (number 8) presents a rather large pointed process at the anterior margin of the semilunar (trochlear) notch (number 5) called the *coronoid process* (number 6). The olecranon process is identified as number 4, and the radial notch of the ulna is number 7. Distally, the ulnar head is number 9, and the styloid process is labeled 10. The radius (number 12) is the lateral bone of the forearm. The radial head is number 3, the radial neck is number 2, and the radial tuberosity is number 1. Distally, the radial styloid process is labeled 11. *(Tortora and Derrickson, 11th ed., p. 237)*

166. **(D)** The PA axial (Caldwell) projection of the paranasal sinuses is used to demonstrate the frontal and ethmoidal sinuses. The CR is angled caudally 15 degrees to the OML. This projects the petrous pyramids into the lower third of the orbits, thus permitting optimal visualization of the frontal and ethmoidal sinuses. *(Bontrager and Lampignano, 6th ed., p. 439)*

167. **(D)** Lead aprons are worn by occupationally exposed individuals during fluoroscopic and mobile x-ray procedures. Lead aprons are available with various lead equivalents; 0.5- and 1.0-mm lead are the most common. The 1.0-mm lead-equivalent apron will provide close to 100% protection at most kilovoltage levels, but it is used rarely because it weighs anywhere from 12 to 24 lb. A 0.25-mm lead-equivalent apron will attenuate about 97% of a 50-kVp x-ray beam, 66% of a 75-kVp beam, and 51% of a 100-kVp beam. A 0.5-mm lead-equivalent apron will attenuate about 99.9% of a 50-kVp beam, 88% of a 75-kVp beam, and 75% of a 100-kVp beam. *(Bushong, 8th ed., p. 597)*

168. **(D)** Shape distortion is caused by misalignment of the x-ray tube, the body part to be radiographed, and the IR. An object can be falsely imaged (foreshortened or elongated) as a result of incorrect placement of the tube, the part, or the IR. Only one of the three need be misaligned for distortion to occur. *(Selman, 9th ed., pp. 225–226)*

169. **(D)** Because the toes curve naturally downward, the interphalangeal joints are not well demonstrated in the AP (dorsoplantar) projection. To "open" the interphalangeal joints, the CR should be directed 15 degrees cephalad. Another method is to place a 15-degree foam sponge wedge under the foot, elevating the toes 15 degrees from the IR; the CR then would be directed perpendicularly. *(Bushong, 8th ed., p. 137)*

170. **(B)** The most commonly used method of low-flow oxygen delivery is the nasal cannula. It can be used to deliver oxygen at rates from 1 to 4 mL/min at concentrations of 24% to 36%. The nasal cannula also provides increased patient freedom to eat and talk, which a mask does not. Masks are used for higher-flow concentrations of oxygen, over 5 mL/min; depending on the type of mask, they can deliver anywhere from 35% to 60% oxygen. Respirators and ventilators are high-flow delivery mechanisms that are used for patients who are in severe respiratory distress or are unable to breathe on their own. Oxyhoods or tents generally are used for pediatric patients who may not tolerate a mask or cannula. The amount of oxygen delivered is somewhat unpredictable, especially if the opening is accessed frequently. Oxygen delivery may be between 20% and 100%. *(Adler and Carlton, 4th ed., p. 204)*

171. **(C)** The landmarks that can be used in radiography of the bony pelvis are the iliac crest, the ASIS, the pubic symphysis, the greater trochanter, the ishchial tuberosity, and the tip of the coccyx. With the patient in the anatomic position, the femoral neck is located 2½ in. distal on a line drawn perpendicular to the midpoint of a line drawn between the ASIS and the pubic symphysis. It is recommended to rotate the legs inward about 15 degrees, whenever possible, to place the femoral neck parallel to the IR. *(Frank, Long, and Smith, 11th ed., vol. 1, p. 354)*

172. **(C)** A signed consent form (informed consent) is not necessary prior to performing an upper GI series. Informed consent is necessary before performing any procedure that is considered invasive or that carries considerable risk. A myelogram, a cardiac catheterization, and an interventional vascular procedure are all invasive procedures, and all carry some degree of risk. A physician should explain to the patient what those risks are as well as the risk of not having the procedure. In addition, the patient should be made aware of alternative procedures and the risks associated with the alternatives. Only after the patient has been made aware and all questions have been answered appropriately should the informed consent be signed. A radiographer is not responsible for obtaining informed consent. However, in some institutions, it may be

departmental procedure for the radiographer to check the chart and see whether there is a signed consent form in place. *(Adler and Carlton, 4th ed., p. 377)*

173. (D) Improper support of a patient's fractured lower leg (tibia/fibula) while performing radiography could result in movement of the fracture fragments, which can cause tearing of the soft tissue, nerves, and blood vessels. In addition, lack of support may cause muscle spasm, which can make closed reduction of some fractures difficult. *(Frank, Long, and Smith, 11th ed., vol. 2, p. 54)*

174. (D) According to state and federal law, personal radiation monitor reports must be retained as legal documents. Information that must be included in these documents includes the user's personal data, that is, name, birth date, sex, identification number (usually, Social Security Number), type of monitor (e.g., film badge, TLD, or OSL dosimeter), radiation quality, dose equivalent (i.e., deep, eye, and shallow) for that exposure period (usually one month), the quarterly accumulated dose equivalent (i.e., deep, eye, and shallow), year-to-date dose equivalent (i.e., deep, eye, and shallow), lifetime dose equivalent (i.e., deep, eye, and shallow), number of monitors received year to date, and inception date (month and year) of the dosimeter. *(Sherer, 5th ed., p. 254)*

175. (A) The femur is the longest and strongest bone in the body. The femoral shaft is bowed slightly anteriorly and presents a long, narrow ridge posteriorly called the *linea aspera*. The proximal femur consists of a head that is received by the pelvic acetabulum. The femoral neck, which joins the head and shaft, normally angles upward about 120 degrees and forward (in anteversion) about 15 degrees. The greater and lesser trochanters are large processes on the posterior proximal femur. The intertrochanteric crest runs obliquely between the trochanters posteriorly; the intertrochanteric line parallels the intertrochanteric crest on the anterior femoral surface. The intercondyloid fossa, a deep notch found on the distal posterior femur between the large femoral

condyles and the popliteal surface, is a smooth surface just superior to the intercondyloid fossa. *(Frank, Long, and Smith, 11th ed., vol. 1, p. 337)*

176. (C) Fidelity, veracity, nonmalficence, and beneficence are all ethical principles. *Nonmalficence* is the principle that refers to the prevention of harm. *Beneficence* is the ethical principle that refers to bringing about good or benefiting others. *Fidelity* refers to faithfulness, and *veracity* refers to truthfulness. *(Adler and Carlton, 4th ed., p. 352)*

177. (C) A radiographer who fails to wear a lead apron when performing portable radiography is in direct violation of the ARRT *Code of Ethics for the Profession of Radiologic Technology.* Although this may seem to some to be a personal decision, the fact is that our profession demands that we protect not only others but ourselves as well from unnecessary radiation exposure. Participating in continuing education is every radiographer's duty and not only is in keeping with the ARRT *Code of Ethics* but now is also mandatory for renewal of ARRT certification. Under normal circumstances, patient confidentiality is of the utmost importance, and radiographers always must respect a patient's right to privacy. There are special circumstances, however, where a radiographer is negligent if he or she does not communicate confidential information to the proper individuals. These cases include suspected cases of child abuse and any instance where the welfare of an individual or community is at risk. The professional radiographer is encouraged to investigate new and innovative techniques. As technology continues to grow, we must grow with it. There are often new and better ways to perform procedures, especially as equipment changes occur. *(Torres et al., 6th ed., pp. 8–9)*

178. (C) Hospital information systems must ensure confidentiality in compliance with Health Insurance Portability and Accountability Act of 1996 (HIPAA) regulations. Most institutions now have computerized, paperless systems that accomplish the same information transmittal; these systems must ensure confidentiality in compliance with HIPAA regulations. The health care professional generally has access to the computerized system only via personal password, thus helping to ensure confidentiality of patient information. All medical records and other individually identifiable health information, whether electronic, on paper, or oral, are covered by HIPAA legislation and by subsequent Department of Health and Human Services (HHS) rules that took effect in April of 2001. *(Torres et al., 6th ed., p. 20)*

179. **(B)** *Dysplasia* refers to abnormal development of tissue—often demonstrated radiographically in skeletal imaging. Difficulty in speaking is termed *dysphasia. Malposition* refers to an anatomic structure located in a place other than the norm, for example, situs inversus. Difficult or painful breathing is termed *dyspnea. (Taber, 20th ed., p. 652)*

180. **(D)** Fidelity, veracity, nonmalficence, and beneficence are all ethical principles. *Nonmalficence* is the principle that refers to the prevention of harm. *Beneficence* is the ethical principle that refers to bringing about good or benefiting others. *Fidelity* refers to faithfulness, and *veracity* refers to truthfulness. *(Adler and Carlton, 4th ed., p. 352)*

181. **(C)** There is no preparation required for an abdominal survey. For an upper GI series and a lower GI series (BE), the patient should be NPO, or have nothing by mouth, for 8 to 10 hours prior to the examination. In addition, a low-residue diet may be imposed, fluid intake may be increased, and cleansing enemas and laxatives may be prescribed to rid the colon of fecal matter. *(Adler and Carlton, 4th ed., p. 269)*

182. **(B)** The pregnant radiographer poses a special radiation protection consideration because the safety of the unborn individual must be considered. It must be remembered that the developing fetus is particularly sensitive to radiation exposure. Established guidelines state that the occupational radiation exposure to the fetus must not exceed 0.5 rem (500 mrem, or 5 mSv) during the entire gestation period. *(Bushong, 8th ed., p. 557)*

183. **(D)** Epidemiologic studies indicate that AIDS can be transmitted only by intimate contact with body fluids of an infected individual. This can occur through the sharing of contaminated needles, through sexual contact, and from mother to baby at childbirth (perinatal). AIDS can also be transmitted by transfusion of contaminated blood. *(Torres et al., 6th ed., p. 116)*

184. **(B)** Venous blood is returned to the right atrium of the heart via the superior (from the upper part of the body) and inferior (from the lower body) venae cavae and the coronary sinus (from the heart substance). During atrial systole, the blood passes through the tricuspid valve into the right ventricle. During ventricular systole, the blood is pumped through the pulmonary semilunar valve into the pulmonary artery (the *only* artery to carry unoxygenated blood) to the lungs for oxygenation. Blood is returned via the pulmonary veins (the *only* veins to carry oxygenated blood) to the left atrium. During atrial systole, blood passes through the mitral (bicuspid) valve into the left ventricle. During ventricular systole, the oxygenated blood is pumped through the aortic semilunar valve into the aorta. The coronary arteries supply oxygenated blood to the myocardium. The chordae tendineae are connective tissue fibers that help to limit the movement of valve flaps, preventing backflow of blood. *(Tortora and Grabowski, 11th ed., pp. 706, 792)*

185. **(A)** Mature white blood cells (*lymphocytes*) are considered the most radiosensitive cells. *Ova* (female germ cells) are very radiosensitive, but not to the same degree as lymphocytes. *Myocytes* (muscle cells) and especially *neurons* (nerve cells) are actually radioresistant. *(Gurley and Callaway, 6th ed., p. 254)*

186. **(A)** Proper body mechanics includes a wide base of support. The *base of support* is the portion of the body that is in contact with the floor or some other horizontal plane. The *center of gravity* is the midpoint of the pelvis or lower abdomen, depending on body build. The *line of gravity* is the abstract line passing vertically through the center of gravity.

Proper body mechanics can help to prevent painful back injuries by making proficient use of the muscles in the arms and legs. *(Torres et al., 6th ed., pp. 82–83)*

187. **(B)** The input phosphor of image intensifiers is usually made of cesium iodide. For each x-ray photon absorbed by cesium iodide, approximately 5,000 light photons are emitted. As the light photons strike a photoemissive *photocathode*, a number of electrons are released from the photocathode and focused toward the output side of the image tube by voltage applied to the negatively charged *electrostatic focusing lenses*. The electrons are then accelerated through the neck of the tube where they strike the small (0.5–1 in.) *output phosphor* that is mounted on a flat glass support. The entire assembly is enclosed within a 2–4-mm thick vacuum glass envelope. Remember that the image on the output phosphor is *minified, brighter,* and *inverted* (electron focusing causes image inversion).

Input screen diameters of 5–12 in. are available. Although smaller diameter input screens improve resolution, they do not permit a large FOV, that is, viewing of large patient areas.

Dual- and triple-field image intensifiers are available that permit *magnified* viewing of fluoroscopic images. To achieve magnification, the *voltage* to the focusing lenses is increased and a *smaller* portion of the input phosphor is used, thereby resulting in a smaller FOV. Because minification gain is now decreased, the image is not as bright. The mA is automatically increased to compensate for the loss in brightness when the image intensifier is switched to magnification mode. Entrance skin exposure (ESE) can increase dramatically as the FOV decreases (i.e., as magnification increases).

As FOV decreases, *magnification* of the output screen image increases, there is less *noise* because increased mA provides a greater number of x-ray photons, and *contrast* and *resolution* improve. The focal point in the magnification mode is *further away from* the output phosphor (as a result of increased voltage applied to the focusing lenses) and therefore the output image is magnified. *(Fosbinder and Orth, p. 191)*

188. **(C)** *Idiopathic* refers to a disease of unknown or unclear cause. The term *systemic* refers to or concerns a (body) system. An *epidemic* describes a disease that swiftly affects a large number of people in a particular geographic region. Anything that is or can be disease-producing is termed *pathogenic. (Taber, 20th ed., p. 1064)*

189. **(A)** The velocity and charge of particulate radiation determine the amount of energy transferred (and, therefore, the number of ionizations) to the tissue traversed. A greater LET (number of ionizations) is delivered by particles with a slower velocity and greater charge. The greater the LET and the number of ionizations, the greater is the biologic effect. The unit of absorbed dose is the *rad* (radiation *ab*sorbed *dose*). *Rem* is the acronym for *radiation equivalent man*—the unit of dose equivalent. *(Bushong, 8th ed., p. 495)*

190. **(D)** Most needle sticks occur while attempting to recap a needle. Several diseases, including hepatitis and human immune-deficiency virus (HIV) infection, can be transmitted via a needle stick. Therefore, do not attempt to recap a needle, but rather dispose of the entire syringe with needle attached in the special container that is available. *(Torres et al., 6th ed., pp. 63–66)*

191. **(C)** *Angina pectoris* is a spasmodic chest pain that is frequently due to oxygen deficiency in the myocardium. The pain often radiates down the left arm and up to the left jaw. Angina pectoris attacks frequently are associated with exertion or emotional stress in individuals with coronary artery disease. Pain may be relieved with a vasodilator such as *nitroglycerin* given sublingually or transdermally. *Digitalis* is used to treat congestive heart failure. *Dilantin* is used in the control of seizure disorders, and *cimetidine* (Tagamet) is used to treat duodenal ulcers. *(Torres et al., 6th ed., p. 282)*

192. **(A)** As the kilovoltage is increased, more penetration will occur, and a greater range of densities (grays) will be apparent in film/screen imaging. This is termed *long scale* or *low contrast*. In addition, as the kilovoltage and scale of grays increase, the exposure latitude increases

in film/screen imaging; the margin for error in technical factors becomes greater. As the mAs value is decreased in film/screen imaging to compensate for the increased kV, density should remain the same. *(Shephard, p. 204)*

193. **(C)** The occupational dose limit is valid for beta, x-, and gamma radiations. Because alpha radiation is so rapidly ionizing, traditional personal monitors will not record alpha radiation. Because alpha particles are capable of penetrating only a few centimeters of air, they are practically harmless as an external source. *(Selman, 6th ed., p. 395)*

194. **(A)** With three-phase equipment, the voltage never drops to zero, and x-ray intensity is significantly greater. When changing from single-phase to three-phase, six-pulse equipment, two-thirds of the original milliampere-seconds are required to produce a radiograph with similar density. (When going from three-phase, six-pulse to single-phase, add one-third more milliampere-seconds.) When changing from single-phase to three-phase, 12-pulse equipment, only one-half of the original milliampere-seconds is required. (Going from three-phase, 12-pulse to single-phase requires twice the milliampere-seconds.) In this instance, we are changing from single-phase to three-phase, 12-pulse equipment; therefore, the new milliampere-seconds value should be half the original 50 mAs, or 25 mAs. The only selection that will provide 25 mAs is (A), 200 mA. (B) will produce 75 mAs (600 mA × ⅛ s = 75 mAs); (C) will produce 50 mAs (400 mA × 0.125 s = 50 mAs); (D) will produce 100 mAs (400 × 0.25 = 100 mAs). *(Carlton and Adler, 4th ed., p. 96)*

COMPARISON OF TECHNICAL FACTORS REQUIRED

Single phase	Three phase	Three phase
	6-pulse	12-pulse
x mAs	⅔ x mAs	⅔ x mAs

195. **(A)** When a patient's elbow needs to be examined in partial flexion, the lateral projection offers little difficulty, but the AP projection requires special attention. If the AP projection is made with a perpendicular CR and the olecra-

non process resting on the table-top, the articulating surfaces are obscured. With the elbow in partial flexion, *two exposures are necessary* to achieve an AP projection of the elbow joint articular surfaces. One is made with the forearm parallel to the IR (humerus elevated), which demonstrates the proximal forearm. The other is made with the humerus parallel to the IR (forearm elevated), which demonstrates the distal humerus. In both cases, the CR is perpendicular if the degree of flexion is not too great or angled slightly into the joint space with greater degrees of flexion. *(Bontrager and Lampignano, 6th ed., p. 169)*

196. **(D)** The S-shaped clavicle ("collar bone") is usually the last bone to completely ossify, at about age 21, and is one of the most commonly fractured bones in young people. Its medial end articulates with the sternum to form the sternoclavicular joint; the clavicle articulates laterally with the scapula's acromion process, forming the acromioclavicular joint. Superior dislocation of the acromioclavicular joint is a common athletic injury. *(Tortora and Derrickson, 11th ed., p. 233)*

197. **(B)** Standard blood and body fluid precautions serve to protect health care workers and patients from the spread of diseases such as AIDS and AIDS-related complex. Although the precautions are indicated for *all* patients, special care must be emphasized when working with patients whose infectious status is unknown (e.g., the emergency trauma patient). Gloves must be worn if the radiographer may come in contact with blood or body fluids. A gown should be worn if the clothing may become contaminated. Blood spills should be cleaned with a solution of 1 part bleach to 10 parts water. *(Torres et al., 6th ed., pp. 62–65)*

198. **(C)** X-ray tube life may be extended by using exposure factors that produce a minimum of heat (a lower milliampere-seconds and higher kilovoltage combination) whenever possible. When the rotor is activated, the filament current is increased to produce the required electron source (thermionic emission). Prolonged rotor time, then, can lead to shortened fila-

ment life owing to early vaporization. Large exposures to a cold anode will heat the anode surface, and the temperature difference between surface and interior can cause cracking of the anode. This can be avoided by proper warming of the anode prior to use, thereby allowing sufficient dispersion of heat through the anode. *(Selman, 9th ed., pp. 147–148)*

199.   **(D)** The thoriated tungsten filament of the cathode assembly is heated by its own filament circuit. This circuit provides current and voltage to heat the filament to incandescence, at which time it undergoes thermionic emission (the liberation of valence electrons from filament atoms). The greater the number of electrons flowing between the cathode and the anode, the greater is the tube current (mA). *Rectification* (single- or three-phase) is the process of changing alternating current to unidirectional current. A greater number of secondary transformer turns functions to increase voltage and decrease current. *(Bushong, 8th ed., pp. 132–133)*

200.   **(D)** *Technique charts* are exposure factor guides that help technologists produce radiographs with consistent density and contrast. They suggest a group of exposure factors to be used at a particular SID with a particular grid ratio, focal-spot size, and CR angulation. *Technique charts do not take into account the nature of the part* (disease and atrophy). *(Shephard, p. 298)*

Subspecialty List

1. Patient care and education
2. Image acquisition and evaluation
3. Patient care and education
4. Image acquisition and evaluation
5. Image acquisition and evaluation
6. Radiation protection
7. Image procedures
8. Radiation protection
9. Radiation protection
10. Radiation protection
11. Image procedures
12. Patient care and education
13. Image procedures
14. Image procedures
15. Equipment operation and quality control
16. Patient care and education
17. Equipment operation and quality control
18. Image procedures
19. Image procedures
20. Patient care and education
21. Image procedures
22. Image procedures
23. Radiation protection
24. Radiation protection
25. Image procedures
26. Image procedures
27. Equipment operation and quality control
28. Image acquisition and evaluation
29. Patient care and education
30. Patient care and education
31. Image procedures
32. Image procedures
33. Radiation protection
34. Patient care and education
35. Image procedures
36. Image acquisition and evaluation
37. Equipment operation and quality control
38. Equipment operation and quality control
39. Patient care and education
40. Image acquisition and evaluation
41. Equipment operation and quality control
42. Image acquisition and evaluation
43. Image procedures
44. Image procedures
45. Image procedures
46. Image acquisition and evaluation
47. Radiation protection
48. Equipment operation and quality control
49. Image procedures
50. Equipment operation and quality control
51. Image procedures
52. Equipment operation and quality control
53. Patient care and management
54. Radiation protection
55. Equipment operation and quality control
56. Radiation protection
57. Image acquisition and evaluation
58. Image procedures
59. Equipment operation and quality control
60. Image acquisition and evaluation
61. Radiation protection
62. Image procedures
63. Image acquisition and evaluation
64. Image acquisition and evaluation

65. Image acquisition and evaluation
66. Image acquisition and evaluation
67. Radiation protection
68. Radiation protection
69. Radiation protection
70. Image acquisition and evaluation
71. Radiation protection
72. Image procedures
73. Equipment operation and quality control
74. Image procedures
75. Image procedures
76. Image acquisition and evaluation
77. Image procedures
78. Radiation protection
79. Image acquisition and evaluation
80. Image acquisition and evaluation
81. Radiation protection
82. Image acquisition and evaluation
83. Image acquisition and evaluation
84. Radiation protection
85. Patient care and education
86. Image acquisition and evaluation
87. Image acquisition and evaluation
88. Equipment operation and quality control
89. Radiation protection
90. Image procedures
91. Image acquisition and evaluation
92. Patient care and education
93. Radiation protection
94. Equipment operation and quality control
95. Equipment operation and quality control
96. Radiation protection
97. Image procedures
98. Image procedures
99. Image acquisition and evaluation
100. Image acquisition and evaluation
101. Radiation protection
102. Image acquisition and evaluation
103. Image acquisition and evaluation
104. Equipment operation and quality control
105. Image procedures
106. Image acquisition and evaluation
107. Equipment operation and quality control
108. Equipment operation and quality control
109. Image acquisition and evaluation
110. Equipment operation and quality control
111. Image procedures
112. Image procedures
113. Image procedures
114. Patient care and education
115. Equipment operation and maintenance
116. Image procedures
117. Equipment operation and quality control
118. Image procedures
119. Image procedures
120. Image procedures
121. Equipment operation and quality control
122. Patient care and education
123. Image acquisition and evaluation
124. Image procedures
125. Image procedures
126. Radiation protection
127. Patient care and education
128. Image procedures
129. Image acquisition and evaluation
130. Image procedures
131. Image procedures
132. Patient care and education
133. Image procedures
134. Image acquisition and evaluation
135. Image procedures
136. Radiation protection
137. Image procedures
138. Image procedures
139. Patient care and education
140. Equipment operation and quality control
141. Radiation protection
142. Image procedures
143. Image procedures
144. Image procedures
145. Patient care and education
146. Image procedures
147. Image procedures
148. Radiation protection
149. Patient care and education
150. Radiation protection
151. Image procedures
152. Image procedures
153. Image procedures
154. Image acquisition and evaluation
155. Image acquisition and evaluation
156. Image procedures
157. Equipment operation and quality control
158. Image procedures
159. Image procedures
160. Image procedures
161. Radiation protection
162. Equipment operation and quality control
163. Image acquisition and evaluation
164. Image procedures
165. Image procedures
166. Image procedures

167. Radiation protection
168. Image acquisition and evaluation
169. Image procedures
170. Patient care and education
171. Image procedures
172. Image procedures
173. Patient care and education
174. Radiation protection
175. Patient care and education
176. Patient care and education
177. Patient care and education
178. Patient care and education
179. Image procedures
180. Patient care and education
181. Image procedures
182. Radiation protection
183. Patient care and education
184. Image procedures

185. Radiation protection
186. Patient care and education
187. Equipment operation and quality control
188. Image procedures
189. Radiation protection
190. Patient care and education
191. Patient care and education
192. Image acquisition and evaluation
193. Radiation protection
194. Image acquisition and evaluation
195. Image procedures
196. Image procedures
197. Patient care and education
198. Equipment operation and quality control
199. Image acquisition and evaluation
200. Image acquisition and evaluation

CHAPTER 7

Practice Test 2
Questions

1. Europium-activated barium fluorohalide is associated with

    (A) rare earth intensifying screens
    (B) image intensifiers
    (C) PSP storage plates
    (D) filament material

2. For which of the following can a radiographer be found liable for a negligent tort?

    1. Radiographer images the wrong forearm.
    2. Patient is injured while being positioned on the x-ray table.
    3. Radiographer fails to question patient about possible pregnancy before performing x-ray examination.

    (A) 1 only
    (B) 1 and 2 only
    (C) 2 and 3 only
    (D) 1, 2, and 3

3. Which of the lines indicated in Figure 7–1 correctly demonstrates the relationship between the exposure received by the PSP and its resulting luminescence as it is laser scanned?

    (A) Line A is representative of PSP exposure.
    (B) Line B is representative of PSP exposure.
    (C) Neither line is representative of PSP exposure.
    (D) Both lines are representative of PSP exposure.

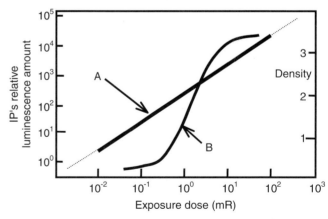

Figure 7–1. Courtesy FUJIFILM Medical Systems USA, Inc.

4. The image intensifier's input phosphor differs from the output phosphor in that the input phosphor

   (A) is much larger than the output phosphor
   (B) emits electrons, whereas the output phosphor emits light photons
   (C) absorbs electrons, whereas the output phosphor absorbs light photons
   (D) is a fixed size, and the size of the output phosphor can vary

5. As the CR laser scanner/reader recognizes the phosphostimulated luminescence (PSL) released by the PSP storage plate, it constructs a graphic representation of pixel value distribution called a

   (A) processing algorithm
   (B) histogram
   (C) lookup table
   (D) exposure index

6. An accurately positioned oblique projection of the first through fourth lumbar vertebrae will demonstrate the classic "Scotty dog." What bony structure does the Scotty dog's neck represent?

   (A) Superior articular process
   (B) Pedicle
   (C) Transverse process
   (D) Pars interarticularis

7. How is source-to-image distance (SID) related to exposure rate and radiographic density?

   (A) As SID increases, exposure rate increases and radiographic density increases.
   (B) As SID increases, exposure rate increases and radiographic density decreases.
   (C) As SID increases, exposure rate decreases and radiographic density increases.
   (D) As SID increases, exposure rate decreases and radiographic density decreases.

8. What information *must* be included on an x-ray image for it to be considered as legitimate legal evidence?

   1. Name of facility where examination performed
   2. Examination date
   3. Date of birth

   (A) 1 only
   (B) 1 and 2 only
   (C) 2 and 3 only
   (D) 1, 2, and 3

9. Figure 7–2 illustrates a sectional image of the abdomen. Which of the following is represented by the number 13?

   (A) Gallbladder
   (B) Portal vein
   (C) Inferior vena cava
   (D) Aorta

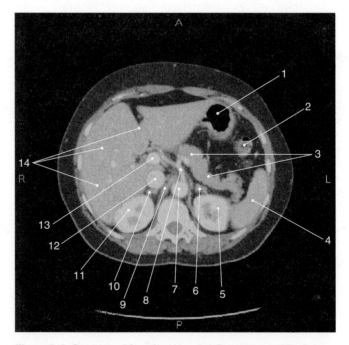

Figure 7–2. Courtesy of Stamford Hospital, Department of Radiology.

10. The principal late effects of ionizing radiation on humans include

 1. local tissue damage
 2. genetic effects
 3. malignant disease

 (A) 1 only
 (B) 1 and 2 only
 (C) 2 and 3 only
 (D) 1, 2, and 3

11. Which of the following procedures requires that contrast medium be injected into the ureters?

 (A) Cystogram
 (B) Urethrogram
 (C) Retrograde pyelogram
 (D) Cystourethrogram

12. The *roentgen* is the unit of

 (A) radiation dose
 (B) biologic dose
 (C) dose equivalent
 (D) ionization in air

13. Which of the following combinations would pose the *least* hazard to a particular anode?

 (A) 0.6-mm focal spot, 75 kVp, 30 mAs
 (B) 0.6-mm focal spot, 85 kVp, 15 mAs
 (C) 1.2-mm focal spot, 75 kVp, 30 mAs
 (D) 1.2-mm focal spot, 85 kVp, 15 mAs

14. What is the structure indicated by the letter A in Figure 7–3?

 (A) Greater tubercle
 (B) Coronoid process
 (C) Coracoid process
 (D) Acromion process

15. Which of the following indicates the scapular costal surface seen in Figure 7–3?

 (A) D
 (B) H
 (C) K
 (D) M

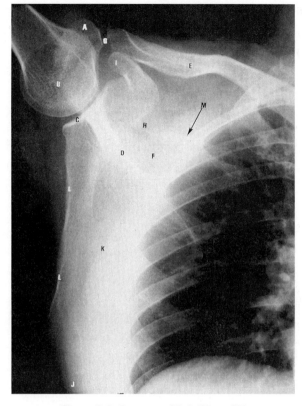

Figure 7–3. Courtesy of Bob Wong, RT.

16. The CR should be directed to the center of the part of greatest interest to avoid

 (A) rotation distortion
 (B) magnification
 (C) foreshortening
 (D) elongation

17. Federal regulations regarding infection control in the workplace, as amended by the Occupational Safety and Health Administration (OSHA), make which of the following requirements?

 1. Hepatitis B immunizations must be made available to all hospital employees.
 2. Puncture-proof containers must be provided for all used needles.
 3. Follow-up care must be provided to any staff accidentally exposed to blood splash/needle stick.

 (A) 1 only
 (B) 1 and 2 only
 (C) 2 and 3 only
 (D) 1, 2, and 3

18. Imperfect expansion of the lungs, often accompanied by dyspnea, is called

   (A) atelectasis
   (B) pneumothorax
   (C) pneumonia
   (D) COPD

19. Which of the following radiologic examinations requires preparation consisting of a low-residue diet, cathartics, and enemas?

   (A) Upper GI series
   (B) Small bowel series
   (C) Barium enema (BE)
   (D) Intravenous (IV) cystogram

20. The exposure timer settings on three-phase radiographic equipment must be tested annually and must be accurate to within

   (A) +/− 2%
   (B) +/− 5%
   (C) +/− 10%
   (D) +/− 20%

21. Which of the following is (are) feature(s) of fluoroscopic equipment that are designed especially to eliminate unnecessary radiation to patient and personnel?

   1. Protective curtain
   2. Filtration
   3. Collimation

   (A) 1 only
   (B) 1 and 2 only
   (C) 1 and 3 only
   (D) 1, 2, and 3

22. Which of the following will *best* demonstrate the lumbosacral junction in the AP position?

   (A) CR perpendicular to L3
   (B) CR perpendicular to L5–S1
   (C) CR caudad 30–35 degrees
   (D) CR cephalad 30–35 degrees

23. Which of the following projections require(s) that the shoulder be placed in external rotation?

   1. AP humerus
   2. Lateral forearm
   3. Lateral humerus

   (A) 1 only
   (B) 1 and 2 only
   (C) 2 and 3 only
   (D) 1, 2, and 3

24. During endoscopic retrograde cholangiopancreatography (ERCP) examination, contrast medium is injected into the

   (A) hepatic duct
   (B) cystic duct
   (C) pancreatic duct
   (D) common bile duct

25. Which of the following is (are) well demonstrated in the oblique position of the cervical vertebrae?

   1. Intervertebral foramina
   2. Disk spaces
   3. Apophyseal joints

   (A) 1 only
   (B) 1 and 2 only
   (C) 1 and 3 only
   (D) 1, 2, and 3

26. Which of the following is *most likely* to produce a high-quality image?

   (A) Small image matrix
   (B) High signal-to-noise ratio (SNR)
   (C) Large pixel size
   (D) Low resolution

27. A decrease from 90 to 77 kVp will result in a decrease in which of the following?

1. Wavelength
2. Scale of grays
3. Optical density

(A) 1 only
(B) 1 and 2 only
(C) 2 and 3 only
(D) 1, 2, and 3

28. The image shown in Figure 7–4 was made in the following recumbent position

(A) RAO
(B) Lateral
(C) LPO
(D) PA

29. Terms that refer to size distortion include

1. magnification
2. attenuation
3. elongation

(A) 1 only
(B) 1 and 2 only
(C) 1 and 3 only
(D) 1, 2, and 3

30. Advantages of high-frequency generators include

1. small size
2. decreased patient dose
3. nearly constant potential

(A) 1 only
(B) 1 and 2 only
(C) 2 and 3 only
(D) 1, 2, and 3

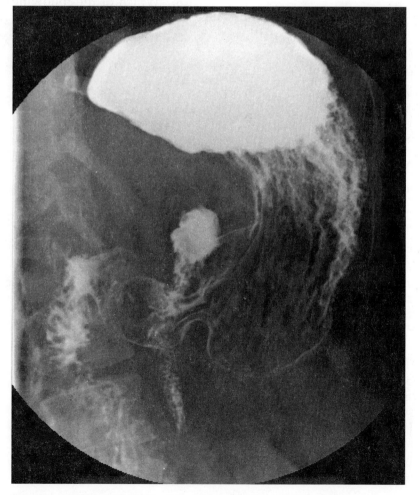

Figure 7–4. Courtesy of Stamford Hospital, Department of Radiology.

31. Biologic material is most sensitive to radiation exposure under which of the following conditions?

    (A) Anoxic
    (B) Hypoxic
    (C) Oxygenated
    (D) Deoxygenated

32. Which of the following is the *preferred* scheduling sequence?

    (A) Lower GI series, abdomen ultrasound, upper GI series
    (B) Abdomen ultrasound, lower GI series, upper GI series
    (C) Abdomen ultrasound, upper GI series, lower GI series
    (D) Upper GI series, lower GI series, abdomen ultrasound

33. The RAO position is used to project the sternum to the left of the thoracic vertebrae in order to take advantage of

    (A) pulmonary markings
    (B) heart shadow
    (C) posterior ribs
    (D) costal cartilages

34. How would the introduction of a 6-in. OID affect image contrast?

    (A) Contrast would be increased.
    (B) Contrast would be decreased.
    (C) Contrast would not change.
    (D) The scale of contrast would not change.

35. The AP axial projection of the chest for pulmonary apices

    1. requires 15 to 20 degrees of cephalad angulation
    2. projects the apices above the clavicles
    3. should demonstrate the medial ends of the clavicles equidistant from the vertebral column

    (A) 1 only
    (B) 1 and 2 only
    (C) 1 and 3 only
    (D) 1, 2, and 3

36. Rapid onset of severe respiratory or cardiovascular symptoms after ingestion or injection of a drug, vaccine, contrast agent, or food or after an insect bite *best* describes

    (A) asthma
    (B) anaphylaxis
    (C) myocardial infarction
    (D) rhinitis

37. Figure 7–5 illustrates which of the following?

    (A) Screen resolution test
    (B) Nine-penny test
    (C) Collimator accuracy test
    (D) Focal-spot size test

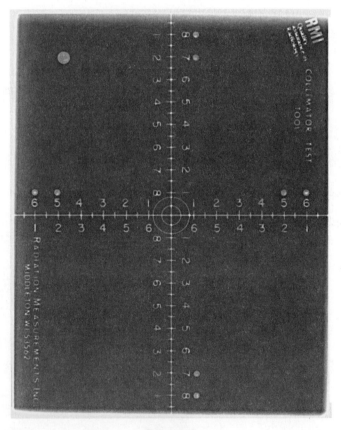

Figure 7–5.

38. Electronic imaging terms used to indicate the intensity of radiation reaching the IR include

    1. exposure index
    2. sensitivity (S) number
    3. field of view (FOV)

    (A) 1 only
    (B) 1 and 2 only
    (C) 2 and 3 only
    (D) 1, 2, and 3

39. The patient usually is required to drink barium sulfate suspension in order to demonstrate which of the following structures?

    1. Descending duodenum
    2. Ilium
    3. Splenic flexure

    (A) 1 only
    (B) 1 and 3 only
    (C) 2 and 3 only
    (D) 3 only

40. What lies immediately under the phosphor layer of a PSP storage plate?

    (A) Reflective layer
    (B) Base
    (C) Antistatic layer
    (D) Lead foil

41. Which of the following positions would *best* demonstrate the lumbar intervertebral joints and foramina?

    (A) LPO
    (B) RPO
    (C) Lateral
    (D) PA

42. The National Council on Radiation Protection and Measurements (NCRP) has recommended what total equivalent dose limit to the embryo/fetus?

    (A) 0.5 mSv
    (B) 5.0 mSv
    (C) 50 mSv
    (D) 500 mSv

43. Fluids and medications are administered to patients intravenously for which of the following reasons?

    1. To promote rapid response
    2. To administer parenteral nutrition
    3. To achieve a local effect

    (A) 1 only
    (B) 1 and 2 only
    (C) 1 and 3 only
    (D) 1, 2, and 3

44. Which of the following is (are) tested as part of a QC program?

    1. Beam alignment
    2. Reproducibility
    3. Linearity

    (A) 1 only
    (B) 1 and 2 only
    (C) 1 and 3 only
    (D) 1, 2, and 3

45. The line-focus principle refers to the fact that

    (A) the actual focal spot is larger than the effective focal spot
    (B) the effective focal spot is larger than the actual focal spot
    (C) x-rays travel in straight lines
    (D) x-rays cannot be focused

46. Which of the following positions will move the fundus of the gallbladder shown in Figure 7–6 away from the superimposed transverse process?

    (A) RAO
    (B) LAO
    (C) LPO
    (D) Left lateral decubitus

47. Which of the following effects does an antibiotic have on the body?

    (A) Decreases pain
    (B) Helps delay clotting
    (C) Increases urine output
    (D) Combats bacterial growth

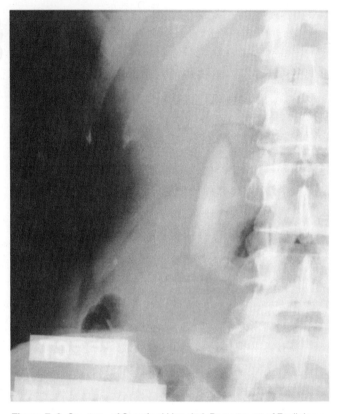

Figure 7–6. Courtesy of Stamford Hospital, Department of Radiology.

48. The roentgen, as a unit of measurement, expresses

    (A) absorbed dose
    (B) exposure in air
    (C) dose equivalent
    (D) dose to biologic material

49. Which of the following can affect histogram appearance?

    1. Centering accuracy
    2. Positioning accuracy
    3. Processing algorithm accuracy

    (A) 1 only
    (B) 1 and 2 only
    (C) 2 and 3 only
    (D) 1, 2, and 3

50. Bone densitometry is often performed to

    1. measure degree of bone (de)mineralization
    2. evaluate results of osteoporosis treatment/therapy
    3. evaluate condition of soft tissue adjacent to bone

    (A) 1 only
    (B) 1 and 2 only
    (C) 2 and 3 only
    (D) 1, 2, and 3

51. Indirect modes of disease transmission include

    1. airborne
    2. fomite
    3. vector

    (A) 1 only
    (B) 1 and 2 only
    (C) 1 and 3 only
    (D) 1, 2, and 3

52. If a patient received 0.9 rad during a 3-minute fluoroscopic examination, what was the dose rate?

    (A) 3 mrad/min
    (B) 30 mrad/min
    (C) 300 mrad/min
    (D) 3,000 mrad/min

53. An increase from 78 to 92 kVp will result in a decrease in which of the following?

    1. Wavelength
    2. Beam intensity
    3. Scale of grays

    (A) 1 only
    (B) 1 and 2 only
    (C) 2 and 3 only
    (D) 1, 2, and 3

54. The total number of x-ray photons produced at the target is contingent on the

1. tube current
2. target material
3. square of the kilovoltage

(A) 1 only
(B) 1 and 2 only
(C) 2 and 3 only
(D) 1, 2, and 3

55. Major effect(s) of irradiation of macromolecules include(s)

1. point lesions
2. cross-linking
3. main-chain scission

(A) 1 only
(B) 1 and 2 only
(C) 1 and 3 only
(D) 1, 2, and 3

56. All of the following cells/tissue are correctly described as somatic *except*

(A) muscle
(B) bone
(C) spermatozoa
(D) neuron

57. An animal host of an infectious organism that transmits the infection via a bite or sting is a

(A) vector
(B) fomite
(C) host
(D) reservoir

58. If the exposure rate at 2.0 m from a source of radiation is 18 mR/min, what will be the exposure rate at 5 m from the source?

(A) 2.8 mR/min
(B) 4.5 mR/min
(C) 18 mR/min
(D) 85 mR/min

59. Which of the following will increase patient dose during fluoroscopy?

1. Decreasing the SSD
2. Using 2.5 mm Al filtration
3. Restricting tabletop intensity to less than 10 R/min

(A) 1 only
(B) 1 and 2 only
(C) 2 and 3 only
(D) 1, 2, and 3

60. An axial projection of the clavicle is often helpful in demonstrating a fracture that is not visualized using a perpendicular CR. When examining the clavicle in the PA position, how is the CR directed for the axial projection?

(A) Cephalad
(B) Caudad
(C) Medially
(D) Laterally

61. An exposure was made using 600 mA, 0.04-s exposure, and 85 kVp. Each of the following changes will serve to decrease the radiographic density by one-half *except* change to

(A) 1/50-s exposure
(B) 72 kVp
(C) 18 mAs
(D) 300 mA

62. All the following are rules of good body mechanics *except*

(A) keep back straight, avoid twisting
(B) keep the load close to the body
(C) push, do not pull, the load
(D) keep a narrow base of support

63. Which of the following is (are) accurate positioning or evaluation criteria for an AP projection of the normal knee?

1. Femorotibial interspaces equal bilaterally.
2. Patella superimposed on distal tibia.
3. CR enters ½ in. distal to base of patella.

(A) 1 only
(B) 1 and 2 only
(C) 1 and 3 only
(D) 1, 2, and 3

64. The source-to-table distance in fixed/stationary fluoroscopy must

(A) be at least 15 in.
(B) not exceed 15 in.
(C) be at least 12 in.
(D) not exceed 12 in.

65. Which of the following structures will be filled with barium in the AP recumbent position of a sthenic patient during an upper GI examination?

(A) Duodenal bulb
(B) Descending duodenum
(C) Pyloric vestibule
(D) Gastric fundus

66. Which of the following artifacts is occasionally associated with the use of grids in digital imaging?

(A) Incomplete erasure
(B) Aliasing
(C) Image fading
(D) Vignetting

67. Images useful in demonstrating postspinal fusion degree of motion include

1. AP flexion and extension
2. lateral flexion and extension
3. AP right and left bending

(A) 1 only
(B) 1 and 2 only
(C) 2 and 3 only
(D) 1, 2, and 3

68. A blowout fracture usually occurs in which aspect of the orbital wall?

(A) Superior
(B) Inferior
(C) Medial
(D) Lateral

69. What is the name of the structure indicated as number 5 in Figure 7–7?

(A) Coronoid fossa
(B) Coracoid fossa
(C) Olecranon fossa
(D) Trochlear/semilunar notch

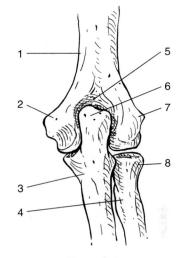

Figure 7–7.

70. Which of the following projections/positions would best demonstrate structure number 6 seen in Figure 7–7?

(A) PA projection
(B) Lateral projection
(C) AP external oblique
(D) AP internal oblique

71. The condition in which pulmonary alveoli lose their elasticity and become permanently inflated, causing the patient to consciously exhale, is

(A) bronchial asthma
(B) bronchitis
(C) emphysema
(D) tuberculosis

72. Tungsten alloy is the usual choice of target material for radiographic equipment because it

    1. has a high atomic number
    2. has a high melting point
    3. can readily dissipate heat

    (A) 1 only
    (B) 1 and 2 only
    (C) 2 and 3 only
    (D) 1, 2, and 3

73. The portion of a hypodermic needle that attaches to the syringe is termed its

    (A) hub
    (B) gauge
    (C) length
    (D) bevel

74. X-ray tube life may be extended by

    1. using low-milliampere-seconds/high-kilovoltage exposure factors
    2. avoiding lengthy anode rotation
    3. avoiding exposures to a cold anode

    (A) 1 only
    (B) 1 and 2 only
    (C) 1 and 3 only
    (D) 1, 2, and 3

75. Gonadal shielding should be provided for male patients in which of the following examinations?

    1. Femur
    2. Abdomen
    3. Pelvis

    (A) 1 only
    (B) 1 and 2 only
    (C) 2 and 3 only
    (D) 1, 2, and 3

76. An automatic exposure control (AEC) device can operate on which of the following principles?

    1. A photomultiplier tube charged by a fluorescent screen
    2. A parallel-plate ionization chamber charged by x-ray photons
    3. Motion of magnetic fields inducing current in a conductor

    (A) 1 only
    (B) 2 only
    (C) 1 and 2 only
    (D) 1, 2, and 3

77. In which of the following projections was the image in Figure 7–8 made?

    (A) AP
    (B) Medial/internal oblique
    (C) Lateral/external oblique
    (D) Acute flexion

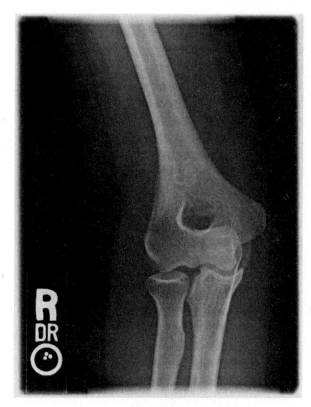

Figure 7–8.

78. Which of the following pathologic conditions require(s) a decrease in exposure factors?

    1. Pneumothorax
    2. Emphysema
    3. Multiple myeloma

    (A) 1 only
    (B) 1 and 2 only
    (C) 2 and 3 only
    (D) 1, 2, and 3

79. Which interaction between x-ray photons and matter involves partial transfer of the incident photon energy to the involved atom?

    (A) Photoelectric effect
    (B) Compton scattering
    (C) Coherent scattering
    (D) Pair production

80. In which section of the automatic processor shown in Figure 7–9 are the exposed silver halide crystals changed to black metallic silver?

    (A) Section 1
    (B) Section 2
    (C) Section 3
    (D) Section 4

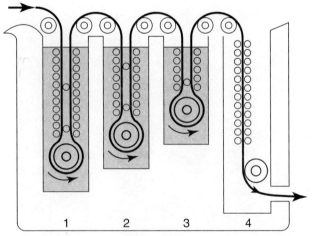

Figure 7–9.

81. It is essential to question female patients of childbearing age regarding the

    1. date of their last menstrual period
    2. possibility of their being pregnant
    3. number of x-ray examinations they have had in the past 12 months

    (A) 1 only
    (B) 1 and 2 only
    (C) 1 and 3 only
    (D) 1, 2, and 3

82. Geometric unsharpness is influenced by which of the following?

    1. Distance from object to image
    2. Distance from source to object
    3. Distance from source to image

    (A) 1 only
    (B) 1 and 2 only
    (C) 1 and 3 only
    (D) 1, 2, and 3

83. Which of the following shoulder projections can be used to evaluate the lesser tubercle in profile?

    (A) External rotation position
    (B) Internal rotation position
    (C) Neutral rotation position
    (D) Inferosuperior axial position

84. Which of the following radiologic examinations would deliver the greatest ESE?

    (A) Chest
    (B) Skull
    (C) Abdomen
    (D) Thoracic spine

85. Combinations of milliamperage and exposure time that produce a particular milliampere-seconds value will produce identical radiographic density. This statement is an expression of the

    (A) inverse-square law
    (B) line-focus principle
    (C) reciprocity law
    (D) D log E curve

86. The AP projection of the scapula requires that the

    1. affected arm be abducted
    2. CR enters approximately 2 in. inferior to the coracoid process
    3. thorax be rotated about 15 degrees toward the affected side

    (A) 1 only
    (B) 1 and 2 only
    (C) 2 and 3 only
    (D) 1, 2, and 3

87. How can OID be reduced for a PA projection of the wrist?

    (A) Extend the fingers.
    (B) Flex the metacarpophalangeal joints.
    (C) Extend the forearm.
    (D) Oblique the metacarpals 45 degrees.

88. When medications are administered *parenterally*, they are given

    (A) orally
    (B) orally or intravenously
    (C) intravenously or intramuscularly
    (D) by any route other than orally

89. During an intravenous urogram (IVU), the RPO position is used to demonstrate the

    1. left kidney parallel to the IR
    2. right kidney parallel to the IR
    3. right kidney perpendicular to the IR

    (A) 1 only
    (B) 2 only
    (C) 1 and 2 only
    (D) 1 and 3 only

90. Impingement on the wrist's median nerve causing pain and disability of the affected hand and wrist is known as

    (A) carpal boss syndrome
    (B) carpal tunnel syndrome
    (C) carpopedal syndrome
    (D) radioulnar syndrome

91. All other factors remaining the same, if a 14 × 17 in. field is collimated to a 4-in.-square field, the radiographic image will demonstrate

    (A) more density
    (B) less density
    (C) more detail
    (D) less detail

92. A term that is often used to describe computer programs, or software functioning, in medical imaging is

    (A) hardware
    (B) algorithm
    (C) histogram
    (D) modem

93. The legal doctrine *respondeat superior* relates to which of the following?

    (A) Let the master answer.
    (B) The thing speaks for itself.
    (C) A thing or matter settled by justice.
    (D) A matter settled by precedent.

94. What should be done to correct for magnification when using air-gap technique?

    (A) Decrease OID
    (B) Increase OID
    (C) Decrease SID
    (D) Increase SID

95. In the AP projection of an asthenic patient whose knee measures less than 19 cm from the anterosuperior iliac spine (ASIS) to table-top, the CR should be directed

    (A) perpendicularly
    (B) 5 degrees medially
    (C) 5 degrees cephalad
    (D) 5 degrees caudad

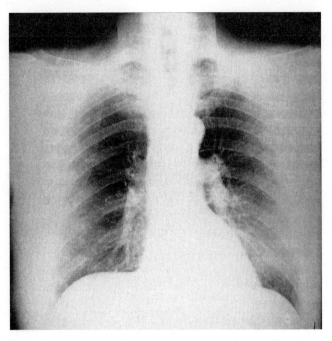

Figure 7–10. Courtesy of Stamford Hospital, Department of Radiology.

96. Which of the following statements is (are) true regarding Figure 7–10?

    1. Excessive kilovoltage was used.
    2. High contrast is demonstrated.
    3. Insufficient penetration is evident.

    (A) 1 only
    (B) 1 and 2 only
    (C) 2 and 3 only
    (D) 1, 2, and 3

97. The x-ray image seen on the computer display monitor is a (an)

    (A) analog image
    (B) digital image
    (C) phosphor image
    (D) emulsion image

98. During measurement of blood pressure, which of the following occurs as the radiographer controls arterial tension with the sphygmomanometer?

    (A) The brachial vein is collapsed.
    (B) The brachial artery is temporarily collapsed.
    (C) The antecubital vein is monitored.
    (D) Oxygen saturation of arterial blood is monitored.

99. Which of the following groups of organs/structures are located in the left upper quadrant?

    (A) Left kidney, left suprarenal gland, and gastric fundus
    (B) Left suprarenal gland, pylorus, and duodenal bulb
    (C) Hepatic flexure, cecum, and pancreas
    (D) Gastric fundus, liver, and cecum

100. Unlawful touching of a person without his or her consent is termed

    (A) assault
    (B) battery
    (C) false imprisonment
    (D) invasion of privacy

101. Exposure factors of 100 kVp and 6 mAs are used with a 6:1 grid for a particular exposure. What should be the new milliampere-seconds value if a 12:1 grid is substituted?

    (A) 7.5 mAs
    (B) 10 mAs
    (C) 13 mAs
    (D) 18 mAs

102. A diabetic patient who has not taken insulin while preparing for a fasting radiologic examination is susceptible to a hypoglycemic reaction. This is characterized by

1. fatigue
2. cyanosis
3. restlessness

(A) 1 only
(B) 1 and 2 only
(C) 1 and 3 only
(D) 1, 2, and 3

103. Which of the following is (are) located on the proximal aspect of the humerus?

1. Intertubercular groove
2. Capitulum
3. Coronoid fossa

(A) 1 only
(B) 1 and 2 only
(C) 1 and 3 only
(D) 1, 2, and 3

104. If the lumbar apophyseal articulation is not well visualized in the posterior oblique position, and the pedicle is seen on the posterior aspect of the vertebral body, what should be done to correct the position?

(A) Increase the degree of patient rotation.
(B) Decrease the degree of patient rotation.
(C) Flex knees to decrease lordotic curve.
(D) Angle 5 to 7 degrees cephalad.

105. Which of the following is/are associated with magnification fluoroscopy?

1. Less noise
2. Improved contrast resolution
3. Improved spatial resolution

(A) 1 only
(B) 1 and 2 only
(C) 2 and 3 only
(D) 1, 2, and 3

106. A *controlled area* is one that is

(A) restricted to access by nonradiation workers only
(B) monitored by survey meters
(C) occupied by radiation workers
(D) occupied by the general population

107. Exposure factors of 400 mA, 20 ms, 68 kVp at 40-in. SID were used to produce a satisfactory radiographic image. A change to 4 mAs can be *best* compensated for by which of the following?

(A) Increasing the SID to 60 in.
(B) Decreasing the SID to 20 in.
(C) Decreasing the kilovoltage to 60
(D) Increasing the kilovoltage to 78 kVp

108. Which of the following statements referring to Figure 7–11 is (are) correct?

1. Image A was performed AP.
2. Image B was performed AP.
3. The AP image was obtained using ureteral compression.

(A) 1 only
(B) 2 only
(C) 1 and 3 only
(D) 2 and 3 only

109. The process of radiation passing through tissue and depositing energy through ionization processes is known as

(A) the characteristic effect
(B) Compton scatter
(C) linear energy transfer
(D) the photoelectric effect

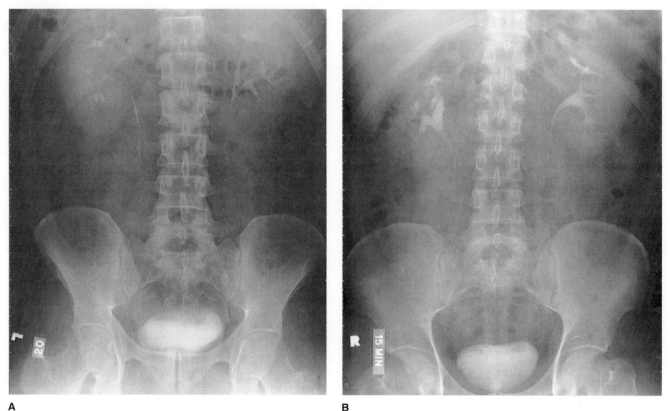

A   B

Figure 7–11. Courtesy of Stamford Hospital, Department of Radiology.

110. The radiograph shown in Figure 7–12 can be produced with the

1. long axis of the plantar surface perpendicular to the IR
2. CR 40 degrees cephalad to the base of the third metatarsal
3. CR 20 degrees cephalad to the talotibial joint

(A) 1 only

(B) 2 only

(C) 1 and 2 only

(D) 1 and 3 only

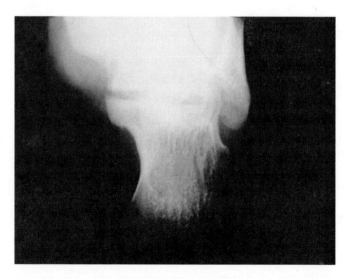

Figure 7–12. Courtesy of Stamford Hospital, Department of Radiology.

111. Which of the following interactions between x-ray photons and matter is *most responsible* for patient dose?

    (A) The photoelectric effect
    (B) Compton scatter
    (C) Classic scatter
    (D) Thompson scatter

112. The collimator light and actual irradiated area must be accurate to within what percentage of the SID?

    (A) 2%
    (B) 5%
    (C) 10%
    (D) 15%

113. The brightness level of the fluoroscopic image can vary with changes in

    1. milliamperage
    2. kilovoltage
    3. patient thickness

    (A) 1 only
    (B) 1 and 2 only
    (C) 1 and 3 only
    (D) 1, 2, and 3

114. Which of the following methods can be used effectively to decrease differential absorption, providing a longer scale of contrast in the diagnostic range?

    1. Using high peak kilovoltage and low milliampere-seconds factors
    2. Using compensating filtration
    3. Using factors that increase the photoelectric effect

    (A) 1 only
    (B) 1 and 2 only
    (C) 2 and 3 only
    (D) 1, 2, and 3

115. The line-focus principle expresses the relationship between

    (A) actual and effective focal spot
    (B) SID used and resulting density
    (C) exposure given the IR and resulting density
    (D) kilovoltage used and the resulting contrast

116. Compared with that of the hypersthenic and sthenic body types, the gallbladder of an asthenic patient is *most likely* to be located

    (A) higher and more medial
    (B) lower and more medial
    (C) higher and more lateral
    (D) lower and more lateral

117. Which of the following correctly identifies the letter *T* in the radiograph shown in Figure 7–13?

    (A) Gliding joint
    (B) Pivot joint
    (C) Diarthrotic joint
    (D) Amphiarthrotic joint

118. Which of the following correctly identifies the letter *L* in the radiograph shown in Figure 7–13?

    (A) Hamate
    (B) Lunate
    (C) Scaphoid
    (D) Trapezium

119. The RPO position of the cervical spine requires which of the following combinations of tube angle and direction?

    (A) 15 to 20 degrees caudad
    (B) 15 to 20 degrees cephalad
    (C) 25 to 30 degrees caudad
    (D) 25 to 30 degrees cephalad

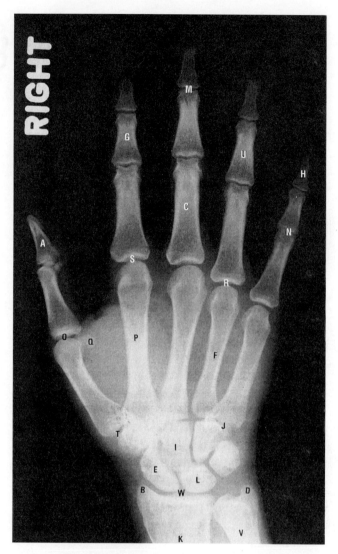

Figure 7–13. Courtesy of Bob Wong, R.T.(R).

120. Crescent-shaped black marks on a chemically processed x-ray film are usually due to

    (A) bending the film acutely
    (B) improper development
    (C) improper film storage
    (D) static electricity

121. If 300 mA has been selected for a particular exposure, what exposure time should be selected to produce 18 mAs?

    (A) 40 ms
    (B) 60 ms
    (C) 400 ms
    (D) 600 ms

122. If the center photocell were selected for a lateral projection of the lumbar spine that was positioned with the spinous processes instead of the vertebral bodies centered to the grid, how would the resulting radiograph look?

    (A) The image would be underexposed.
    (B) The image would be overexposed.
    (C) The image would be correctly exposed.
    (D) An exposure could not be made.

123. What type of shock results from loss of blood?

    (A) Septic
    (B) Neurogenic
    (C) Cardiogenic
    (D) Hypovolemic

124. What is the most superior structure of the scapula?

    (A) Apex
    (B) Acromion process
    (C) Coracoid process
    (D) Superior angle

125. Which of the following contribute(s) to x-ray film base-plus fog?

    1. Chemical fog
    2. Base tint
    3. Background radiation

    (A) 1 only
    (B) 1 and 2 only
    (C) 1 and 3 only
    (D) 1, 2, and 3

126. Examples of primary radiation barriers include

    1. radiographic room walls
    2. lead aprons
    3. radiographic room floor

    (A) 1 only
    (B) 1 and 2 only
    (C) 1 and 3 only
    (D) 1, 2, and 3

127. Inadequate collimation in CR imaging can result in an image that is too

    1. light
    2. dark
    3. noisy

    (A) 1 only
    (B) 1 and 2 only
    (C) 2 and 3 only
    (D) 1, 2, and 3

128. Which of the following cell types has the *lowest* radiosensitivity?

    (A) Nerve cells
    (B) Muscle cells
    (C) Spermatids
    (D) Lymphocytes

129. An emetic is used to

    (A) induce vomiting
    (B) stimulate defecation
    (C) promote elimination of urine
    (D) inhibit coughing

130. Although the stated focal-spot size is measured directly under the actual focal spot, focal-spot size in fact varies along the length of the x-ray beam. At which portion of the x-ray beam is the effective focal spot the largest?

    (A) At its outer edge
    (B) Along the path of the CR
    (C) At the cathode end
    (D) At the anode end

131. Extravasation occurs when

    (A) there is an absence of collateral circulation
    (B) there is a multitude of vessels supplying one area
    (C) excessive contrast medium is injected
    (D) contrast medium is injected into surrounding tissue

132. What is the *best* position/projection to demonstrate the longitudinal arch of the foot?

    (A) Mediolateral
    (B) Lateromedial
    (C) Mediolateral weight-bearing lateral
    (D) Lateromedial weight-bearing lateral

133. Both radiographic images shown in Figure 7–14 were made of the same subject using identical exposure factors. Which of the following statements correctly describe(s) these images?

    1. Image A demonstrates less optical density because a shorter SID was used.
    2. Image A demonstrates more optical density because the subject was turned PA.
    3. Image B demonstrates more optical density because a shorter SID was used.

    (A) 1 only
    (B) 2 only
    (C) 3 only
    (D) 1 and 2 only

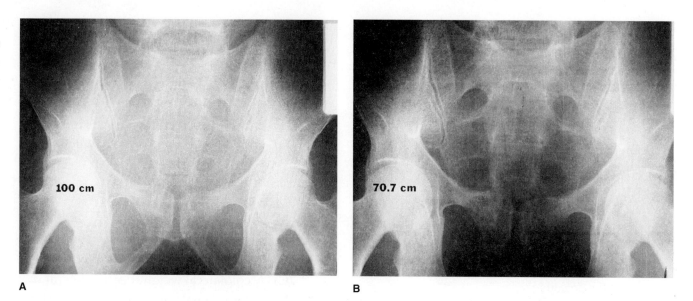

A   B

Figure 7–14. From the American College of Radiology Learning File. Courtesy of the ACR.

134. What is the minimum requirement for lead aprons, according to CFR 20?

(A) 0.05 mm Pb
(B) 0.50 mm Pb
(C) 0.25 mm Pb
(D) 1.0 mm Pb

135. Which of the following would be *most likely* to cause the greatest skin dose (ESE)?

(A) Short SID
(B) High kilovoltage
(C) Increased filtration
(D) Increased milliamperage

136. Stochastic effects of radiation include

(A) blood changes
(B) genetic alterations
(C) cataractogenesis
(D) reduced fertility

137. The cycle of infection includes which of the following components?

1. Reservoir of infection
2. Pathogenic organism
3. Means of transmission

(A) 1 only
(B) 1 and 2 only
(C) 1 and 3 only
(D) 1, 2, and 3

138. Which of the following conditions will require an increase in x-ray photon energy/penetration?

(A) Fibrosarcoma
(B) Osteomalacia
(C) Paralytic ileus
(D) Ascites

139. A diuretic is used to

(A) induce vomiting
(B) stimulate defecation
(C) increase urine output
(D) inhibit coughing

140. Which of the following positions is *most likely* to offer the best visualization of the pulmonary apices?

 (A) Lateral decubitus
 (B) Dorsal decubitus
 (C) Erect lateral
 (D) AP axial lordotic

141. Which of the following is used to obtain a lateral projection of the upper humerus on patients who are unable to abduct their arm?

 (A) Bicipital groove projection
 (B) Superoinferior lateral
 (C) Inferosuperior axial
 (D) Transthoracic lateral

142. The term *differential absorption* is related to

 1. beam intensity
 2. subject contrast
 3. pathology

 (A) 1 only
 (B) 1 and 2 only
 (C) 2 and 3 only
 (D) 1, 2, and 3

143. Which of the following is (are) demonstrated in the lateral projection of the thoracic spine?

 1. Intervertebral spaces
 2. Apophyseal joints
 3. Intervertebral foramina

 (A) 1 only
 (B) 2 only
 (C) 1 and 3 only
 (D) 1, 2, and 3

144. Which of the following positions would demonstrate the right lumbar apophyseal articulations closest to the IR?

 (A) LAO
 (B) RAO
 (C) LPO
 (D) RPO

145. All the following are related to recorded detail *except*

 (A) motion
 (B) focal-spot size
 (C) OID
 (D) scattered radiation

146. Grid interspace material can be made of

 1. plastic
 2. lead
 3. aluminum

 (A) 1 only
 (B) 1 and 2 only
 (C) 1 and 3 only
 (D) 1, 2, and 3

147. What is the annual TEDE limit for radiation workers?

 (A) 5 mSv
 (B) 500 mSv
 (C) 5,000 mSv
 (D) 50 mSv

148. All the following statements regarding beam restriction are true *except*

 (A) beam restriction improves contrast resolution
 (B) beam restriction improves spatial resolution
 (C) field size should never exceed IR dimensions
 (D) beam restriction reduces patient dose

149. An increase in exposure factors usually is required in which of the following circumstances?

 1. Edema
 2. Ascites
 3. Acromegaly

 (A) 1 only
 (B) 1 and 2 only
 (C) 1 and 3 only
 (D) 1, 2, and 3

150. Verbal disclosure of confidential information that is detrimental to the patient is referred to as

(A) invasion of privacy
(B) slander
(C) libel
(D) assault

151. Which of the following medications commonly found on emergency carts functions to raise blood pressure?

(A) Heparin
(B) Norepinephrine
(C) Nitroglycerin
(D) Lidocaine

152. Focal-spot blur is greatest

(A) toward the anode end of the x-ray beam
(B) toward the cathode end of the x-ray beam
(C) directly along the course of the CR
(D) as the SID is increased

153. An advantage of coupling the image intensifier to the TV camera or CCD via a fiber-optic coupling device is its

1. compact size
2. durability
3. ability to accommodate auxilary imaging devices

(A) 1 only
(B) 1 and 2 only
(C) 1 and 3 only
(D) 1, 2, and 3

154. Occupational exposure received by the radiographer is *mostly* from

(A) Compton scatter
(B) the photoelectric effect
(C) coherent scatter
(D) pair production

155. The bone labeled number 3 in Figure 7–15 is the

(A) talus
(B) cuboid
(C) navicular
(D) lateral cuneiform

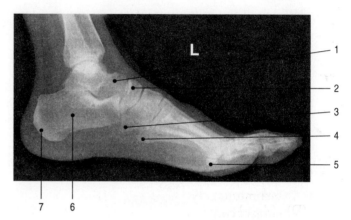

Figure 7–15. Courtesy of Stamford Hospital, Department of Radiology.

156. Sternal compressions during CPR are made with the heels of the hands located about

(A) 1½ in. superior to the xiphoid tip
(B) 1½ in. inferior to the xiphoid tip
(C) 3 in. superior to the xiphoid tip
(D) 3 in. inferior to the xiphoid tip

157. As window level decreases

(A) contrast scale increases
(B) contrast scale decreases
(C) brightness increases
(D) brightness decreases

158. Which of the following may be used as landmark(s) for an AP projection of the hip?

1. 2 in. medial to the ASIS
2. Prominence of the greater trochanter
3. Midway between the iliac crest and the pubic symphysis

(A) 1 only
(B) 1 and 2 only
(C) 1 and 3 only
(D) 1, 2, and 3

159. If 32 mAs was used to produce a particular screen/film x-ray image, what new mAs value would be required to produce a similar image if the kV was increased by 15%?

(A) 8 mAs
(B) 16 mAs
(C) 32 mAs
(D) 64 mAs

160. Recommended method(s) of minimizing motion unsharpness include

1. suspended respiration
2. short exposure time
3. patient instruction

(A) 1 only
(B) 1 and 2 only
(C) 1 and 3 only
(D) 1, 2, and 3

161. Which of the following is *most useful* for bone age evaluation?

(A) Lateral skull
(B) PA chest
(C) AP pelvis
(D) PA hand

162. The function of the developer solution chemicals is to

(A) reduce the manifest image to a latent image
(B) increase production of silver halide crystals
(C) reduce the latent image to a manifest image
(D) remove the unexposed crystals from the film

163. An acute reaction caused by ingestion or injection of a sensitizing agent describes

(A) asthma
(B) anaphylaxis
(C) myocardial infarction
(D) rhinitis

164. A minor reaction to the IV administration of a contrast agent can include

1. a few hives
2. nausea
3. a flushed face

(A) 1 only
(B) 1 and 2 only
(C) 1 and 3 only
(D) 1, 2, and 3

165. In an AP abdomen radiograph taken at 105-cm SID during an IVU series, one renal shadow measures 9 cm in width. If the OID is 18 cm, what is the actual width of the kidney?

(A) 5 cm
(B) 7.5 cm
(C) 11 cm
(D) 18 cm

166. Which of the following affect(s) both the quantity and quality of the primary beam?

1. Half-value layer (HVL)
2. Kilovoltage
3. Milliamperage

(A) 1 only
(B) 2 only
(C) 1 and 2 only
(D) 1, 2, and 3

167. A lesion with a stalk projecting from the intestinal mucosa into the lumen is a(n)

(A) fistula
(B) polyp
(C) diverticulum
(D) abscess

168. Which of the x-ray circuit devices shown in Figure 7–16 operates on the principle of self-induction?

1. Number 1
2. Number 2
3. Number 3

(A) 1 only
(B) 1 and 2 only
(C) 2 and 3 only
(D) 1, 2, and 3

169. Referring to the simplified x-ray circuit shown in Figure 7–16, what is indicated by the number 4?

(A) Step-up transformer
(B) Kilovoltage meter
(C) Grounded milliamperage meter
(D) Rectification system

170. Which of the following pathologic conditions are considered *additive* conditions with respect to selection of exposure factors?

1. Osteoma
2. Bronchiectasis
3. Pneumonia

(A) 1 and 2 only
(B) 1 and 3 only
(C) 2 and 3 only
(D) 1, 2, and 3

171. The type of isolation practiced to prevent the spread of infectious agents in aerosol form is

(A) respiratory isolation
(B) protective isolation
(C) contact isolation
(D) strict isolation

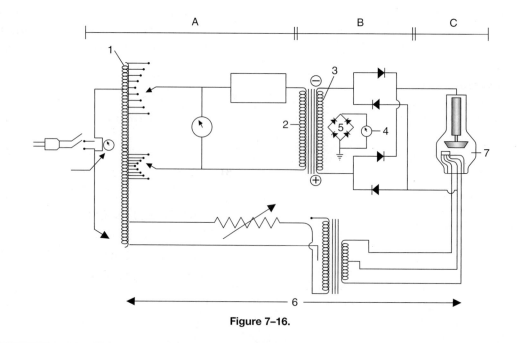

Figure 7–16.

172. Which of the following is (are) essential to high-quality mammographic examinations?

1. Small-focal-spot x-ray tube
2. Short-scale contrast
3. Use of a compression device

(A) 1 only
(B) 1 and 2 only
(C) 1 and 3 only
(D) 1, 2, and 3

173. How often are radiographic equipment collimators required to be evaluated?

(A) Annually
(B) Biannually
(C) Semiannually
(D) Quarterly

174. If 84 kV and 8 mAs were used for a particular abdominal exposure with single-phase equipment, what milliampere-seconds value would be required to produce a similar radiograph with three-phase, 12-pulse equipment?

(A) 24 mAs
(B) 16 mAs
(C) 8 mAs
(D) 4 mAs

175. A focal-spot size of 0.3 mm or smaller is essential for which of the following procedures?

(A) Bone radiography
(B) Magnification radiography
(C) Tomography
(D) Fluoroscopy

176. What type of x-ray imaging uses an area beam and a photostimulable phosphor as the IR?

(A) Traditional radiography
(B) Computed radiography
(C) Digital radiography
(D) Cineradiography

177. The term used to describe the gradual decrease in exposure rate as an x-ray beam passes through matter is

(A) attenuation
(B) absorption
(C) scattered radiation
(D) secondary radiation

178. The principal function of filtration in the x-ray tube is to reduce

(A) patient skin dose
(B) operator exposure
(C) scattered radiation
(D) image noise

179. The effects of radiation on biologic material depend on several factors. If a quantity of radiation is delivered to a body over a long period of time, the effect

(A) will be greater than if it is delivered all at one time
(B) will be less than if it is delivered all at one time
(C) has no relation to how it is delivered in time
(D) solely depends on the radiation quality

180. Which of the following adult radiographic examinations usually require(s) use of a grid?

1. Ribs
2. Vertebrae
3. Shoulder

(A) 1 only
(B) 1 and 2 only
(C) 1 and 3 only
(D) 1, 2, and 3

181. The x-ray beam and collimator light field must coincide to within

(A) 10% of the OID
(B) 2% of the OID
(C) 10% of the SID
(D) 2% of the SID

182. The use of which of the following is (are) essential in magnification radiography?

1. High-ratio grid
2. Fractional focal spot
3. Direct exposure technique

(A) 1 only
(B) 2 only
(C) 1 and 3 only
(D) 1, 2, and 3

183. A minimum total amount of aluminum filtration (inherent plus added) of 2.5 mm is required in equipment operated

(A) above 50 kVp
(B) above 60 kVp
(C) above 70 kVp
(D) above 80 kVp

184. Which type of error results in grid cutoff at the periphery of the radiographic image?

(A) Off-focus
(B) Off-center
(C) Off-level
(D) Off-angle

185. Each of the following statements regarding respiratory structures is true *except*

(A) the left lung has two lobes
(B) the lower portion of the lung is the base
(C) each lung is enclosed in peritoneum
(D) the main stem bronchus enters the lung hilum

186. The positive electrode of the x-ray tube is the

(A) capacitor
(B) grid
(C) cathode
(D) anode

187. Which of the following techniques might have been employed in the production of Figure 7–17?

1. Motion
2. Anode heel effect
3. Compression

(A) 1 only
(B) 1 and 2 only
(C) 1 and 3 only
(D) 1, 2, and 3

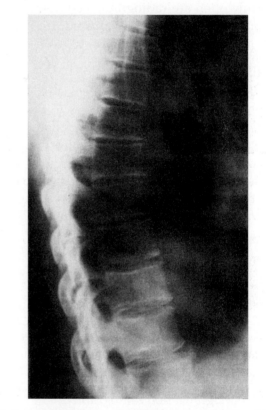

Figure 7–17. Reproduced, with permission, from Shephard CT. *Radiographic Image Production and Manipulation*. New York: McGraw-Hill; 2003.

188. Which of the following statements is (are) true with respect to the differences between the male and female bony pelvis?

1. The female pelvic outlet is wider
2. The pubic angle is 90 degrees or less in the male
3. The male pelvis is more shallow

(A) 1 only
(B) 1 and 2 only
(C) 2 and 3 only
(D) 1, 2, and 3

189. The medical term used to describe the vomiting of blood is

    (A) hematemesis
    (B) hemoptysis
    (C) hematuria
    (D) epistaxis

190. An exposed image plate will retain its image for about

    (A) 2 hours
    (B) 8 hours
    (C) 24 hours
    (D) 48 hours

191. In the 45-degree medial oblique projection of the ankle, the

    1. talotibial joint is visualized
    2. tibiofibular joint is visualized
    3. plantar surface should be vertical

    (A) 1 only
    (B) 1 and 2 only
    (C) 2 and 3 only
    (D) 1, 2, and 3

192. Which of the following formulas would the radiographer use to determine the total number of heat units (HU) produced with a given exposure using three-phase, 12-pulse equipment?

    (A) mA × kVp × s
    (B) mA × kVp × s × 3.0
    (C) mA × kVp × s × 1.35
    (D) mA × kVp × s × 1.41

193. Body substances and fluids that are considered infectious or potentially infectious include

    1. sputum
    2. synovial fluid
    3. cerebrospinal fluid

    (A) 1 only
    (B) 1 and 2 only
    (C) 2 and 3 only
    (D) 1, 2, and 3

194. The *control* dosimeter that comes from the monitoring company should be

    (A) stored in a radiation-free area
    (B) kept in a designated control booth
    (C) kept in the film-processing area
    (D) used as an extra badge for new personnel

195. What is the *appropriate* action if a patient has signed consent for a procedure but, once on the radiographic table, refuses the procedure?

    (A) Proceed—the consent form is signed.
    (B) Send the patient back to his or her room.
    (C) Honor the patient's request and proceed with the next patient.
    (D) Immediately stop the procedure and inform the radiologist and the referring physician of the patient's request.

196. To maintain image clarity, the path of electron flow from photocathode to output phosphor is controlled by

    (A) the accelerating anode
    (B) electrostatic lenses
    (C) the vacuum glass envelope
    (D) the input phosphor

197. Which of the following terms is used to express resolution/recorded detail?

   (A) Kiloelectronvolts (keV)
   (B) Modulation transfer function (MTF)
   (C) Relative speed
   (D) Latitude

198. What is the function of the x-ray tube component numbered 2 in Figure 7–18?

   (A) To release electrons when heated
   (B) To release light when heated
   (C) To direct electrons to the focal track
   (D) To direct light to the focal track

199. Of what material is the x-ray tube component numbered 5 in Figure 7–18 made?

   (A) Cesium
   (B) Copper
   (C) Molybdenum
   (D) Tungsten

200. Of what material is the x-ray tube component numbered 2 in Figure 7–18 made?

   (A) Cesium
   (B) Copper
   (C) Molybdenum
   (D) Tungsten

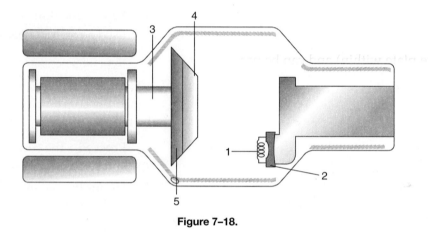

Figure 7–18.

Answers and Explanations

1. **(C)** Computed radiography (CR) cassettes use no intensifying screens or film—hence, the term *filmless radiography*. The Image Plates (IPs) have a protective function (for the PSP/storage plate within) and can be used in the Bucky tray or directly under the anatomic part; they need not be light-tight because the PSP is not light sensitive. The IP has a thin lead-foil backing (similar to traditional cassettes) to absorb backscatter. Inside the IP is the photostimulable phosphor (PSP) storage plate. This PSP storage plate within the IP has a layer of europium-activated barium fluorohalide that serves as the IR as it is exposed in the traditional manner and receives the latent image. The PSP can store the latent image for several hours; *after about 8 hours, noticeable image fading will occur. (Carlton and Adler, 4th ed., p. 358)*

2. **(D)** For negligent tort liability, four elements must be present—duty (what should have been done), breach (deviation from duty), injury sustained, and cause (as a result of breach). The assessment of duty is determined by the professional standard of care. Examples of negligent torts include patient injury as a result of a fall while unattended on an x-ray table, in a radiographic room, or on a stretcher without side rails or safety belt. Radiographing the wrong patient and radiographing the opposite limb are other examples of negligence. If patient injury results from misperformance of a duty in the routine scope of practice of the radiographer, most courts will apply *res ipsa loquitur;* that is, "the thing speaks for itself." If the patient is obviously injured as a result of the radiographer's actions, it becomes the radiographer's burden to disprove negligence. In many instances, the hospital and/or radiologist also will be held responsible according to *respondeat superior*, or "the master speaks for the servant." *(Adler and Carlton, 4th ed., p. 374)*

3. **(A)** One of the biggest advantages of CR/DR is the *latitude* it offers. The characteristic curve of typical film emulsion has a "range of correct exposure" limited by the toe and shoulder of the curve. In CR/DR, there is a *linear* relationship between the exposure given the PSP and its resulting luminescence as it is scanned by the laser, as illustrated in the figure shown. This affords much greater exposure latitude; technical inaccuracies can be effectively eliminated. Overexposure of up to 500% and underexposure of up to 80% are reported as recoverable, thus eliminating most retakes. *This surely affords increased efficiency; however, this does not mean that images can be exposed arbitrarily.* The professional radiographer has a responsibility to keep dose reduction to a minimum. The same exposure factors as screen–film systems or less generally are recommended for CR/DR. *(Shephard, p. 332)*

4. **(A)** The image intensifier's input phosphor is 6 to 9 times larger than the output phosphor.

It receives the remnant radiation emerging from the patient and converts it into a fluorescent light image. Very close to the input phosphor, separated only by a thin, transparent layer, is the photocathode. The photocathode is made of a photoemissive alloy, usually a cesium and antimony compound. The fluorescent light image strikes the photocathode and is converted to an electron image, which is focused by the electrostatic lenses to the small output phosphor. *(Bushong, 8th ed., pp. 360–363)*

5. **(B)** As the CR laser scanner/reader recognizes the phosphostimulated luminescence (PSL) released by the PSP storage plate, it constructs a graphic representation of pixel value distribution called a histogram.

The photostimulable storage phosphor (PSP) within the IP is the image receptor (IR). The PSP is a europium-doped barium fluorohalide coated storage plate. When the PSP is exposed by x-ray photons, the x-ray energy interacts with the crystals and a small amount of visible light is emitted, *but most of the x-ray energy is stored* (hence, the term *storage plate*). This stored energy represents the latent image.

The IP is placed in the CR scanner/reader where a helium–neon, or solid-state, laser beam scans the PSP and its stored energy is released as blue-violet light (phosphostimulated luminescence [PSL]). This light signal represents varying tissue densities and the latent image that is then transferred to an *analog-to-digital converter* (ADC) — converting the signal to a digital (electrical) one to be displayed on a monitor.

The PSL values will result in numerous image *density/brightness values* that represent various *tissue densities* (i.e., x-ray attenuation properties), for example, bone, muscle, blood-filled organs, air/gas, pathologic processes, and so on. The CR scanner/reader recognizes all these values and constructs a representative gray-scale *histogram* of them corresponding to the anatomical characteristics of the imaged part. Thus, all PA chest histograms will be similar, all lateral chest histograms will be similar, all pelvis histograms will be similar, and so on.

A histogram is a *graphic representation* of pixel-value distribution. The histogram analyzes all the densities from the PSP and represents them graphically—demonstrating the quantity of exposure, the number of pixels, and their value. Histograms are generated that are unique to each body part that can be imaged.

After a part is exposed/imaged, its PSP is read/scanned and its own histogram is developed and analyzed. The resulting analysis, and histogram of the *actual* imaged part, is compared to the programmed representative histogram for that part. Over time, if required diagnostic image characteristics change, a histogram can be updated to reflect the latest required characteristics. *(Carlton and Adler, 4th ed., pp. 361–362)*

6. **(D)** The 45-degree oblique position of the lumbar spine generally is performed for demonstration of the *apophyseal joints*. In a correctly positioned oblique lumbar spine, "Scotty dog" images are demonstrated. The Scotty's *ear* corresponds to the superior articular process, his *nose* to the transverse process, his *eye* to the pedicle, his *neck* to the pars interarticularis, his *body* to the lamina, and his *front foot* to the inferior articular process. *(Frank, Long, and Smith, 11th ed., vol. 1, p. 432)*

7. **(D)** According to the inverse-square law of radiation, the intensity or exposure rate of radiation from its source is inversely proportional to the square of the distance. Thus, as distance from the source of radiation increases, exposure rate decreases. Because exposure rate and radiographic density are directly proportional, if the exposure rate of a beam directed to the IR is decreased, the resulting radiographic density would be decreased proportionally. *(Selman, 9th ed., p. 117)*

8. **(B)** X-ray images are often subpoenaed as court evidence in cases of medical litigation. In order to be considered as legitimate legal evidence, each x-ray image must contain certain essential and specific patient information. Essential information that must be included on each image is patient identification, the identity of the facility where the x-ray study

was performed, the date that the study was performed, and a right- or left-side marker.

Other useful information that may be included, but that is not considered essential, is additional patient demographics such as their date of birth, the identity of the referring physician, the time of day that the study was performed, and the identity/initials of the radiographer performing the examination.

9. **(B)** A cross-sectional image of the abdomen is shown in the figure. The large, homogeneous structure on the right, labeled 14, is the *liver*. The gallbladder is often seen as a darker density on the medial border of the liver but is not visualized here. The left kidney is labeled 5; the right kidney is seen clearly on the opposite side labeled 11. The vertebra is seen in the center, and the psoas muscles are seen just posterior to the vertebra. Just anterior to the body of the vertebra is the circular *aorta*, labeled 7. The *inferior vena cava* (number 12) is seen to the left of the aorta. The circular structure just anterior to the inferior vena cava is the *portal vein* (number 13). Number 1 is the stomach, number 2 is the splenic/left colic flexure, number 3 is the pancreas, and number 4 is the spleen. Numbers 6 and 10 are portions of the left and right adrenal glands—not normally seen at this level. Number 8 is the celiac trunk; the common hepatic artery is seen branching to the right, and the splenic artery is seen branching to the left. Number 9 is a part of the diaphragmatic crura connecting the vertebrae and diaphragm. *(Bontrager and Lampignano, 6th ed., p. 114)*

10. **(C)** Late or long-term effects of radiation can occur in tissues as a result of chronic exposure or tissues that have survived a previous irradiation months or years earlier. These late effects, such as carcinogenesis and genetic effects, are "all-or-nothing" effects—either the organism develops cancer or it does not. Most late effects do not have a threshold dose; that is, any dose, however small, can induce an effect (thus, the importance of radiation protection). Increasing that dose will increase the *likelihood* of the occurrence but will not affect its severity; these effects are termed *stochastic*. *Nonstochastic* effects are those that will not occur below a particular threshold dose and

that increase in severity as the dose increases. Early effects of radiation exposure are in response to relatively high radiation doses. These never should occur in diagnostic radiology; they occur only in response to doses much greater than those used in diagnostic radiology. One of the effects that may be noted in such a circumstance is the hematologic effect—reduced numbers of white blood cells, red blood cells, and platelets in the circulating blood. Immediate local tissue effects can include effects on the gonads (temporary infertility) and on the skin (e.g., epilation and erythema). Acute radiation lethality, or radiation death, occurs after an acute exposure and results in death in weeks or days. *(Bushong, 8th ed., p. 532)*

11. **(C)** Contrast-medium injection into the ureters can be achieved only by first catheterizing the bladder, locating the ureteral orifices, and then injecting the contrast agent into the ureters. This procedure is called a *retrograde* (because contrast is being introduced against the normal direction of flow) *pyelogram*. A *cystogram* is an examination of the bladder. A *cystourethrogram* is an examination of the bladder and urethra. *(Frank, Long, and Smith, 11th ed., vol. 2, p. 228)*

12. **(D)** There are several radiation units that are used to express quantity and effects of radiation. *Rad* (radiation *a*bsorbed *d*ose) expresses energy deposited (as a result of ionizations) in any kind of absorber. The unit of exposure, the *roentgen*, is used to express the quantity of ionization in air. The unit of dose equivalent is the *rem* (radiation *e*quivalent *m*an), which expresses dose to biologic material. *(Selman, 9th ed., p. 131)*

13. **(D)** Radiographic rating charts enable the operator to determine the maximum safe milliamperage, exposure time, and peak kilovoltage for a particular exposure using a particular x-ray tube. An exposure that can be made safely with the large focal spot may not be safe for use with the small focal spot of the same x-ray tube. The total number of heat units that an exposure generates also influences the amount of stress (in the form of heat) imparted to the anode. The product of milliampere-second and

peak kilovolts determines HU. Groups (A) and (C) produce 2250 HU; groups (B) and (D) produce 1275 HU. Groups (B) and (D) deliver less heat load, but group (D) delivers it to a larger area (actual focal spot), making this the least hazardous group of technical factors. The *most* hazardous group of technical factors is group (A). *(Selman, 9th ed., p. 145)*

14–15. **(14, D; 15, C)** The radiograph illustrates an AP projection of the scapula; abduction of the arm moves the scapula away from the rib cage, revealing a greater portion of the scapula than would be visualized with the arm at the side. A number of bony structures are identified: the acromion process (A), the humeral head (B), glenoid fossa (C), scapular spine (D), clavicle (E), supraspinatus fossa (F), acromioclavicular joint (G), scapular notch (H), coracoid process (I), inferior angle/apex (J), body/costal surface (K), lateral/axillary border (L).

16. **(A)** Image details placed away from the path of the CR will be exposed by more divergent rays, resulting in *rotation distortion*. This is why the CR must be directed to the midpoint of the part of greatest interest. For example, if bilateral hands are requested, they should be examined individually; if imaged simultaneously, the CR will be directed to no anatomic part (between the two hands) and rotation distortion will occur.

    Magnification occurs when an OID is introduced, or with a decrease in SID. Foreshortening and elongation are the two types of shape distortion—caused by nonalignment of the x-ray tube, part/subject, and IR. *(Bontrager and Lampignano, 6th ed., p. 46 and 147)*

17. **(C)** Federal regulations regarding infection control in the workplace, as amended by OSHA, require development of policies conforming to OSHA guidelines and instruction in their application/use. These regulations also require provision of hepatitis B immunization (free of charge) for all staff *who might be exposed to blood/body substances*, follow-up care for any staff accidentally exposed to blood/body fluids and/or needle stick injuries, and readily accessible personal protective equipment (PPE) and impermeable puncture-proof containers for used needles/syringes. It also requires that all health care workers and their employers follow/enforce standard precautions, transmission-based precautions, and these OSHA guidelines under penalty of law. *(Torres et al., 6th ed., p. 63)*

18. **(A)** *Atelectasis* is partial or complete collapse (i.e., imperfect expansion) of a lung or lobe of a lung. *Pneumonia* is an acute infection of the lung parenchyma characterized by productive cough, chest pain, fever, and chills and frequently accompanied by rales. *Pneumothorax* is the condition of air or gas in the pleural space. *Chronic obstructive pulmonary disease* (COPD) is the name given to a number of disease processes that decrease the lung's ability to perform its function of ventilation. *(Tortora and Derrickson, 11th ed., p. 888)*

19. **(C)** To have high diagnostic quality, a barium enema (BE) examination requires rigorous and complete patient preparation. This usually consists of a modified low-residue diet for a few days before the examination, cathartics the day before, and cleansing enemas the morning of the examination. Instructions for a upper GI series, small bowel series, and IV cystogram are usually to be NPO after midnight. *(Frank, Long, and Smith, 11th ed., vol. 2, p. 159)*

20. **(B)** Quality Control refers to our equipment and its safe and accurate operation. Various components must be tested at specified intervals and test results must be within specified parameters. Any deviation from those parameters must be corrected. Examples of equipment components that are tested annually are the focal spot size, linearity, reproducibility, filtration, kV, and exposure time. Three-phase x-ray generators should be able to time exposures to $+/-5\%$ accuracy. Radiographic equipment collimators should be inspected and verified as accurate semiannually (twice a year); the relationship between the collimator light field and the actual x-ray field must be congruent to within 2% of the SID. Kilovoltage settings can most effectively be tested using an electronic kV meter; to meet required standards, the kV should be accurate to within $+/-4$ kV. Reproducibility testing should specify that radiation output be consistent to within $+/-5\%$. *(Fosbinder and Orth, pp. 223–225; NCRP Report No. 99, p. 70)*

21. **(D)** The *protective curtain,* usually made of leaded vinyl with at least 0.25-mm Pb equivalent, must be positioned between the patient and the fluoroscopist to greatly reduce exposure of the fluoroscopist to energetic scatter from the patient. As with overhead equipment, fluoroscopic total *filtration* must be at least 2.5-mm Al equivalent to reduce excessive exposure to soft radiation. Collimator/beam alignment must be accurate to within 2%. *(Bushong, 8th ed., p. 569)*

22. **(D)** In the AP projection of the lumbar spine, the disk spaces of L1 to L4 are perpendicular to the IR and well visualized, but the L5 to S1 disk space is angled 30 to 35 degrees cephalad to the perpendicular. If the CR is directed 30 to 35 degrees cephalad midway between the ASIS and the publis symphysis, the L5 to S1 interspace will be well demonstrated. *(Bontrger and Lampignano, 6th ed., p. 337)*

23. **(A)** When the arm is placed in the AP position, the epicondyles are parallel to the plane of the cassette, and the shoulder is placed in external rotation. In this position, an AP projection of the humerus, elbow, and forearm can be obtained. For the lateral projection of the humerus, elbow, or forearm, the epicondyles must be perpendicular to the plane of the cassette. *(Frank, Long, and Smith, 11th ed., vol. 1, p. 159)*

24. **(D)** Endoscopic retrograde cholangiopancreatography (ERCP) is performed to diagnose disease of the biliary and/or pancreatic organs. Fluoroscopic control is used to introduce the fiber-optic endoscope through the mouth and into the duodenum. The hepatopancreatic ampulla (of Vater) then is located and cannulated, and contrast medium is injected into the common bile duct. *(Frank, Long, and Smith, 11th ed., vol. 2, p. 116)*

25. **(A)** The cervical intervertebral foramina form a 45-degree angle with the MSP and, therefore, are well visualized in a 45-degree oblique position. Apophyseal joints are formed by articulating surfaces of the inferior articular facet of one vertebra with the superior articular facet of the vertebra below; they are well demonstrated in the lateral position of the cervical

spine. The intervertebral disk spaces are best demonstrated in the lateral position. *(Bontrager and Lampignano, 6th ed., p. 298)*

26. **(B)** SNR can refer to home television images, magnetic resonance images (MRIs), ultrasound images, x-ray images, and so on. Noise interferes with visualization of image details, for example, scattered radiation fog, graininess from quantum mottle, and so no. The actual signal can be from x-rays, sound waves, and so on. The signal is desirable, the noise is not, therefore, a higher SNR produces a higher-quality image. Low SNR severely impairs contrast resolution. *(Bushong, 8th ed., p. 412)*

27. **(C)** As kilovoltage is increased, more electrons are driven to the anode with greater speed and energy. More high-energy electrons will result in production of more (i.e., increased exposure rate) high-energy (i.e., short-wavelength) x-rays. Thus, peak kilovoltage affects both quantity and quality of the x-ray beam. However, although peak kilovoltage and radiographic density are directly related, they are not directly proportional; that is, twice the radiographic density does not result from doubling the kilovoltage. With respect to the effect of peak kilovoltage on image density, there is a convenient rule (15% rule) that can be followed. If it is desired to double the radiographic density yet impossible to adjust the milliampere-seconds, a similar effect can be achieved by increasing the kilovoltage by 15%. Conversely, the density may be cut in half by decreasing the kilovoltage by 15%. *(Shephard, pp. 194–197)*

28. **(C)** The stomach is generally not parallel with the long axis of the body—its fundus/superior portion lies more posterior, and the pylorus/inferior portion lies more anterior. Consequently, in the recumbent position, barium will gravitate to the fundus when the patient is supine and to the pylorus when the patient is prone. Since the image shows a barium-filled fundus, it must have been made in the AP projection or LPO position. A look at the vertebrae indicates that the body is somewhat obliqued, indicating an LPO position. Note the double-contrast demonstration of rugal folds in the body of the stomach and

double-contrast delineation of the pylorus and duodenal bulb.

29. **(A)** *Distortion* is misrepresentation of the actual size or shape of the object being imaged. Size distortion is magnification. Shape distortion is a result of improper alignment of the x-ray tube, the part being radiographed, and the IR; the two types of shape distortion are foreshortening and elongation. The shapes of various structures can be misrepresented radiographically as a result of their position in the body, when the part is out of the central axis of the x-ray beam, or when the CR is angled (Figure 7–19). Parts sometimes are elongated intentionally for better visualization (e.g., sigmoid colon). Some body parts, because of their position in the body, are foreshortened, such as the carpal scaphoid. *Attenuation* refers to decreasing beam intensity and is unrelated to distortion. *(Shephard, pp. 228–231)*

30. **(D)** Conventional 60-Hz full-wave rectified power is converted to a higher frequency of 500 to 25,000 Hz in the most recent generator design—the *high-frequency generator*. The high-frequency generator is small in size, in addition to producing an almost constant potential waveform. High-frequency generators first appeared in mobile x-ray units and were then adopted by mammography and CT equipment. Today, more and more radiographic equipment uses high-frequency generators. Their compact size makes them popular, and the fact that they produce nearly constant potential voltage helps to improve image quality and decrease patient dose (fewer low-energy photons to contribute to skin dose)

31. **(C)** Tissue is most sensitive to radiation exposure when it is in an oxygenated condition. *Anoxic* refers to a general lack of oxygen in tissue; *hypoxic* refers to tissue with little oxygen. Anoxic and hypoxic tumors typically are avascular (with little or no blood supply) and, therefore, more radioresistant. *(Bushong, 8th ed., p. 496)*

32. **(B)** Diagnostic imaging examinations must be scheduled appropriately. Retained barium sulfate contrast medium can obscure necessary anatomic details in x-ray or ultrasound studies that are scheduled later. Therefore, the ultrasound examination should come first, followed by the lower GI series (BE), and finally the upper GI series. Retained barium from the lower GI series probably will not obscure upper GI structures. *(Torres et al., 6th ed., pp. 233–234)*

33. **(B)** The heart superimposes a homogeneous density over the sternum in the RAO position, thus providing clearer radiographic visualization of its bony structure. If the LAO position were used to project the sternum to the right

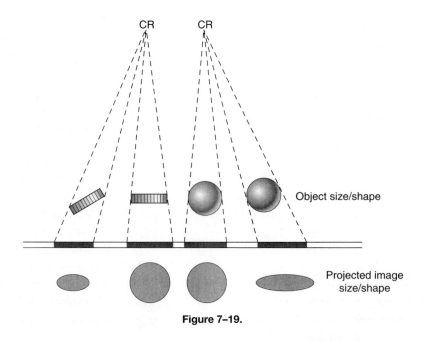

Figure 7–19.

of the thoracic vertebrae, the posterior ribs and pulmonary markings would cast confusing shadows over the sternum because of their differing densities. Prominent pulmonary markings can be obliterated using a "breathing technique," that is, using an exposure time long enough (with appropriately low milliamperage) to equal at least a few respirations. (*Frank, Long, and Smith, 11th ed., vol. 1, pp. 472–473*)

34. **(A)** OID can affect contrast when it is used as an air gap. If a 6-in. air gap (OID) is introduced between the part and IR, much of the scattered radiation emitted from the body will not reach the IR, as shown in Figure 7–20. The OID thus is acting as a low-ratio grid and increasing image contrast. (*Shephard, p. 205*)

35. **(C)** The AP axial projection is used to prevent the clavicles from superimposition on the pulmonary apices. A 15- to 20-degree cephalad angle projects the clavicles above the apices.

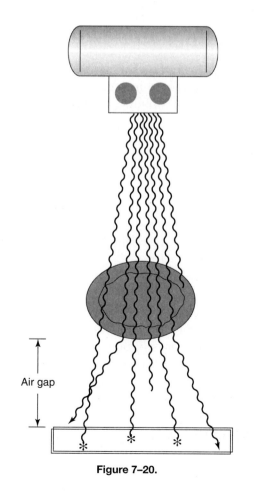

Figure 7–20.

The radiograph is evaluated for rotation by checking the distance between the medial ends of the clavicles and the lateral border of the vertebral column. (*Frank, Long, and Smith, 11th ed., vol. 1, pp. 534–535*)

36. **(B)** *Anaphylaxis* is an acute reaction characterized by sudden onset of urticaria, respiratory distress, vascular collapse, or systemic shock; it sometimes leads to death. It is caused by ingestion or injection of a sensitizing agent such as a drug, vaccine, contrast agent, or food or by an insect bite. Asthma and rhinitis are examples of allergic reactions. Myocardial infarction results from a blocked coronary artery. (*Adler and Carlton, 4th ed., p. 279*)

37. **(C)** The figure is that of a collimator accuracy test. The collimator is, overall, the most efficient beam-restricting device. It is attached to the tube head, and its upper aperture, the first set of shutters, is placed as close as possible to the x-ray-tube port window. This is done to control the amount of image degrading off-focus radiation leaving the x-ray tube (i.e., radiation produced when electrons strike surfaces other than the focal track). The next set of lead shutters (blades or leaves) actually consists of two pairs of adjustable shutters—one pair for field length and another pair for field width. It is these shutters that the radiographer adjusts when changing the field size and shape. Another important part of the collimator assembly is the light-localization apparatus. It consists of a small light bulb (to illuminate the field) and a mirror. For the light field and x-ray field to correspond accurately, the x-ray-tube focal spot and the light bulb must be exactly at the same distance from the center of the mirror. If the light and x-ray fields do not correspond, IR alignment can be off enough to require a repeat examination. Collimator accuracy should be checked regularly as part of the QA program. NCRP guidelines state that collimators must be accurate to within 2% of the SID. The nine-penny test can also be used to evaluate collimator accuracy, but it has been replaced by the ruled measuring device shown in the figure. (*Bushong, 8th ed., p. 461*)

38. **(B)** Computed radiography (CR) offers wide latitude and automatic optimization of the radiologic image. When AEC is not used, CR can compensate for about 80% underexposure and 500% overexposure. This can be an important advantage in trauma and mobile radiography. The radiographer still must be vigilant in patient dose considerations—overexposure, though correctable, results in increased patient dose; underexposure results in decreased image quality owing to increased image noise. CR systems provide an exposure indicator: an *S* (sensitivity) number, exposure index *EI*, or other relative exposure index depending on the manufacturer used. The manufacturer usually provides a chart identifying the acceptable range the exposure indicator numbers should be within for various examination types. For example, a high *S* number often is related to underexposure, whereas a high *EI* number is related to overexposure. *Field of view* (FOV) refers to the anatomic area being visualized. *(Bontrager and Lampignano, 6th ed., p. 52)*

39. **(A)** Oral administration of barium sulfate is used to demonstrate the upper digestive system, esophagus, fundus, and body and pylorus of the stomach and barium progression through the small bowel/intestine. The small intestine is composed of the duodenum, jejunum, and ileum. The duodenum is the shortest portion, beginning just beyond the pyloric sphincter and dividing into four portions—the duodenal cap or bulb, the descending duodenum, the transverse duodenum, and the ascending duodenum. These portions form a C-shaped loop that is occupied by the head of the pancreas. The descending portion receives the hepatopancreatic ampulla and duodenal papilla. The ascending portion terminates at the duodenojejunal flexure (angle of Treitz). Whereas the position of the short (9 in.) duodenum is fixed, the jejunum (9 ft) and ileum (13 ft) are very mobile. The large bowel, including the cecum, usually is demonstrated via rectal administration of barium. The approximately 5-ft-long large intestine (colon) begins at the terminus of the small intestine; its first portion is the dilated saclike cecum, located inferior to the ileocecal valve. Projecting posteromedially from the cecum is the short vermiform appendix. The ascending colon is continuous with the cecum, bending and forming the right colic (hepatic) flexure. The colon traverses the abdomen as the transverse colon and bends to form the left colic (splenic) flexure. The descending colon continues down the left side and moves medially to form the S-shaped sigmoid colon. The rectum is that part of the large intestine, approximately 5 in. in length, between the sigmoid and the anal canal. The ilium is the bony pelvis, whereas the ileum is the small bowel—which would be demonstrated by oral administration of barium. *(Frank, Long, and Smith, vol. 2, 11th ed., p. 140)*

40. **(A)** The PSP storage plate within the IP has a layer of europium-activated barium fluorohalide (BaFX : Eu²⁺; X = halogen) mixed with a binder substance. This layer serves as the *image receptor* when exposed in the traditional manner; it looks very much like an x-ray cassette intensifying screen.

    The barium fluorohalide is usually granular or turbid phosphors. Other examples of turbid phosphors are gadolinium oxysulfide and rubidium chloride. "Needle"-shaped, or columnar phosphors (usually, cesium iodide), have the advantage of better x-ray absorption and less light diffusion.

    Just under the barium fluorohalide layer is a *reflective layer* that helps direct emitted light up toward the CR reader. Below the reflective layer is the *base*, behind that is an *antistatic layer*, and then the *lead foil* to absorb backscatter. Over the *top* of the barium fluorohalide is a *protective layer*.

41. **(C)** The lateral lumbar position is useful to demonstrate the intervertebral disk spaces, intervertebral foramina, and spinous processes. The posterior oblique positions (i.e., LPO and RPO) of the lumbar vertebrae demonstrate the apophyseal articulations closer to the IR. The left apophyseal articulations are demonstrated in the LPO position, whereas the right apophyseal articulations are demonstrated in the RPO position. *(Bontrager and Lampignano, 6th ed., pp. 334–335)*

42. **(B)** The NCRP recommends a total equivalent dose limit to the embryo/fetus of 5 mSv (500 mrem, 0.5 rem). This dose limit is the total for the entire gestational period. The dose limit for 1 month during pregnancy is 0.5 mSv (50 mrem, 0.05 rem). *(Bushong, 8th ed., p. 557)*

43. **(B)** Fluids and medications are administered to patients intravenously to achieve a more rapid response to the medication than if it were delivered orally or intramuscularly. The IV route is also often used to deliver parenteral nutrition to patients who cannot take their meals by mouth. Medications that are administered topically, such as calamine lotion, achieve a local effect. *(Ehrlich et al., 6th ed., p. 192)*

44. **(D)** Each of the three is included in a good QC program. Beam alignment must be accurate to 2% of the SID. *Reproducibility* means that repeated exposures at a given technique must provide consistent intensity. *Linearity* means that a given milliampere-seconds value, using different milliamperage stations with appropriate exposure-time adjustments, will provide consistent intensity. *(Bushong, 8th ed., pp. 460–464)*

45. **(A)** A distinction is made between the actual focal spot and the effective, or projected, focal spot. The *actual focal spot* is the finite area on the tungsten target that is actually bombarded by electrons from the filament. The *effective focal spot* is the foreshortened size of the focus as it is projected down toward the image receptor. This is called line focusing or the *line-focus principle*. The quoted focal-spot size is the effective focal-spot size. *(Carlton & Adler, 4th ed., pp. 112–114)*

46. **(B)** The image shown is an erect PA projection of a patient of hyposthenic body habitus. Note the low position of the gallbladder. It is a result of body habitus and position (viscera assume a lower position in the erect position). The gallbladder may be moved away from the spine by using the LAO position. The right lateral decubitus position also will move the gallbladder away from the spine. *(Bontrager and Lampignano, 6th ed., p. 528)*

47. **(D)** An *analgesic* is any drug, such as aspirin, which functions to relieve pain. An *anticoagulant* (e.g., heparin) is used to prevent clotting of blood. A *diuretic* is used to increase urine output. And an *antibiotic* (e.g., penicillin) fights the growth of bacterial microorganisms. *(Torres et al., 6th ed., p. 291)*

48. **(B)** There are several radiation units that are used to express quantity and effects of radiation. Radiation ionizes air, and the unit of measurement used to describe the amount of ionization (and, therefore, the quantity of radiation present) is the *roentgen*. The *rad* is the unit of absorbed dose. The *rem* is the unit of dose equivalent, which expresses radiation dose to biologic material. *(Bontrager and Lampignano, 6th ed., p. 65)*

49. **(D)** The computed radiography (CR) laser scanner recognizes the various tissue-density values and constructs a representative grayscale histogram. A *histogram* is a graphic representation showing the distribution of pixel values. Histogram analysis and use of the appropriate LUT together function to produce predictable image quality in CR. Histogram appearance can be affected by a number of things. Degree of accuracy in positioning and centering can have a significant effect on histogram appearance (as well as patient dose). Change is effected in average exposure level and exposure latitude; these changes will be reflected in the images informational numbers (i.e., S number and exposure index). Other factors affecting histogram appearance, and therefore these informational numbers, include selection of the correct processing algorithm (e.g., chest vs. femur vs. cervical spine) and changes in scatter, SID, OID, and collimation. Figure 7–21 illustrates the effect of incorrect collimation on histogram appearance—in short, anything that affects scatter and/or dose. *(Carlton and Adler, 4th ed., pp. 361–362)*

50. **(B)** Dual x-ray absorptiometry (DXA) imaging is used to evaluate bone mineral density (BMD). Bone densitometry/DXA can be used to evaluate bone mineral content of the body, or part of it, to diagnose osteoporosis, or to

Example A   **Example B**

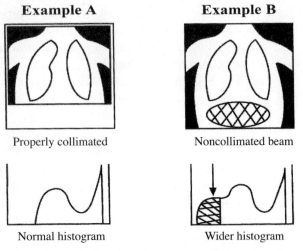

Properly collimated   Noncollimated beam

Normal histogram   Wider histogram

Figure 7–21. Courtesy FUJIFILM Medical Systems USA, Inc.

evaluate the effectiveness of treatments for osteoporosis. It is the most widely used method of bone densitometry—it is low dose, precise, and uncomplicated to use/perform. DXA uses two photon energies—one for soft tissue and one for bone. Since bone is denser and attenuates x-ray photons more readily, the attenuation is calculated to represent the degree of bone density. Soft tissue attenuation information is not used to measure bone density. *(Frank, Long, and Smith, 11th ed., vol. 3, pp. 454–455)*

51. **(D)** Airborne, fomite, and vector are all indirect modes of transmitting microorganisms. Direct contact involves actual touching of the infected person. A *fomite* is an inanimate object that has been in contact with an infectious microorganism (e.g., doorknobs or x-ray tables). Although an inanimate object may serve as a temporary host for microbes, microbes flourish on and in the human host, where plenty of body fluids and tissues nourish and feed them. A *vector* is an animal host of an infectious organism that transmits the infection via a bite or sting, such as the mosquito or deer tick. *Airborne* contamination occurs via droplets (sneeze) or dust. *(Adler and Carlton, 4th ed., pp. 225–226)*

52. **(C)** If 0.9 rad were delivered in 3 minutes, then the dose rate would be 0.9/3, or 0.3 rad/min. Three-tenths rad is equal to 300 mrad. *(Selman, 9th ed., p. 528)*

53. **(A)** As kilovoltage is increased, more electrons are driven to the anode with greater speed and energy. These high-energy electrons will result in production of a *greater* quantity (i.e., increased exposure rate/*intensity*) of high-energy (i.e., short/*decreased* wavelength) x-rays. Thus, kilovoltage affects both quantity and quality of the x-ray beam. Since kilovoltage impacts penetration and contrast scale, higher kV is more likely to produce an *increase* in the scale of contrast *in film/screen imaging. (Shephard, pp. 194–197)*

54. **(D)** The greater the number of electrons making up the electron stream and bombarding the target, the greater is the number of x-ray photons produced. Although kilovoltage usually is associated with the energy of the x-ray photons because a greater number of more energetic electrons will produce more x-ray photons, an increase in kilovoltage will also increase the number of photons produced. Specifically, the quantity of radiation produced increases as the square of the kilovoltage. The material composition of the tube target also plays an important role in the number of x-ray photons produced. The higher the atomic number, the denser and more closely packed are the atoms making up the material, and therefore, the greater is the chance of an interaction between a high-speed electron and the target material. *(Selman, 9th ed., pp. 112–115)*

55. **(D)** A *point lesion* is a disturbance of a single chemical bond that can result in malfunction within the affected cell. Following irradiation, a small extension-type molecule can develop, extending from the main chain. This molecule can attach to a neighboring molecule or to another portion of the same molecule; this is referred to as *cross-linking. Main-chain scission* is breakage of the molecule's principal connection so that the molecule is broken into smaller molecules. Each of these radiation effects on macromolecules is repairable. *(Bushong, p. 505)*

56. **(C)** The human body is composed of approximately 80% water; the remaining 20% is a combination of substances such as proteins,

carbohydrates, and lipids. The smallest functional unit of the body is the cell; the structure/content of a cell often determines its function. Cells form tissues and organs that also have functional characteristics. The two basic types of cells are *somatic* and *genetic*. Somatic cells are all the body's cells (bone, muscle, nerve, etc.), except those concerned with reproduction—those cells are termed genetic. *(Fosbinder and Orth, p. 287)*

57. **(A)** A *vector* is an animal host of an infectious organism that transmits the infection via a bite or sting, such as the mosquito (malaria) and the deer tick (Lyme disease). A *fomite* is an inanimate object that has been in contact with an infectious microorganism. A *reservoir* is a site where an infectious organism can remain alive and from which transmission can occur. Although an inanimate object can be a reservoir for infection, living objects (such as humans) can also be reservoirs. For infection to spread, there must be a *host* environment. Although an inanimate object may serve as a temporary host for microbes to grow, microbes flourish on and in the human host, where plenty of body fluids and tissue nourish and feed the microbes. *(Adler and Carlton, 4th ed., p. 226)*

58. **(A)** The relationship between x-ray intensity and distance from the source is expressed in the inverse-square law of radiation. The formula is

$$\frac{I_1}{I_2} = \frac{D_2^2}{D_1^2}$$

Substituting known values:

$$\frac{18}{x} = \frac{25}{4}$$
$$2.5x = 72$$

Thus, $x = 2.88$ mR/min at 5 m. Distance has a profound effect on dose received and, therefore, is one of the cardinal factors considered in radiation protection. As distance from the source increases, dose received decreases. *(Bushong, 8th ed., pp. 68–70)*

59. **(A)** Patient dose during fluoroscopy can be considerable because the x-ray tube is in close proximity to the patient. Therefore, we can decrease patient dose by increasing the SSD as much as possible. The law states that the SSD must be at least 15 in. with fixed fluoroscopic equipment and at least 12 in. with mobile fluoroscopic equipment. The use of 2.5-mm-Al-equivalent filtration in equipment operated above 70 kVp is also required by law to reduce patient skin dose. Another requirement of fluoroscopic equipment is that the tabletop intensity not exceed 10 R/min. *(Bushong, 8th ed., p. 569)*

60. **(B)** With the patient in the AP position, the CR is directed cephalad 25 to 30 degrees. This serves to project the clavicle away from the pulmonary apices and ribs, projecting most of the clavicle above the thorax. The reverse is true when the patient is examined in the PA position. The PA projection can be useful to obtain better recorded detail because of reduced OID. *(Bontrager and Lampignano, 6th ed., p. 202)*

61. **(C)** Radiographic density is directly proportional to milliampere-seconds. If exposure time is halved from 0.04 s to 0.02 s, radiographic density will be cut in half. Changing to 300 mA also will halve the milliampere-seconds, effectively halving the radiographic density. If the kilovoltage is decreased by 15%, from 85 to 72 kVp, radiographic density will be halved according to the 15% rule. To cut the density in half, the milliampere-seconds must be reduced to 12 mAs (rather than to 18 mAs). *(Selman, 9th ed., p. 214)*

62. **(D)** Proper body mechanics can help to prevent painful back injuries by making proficient use of the muscles in the arms and legs. Proper body mechanics includes a wide base of support. The *base of support* is the part of the body in touch with the floor or other horizontal plane. The back always should be kept straight; twisting increases the chance of injury. When lifting a load, keep it as close to the body as possible to avoid back strain. Always push a load (such as a mobile x-ray machine) rather than pull it. *(Torres et al., 6th ed., pp. 82–83)*

63. **(B)** In the AP projection of the normal knee, the space between the tibial plateau and the femoral condyles is equal bilaterally. It is, therefore, important that there be no pelvic rotation that could change the appearance of an otherwise normal relationship. The AP projection of the knee superimposes the patella and femur. The CR should enter at the knee joint, located ½ in. distal to the patellar apex. *(Frank, Long, and Smith, 11th ed., vol. 1, p. 302)*

64. **(A)** Lead and distance are the two most important ways to protect from radiation exposure. Fluoroscopy can be particularly hazardous because the SID is so much shorter than in overhead radiography. Therefore, it has been established that mobile fluoroscopic equipment must provide at least 12 in. source-to-tabletop/skin distance for the protection of the patient, and fixed or stationary fluoroscopic equipment must provide at least 15 in. source-to-tabletop/skin distance. *(Bushong, 8th ed., p. 569)*

65. **(D)** The stomach is normally angled with the fundus lying posteriorly and the body, pylorus, and duodenum inferior to the fundus and angling anteriorly. Therefore, when the patient ingests barium and lies AP recumbent, the heavy barium gravitates easily to the fundus and fills it. With the patient PA recumbent, barium gravitates inferiorly to the body, pylorus, and duodenum, displacing air into the fundus. *(Frank, Long, and Smith, 11th ed., vol. 2, pp. 144–145)*

66. **(B)** An artifact associated with digital imaging and grids is *"aliasing"* or the *"Moiré effect."* If the direction of the lead strips and the grid lines per inch (i.e., grid frequency) matches the scan frequency of the scanner/reader, this artifact can occur. Aliasing (or Moiré effect) appears as superimposed images slightly out of alignment, an image "wrapping" effect. This most commonly occurs in mobile radiography with stationary grids and can be a problem with DR flat panel detectors.

67. **(C)** Arthrodesis, or spinal fusion, is a surgical procedure that might be employed in cases of certain fractures, degenerative disc disease, spinal stenosis, degenerative spondylolisthesis, and other vertebral conditions. It is most often seen in the lumbar region. Implants might be employed to hold vertebrae in position/alignment. After approximately 6 months post surgery imaging is often helpful in demonstrating the degree of motion permitted at the site(s) of fusion. The images can include AP left and right bending to demonstrate degree of lateral motion, and lateral in flexion and extension to demonstrate degree of AP motion. *(Frank et al., 11th ed., vol. 1, pp. 454–457)*

68. **(B)** The bony walls of the orbit are thin, fragile, and subject to fracture. A direct blow to the eye results in a pressure that can cause fracture. That fracture is usually to the orbital floor (the inferior aspect of the bony orbit). Because the fracture results from increased pressure within the eye, it is referred to as a *blowout fracture. (Frank, Long, and Smith, 11th ed., vol. 2, p. 335)*

69–70. **(69, C; 70, B)** The figure shows a posterior view of the elbow. The distal posterior humerus (number 1) is seen, as well as the proximal posterior radius (number 4) and ulna (number 3). Additional structures identified are the medial epicondyle (number 2), the olecranon fossa (number 5), olecranon process (number 6), lateral epicondyle (number 7), and radial head (number 8) The olecranon process (number 6) can best be demonstrated in the lateral projection; it can also be demonstrated in the acute flexion position. The AP internal oblique will demonstrate the coronoid process; the AP external oblique will demonstrate the radial head free of superimposition.

71. **(C)** *Emphysema* is a progressive disorder caused by long-term irritation of the bronchial passages, such as by air pollution or cigarette smoking. Emphysema patients are unable to exhale normally because of the loss of elasticity of the alveolar walls. If emphysema patients receive oxygen, it is usually administered at a very slow rate because their respirations are controlled by the level of carbon

dioxide in the blood. *(Tortora and Derrickson, 11th ed., p. 887)*

72. **(D)** The x-ray anode may be a molybdenum disk coated with a tungsten–rhenium alloy. Tungsten, with a high atomic number (74), produces high-energy x-rays quite efficiently. Since a great deal of heat is produced at the target, its high melting point (3410°C) helps to avoid damage to the target surface. Heat produced at the target should be dissipated readily, and tungsten's conductivity is similar to that of copper. Therefore, as heat is applied to the focus, it can be conducted throughout the disk to equalize the temperature and thus avoid pitting, or localized melting, of the focal track. *(Selman, 9th ed., p. 138)*

73. **(A)** The diameter of a needle is the needle's *gauge*. The higher the gauge number, the thinner is the diameter. For example, a very tiny-gauge needle such as 25-gauge needle may be used on a pediatric patient for IV injection, whereas a large-gauge needle such as 16-gauge needle may be used for donating blood. The *hub* of the needle is the portion of the needle that attaches to a syringe. The *length* of the needle varies depending on its use. A longer needle is needed for intramuscular injections; a shorter needle, for a subcutaneous injection. The *bevel* of the needle is the slanted tip of the needle. For IV injections, the bevel should always face up. *(Adler and Carlton, 4th ed., p. 308)*

74. **(D)** X-ray tube life may be extended by using exposure factors that produce a minimum of heat, that is, a lower milliampere-seconds and higher kilovoltage combination, whenever possible. When the rotor is activated, the filament current is increased to produce the required electron source (thermionic emission). Prolonged rotor time, then, can lead to shortened filament life as a result of early vaporization. Large exposures to a cold anode will heat the anode surface, and the big temperature difference can cause cracking of the anode. This can be avoided by proper warming of the anode prior to use, thereby allowing sufficient dispersion of heat through the anode. *(Selman, 9th ed., pp. 143–145)*

75. **(D)** Gonadal shielding should be used when the gonads lie within 5 cm of the collimated primary beam, when the patient has reasonable reproductive potential, and when clinical objectives permit. Because their reproductive organs lie outside the abdominal cavity, male patients are more easily and effectively shielded than are female patients, whose reproductive organs lie within the abdominal cavity. Therefore, radiographic examinations of the male abdomen and pelvic structures should include evidence of gonadal shielding. *(Sherer, 5th ed., p. 177)*

76. **(C)** A *phototimer* is one type of automatic exposure control (AEC) that actually measures light. As x-ray photons penetrate and emerge from a part, a fluorescent screen beneath the cassette glows, and the fluorescent light charges a photomultiplier tube. Once a predetermined charge has been reached, the exposure terminates automatically. A parallel-plate *ionization chamber* is another type of AEC. A radiolucent chamber is beneath the patient (between the patient and the IR). As photons emerge from the patient, they enter the chamber and ionize the air within it. Once a predetermined charge has been reached, the exposure is terminated automatically. Motion of magnetic fields inducing a current in a conductor refers to the principle of *mutual induction. (Fauber, 2nd ed., pp. 232–233)*

77. **(C)** The image illustrates an oblique view of the proximal radius and ulna and distal humerus with epicondyles 45 degrees to the IR—the external oblique (lateral rotation) projection is shown demonstrating the radial head free of superimposition as well as the radial neck, tuberosity, and the humeral capitulum.

The *medial oblique (internal rotation)* projection of the elbow is particularly useful to demonstrate the *coronoid process* in profile, the *trochlea*, and the *medial epicondyle*.

The acute flexion projection (Jones method) of the elbow is a two-projection method demonstrating the elbow anatomy when the part cannot be extended for an AP projection. *(Bontrager and Lampignano, 7th ed., p. 164)*

78. **(D)** All three pathologic conditions involve processes that render tissues more easily penetrated by the x-ray beam. *Pneumothorax* is a collection of air or gas in the pleural cavity. *Emphysema* is a chronic pulmonary disease characterized by an increase in the size of the air-containing terminal bronchioles. These two conditions add air to the tissues, making them more easily penetrated. *Multiple myeloma* is a condition characterized by infiltration and destruction of bone and marrow. Each of these conditions requires that factors be decreased from the normal to avoid overexposure. *(Carlton and Adler, 4th ed., pp. 251–252)*

79. **(B)** The photoelectric effect and Compton scattering are the two predominant interactions between x-ray photons and matter in diagnostic x-ray. In *Compton scatter,* the high-energy incident photon uses only *part* of its energy to eject an outer-shell electron. It retains most of its original energy in the form of a scattered x-ray. The outer-shell electron leaves the atom and is called a *recoil electron.* Compton scatter is the interaction between x-ray photons and matter that occurs most frequently in diagnostic x-ray and is the major contributor of scattered radiation fog. In the *photoelectric effect,* the low-energy incident photon uses all its energy to eject an atom's inner-shell electron. When photon ceases to exist, it means it has used all its energy to ionize the atom. The part has absorbed the x-ray photon. This interaction contributes to patient dose and produces short-scale contrast. *(Bushong, 8th ed., pp. 176–177)*

80. **(A)** As the exposed film enters the processor from the feed tray, it first enters the developer section (number 1), where the emulsion's exposed silver bromide crystals are reduced to black metallic silver. The film then enters the fixer (number 2), where the unexposed silver grains are removed from the film by the clearing agent (hypo). The film then enters the wash section (number 3), where chemicals are removed from the film to preserve the image. From the wash section, the film enters the dryer section (number 4). *(Fauber, 2nd ed., p. 163)*

81. **(B)** It is the radiographer's responsibility to keep radiation exposure to patients and to himself or herself to a minimum. The embryo/fetus is particularly radiosensitive. One way to avoid irradiating a newly fertilized ovum is to inquire about the possibility of a female patient being pregnant or to ask her for the date of her last menstrual period. The safest time for a woman of childbearing age to have elective radiographic examinations is during the first 10 days following the onset of menstruation. *(Bushong, 8th ed., p. 559)*

82. **(D)** Geometric unsharpness is affected by all three factors listed. As OID increases, so does magnification. As focal-object distance and SID decrease, so does magnification. OID may be said to be directly proportional to magnification. Focal-object distance and SID are inversely proportional to magnification. *(Shephard, pp. 214–217)*

83. **(B)** The internal rotation position places the humeral epicondyles perpendicular to the IR, the humerus in a true lateral position, and the lesser tubercle in profile. The external rotation position places the humeral epicondyles parallel to the IR, the humerus in a true AP position, and the greater tubercle in profile. The neutral position is used often for the evaluation of calcium deposits in the shoulder joint. *(Frank, Long, and Smith, 11th ed., vol. 1, p. 178)*

84. **(C)** The quantity of radiation absorbed by the skin from the primary beam is referred to as the ESE. Although the primary x-ray beam is filtered, it is still quite heterogeneous, containing x-ray photons of low energy that do not contribute to image formation but do contribute to patient skin dose. Thus, the greater the intensity of the initial primary beam, the greater the ESE will be. Therefore, the chest delivers the lowest ESE (12–26 mR); the next is the skull (105–240 mR), then the thoracic spine (290–485 mR), and the examination delivering the greatest ESE is the abdomen (375–698 mR). *(Frank, Long, and Smith, 11th ed., vol. 1, p. 47)*

85. **(C)** A number of milliamperage and exposure time settings can produce the same milliampere-seconds value. Each of the following milliamperage and time combinations produces 10 mAs: 100 mA and 0.1 s, 200 mA and 0.05 s, 300 mA and , and 400 mA and 0.025 s. These milliamperage and exposure-time combinations should produce identical radiographic density. This is known as the *reciprocity law*. The radiographer can make good use of the reciprocity law when manipulating exposure factors to decrease exposure time and decrease motion unsharpness. *(Selman, 9th ed., p. 214)*

86. **(B)** Abduction of the arm of the affected side serves to free the scapula of some of its superimposition on the ribs. The affected arm should be perpendicular to the long axis of the body, with the elbow flexed and hand supported. The thorax should not be rotated toward the affected side, as that would defeat the purpose of arm abduction and move the ribs over the scapula. The CR should be directed to the mid-scapula, approximately 2 in. inferior to the coracoid process. *(Frank et al., 11th ed., vol. 1, pp. 212–213)*

87. **(B)** When the hand is pronated and the fingers are extended for a PA projection of the wrist, the wrist arches, and an OID is introduced between the wrist and the cassette. To reduce this OID, the metacarpophalangeal joints should be flexed slightly. This maneuver will bring the anterior surface of the wrist into contact with the cassette. *(Frank, Long, and Smith, 11th ed., vol. 1, p. 124)*

88. **(D)** Some medications cannot be taken orally. They may be destroyed by the GI juices or may irritate the GI tract. Medications that are administered by any route other than orally are said to be given *parenterally*. This can include intravenous, intramuscular, topical, intrathecal, or subcutaneous modes of medication administration. *(Torres et al., 6th ed., p. 270)*

89. **(D)** Since the kidneys do not lie parallel to the IR in the AP position, the oblique positions are used during IVU to visualize them better.

With the AP oblique projections (i.e., RPO and LPO), the kidney that is farther away is placed parallel to the IR, and the kidney that is closer is placed perpendicular to the IR. Therefore, in the RPO position, the right kidney, being closer, is perpendicular to the IR. The left kidney, the one farther away, is placed parallel to the IR. *(Frank, Long, and Smith, 11th ed., vol. 2, p. 220)*

90. **(B)** *Carpal tunnel syndrome* involves pain and numbness to some parts of the median nerve distribution (i.e., palmar surface of the thumb, index finger, and radial half of the fourth finger and palm). Carpal tunnel syndrome occurs frequently in those who continually use vibrating tools or machinery. *Carpopedal spasm* is spasm of the hands and feet, commonly encountered during hyperventilation. *Carpal boss* is a bony growth on the dorsal surface of the third metacarpophalangeal joint. *(Bontrager and Lampignano, 6th ed., p. 142)*

91. **(B)** As field size decreases, the volume of tissue being irradiated decreases, and consequently, the production of scattered radiation decreases. When less scattered radiation contributes to the image, the result is higher contrast and lower density. Restriction of field size is an important way to reduce patient dose and improve image quality. Field size and scattered radiation are unrelated to recorded detail. *(Shephard, p. 185)*

92. **(B)** Computer *hardware* describes the actual computer equipment (CPU, keyboard, memory chips, etc.). The *software* are the computer programs—*algorithms*, or programmed instructions, that are needed to perform specific tasks.

A *modem* converts a computer's outgoing digital signal to an analog signal, which is then transmitted via telephone line to another computer where it must first be changed back to a digital signal for computer processing.

A *histogram* is a graphic representation of pixel value distribution. The histogram is an analysis and graphic representation of all the densities from the PSP screen, demonstrating the quantity of exposure, the number of pixels, and their value. *(Seeram, pp. 201–202)*

93. **(A)** The legal doctrine *res ipsa locquitur* relates to "a matter that speaks for itself." For instance, if a patient were admitted to the hospital to have a kidney stone removed and incorrectly was given an appendectomy, "that speaks for itself," and negligence could be proven. *Respondeat superior* is the phrase meaning "let the master answer" or "the one ruling is responsible." If a radiographer is negligent, there may be an attempt to prove that the radiologist was responsible because the radiologist oversees the radiographer. *Res judicata* means "a thing or matter settled by justice." *Stare decisis* refers to "a matter settled by precedent." *(Adler and Carlton, 4th ed., p. 376)*

94. **(D)** OID is used to effect an increase in contrast in the absence of a grid, usually in chest radiography. If a 6-in. air gap (OID) is introduced between the part and the IR, much of the scattered radiation emitted from the body will not reach the IR; thus, the OID acts as a low-ratio grid and increases image contrast. However, the 6-in. OID air gap will make a very noticeable increase in magnification. To correct for this, the SID must be increased. Generally speaking, the SID needs to be increased 7 in. for every 1 in. of OID. With a 6-in. OID, the SID usually is increased from 6 to 10 ft (120 in.). *(Shephard, pp. 263, 264)*

95. **(D)** In the AP projection of the knee, the position of the joint space is significantly affected by the patient's overall body habitus and the distance between the ASIS and tabletop. When the patient is of sthenic habitus with a distance of 19 to 24 cm between the ASIS and tabletop, the CR is directed perpendicularly. When the patient is of asthenic habitus with a distance of less than 19 cm between the ASIS and tabletop, the CR is directed 5 degrees caudad. With a patient with a hypersthenic habitus and an ASIS-to-table measurement of greater than 24 cm, the CR is directed 5 degrees cephalad. *(Frank, Long, and Smith, 11th ed., vol. 1, p. 302)*

96. **(C)** The radiograph shows evidence of very few grays; this is short scale, or high, contrast. There is inadequate penetration of the denser structures—the heart and the lung bases and apices. Penetration and contrast are a function of kilovoltage. Inadequate penetration and high contrast are a result of insufficient peak kilovoltage. *(Shephard, pp. 203–304)*

97. **(A)** Remnant x-rays emerging from the patient/part are converted to electrical signals. This is an analog image. These electrical signals are sent to the ADC (analog-to-digital converter) to be converted to digital data (in binary digits or bits). Then the digital image data is transferred to a DAC (digital-to-analog converter) to be converted to a perceptible analog image on the display monitor. The monitor image can be manipulated, postprocessed, stored, or transmitted. *(Seeram, pp. 7–8)*

98. **(B)** A stethoscope and a sphygmomanometer are used together to measure blood pressure. The sphygmomanometer's cuff is placed around the midportion of the upper arm. The cuff is inflated to a value higher than the patient's systolic pressure to temporarily collapse the brachial artery. As the inflation is gradually released, the first sound heard is the systolic pressure; the normal range is 110 to 140 mmHg. When no more sound is heard, the diastolic pressure is recorded. The normal diastolic range is 60 to 90 mm Hg. Elevated blood pressure is called *hypertension*. *Hypotension*, low blood pressure, is not of concern unless it is caused by injury or disease; in that case, it can result in shock. *(Adler and Carlton, 4th ed., pp. 200–201)*

99. **(A)** The abdomen is divided anatomically into nine regions and four quadrants. The region designation usually is used for anatomic studies, whereas the quadrant designation is used most often to describe the location of a lesion, pain, tumor, or other abnormality. Some of the structures found in the left upper quadrant (LUQ) are the fundus of the stomach, the left kidney and suprarenal gland, and the splenic flexure. *(Tortora and Derrick-son, 11th ed., p. 20)*

100. **(B)** *Battery* refers to the unlawful laying of hands on a patient. Battery could be charged if a patient were moved about roughly or touched in a manner that is inappropriate or without the patient's consent. *Assault* is the threat of touching or laying hands on. If a

patient feels threatened by a health care provider either because of the provider's tone or pitch of voice or because of words that are threatening, an assault charge may be made. *False imprisonment* may be considered if a patient states that he or she no longer wishes to continue with a procedure and is ignored or if restraining devices are used improperly or used without a physician's order. *Invasion-of-privacy* issues arise when there has been a disclosure of confidential information. *(Adler and Carlton, 4th ed., p. 374)*

101. **(B)** To change nongrid to grid exposure, or to adjust exposure when changing from one grid ratio to another, recall the factor for each grid ratio:

$$
\begin{aligned}
\text{No grid} &= 1 \times \text{original mAs} \\
\text{5:1 grid} &= 2 \times \text{original mAs} \\
\text{6:1 grid} &= 3 \times \text{original mAs} \\
\text{8:1 grid} &= 4 \times \text{original mAs} \\
\text{12:1 grid} &= 5 \times \text{original mAs} \\
\text{16:1 grid} &= 6 \times \text{original mAs}
\end{aligned}
$$

The grid conversion formula is

$$
\frac{\text{mAs}_1}{\text{mAs}_2} = \frac{\text{grid factor}_1}{\text{grid factor}_2}
$$

Substituting known quantities:

$$
\frac{6}{x} = \frac{3}{5}
$$
$$
3x = 30
$$

Thus, $x = 10$ mAs with a 12:1 grid. *(Shephard, p. 248)*

102. **(C)** Hypoglycemic reactions can be very severe and should be treated with an immediate dose of sugar in the form of juice or candy. Symptoms of hypoglycemia include fatigue, restlessness, irritability, and weakness. Diabetic patients who have not taken their insulin prior to a fasting examination should be given priority, and their examinations should be expedited as quickly as possible. *(Torres et al., 6th ed., pp. 169–170)*

103. **(A)** The intertubercular (bicipital) groove is located on the proximal humerus, distal to the head, between the greater and lesser tubercles. The distal humerus articulates with the radius and ulna to form the elbow joint. The lateral aspect of the distal humerus presents a raised, smooth, rounded surface, the capitulum, which articulates with the superior surface of the radial head. The trochlea is on the medial aspect of the distal humerus and articulates with the semilunar notch of the ulna. Just proximal to the capitulum and the trochlea are the lateral and medial epicondyles; the medial is more prominent and palpable. The coronoid fossa is found on the anterior distal humerus and functions to accommodate the coronoid process with the elbow in flexion. *(Tortora and Derrickson, 11th ed., p. 325)*

104. **(B)** The posterior oblique positions (LPO, RPO) are used to demonstrate the apophyseal articulations of L1 through L4. When correctly positioned, the classic "Scottie Dog" would be visualized. If the apophyseal articulations are not "open", that is, clearly visualized, and the pedicle is seen on the posterior aspect of the vertebral body, patient rotation should be decreased.

If the apophyseal articulations are not clearly visualized, and the pedicle is seen on the anterior aspect of the vertebral body, patient rotation should be increased. *(Frank et al., 11th ed., vol. 1, p. 433)*

105. **(D)** The input phosphor of image intensifiers is usually made of cesium iodide. For each x-ray photon absorbed by cesium iodide, approximately 5,000 light photons are emitted. As the light photons strike a photoemissive *photocathode*, a number of electrons are released from the photocathode and focused toward the output side of the image tube by voltage applied to the negatively charged *electrostatic focusing lenses*. The electrons are then accelerated through the neck of the tube, where they strike the small (0.5–1 in.) *output phosphor* that is mounted on a flat glass support. The entire assembly is enclosed within a 2–4-mm thick vacuum glass envelope. Remember that the image on the output phosphor is *minified, brighter,* and *inverted* (electron focusing causes image inversion).

Input screen diameters of 5–12 in. are available. Although smaller diameter input screens improve resolution, they do not permit a large FOV, that is, viewing of large patient areas.

Dual- and triple-field image intensifiers are available that permit *magnified* viewing of fluoroscopic images. To achieve magnification, the *voltage* to the focusing lenses is increased and a *smaller* portion of the input phosphor is used, thereby resulting in a smaller FOV. Because minification gain is now decreased, the image is not as bright. The mA is automatically increased to compensate for the loss in brightness when the image intensifier is switched to magnification mode. Entrance skin exposure (ESE) can increase dramatically as the FOV decreases (i.e., as magnification increases).

As FOV decreases, *magnification* of the output screen image increases, there is less *noise* because increased mA provides a greater number of x-ray photons, and *contrast* and *resolution* improve. The *focal point* in the magnification mode is *further away from* the output phosphor (as a result of increased voltage applied to the focusing lenses) and therefore the output image is magnified. (*Fosbinder and Orth, pp. 191–192*)

106. **(C)** A *controlled area* is one that is occupied by radiation workers; the exposure rate in a controlled area must not exceed 100 mR/week. An *uncontrolled area* is one that is occupied by the general population; the exposure rate must not exceed 10 mR/week. Shielding requirements vary according to several factors, one of them being occupancy factor. (*Bushong, 8th ed., p. 573*)

107. **(D)** The milliampere-seconds value used was 8 (400 mA × 0.02 s); the new milliampere-seconds value is half that—4 mAs—which will result in half the original density. An increase in SID, as suggested by choice (A), would further decrease density. The decrease in milliampere-seconds could be compensated for by a decrease in SID—but according to the density-maintenance formula, that distance should be 18 in. Decreasing the kilovoltage to 60 would also decrease the density by another half. Increasing the kilovoltage by 15%, as suggested by choice (D), will best simulate the original density. (*Shephard, pp. 178–181*)

108. **(B)** *Radiograph A* was performed PA, and *radiograph B* performed AP, as evidenced by the bony pelvis anatomy. The PA projection (image *A*) shows the ilia more foreshortened,

giving the pelvis a "closed" appearance, whereas in the AP projection the ilia and bladder area appears more "open." There was an appropriate selection of exposure factors, for the required anatomic structures are well visualized—renal shadows, psoas muscle, lumbar transverse processes, and inferior margin of the liver. There is no evidence of ureteral compression, which would be seen as air-filled bladders, or some other type of compression device, placed over the distal ureters. (*Ballinger and Frank, 11th ed., vol. 2, p. 124*)

109. **(C)** As radiation passes through tissue, different types of ionization processes can take place depending on the photon energy and the type of material being irradiated. The photoelectric effect (whose end products include a characteristic ray) and Compton scatter are the two major interactions that take place in the diagnostic x-ray peak kilovoltage range. The rate at which energy is deposited in (or transferred to) tissue during these interactions is termed *linear energy transfer* (LET). The greater the LET, the greater is the potential biologic effect. Diagnostic x-ray is considered low-LET radiation. (*Bushong, 8th ed., p. 495*)

110. **(C)** The radiograph illustrates a plantodorsal projection of the calcaneus. The patient usually is positioned with the leg extended and the long axis of the plantar surface perpendicular to the tabletop/IR. The CR is directed 40 degrees cephalad to the base of the third metatarsal. Structures that should be visualized include the sustentaculum tali, trochlear process, and calcaneal tuberosity. (*Bontrager and Lampignano, 6th ed., p. 236*)

111. **(A)** As radiation passes through tissue, different types of ionization processes can take place depending on the photon energy and the type of material being irradiated. In the *photoelectric effect*, a relatively low-energy photon uses all its energy to eject an inner-shell electron from the target atom, leaving a vacancy in that shell. An electron from the shell beyond drops down to fill the vacancy and in so doing emits a characteristic ray. This type of interaction contributes most to patient dose because all the x-ray photon energy is being transferred to tissue.

In *Compton scatter,* a high-energy-incident photon uses some of its energy to eject an outer-shell electron. In so doing the incident photon is deflected with reduced energy but usually retains most of its original energy and exits the body as an energetic scattered photon. In Compton scatter, the scattered radiation will either contribute to image fog or pose a radiation hazard to personnel depending on its direction of exit. In *classic scatter,* a low-energy photon interacts with an atom but causes no ionization; the incident photon disappears in the atom and then immediately reappears and is released as a photon of identical energy but with changed direction. *Thompson scatter* is another name for classic scatter. *(Selman, 9th ed., pp. 125–128)*

112. **(A)** Restriction of field size is one important method of patient protection. However, the accuracy of the light field must be evaluated periodically as part of a QA program. Guidelines set forth for patient protection state that the collimator light and actual irradiated area must be accurate to within 2% of the SID. *(Thompson et al., p. 403)*

113. **(D)** The thicker and more dense the anatomic part being studied, the less bright will be the fluoroscopic image. Both milliamperage and kilovoltage affect the fluoroscopic image in a way similar to the way they affect the radiographic image. For optimal contrast, especially taking patient dose into consideration, higher kilovoltage and lower milliamperage generally are preferred. *(Carlton and Adler, 4th ed., p. 572)*

114. **(B)** When differences in absorption characteristics are decreased, body tissues absorb radiation more uniformly, and as a result, more grays are seen on the radiographic image. A longer scale of contrast is produced. High-kilovoltage and low-milliamperage factors achieve this. Compensating filtration is also used to "even out" densities in uneven anatomic parts, such as the thoracic spine. The photoelectric effect is the interaction between x-ray photons and matter that occurs at low-peak kilovoltage levels—levels that tend to produce short-scale contrast. *(Shephard, pp. 193, 197, 199)*

115. **(A)** The *line-focus principle* is a geometric principle illustrating that the actual focal spot is larger than the effective (projected) focal spot. The actual focal spot (target) is larger, to accommodate heat over a larger area, and angled so as to project a smaller focal spot, thus maintaining recorded detail by reducing blur. The relationship between the exposure given the IR and the resulting density is expressed in the inverse-square law. The relationship between the kilovoltage used and the resulting contrast may be illustrated using an aluminum step wedge. *(Selman, 9th ed., pp. 138–139)*

116. **(B)** The four types of body habitus describe differences in visceral shape, position, tone, and motility. One body type is *hypersthenic,* the very large individual with short, wide heart and lungs, high transverse stomach and gallbladder, and peripheral colon. The *sthenic* individual is the average, athletic, most predominant type. The *hyposthenic* patient is somewhat thinner and a little more frail, with organs positioned somewhat lower. The *asthenic* type is smaller in the extreme, with a long thorax, a very long, almost pelvic stomach, and a low medial gallbladder. The asthenic colon is medial and redundant. *(Frank, Long, and Smith, 11th ed., vol. 1, p. 64)*

117. **(C)** The radiograph is a PA projection of the hand and wrist; an oblique projection of the thumb is obtained. The letter *T* is pointing out the first carpometacarpal joint, formed by the base of the first metacarpal and the trapezium. This is classified as a saddle-*type* diarthrotic joint. Diarthrotic joints are freely movable joints and the most plentiful type of joint in the human body. Amphiarthrotic joints are partially movable; synarthrotic joints are immovable. *(Frank, Long, and Smith, 11th ed., vol. 1, p. 73)*

118. **(B)** The eight carpal bones are well visualized in this PA projection of the hand and wrist. The letters *E* (scaphoid) and *L* (lunate) are in the proximal carpal row. The capitate (*I*) is seen in the distal carpal row; just lateral to the capitate is the carpal trapezium, seen articulating with the base of the first metacarpal. The PA projection of the hand provides an

oblique projection of the first finger (thumb). (*Frank, Long, and Smith, 11th ed., vol. 1, p. 116*)

119. **(B)** The cervical intervertebral foramina lie 45 degrees to the midsagittal plane (MSP) and 15 to 20 degrees to the transverse plane. When the posterior oblique position (i.e., LPO or RPO) is used, the CR is directed 15 to 20 degrees cephalad, and the cervical intervertebral foramina demonstrated are those farther from the IR. There is, therefore, some magnification of the foramina (because of the OID). In the anterior oblique position (i.e., LAO or RAO), the CR is directed 15 to 20 degrees caudad, and the foramina disclosed are those closer to the IR. (*Frank, Long, and Smith, 11th ed., vol. 1, pp. 404–406*)

120. **(A)** X-ray film is sensitive and requires proper handling and storage. Careless handling during production of the radiographic image can produce several kinds of artifacts. Crescent-shaped artifacts (crinkle marks) are a result of bending the film acutely over the fingertip while loading or unloading the cassette. A black crescent usually results from bending after exposure, whereas a white crescent occurs if the film is bent before exposure. Tree-like branching black marks on a radiograph are usually due to static electrical discharge. Problems with static electricity are especially prevalent during cold, dry weather and can be produced simply by removing a sweater in the darkroom. (*Selman, 9th ed., p. 197*)

121. **(B)** The exposure factor that regulates radiographic density is milliampere-seconds (mAs). The equation used to determine mAs is mA × s = mAs. Substituting known factors:

$$300x = 18 \text{ mAs}$$
$$x = 0.06 \text{ s (60 ms)}$$

(*Selman, 9th ed., p. 214*)

122. **(A)** If the photocell were centered more posteriorly to a thinner and less dense structure, then the exposure received would be correct for that less-dense structure. The spinous processes would be well visualized, but the denser vertebral bodies and surrounding structures (pedicles and lamina) *would be underexposed*. Accurate selection of photocells and precise positioning are critical with the use of automatic exposure devices. (*Carlton and Adler, 4th ed., p. 540*)

123. **(D)** Shock caused by an abnormally low volume of blood in the body is termed *hypovolemic shock*. *Neurogenic shock* can be caused by some kind of trauma to the nervous system, that is, spinal cord injury or extreme psychological stress. *Cardiogenic shock* is related to the heart and caused by failure of the heart to pump adequate blood to the body's vital organs. *Septic shock* can result when the body is invaded by bacteria; there are signs of acute septicemia and hypotension. (*Torres et al., 6th ed., p. 163*)

124. **(B)** It is easy to determine the highest point of the scapula when it is viewed laterally. The coracoid process projects anteriorly and is quite superior. However, the acromion process, which is an anterior extension of the scapular spine, projects considerably more superior than the coracoid. (*Frank, Long, and Smith, 11th ed., vol. 1, p. 168*)

125. **(D)** Base-plus fog is the small amount of measurable density on unexposed and processed x-ray film. This fog is a result of environmental background radiation that is present during film manufacture, transportation, and storage. The (usually blue) tint, given the base to enhance contrast, adds more density. Finally, the emulsion receives further fog as the film is chemically processed. Base-plus fog should not exceed 0.2D. (*Carlton and Adler, 4th ed., p. 307*)

126. **(C)** Primary radiation barriers are barriers that protect from the primary, or useful, x-ray beam. Secondary radiation barriers are those that protect from secondary or scattered radiation. Examples of primary barriers are the radiographic room walls, doors, and floors because the primary beam often can be directed toward them. Secondary radiation barriers include lead aprons, gloves, thyroid shields, and the radiographic room ceiling. These will protect from exposure to scattered radiation only. Secondary radiation barriers will not protect from the useful beam. (*Bushong, 8th ed., p. 553*)

127. **(D)** It is important to note that *histogram appearance* as well as *patient dose* can be affected by the radiographer's knowledge and skill using digital imaging, in addition to his or her degree of accuracy in positioning and centering. Collimation is exceedingly important to avoid histogram analysis errors. Lack of adequate collimation can result in signals outside the anatomical area being included in the exposure data recognition/histogram analysis. This can result in a variety of histogram analysis errors, including excessively light, dark, or noisy images.

128. **(A)** Muscle cells have a fairly low radiosensitivity, and nerve cells are the least radiosensitive in the body (in fetal life, however, nerve cells are highly radiosensitive). Lymphocytes, a type of white blood cell concerned with the immune system, have the greatest radiosensitivity of all body cells. Spermatids are also highly radiosensitive, although not to the same degree as lymphocytes. *(Dowd and Tilson, 2nd ed., p. 135)*

129. **(A)** *Emetics,* such as ipecac, function to induce vomiting. *Cathartics* are used to stimulate defecation (bowel movements). *Diuretics* are used to promote urine elimination in individuals whose tissues are retaining excessive fluid. And *antitussives* are used to inhibit coughing. *(Ehrlich et al., 6th ed., p. 188)*

130. **(C)** X-ray tube targets are constructed according to the *line-focus principle*—the focal spot is angled (usually 12–17 degrees) to the vertical. As the actual focal spot is projected downward, it is foreshortened; thus, the effective focal spot is smaller than the actual focal spot. As the focal spot is projected toward the cathode end of the x-ray beam, it becomes larger and approaches its actual size. Figure 7–22 illustrates the variation of the effective focal-spot size along the longitudinal tube axis. As the effective focal spot becomes larger toward the cathode end, the images of the phalanges illustrate gradual loss of recorded detail. *(Bushong, 8th ed., p. 140)*

131. **(D)** Extravasation occurs when medication or contrast medium is injected into the tissues surrounding a vein rather than into the vein itself. It can happen when the patient's veins are particularly deep and/or small. If this happens, the needle should be removed, pressure applied to prevent formation of a hematoma, and then hot packs applied to relieve pain. *(Torres et al., 6th ed., p. 324)*

132. **(D)** Weight-bearing lateral projections of the foot are requested often to evaluate the longitudinal arch structure of the foot. The patient stands on a small platform. The x-ray cassette is placed between the feet, in a slot provided on the platform, with the top of the cassette against the medial aspect of the foot. The CR is directed to enter the lateral aspect of the foot perpendicular to the base of the fifth metatarsal and to exit the medial side of the foot. *(Frank, Long, and Smith, 11th ed., vol. 1, pp. 268–269)*

133. **(C)** In the figure, image *B* is darker and, therefore, has more optical (radiographic) density. Radiographic density is significantly affected by milliampere-seconds, SID, and exposure rate. In this case, there is a difference in SID between the two images. As SID decreases, exposure rate increases and radiographic density increases. Image *B* is darker (has more optical density) than image *A* because image *B* was exposed at a shorter SID (and, therefore, a higher exposure rate). *(Bushong, 8th ed., pp. 300–303)*

134. **(C)** Lead aprons are secondary radiation barriers and must contain at least 0.25-mm Pb equivalent, usually in the form of lead-impregnated vinyl (according to CFR 20). Many radiology departments routinely use lead aprons containing 0.5 mm Pb (the NCRP recommends 0.5-mm Pb equivalent minimum). These aprons are heavier, but they attenuate a higher percentage of scattered radiation. *(Bushong, 8th ed., p. 560)*

135. **(A)** The shorter the SID, the greater is the skin dose (ESE). This is why there are specific SSD restrictions in fluoroscopy. X-ray beam quality has a significant effect on patient skin dose. The use of high kilovoltage produces more high-energy penetrating photons, thereby decreasing skin dose. Filtration is used to remove the low-energy photons that contribute to skin dose from the primary

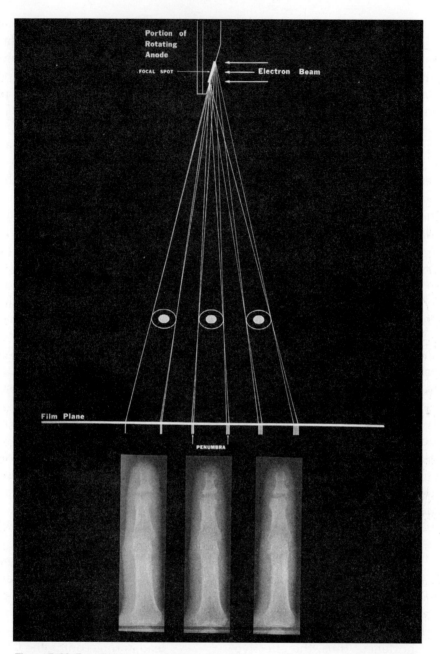

Figure 7–22. From the American College of Radiology Learning File. Courtesy of the ACR.

beam. Although milliamperage regulates the number of x-ray photons produced, it does not affect photon quality. *(Bushong, 8th ed., pp. 300–303)*

136. **(B)** *Stochastic* effects of radiation are non-threshold and randomly occurring. Examples of stochastic effects include carcinogenesis and genetic effects. The chance of occurrence of stochastic effects is directly related to the radiation dose; that is, as radiation dose increases, there is a greater likelihood of genetic alterations or development of cancer. *Nonstochastic* effects are predictable threshold responses; that is, a certain quantity of radiation must be received before the effect will occur, and the greater the dose, the more severe is the effect. *(Bushong, 8th ed., p. 532)*

137. **(D)** The cycle of infection includes four components—a susceptible host, a reservoir of infection, a pathogenic organism, and a means of transmission. *Pathogenic organisms* are microscopic and include bacteria, fungi,

and viruses. The *reservoir of infection* is the environment in which the microorganism thrives; this can be the human body. A *susceptible host* may have reduced resistance to infection. The means of transmission is either direct (touch) or indirect (vector, fomite, airborne). *(Torres et al., 6th ed., p. 53)*

138. **(D)** The ability of x-ray photons to penetrate a body part has a great deal to do with the composition of that part (e.g., bone vs. soft tissue vs. air) and the presence of any pathologic condition. Pathologic conditions can alter the normal nature of the anatomic part. Some conditions, such as osteomalacia, fibrosarcoma, and paralytic ileus (obstruction), result in a decrease in body tissue density. When body tissue density decreases, x-rays will penetrate the tissues more readily; that is, there is more x-ray penetrability. In conditions such as ascites, where body tissue density increases as a result of the accumulation of fluid, x-rays will not readily penetrate the body tissues; that is, there is less x-ray penetrability. *(Carlton and Adler, 4th ed., p. 250)*

139. **(C)** *Diuretics* are used to promote urine elimination in individuals whose tissues are retaining excessive fluid. They are used in treating hypertension, congestive heart failure, and edema. *Cathartics* are used to stimulate defecation (bowel movements); they are used as preparation for some x-ray examinations such as barium enemas. *Emetics* function to induce vomiting, and *antitussives* are used to inhibit coughing. *(Torres et al., 6th ed., p. 288)*

140. **(D)** The pulmonary apices are often at least partially obscured by the clavicles. To visualize the entire lung apex and any suspicious areas, the clavicles must be "removed." This can be accomplished with the AP axial lordotic position. Through the arching of the patient's back and the cephalad angulation, the clavicles are projected upward and out of the pulmonary apices. Decubitus positions are used primarily to see air–fluid levels. Lateral and dorsal decubitus positions show fluid in the side that is down and air in the side that is up. *(Frank, Long, and Smith, 11th ed., vol. 1, p. 534)*

141. **(D)** A transthoracic projection is used to obtain a lateral projection of the upper half to two-thirds of the humerus when the arm cannot be abducted. The affected arm is placed next to the upright Bucky, the unaffected arm rests on the head, and the CR is directed horizontally through the thorax, exiting the upper humerus. The superoinferior and inferosuperior projections of the shoulder both require abduction of the arm. *(Bontrager and Lampignano, 6th ed., p. 198)*

142. **(C)** The radiographic subject, the patient, is composed of many different tissue types of varying densities (i.e., subject contrast), resulting in varying degrees of photon attenuation and absorption. This differential absorption contributes to the various shades of gray (i.e., scale of radiographic contrast) on the finished image. Normal tissue density may be significantly altered in the presence of pathology. For example, destructive bone disease can cause a dramatic decrease in tissue density. Abnormal accumulation of fluid (as in ascites) will cause a significant increase in tissue density. Muscle atrophy or highly developed muscles similarly will decrease or increase tissue density. *(Carlton and Adler, 4th ed., p. 245)*

143. **(C)** The thoracic intervertebral (disk) spaces are demonstrated in the AP and lateral projections, although they are probably best demonstrated in the lateral projection. The thoracic apophyseal joints are 70 degrees to the MSP and are demonstrated in a steep (70-degree) oblique position. The thoracic intervertebral foramina, formed by the vertebral notches of the pedicles, are 90 degrees to the MSP. They are, therefore, well demonstrated in the lateral position. *(Bontrager and Lampignano, 6th ed., p. 316)*

144. **(D)** The posterior oblique positions (i.e., LPO and RPO) of the lumbar vertebrae demonstrate the apophyseal joints closer to the IR. The left apophyseal joints are demonstrated in the LPO position, whereas the right apophyseal joints are demonstrated in the RPO position. The lateral position is useful to demonstrate the intervertebral disk spaces, intervertebral foramina, and spinous processes. *(Bontrager and Lampignano, 6th ed., pp. 334–335)*

145. **(D)** Motion is said to be the greatest enemy of recorded detail because it completely obliterates image sharpness. Focal-spot size affects recorded detail as a result of blur—the smaller the focus, the less is the focal-spot blur and the better is recorded detail. A decrease in OID reduces magnification and improves recorded detail. Scattered radiation is not related to recorded detail. *(Shephard, pp. 213–217)*

146. **(C)** A grid is a thin wafer placed between the patient and the IR to collect scattered radiation. It is made of alternating strips of lead and a radiolucent material such as plastic or aluminum. If the interspace material also were made of lead, little or no radiation would reach the IR, and no image would be formed. *(Shephard, pp. 244–245)*

147. **(D)** Whenever a radiation worker could receive 10% or more of the annual TEDE limit, that person must be provided with a radiation monitor. The annual TEDE limit for radiation workers is 50 mSv (5 rem, 5,000 mrem), but it is the responsibility of the radiographer to practice the ALARA principle, that is, to keep radiation dose as low as reasonably achievable. *(Sherer et al., 5th ed., p. 250)*

148. **(B)** Beam restriction is used to determine the size of the x-ray field. This size never should be larger than the IR size. Because the size of the irradiated area can be made smaller, patient dose is reduced. Beam restriction reduces the production of scattered radiation that leads to fog and, therefore, improves contrast resolution. Spatial resolution is related to factors affecting recorded detail, not contrast resolution. *(Bushong, 8th ed., pp. 243, 244)*

149. **(D)** An increase in exposure factors will be required when imaging pathologic conditions that cause greater attenuation of the x-ray beam. The x-ray beam suffers more attenuation as the thickness and/or density of the tissues increases. Examples include conditions involving an increase in part size as a result of fluid accumulation (*edema*) following trauma, an accumulation of fluid in the abdomen (*ascites*), or an increase in bone size and density (*acromegaly*) as a result of an endocrine disorder. The radiographer needs a good working knowledge of pathologic conditions, their effect on the body, and the resulting modifications in technical factors required. *(Carlton and Adler, 4th ed., p. 245)*

150. **(B)** A radiographer who discloses confidential information to unauthorized individuals may be found guilty of invasion of privacy. If the disclosure is in some way detrimental or otherwise harmful to the patient, the radiographer may be accused of defamation. Spoken defamation is slander; written defamation is libel. Assault is to threaten harm; battery is to carry out the threat. *(Torres et al., 6th ed., p. 11)*

151. **(B)** All four medications are found routinely on the typical emergency cart. *Heparin* is used to decrease coagulation and often used in the cardiovascular imaging suite to inhibit coagulation on catheters. *Norepinephrine* functions to raise the blood pressure, whereas *nitroglycerin* functions as a vasodilator, relaxing the walls of blood vessels and increasing circulation. *Lidocaine* is used as a local anesthetic or antidysrhythmic. *(Adler and Carlton, 4th ed., p. 278)*

152. **(B)** Focal-spot blur, or geometric blur, is caused by photons emerging from a large focal spot. Because the projected focal spot is greatest at the cathode end of the x-ray tube, geometric blur is also greatest at the corresponding part (cathode end) of the radiograph. The projected focal-spot size becomes progressively smaller toward the anode end of the x-ray tube. *(Bushong, 8th ed., p. 140)*

153. **(B)** The image intensifier can be coupled to the TV camera via a fiber-optic bundle or via a lens coupling device. The fiber-optic connection offers less fragility, more compactness, and ease of maneuverability. The big advantage of the objective lens is that it allows the use of auxiliary imaging devices such as a cine camera or spot-film camera. *(Bushong, 8th ed., p. 366)*

154. **(A)** The photoelectric effect and Compton scattering are the two predominant interactions between x-ray photons and matter in diagnostic radiology. In the photoelectric effect, the low-energy-incident photon is absorbed by the tissues being radiographed. In Compton scatter, the high-energy-incident photon uses only part of its energy to eject an outer-shell electron. It retains much of its original energy in the form of a scattered x-ray. Radiologic personnel can be exposed to that high-energy scattered radiation, especially in fluoroscopy and mobile radiography. Lead aprons are used to protect us from exposure to scattered radiation during these procedures. *(Bushong, 8th ed., p. 174)*

155. **(B)** The bones of the foot include the 7 tarsal bones, 5 metatarsal bones, and 14 phalanges. The calcaneus (os calsis), or heel bone, is the largest tarsal (numbers 6 and 7). It serves as attachment for the Achilles tendon posteriorly, articulates anteriorly with the cuboid bone (number 3), presents three articular surfaces superiorly for its articulation with the talus (number 1), and has a prominent shelf on its anteromedial edge called the *sustentaculum tali*. The inferior surface of the talus (astragalus) articulates with the superior calcaneus to form the three-faceted subtalar joint. The talus also articulates anteriorly with the navicular (number 2). Articulating anteriorly with the navicular are the three cuneiform bones—medial/first, intermediate/second, and lateral/third. The navicular articulates laterally with the cuboid. *(Bontrager and Lampignano, 6th ed., p. 234)*

156. **(A)** Location of the heels of the hands is of great importance during CPR. They should be placed about 1½ in. superior to the xiphoid tip. In this way, the heart will receive the compressions it requires without causing internal injuries. Rib fractures can depress and cause injury to the lung tissues within the rib cage. *(Torres et al., 6th ed., pp. 172–176)*

157. **(D)** In electronic/digital imaging, changes in window width affect changes in contrast scale, while changes in window level affect changes in brightness (in analog terms, density). As window width decreases, the scale of contrast decreases (i.e., contrast increases). As window level decreases, brightness decreases. It should be noted that, to describe a decrease in brightness, our analog terminology would say that density increases. This can be easily illustrated as you postprocess/window your personal digital photographs or scanned documents. As you slide the brightness scale to decrease brightness, the photo/image gets lighter/brighter, that is, density decreases. *(Fosbinder and Orth, p. 208)*

158. **(B)** For an AP projection of the hip, two bony landmarks are used. The CR is directed perpendicular to a point located 2 in. medial to the ASIS at the level of the greater trochanter. A point midway between the iliac crest and the pubic symphysis is too superior and medial to coincide with the hip articulation. *(Frank, Long, and Smith, 11th ed., vol. 1, p. 354)*

159. **(B)** In film/screen imaging, a 15% change in kilovoltage, one way or the other, can have significant radiographic impact according to the *15% rule*. An increase of 15% in kV will effectively double the density; a decrease of 15% will reduce the density by one half. So, in this instance, if the kV is increased by 15%, exposure to the image receptor will be doubled—therefore, the mAs should be reduced by half (changed from 32 to 16 mAs) to compensate for the exposure change. *(Bushong, 9th ed., p. 254)*

160. **(D)** The shortest possible exposure time should be used to minimize motion unsharpness. Motion causes unsharpness that destroys detail. Careful and accurate patient instruction is essential for minimizing voluntary motion. Suspended respiration eliminates respiratory motion. Using the shortest possible exposure time is essential to decreasing involuntary motion. Immobilization also can be useful in eliminating motion unsharpness. *(Selman, 9th ed., p. 210)*

161. **(D)** A PA projection of the left hand and wrist is obtained most often to evaluate skeletal maturation. These images are compared with standard normal images for the age and sex of

the child. Additional supplemental images may be requested. *(Bontrager and Lampignano, 6th ed., p. 654)*

162. **(C)** The *latent image* is the invisible image produced within the film emulsion as a result of exposure to radiation. The developer solution converts this to a visible *manifest image*. The exposed silver halide grains in the emulsion undergo chemical change in the developer solution, and the unexposed crystals are removed from the film during the fixing process. *(Fauber, 2nd ed., p. 163)*

163. **(B)** *Anaphylaxis* is an acute reaction characterized by sudden onset of urticaria, respiratory distress, vascular collapse, or systemic shock; it sometimes leads to death. It is caused by ingestion or injection of a sensitizing agent such as a drug, vaccine, contrast agent, or food or by an insect bite. *Asthma* is characterized by difficulty in breathing, causing bronchospasm. It is often precipitated by stress, and although dyspnea is a symptom, oxygen is not administered. Asthmatics carry a nebulizer that contains a medication to relieve the bronchospasm, thereby relieving their breathing distress. Asthma and rhinitis are examples of allergic reactions. *(Bontrager and Lampignano, 6th ed., p. 656)*

164. **(D)** Adverse reactions to the intravascular administration of iodinated contrast medium are not uncommon, but although the risk of a life-threatening reaction is relatively rare, the radiographer must be alert to recognize and deal effectively with a serious reaction should it occur. Flushed appearance and nausea, occasionally vomiting, and a few hives characterize a minor reaction. Early symptoms of a possible anaphylactic reaction include constriction of the throat, possibly owing to laryngeal edema, dysphagia (difficulty in swallowing), and itching of the palms and soles. The radiographer must maintain the patient's airway, summon the radiologist, and call a "code." *(Ehrlich et al., 6th ed., p. 234)*

165. **(B)** As OID increases, magnification increases. Viscera and structures within the body will be

varying distances from the IR depending on their location within the body and the position used for the exposure. The size of a particular structure or image can be calculated using the following formula:

$$\frac{\text{Image size}}{\text{Object size}} = \frac{\text{SID}}{\text{SOD (SOD = SID - OID)}}$$

Substituting known quantities:

$$\frac{9 \text{ cm}}{x \text{ cm}} = \frac{105 \text{ cm}}{87 \text{ cm}}$$

$$105x = 783$$

Thus, $x = 7.45$ cm (approximate actual size). The relationship between SID, SOD, and OID is illustrated in Figure 7–23. *(Bushong, 8th ed., p. 284)*

166. **(C)** Kilovoltage (kVp) and half-value layer (HVL) change both the quantity and the quality of the primary beam. The principal qualitative factor of the primary beam is peak kilovoltage, but an increase in kilovoltage will also effect an increase in the number of photons produced at the target. HVL is defined as the amount of material necessary to decrease the intensity of the beam to one-half its original value, thereby effecting a change in both beam quality and quantity. The milliampere-seconds

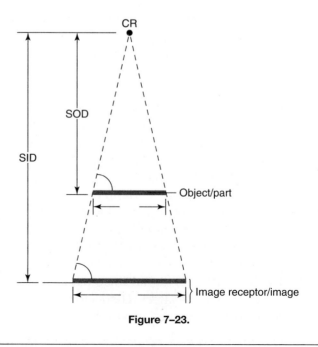

Figure 7–23.

value is adjusted to regulate the number of x-ray photons produced at the target. X-ray beam quality is unaffected by changes in milliampere-seconds. *(Bushong, 8th ed., p. 165)*

167. **(B)** A *polyp* is a tumor with a pedicle (stalk) that is found commonly in vascular organs projecting inward from its mucosal wall. Polyps usually are removed surgically because, although usually benign, they can become malignant. A *diverticulum* is an outpouching from the wall of an organ, such as the colon. A *fistula* is an abnormal tube-like passageway between organs or between an organ and the surface. An *abscess* is a localized collection of pus as a result of inflammation. *(Bontrager and Lampignano, 6th ed., p. 499)*

168. **(A)** The *autotransformer* (number 1) controls/selects the amount of voltage sent to the primary winding of the high-voltage transformer and operates on the principle of self-induction. The *step-up* (high-voltage) *transformer* (primary coil is number 2; secondary coil is number 3) operates on the principle of mutual induction. The step-up transformer functions to change low voltage to the high voltage necessary to produce x-ray photons. The x-ray tube is identified as number 7. *(Selman, 9th ed., pp. 83–84)*

169. **(C)** In the simplified x-ray circuit shown, the *autotransformer* is labeled number 1, the primary coil of the *high-voltage transformer* is number 2, and the *secondary coil* is labeled number 3. The autotransformer selects the voltage that will be sent to the high-voltage transformer to be stepped up to the thousands of volts required for x-ray production. At the midpoint of the secondary coil is the *grounded milliamperage meter* (number 4). Since the milliamperage meter is in the control panel and is associated with high voltage, it must be grounded. The *rectification system*, which is used to change alternating current to unidirectional current, is indicated by the number 5. The rectification system is located between the secondary coil of the high-voltage transformer (number 3) and the x-ray tube (number 7). *(Selman, 9th ed., pp. 159, 161)*

170. **(D)** All these conditions are considered technically additive because they all involve an increase in tissue density. *Osteoma,* or *exostosis,* is a (usually benign) bony tumor that can develop on bone. *Bronchiectasis* is a chronic dilatation of the bronchi with accumulation of fluid. *Pneumonia* is inflammation of the lung(s) with accumulation of fluid. Additional bony tissues and the pathologic presence of fluid are additive pathologic conditions and require an increase in exposure factors. Destructive conditions such as *osteoporosis* require a decrease in exposure factors. *(Carlton and Adler, 4th ed., p. 249)*

171. **(A)** The type of isolation practiced to prevent the spread of infectious agents in aerosol form is *respiratory isolation*. A mask is sufficient protection from aerosol transmission of pathogens. *Protective isolation,* also referred to as *reverse isolation,* is used to protect patients whose immune systems are compromised. Patients receiving chemotherapy, burn patients, or patients who are human immunodeficiency virus (HIV)–positive all may have compromised immune systems. *Contact isolation* is used when there is a chance that infection may be spread by contact with body fluids. Gloves and a gown are used, and goggles and masks may be necessary if there is a chance of fluids spraying, such as in biopsy or drainage. *Strict isolation* is practiced with highly contagious diseases or viruses that may be spread by air and/or contact. *(Adler and Carlton, 4th ed., p. 233)*

172. **(D)** Breast tissue has very low subject contrast, but it is imperative to visualize microcalcifications and subtle density differences. Fine detail is necessary to visualize any microcalcifications; therefore, a small-focal-spot tube is essential. High, short-scale contrast (and, therefore, low kilovoltage) is needed to accentuate minute differences in tissue density. A compression device serves to even out differences in tissue thickness (thicker at the chest wall, thinner at the nipple) and decrease OID and helps to decrease the production of scattered radiation. *(Selman, 9th ed., pp. 288–289)*

173. (C) Quality Control refers to our equipment and its safe and accurate operation. Various components must be tested at specified intervals and test results must be within specified parameters. Any deviation from those parameters must be corrected. Examples of equipment components that are tested annually are the focal spot size, linearity, reproducibility, filtration, kV, and exposure time. Congruence is a term used to describe the relationship between the collimator light field and the actual x-ray field—they must be congruent (i.e., match) to within 2% of the SID. Radiographic equipment collimators should be inspected and verified as accurate semiannually, that is, twice a year. Kilovoltage settings can most effectively be tested using an electronic kV meter; to meet required standards, the kV should be accurate to within +/−4 kV. Reproducibility testing should specify that radiation output be consistent to within +/−5%. *(Fosbinder and Orth, pp. 223–225; NCRP Report No. 99, p. 64)*

174. (D) Single-phase radiographic equipment is much less efficient than three-phase equipment because it has a 100% voltage ripple. With three-phase equipment, voltage never drops to zero, and x-ray intensity is significantly greater. To produce similar density, only two-thirds of the original milliampere-seconds would be used for three-phase, six-pulse equipment ($\frac{2}{3} \times 8 = 5.3$ mAs). With three-phase, 12-pulse equipment, the original milliampere-seconds would be cut in half ($\frac{1}{2} \times 8 = 4$ mAs). *(Bushong, 8th ed., p. 124)*

175. (B) A fractional focal spot of 0.3 mm or smaller is essential for reproducing fine detail without focal-spot blurring in magnification radiography. As the object image is magnified, so will be the associated blur unless the fractional focal spot is used. Fluoroscopic procedures probably would cause great wear on a fractional focal spot. Use of the fractional focal spot is not essential in bone radiography, although magnification of bony structures often is helpful in locating hairline fractures. *(Selman, 9th ed., pp. 226–228)*

176. (B) Traditional radiography uses an area x-ray beam, but the IR is film emulsion sandwiched between intensifying screens in a cassette. Computed radiography (CR) also uses an area x-ray beam, but the IR is a photostimulable phosphor such as europium-activated barium fluorohalide coated on an image plate. Digital radiography (DR) can use an area x-ray beam detected by a direct-capture solid-state device—there are no traditional cassette-like devices. DR can also use a fan-shaped x-ray beam. The fan-shaped beam is "read" by a linear array of detectors. *(Bushong, 8th ed., pp. 401, 403)*

177. (A) The gradual decrease in exposure rate as radiation passes through matter is called *attenuation*. Attenuation is attributed to the two major types of interactions that occur in tissue between x-ray photons and matter in the diagnostic x-ray range. In the photoelectric effect, absorption and secondary radiation occur. In the Compton effect, scattered radiation is produced. With each of these occurrences, there is a decrease in the exposure rate that is referred to as *attenuation. (Bushong, 8th ed., p. 185)*

178. (A) X-rays produced in the x-ray tube make up a heterogeneous beam. There are many low-energy, or "soft," photons that do not contribute to the radiographic image because they never reach the IR. Instead, they stay in the patient, contributing to skin dose. It is these photons that are removed by (aluminum) filtration. *(Bushong, 8th ed., p. 12)*

179. (B) The effects of a quantity of radiation delivered to a body depend on several factors—the amount of radiation received, the size of the irradiated area, and how the radiation is delivered in time. If the radiation is delivered in portions over a period of time, it is said to be *fractionated* and has a less harmful effect than if the radiation were delivered all at once. With fractionation, cells have an opportunity to repair, so some recovery occurs between doses. *(Bushong, 8th ed., p. 496)*

180. (D) Generally speaking, anatomic parts measuring in excess of 10 cm require a grid. (The major exception to this rule can be the chest). The larger the part, the more scattered radiation is generated. To avoid degradation of the image as a result of scattered radiation fog, a grid is used to absorb scatter. Parts generally requiring the use of a grid include the skull, spine, ribs, pelvis, shoulder, and femur. *(Shephard, p. 245)*

181. **(D)** There are many radiation protection devices and laws associated with today's x-ray equipment. For example, the collimator light must accurately indicate the size and location of the x-ray beam to within 2% of the SID. Equipment that does not function properly contributes to excessive patient exposure, in the form of repeat examinations, and to poor image quality. *(Bushong, 8th ed., p. 568)*

182. **(B)** Magnification radiography is used to enlarge details to a more perceptible degree. Hairline fractures and minute blood vessels are candidates for magnification radiography. The problem of magnification unsharpness is overcome by using a fractional focal spot; larger focal-spot sizes will produce excessive blurring unsharpness. Grids are usually unnecessary in magnification radiography because of the air-gap effect produced by the OID. Direct-exposure technique probably would not be used because of the excessive exposure required. *(Selman, 9th ed., pp. 226–228)*

183. **(C)** The x-ray tube's glass envelope and oil coolant are considered inherent (built-in) filtration. Thin sheets of aluminum are added to make a total of at least 2.5-mm-Al-equivalent filtration in equipment operated above 70 kVp. The function of the filtration is to remove the low-energy photons that serve only to contribute to skin dose. *(Bushong, 8th ed., p. 568)*

184. **(A)** The lead strips in a focused grid are made to parallel the x-ray beam. Therefore, scattered radiation, which radiates in directions other than that of the primary beam, will be absorbed by the grid. When the x-ray beam does not parallel the lead strips, some type of grid cutoff occurs. If the x-ray beam is not centered to the grid, or if the x-ray tube and grid surface are not parallel (level), there will be a fairly uniform decrease in radiographic density across the entire image. However, if the grid is not used within its recommended SID (focus) range (i.e., if the SID is too great or too

little), there will be a decrease in density at the periphery of the image. *(Carlton and Adler, 4th ed., pp. 263–266)*

185. **(C)** The trachea (windpipe) bifurcates into left and right main stem bronchi, each of which enters its respective lung hilum. The left bronchus divides into two portions—one for each lobe of the left lung. The right bronchus divides into three portions—one for each lobe of the right lung. The lungs are conical in shape, consisting of upper pointed portions, termed the *apices* (plural of apex), and broad lower portions (or *bases*). The lungs are enclosed in a double-walled serous membrane called the *pleura*. *(Tortora and Derrickson, 11th ed., p. 857)*

186. **(D)** X-ray tubes are diode tubes; that is, they have two electrodes—a positive electrode called the *anode* and a negative electrode called the *cathode*. The cathode filament is heated to incandescence and releases electrons, a process called *thermionic emission*. During the exposure, these electrons are driven by thousands of volts toward the anode, where they are suddenly decelerated. This deceleration is what produces x-rays. Some x-ray tubes, such as those used in fluoroscopy and in capacitor-discharge mobile units, are required to make short, precise—sometimes, multiple—exposures. This need is met by using a grid-controlled tube. A grid-controlled tube uses the molybdenum focusing cup as the switch, permitting very precise control of the tube current (flow of electrons between cathode and anode). *(Bushong, 8th ed., p. 132)*

187. **(B)** The figure illustrates a lateral thoracic spine. Motion from "breathing technique" has been employed to blur out the superimposed pulmonary vascular markings and bony rib details in order to better demonstrate the bony structure of the thoracic spine. This is often referred to as *autotomography*; that is, the part moves itself rather than actual tomographic apparatus being employed. Since the shoulder area of the upper thoracic spine is so much thicker and more dense than the lower thoracic area, employment of the anode heel effect is also a valuable tool here. The thicker

shoulder area is placed under the more intense cathode end of the x-ray beam, and the thinner anatomic part is placed under the anode end of the x-ray beam. *(Frank, Long, and Smith, 11th ed., vol. 1, pp. 418, 420)*

188. **(B)** The female pelvis differs from the male pelvis in that it is shallower and its bones generally are lighter and more delicate (Figure 7–24). The pelvic outlet is wider and more circular in the female, and the ischial tuberosities and acetabula are farther apart; the angle formed by the pubic arch is also greater (more than 100 degrees) in the female. All these bony characteristics facilitate childbearing and birth. *(Frank, Long, and Smith, 11th ed., vol. 1, p. 340)*

189. **(A)** *Hematemesis* refers to vomiting blood. If the blood is dark in color, it is probably gastric in origin; if it is bright red, it is most likely pharyngeal in origin. Expectoration (coughing or spitting up) of blood is called *hemoptysis*. Blood is originating from the mouth, larynx, or respiratory structure. *Hematuria* is the condition of blood in the urine. *Epistaxis* is the medical term for nosebleed. *(Taber, p. 954)*

190. **(B)** Computed radiography (CR) cassettes use no intensifying screens or film—hence, the term *filmless radiography*. The cassettes have a protective function (for the image plate within) and can be used in the Bucky tray or directly under the anatomic part; they need not be light-tight because the image plate is not light sensitive. The cassette has a thin lead-foil backing (similar to traditional cassettes) to absorb backscatter. Inside the cassette is the photostimulable phosphor (PSP) image plate, sometimes referred to simply as an *image plate* (IP). This PSP or IP within the cassette has a layer of europium-activated barium fluorohalide that serves as the IR as it is exposed in the traditional manner and receives the latent image. The PSP can store the latent image for several hours; after about 8 hours, noticeable image fading will occur. *(Carlton and Adler, 4th ed., p. 358)*

191. **(C)** The medial oblique projection of the ankle can be performed either as a 15- to 20-degree oblique or as a 45-degree oblique. The 15- to 20-degree oblique projection demonstrates the ankle mortise, that is, the articulations between the talus, tibia, and fibula. The 45-degree oblique opens the distal tibiofibular joint. In all three cases, although the MSP can change the plantar surface must be vertical. *(Frank, Long, and Smith, 11th ed., vol. 1, p. 291)*

192. **(D)** The number of heat units produced during a given exposure with single-phase equipment is determined by multiplying mA × time × kVp. Correction factors are required with three-phase equipment. Unless the equipment manufacturer specifies otherwise,

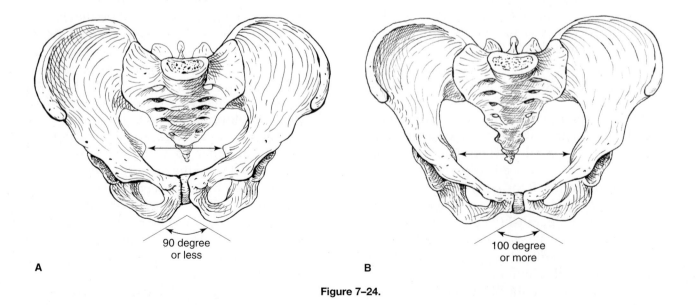

A   B

Figure 7–24.

three-phase, six-pulse heat units are determined by multiplying mA × time kVp × 1.35. Three-phase, 12-pulse heat units are determined by multiplying mA × time × kVp × 1.41. (*Selman, 9th ed., p. 145*)

193. **(D)** Body substance precaution procedures identify various body fluids as infectious or potentially infectious. These body substances include pleural, pericardial, peritoneal, and amniotic fluids; synovial fluid; CSF; breast milk; and vaginal secretions, as well as semen, nasal secretions, tears, saliva, sputum, feces, urine, and wound drainage. (*Torres et al., 6th ed., p. 63*)

194. **(A)** The control badge that comes with the month's supply of dosimeters is used as a standard for comparison with the used personal badges. The control badge should be stored in a radiation-free area, away from the radiographic rooms. When it has been processed, its density is compared with the densities of the monitors worn in radiation areas. Densities greater than the density of the radiation-free monitor are reported in millirem units. (*Bushong, 8th ed., p. 596*)

195. **(D)** According to the patient's bill of rights, the patient's verbal request supersedes any prior written consent. It is not appropriate to dismiss the patient without notifying the referring physician and the radiologist. The patient may very well need a particular radiographic examination to make a proper diagnosis or for preoperative planning, and the radiographer must inform the physician of the patient's decision immediately. (*Ehrlich et al., 6th ed., pp. 54–55*)

196. **(B)** The *input phosphor* of an image intensifier receives remnant radiation emerging from the patient and converts it to a fluorescent light image. Directly adjacent to the input phosphor is the *photocathode*, which is made of a photoemissive alloy (usually, a cesium and antimony compound). The fluorescent light image strikes the photocathode and is converted to an electron image. The electrons are carefully focused, to maintain image resolution, by the *electrostatic focusing lenses*, through the *accelerating anode* and to the *output phosphor* for conversion back to light. (*Bushong, p. 361*)

197. **(B)** *Resolution* describes how closely fine details may be associated and still be recognized as separate details before seeming to blend into each other and appear as one. The degree of resolution transferred to the image receptor is a function of the resolving power of each of the system components and can be expressed in line pairs per millimeter (lp/mm), line-spread function (LSP), or modulation transfer function (MTF). Line pairs per millimeter can be measured using a resolution test pattern; a number of resolution test tools are available. LSP is measured using a 10-μm x-ray beam; MTF measures the amount of information lost between the object and the IR. (*Carlton and Adler, 4th ed., p. 334*)

198–200. **(198, C; 199, D; 200, C)** The figure illustrates the x-ray tube component parts. Number 1 indicates the thoriated tungsten filament, which functions to release electrons when heated. Number 2 is the molybdenum focusing cup, which directs these electrons toward the anode's focal track. Number 4 is the rotating anode, and number 5 is the anode's focal track. The focal track is made of thoriated (for extra protection from heat) tungsten. When high-speed electrons are suddenly decelerated at the target, their kinetic energy is changed to x-ray photon energy. (*Bushong, 8th ed., pp. 132–135*)

Subspecialty List

65. Image procedures
66. Image acquisition and evaluation
67. Image procedures
68. Image procedures
69. Image procedures
70. Image procedures
71. Equipment operation and maintenance
72. Equipment operation and quality control
73. Patient care and education
74. Equipment operation and quality control
75. Radiation protection
76. Equipment operation and quality control
77. Image procedures
78. Image acquisition and evaluation
79. Radiation protection
80. Image acquisition and evaluation
81. Radiation protection
82. Image acquisition and evaluation
83. Image procedures
84. Radiation protection
85. Image acquisition and evaluation
86. Image procedures
87. Image procedures
88. Patient care and education
89. Image procedures
90. Image procedures
91. Image acquisition and evaluation
92. Equipment operation and quality control
93. Patient care and education
94. Image acquisition and evaluation
95. Image procedures
96. Image acquisition and evaluation
97. Equipment operation and quality control
98. Patient care and education
99. Image procedures
100. Patient care and education
101. Image acquisition and evaluation
102. Patient care and education
103. Image procedures
104. Image procedures
105. Equipment operation and quality control
106. Radiation protection
107. Image acquisition and evaluation
108. Image procedures
109. Radiation protection
110. Image procedures
111. Radiation protection
112. Radiation protection
113. Equipment operation and quality control
114. Image acquisition and evaluation
115. Image acquisition and evaluation
116. Image procedures
117. Image procedures
118. Image procedures
119. Image procedures
120. Image acquisition and evaluation
121. Image acquisition and evaluation
122. Equipment operation and quality control
123. Patient care and education
124. Image procedures
125. Image acquisition and evaluation
126. Radiation protection
127. Image acquisition and evaluation
128. Radiation protection
129. Patient care and education
130. Image acquisition and evaluation
131. Patient care and education
132. Image procedures
133. Image acquisition and evaluation
134. Radiation protection
135. Radiation protection
136. Radiation protection
137. Patient care and education
138. Image acquisition and evaluation
139. Patient care and education
140. Image procedures
141. Image procedures
142. Image acquisition and evaluation
143. Image procedures
144. Image procedures
145. Image acquisition and evaluation
146. Image acquisition and evaluation
147. Radiation protection
148. Image acquisition and evaluation
149. Image acquisition and evaluation
150. Patient care and education
151. Patient care and education
152. Equipment operation and quality control
153. Equipment operation and quality control
154. Radiation protection
155. Image procedures
156. Patient care and education
157. Image acquisition and evaluation
158. Image procedures
159. Image acquisition and evaluation
160. Image acquisition and evaluation
161. Image procedures
162. Image acquisition and evaluation
163. Patient care and education
164. Patient care and education
165. Image procedures
166. Radiation protection

167. Patient care and education
168. Equipment operation and quality control
169. Equipment operation and quality control
170. Image acquisition and evaluation
171. Patient care and education
172. Image procedures
173. Equipment operation and quality control
174. Image acquisition and evaluation
175. Equipment operation and quality control
176. Image acquisition and evaluation
177. Radiation protection
178. Radiation protection
179. Radiation protection
180. Image acquisition and evaluation
181. Equipment operation and quality control
182. Image acquisition and evaluation
183. Radiation protection

184. Image acquisition and evaluation
185. Radiation protection
186. Equipment operation and quality control
187. Image procedures
188. Image procedures
189. Patient care and education
190. Equipment operation and quality control
191. Image procedures
192. Equipment operation and quality control
193. Patient care and education
194. Radiation protection
195. Patient care and education
196. Equipment operation and quality control
197. Image acquisition and evaluation
198. Equipment operation and quality control
199. Equipment operation and quality control
200. Equipment operation and quality control

Index

Note: Page numbers followed by *f* refer to figures; page numbers followed by *t* refer to tables.